STEEPLES AND SMOKESTACKS

A collection of essays on

The Franco-American Experience
in New England

Edited by

Claire Quintal

Institut français
Assumption College
Worcester, Massachusetts
1996

Cover photo of New Bedford's St. Antoine Church and the Wamsutta Mills by Joseph D. Thomas, Publisher/Editor of *Spinner—People and Culture in Southeastern Massachusetts.*

Typesetting: Maggy Groccia

© Éditions de l'Institut français
Assumption College
500 Salisbury Street
Worcester, Massachusetts 01615-0005

ISBN 1-880261-03-0

The publication of this book having been made possible in great measure by the generosity of Roger Proulx, D.C., in honor of his parents and to commemorate their life together, we gladly dedicate this book in their memory.

*A la douce mémoire de Joseph-G. Proulx (1900-1991)
et de Juliette-M. Péloquin Proulx (1908-1994)*

*Leur amour l'un pour l'autre, leur foi à toute épreuve,
leur sens du devoir envers tous ceux qui leur étaient chers
vivront à jamais dans le souvenir de leur fils, Roger Proulx.*

Faith best describes Joseph and Juliette Proulx,
faith in God, fidelity to their cultural heritage,
and total allegiance to one another.
Faire son devoir was the motto they lived by,
duty to God and to family
in spite of great hardships and against all odds.

Table of Contents

VIII.   The View From Within

Preface

Etched into the mind's eye of most Franco-Americans is an urban landscape from which emerge one or many steeples and just as many, if not more, smokestacks. Steeples and smokestacks together were a fact of life for French-Canadian immigrants in the United States. Their lives were spent not only within view of them both, but also within their purview. They labored below the smokestack and prayed beneath the steeple, the two poles of the lives of so many migrants to this country.

The steeples invariably impress the passerby by their grandeur, and the soaring nature of their reason for being. They embody both beauty of form as well as function, standing for the high-mindedness which made their construction possible. Smokestacks exist for another purpose. Their own function, however, is as evident as is that of the steeple. They are the icon of the industrial age, the most visible symbol of the factories which "pulled" so many migrants out of French Canada to settle in New England.

French-speaking immigrants from Quebec and the Maritime Provinces settled in the shadow of those smokestacks of the textile and shoe mills. There, they built ethnic enclaves known as Little Canadas. As soon as enough of them had settled in a given place, they set about building churches where they could worship in their own language, much as they had done from time immemorial. Offsetting the stark reality of the smokestacks, these steeples provided the soul-lifting atmosphere of religious ceremonies and the comfort of prayer in one's mother tongue. They brightened the bleakness of the workaday lives of hundreds of thousands of new settlers whose very subsistence depended upon the smokestacks.

Claire Quintal

Acknowledgments

We wish here to express our deep-seated gratitude to Leslie Choquette, Ph.D., our collaborator in the choice of texts for this book, who graciously and with great generosity re-read all the essays, both the translations and those which had originally been written in English. She placed at our disposal her time and her expertise in these matters. Without her input, this book would have been less worthy of its reason for being published at all.

We wish also to acknowledge our heartfelt appreciation to all of our collaborators, especially to those who accepted the unenviable task of translating the French texts into English and to do so without remuneration, from a personal conviction in the validity of the undertaking. Given the French Institute's limited budget, this book would never have been published without this splendid gift of their time and their knowledge of both languages.

To the Assumptionists, Rev. Alexis A. Babineau, Rev. Louis F. Dion, and Rev. Wilfrid J. Dufault, who read the final copy, under less than ideal conditions, we also owe our sincere thanks. Father Babineau, who translated all of the Acadian texts but one in this volume, deserves a special *merci.*

And, finally, to Maggy Groccia, without whom all of this material would still be scattered among the several previous publications of the French Institute, we wish to profess our unending gratitude for the many talents she places, each and every day, at the disposal of the French Institute and its directress.

Introduction

Claire Quintal

By the time of the Civil War, when industrial expansion was in full swing in the United States, the French Canadians of Quebec and the Acadians of the Maritime Provinces were struggling to feed their large families on small farms where depleted soil, a poor road network, and a harsh climate contributed to a sense of hopelessness about the future. Although they were by turns cajoled and berated into staying in Canada, they chose, nonetheless, to emigrate, to leave behind what their forefathers had painstakingly built over the centuries, since the founding of Port Royal in 1605 and Quebec City in 1608.

Because the border with the United States was not very far away, and because in the collective memory of both Quebecers and Acadians there remained the remembrance of that country—of the forced exile of their Acadian forebears to the cities and towns of the Eastern Seaboard—of the exploration of large portions of the American continent by their Quebec forefathers—the United States did not seem to be so much a foreign land as part of a continent which the French knew already, and had made their own, especially along the Mississippi River, in cities like St. Louis and New Orleans.

The story told here deals with a later period, that of the last half of the nineteenth century and the early part of the twentieth. It tells of farmers who struggled mightily, but unsuccessfully, against the forces arrayed against them—the loss of protective tariffs, usurious lenders, an industrial expansion which lagged woefully behind that of the United States, a government that, although well-informed about the nefarious effects of the departure of so many, did little to stem the torrent. And so, they left in desperation, left their ancestral homeland to come south into the mill cities and towns of New England where they would only be tolerated because they were known to work hard and well and because they did not complain about harsh labor conditions.

This book does not tell the story of all the cities where they settled—in such large numbers in certain neighborhoods that these areas often became known as Little Canadas—but it does describe a handful of communities of varying sizes that are both similar to all the rest and quite different, each in its own way.

We need not here insist upon the importance of religion in the lives of French-Canadian immigrants. Religion was the great supporting pillar of *la survivance* on American soil. Because these men and women were the descendants of one of the founding nations of the New World—along with England and Spain—the preservation of their French identity weighed more heavily upon them than upon other immigrant groups. *Survivance* had been maintained in Canada against overwhelming odds, ever since the defeat of the French by the British in the mid-eighteenth century. That determination to remember the role played by the French in the development of the North American continent, that sense of obligation to their ancestors, of not letting go of something for which so much had been sacrificed, that need to survive, for their sake, as a distinct entity, has to be understood if one hopes to comprehend the attitudes, the actions, and the reactions of these immigrants.

Along with religion, language was a key component of the group's distinctive identity. The explorers had directed their men in French, the missionaries had left behind a legacy of praying in that same language, the *coureurs de bois* and the *voyageurs* had kept up their paddling rhythms with French songs, the military victories had been toasted with a Gallic accent and the defeats deplored in that same language. The mother tongue, transmitted from generation to generation, had been passed on as a quasi-sacred relic. Life on the farms, in the villages, on the roads and rivers of French North America had been lived *en français* for three centuries. Would it, could it continue to be spoken in a country where life was lived in English? To ensure that it both could and would, a heroic effort was undertaken by the Church and its religious communities of women and men who came into New England, from Canada and France, to teach the French language, and inculcate the tenets of Catholicism in that same tongue, to generations of school children being raised in a Protestant land. An overview of that herculean enterprise—to establish parishes, where homilies were preached and prayers were recited in French, and parochial schools, where one-half of the school day was taught in French—can be found in these pages.

The trials and tribulations attendant upon such an undertaking are also described here. For this was, alas, a land where even Catholic bishops tried to thwart the efforts made on behalf of *survivance* by these descendants of a people whose bishops had been the first occupants of so many American dioceses, including that of Boston. In their stated goal of accelerating the acculturation of non-English-speaking Catholic immigrants to the United States, the hierarchy at times paid little heed and displayed no apparent regard for the long and impressive religious history and missionary zeal of French-speakers on this continent.

These hundreds of thousands of immigrant workers, who had been followed into New England by doctors, lawyers, small businessmen, and especially by *curés* and religious teaching congregations, even managed somehow to support, albeit precariously, a French-language press, the sheer numbers of which remain impressive to this day. Some two hundred newspapers were founded during the period—from 1874, when Ferdinand Gagnon began publishing *Le Travailleur* in Worcester, Massachusetts, to 1978 when Wilfrid Beaulieu's own *Le Travailleur* (1931), so-named in homage to its predecessor, passed out of existence with the death of its founder-director. In spite of the day-to-day struggle to maintain a foreign-language daily or weekly, a goodly number of these newspapers managed to hang on—guiding their readers, defending their religious and civic rights, pleading with the authorities on their behalf, keeping them informed of events in Canada and even in France, while upholding the belief of their readership in the correctness of the cause of *survivance*. The editors condemned those who were lukewarm in this religious-linguistic battle, arming the more ardent with the facts they needed to maintain their distinct identity even in the face of mounting opposition or indifference. These newspapers even provided a haven for fledgling writers who preferred to express themselves in their mother tongue, and whose voices might otherwise never have been heard.

And what of these writers? Can it be stated that there exists a body of works which, taken together, can be called Franco-American Literature? A perusal of the table of contents will go some way toward answering that question and will enable the reader to discover writers who deserve to be better known, and well-known writers who have found inspiration in describing their ethnic past. Folklore has also been given pride of place here. What these people sang, and the stories they told constitute a revealing component of their ties with the past. To be able to sing—in a drab mill town in New England—a song sung by the *voyageurs* surely makes for connectedness, and must, of necessity, enhance one's ethnic identity, in addition to having an energizing effect upon the singer!

This book also brings Franco-American women out of the shadows of home, convent, and factory to shine a bright light on the importance of the roles played by them in the battle for *survivance*. Franco-American women are described in various guises in these pages—as the foundresses of religious communities and lay organizations, as the teachers of French and religion—those buttresses of *survivance* which could never have been maintained without these consecrated women—and, of course, as the mill workers whose deft fingers helped in great measure to support their families.

Do Franco-Americans still speak French? Do they remember their past—both the distant one, as founders of New France, as well as their more immediate history as founders of parishes and schools in immigrant communities? These are the questions that the essays on "Franco-Americans Today" attempt to answer.

It is in the final section, entitled "The View From Within," that the transformation of a people from past to present can best be gauged—in the reminiscences of an immigrant childhood and through the problems created by cultural fragmentation and the difficulties this created for succeeding generations. The book closes on an evocation of "Mémère's kitchen," a place for gathering, for eating, for telling stories, and for remembering —remembering all that was and taking stock of what remains of the experience of these hundreds of thousands of men and women whose lives were spent beneath both the steeple and the smokestack.*

---

* Additional information on the various topics analyzed in these pages can be found in the books published by the *Institut français*/French Institute since 1980. These titles, in order of publication, are:

La Situation de la recherche sur les Franco-Américains
L'Émigrant québécois vers les États-Unis
The Little Canadas of New England
Le Journalisme de langue française aux États-Unis
L'Émigrant acadien aux États-Unis
Le Patrimoine folklorique des Franco-Américains
Les Franco-Américains et leurs institutions scolaires
Franco-American Literature: Writers and Their Writings
Franco-Americans and Religion: Impact and Influence
The Franco-American Woman

I
EMIGRATION

The Economic Evolution of Quebec and the Emigrant (1850-1929)

Yves Roby

From 1850 to 1930, more than 850,000 persons left Quebec for the United States.[1] The majority of them settled in New England. How can we explain the scale of this phenomenon? Quebec did not experience religious persecutions, political upheavals, or great famines which, in other areas of the world, have been the cause of dramatic population displacements. Generally speaking, poverty, discouragement, and unemployment are the factors which pushed so many French Canadians, at that time, to leave behind family and friends to crowd themselves into the working-class neighborhoods of New England cities. In order to understand Franco-Americans, it is essential to know the economic environment from which they came and the factors influencing their migration.

My plan here is to describe the state of the Quebec economy by highlighting its structural transformations and the economic crisis which marked the lives of French Canadians from the middle of the nineteenth century to the beginning of the Great Depression.

Economically speaking, the period consisted of three phases: one of expansion (1851-1873), one of contraction (1873-1896), and again a period of expansion (1896-1929). All three phases contained cyclical movements marked by financial crises which affected the structural transformations of the Quebec economy.

On the structural level, the years 1851-1929 were of major importance in the history of Quebec. One era ended in 1848: that of commercial mercantilism characterized by navigation laws, its preferential tariffs, and the absence of manufacturing. The second half of the nineteenth century constituted a period of transition. Another era came into being at the turn of the century: that of an

---

[1]   Yolande Lavoie, *L'Émigration des Québécois aux États-Unis de 1840 à 1930* (Quebec City: Éditeur officiel du Québec, 1979) p. 45.

industrial economy dominated by an all-encompassing capitalism and characterized, in particular, by the growth of cities and the development of labor unions.

Quebec was sparsely populated. From 1851 to 1931, its population grew from 890,261 to 2,874,662 inhabitants. The people of Quebec were very mobile. While hundreds of thousands found their way to New England, a great number abandoned the countryside for the city. In 1851, the rural population constituted 80% of the total population; by 1931, it represented only 36.9% of the population. This is but one indication, among many others, of the transformations experienced by Quebec's agricultural population.

It is customary, in certain circles, to represent the rural population of the nineteenth, and even of the beginning of the twentieth centuries, as a closed world, turned in on itself and self-sufficient. According to this view, a typical farm sufficed to nourish one family, although with some difficulty. Routine practices, ignorance of the basic principles of agriculture, and soil depletion meant that the land was able to produce only small surpluses which the farmer traded at the local market for three or four manufactured articles. Besides, what did farmers need from outside sources when all the essential needs of rural families were crafted at home by family members?

During the last quarter of the nineteenth century, this picture no longer corresponded to reality, except in certain isolated regions. Agriculture had progressively become a commercial enterprise subject to the ups and downs of the market place. Charles Gagné, a professor at the Sainte-Anne-de-la-Pocatière School of Agriculture, describes the change as follows: "The farmer," he wrote in 1924, "is no longer the one who used to live in great isolation; now he is in almost daily contact with merchants or representatives of industry. For him, it is a matter of exchanging four or five raw farm products for twenty or forty manufactured articles."[2]

How does one explain this transformation from a subsistence to a market economy? With the coming of canals and railroads, Quebec farmers had to face the impossibility of competing with the new and more productive lands of Ontario and the western

---

[2]   Charles Gagné, "Notre problème agricole," *L'Action française*, vol. 11, no. 2 (February 1924), pp. 99-100.

provinces. At first, few choices were open to them. In the regions most distant from the markets, where the soil was often ill-suited to agriculture, wheat lost more and more ground to replacement crops like potatoes, buckwheat, and peas. Farmers there relied on the products of dairy farming, still in its embryonic stage, to replace the meager revenues which they had previously received from the sale of their grains. A great many among the rural class succeeded in clinging to the soil only by consecrating the long winter months to working in the forest or by selling their wood to nearby sawmills. According to observers, this situation prevailed in regions of the Gaspé, Lake St. John, the Lower St. Lawrence, the Valley of the St. Maurice, the Ottawa River Valley, and Quebec. Farmers of the Richelieu River Valley, the Montreal Plain, the Eastern Townships, and, to a lesser degree, the Quebec Region met the challenges of change more easily. They benefited from the fertility of the soil, their proximity to markets and export centers, and the existence of an adequate transportation network. Furthermore, they listened more closely to the information dispensed by agricultural schools and by the advertising agents (the first "agronomists") hired by the government.

After much fruitless groping, the dairy industry became the backbone of Quebec agriculture. It was taken up everywhere but took root mainly in the Richelieu Valley where it became the farmers' main source of revenue. The farmers of the Eastern Townships specialized in animal husbandry and horticulture in addition to dairy farming; those of Chambly County bred horses for the American market. The Beauce, the Quebec Region, the Saint Maurice Valley, and Pontiac County raised hay for the needs of the New England market; the counties of Bellechasse and Montmagny specialized in animal husbandry. The counties around Quebec and Montreal took up truck farming, and the Joliette region began to move toward the growing of tobacco. Agriculture was becoming more and more specialized, and farmers earned additional revenues from the sale of firewood, maple sugar, etc.

Undeniably, Quebec agriculture progressed during this entire period. Many indices support this conclusion. The acreage of occupied lands grew by 3,318,389 acres between the years 1871 and 1901 and by 2,812,837 during the first two decades of the twentieth century. The acreage of improved lands, that is, under cultivation or used for pasture, grew even more rapidly. The production of hay and oats surged in a remarkable manner. Butter and cheese-processing plants mushroomed, their production reaching

54,243,000 and 48,630,000 pounds respectively in 1921. The rise of the dairy industry prompted numerous farmers to improve the drainage of their soil, rotate their crops, use fertilizers, and upgrade their livestock. Finally, agricultural specialization accelerated farm mechanization. This last phenomenon is not well-known due to inadequate statistics. At the very most, we know that for the years 1901, 1911, and 1921 every farm possessed, on average, equipment worth $193, $347, and $813.[3]

In spite of the progress recorded, the agricultural world remained traditional nonetheless. The French-Canadian farmer experienced great difficulty in freeing himself from the weight of custom. Charles Gagné confirmed what some observers had previously noted:

> We believe that we can say, without fear of error, although official statistics reveal nothing on this subject, that 60% of our farmers are not influenced by any scientific notion in the exploitation of their fields and their animals. People farm or believe they are farming in the tradition of their fathers and grandfathers. The principles of soil preparation, seed selection, the rotation of crops, the feeding and the raising of livestock, as well as the means of combating plant and animal diseases, are unknown to them."[4]

Living conditions in the countryside were still difficult. Food, water, lodging, medical care, and leisure bore little resemblance to the idyllic picture painted by certain present-day proponents of the return-to-the-soil movement.

Statistical data referred to here camouflage the high price which the Quebec farmer had to pay for these transformations of agricultural activity. As we shall see, the cost was all the higher given the fact that the transition to a market agriculture, in which the producer was more and more at the mercy of forces over which he had no control, occurred during periods of prolonged decline in agricultural prices (such as the one which lasted from 1873 to 1896) interspersed with extreme cyclical fluctuations. We are

---

[3]   François-Albert Angers, "Documentation statistique," in Esdras Minville, ed., *L'Agriculture* (Montreal: Fides, 1944), p. 500.

[4]   Gagné, *loc. cit.*, pp. 94-95.

reminded in particular of the grave crises from 1873 to 1879 and from 1921 to 1926.

By specializing, farmers increased their dependency on the outside world for products of prime necessity which formerly had been furnished by their own domestic industries. This reliance on the outside world was aggravated by the fact that Quebec agriculture retained many of the characteristics of the past: yields were low, mechanization was insufficiently advanced, and the average area of improved farmland was not very extensive. Furthermore, while the price of crops held or dropped over long periods, that of manufactured goods, which farmers had to purchase, tended to rise in price. To meet ever-growing needs, the more progressive farmers had to improve their methods of cultivation, increase their flocks, procure relatively costly equipment, and augment their farm acreage. In this way, from 1901 to 1921, the average size of the Quebec farm grew from 103.1 acres to 125.4 acres. All this required funds which farmers did not hesitate to borrow at high interest rates of 8%, 10%, and 12%. Where did they find the necessary money? Little is known about this, other than the fact that the banking system was little developed in rural areas.

In a certain number of parishes, the land made possible sufficiently remunerative crops to justify the creation of branch banks. Farmers were no better off for it. They reproached the banks for draining the limited capital of the parishes to accumulate it in larger centers, for not lending to the poor, and, finally, for not meeting their particular needs. For instance, bank loans were made to farmers, but only for short terms of four months with the right of renewal, whereas the minimum lending period should not have been less than six months and should even have extended from nine to twelve months. "What do you expect the farmer to do with money due in three months?" one reads in the *Gazette des campagnes* of December 2, 1861. "The land does not pay us off for a year and often after eighteen months of credit."

Lawyers, persons of independent means, and shopkeepers, who were more than simple intermediaries between urban wholesalers and country dwellers, ensured the credit that was indispensable to the farmers, through promissory notes and mortgages.

The fragile nature of the credit system was well-known and had a great deal to do with the phenomenon of emigration. During prosperous times, when crops were good and prices stable or rising, all went well. Lenders were accommodating and optimism reigned. But, in the event of a bad crop and the lowering of prices, the entire mechanism jammed. Because his income decreased, the borrower had little or nothing to give his creditors, who counted on the harvest for the reimbursement of a mortgage, a promissory note, or payments for merchandise. The borrower then had to renegotiate his loan at a higher interest rate. If bad harvests followed one upon the other, as happened in 1888, 1889, and 1890, the situation was catastrophic. The mortgage holder became impatient and the merchant insisted on payment without delay. Sometimes this resulted in foreclosure, often discouragement, which pushed the farmer to sell his land and leave the countryside. Some also had recourse to less scrupulous money-lenders who profited from hard times by demanding interest rates of 15%, 20%, and sometimes even more. *La Gazette des campagnes* of December 2, 1861, mentions interest rates as high as 72%.

Particularly during the nineteenth century, observers unceasingly condemned the plague of usury in the countryside. In 1868, for example, Pierre Samuel Gendron, the Deputy from Bagot to the Legislative Assembly, cried out:

> It is not enough that the farmer, for lack of agricultural knowledge, draws only meager revenues from his land, his ruin is then ensured by his falling into the greedy hands of men whom the love of profit drives to dishonest speculations. How can a farmer pay 10%, 15% or 20% interest to those who profit from the poor state of his affairs by lending him money at exorbitant rates? The plague of usury which gnaws at the countryside is . . . one of the causes which force the *habitant* to leave the field he has fertilized with his sweat and to take the road to the United States.[5]

The return of good harvests did not settle all the farmer's problems. Before all else, he needed to repay his debts. To avoid narrowing his margin of profit too much, he felt constrained to

---

5   Quoted in Marcel Hamelin, *Les premières années du parlementarisme québécois (1867-1878)* (Quebec City: Presses de l'Université Laval, 1974) p. 92.

Alphonse Desjardins, founder of the *Caisses populaires* [Credit Unions] would make the same observation in 1907. See Yves Roby: *Les Caisses populaires Alphonse Desjardins, 1900-1920* (Levis: La Fédération des Caisses populaires, 1975) p. 20.

produce more. This fact no doubt discouraged many of the young who had the impression of working for nothing. They would next be found in the city or in the United States.

Stability or the prolonged decline in prices which affected Quebec agriculture from 1873 to 1896 and at other times, notably from 1921 to 1926, had an even greater demoralizing effect on the agricultural producer. Here, once again, it meant that he had to produce more to meet his current financial obligations. Consider that if he had to sell 100 pounds of butter at twenty cents a pound to pay a merchant a bill of $20, he would need to sell 134 pounds at fifteen cents to pay the same bill. [6] It sometimes happened that he had no other choice but to borrow and wait for better days. A new inflationary spiral of interest rates, discouragement, and desertion from the countryside would then begin anew.

At other times, the system broke down at the other end of the pyramid. A financial crisis in England, for example, would force an exporter to call in his outstanding loans, unleashing in the process a chain reaction of commercial failures ending at times with the eviction of farmers or the proliferation of lenders against security.

In the more remote regions, the Quebec farmer was not sheltered from the problems we have just described. We should remember that about the middle of the nineteenth century, the young in search of land had to go beyond the St. Lawrence Plain almost totally occupied by then. They progressively colonized the regions of Lake St. John, the Ottawa River Valley, the Témiscamingue, the Lower St. Lawrence, the Gaspé, and the Abitibi. In these areas, even if improvements in the means of transportation enlarged the distribution network, stimulated exchanges, and pushed back subsistence agriculture, agrarian specialization was less advanced—it was logging, during the long winter months, which provided the money necessary for

---

[6]   Some of Charles Gagné's statistics, loc. cit., pp. 99-100, underline the brutality of the phenomenon. "Thus, in 1920, Quebec produced 41,632,511 pounds of butter valued at $23,580,942; in 1921 it produced 48,630,403 pounds valued at $17,652,481. In 1920, Quebec was producing 52,162,771 pounds of cheese valued at $13,372,250; in 1921, 54,242,735 pounds of cheese valued at $9,197,911. Dividing these numbers by the total number of employers of the butter and cheese-making plants of Quebec, it can be stated that each employer made $430 in 1920 and $285.20 in 1921, even though they had produced 409 pounds more in 1921 than in 1920."

aggressive sales techniques, and especially by keeping wages low. Workers, who were still weakly organized, paid the price and often saw their real wages cut.

Alongside these large factories, there were other enterprises even more exploitative of the working classes. A number of entrepreneurs, often with sizeable capital at their disposal, would buy large quantities of raw materials, have them partially transformed in their factories, then turn them over to master craftsmen and workers who finished the product at home. They then collected the finished product for sale to retailers. This "sweating system" was widely used in the textile, shoe, cigar, etc., industries which experienced intense competition during those difficult years. Because the retail merchant bought from whoever granted him the lowest prices, the entrepreneur then attempted to reduce his production costs by lowering salaries or, at the very least, by refusing to increase them.

In normal times, the revenues of a working-class family barely provided for essential needs, allowing only for the basic necessities. Saving money was rarely possible. When illness or death struck a family member, its only recourse was to "charge it" at the general store. During good times, the merchant did not hesitate to extend credit just as he did to stevedores, wagoners, or construction workers during seasonal unemployment. But, in the event of an economic crisis, destitution was inevitable. Unemployment, salary reduction, or the lowering of work hours drained working-class family incomes. Since there was then no social welfare system—family allocations, old-age pensions, unemployment compensation—to soften the blows of the crises, the hellish cycle of indebtedness set in. The current situation became unbearable and the future held no promise. To feed their families and pay the rent, many heads of households were obliged to borrow from exacting and unscrupulous lenders. On April 6, 1897, Michael Quinn, deputy from Montreal-Sainte-Anne to the House of Commons, revealed that "throughout the country, especially in the city of Montreal, there have been cases in which interest equivalent to nearly 3,000% per year was collected. There was," he added, "just a few days ago in Montreal, a remarkable case in which a man who had borrowed $150 was brought to court and condemned to pay $5,000 of interest on the sum of $150."[9] A return to prosperity did not always deliver them from the clutches of the usurer or the lender against security. Discouragement would set in.

---

9   *Débats de la Chambre des Communes*, I (April 6, 1897), pp. 468-469.

The enticing words of recruiting agents for New England factories, the boasting of friends and relatives returning from the "States" gave rise to great hopes among these unfortunates, many of whom took the road to a foreign country.

During those difficult years, the decline in the purchasing power of the workers and farmers and the departures to the United States seriously affected the revenues of retailers, wholesalers, lawyers, *notaires*,[10] doctors, and all persons working in the service sectors. If one adds to this the chronic oversupply of persons in the liberal professions, we can better understand why there appeared a new class of emigrants: the educated unemployed.

As a result of the combined effects of the structural transformations and the economic shifts which affected the Quebec economy from 1850 to 1929, hundreds of thousands of Quebecers left for the United States. They did this hoping that the present would be more bearable and that the future would offer them at least a chance of living with dignity. For, while it is important not to minimize the attraction which New England held for the country and city dweller of Quebec, I believe that it was despair which led most of them to emigrate.

Moreover, emigrants could count only on themselves and their families. What could they expect from their government leaders? Very little! Yet government officials were well informed. Studies, inquiries on the problem abound throughout the period. When convened in the Legislative Assembly, members of Parliament analyzed and speechified *ad nauseam* on the question of emigration to the United States, the difficulties of agriculture, colonization, the lack of jobs, the display of wealth, usury, etc. But the means at the government's disposal to stimulate and orient economic development and to counter the effects of the crises were limited, very limited. Government revenues rose from $1,651,321 in 1869, to $4,178,000 in 1897-1898 and to $39,976,000 in 1928-1929. That was too little to subsidize railroads, encourage colonization, support the exploitation of natural resources, contribute to industrialization, etc. It was also too little to give relief to the impoverished and help families in need. Just think that until the 1920s the government allocated less than 10% of its budget for welfare and public health.

---

10   [The word *notaire* in French is the equivalent of *solicitor* in Britain. The *notaire* is a lawyer who does not plead cases in court.—Editor]

Families hit by unemployment, illness, and destitution had to rely on private organizations who tried to ward off the worst by distributing firewood, food, etc. The Church played a preponderant role in these matters. However, private charity was not a solution. It was inadequate and austere. Why?

For the members of the ruling classes, the essential ingredients for the success and happiness of the working classes were often summed up in a simple equation: work and thriftiness equaled success. Each person was responsible for his own destiny and thus had to learn to pull through on his own. As a result, we can understand with what resolve those in authority denounced vices like laziness, drunkenness, lack of foresight, and luxury which were perceived as hindering the happiness and success of the working classes. Authorities inveighed so much against these vices that they ended up by giving credit to the idea that indebtedness was to be condemned whatever the reasons. In the twentieth century, Joseph-Edouard Caron, Minister of Agriculture in the Gouin and Taschereau cabinets, did not hesitate to declare that "a farmer who borrows ruins himself." Likewise, we can see more clearly why homilists preached the virtues of temperance, foresight, and saving with such insistence. These men believed that by saving tiny sums of money each day, farmers and workers would be less destitute during periods of crisis and could avoid the traps of the usurers. It is not surprising, as a result, that the elite, notably the clergy, so strongly encouraged savings institutions. We should remember, for example, that it was Bishop Ignace Bourget of Montreal who, on May 26, 1846, inspired the foundation of the savings bank and that it was the Society of Saint Vincent de Paul which sponsored the establishment of the savings bank of Notre Dame of Quebec.[11] A number of mutual aid societies were encouraged for the same reasons.

It must be admitted that all this represents a very austere conception of charity. The historian Terry Copp summarizes it in this way:

> The poor presented a delicate problem. A society dedicated to the principles of laissez-faire could not support the idea of pauperism; the obligation of each

---

[11]   Desjardins, the founder of the *Caisses populaires*, observed that these institutions played a useful role, but that they lacked an essential dimension: they did not grant loans.

individual to manage on his own in life constituted the
very foundation of the social order. Yet the poor were
always present. The fear of social disorders, if their basic
needs were not met, as well as a burning conscience
pushed the well-to-do classes to be charitable. But, in
that context, it was necessarily an austere charity . . .
Christian charity commanded one to help one's
neighbor in need, but not to encourage depraved people to
take pleasure in impoverishment.[12]

To summarize, I have tried to indicate the economic factors
which explain the emigration of Quebecers to New England. It
seems to me that those who resigned themselves to this solution
were people for whom the present was intolerable and the future a
dead end. They were also people who accepted the ideas of the
society in which they lived and who judged that the solution to
their problems had to come from themselves. Thus the frenetic
search for means of subsistence which brought them to territories
opened up for colonization, to the lumber camps, to the city, to the
Canadian and American West, and especially to the
manufacturing cities of New England. The result was that for
almost a century, there existed population movements and a
geographic mobility hardly conceivable for the Quebecer of today.

Translated by †Raymond J. Marion

[This article first appeared as "L'évolution économique du Québec et
l'émigrant (1850-1929)," in the French Institute's publication entitled
L'Émigrant québécois vers les États-Unis: 1850-1920. It has been
reviewed by the author for inclusion in this volume.]

---

[12]   Terry Copp, Classe ouvrière et pauvreté. Les conditions de vie des
travailleurs montréalais, 1897-1929 (Montreal: Boréal Express, 1978) p.
115.

The Acadian Background

†Mason Wade

[A friend of the *Institut français*/French Institute from the very start, Mason Wade attended all of its colloquia until his regretted passing. His was an encouraging as well as a knowledgeable presence. His evident approval and ongoing support of our research efforts on behalf of Franco-Americans were as necessary as they were welcome in those early years. It seemed to us, therefore, that we could not publish this collection of essays without including the article—albeit shortened–that he prepared for the institute's colloquium on the migration of Acadians to the United States. Because he remembered us in death as well as in life—bequeathing money as well as books to the French Institute—we wish here to express to him, *in memoriam,* our deeply felt gratitude.]

The Acadians were among the first European settlers in North America. Though the Sieur de Monts' initial establishment at Ile Sainte-Croix (today Dochet Island) in 1604 was a disastrous failure, with nearly half the settlers perishing of cold and scurvy that first winter, the following year a new site across the Baie des Français (Bay of Fundy) at Port Royal (today Annapolis, Nova Scotia) became the lasting center of French settlement in Acadia, so named by Verrazano who thought it Arcadia indeed.

Though this French colony, established some four years before Champlain founded Quebec, changed hands some eight times before finally passing to the English for good in 1713, the fifty or so French families established there during the seventeenth century flourished, increased, and multiplied, producing a population of 13,000 by 1755. Then the English, fearing that the Acadians, who had claimed to be neutral since 1713, would be disloyal to them in the final struggle between England and France for North America, deported more than 6,000 Acadians from Nova Scotia to the English coastal colonies from Massachusetts to Georgia, in what the victims called with remarkable restraint the *Grand Dérangement*. This first expulsion of the Acadians from their homeland was followed by another in 1758, after the capitulation of Louisbourg, of some 3,000 of the 5,000-6,000 fugitives from the first expulsion who had taken refuge in Prince Edward Island and New Brunswick. The Acadian manhunts continued in 1760 and only ceased with the Peace of Paris in 1763. By then the Acadians had been scattered to the four quarters of the North Atlantic world.

Soon after that date, however, some Acadians were allowed to return to Nova Scotia (then including New Brunswick), provided that they took the oath of allegiance to Britain's king and settled in small groups in specified places: the French Shore of Nova Scotia along the Bay of Fundy, the Moncton region of southeastern New Brunswick at the head of the Bay of Fundy, the North Shore of New Brunswick and along the Gulf of St. Lawrence from Shediac to Gaspé, Madawaska, in the northwestern region of New Brunswick, and Isle Madame and Cheticamp on Cape Breton Island. Those exiles who did not return to the Maritimes or go to Quebec, where there were several settlements of Acadian refugees, were concentrated in New England and Louisiana, where some of the original deportees had made their way and were later joined by Acadians who had been deported to France, and eventually turned over to Spain, as colonists for Louisiana, when the mother country grew weary of supporting them.

Until very recently, the Acadians were for the most part fishermen and farmers in the Maritimes. Though the Acadians had prospered as farmers on the fertile marshlands which they had reclaimed from the Bay of Fundy, they were less successful on the poorer lands that were allotted to them after their return, since pro-Loyalist Yankees had taken over their old farms. So they combined fishing and farming in order to survive. Both as fishermen and farmers, they led essentially a subsistence way of life, for they lacked the capital for commerce. In the fisheries they were long exploited by the Channel Island [Jersey] entrepreneurs who took over the fisheries of the Gulf of St. Lawrence, from Cape Breton to Gaspé, after the British conquest. These French-speaking Protestants were forbidden to intermarry with the Acadians. Though they played a considerable part in the resettlement of the Acadians by bringing Acadian refugees from France to settle their Maritime grants, their exploitation of the Acadians by buying cheap and selling dear earned them the enduring name of *les maudits Jersiais* (the damned Jerseymen). It was only with the rise of the fishery cooperatives, after 1908, that the Acadians were to escape from this bondage.

We are concerned here chiefly with the Acadians who emigrated from the Maritimes to the United States. Aside from a few deportees of the *Grand Dérangement* who remained in the English colonies, such as the "John Laundry," presumably *né* Jean Landry, whose name figures in the first census of Manchester, New Hampshire, the first major tide of migration was constituted by the Madawaska settlers of northern Maine, who found themselves American citizens, thanks to the boundary drawn by the Webster-Ashburton Treaty of 1842. These *Brayons* remained farmers and lumbermen for the most part, unlike the later immigrants from the Maritime coastal regions who, in increasing numbers from the 1860s onward, sought in the New England milltowns the jobs that were not available in a depressed Canada. The Acadian clergy sought to check this out-migration by launching colonization movements in the interior of New Brunswick and Prince Edward Island, but fishermen rarely become good farmers, and these efforts proved as ineffective as similar ones in Quebec.

The immigrants tended to go where relatives or friends had already established themselves and formed Acadian communities distinct from the *Québécois* "Little Canadas." This explains how the founding of the Acadian national society, La Société l'Assomption, was first discussed in Fitchburg, Massachusetts, on May 30, 1903, and the organization was finally founded in September of that year at Waltham. Only after developing for ten years in the States was the society's headquarters transferred to Moncton, New Brunswick, since by then it had more Canadian than American members.

Ironically, the effort to destroy the Acadian people in the eighteenth century reinforced its self-consciousness and its sense of separateness from the *Québécois*, who had a less tragic history and came under English rule half a century later and under more favorable conditions. As the Acadians' numbers grew during the latter part of the nineteenth century, they adopted their own symbols of nationality, celebrating the Feast of the Assumption (August 15) as their national day, rather than Quebec's Saint-Jean-Baptiste Day (June 24); displaying the French tricolor with a star in the blue (in honor of their patron Mary—*Stella Maris*) rather than the *drapeau fleurdelisé* invented in the nineteenth century by an *abbé* of the Séminaire de Québec; and the *Ave Maris Stella* as a national anthem, rather than *O Canada*, or *Un Canadien errant*. They held their own national conventions at irregular intervals from the 1880s onward.

The number of Acadians in New England continued to grow,

despite the fact that the clergy and the press back home consistently opposed emigration in vigorous terms. External aid to the cause of Acadian survival came as France and Quebec sought to assist the Acadians, both in the Maritimes and in New England. In 1920 the French historian Emile Lauvrière founded a France-Acadia Committee through which the French government supplied cultural support to the Acadians. For many years it also helped to support *L'Évangéline*, the principal Acadian newspaper. This French support reached its height in the 1960s under General De Gaulle, whose proclamation of cultural unity with the Acadians as well as the *Québécois* disturbed many English Canadians and enraged Mayor Leonard Jones of Moncton, the leader of the "Bulldogs" who waged a rearguard action against growing bilingualism and biculturalism in New Brunswick. Over the years, the Acadians managed to acquire a certain cultural unity; they constituted a people without a country, but with a common consciousness, heritage, and traditions.

Curiously enough, it was outsiders who did most to further this development. Though the New Englanders were largely responsible for *le Grand Dérangement*, since they were land hungry for the rich marsh meadows devoid of rocks of the Acadians, it was a New Englander, Henry Wadsworth Longfellow—inspired by Thomas Chandler Haliburton's *An Historical & Statistical Account of Nova Scotia* (Halifax: 1823 & 1829) and the oral tradition of an Acadian resident in Salem—who immortalized the tragic history of the Acadians with his epic poem, *Evangeline* (1847), which found large audiences in England and France as well as in Canada and the United States.

Then in 1886, the same year as the publication in Quebec of a French translation by Pamphile Lemay, Napoléon Bourassa published his historical novel, *Jacques et Marie: souvenirs d'un peuple dispersé*, while a few years earlier, another French historian, Rameau de Saint-Père, had published his *La France aux colonies*, which called for an Acadian revival and aroused French and French-Canadian interest in Acadian history. Rameau's influence continued strong into the twentieth century, inspiring the *Abbé* Lionel Groulx's novel, *Au cap Blomidon* (1932) and Lauvrière's highly prejudiced *La Tragédie d'un peuple* (1922). The final effect of Rameau's influence might be considered to be Robert Rumilly's *Histoire des Acadiens* (1955), commissioned by the Saint-Jean-Baptiste Society of Montreal to commemorate the bicentennial of *le Grand Dérangement*. This lively, though largely undocumented work, carried on the French tradition of assigning all evils to perfidious Albion, and all responsibility for the expulsion of the Acadians to the English, blame which in truth should be shared by the French and Americans, who all pursued their own interest with little regard for the Acadians who were mere pawns in a great imperial game of chess. Acadian history has been a scholarly battleground since the 1880s, with the *Abbé* Henri-Raymond Casgrain and Francis Parkman feuding vigorously. The feud was continued by Lauvrière, Groulx, and Antoine Bernard, against D.C. Harvey, W. Stewart MacNutt, and Bruce Fergusson. As late as the 1960s it was possible for so reputable a historian as MacNutt to write a history of the Maritime provinces with only a few passing references to the Acadians.

Fortunately, J. B. Brebner, with his *New England's Outpost: Acadia before the Conquest of Canada* (1927) and *The Neutral Yankees of Nova Scotia* (1937), produced two objective and impartial accounts of the French and British conflict in the Maritimes which are accepted as authoritative by both English and French Maritimers. His revelation that the New Englanders had played a major role in the Maritime conflict relieved a racist tendency of some writers to regard it simply as a continuation of the European Hundred Years War.

The Acadians in the United States, like those in the Maritimes, are also geographically divided between New England and Louisiana. [1] The "Cajuns" of Louisiana have higher visibility than the Acadians of New England, for they are largely concentrated in the French parishes of southwestern Louisiana, in the Bayou country. Cultural contacts have now renewed relations among far dispersed groups of Acadians. The Acadian people have once more achieved some unity after their long dispersal.

[A longer version of this article first appeared, in a French translation, as "Les Acadiens d'hier et d'aujourd'hui" in the French Institute's publication entitled *L'Émigrant acadien vers les États-Unis: 1842-1950.*]

---

[1]   [The 1990 Census figures show that, in Louisiana, 1,069,558 persons are of French origin, with 261,678 of these stating that they are French speakers.—Editor]

Acadians and Emigration

Fernand Arsenault

In the Maritime Provinces, the struggle against emigration was long and painful. What was the true extent of the emigration phenomenon of the Acadians to the United States from 1851 to 1931, and what were the factors which caused it? Why were Acadian leaders so strongly opposed to it, and what were the values underlying this exodus? What fueled the struggle against emigration? Was it, as has been stated, the clergy's fear of losing some of its power over this tiny submissive population attached to its priests, quite apart from the fear of the corrupting influence of the city? Were these the real motives behind the expenditure of so much energy by those who did everything they could to suppress what was called the plague of emigration? This study attempts to address these questions.

I.   Acadian Emigration

Exact statistics covering Acadian emigration to the United States are not available, nor does the data we have collected on this topic distinguish between Francophone Acadians and Anglophones from the Maritime Provinces. They also lump together Acadians and Quebecers who came to settle in the United States. In addition, when people speak of Americans of Acadian extraction, they can mean those who have been in the United States since the deportation of 1755 as well as those who became Americans as a result of national boundaries being redrawn, as is the case for numerous citizens of the Madawaska region of Northern Maine, resulting from the Webster-Ashburton Treaty of 1842. Then too, among the Acadians who did enter the United States voluntarily, a very great number returned to their native land. It is therefore difficult, given the current state of research, to provide precise figures on the number of Acadians who emigrated to the United States between 1850 and 1950. That study has yet to be undertaken.

For the moment, we must be content with generalizations and approximate numbers. In an article published in 1889[1] in the newspaper *L'Évangéline*, Thomas F. Anderson estimated that 150,000 people left the Maritime Provinces for New England between 1873 and 1888. It is thought that about 50,000 of them returned to live in Canada.

When we compare the demographic data presented by Muriel K. Roy in *Les Acadiens des Maritimes*[2] with those of Yolande Lavoie in *L'émigration des Canadiens aux États-Unis avant 1930*,[3] it becomes evident that emigration was truly disastrous for the Acadians of Nova Scotia, where the population dropped to 56,000 between 1921 and 1931, while in Prince Edward Island, between 1901 and 1931, the Acadian population only decreased from 13,866 to 12,962. For the demographic growth to have decreased to such an extent, in spite of the high birth rate in Acadian families (around 37% between 1921 and 1931), it is easy to infer, and this is confirmed by abundant testimony, that a great many young people emigrated to the United States. In New Brunswick, the effects of the Acadian emigration were felt most strongly between 1921 and 1931, at the height of the economic crisis. Although the Acadian population did grow during this period, from 121,111 to 136,999, an increase of 15,000 inhabitants—this, nonetheless, represents a notable decrease in the rate of growth compared to previous years. Between 1881 and 1921, the population had grown from 56,635 to 121,111. Emigration from English-speaking communities had also been quite high between 1901 and 1911, years during which the population decreased from 246,221 to 242,705. One can assume that the all-out campaigns of the Acadian leaders to stem the flow of emigration, together with the entire movement favoring colonization, i.e. clearing new land in Acadian territory, had been successful, especially among the Acadians of New Brunswick.

[1]   *L'Évangéline*, September 18, 1889, p. 3.

[2]   Muriel K. Roy, "Peuplement et croissance démographique en Acadie," *Les Acadiens des Maritimes*, Jean Daigle, ed. (Moncton, N.B.: Centre d'études acadiennes, 1980), p. 177 et seq.

[3]   Yolande Lavoie, *L'émigration des Canadiens aux États-Unis avant 1930* (Montreal: Les Presses de l'Université de Montréal, 1972).

Growth of the French-speaking and English-speaking populations in New Brunswick and Nova Scotia from 1881 to 1931[4]

New Brunswick

	Francophone Population	Anglophone Population
1881	56,635	246,775
1901	79,979	246,221
1911	98,795	242,705
1921	121,111	248,789
1931	136,999	261,101

Nova Scotia

	Francophone Population	Anglophone Population
1881	41,219	373,000
1901	45,161	409,839
1911	51,919	424,081
1921	56,619	451,481
1931	56,629	461,671

We should note that in a talk, given at the Acadian Convention held in Waltham, Massachusetts, in 1902, Dr. L. J. Belliveau spoke of 20,000 to 30,000 Acadian men and women then living in the United States.[5] These numbers undoubtedly greatly increased thereafter. In 1923, Rev. Philippe Belliveau stated in Gardner, Massachusetts, that "if Acadia had kept all of her children, we would today be in the majority in the Maritime Provinces."[6]

---

[4]   Table established on the basis of data compiled by Muriel K. Roy, "Peuplement et croissance démographique en Acadie," p. 177, and Yolande Lavoie, *L'émigration des Canadiens aux États-Unis avant 1930*, p. 39.

[5]   *Le Moniteur Acadien*, April 28, 1902, p. 6.

[6]   *L'Évangéline*, October 11, 1923, p. 3.

Who were these Acadian emigrants to the United States? According to several sources, they were usually young, and Thomas F. Anderson, states that there were as many women as men among them. The men were farmers, mechanics, carpenters, boatbuilders, lumberjacks, stevedores, fishermen, or jacks-of-all-trades, who often took jobs left vacant by those who had gone to seek a better life on the West Coast of the United States.[7] The women tended to seek work as domestic servants, as waitresses in restaurants, as cleaning women in hotels, as workers in factories and textile mills. But what forces were at work pushing these Acadian men and women to make their way to the United States?

II.   The Causes of Emigration

Economic difficulties were the primary factor pushing so many Acadians to leave their country for the United States. Although the Maritime provinces were rich in natural resources, Acadians generally lived in dire poverty at the end of the nineteenth and the beginning of the twentieth centuries. Agriculture, forestry, and fishing just barely enabled people to subsist, and industry employed but a very small portion of the population.

A Stagnating Agriculture

Agriculture had been the main occupation of the vast majority of Acadians, although this sector of the economy had never flourished. Except in the northwest region of New Brunswick,[8] Acadians had never encountered much success in this way of life, so greatly extolled by the clergy. Generally, farms were small and almost always subdivided among the sons at the death of the father. Lack of capital prevented Acadian farmers from modernizing their equipment and thus becoming more competitive. Unlike the farms of the Anglophones, those of the Acadians were located far from urban centers and the

---

[7]   *Le Moniteur Acadien*, May 12, 1881, p. 1 and *L'Évangéline*, September 18, 1889, p. 3.

[8]   *Le Moniteur Acadien*, August 24, 1905, p. 3.

railroad, which rendered access to markets difficult.[9] In addition, Acadian methods of farming, cattle raising, and soil fertilization were very old-fashioned and thus inevitably led to soil depletion. Even as late as 1937, Bishop Arthur Melanson, the first Archbishop of Moncton, made the following anguished appeal to Acadian farmers:

> When will these impoverished small farmers, who make up almost our entire population, finally forsake the old beaten paths of routine and finally adopt more enlightened, more practical and more efficient methods?[10]

Although Acadian leaders rejected the argument that it was the lack of "land for everyone" that pressured young people to emigrate,[11] the following statement nevertheless appeared in the report of the *Commission de l'émigration et de la colonisation* given at the National Convention of 1881:

> Our young people, left to their own resources on a small plot of worn-out land, have been constrained to scatter over barren hillsides, or along our seacoasts, or else have eventually left and been lost in the vast American republic where they will never know how to do anything else but vegetate and wither away.[12]

---

[9]   Aurèle Young, "L'économie acadienne, histoire et développement," *Les Acadiens des Maritimes*, Jean Daigle, ed. (Moncton, N.B.: Centre d'études acadiennes, 1980), p. 211 et seq.

[10]   Bishop Arthur Melanson, *Lettre circulaire*, 1:9, December 31, 1937.

[11]   *Le Moniteur Acadien*, May 28, 1881, p. 1. and August 12, 1881, p. 2.

[12]   Ferdinand J. Robidoux, compiler, *Conventions nationales des Acadiens. Recueil des travaux et délibérations des six premières conventions*, vol. 1 (Shediac, N.B.: Imprimerie du *Moniteur Acadien*, 1907), p. 128.

Humiliating Working Conditions

The wretched working conditions of many carpenters, loggers, and boatbuilders seems to have been another reason for the emigration of Acadians to the United States. According to a series of articles entitled *"La Baie-Sainte-Marie et l'émigration,"* published by *Le Moniteur Acadien,* unscrupulous English companies exploited the exceptional talents of the Acadian boatbuilders, making them work long hours and then paying those "poor defenseless souls" with merchandise they did not need at prices set by the companies.

> To ruin Acadians by any means and to keep them in slavery worse than the former persecution, such is the plan that has been and still is being followed to the letter. One can't hide the fact that for a number of Acadians, slavery is complete while the merchants are assured of success. Everything has contributed to this state of affairs, our qualities no less than our defects. The disastrous English influence, or if you prefer, the plundering, by heartless, dishonorable merchants, is the source of all the troubles of Baie-Sainte-Marie, especially emigration, which is the greatest of them all.[20]

These are the very same slave-like conditions imposed by the Robin Company on several generations of Acadian fishermen before the establishment of fishermen's cooperatives. Added to all this was the economic crisis of 1921, which enormously exacerbated the plague of emigration. As in 1881, or thereabouts, many Acadians wished to go to the United States so that they could accumulate savings which would then allow them to return to their country and live out their lives in comfort and independence.[21]

Thomas F. Anderson believes that the real reason which drove Acadians as well as Anglophones toward the U.S. was the desire to join up with a people which seemed to be progressing much more rapidly along the road to riches, comfort, and freedom.[22] Young

---

[20]   Ibid., August 28, 1881, p. 2.

[21]   Young, "L'économie acadienne," p. 212.

[22]   *L'Évangéline,* September 18, 1889, p. 3.

Acadian men and women undoubtedly were attracted by the prospect of the bright future of their neighboring country, which was opening itself up broadly to the industrial era, while the promises for the future engendered by the Acadian revival and the grandiose objectives of the National Conventions seemed so very utopian. Even as late as 1921, Acadia was poor and deprived; everything still needed to be done. We can then hardly be surprised that many young people, full of courage and with a yen for adventure, like their ancestors, wanted to explore other horizons.

III.   Emigration: A Serious Threat to the National Plan

Why was emigration so strongly opposed? The many reasons which prompted Acadian youth to head for the United States and other regions of Canada were really quite obvious: the Acadian leaders could not have been oblivious to them. They knew better than anyone that the Acadians of the Maritimes exercised no control at the economic, political, and religious levels. They knew this, but they had an objective, a dream which they neither wanted to have die out nor could they allow it to do so; a dream whose roots dated back to the earliest hours of colonization in America and that three centuries of tribulation had not succeeded in crushing. That dream, that ideal was described by Philippe Belliveau in the following terms during the national holiday celebration of 1901:

> For us French Acadians, our ideal and our ambition is to make ourselves worthy of our glorious ancestors, to repair the disasters of deportation . . . to retake possession by peaceful means, of that part of our patrimony which was stolen from us by our age-old enemies, to work to the very end at the slow but sure task of expansion in this very country which was the scene of our misfortune—and to take our place in the sun once again in every sphere of activity available to human beings. The struggle is painful, my dear sirs, and the obstacles difficult to overcome, and we need all that is rightfully ours so as not to fail in this undertaking.[23]

Even throughout the darkest periods of Acadian history, the

---

[23]   Ibid., September 19, 1901, p. 2.

fathers of the New Acadia, like prophets of hope, proclaimed this national objective everywhere. "We have but one goal in mind, one mission to accomplish," declared Pierre-A. Landry to the delegates of the National Convention of 1881. "This goal . . . this concept is the development of the French Acadians of Canada; it is the progress of our race . . . We wish to underscore the beautiful character of the Acadian family and to make it better appreciated."[24] And Pascal Poirier declared to the Acadians assembled at Caraquet in 1905:

> Because our origins are French, we wish . . . without isolating ourselves and without keeping only to our own kind . . . that our language, our feelings, and our hearts remain French. We desire, moreover, we, whose ancestors were the first settlers of Canada, . . . to take our place, based on our numbers, among the races which make up the Canadian confederation.[25]

Acadians have never ceased to nurture this great dream in their hearts and to give it expression in eloquent fashion, as has been demonstrated by Marguerite Maillet in her *Histoire de la littérature acadienne.*[26] Acadians sought to become masters of their own destiny, to reconquer in a peaceful manner a part of that land which centuries of injustice had deprived them of. This objective would be achieved through agriculture, colonization, industry, and, above all, education. They would also become their own masters when they abandoned their sad habit of placing themselves in the service of others and became accustomed to depend, first and foremost, upon themselves.[27] As far back as 1881, Rev. Stanislas-J. Doucet, at that time pastor of Pokemouche in New Brunswick, was stating that Acadians had to build their own homeland. He was convinced that they had within themselves the vitality and the strength needed to work out their own recovery, for they had already demonstrated this ability. The progress

---

[24]   Robidoux, *Conventions nationales*, pp. 28-30.

[25]   *Le Moniteur Acadien*, August 24, 1905, p. 2.

[26]   Marguerite Maillet, *Histoire de la littérature acadienne. De rêve en rêve* (Moncton, N.B.: Éditions d'Acadie, 1983.)

[27]   Rev. Philippe Belliveau, Fonds 24, 3-2, Centre d'études acadiennes, Université de Moncton, p. 53.

that had already been achieved would continue if they remained closely united and if they kept the flame of patriotism burning brightly.

Let our growth be natural, not artificial, and let our progress, in whatever direction, result from our own energy and our own efforts. We should, therefore, not locate our base of support elsewhere than in our own land, nor should we pin our expectations for the future on anyone but ourselves . . . taking care nonetheless to manifest our gratitude for favors received and showing our willingness to accept an occasional helping hand . . . If we were to rely too heavily on others, we would never have anything other than a weak-kneed and dependent spirit, which would hamper to some extent our march forward and would prevent us from learning to rely on ourselves. We have been obliged in the past to make do with our own resources, however meager they might be, and we will often enough be obliged to do so again. Our glory and our fame will result from the strength and the courage that we will display and the success that we will achieve by ourselves. Better for us to continue for a time to burn only candles rather than to light our way with the brighter gas lamps of our rich neighbors, even if they are our closest relatives![28]

The objective might appear to be presumptuous, but the courage of the builders was like tempered steel. They met often to spur one another on, to take count of their resources, to work out strategies, to unmask their enemies. Emigration was a formidable adversary, since it threatened to topple both religious and national institutions.

For us Acadians who are only now lifting up our heads after one hundred and fifty years of persecution and neglect, the emigration of our compatriots is a wound which corrodes the vital elements of our organization, which slows down our forward progression, and which, if it is not kept in check, will, in the end, cause our dreams of grandeur and prosperity to die out.[29]

Rev. Philippe Belliveau, not content with denouncing emigration, often journeyed to the New England States to explain to the emigrants

---

[28]   *Le Moniteur Acadien*, September 8, 1881, p. 2.

[29]   Rev. Philippe Belliveau, *Le Moniteur Acadien*, August 31, 1905; cf. also Rev. Marcel-F. Richard, *Le Moniteur Acadien*, January 6, 1897, p. 2.

the importance of the Acadian movement and to invite them to contribute to the construction of Acadia by returning home. At the Waltham Convention in 1902, while acknowledging the beneficial role of Acadians in New England, he showed them clearly that their presence was required in the ancestral land:

> I want you to grasp fully my thinking on the subject and to know once and for all that the departure of just one of you robs the tree of the nation of a part of its sap, thereby weakening the most cherished desire of us all to see you . . . return as soon as possible. The homeland stretches out its arms to you and will leap for joy on the day of your repatriation.[30]

And twenty years later, this untiring apostle would renew the same appeal to the Acadians assembled at a convention in Gardner.

> I would like to retain for our dear Acadia all of its hands and all of its hearts in order to make it great and prosperous . . . Acadia, like all of French Canada for that matter, needs all its children to survive—otherwise it will decline little by little and disappear in the end.[31]

The era of the Gardner Convention coincides with the years when emigration was bleeding especially New Brunswick dry. There was widespread economic crisis. It was thus necessary to redouble efforts to stop this potentially fatal hemorrhage. What was important was the survival of the Acadian nation, that Acadians be able to stand on their own two feet, in a highly visible fashion, so that they could take on the role which Providence had assigned to them among the nations: namely, to contribute in a unique way to Canadian civilization and to the world.[32] Understandably then, according to Rev. Philippe Belliveau and the Acadian leaders of the Maritimes, it was not in the States that Acadians would best be able to bear witness to the richness of Acadian culture. In Canada, Acadians were identified as such in each census, and their influence increased in proportion to their numbers:

---

[30]   *L'Évangéline*, September 4, 1902, p. 1.

[31]   Ibid., October 11, 1923, p. 3.

[32]   Rev. François Bourgeois, *L'Évangéline*, April 7, 1915, p. 1.

While you, compatriots of the United States, you are not classified as Acadians in the census. The State does not recognize you as such and so your absence results in a total loss for old Acadia. Because of the constitution and structure of these United States, your numbers here, large though they be, count for very little in your adopted country, submerged as you are in this vast American entity.[33]

In 1902, Rev. Belliveau had even been somewhat harsher when he reminded the Acadians of Waltham that, in spite of the admirable state of liberty and the great freedom enjoyed by American citizens, Acadians were nonetheless submerged in the midst of seventy-five million inhabitants of whom "you are to a great extent the servants" and condemned to count for very little in such an immense country.[34]

IV. Emigration: A Challenge to National Values

In order to keep Acadian men and women in the Acadian work force, the spokespersons of the New Acadia would use all possible means, even those which sometimes bordered on manipulation! A certain orator, who did not lack a sense of humor, would go so far as to ask young girls and Acadian women to use their powers of seduction to keep men close to home, especially the young ones: "And you, ladies, whose dominion over the homely sex has always been so great, keep your husbands, keep your sons, keep your lovers in our land; you can do this—a word, a glance from you can accomplish more than all the speeches and all the sermons in the world!"[35]

For Rev. Philippe Belliveau, however, it was the charms of Lady Acadia herself that would succeed in seducing Acadians: the beauty of her countryside, the perfumed aroma of her forests and fields, the breezes over her rivers, her bays, and her seas:

This is where we find vigorous health, the rosy cheeks that require

---

33   *L'Évangéline*, October 11, 1923, p. 3.

34   Ibid., September 4, 1902, p. 1.

35   Robidoux, *Conventions nationales*, p. 39.

no artifice of paint to appear wholesome; this is where one can raise children in the fear of God and sheltered from the vices that flood the streets of the city. It is here, finally, that one can breathe deeply God's pure air which vivifies, which gives the body energy and the soul contentment and serenity.[36]

These are the poetic words, inspired by patriotic love, of an indefatigable warrior, but the fact remains that it was by appealing to the national pride of Acadians and their love of the motherland that their leaders tried to keep them from abandoning the old Acadian dream.

Dignity and Pride

Deprived as they had been for almost a century of the most basic human rights, can we be surprised that Acadians had so profoundly internalized a fear of the English, a timidity, an inveterate lack of confidence in themselves, both as persons and as a people, and that consequently they were lagging behind in all fields?

These grievous psychological handicaps were quickly perceived as the worst enemies of national reconstruction. Acadian leaders mercilessly waged war against them. Rev. A.-E. Mombourquet compared the hesitations of the Acadian people to the fears of the child who would like to take his first steps:

> The development of a people is subject to the same laws as that of an individual. A people which takes its first steps along the path of progress resembles the infant who begins to walk. Like the infant who hesitates, who falters, whose steps are not steady, they have no confidence in themselves. That shortcoming does little harm to a child, but it does incalculable harm to a people. Brethren, we have to admit that the Acadian people are afflicted with that sickness. If I rightly grasp the ingrained feeling of a great number of my compatriots, I read there the word mistrust. All other peoples avidly seize upon all that science and civilization places at their

---

[36]   *L'Évangéline*, October 11, 1923, p. 3.

fingertips; the Acadian people languish woefully behind. We lack self-confidence.[37]

Their leaders would tenaciously seek to convince the Acadians of their dignity and worth by recalling to them the glorious pages of their history and the amazing resurrection of their people, thanks to the courage and audacity of their ancestors and to the expectations of God regarding Acadia.

Let us stop bowing our heads! Let us show the kind of pride that will make us lift up our eyes and look at the people around right in the eye! We are not a people to be merely tolerated. We are the descendants of a race of apostles and knights; we opened up this land to the benefits of civilization; our customs are sanctioned by treaties. We bring a special cachet to Canadian civilization. We need apologize to no one, we are proud of our people![38]

Thus, Acadians needed to convince themselves that there was a place for them in Canada and that without them the country would be less beautiful. This was the same conviction that Pierre-Armand Landry wanted to instill in Acadians at the First Convention of 1881 at Memramcook:

History teaches us that, when our forebears landed on the shores of Acadia, they possessed all the qualities required to ensure success and happiness in this life: their courage amid difficulties, their patience under trial, their dedication and heroism in defending what was dear to them, are far from belying history. Is it possible that we who are their descendants have lost those wonderful qualities that characterized them? We say that this is not so; we declare that we are the heirs of their virtues and their heroism . . .

Every page of our history yields up something to admire and make us feel proud. As a people we yield to none of our English fellow-citizens when it comes to the qualities that constitute a good citizen

---

[37]   Rev. A.-E. Mombourquet, Homily given on August 15, 1902 at Chéticamp. Reprinted in *Le Moniteur Acadien* of September 11, 1902. A.-E. Mombourquet was the pastor at Margaree on Cape Breton.

[38]   *L'Évangéline*, April 7, 1915, p. 1.

and a good Christian. Divine Providence has endowed us with as much intelligence; we are their equals in physical strength, courage, integrity, hospitality, honesty, and heroism. We lack only the same opportunities to develop these natural talents that would enable us to compete with them on an equal footing.[39]

Rev. Philippe Belliveau was saying nearly the same thing to the Acadians in the United States. Acadian pride was a guarantee of survival. Acadians must learn to assert their rights; they must proclaim their identity by proudly speaking their language at every occasion.

In other words, our greatest desire is that you show yourselves proud to be Acadians from this day forward. The Acadian is the equal of any man, whatever his nationality, his merits, and his titles, and he need not humble himself before anyone. The true Acadian will use his mother tongue with care and speak it at every opportunity instead of being ashamed of it. He will speak it without fail at home and in public, he will take care to have his children learn it at school, and he will speak English only to the English to be understood in the transaction of business, and this will always be by way of a concession to the ignorance of his listener.[40]

In 1912, Rev. Stanislas-J. Doucet, for his part, asserted that the majority of Acadians prized their mother tongue, habitually spoke it to one another, and, even though a very large number of them knew English, only a tiny minority made a habit of speaking it on a regular basis.[41] Nonetheless, he regretted that Acadians too easily accepted to speak English with their fellow English-speaking citizens. He saw in that the reason why so few Anglophones learned French. In this matter, as in many others, Acadians were much too accommodating

---

[39]   Robidoux, *Conventions nationales,* pp. 29 and 32.

[40]   Fonds 24, 31-1, Centre d'études acadiennes, Université de Moncton, p. 40.

[41]   Fonds 1915 A, Centre d'études acadiennes, Université de Moncton, p. 590.

toward the English. "They too often bow and scrape and do not receive the same in return."[42]

Rev. François Bourgeois was more outspoken. He thought that Acadians had to avoid considering a virtue what was often nothing but cowardice and servility in seeking understanding at any price when confronted by a certain degree of power.

> Only enslaved peoples are ashamed of their nationality or take the risk of admitting to it only with many apologies so as not to provoke the fury of fanaticism.
> What goads me to the highest degree of indignation is that these slaves try to mask their servility and cowardice under the guise of practicing the beautiful and necessary virtue of prudence.
> As if it were prudent to repress feelings of dignity and self-respect to gain some slight passing and immediate advantages or else to receive a few small compliments on one's foresight.
> Oh, what vulgar traffickers of a race's national patrimony![43]

For a long time, the great obstacle to the progress of Acadians was this lack of national pride. In 1905, the members of the Société nationale l'Assomption from the Moncton region chose the instilling of national pride as their main objective, in order to stop the anglicization of Acadians.[44] As for Rev. Stanislas-J. Doucet, when the Monument to Our Lady of Assumption was being blessed at Rogersville in 1912, he did not hesitate to use the voice of Our Lady, patroness of Acadian people, to implore his fellow citizens to choose the road of dignity and progress.

> Does this monument not tell us, nay, cry out to us: "Forward?" Do you not hear the sweet voice of Our Lady speaking to you behind the symbolic veil, telling you, indeed telling us all: "Rise up, Acadians, always rise; never crawl. Raise your heads and stride forward as should the sons of heroes, of confessors of the faith! Forward! Climb the mountain of genuine progress, of that progress

---

[42]   *L'Évangéline*, July 3, 1912, p. 4.

[43]   Ibid., August 26, 1915, p. 1.

[44]   Henri-P. LeBlanc, Fonds HPL24, 3-9, Centre d'études acadiennes, Université de Moncton.

which is good, which is beautiful, which promotes, which
ennobles, which enhances . . . life.
Thereby will you prove yourselves worthy of my maternal and
powerful protection.[45]

In the eyes of the leaders, Acadia had a position to occupy and a
role to play in Canada and North America. That position and that role
were based upon the concerted efforts of all Acadians. That is why
those who yielded to the temptation to give their lives to a different
homeland were judged very harshly. Those who emigrated were
nothing but "vile mercenaries," who spent their energy and
undermined their health in the service of strangers, for the profit of
Yankee industrialists who treated them like real slaves.[46] If Acadians
were to take cognizance of their dignity, they would never again be
willing to hire themselves out to foreigners. Their bodies and their
souls carried the wounds of long centuries of struggle, but they would
always be the "descendants of a virile race" hammered into shape by
great challenges—the descendants of a race "which cannot perish."[47]

Love for Acadia

It was, therefore, by appealing to the national pride of Acadians, to
their faithful commitment to the land of their ancestors, and to their
great dream of becoming masters of their own land that Acadian
leaders made manifest their strong opposition to the expatriation of
the youth of Acadia, of those on whom they counted to make their
dream come true. Such pride and commitment had their natural roots
in love. In the final analysis, it was in the name of love that Acadians
were urged to remain in Acadia. Love of Acadia appeared to be the
greatest of all Acadian values, at least for those who became conscious
of their history and their identity. This love was inextricably woven

[45]   Fonds 1451A, Centre d'études acadiennes, Université de Moncton, p.
590.

[46]   Robidoux, *Conventions nationales*, p. 32; *Le Moniteur Acadien*, March
24, 1881, p. 2; *Le Moniteur Acadien*, October 1, 1908, p. 3.

[47]   Dr. L.-J. Belliveau, Lecture delivered at the Convention in Waltham,
Massachusetts. Reprinted in *Le Moniteur Acadien*, August 28, 1902, p. 6.

into the fabric of a deep attachment to religion, the French language, the family, and ancestral traditions. For this reason, it is sometimes very difficult to discern whether religion or patriotism more strongly motivated the Philippe Belliveaus, the Pascal Poiriers, the Stanislas-J. Doucets, the Marcel-François Richards and so many others. Quoting Rev. Rozier, Rev. Marcel-François Richard declared to the Acadians gathered at a Convention in Waltham in 1902:

> In all human languages three words have a very great importance, as they also have in the life of nations: altar, flag, home. The altar stands for religion; the home for family; the flag for the homeland. Of these three words, I shall retain but one—homeland, because this word includes the two others.[48]

This triple love: for religion, hearth, and homeland—these three values—were very much linked in the minds of the builders of Acadia. Rev. Richard further developed his thought by asserting the following, in the same address to his American compatriots:

> The love Acadians feel for their homeland has sustained them and has allowed them to rebuild it again. Today that edifice rests on solid and durable foundations and nothing can tear it down or destroy it, because it is protected by a vigorous race, decided and determined to defend it unto death.
>
> The Acadians, therefore, have a homeland; it is Acadia. There is no need to recall to the present generation all that their fathers endured and suffered to bequeath this sacred heritage to their descendants. Would it not constitute an apostasy, which would forever dishonor the Acadian name, were one to refuse to transmit the memory of it?[49]

Thus, the Acadian has a homeland he loves and wishes to serve. This homeland is located mainly in the ancestral lands, in the Maritime Provinces; that is where Acadia must become great and prosperous. "It is there that Acadians justly claim the right to exist as

---

[48]   *Le Moniteur Acadien*, August 28, 1902, p. 2.

[49]   Ibid.

a nationality with the privileges thereunto pertaining, in the land which they founded and established."[50]

This love for Acadia, recalled Rev. Richard, is endowed with the same tenderness and the same devotion that Acadians have always pledged to Mary and to their own mothers. They are all the more attached to this Acadia that it has suffered so much; their duty and their happiness will derive from their dedication to bringing about the recognition of its rights and legitimate aspirations.[51]

A Love That Makes Light of Borders

In spite of those vibrant appeals to fidelity, pride, and love of Acadia, thousands of young Acadian men and women went to the United States in search of better living conditions. As their numbers increased, they grouped together in a number of New England cities where they constituted truly Acadian colonies. At the turn of the century, Little Acadias came into being in Waltham, Gardner, Worcester, Fitchburg, Lynn, and Boston, Massachusetts, as well as Old Town, Maine. Having progressed in financial status and education, and motivated by the proposals of National Conventions and Acadian patriots, these emigrants suddenly realized that they had not really left Acadia behind. After many years of separation, very strong bonds continued to keep them tied to old Acadia.

Even the fiercest opponents of emigration, either through necessity or enlightenment, began to soften their language and value the presence of their brothers and sisters on American soil. In great part due to these Acadians, who had remained faithful to their values, Acadia was extending beyond its geographical limits. Love was once again encompassing its own; in this case, it transformed traitors and mercenaries into patriots. So taught Rev. Marcel-François Richard, one of the most authoritative spokesmen of the great Acadian vision, at the 1902 rally in Waltham.

---

50   Ibid., August 28, 1908.

51   Ibid., September 11, 1902, p. 2.

The homeland is to be found wherever live those of its children who have preserved the ancestral faith, the national language, the family traditions, and the love of the religion of their forefathers. So, I maintain that there is not on this American continent a race which has a better right to a national existence than the tiny Acadian people because, true to the traditions they brought with them from old France, Acadians have remained steadfastly faithful to the altar, the home, the flag, to religion, the family, and the homeland . . . Acadia, the homeland, is in exile, but she is not dead; . . . suffering, plundering, exile, martyrdom have not succeeded in making Acadians become turncoats and apostates. Their bonds to the Church, the flag, and the home have given them strength and heroism, and they have again rebuilt their homeland, more beautiful, more spacious, and more glorious.[52]

So it is that Acadia was really and truly present in these United States at the start of the twentieth century. Many Acadian immigrants had brought with them, along with their bags and old suitcases, a genuine love of Acadia, which they religiously maintained. Numerous witnesses strongly affirmed as much at the turn of the century. Pierre-Armand Landry declared to the National Convention at Caraquet [New Brunswick] in 1905:

In former times, when I saw some of our compatriots leaving their land to settle in the United States, I considered such cases to be a calamity and a great loss to the Acadian cause. Now, I realize that those who went there brought with them a love of their homeland which does not weaken abroad, but instead grows stronger and more organized; I have modified many of my first impressions. The splendid example set by our brothers in the United States through their intelligent and tenacious efforts to maintain the use of their language, keep alive the love of their homeland, and continue to preserve intact their links to us is a source of great edification for me and gives me hope that they are not lost to Acadia.[53]

Jean-H. LeBlanc, spokesman for the *Commission des Acadiens des États-Unis* at that same convention in Caraquet, reported that "The

---

[52] Ibid. [In 1905, Rev. Richard was appointed a domestic prelate and was thereafter known as Monsignor Richard. He passed away in 1915.—Editor]

[53] Ibid., August 24, 1905, p. 5.

Acadians of Massachusetts and neighboring states are happy, and indeed almost astonished at their gigantic progress in consolidating and preserving both their French language and their Acadian nationality."[54] And, in a series of articles entitled "Echoes from Lynn, Mass.," published in *Le Moniteur Acadien*, there appeared more than once the following kind of statement: To raise our children to be good citizens, let us instill in them "a solid and genuine faith, a love and veneration of their glorious ancestors, a pride in their name and race, a devotion and generosity to their country."[55] In 1906, an attempt was made to reassure the Canadian cousins. One reads in *Le Moniteur*: "Rest assured . . . there have been some defections, it is true, but we notice also on the part of the near totality of our colony, a generous *élan* for matters of religion and nationality."[56]

As for the spirited Rev. Philippe Belliveau who, until his death, always fought against the emigration of his compatriots, he enthusiastically declared at Waltham in 1902 that the Acadians of the United States had given the lie to his pessimistic predictions and that they had maintained the constituent elements of the Acadian nation: faith and patriotism.

> In the annals of history can the world offer a happening such as this, that of a handful of brave men who dared to lift up their heads in the midst of a region numbering seventy-five to eighty million inhabitants and fearlessly demand the right to maintain their distinctive nationality, with all that this includes? No, gentlemen, it is only among a people tried by fire, sword, blood, and tears, that you will find such tenacity, courage, and, might I say, audacity!"[57]

Pascal Poirier went further yet when he declared to the Convention at Caraquet: the patriotism "enlightened and zealous, fearless and

---

54   Ibid., September 7, 1905, p. 5.

55   Ibid., June 21, 1898, p. 1; Ibid., September 11, 1902, p. 3.

56   Ibid., April 12, 1906, p. 2.

57   *L'Évangéline*, September 4, 1902, p. 1.

blameless, of our brothers in the United States can serve today as an example to those of us who have remained at home."[58]

A Contribution to the "National" Plan

Without easing up on their efforts to stem the tide of emigration to the United States, the Acadian leaders, as early as the end of the nineteenth century, came to realize that their compatriots on the other side of the border were a powerful element among French-speaking peoples and were, by that very fact, contributing to making manifest the values of Catholicism and French civilization in the world. The fathers of the new Acadia admitted the fact that these brothers and sisters, whom they had always loved, but often judged very harshly, had very likely responded to the plan of Divine Providence which, for good reasons, had placed on this earth "the diversity of races with their respective idioms."[59] In the opinion of Judge Pierre-A. Landry, the Acadians of the United States were amply contributing to the success of the mission of Acadia in North America and the world.

> Yes, ladies and gentlemen, your numbers here, your rapid growth in the cities of this State of Massachusetts, the progress you are making here, your taking hold in the industries of this beautiful country, the esteem and trust that you inspire, first of all in your clergy and then in your employers, the peace and contentment that you enjoy here, all this indicates to me that Divine Providence, in its sometimes mysterious but always equitable plan, did not send you here to destroy the tiny Acadian race. You have not abandoned the homeland, you have enlarged it, you have not weakened it, you have strengthened and invigorated it, and made it better able to fulfill the plan of Divine Providence for it.[60]

Like Marcel-François Richard, Pierre-Armand Landry thus saw the borders of Acadia expanding due to the dynamism of his American

---

[58]   *Le Moniteur Acadien*, April 24, 1905, p. 2.

[59]   *L'Évangéline*, October 18, 1923, p. 3.

[60]   *Le Moniteur Acadien*, September 4, 1902, p. 1.

compatriots: "We are brothers . . . and members of the great and proud French family,"[61] he stated forcefully at that memorable meeting in Waltham. Rev. Philippe Belliveau would add, "the most closely knit unity between us is a necessity if we wish to fulfill the mission assigned to us, among ourselves, and with our French-Canadian brothers."[62]

The Acadians of the United States heard the message clearly. Several weeks after the festivities in Waltham, they founded, in September 1902, the Société Mutuelle l'Assomption, whose goal was "to unite and help all Acadian Catholics no matter where they live; to make ardent and enlightened patriots of them." According to Jean-H. LeBlanc, it was to this society that the Acadians of the United States attributed a great many of their accomplishments. He added, "Allow me to tell you (in the name of your compatriots of the neighboring republic) that they do not forget the memories of the homeland, that they are always ready to extend a fraternal and helping hand to you in the execution of national duties."[63] In Acadia, the newspapers considered it a duty to inform the Maritime Acadians on a regular basis of the principal events affecting the lives of their American cousins. For their part, the Acadian leaders felt liked and appreciated in the New England States, and they never let pass an opportunity to go there and fan the flame of Acadian patriotism.

Better Acadians Make Better Americans

But what would happen if the Acadians did not fulfill their dream of establishing a New France in America? Would all those efforts and struggles be for naught? Not according to Pascal Poirier. Even though they remained but a minority, Poirier stated at Lynn, Massachusetts, during the Lafayette Celebration of 1898, that the Acadians of the United States and Canada had an important role to play if they knew enough to remain French and Catholic: "On account of the qualities of

---

61   Ibid.

62   Ibid.

63   Ibid., September 7, 1905, p. 5.

our race and because of our sweet divine religion, we will, all together, constitute the sap . . . of the country to which we will bear allegiance and which will have extended to us the protection of its flag." In his customary witty style, the senator then proceeded to explain what it means to be Catholic and French.

> As I understand it, to be Catholic does not consist in believing oneself to be better than the Protestants, for example; but rather, if that be possible, to **be** better. To be Catholic does not consist in saying: "Lord, Lord, I thank you for not being like those Methodist Salvation Army, P.P.A. publicans, but to try within the humility of one's heart to **be** better than these brothers to whom the Kingdom of God belongs as it does to us and whom we are expressly commanded to love as we love ourselves . . .

> To be French and to remain so forever, means to practice those virtues which are more especially characteristic of the French: politeness, urbanity, sincerity, honesty in business dealings, avoidance of fraud and deliberate bankruptcy as dishonorable deeds, some enthusiasm, even a lot of it, tremendous loyalty in all things, courage, cheerfulness, wit, and withall the jealous preservation of French as one's mother tongue.

> But, you will tell me, Americans have all these qualities except for the language. True. But do they have them in the same degree, and do they have them in the same manner?[64]

Thus, by becoming fully Catholic and French, Acadians would create a lineage which would be "strong," healthy, and beneficent.[65] This would be their greatest contribution to the American nation. As for Rev. Philippe Belliveau, he concluded his address to the Convention at Waltham with the following statement, which he would have liked every United States citizen to hear: "The more you preserve these treasures [your Catholic faith, the beautiful French language, our customs and traditions], the more will you take pride in being

---

[64]   Pascal Poirier, "Discours aux Franco-Américains." Convention at Waltham, Massachusetts. Reprinted in *Le Moniteur Acadien*, November 8, 1898, p. 1.

[65]   *Le Moniteur Acadien*, November 8, 1898, p. 1.

Boatbuilding among the Acadians of the Nova-Scotian southwest experienced a rather prosperous period during the 1860s and 1870s. The interior of the two counties contained rich reserves of wood, and the many rivers furnished the water power needed by the sawmills. This allowed the Acadians to use their boatbuilding talent. This ability, recognized not only by the Acadians, but coveted by the Anglophone entrepreneurs of Yarmouth, was such that Acadian villages such as Wedgeport, Meteghan, Anse-des-Belliveau, etc., emerged as important boatbuilding centers.[7] The international reputation of Yarmouth as a sizeable port was largely due to the Acadians.

If the preindustrial period had been profitable for these Acadian communities, the positive economic consequences of this era would soon collapse. It began with the repeal of the Treaty of Reciprocity with the United States. Since 1854, this commercial agreement had allowed the Acadians of Digby and Yarmouth free access to the American market for certain foodstuffs such as fish, butter, eggs, and potatoes.[8] The treaty had also taken away the tariff rights on imported wood which had further stimulated the local forest industry. But, in 1866, when the treaty was revoked, the profitable American market was also taken away. Prices experienced a sudden decline and the rural economy rapidly fell into a recession. At the end of the century, a correspondent from Meteghan was still bemoaning the consequences of the end of the treaty: "the price of wood still keeps very low in [the] U.S. market, making it hardly worthwhile to send any there."[9]

Boatbuilding, which had known a golden age during the preindustrial period, would also drop precipitously during the last decades of the century. An industrial and continental vision would arise in opposition to the former maritime approach. The national political approach of Prime Minister Macdonald would encourage industrialization by a series of tariffs imposed on imported commodities and by a railway system the length of the

---

[7]   David Alexander and Gerry Panting, "The Mercantile Fleet and its Owners: Yarmouth, Nova Scotia, 1840-1889," in P. A. Buckner and David Frank, eds., *Acadiensis Reader*, vol. 1 (Fredericton: Acadiensis Press, 1985), pp. 311-312.

[8]   Under the direction of J. Alphonse Deveau, *Clare—La Ville Française*, vol. 2 (Yarmouth: Imprimerie Lescarbot Limitée, 1985), p. 253.

[9]   *Digby Weekly Courier*, October 5, 1894, p. 1.

country that would bring about the downfall of the shipyards. [See Figure 5]

Cities such as Yarmouth, formerly centers of traffic based on maritime commercial activity, became almost stagnant. Yarmouth would drag along in her decline the Acadian centers of construction in the hinterland which had largely furnished the boats during the periods of soaring commercial activity.

But would not the new national objective of industrialization furnish employment for the Acadians affected by the recent economic changes? In principle, yes, and, during the decade 1880-1890, the manpower of Yarmouth would more than quadruple,[10] and many of the new arrivals would be Acadians[11] in search of employment in the mills, especially in the textile factory of the Yarmouth Duck Yarn Company. But, regardless of the promising impetus at the outset, by the turn of the century, industrialization had already begun to decline. High freight tariffs on the railway line, a saturated market, and the lack of what Acheson calls a "viable regional metropolis . . . to provide the financial leadership"[12] are partial reasons for this downfall throughout the Maritimes. Again the Acadians found themselves searching for steady employment that could ensure a decent standard of living. The repeal of the Treaty of Reciprocity, the end of the boatbuilding era, and the collapse of the industrial firms forced many of the Acadians of southwestern Nova Scotia to make important decisions regarding their personal and collective future. Even the clearing of land was no longer a valid option to counter economic distress. The infertile lands on which these Acadians lived could not meet the family needs, and it was only by dint of great difficulty that they succeeded in having a kitchen garden behind the house. Father Ange Le Doré, superior of the Eudist congregation, which had recently founded the Collège Sainte-Anne at Church Point, expressed, with a certain humor, what befell any and all future farmers at Baie Sainte-Marie.

---

10   T. W. Acheson, "The National Policy and the Industrialization of the Maritimes, 1880-1910," *Acadiensis Reader*, vol. 1, p. 178.

11   Del Muise, "The Great Transformation: Changing the Urban Face of Nova Scotia, 1871-1921," in *Nova Scotia Historical Review*, vol. 2, no. 2, 1991, p. 15.

12   T. W. Acheson, *op. cit.* p. 200.

Brother Henri spent almost a year clearing, in the middle of a
wood, a sort of garden the size of one of the patches of the Rock.
On the other hand, the stones that he had removed allowed him
to form a complete enclosure of walls high enough to protect
his vegetables against the north winds.[13]

In such a situation, the attraction of the American factories
was strong, sometimes too strong to resist, even though this meant
abandoning what was most familiar and most dear. Father
Dagnaud, superior of the Collège Sainte-Anne, at the turn of the
century, grasped the core of the dilemma when he asked himself,
"How can it be stopped? No work in the fields, little at home, no
servants, one must, nevertheless, live."[14] And when the
newspaper, L'Évangéline, announced modern rapid steamships[15]
that could make the crossing between Yarmouth and Boston in
seventeen hours, all obstacles to departure seemed to fade away.

Opposing Forces

According to Fernand Arsenault, Acadian emigration, which
posed a challenge to the national ideal, motivated the Acadian
leadership to embark upon a campaign to encourage people to
remain in Acadia.[16] The members of the "national" elite,
especially the clergy, threw themselves into this combat because
they saw in the exodus the possible loss of the two pillars of the
Acadian identity—language and faith. The clergy at this time
thought that these entities existed in a symbiotic relationship,
which meant that the loss of the first would necessarily bring
about the loss of the second.[17] Thus, the clergy, conscious of its

---

13   Father Ange LeDoré, May 30, 1893, in Le Saint Coeur de Marie,
August 15, 1893, copy at MG 1, vol. 1, f (2), Archives of the Acadian Center
at Université Sainte-Anne.

14   "Father Pierre-Marie Dagnaud to Father Ange LeDoré, April 8, 1900,"
Church Point College, 1897-1917, Archives of the Eudist Congregation.
Copy in the Archives du Centre acadien, Université Sainte-Anne.

15   L'Évangéline, August 8, 1888, p. 4.

16   Fernand Arsenault, op. cit.

17   See Neil Boucher, "Le bon Dieu parle français," Cahiers de la société
historique acadienne, vol. 23, nos. 3 and 4, 1992, pp. 135-142.

mission, had to intervene. In New Brunswick, pastors like Monsignor Marcel-François Richard, and priests like Father Stanislas Doucet and Father Philippe Belliveau went to great lengths to denounce the calamity of the emigration of Acadians towards the urban centers of New England. It is no mere coïncidence that Monsignor Richard was the first president of the Société de colonisation acadienne-française [French-Acadian Colonization Society], whose mandate was to encourage Acadians to remain at home and take possession of the land. Did southwest Nova Scotia have as energetic a leadership, one that would allow it to make this region of Acadia duplicate what was going on in New Brunswick? Unfortunately, it is impossible for us to answer this question in a categorical fashion.

In the formation of a professional elite, lay as well as clerical, southwest Nova Scotia fell behind New Brunswick. The question of institutions of higher education is largely responsible for this state of affairs. In 1864, the Acadians of New Brunswick were endowed with a college when the Holy Cross Fathers founded Saint Joseph's in the Memramcook Valley in the southeast of that province. Ten years later, Monsignor Marcel-François Richard founded his own institution at St. Louis, in Kent County. But it was not until the end of the century, that is to say, in 1890, that the Eudist Fathers opened Sainte-Anne's at Church Point. During this interval of a quarter of a century, between the founding of Saint Joseph's College and that of Sainte-Anne, certain Acadians of the southwest had attended the college at Memramcook, but these were but a handful of people. Thus, while the professional Acadian elite took root in New Brunswick, it was merely at the embryonic stage in Nova Scotia. This state of affairs becomes particularly evident if we examine the clergy. Fathers Richard, Doucet, and Belliveau had been preaching the anti-emigration theme[18] long before the Acadian parishes in southwest Nova Scotia even saw one of their own ordained a priest. It was only at the turn of the century that Acadian priests from the southwest would come to settle in their native region as pastors of parishes.[19] Before this time, these Acadians had been served by foreign priests, especially

---

18   Marcel-François Richard and Stanislas Doucet were ordained to the priesthood in 1870, while Philippe Belliveau had been ordained in 1855.

19   In 1898 Edouard LeBlanc and Désiré Comeau were ordained, the first two from Sainte-Marie. In Yarmouth County, the first was Augustin Amirault of Pubnico-East in 1901.

by those of Irish and Scottish origin.[20] Could this clergy really comprehend the havoc that emigration could inflict on this population already living in a minority situation in Nova Scotia? The *Moniteur Acadien* seemed to have seized upon the essentials of the situation when it wrote:

> It must be remembered that in recent times, the Church has not been represented at Baie Ste-Marie in a manner really useful to the Acadian population. The clergy that formerly . . . had been the glory and honor of Acadia ended up being composed solely of priests who are strangers to our nation . . . and consequently, [they are] without concern for the true interests of their flock, without serious regard for their needs, and perhaps also without sufficient influence to direct their temporal and spiritual progress.[21]

But even in this bleak situation, an exception can *perhaps* be found. I emphasize *perhaps,* for it concerns a person who was vehemently opposed to the Acadian emigration, as he expressed it in the local press, but who never identified himself, preferring to use the pseudonym of "Alpha." In the inventory of the newspaper, *L'Évangéline*, prepared by the historian-archivist Thérèse Roy, the probable identity of "Alpha" is attributed to Father Alphonse Parker. We have good reasons to support this theory.

Of Irish origin, Alphonse Parker received his training in the classics in France and England, and he completed his studies in theology at the Grand Séminaire of Montréal. As soon as he arrived in the Acadian parishes of the southwest, he quickly gained the esteem of his flock, for he seemed more supportive of their cause than his predecessors had been. When Alpha's articles started to appear in *L'Évangéline*, Father Parker was pastor of Saint-Bernard, a village next to Weymouth where the newspaper of Valentin Landry was printed. He quickly became interested in this weekly newspaper, as was borne out by a biography of Father Parker written shortly after his death:

> . . . Father Parker was quite actively involved in Acadian

---

20   To better understand the size of this phenomenon see Neil Boucher, "Acadian Nationalism and the Episcopacy of Mgr. Edouard Alfred LeBlanc, Bishop of Saint John, New Brunswick (1912-1935): A Maritime Chapter of Canadian Ethno-Religious History" (Doctoral dissertation, Dalhousie University, 1992).

21   *Le Moniteur Acadien*, June 23, 1881, p. 2

journalism. *L'Évangéline* had recently been founded in Weymouth . . . From his rectory at Saint-Bernard's, Father Parker was a vigilant sentry. He encouraged this work of the press that he wanted to see as being Catholic above all else.[22]

Here then is one possible link between Father Parker, Alpha, and *L'Évangéline*. But other factors lead us to believe that Father Parker and Alpha are one and the same person. First of all, Alpha and Alphonse, the given name of this priest are somewhat alike. Secondly, the articles of Alpha appeared in two languages, thus pointing to a bilingual author, which Father Parker was. Also, the articles are very frequently strewn with religious metaphors recalling the time of innocence before the exodus and often clinging to the idea that the loss of faith is the greatest risk facing the emigrant, a topic which would have preoccupied a member of the clergy above all. But it is perhaps the editor of the newspaper himself who confirms this hypothesis. In an editorial of that time, Valentin Landry declared, ". . . our valued correspondent Alpha, *who is a priest*, has made some suggestions . . ."[23]

Many facets of Alpha's thesis are comparable to those being proclaimed by other Acadian "nationalists" during this period. Three principal themes can be found in Alpha's ideology, the first being the innate physical and spiritual ills of the American factory, which inevitably brought about the ruin and destruction of naïve Acadians faced with the dangers lurking there: "Working in the ill-ventilated and morally tainted atmosphere of the factory, how can the young Acadian become physically or morally strong?" Alpha asked. He warned of the possible consequences. "Learning a strange tongue and forgetting his own, mocked at if he uses the signs and symbols of his Holy Religion; acquiring the vices as well as the expensive habits of a new civilization, the place he works in is surely his ruin."[24]

The second theme which can be found in Alpha's articles, just as in those of many Acadian "patriots" of the era, was a return to the lifestyle of the ancestors as a model, in opposition to the tide of emigration which was growing ever stronger. It was in the

[22]   Rev. J. M. Doucet, "Un noble fils de la Verte Erin," *L'Évangéline*, March 3 1927, p. 7.

[23]   *L'Évangéline*, July 10, 1889, p. 2. The emphasis is ours.

[24]   *L'Évangéline*, April 10, 1889, p. 3.

Figure 1

Principal Acadian Villages of
Southwest Nova Scotia

Saint-Bernard

Meteghan

Rivière-aux-Saumons

Yarmouth

Sainte-Anne-du-Ruisseau

Wedgeport

Pubnico

Figure 2

The Widely Dispersed Acadian Villages of
Southwest Nova Scotia

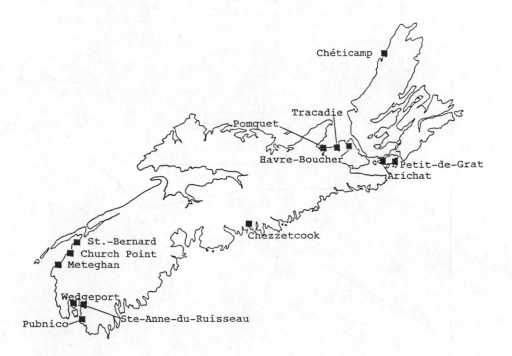

Figure 3

Acadian and "Other" Populations
of Digby and Yarmouth Counties

1827-1931

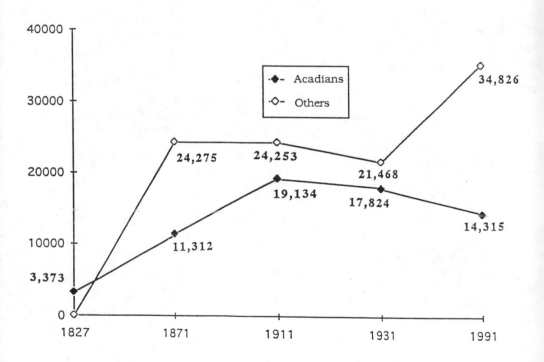

Sources: *Census of Nova Scotia*: 1827
           Census of Canada, 1871, 1911, 1931, and 1991

Figure 4

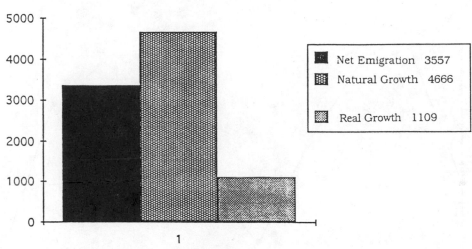

Digby County
1871-1911

Net Emigration   3557
Natural Growth   4666

Real Growth   1109

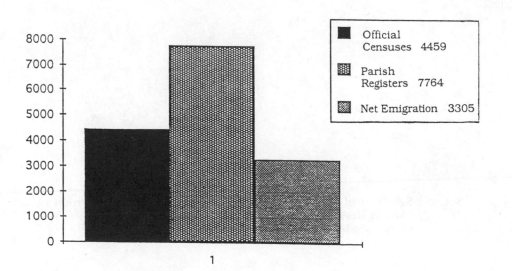

Yarmouth County
1871-1911

Official Censuses   4459

Parish Registers   7764

Net Emigration   3305

Figure 5

Naval Construction in Clare
1876-1885

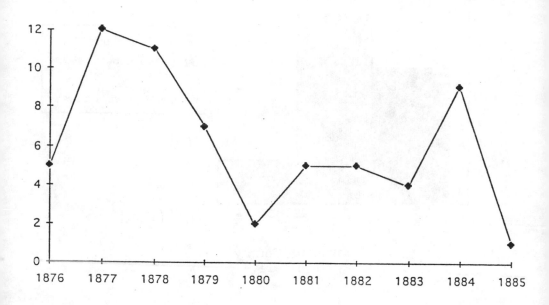

Source: See "List of Vessels on the Registry Books of the Dominion of
Canada the 31st day of December 1886," *Sessional Papers*, Vol.
14, No. 15, 1887, pp. 2-396.

II

FRANCO-AMERICAN
COMMUNITIES

«FRANCO-AMÉRICANIE» IN 1900

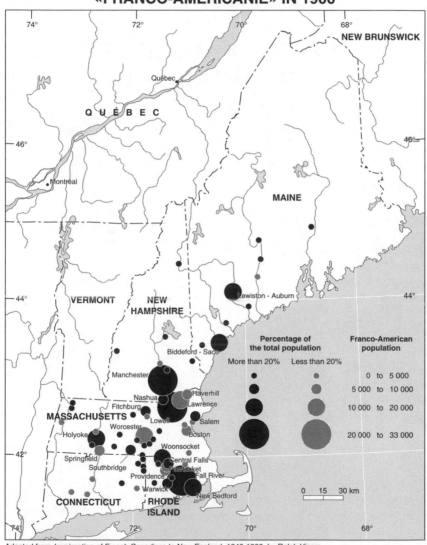

NEW BRUNSWICK

QUÉBEC

Québec

Montréal

MAINE

VERMONT

NEW HAMPSHIRE

Lewiston - Auburn

Biddeford - Saco

Manchester

Nashua   Haverhill
Fitchburg   Lawrence

MASSACHUSETTS   Lowell
Worcester   Salem
Holyoke   Boston

Woonsocket

Springfield
Southbridge   Central Falls
Providence   Pawtucket
Warwick   Fall River

CONNECTICUT   RHODE
ISLAND   New Bedford

Percentage of the total population

More than 20%   Less than 20%

Franco-American population

0 to 5 000
5 000 to 10 000
10 000 to 20 000
20 000 to 33 000

0   15   30 km

Adapted from *Immigration of French Canadiens to New England, 1840-1900*, by Ralph Vicero.

An Overview of Studies Relating to Franco-American Communities in New England

Gerard J. Brault

The French Canadians of New England and parts of New York State share a common national origin, mother tongue, and religion and are the only people who have referred to themselves consistently for the past eighty years or so as Franco-Americans. Americans of French ancestry do not, as a rule, identify with this group and French Canadians residing outside the New England area have evolved differently.

Ralph D. Vicero's research enables us to pinpoint scores of New England French-Canadian settlements in 1900. While there have been changes since then, Franco-Americans are largely concentrated in the same areas today. Vicero identifies eleven regions that account for ninety percent of the group at the turn of the century. For the most part, these are small and medium-sized cities and towns situated on rivers that provided power for the textile industry. Some, like Chicopee, Massachusetts, were old Yankee settlements that, as Vera Shlakman has shown, were transformed into factory towns. Others, for example Lowell, Massachusetts and Manchester, New Hampshire, were planned industrial communities.

Richard S. Sorrell has suggested that, among other factors, a large Franco-American population constituting a high percentage of the total population in Woonsocket, Rhode Island, set it apart from other such communities in the 1920s. Writing independently, Peter Haebler has observed that a relatively lower percentage of French Canadians combined with other circumstances to accelerate social integration of the group in Holyoke, Massachusetts, beginning in the mid-1880s. It appears possible, then to classify Franco-American communities on the basis of regional considerations and of relative size and percentage of the population.

Region 1: northern Maine, principally the Upper Saint John Valley. This area along the Canadian border became part of the

United States by the terms of the Webster-Ashburton Treaty in 1842. It is still largely agricultural today.

Region 2: western Vermont and northeastern New York State. This is a string of small communities, most of them rural, along the Vermont/New York State border but extending as far west as Ogdensburg, N.Y. Historically, these towns served as way stations for French-Canadian immigrants who eventually settled elsewhere in New England. However, industrial Burlington and Winooski, Vermont, as well as Cohoes, New York, bear much resemblance to the next category of communities.

Region 3: middle and southeastern New England (including southern Maine). The vast majority of Franco-Americans have resided in this area since the latter part of the nineteenth century. It is possible to distinguish four subgroups in this region. Here the relative size and percentage of the Franco-American population rather than the size of the city or town itself or its location are the main determinants. There have been demographic changes since 1900 but probably not enough to alter the following general classification. The cutoff between subcategories A, B, C, and D and the notion of "high" and "low" percentages are admittedly somewhat arbitrary.

A. **High Franco-American population (more than 5,000) and high percentage (more than 20%) of total population in 1900.**[1]

Fall River, Mass.	33,000 (32%)	*Biddeford-Saco, Me.	10,650 (62/16%)
Lowell, Mass.	24,800 (26%)	Nashua, N.H.	8,200 (34%)
*Manchester, N.H.	23,000 (40%)	Warwick, R.I.	7,700 (36%)
*Woonsocket, R.I.	17,000 (60%)	Fitchburg, Mass.	7,200 (23%)
Holyoke, Mass.	15,500 (34%)	Salem, Mass.	6,900 (20%)
New Bedford, Mass.	15,000 (24%)	Southbridge, Mass.	6,027 (60%)
*Lewiston-Auburn, Me.	13,300 (46/18%)	Central Falls, R.I.	6,000 (33%)

* Very high Franco-American population as well as very high percentage of total population.

---

1   All of the following statistics, including percentages, in Tables A through D, are taken from Ralph D. Vicero, "Immigration of French Canadians to New England, 1840-1900: A Geographical Analysis" (Ph.D. dissertation, University of Wisconsin, 1968).

B. Medium-sized Franco-American population (1,500-5,000) and high percentage (more than 20%) of total population in 1900.

Lincoln, R.I.	5,000 (56%)	Thompson, Ct.	2,500 (39%)
No. Adams, Mass.	5,000 (20%)	Westbrook, Me.	2,400 (33%)
Waterville, Me.	4,300 (45%)	Willimantic, Ct.	2,400 (27%)
Chicopee, Mass.	4,200 (22%)	Gardner, Mass.	2,400 (22%)
Spencer, Mass.	4,000 (52%)	Suncook, N.H.	2,200 (60%)
Marlboro, Mass.	4,000 (29%à	Sanford, Me.	2,100 (35%)
Webster-Dudley, Mass.	3,650 (28/32%)	Palmer, Mass.	2,100 (27%)
Ware, Mass.	3,200 (39%)	Warren, R.I.	2,000 (39%)
Killingly-Brooklyn, Ct.	3,100 (34%)	Claremont, N.H.	2,000 (31%)
Old Town, Me.	3,000 (52%)	Laconia, N.H.	2,000 (25%)
Berlin, N.H.	3,000 (34%)	Sutton, Mass.	1,900 (57%)
Adams, Mass.	3,000 (20%)	Skowhegan, Me.	1,850 (36%)
Somersworth, N.H.	2,840 (40%)	Danielson, Ct.	1,800 (64%)
Plainfield, Ct.	2,800 (58%)	Coventry, R.I.	1,800 (34%)
Brunswick, Me.	2,800 (54%)	Millbury, Mass.	1,700 (38%)
Putnam, Ct.	2,800 (42%)	Grafton, Mass.	1,600 (33%)
Burrillville, R.I.	2,500 (40%)		

C. Medium-sized Franco-American population (1,500-5,000) and low percentage (less than 20%) of total population in 1900.

Taunton, Mass.	4,200 (14%)	Leominster, Mass.	2,000 (16%)
Waterbury, Ct.	4,000 (9%)	Augusta, Me.	1,900 (16%)
Cambridge, Mass.	3,200 (4%)	Pittsfield, Mass.	1,700 (8%)
Northampton, Mass.	2,800 (15%)	Meriden, Ct.	1,700 (7%)
Lynn, Mass.	2,700 (4%)	Hartford, Ct.	1,650 (2%)
Concord, N.H.	2,000 (18%)	Brockton, Mass.	1,600 (4%)

D. High Franco-American population (more than 5,000) and low percentage (less than 20%) of total population in 1900.

Worcester, Mass.	15,300 (13%)	Boston, Mass.	5,800 (1%)
Lawrence, Mass.	11,500 (18%)	Haverhill, Mass.	5,500 (15%)
Providence, R.I.	8,000 (5%)	Pawtucket, R.I.	5,200 (13%)
Springfield, Mass.	6,500 (11%)		

James Vander Zanden sees a correlation between the rate of assimilation and the ratio of the incoming group to the resident population, concentration in the same area, rapidity of influx, and proximity to homeland. Plainly, more research is needed before the question of the relative rate of assimilation in Franco-American cities and towns can be settled. For the time being I am merely suggesting that Franco-American life evolved somewhat differently in the regions and in the types of communities classified here.

*   *   *

There is much information about Franco-American communities in parish histories. These accounts stress the role of priests and other notables—chiefly doctors and lawyers—who led parishes through the early and middle phases of their development. The best narratives provide anecdotal and illustrative material of great interest to the cultural and social historian. Monsignor Adrien Verrette's monumental history of Sainte-Marie Parish in Manchester, New Hampshire, is an outstanding example of the genre.

Early on, Franco-American leaders developed a well thought-out ideology balancing French-Canadian values and traditions—notably loyalty to Roman Catholicism and to the French language—with American beliefs and customs. Robert Rumilly's indispensable *Histoire des Franco-Américains* chronicles the many battles waged by the group's leaders to build strong parishes and to preserve these ideals.

These narratives often list the achievements of prominent individuals, but usually furnish few details about the living and working conditions of ordinary Franco-Americans. We must turn, then, to other ources for this information. What follows is an survey of studies—many of them quite recent and mainly by historians and social scientists—which consider Franco-Americans not only as parishioners but also as individuals earning a living and relating to other members of the community. Most do not deal exclusively with Franco-Americans and offer useful comparisons with other ethnic groups which settled in the same localities.

Region 1: northern Maine. James P. Allen analyzes all ethnic and religious groups in Maine from the earliest settlements to the 1960s from a geographical perspective. His maps show the pattern of Acadian and French-Canadian migration and early expansion in the Upper St. John Valley. He notes that, by the 1920s, professionals in northern Maine were predominantly Franco-American and that many small businesses were owned by members of this group. However, in the late 1960s, the overwhelming majority of the descendants of the Acadian and French-Canadian settlers in the area were still living in poverty. Many left the region for other parts of Maine and New England during and after World War II.

Region 2: western Vermont and northeastern New York State. Vicero has charted French-Canadian migration patterns in Vermont but we do not have a comparable analysis for New York State.

In the summer of 1933, Elin L. Anderson took a census of Burlington and also had two-to-three-hour interviews with a representative sample of 459 persons including 144 Franco-Americans. She noted modest residential mobility in the second generation. Burlington's Franco-Americans made up 75% of the work force in the cotton and woolen mills. Though considerable occupational strides had been made by the city's Irish and Jewish populations, slower progress had been realized by the French Canadians.

David J. Blow's account of the development of the French-Canadian community in Winooski, across the river from Burlington, varies very little from that found in most parish histories. The author pays attention to eight community leaders, some of whom became active in local government and politics from 1867 to 1900, but the occupations of the majority of the settlers from Quebec must be deduced from the presence of a large woolen mill in that town. By 1900, erosion of French-Canadian manners and mores is said to have been well under way with the acculturation and occupational mobility of the second generation.

Daniel J. Walkowitz analyzes worker protests in two adjacent cities in New York State, Troy and Cohoes, from 1855 to 1884. During the 1870s, there was a large influx of French Canadians in Cohoes, a one-company town controlled by textile interests. Typically, fathers worked as laborers, mothers kept house, and unmarried children, especially females, found jobs in the mill. In 1880, two-thirds of the cotton mill workers in Cohoes were living in poverty. Stigmatized in New England as anti-labor, French-Canadian cotton mill operatives played a different role in Cohoes. Ably organized by Samuel Sault, they were successful in a nine-day walkout in 1880, but defeated in a bitter four-month strike two years later. Walkowitz underscores the importance of kinship and neighborhood ties, and French-Canadian/Irish solidarity in this unique experience.

Region 3: middle and southeastern New England (including southern Maine). Most studies concern localities that I have categorized as **A.** Other communities include: **B.** Brunswick and Old Town; **C.** Augusta; and **D.** Lawrence. Finally, the Franco-American population of one city (Newburyport) is slightly lower than the minimum size (1,500) I considered in my tabulation.

Augusta. Maurice Violette analyzes the upwardly mobile Franco-American elite, chiefly businessmen and professionals, in this city. From 1880 to 1920, nearly 300 small businesses were started by Franco-Americans, but not a single one survived. However, there was marked improvement after that date. In 1922, *Le Club Calumet* was founded and eventually became a leading civic and social organization. Until World War II, membership was strictly limited and no one engaged in an *occupation salissante* [dirty work] was permitted to join. *Le Club Calumet* sponsored many social events and entertained prominent political and sports personalities. Violette believes life was easier for Franco-Americans in other areas where they predominated. He considers that the club did much to overcome local prejudice.

Biddeford. Michael J. Guignard estimates that in 1969 the number of Franco-Americans in this city was nearly 15,000, or 75% of the total population, one of the highest percentages of any industrial center in New England. This is one of the few studies that includes autobiographical information, especially about growing up in a Franco-American community. Guignard also analyzes the editorial and news content of *La Justice,* a newspaper which ran for fifty-five years and, at its peak, in 1930, was read by at least half of Biddeford's Franco-Americans. The group in this locality produced a modicum of successful businessmen, politicians, and professionals, but the vast majority remained working class. In the 1960s, many Franco-American high-school-aged youths were still following in the footsteps of their parents and grandparents in Biddeford's mills.[2]

Brunswick. William N. Locke chronicles the steady growth of the local French-Canadian population that was attracted to this community by the Cabot cotton mill. By 1877, the company owned 100 tenements that were soon regarded by the town as a breeding-place for disease. In 1886, a diptheria epidemic claimed the lives of seventy-four French Canadians, nearly all of them children. From naturalization records, Locke concludes that a majority of Brunswick's French Canadians emigrated from four contiguous counties on the south shore of the St. Lawrence. As late as 1940, Franco-Americans, who comprised nearly one half of the town's population, owned only one-fourth of its property.

Fall River. A 104-page chapter of Philip T. Silvia, Jr.'s dissertation focuses on labor, politics, and religion as it affected French Canadians in this city at the end of the nineteenth century. The new arrivals were shocked by labor violence and were instructed by their pastor not to participate in strikes. English and Irish mill workers controlled higher paying jobs and forced French-Canadian males to seek employment in other occupations. The immigrants from Quebec never actually forced down wages and were merely the scapegoats until other groups arrived to bear the brunt of such attacks. French Canadians had enterprising religious and lay leaders, but lagged behind other nationalities in becoming naturalized. Other chapters detail operative dissatisfaction with living and working conditions in Fall River.[3]

Holyoke. Constance M. Green found much data relating to this city's French Canadians in the Lyman Mills Papers preserved

---

2   [For additional information on Biddeford see Michael J. Guignard's article entitled "The Franco-Americans of Biddeford, Maine" in this volume.—Editor]

3   [For additional information on Fall River, see Philip T. Silvia's article, entitled "Neighbors From the North: French-Canadian Immigrants vs. Trade Unionism in Fall River, Massachusetts" in this volume.—Editor]

in the Baker Library at Harvard University. She also quotes newspaper accounts describing the arrival of these immigrants and the anxious reaction of other workers. According to the author, even third-generation Franco-Americans do not socialize with other groups.

Kenneth W. Underwood describes the various ecological areas of the city including the workers' wards consisting mostly of tenement buildings built before 1900. The French Canadians experienced some residential and social mobility but lagged considerably behind other groups.

In his study of Holyoke's French-Canadian community from 1865 to 1910, Peter Haebler argues that the process of social integration here was accelerated because the group never represented more than a third of the local population. He also points out that the city offered more diversified employment opportunities. By the mid-1880s and with the arrival of other groups, French Canadians began to show greater employment flexibility but developed no occupational specialization except in the textile industry. After 1890, many joined labor organizations notably the carpenters' union where they formed a French-speaking local in 1889. By 1910, more than half the group's children were attending Franco-American parochial shcools. There was a significant increase in intermarriage in the second generation.

Ernest B. Guillet gives a detailed account of Franco-American literary activity in the Paper City. Theatrical productions of light comedies, melodramas, and religious plays were enjoyed by all classes of society especially after the turn of the century. More than twenty dramatic groups are known to have been active between the two World Wars and fifteen troupes visited the city during this period. Appendices list various theatrical events and the local literary production including works by the poets Joseph Lussier and Gabriel Crevier.

Lawrence. In 1912, this textile city gained international notoriety as the scene of a strike involving 30,000 workers led by the Industrial Workers of the World, or Wobblies, and the American Federation of Labor. Donald B. Cole describes the events leading up to this dramatic confrontation between capital and labor. The city was regarded as a hotbed of Anarchists and Socialists but, the author points out, its reputation for violence was mainly due to Italian immigrants and outside strike organizers. The strike was over in eight weeks and was a major victory for labor. In 1911, one survey showed that people were crowded 300 to 600 per acre in certain areas; one mill had 1,000 accidents in less than five years. About the time the French Canadians began arriving in the city in large numbers, life expectancy was twenty-five years. Irish workers showered much abuse upon the new arrivals, but later shifted their attention to the more recent immigrants from southern Europe.

Lowell. George F. Kenngott's social survey provides an arresting picture of appalling living and working conditions in this city at the turn of the century. Street maps, color-coded for different kinds of dwellings, show the precise location of French-Canadian and other districts. Photographs tell a good deal about crowded and unsanitary housing in certain quarters although not everyone lived in such squalor. The author anaylyzes 287 family budgets including 69 by French Canadians and finds the latter to be poorer than other immigrants.

Frances H. Early concentrates on the early years of the French-Canadian colony here from 1868 to 1886. She does not rule out the possibility that a number of immigrants worked in industry in Quebec cities before moving to New England. Early has verified the identity of 1,448 French Canadians in Lowell in 1870. Nearly 75% of the group consisted of nuclear families headed by two parents. One out of every three families took in at least one additional person, usually a boarder. The author provides maps showing the exact location of residences. French Canadians did not immediately settle in a single quarter but in widely-scattered locations throughout the central part of the city. The district known as Little Canada developed into a ghetto in the 1880s and 1890s. In 1875, 41% of the French Canadians were living below the poverty line while another 11% were just breaking even. Families headed by a skilled worker and with working children fared much better.[4]

In 1936, Camille Lessard published *Canuck*, a novel set in Lowell in 1900. It is the harrowing tale of a young woman forced to work in the mill for three years by a tyrannical father and it has a certain documentary value. The author was employed for four

---

[4]   [For a more complete analysis, see Frances Early's article in this volume entitled "The Settling-In Process: The Beginnings of the Little Canada in Lowell, Massachusetts, in the Late Nineteenth Century."—Editor]

years in a textile mill in Lewiston, Maine, at the beginning of the
present century before landing a job at *Le Messager*, the local
Franco-American newspaper.[5]

Manchester. The personnel records of the Amoskeag
Manufacturing company from 1911 to 1935, a file of some 80,000
individuals—including my father, Philias J. Brault, who worked
there as a tentering machine hand, then as a trucker, from 1910 to
1916—are preserved in the Manchester Historic Association. Once
the largest textile mill in the world, the Amoskeag began to show
losses in 1921 and shut down permanently in 1935 leaving more
than 11,000 persons unemployed. Toward the end, about half of its
employees were French-Canadian. Daniel Creamer and Charles
W. Coulter analyze the effects of the shutdown based on a 10%
sample of the Amoskeag files and on interviews with 227 former
employees. The report includes data about the attitudes, migratory
habits, and social characteristics of laid-off workers.

Tamara K. Hareven studies the laborers of Manchester from
1880 to 1940 based on a sample of 2,000 individuals identified by
Amoskeag records and on 100 oral interviews. Hareven and her
husband Randolph Langenbach published several of these
interviews in 1978. The recollections of French Canadians
predominate in this volume. In two articles, Hareven finds that
Manchester's Franco-Americans exercised a good deal more
control over their lives than was earlier believed. Workers left
their jobs very casually, virtually certain that they would be
rehired by the company. Few participated in educational and
recreational programs designed by the Amoskeag to create a loyal
labor force. Discriminated against in the 1870s and 1880s, French
Canadians were able, early in the twentieth century, to develop
their own informal network of contacts along kinship and ethnic
lines to obtain better jobs and treatment in the mill. In 1922, a
disastrous nine-month strike had serious repercussions on the
Franco-American community. Two-thirds of work separations
had been voluntary before the strike; now most became dismissals
or layoffs.

Nashua. Writing in the 1950s, when about half of this city's
population was of French-Canadian origin, George F. Theriault
underscores the growing social differentiation between older and

---

5   [For a study of this novel, see Janet Shideler's article entitled
"Camille Lessard-Bissonnette (1883-1970)—Immigrant Author and
Itinerant Journalist," in this volume.—Editor]

younger Franco-Americans. He traces the beginnings of this transformation to the years 1910 to 1930, a period marked by gradual upward occupational mobility and a move to less congested middle-class neighborhoods. The younger generation's attitudes and outlook changed even more significantly after 1930 as a result of intermarriage, military service, television, and travel. There was little popular or clerical resistance to this evolution. Theriault estimates that, by the early 1950s, 13,000 of the city's approximately 17,000 Franco-Americans identified closely with the group. During the period 1930 to 1950, Nashua's Franco-American community grew in size but, from an ethnic point of view, merely held its own.

Newburyport. This locality in Massachusetts, designated by a team of social anthropologists at Harvard as Yankee City, had a population of 17,000 at the time of the investigation in 1930-1935. The six-volume work reporting on various aspects of community life is regarded as a classic today. However, Newburyport's Franco-American group—1,466 persons—constituted only 8.6% of the population. Warner and Lunt are perhaps best known for their diagram distinguishing six levels of social stratification, Upper Upper Class to Lower Lower Class, and for mapping the city's twelve ecological areas. The authors found that 40.1% of the French Canadians were Lower Lower Class, 23.8% Upper Lower Class, and 15.3% Lower Middle Class.

Details about French-Canadian residential patterns, social stratification, family, church, language, school, and associations were given by Warner and Srole in a separate volume concerning Yankee City's eight ethnic groups. The authors ascribed the French Canadians' generally lower status to the fact that many still planned to return to Quebec (hence were not as interested in upward occupational mobility as one might have expected), to the group's patriarchal family structure, and to the role of the Church.

Old Town. Marcella Sorg has recently completed a computer-assisted study of this community numbering more than 3,000 Franco-Americans. She has linked names found in parish baptismal and marriage records to federal and city records from 1840 to 1900. According to Sorg, Old Town, known for its pulp mills, had an essentially transient French-Canadian population until the 1870s and 1880s at which point it became a more stable community.[6]

Allen observes that Old Town drew its French-speaking immigrants from Beauce County in Quebec, but also from the Upper St. John Valley and the Maritime Provinces.

Woonsocket. Marie-Louise Bonier's history includes a list of 117 French-Canadian families who arrived in this city from about 1815 to 1861, twenty-three of them from St. Ours. Data was gathered from a census made in 1846, addresses on unclaimed mail at the post office, as reported in the local newspaper, county birth and marriage records, and burials in the Baptist cemetery.

In 1926, Bessie B. Wessel undertook a survey of Woonsocket's public school population. She determined that French Canadians intermarried at a lower rate than other nationalities, but that the percentage increased significantly with the third generation (first, 7.8%; second, 8.8%; third, 35%). The group's most distinguishing feature was its loyalty to its mother tongue. Occupational mobility showed steady signs of improvement. Parochial schools, which enrolled more than half of the city's Franco-American children, refused to cooperate in this survey. In 1926, the "Sentinelle Affair" was working up to a climax.

Richard S. Sorrell has studied this controversy which kept Woonsocket in a turmoil in the 1920s. He shows that this struggle pitted not only certain Franco-Americans led by Elphège Daignault, the editor of a local French-language newspaper, *La Sentinelle*, against the Irish Catholic hierarchy in the Diocese of Providence, but also militant against moderate Franco-American nationalists. The author relates the incident to nineteenth-century Canadian history and to the contemporary American scene. He concludes that the *Sentinellistes* attracted a number of prominent Franco-Americans but gained little support among the group's clergy. Nevertheless, they were able, in 1927, to turn out some 10,000 persons at one protest rally. The movement collapsed when its leaders were excommunicated and its newspaper banned. Sorrell shows that this episode can serve as a prism for analyzing

---

6   [For more detailed information on Old Town, see Marcella Harnish Sorg's study in this volume entitled "Community Formation in Old Town, Maine, 1835-1930: Endogamy and Natal Origins Among the Acadians."—Editor]

key elements in Franco-American culture and community life.[7]

In his Ph.D. thesis, Pierre Anctil offers a revisionist interpretation of Franco-American history and ideology. In the latter part of the nineteenth century, the emerging French-Canadian petty bourgeoisie in Woonsocket, consisting mainly of tradesmen and professionals, developed the *survivance* ideology to create a kind of state within a state in order to further its own interests. These middle-class entrepreneurs fought assimilation because it would destroy their monopoly over their working-class clientele. The Franco-American petty bourgeoisie was on the ascendancy until it was ruined by the Great Depression. Anctil views the *Sentinelliste* crisis as a phase in the long struggle within the Catholic hierarchy over the papacy's temporal and spiritual power. However, he believes that this dispute played a far less important role in shaping the ideology of Franco-American working-class people than did, say, Brother André, who made repeated visits to New England at the turn of the century, and Marie-Rose Ferron, a celebrated stigmatic in Woonsocket in the 1920s and 30s. Anctil reminds us that Jack Kerouac describes a similar kind of Franco-American mysticism in his *Visions of Gerard.*

Marcel J. Bellemare examines Woonsocket's Social neighborhood in the 1960s, an inner-city area with about 10,000 residents, and the site of an Urban Renewal Project. The section has long been a French-Canadian stronghold and, at the time of the investigation, had a heavy blue-collar majority. Bellemare spent a year, mostly in a neighborhood variety store, observing people's behavior, and eventually focused on twenty-three, then on seven individuals (four males, three females). He found the old tenements in this blighted area to be surprisingly comfortable and pleasant. There were a large number of young families with small children; 43% of the district's residents were high-school dropouts, 22.3% earned less that $4,000 per year. According to the author, the Social neighborhood is not so much a place as a network of relationships between persons who are feebly and loosely held together by a parish (St. Ann's). There is a conflict between the older and younger generations arising out of the clash of French-Canadian and American values.

---

[7]   [For a more detailed analysis, see Richard Sorrell's article in this volume entitled "*La Sentinelle* and *La Tribune*: The Role of Woonsocket's French-Language Newspapers in the Sentinelle Affair of the 1920s."—Editor]

The authors cited here base themselves on different kinds of evidence, making comparisons difficult, and several works are unpublished doctoral dissertations, and thus have not yet been subjected to critical review in scholarly journals.

One thing is clear: we have begun to view Franco-American communities in a different light. There was and there is a remarkable French-Canadian *survivance* in New England but there was also an extraordinary survival. French Canadians suffered enormous hardships in Quebec and in their adoptive land. Until recently, this story remained largely untold.

Translated by the author

[This article first appeared as "État présent des études sur les centres franco-américains de la Nouvelle-Angleterre" in the French Institute's publication entitled *La situation de la recherche sur les Franco-Américains*. It has been reviewed by the author for inclusion in this volume.]

Bibliography

Allen, James P. "Catholics in Maine: A Social Geography." Ph.D. dissertation, Syracuse University , 1970.

Anctil, Pierre. "Aspects of Class Ideology in a New England Ethnic Minority: The Franco-Americans of Woonsocket, Rhode Island (1865-1929)." Ph.D. dissertation, New School for Social Research, 1980.

Anderson, Elin L. *We Americans: A Study of Cleavage in an American City.* New York: Russell & Russell, 1964. Appeared originally in 1937.

Bellemare, Marcel. "Social Networks in an Inner-City Neighborhood: Woonsocket, Rhode Island." Ph.D. dissertation, Catholic University of America, 1974.

Blow, David J. "The Establishment and Erosion of French-Canadian culture in Winooski, Vermont, 1867-1900," *Vermont History,* 43 (Winter, 1975), 59-74.

Bonier, Marie Louise. *Débuts de la colonie franco-américaine de Woonsocket, Rhode Island.* Framingham, Mass.: Lakeview Press, 1920.

Cole, Donald B. *Immigrant City: Lawrence, Massachusetts, 1845-1921.* Chapel Hill: University of North Carolina Press, 1963.

Creamer, Daniel and Coulter, Charles W. *Labor and the Shut-Down of the Amoskeag Textile Mills.* Philadelphia: Work Projects Administration, 1939.

Early, Frances H. "French-Canadian Beginnings in an American Community: Lowell, Massachusetts, 1868-1886." Ph.D. dissertation, Concordia University,1979.

Green, Constance M. *Holyoke, Massachusetts: A Case History of the Industrial Revolution in America.* New Haven: Yale University Press, 1939.

Guignard, Michael J. "Ethnic Survival in a New England Mill Town: The Franco-Americans of Biddeford, Maine." Ph.D. dissertation, Syracuse University, 1976. Published by the author as *La foi, la langue et la culture: the Franco-Americans of Biddeford, Maine* in 1982.

Guillet, Ernest B. "French Ethnic Literature and Culture in an American City: Holyoke, Massachusetts." Ph.D. dissertation, University of Massachusetts, 1978.

Haebler, Peter. "*Habitants* in Holyoke: The Development of the French-Canadian Community in a Massachusetts City, 1865-1910." Ph.D. dissertation, University of New Hampshire, 1976.

Hareven, Tamara K. "Family Time and Industrial Time: Family and Work in a Planned Corporation Town, 1900-1924." *Journal of Urban History* 1, No. 3 (1975): 365-389.

_____. "The Laborers of Manchester, New Hampshire, 1912-1922: The Role of Family and Ethnicity in Adjustment to Industrial Life." *Labor History* 16, No. 2 (1975): 249-265.

Hareven, Tamara K., and Langenbach, Randolph. *Amoskeag: Life and Work in an American Factory City*. New York: Pantheon, 1978.

Kenngott, George F. *The Record of a City: A Social Survey of Lowell, Massachusetts*. New York: Macmillan, 1912.

Lessard, Camille. *Canuck*. Lewiston, Maine: Le Messager, 1936.

Locke, William N. *Pronunciation of the French Spoken at Brunswick, Maine*. Greensboro, N.C.: American Dialect Society, 1949. Publication of the American Dialect Society, No. 12.

_____. "The French Colony at Brunswick, Maine: A Historical Sketch." *Les Archives de Folklore* 1 (1946): 97-111.

Rumilly, Robert. *Histoire des Franco-Américains*. Montreal: L'Union Saint-Jean-Baptiste d'Amérique, 1958.

Shlakman, Vera. *Economic History of a Factory Town: A Study of Chicopee, Massachusetts.* Northampton, Mass: Department of History, Smith College, 1935. Smith College Studies in History 20, nos. 1-4.

Silvia, Philip T. Jr. "The Spindle City: Labor, Politics and Religion in Fall River, Massachusetts, 1870-1905." Ph.D. dissertation, Fordham University, 1973.

Sorg, Marcella Harnish. "Genetic Demography of the Franco-American Community of Old Town, Maine: Community Formation, 1840-1903." Paper read before the Franco-American Studies section, Northeast Modern Language Association Convention, March 30, 1979.

Sorrell, Richard S. "The Sentinelle Affair (1924-1929) and Militant *Survivance*: the Franco-American Experience in Woonsocket, Rhode Island." Ph.D. dissertation, State University of New York at Buffalo, 1975.

Theriault, George F. "The Franco-Americans in a New England Community: An Experiment in Survival." Ph.D. dissertation, Harvard University, 1951.

_____. "The Franco-Americans of New England." In *Canadian Dualism: Studies of French-English Relations*, Mason Wade, Ed. Toronto: University of Toronto Press, and Quebec City: Presses Universitaires Laval, 1960: 392-411.

Underwood, Kenneth W. *Protestant and Catholic: Religious and Social Interaction in an Industrial Community.* Boston: Beacon, 1957.

Vander Zanden, James. *American Minority Relations.* New York: Ronald, 1963.

Verrette, Adrien. *Paroisse Sainte-Marie, Manchester, New Hampshire. Cinquantenaire, 1880-1930.* Manchester, N.H.: Imprimerie Lafayette, 1931.

Vicero, Ralph D. "Immigration of French Canadians to New England, 1840-1900: A Geographical Analysis." Ph.D. dissertation, University of Wisconsin, 1968.

Violette, Maurice. *The Franco-Americans: A Franco-American's Chronicle of Historical and Cultural Environment: Augusta Revisited.* New York: Vantage, 1976.

Walkowitz, Daniel J. *Worker City, Company Town. Iron and Cotton-Worker Protest in Troy and Cohoes, New York, 1855-84.* Urbana: University of Illinois Press, 1978.

Warner, W. Lloyd, and Lunt, Paul S. *The Social Life of a Modern Community.* New Haven: Yale University Press, 1941. Yankee City, 1.

Warner, W. Lloyd, and Srole, Leo. *The Social Systems of American Ethnic Groups.* New Haven: Yale University Press, 1945. Yankee City, 3.

Wessel, Bessie B. *An Ethnic Survey of Woonsocket, Rhode Island.* Chicago: University of Illinois Press, 1931.

The Settling-In Process:
The Beginnings of the Little Canada in Lowell, Massachusetts, in the Late Nineteenth Century

Frances H. Early

By the turn of the century, the neighborhood known as "Little Canada" in Lowell, Massachusetts, was the center of familial and community life for many French Canadians. Massachusetts government officials somewhat stridently decried the overcrowded, unsanitary living conditions in Little Canada at this time and reported—with a certain nativist indignation—on the "fearful mortality" among French-Canadian children in this ethnically exclusive neighborhood.[1] However, one French-Canadian woman, interviewed in 1975, recalled her childhood days in Little Canada in the early twentieth century with much pleasure and little regret:

> The population was so big in Little Canada that the blocks were real close. But all families got along beautiful and we were all French people . . . . Everybody helped everybody, which is not done nowadays like it was then, but, people that had the money—if one needed help that means they would get together and they would come over and help. The whole thing was that there were too many people in a small area. But if you look back to it, I still think I'd like to be there.[2]

Two related questions readily spring to mind. How do we come to terms with the two conflicting views of Little Canada presented here? And, what was the French-Canadian community experience in Little Canada really like? To understand the true meaning of community for French Canadians, as well as the

---

[1]   George F. Kenngott, *Record of a City: A Social Survey of Lowell, Massachusetts* (New York: The Macmillan Co., 1912), p. 71.

[2]   C. L., "Little Canada," oral interview, Lowell, May 3, 1975, typewritten transcript, pp. 5 and 22.

response of non-French Canadians to Little Canada, we must seek to uncover the whole process of social change which led French Canadians first to leave their homeland in Quebec, then to choose Lowell as their new home, and finally to re-create and adapt their inherited culture and way of life to a new, alien, and at times hostile society and culture.

French Canadians first began settling in Lowell in appreciable numbers in the late 1860s and 1870s. In those early years, before Little Canada existed, textile corporation recruiting agents scoured agriculturally depressed regions of rural Quebec in search of factory hands. These agents were in many cases French Canadians themselves. In addition to convincing people to migrate, agents frequently made travel arrangements, introduced newcomers to already-settled immigrants, and helped them to find temporary lodgings. In Lowell, Samuel P. Marin, destined to become one of the French-Canadian community's leading citizens, got his start as a recruiting agent in 1865. He performed his job effectively:

> There were but few French-Canadians here prior to 1865, when Mr. S. P. Marin was employed by some of the manufacturing companies to visit his native Province of Quebec, to present to the people the advantages to be derived from "a change of base," as well as of occupation, and to induce them to remove with their families from the Valley of the St. Lawrence to the Valley of the Merrimack. They have since come in greater numbers than any other class of immigrants, and have effected a permanent foothold here, and the cry is, "Still they come."[3]

French Canadians frequently heard about towns like Lowell from neighbors, friends, and relatives, people who had already lived and worked in or visited New England. For instance, Félix Albert, one such immigrant, came to Lowell accompanied by his wife, Desneiges, and their nine children, on the advice of a brother and with the consent of his parish priest.[4] A woman born in

---

[3]   Charles Cowley, "The Foreign Colonies of Lowell," *Contributions of the Old Residents' Historical Association*, vol. 2 (Lowell, 1883), p. 175.

[4]   See Félix Albert, *Immigrant Odyssey: A French-Canadian Habitant in New England*, edited and introduced by Frances H. Early; translated by Arthur L. Eno, Jr. (Orono: University of Maine Press, 1991). This edition

Lowell in 1908 and interviewed in 1975, remembered that families already established in Lowell often encouraged their kin back in Quebec to migrate to Lowell.[5]

In the 1860s, French Canadians sometimes travelled to Lowell in carts or wagons. One woman related a story, part of her family history mythology, of how her cousin had come to Lowell in the nineteenth century:

> Napoléon Lord lived in St. Hilaire, where he was the town baker. When his clients started leaving him to go to the States, 'Poléon thought he might as well follow. He hitched his chestnut mare to his baker's cart and, telling his wife and children that he would be back for them as soon as he was settled, set out with some of the family belongings to find a new home.[6]

After a five-week journey to Lowell, Napoléon secured temporary work. But because he "had the soul of a baker," he went back to his trade as soon as he had amassed a little savings. "Then began another long trek, back to Canada this time, to fetch his family. . . With the coming of his family and the opening of his bakery, 'Poléon sank into the oblivion of the small merchant."[7]

By the post-Civil War era, few French Canadians made the trip to Lowell in a baker's cart. They took the train. Louis Biron, the publisher of *L'Etoile,* Lowell's French-language newspaper, describes the French-Canadian immigrant arrival scene in the last century:

> I can remember the old days. We used to see the

---

contains both the original French version, published in 1909 under the title *Histoire d'un enfant pauvre*, and an English translation.

[5]   C. L., "Little Canada," p. 10. For a similar but more colorful rendition of this practice, see Louis Hémon, *Maria Chapdelaine* (Toronto: The MacMillan Co., 1938), p. 62. [This is an English edition. There are many French-language editions of this novel, written in 1912, serialized by *Le Temps* in Paris from 27 January to 19 February 1914. It was first published in Montreal in 1916.—Editor]

[6]   Jacques Ducharme, *The Shadows of the Trees* (New York: Harper and Bros., 1943), p. 47.

[7]   Ibid., pp. 47-48.

Canadians arrive at the railroad station. There would be the father, with a burlap bag on his shoulder containing the spare clothes. His wife would walk beside him carrying some household article, like a clock. Then children would follow, each one carrying something. They would walk into town, and if they hadn't seen anyone they knew, would stop each person they met to find out where such and such a one lived whom they had known in Canada. Generally they came from the same town as those already here. When they would find the house they were looking for, they would spend a few nights there, until the father and the oldest children found work. Then they would take an apartment of their own.[8]

In 1975 a descendant of *Canadiens* confirmed Biron's story: "Every week there were some arrivals at the depot, the old depot. They would come in by the hundreds."[9] The Albert family, mentioned earlier, were part of this influx. Félix Albert described the arrival experience in his reminiscences:

When we arrived at the depot, I met a Mr. Jules Tremblay, who offered to let us stay with him for a few days until I could find us a place of our own. He too had a large family, and we made a jolly crowd in one apartment. Then we found a tenement.[10]

When French-Canadian immigrants, usually as part of a nuclear-family circle, arrived in Lowell after the end of the American Civil War (1865), they found themselves in a typical American industrial city—grimy and drab with huge prison-like mill complexes and mushrooming tenement slum neighborhoods. Over two-thirds of the working people of Lowell held jobs in industry, mostly as factory hands; many of the rest earned wages as common laborers. Wages were low and working-class families—Yankee, Irish, English, and Scotch—struggled to escape poverty; secondary wage earners in a family, usually children, occasionally wives and mothers, often meant the difference

---

8   Ibid., pp. 44-45.

9   F. A. M., oral interview, Lowell, May 7,1975, typewritten transcript, p. 3.

10   Albert, *Immigrant Odyssey*, p. 68.

between absolute want and basic subsistence.[11]

The influx of people into Lowell from the mid-1860s, while welcomed by the textile corporations which required factory hands, dismayed the well-established, middle-class Yankees who owned stock in the town's main industry, textiles, and who also controlled the secondary and larger service industries and professions, and who sat in the key positions of the municipal government. For example, in 1866, in its annual report, the Ministry-at-Large of Lowell, a non-denominational middle-class charity organization, noted with consternation that in the two years preceding over ten thousand persons, many of whom were "utterly destitute," had entered Lowell. Many of the persons arriving were "wretchedly poor," and, in the eyes of the Ministry, even worse—a significant portion of the newcomers were foreigners, French Canadians from Quebec. The Ministry report described these immigrants in a highly unflattering manner:

They are nearly all Catholic, do not speak English, are in a low, sensual condition of life, and are less disposed than others to improve themselves. They are not so accessible to our influence. Not mingling freely with society, they do not catch the dominant spirit.[12]

This statement by the Ministry-at-Large expressed more than a nativist attitude towards foreigners (similar statements may, by the way, be found in various sources on the Irish, especially for an earlier period, the 1840s and 1850s).[13] It also expressed the middle-class Yankee fear that the promise of America as an open society would soon go awry. For Yankee Lowellians believed in the American Dream or "dominant spirit" of their era: through hard work, frugality, and self-improvement, people who began in humble stations of life could better

---

[11]   Frances H. Early, "Mobility Potential and the Quality of Life in Working-Class Lowell, Massachusetts, ca. 1870," *Labour/Le Travailleur*, pp. 214-228.

[12]   *Twenty-Second Annual Report of the Ministry-at-Large* (Lowell, 1867), p. 5.

[13]   See Barbara M. Solomon, *Ancestors and Immigrants: A Changing New England Tradition* (Chicago: University of Chicago Press, 1972), and Albert Gibbs Mitchell, Jr., "Irish Family Patterns in Nineteenth-Century Ireland and Lowell, Massachusetts" (Ph.D. dissertation, Boston University, 1976).

themselves materially, achieve status in society, and respect from other upwardly striving Americans. By the late 1860s and 1870s, middle-class Lowell citizens, like the members of the Ministry-at-Large, had begun to question the validity of this dream, particularly as it applied to immigrants. Perhaps America would, after all, follow in Europe's footsteps and end up creating a permanent proletariat. In 1873, local historian Charles Cowley stated glumly:

> We are gradually creating—what the founders of Lowell never looked for—a permanent body of factory employees, composed in part of American stock, but more largely of Irish and French-Canadian elements, with English, Scotch, and German blood commingled. What this fact forebodes I will not venture to conjecture. But perhaps we are to have here a class of resident laborers, similar to that of the manufacturing cities of Europe.[14]

As the 1870s progressed and Lowell's population mushroomed, middle-class people like Cowley became convinced that it was no longer possible to believe that *all* people of lowly social origins would or could realize the American promise of individual betterment. Indeed, in addition to a shiftless, hobo group, the work of the Ministry-at-Large revealed the existence of a large and growing number of "laboring poor" who were unable to improve their condition despite hard work, who eked out bare subsistence lives in flush times, and who needed some form of private or public charity or relief to survive in times of job scarcity and business recession or depression. In other words, people could be poor and remain so through no fault of their own. One Ministry clergyman described in graphic detail the lives of "laboring poor" people who were entrapped in an interminable round of work and want:

> A large class of our laboring poor are men of large families with very small pay. Very few earn more than $500 a year, and many of them not more than $300. There are families of seven or eight persons within my knowledge living on six or seven dollars a week, and some of three or four in a family living on less than two dollars a week. Both men and women go to their work

---

14   Massachusetts Bureau of the Statistics of Labor, *Fourth Annual Report*, 1873, pp. 281-282.

day after day with nothing but a few dry crackers and a
little black molasses to eat, and sometimes with not so
much as that. Frequently I have learned of their having
gone to their work without a mouthful of anything to
strengthen their failing energies. And there are those
who never see a morsel of meat upon the table for weeks
together. And they are driven to accept tenements at
high rates in filthy streets and alleys, in uncomfortable
attics or damp basements. Thus with poor food,
uncomfortable houses and scanty clothing, their
vitality is forced down almost to the freezing point.[15]

French Canadians who settled in Lowell in the 1870s and
1880s were both hard-working and poor. Yet they shunned public
charity and accepted private charity only from their own
community institutions. Except for the disparaging remarks in
the already-quoted 1866 Report of the Ministry-at-Large, the
clergymen working for this organization make scant reference to
French Canadians during the 1870s. However, it is worth noting
that in its report published in 1873, the Ministry comments on
anonymous newcomers to Lowell who "though poor in purse" were
"rich in honesty of purpose and genuine goodness of heart," who
"when settled into work" became "excellent citizens, adding to the
wealth of the city by their industry and economy."[16] Could this
report be referring to French Canadians? Since these recently
arrived immigrants composed part of the "laboring poor" of
Lowell, we would expect many Lowell Yankees to take the
Ministry's point of view and to be sympathetic to French
Canadians. For within the context of the Ministry's value
orientation, which matched that of other middle-class citizens,
Lowell French Canadians in the 1870s led respectable working-
class lives.

Nevertheless, French Canadians were foreigners. Although
negative comments about French Canadians were infrequent in
Lowell in the 1870s—indeed, references to French Canadians are
almost nonexistent in newspapers, city records, and the like—in
the broader New England society a certain ethnic stereotype was
developing of which Lowellians could hardly have been unaware.

---

[15]   *Twenty-Seventh Annual Report of the Ministry-at-Large* (Lowell,
1872), pp. 14-15.

[16]   *Twenty-Eighth Annual Report of the Ministry-at-Large* (Lowell,
1873), p. 4.

French Canadians and Irish people were often seen as possessing a similar, and negative, set of characteristics: they were purportedly unskilled workers with low living standards and lower morals; they were under the power of priests, and they avoided schooling for their children. [17] French Canadians, according to this view, in contradistinction to the Irish, also tended to pick up stakes on a moment's whim; they were, then, unreliable employees. [18]

A less invidious but nonetheless patronizing stereotype was also used to describe French Canadians, one that portrayed them as carefree, somewhat crafty peasants of Norman ancestry. Novelist William Dean Howells, seeing French Canadians at work in a Cambridge brickyard, described them as "windy-voiced [and] good-humoured." He marveled that French-Canadian customers were capable of "sharp bargains struck without the help of a common language" when they came into contact with Yankee shopkeepers. [19] Nathaniel Shaler, a naturalist, agreed with some of Howells' points and denied that French Canadians were shiftless; he even found them to possess certain qualities associated with the Protestant ethic:

> Mingled with the Yankee population, the Canadians become a frugal, industrious, even hard-working people, somewhat given to drink and rather immoral, but with none of that shiftlessness which belongs to the Irishman of the same grade. Our hostler is a "Kanuk" of the Canada region. He is a little fellow, but very vigorous, energetic, plausible, able to make his way with his tongue to much advantage, careful of his money and anxious to get it. With a name which might once have been noble, and a person which looks gentlemanly with the slightest aid of dress, he is still only a good specimen of the peasant-folk of his race. [20]

The stereotype of the French Canadian, then, appears to have

---

[17]   Solomon, *Ancestors and Immigrants,* pp. 160-161.

[18]   Ibid.

[19]   William Dean Howells, *Suburban Sketches* (Boston: Houghton Mifflin, 1884), Reprint pp. 62 and 84.

[20]   Nathaniel Shaler, "The Summer Journey of a Naturalist I," *Atlantic Monthly,* May 1873, vol. 31, no. 187, p. 713.

had two sides in this era, that of the shiftless, morally weak, non-individualistic worker versus that of the amiable, fun-loving, shrewd, reliable peasant. By the 1880s, though, the attitude towards French Canadians had hardened considerably. This was due in large part to difficult socio-economic realities. In one decade, the 1870s, many French Canadians—roughly sixty thousand—spilled over the border into New England in search of work.[21] Most settled in industrial towns like Lowell where their labor power was in demand.[22] As has been the case with every immigrant group coming to America, French Canadians, as working-class newcomers, faced resentment from other working-class people, in this case, particularly Americans and Irish, who already had a stake in the communities French Canadians entered. Although the depression of 1873 resulted in a reverse migration of many French Canadians back to Canada, a large number remained in New England to compete with others in a job market which could not employ everyone.[23] And the very qualities which employers, especially in the textile industry, found so appealing in French Canadians—their willingness to work, like the Irish before them, long hours for low wages—created serious problems for French Canadians in relation to other working-class people.

By the 1880s, leaders in the labor movement, as well as many public officials and politicians, were blaming French Canadians for the inability of labor to win a ten-hour day in the textile

---

21   Ralph D. Vicero, "Immigration of French Canadians to New England, 1840-1900: A Geographical Analysis" (Ph.D. dissertation, University of Wisconsin, 1968), p. 275.

22   Ibid., p. 316.

23   Canada, House of Commons, Report of the Select Committee on the Causes of the Present Depression of the Manufacturing, Mining, Commercial, Shipping, Lumber, and Fishing Interests, *Journal of the House*, Appendix 3, 1876, p. 146. In 1874, the Ministry-at-Large report stated that a Montreal paper had noted that by the first of December, 1873, 30,000 French Canadians had returned from New England to Canada. *Twenty-Ninth Annual Report of the Ministry-at-Large* (Lowell, 1874), p. 4. Regarding permanent residency in New England, see Massachusetts Bureau of the Statistics of Labor, *Thirteenth Annual Report*, 1882, pp. 74 and 80. On permanent vs. temporary residence in New England, see also Gerard Blazon, "A Social History of the French-Canadian Community of Suncook, New Hampshire (1870-1920)" (Master's thesis, University of New Hampshire, 1974), pp. 67-68.

industry.[24] Illustrative of this attitude is the Massachusetts Bureau of Statistics of Labor Report for 1881 which labelled French Canadians the "Chinese of the Eastern States." The Bureau accused French Canadians of being a "horde of industrial invaders" who "care nothing for [American] institutions." The report concluded caustically:

> Now, it is not strange that so sordid and low a people should awaken corresponding feelings in the managers, and that these should feel that, the longer the hours for such people, the better, and that to work them to the uttermost is about the only good use they can be put to. Nor is it strange that this impression is so strong, that the managers overlook for the time being all the rest of the operatives, and think that everything should be shaped to these lowest ones.[25]

The comment that French Canadians were a "sordid and low" people recalls the Lowell Ministry-at-Large reference to them in 1866 as "low" and "sensual." The portrayal of French Canadians in this bureau report is a far cry from the Lowell middle-class ideal of socially responsible, educated working-class individuals and families who could improve their position in society. Neither does this image of French Canadians tally with the description of "laboring poor" people, seemingly caught in a poverty-stricken life through no fault of their own. Instead, as the "Chinese of the Eastern States," French Canadians as a group are made to resemble a collective hobo populace—a menace to the values and institutions and economic well-being of New England society.

---

24   Blazon, "Social History of the French-Canadian Community of Suncook," p. 140; Peter Haebler, "*Habitants* in Holyoke: The Development of the French-Canadian Community in a Massachusetts City, 1865-1910" (Ph.D. dissertation, University of New Hampshire, 1976), pp. 66-67; Philip T. Silvia, "The Spindle City: Labor, Politics and Religion in Fall River, Massachusetts, 1870-1905" (Ph.D. dissertation, Fordham University, 1973); and Daniel J. Walkowitz, *Worker City, Company Town: Iron and Cotton Worker Protest in Troy and Cohoes, New York, 1855-1884* (Urbana, Illinois: University of Illinois Press, 1978), pp. 191-192 and 219-229. Walkowitz's study shows that French Canadians could and did organize (in the 1880s) with other workers in the textile industry to improve their wages and working conditions.

25   Massachusetts Bureau of the Statistics of Labor, *Twelfth Annual Report*, 1881, pp. 469-470.

Nonetheless, in 1881 a number of Lowell citizens came forward to vouch for the integrity and respectability of French Canadians in their town. An overseer of the Lawrence Manufacturing Company, a textile corporation, stated: "I employ about seventy-five French-Canadian people, mostly males. I find them as a rule, punctual and steady in their work, and not given to drunkenness."[26] Another textile mill overseer of the Tremont and Suffolk Company also described French-Canadian operatives positively:

It is my opinion, that as regards thrift, sobriety, and general good behavior and application to their labors, they compare, as a class, favorably with either of the other classes—viz. American and Irish—employed on this corporation.[27]

Owners of a grocery store certified that "French Canadians as a class do like and use the best kind of meats and provisions, and don't live as paupers."[28]

Despite these testimonies, which show that French Canadians were earning a certain respect among some Lowell businessmen and corporation supervisors, it seems reasonable to assume that the resentments expressed in the 1881 Bureau of Statistics report were shared by at least some working-class people in Lowell. Still, Yankee and Irish workers in the mills generally held better jobs than French Canadians, which would have mitigated hostility towards the newcomers. Since work was organized according to skill level into different departments in different areas of the mills, French Canadians in the less-skilled jobs, might have been somewhat segregated from operatives of other nationalities who worked in more highly-skilled jobs.[29] This situation would have helped to keep antagonisms between ethnic groups in check.

---

[26]   Massachusetts Bureau of the Statistics of Labor, *Thirteenth Annual Report,* 1882, p. 44.

[27]   Ibid., p. 47.

[28]   Ibid.

[29]   Thomas Louis Dublin, "Women at Work: The Transformation of Work and Community in Lowell, Massachusetts, 1826-1860" (Ph.D. dissertation, Columbia University, 1974), p. 182.

Nevertheless, smoldering animosity and distrust existed and could erupt easily when various ethnic groups in working-class occupations were brought together into close proximity. By the 1860s, textile corporations were losing interest in providing boarding houses for the now largely immigrant work force, partly because of the squabbles and physical fights which broke out regularly when people of different ethnic origins lived in the same residences.[30]

Since one in five people in Lowell in 1870 was Irish, it is important to have a fuller sense of how French Canadians and Irish people related to each other. Contemporary sources and oral interviews with long-time residents in Lowell demonstrate that the French Canadians and the Irish harbored feelings of ill-will towards each other from the very beginning. The French-Canadian quarrel with and resentment of the Irish revolved, in part, around different attitudes towards Catholic Church polity, with the Irish favoring a unified, American, English-speaking Church and the French Canadians favoring separate national parishes within the larger Church structure. Plain jealousy entered the picture, too. As already mentioned, Irish people, as older settlers, had better jobs than did French Canadians in the factories.[31]

Nonetheless, a countervailing tendency in French-Canadian-Irish relations existed in the 1870s and 1880s. Religious leaders in both communities endeavored to create a cooperative spirit among their parishioners, and their efforts met with a certain degree of success. One Irish Catholic priest, Father O'Brien, extended his services to Fathers Garin and Lagier, when they first came to Lowell to establish the first French-Canadian parish church, St. Joseph's.

A little over two months after Rev. André-Marie Garin's arrival, the Provincial of the Oblates of Mary Immaculate officially established as a community the group of Oblates in

30   Fidelia O. Brown, "Decline and Fall: The End of the Dream," in *Cotton Was King: A History of Lowell, Massachusetts*, Ed. by Arthur L. Eno, Jr. (Lowell: Lowell Historical Society and New Hampshire Publishing Co., 1976), p. 142; and Kenngott, *Record of a City*, pp. 45-49.

31   Frances H. Early, "French-Canadian Beginnings in an American Community: Lowell, Massachusetts, 1868-1886" (Ph.D. dissertation, Concordia University, 1980), especially chapter four, "Earning a Living," pp. 93-128.

Lowell which had under its jurisdiction two parishes, St. Joseph's for the French Canadians and St. John's for the Irish.[32] In 1880, the Oblates established a small parochial school with six classrooms for children whose parents belonged to St. Joseph's or St. John's; four classes were taught in English, two in French.[33] Irish priests in the other churches—St. Patrick's, St. Peter's, and St. Mary's—worked closely with the Oblates when occasions for cooperation arose. In 1868, the French-Canadian parish, along with the Irish ones, participated in a fair sponsored to raise money for St. John's Hospital, an Irish charity institution founded in 1867.[34] In 1874, when Father O'Brien—"the first friend of the French Canadians in Lowell"—died, a delegation from St. Joseph's attended the funeral.[35]

French-Canadian and Irish community leaders, lay as well as religious, also organized other formal contacts between the two nationalities. St. Patrick's Day had for long been celebrated in Lowell. Already in 1870, Saint Jean-Baptiste Day, the national holiday of Quebec, was an established event in Lowell. The Lowell *Daily Citizen* reported favorably on the festivities. The Irish Erin Concert Band contributed to the day's entertainment. Members of the band doubtless partook of the refreshments offered at the close of the day and socialized with French Canadians. Other Lowellians, too, might have participated in the event.[36]

Such well-intentioned, apparently pleasant group encounters between Irish and French-Canadian people were not so frequent at a one-to-one level. As individuals, the French Canadians and the Irish tended to shun overly close contact with each other, which is well demonstrated in their differential residence patterns. As Maps 1 and 2 show, French Canadians, when they first began settling in Lowell in large numbers in the

---

[32]   Richard Santerre, *La paroisse Saint-Jean-Baptiste et les Franco-Américains de Lowell, Massachusetts, 1868-1968* (Manchester, N.H.: Éditions Lafayette, 1993), pp. 43-44.

[33]   In 1882, the Oblates, following Rev. Garin's suggestion, opened a separate French-Canadian parochial school. Santerre, *La paroisse Saint-Jean-Baptiste*, pp. 62 and 67.

[34]   *Lowell Daily Citizen and News*, November 27-30, 1868.

[35]   Santerre, *La paroisse Saint-Jean-Baptiste*, p. 48.

[36]   *Lowell Daily Citizen and News*, June 25, 1870.

late 1860s and 1870s, before Little Canada existed, clustered in two neighborhoods, one fanning out from the old Railroad Depot, along and around Merrimack Street, and the other encircling the area of the new Railroad Depot on Middlesex Street. Irish clustering occurred in the Acre in central Lowell or in the Chapel Hill area. When French Canadians and the Irish shared the same neighborhood, a rough balance in numbers between the two usually existed. It is interesting, too, as Maps 3 and 4 indicate, that in 1880, when the flimsy, poorly-ventilated tenements in Little Canada were just going up, most French Canadians still resided in their old neighborhoods; those who did live in Little Canada, though, clustered in the upper part, while the Irish, the English, and the Yankees clustered in the lower part.

Children in this era appear to have assumed the attitudes and racial prejudices of their parents. Tensions related to occupational competitiveness between French-Canadian and Irish boys erupted rather easily into brawling and street fighting.[37] And, according to one eye-witness, a commitment to ethnic exclusiveness triggered aggressive behavior between French-Canadian and Irish youths:

> . . . There's always the matter of when you stick together too much . . . all the other groups are your enemies. It starts with fights or insults and so on to throwing rocks. The North Common was the battleground between the Irish and the French. Of course, the Irish were here first, too, so they had their troubles when they first came in . . . [38]

Further, job competitiveness and *a priori* loyalty to the idea of ethnic exclusiveness kept inter-ethnic marriages between French-Canadian and Irish young people at a bare minimum; a strong aversion to Protestantism, the religious orientation of most other Lowellians, reinforced French-Canadian commitment to choose marriage partners from within their own ethnic group.[39]

*   *   *

---

[37]   Peter F. Blewett, "The New People," in *Cotton was King*, ed. Arthur L. Eno (New Hampshire Publishing Company, 1976), pp. 212-213.

[38]   F. A. M., oral interview, p. 11.

[39]   Lowell Marriage Records, 1870, 1872, 1874, 1876, 1878, and 1880.

By way of summary, we have seen that French Canadians in their early years of settlement in Lowell faced the hardships and deprivations of working-class existence bravely and stoically. All members of the family circle contributed their share of "industry" to family survival. As the person quoted at the beginning of this paper stated, "Everybody helped everybody." This was true whether people needed to find a home, secure a job, or accept temporary charity from kin or community to weather hard times. French Canadians as a group held themselves somewhat aloof from the larger ethnically mixed populace surrounding them, most obviously, perhaps, from the Irish. Understandably, as strangers in a new land, they preferred to live with their own kind, and as a group they resisted dependence upon the public or private relief agencies which other Lowellians, including the Irish, chose not to shun. A mantle of otherness or separateness both sheltered and hid French Canadians from the larger Lowell community. As a result, the Lowell citizenry, particularly the Yankee middle class, felt ambivalent towards the newcomers in their midst. On the one hand, French Canadians appeared to have solid work habits and to take care of themselves in difficult economic times. On the other hand, French Canadians had a commitment to family (rather than individual) survival and well-being which was out of step with the individualistic success ethic of upwardly striving working-class or middle-class Yankees and partially assimilated Irish people. Then, too, their allegiance to *survivance*, the survival of their ethnic identity, disturbed Lowell's Yankee citizenry: Would French Canadians, they asked themselves, learn America's "dominant spirit?"

We began our inquiry by placing in juxtaposition the views of Yankee officials and a Franco-American woman on conditions in Little Canada. The officials complained, with barely concealed nativist assumptions, about material conditions in Little Canada—overcrowding, lack of sanitation, and high disease and mortality rates. The Franco-American woman, however, downplayed material conditions. She spoke instead of what Little Canada had meant to her as a child—she portrayed a warm, comforting place, where people felt united through family and community bonds.

How, then, do we reconcile these very different views of Little Canada and, by extension, of the whole French-Canadian immigrant experience in New England during this period? It appears that we begin by recognizing that there are indeed more realities than are dreamt of in our present-day historical concepts and methodologies. In this instance of Little Canada, we can "prove" that officials were at one level correct in their description of Little Canada—it did constitute a health hazard and people who lived in this neighborhood risked sickness or even death, especially children. However, we also sense that these officials were *biased*: they expected to find French Canadians in such circumstances. The Franco-American woman expressed another reality, one that has validity, although we know that, by 1975, the date of the interview, it was tinged with nostalgia. People found emotional sustenance, psychological security, and a sense of meaning in the Little Canada of the late nineteenth and early twentieth centuries, a truth which will never "show up" in government reports and vital statistics records.

Our job as historians—ultimately—is to understand the two levels, or planes of reality, the objective and the subjective, which are always united in the actual experience of people in the past. Hopefully, this essay on the settling-in process and the beginnings of Little Canada in Lowell in the latter part of the nineteenth century can serve as a helpful reminder of what our true task really is.

[This article first appeared in the French Institute's publication entitled *The Little Canadas of New England*. It has been reviewed by the author for inclusion in this volume.]

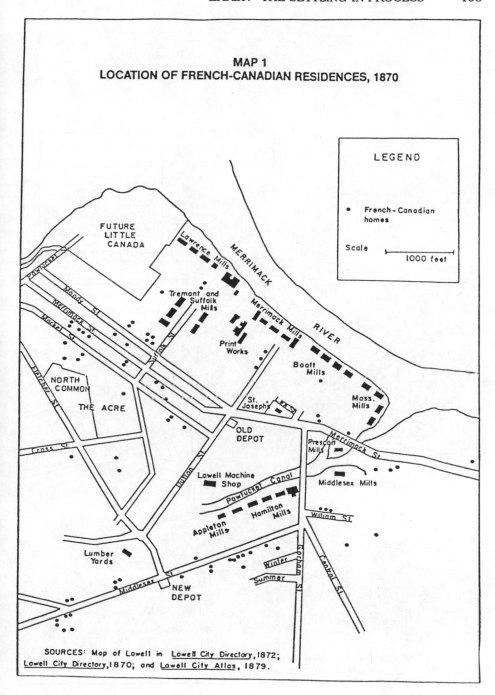

MAP 1
LOCATION OF FRENCH-CANADIAN RESIDENCES, 1870

LEGEND

• French-Canadian homes

Scale |————| 1000 feet

FUTURE LITTLE CANADA

Lawrence Mills

MERRIMACK

Merrimack Mills

RIVER

Pawtucket St.

Moody St.

Merrimack St.

Market St.

Suffolk St.

Tremont and Suffolk Mills

Print Works

Boott Mills

NORTH COMMON

THE ACRE

Fletcher St.

St. Joseph's

Mass. Mills

OLD DEPOT

Cross St.

Prescott Mills

Merrimack St.

Lowell Machine Shop

Pawtucket Canal

Middlesex Mills

Worthen St.

Appleton Mills

Hamilton Mills

William St.

Lumber Yards

Winter

Summer

Gorham St.

Central St.

Middlesex St.

NEW DEPOT

SOURCES: Map of Lowell in *Lowell City Directory*, 1872; *Lowell City Directory*, 1870; and *Lowell City Atlas*, 1879.

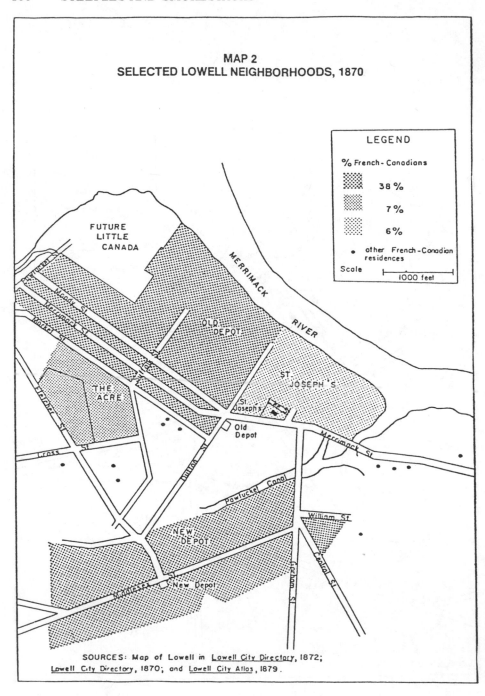

MAP 2
SELECTED LOWELL NEIGHBORHOODS, 1870

LEGEND

% French - Canadians

38 %

7 %

6 %

•   other French-Canadian
     residences

Scale ⊢————————⊣
        1000 feet

FUTURE
LITTLE
CANADA

MERRIMACK

RIVER

OLD
DEPOT

ST. JOSEPH'S

THE
ACRE

St.
Joseph's

Old
Depot

Merrimack St.

Pawtucket Canal

William St.

NEW
DEPOT

New Depot

SOURCES: Map of Lowell in Lowell City Directory, 1872;
Lowell City Directory, 1870; and Lowell City Atlas, 1879.

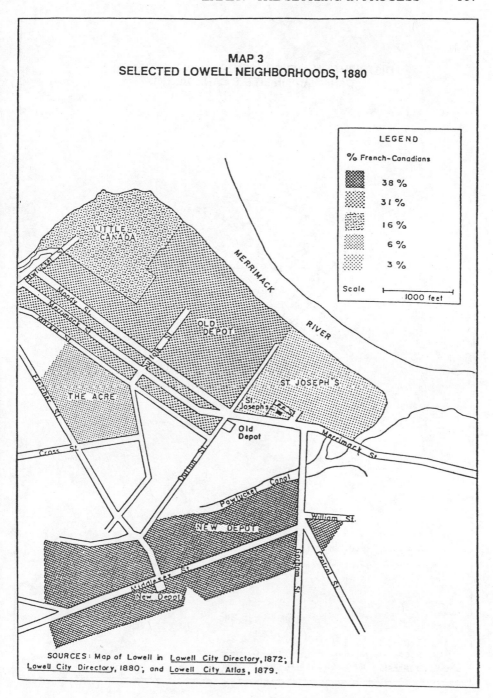

MAP 3
SELECTED LOWELL NEIGHBORHOODS, 1880

LEGEND

% French-Canadians

38 %
31 %
16 %
6 %
3 %

Scale |———————| 1000 feet

LITTLE CANADA

MERRIMACK

RIVER

OLD DEPOT

ST. JOSEPH'S

St. Joseph's

THE ACRE

Old Depot

Cross St.

Merrimack St.

Pawtucket Canal

William St.

NEW DEPOT

New Depot

Middlesex St.

SOURCES: Map of Lowell in Lowell City Directory, 1872;
Lowell City Directory, 1880; and Lowell City Atlas, 1879.

MAP 4
DISTRIBUTION AND CONCENTRATION OF FRENCH
CANADIANS IN LITTLE CANADA, 1880

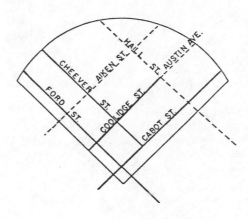

————— streets which have $\frac{1}{3}$ or less Identified French Canadians
– – – – – – streets which have $\frac{2}{3}$ or more Identified French Canadians

SOURCES: Map of Lowell in _Lowell City Directory_, 1872 ;
Lowell City Directory, 1880; and _Lowell City Atlas_, 1879.

Community Formation in Old Town, Maine, 1835-1930: Endogamy and Natal Origins Among the Acadians

Marcella Harnish Sorg

Introduction

Although it is an important and even critical component of Franco-American history, research on the Acadian immigrants to New England has lagged behind work on French Canadians. Even in community studies such as those by Hareven on Manchester, New Hampshire,[1] by Early on Lowell, Massachusetts,[2] and my own earlier studies of Old Town, Maine,[3] Franco-Americans are frequently treated as a homogeneous aggregate. In some studies of Franco-American communities the assumption is made that all originated from Quebec. Although this is sometimes warranted, in fact, Acadians from the Maritime Provinces formed a significant population throughout New England. The work done recently by LeBlanc on the Acadians of Fitchburg represents an important step in bridging the gap in our knowledge of the New England Acadian heritage.

Perhaps the single most important factor limiting historical research on New England Acadians is the difficulty in identifying them. Although they differ in ultimate geographical origin, in language, and in custom, these distinctions become increasingly blurred after the mid-eighteenth century, and especially after the

---

[1]   Tamara K. Hareven, *Family Time and Industrial Time: The Relationship Between the Family and Work in a New England Industrial Community* (New York: Cambridge University Press, 1982).

[2]   Frances H. Early, "The French-Canadian Family Economy and Standard-of-Living in Lowell, Massachusetts, 1870," *Journal of Family History* (Summer 1982), pp. 180-199.

[3]   Marcella Harnish Sorg, "Genetic Demography of Deme Formation in a Franco-American Population: 1830-1903" (Ph.D. dissertation, The Ohio State University, 1979).

1755 expulsion. Besides their mobility and intermarriage with French Canadians, as illustrated by Craig's research on Madawaska,[4] the process of adaptation to the New World over the centuries has modified both language and custom.

So the question will return again and again to haunt our historical research: Who is the Acadian? Is she the person who is directly descended from original Acadian settlers around the Bay of Fundy, but who calls herself only an American? Or is he the direct descendant of the early settlers of the St. Lawrence, who is only partly Acadian by descent, but who calls himself Acadian? There is no easy answer. If we use surname analysis, we will miss many who are fully Acadian on their mother's side. If we use genealogy, we will miss those who have become fully assimilated to the Acadian culture, but who may not be biologically Acadian. If we use place of birth in a migrant community, we may miss those who are second generation, or who happened to have been born in a non-Acadian location. The best approach is probably a combination of methods as well as a good knowledge of a particular community's history.

Background

In this article I will be looking specifically at the Franco-American population of Old Town, Maine and its relationship to the primarily Acadian Madawaska population in the upper St. John River Valley along the Maine-New Brunswick border. Family reconstitution of the Old Town community which I did in the late 1970s, and the family reconstitution done by Beatrice Craig for the Madawaska population have been used in studying the rather significant migratory links between the two groups.

The connections between the two communities are to be expected, given the establishment of railroad links after the 1850s. Old Town was one of the earliest towns to receive French-Canadian or Acadian immigrants in New England; a community began forming in that area during the 1830s. Many of the earliest migrants came either from, or at least via, the upper St. John Valley. In the nineteenth century, the "pull" factor to the Old Town area was almost exclusively due to the lumber industry; textile

---

4   Beatrice Chevalier Craig, "Family, Kinship and Community Formation on the Canadian-American Border: Madawaska 1785-1842" (Ph.D. dissertation, Universtiy of Maine at Orono, 1983).

manufacture came in around the turn of the twentieth century.

Immigrants to Old Town were similar to other New England-bound migrants in that they came in family groups. Although a large portion of the French population consisted of single men involved in seasonal labor, those men often had relatives in town, or they later brought families to the area. Single women came with other single women to work as domestics, or with their parents. Married women tended not to work outside the home until the arrival in the area of textile and shoe factories in the early 1900s.

The Old Town French population during the nineteenth century was remarkably fluid, with only about 25% of the census population remaining for ten or more years. This mobility reduces the efficacy of family reconstitution techniques in answering questions about the "unstable" migrants. Nevertheless, we often have enough information to link such earlier migrants with their communities of origin, including Madawaska.

Methods and Results

Family reconstitution was done for the entire Old Town area French population (Old Town, Orono, Bradley, and Milford), using record linkage techniques including: parish marriage, baptism, and death records, 1848-1900; civil birth, marriage, and death records, 1830-1900; federal manuscript census records, 1840-1880 and 1900; and a parish census of 1903-1907. Orono was included until it formed a separate parish in 1880; Milford and Bradley were included in the entire study period. In addition, the parish marriage records for 1900-1930 were analyzed, but were not included in the record linkage process.

The first part of the analysis focuses on the marriage patterns among Acadians from Madawaska who migrated to the Old Town area. I utilized the birth place of the bride and groom as well as the birth place of their parents if known.

As mentioned above, the use of birth place has a number of problems. There is a high degree of ambiguity in the Old Town records during the nineteenth century. It is not rare to find an individual's birthplace listed variously as New Brunswick, Madawaska, and/or Grand Falls. A further complication is the fact that "Madawaska" is a town on the St. John River's southern side, a county of New Brunswick on the river's northern side, and a term for the region including both sides of the valley. I included in my study any that indicated a birthplace of Madawaska or any of the parishes or towns on either side of the upper St. John Valley. Obviously, this excludes Acadians from other areas from this part of the analysis.

Beatrice Craig's research has described the characteristics of the people who tended to migrate away from Madawaska to Old Town. I will build on the results of her work and support the idea that the Madawaska Acadian migrants experienced an assimilation to a regional Franco-American culture followed by an assimilation to the Anglo culture of the area. This assimilation process is still taking place in the Old Town area.

The families who migrated from Madawaska were a biologically mixed population consisting of French Canadians and Acadians. On the other hand, those who had resided in the Madawaska area long enough and who had married into the community were likely to be culturally Acadian. Madawaska, however, was used as a "way station" for many migrants from the St. Lawrence Valley to New England. Thus some Old Town in-migrants who listed towns in Madawaska as their birthplace were simply children of French Canadians who stayed in the St. John Valley a short time.

During the period 1860-1900, Old Town marriage records sometimes, but not often, listed the birthplace of the bride and groom. Table 1 shows the distribution of the marriages in which Madawaska was listed as a birth place for one or both spouses. This method underestimates the actual number of Madawaska area spouses since many marriage records did not include birth place. The top line presents the total number of marriages between persons with French surnames, with and without a reported birth place. The second line shows the number of marriages recording one or both spouses as born in the Madawaska area. The percent involving a Madawaska spouse increased from 10% in the 1860s to 27% in the 1890s due to two factors. First, the marriage records are more complete for the 1880s and 1890s than for the 1860s and 1870s. Second, there is an actual increase in the number of Madawaska migrants in the 1890s compared to earlier decades. Thus, although migrants from the Madawaska area began coming to the Old Town area as early as 1835, they continued to form a steady proportion of the in-migrant population in succeeding decades, their numbers peaking during the 1890s. On average,

Madawaska-related marriages constituted at least 16% of all marriages among French-named spouses.

Endogamy is a term that refers to marriage within some socially defined boundary. Exogamy is the term referring to marriage across that boundary. Endogamy usually characterizes populations that prefer to marry within their own group. This research addresses the question of whether Acadians from the Madawaska area preferred to marry others from that area, or whether they sought out marriage partners who were simply French-speaking. If the latter is true, it would have produced some reduction in the intensity of the Acadian cultural identity. Given the heterogeneity of Franco-American origins within Canada and Acadia, one might expect that Franco-Americans would have had to create a new cultural identity anyway—one that was appropriate for an urban, industrial environment, one where speaking French was important and whether one was French Canadian or Acadian much less important.

Table 2 shows the marriage patterns for the 103 Old Town area marriages involving one or both spouses from the Madawaska area from 1860 to 1899. Just under a third, 28%, involved couples where both bride and groom were from Madawaska. In 33% of the marriages one spouse was from Madawaska, and the other was recorded as being from "Canada." From the pattern of records in the Old Town area, it is most likely that "Canada" refers to French Canada or Quebec, but there is no way to be sure in every case.

Over 90% of the marriages during this period involved couples who were both French-surnamed. This indicates a clear marriage preference for endogamous marriages within the French-speaking community. On the other hand, the data presented in Table 2 show a range of variation of marriage choices within the Franco-American community. For example, migrants from Madawaska were just about as likely to marry someone from Quebec, Old Town, or "other" as they were to marry a fellow migrant from Madawaska. Although important, endogamy among Madawaskans is not the predominant pattern during the period 1860-1899.

But what about the 1900s? During the period 1900-1930 the marriage records specify the town of baptism for virtually every bride and groom. This offers the chance of checking the assumptions mentioned above; for example, the period 1900-1909 might be expected to be fairly similar to the period 1860-1899. Table 3 shows the results of the analysis. Marriages involving at least one spouse from Madawaska constitute 15 to 19% of marriages, very similar to the previous decades.

The number of endogamous marriages between Madawaska spouses drops drastically, however, from 28% in the period 1860-1899 to 0% to 11% from 1900-1929. The greatest proportion of marriages after 1900 are between Madawaska-born in-migrants and Old Town-born Francos.

At first I suspected that these Old Town-born spouses might be children of Madawaska in-migrants. However, during the period 1900-1909, the marriage records also list parents' birth places. Only 24% of the Old Town-born spouses had one or both parents who were Madawaska-born, suggesting a level of endogamy between people of Madawaska origin (first and second generation) somewhat less than the 28% estimated for the nineteenth century.

An analysis of the overall Old Town Franco-American population marriage patterns from 1900 to 1929[5] is summarized in Figure 1. Near the bottom of the figure, the percent of local ethnic endogamy is shown. This includes marriages between French-surnamed spouses born in Old Town only; it ranges from 17% during 1990-1909 to a high of only 27% during 1915-1919. The middle sector of the figure includes marriages either between two in-migrants or between a native and an in-migrant. The shaded sector at the top of the figure represents the percent of ethnic exogamy. This includes marriages between French-surnamed and non-French-surnamed persons.

A preference for French-surnamed spouses is clear throughout the first three decades of the twentieth century, including two-thirds or more of marriages. However, there is an obvious trend from a high of 87% in the first decade to only 68% between 1925-1929. The turning point seems to be at about 1920.

For this transitional time during the early twentieth century, there was an exceptional diversity of birth places recorded for

5   Marcella Harnish Sorg, "Contrasting Local Ethnic Endogamy with Natal Origins: Is Language the Key?" Paper read at the University of Maine Franco-American Faculty Seminar: "Franco-American Studies: A Social Science Approach," 1980.

spouses (those involving at least one French-surnamed spouse). Table 4 summarizes the pattern of natal origins for in-migrants marrying in Old Town between 1900 and 1929. Out of 866 marriages involving 1742 individuals, 770 or 44% of the spouses were born outside of Old Town. These 770 in-migrants were born in 170 different towns. The majority, 54%, were from Canada, with the majority of these from New Brunswick.

Table 5 displays the most important in-migrant sources. It includes only towns that contributed five or more migrants during the period. The major contributors, sending twenty-five or more, include: Orono, Caribou, Van Buren, Chatham, Petit Rocher, and St. Leonard, the latter four of which are primarily Acadian. People from towns in the upper St. John Valley constitute a full 41% of the in-migrants from the 394 sources itemized in this table, and 21% of the 770 in-migrant spouses.

Conclusion

In conclusion, Old Town, Maine, during the period 1860 to 1930, was an important destination for migrants from the primarily Acadian settlement of Madawaska, as well as other Acadian communities in New Brunswick. Marriages involving persons born in the Madawaska area averaged about 15 to 18% of Old Town Franco-American marriages through the study period. However, endogamy between persons born in Madawaska constituted a minority of Madawaska in-migrant marriages. The overall marriage patterns suggest that, although community/ region of origin was important, it was not as important as linguistic factors in marriage choices. However, it does appear that region of origin was more important before than after the turn of the century. Before 1900, about 28% of marriages involving Madawaska natives were with each other; after 1900 they averaged only about 7%, slightly higher if one includes children of Madawaska natives.

The Madawaska region has always had a strong Acadian cultural identity, despite the influx of in-migrants from Quebec. To some extent, therefore, the Acadian cultural identity is directly associated with Madawaska natal origins. The diminishing importance of regional origin in determining marriage choice after 1900 probably reflects a decrease in the importance of Acadian ethnic identity as well. This change in values was followed about twenty years later by a sharp decrease in the importance of Franco-American status in the choice of marriage partners; ethnic endogamy dropped from 87% in 1900 to 68% by the 1920s.

If one can generalize from these findings to other New England Franco-American communities with strong Acadian components, one can hypothesize the existence of a growing regional Franco-American ethnic identity to which in-migrants were assimilating during the late nineteenth and early twentieth centuries. This process of assimilation would have diluted cultural differences between Acadians and French Canadians. This initial phase was then succeeded, just after World War I, by a sharp increase in assimilation to the Anglo culture. By 1930, the change in values, reflected in marriage choices, would have affected about a third of all Franco marriages and probably would have begun to have a noticeable effect on family life.

Although the Acadian experience in New England was a distinct component of Franco-American history, it may have been more similar than different from the French-Canadian experience, especially after 1900. That is, the experience included two levels of assimilation, one following the other. In some sense, then, there was a loss of cultural identity on two levels, resulting in a complex social and psychological response. One might expect to find an intensification of resistance to loss of ethnic identity paralleling these changes, especially just after 1920. Little is known, however, of the effects of assimilation to a regional francophone identity and the dilution of specifically Acadian (or French-Canadian) values that accompanied it.

The difficulties in obtaining historical information about these Acadian Franco-Americans are great. Efforts to identify the Acadians by surname, by genealogy, or by birth place all have weaknesses, weaknesses also inherent in the present study. These should, one hopes, present a challenge to others and stimulate further research.

[This article first appeared in a French translation as "La formation d'une communauté à Old Town, Maine, 1835-1930: endogamie et origines natales parmi les Acadiens," in the French Institute's publication entitled *L'Émigrant acadien vers les États-Unis: 1842-1950*. It has been reviewed by the author for inclusion in this volume.]

Table 1

Proportion of Old Town Franco marriages involving known
Madawaska-born migrants, 1860-1899

	1860s	1870s	1880s	1890s	1860-1899
Total number of Franco marriages with or without recorded birthplace of spouses	84	164	198	192	638
Total number of Franco marriages recording one or both spouses born in the Madawaska area	10	14	28	51	103
Percent	12%	9%	14%	27%	16%

Table 2

Marriage patterns of Madawaska-born Old Town in migrants,
1860-1899

Both spouses from Madawaska area	29	(28%)
One spouse from Madawaska area, one from "Canada"	34	(33%)
One spouse from Madawaska area, one from Quebec	6	(6%)
One spouse from Madawaska area, one from New Brunswick	8	(8%)
One spouse from Madawaska area, one from Old Town area	12	(12%)
One spouse from Madawaska area, one from place other than above (France, Ireland, Italy, New Hampshire, or other Maine town)	14	(14%)
TOTAL	103	(100%)

Table 3.

Marriage patterns of Madawaska-born Old Town in-migrants,
1860-1929

	1860-1899	1900-1909	1910-1919	1920-1929
Total number of Franco marriages	638	116	250	370
Total Franco marriages with one or both spouses from Madawaska area	103	21	39	57
Percent of Franco marriages with Madawaska spouse	16%	18%	16%	15%
Both spouses from Madawaska area	29 (28%)	0 (0%)	2 (5%)	6 (11%)
One spouse from Madawaska area, one from "Canada"	34 (33%)	—	—	—
One spouse from Madawaska area, one from Quebec	6 (6%)	0 (0%)	5 (13%)	1 (2%)
One spouse from Madawaska area, one from New Brunswick	8 (8%)	0 (0%)	3 (8%)	7 (12%)
One spouse from Madawaska, one from Old Town area	12 (12%)	21 (100%)*	24 (62%)	29 (51%)
One spouse from Madawaska, one from place other than above	14 (14%)	0 (0%)	5 (13%)	14 (25%)
TOTAL FRANCO MARRIAGES WITH MADAWASKA SPOUSE (S)	103 (100%)	21 (100%)	39 (100%)	57 (100%)

* Of these 21, only 5 had one or both parents who were born in Madawaska.

Table 4.

Natal origins for Franco in-migrants marrying in Old Town
1900-1929

Number	Percent	Source
59	35%	Maine towns
48	28%	New Brunswick towns
32	19%	Quebec towns
6	4%	Nova Scotia towns
5	3%	Prince Edward Island towns
13	8%	Massachusetts towns
7	4%	Other New England towns
92	54%	Canada
78	46%	U.S.
170	100%	Total number of towns

Table 5.

Towns contributing five or more in-migrants to
Old Town Franco marriages, 1900-1929

Source	Town	Number
Maine	Acadia	5
	Augusta	5
	Bangor	12
	Brewer	5
	Caribou	37
	Fairfield	10
	Frenchville	7
	Kingman	6
	Lewiston	11
	Orono	58
	St. David	5
	Skowhegan	5
	Van Buren	55
	Waterville	9
	Winn	5
New Brunswick	Cape Bald	12
	Chatham	30
	Grand Sault	10
	Kent	5
	Petit Rocher	29
	St. Anne de Madawaska	8
	St. Hilaire de Madawaska	6
	St. Leonard	30
Prince Edward Island	Mt. Carmel	5
Quebec	Cacouna	14
	Lac Mégantic	5
"Madawaska"	(probably Madawaska, ME)	5
TOTAL		394

Figure 1

Changes in ethnic endogamy among
Old Town francophone natives and in-migrants, 1900-1929

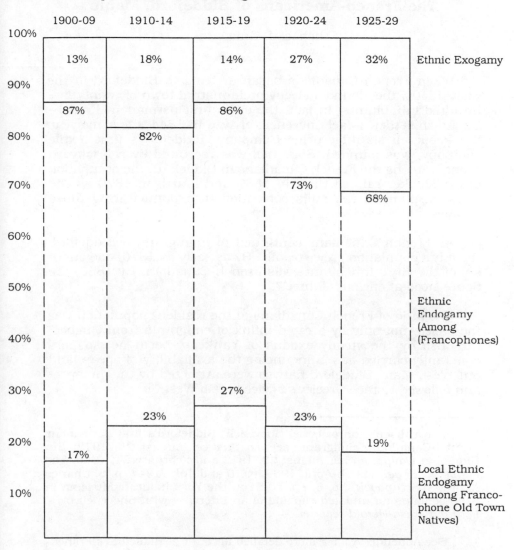

The Franco-Americans of Biddeford, Maine

Michael J. Guignard

When French Canadians began arriving in Biddeford in the early 1840s, they found a sleepy preindustrial town of twenty-five hundred inhabitants. In fact, the city's first permanent French-Canadian settler, Israel Shevenell, arrived in 1844, the same year the Pepperell Manufacturing Company, Biddeford's first textile company, was founded. Shevenell was recruited by a brickyard agent.[1] Among the French Canadians in Biddeford, the occupation of brickmaker ranked third in 1860 and fourth in 1870 as the physical plant of the mills continued to expand during those decades.

As French Canadians continued to immigrate to Biddeford, the city's population grew steadily. By as early as 1870, one out of six of the city's inhabitants was French-Canadian. By 1880, the figure stood at one out of three.[2]

The ratio of French Canadians to the resident population was increased, not only by a rapid influx of emigrants from Quebec, but also by the steady exodus of Yankees. Local newspapers constantly carried ads announcing the availability of cheap land out West. Many Biddeford natives were attracted by the prospect and followed Horace Greeley's advice to "Go West."[3]

---

[1] For a discussion of Israel Shevenell, Biddeford's first permanent French-Canadian immigrant, see *La Justice*, August 26, 1912; the *Biddeford Daily Journal*, August 23, 1912 and February 24, 1940; *The Pepperell Sheet*, March-April, 1939, p. 10 and July, 1944, p. 8. Charles Andrews' *Scrapbook*, No. 6, pp. 50-51 at the York Institute Museum in Saco contains an undated clipping of an interview with Shevenell by a *Portland Press Herald* reporter.

[2] See Appendix A for a more detailed account of Biddeford's Franco-American population percentages.

[3] Stewart H. Holbrook, *The Yankee Exodus* (New York: Macmillan and Co., 1950). Ralph D. Vicero, "Immigration of French Canadians to New England 1840-1900: A Geographical Analysis" (Ph.D. dissertation,

Taking into consideration the continued migration and high birth rates of French Canadians, as well as the Yankee exodus, it is not surprising that the ratio of the French-Canadian population increased dramatically after 1880. In 1890, according to Ralph Vicero, in his Ph.D. dissertation on French-Canadian migration into New England in the nineteenth century, Biddeford had the highest concentration of Francos in New England among cities with a population of over 14,000—56%. In 1900, the percentage of Franco-Americans—as they were now called— reached 60% in Biddeford and remained at that figure until 1920. In 1930, according to the best available figures, 75% of Biddeford's population was of French-Canadian origin. By 1970, that figure had remained the same, according to statistics I gathered from the two French parishes in the city. The 1970 Census shows Biddeford with a French-mother-tongue population of 61.4%, which is quite likely an underestimation since, by 1970, a not-insignificant number of French-surnamed inhabitants in Biddeford probably failed to claim French as their mother tongue. In any case, and this is the important point, Biddeford had the highest percentage of Francos among New England cities with a population of over ten thousand, according to the 1970 Census.[4]

The geographic concentration of Francos in Biddeford was reinforced by the residential concentration within the city itself. The French-Canadian population in the city, as in so many other New England mill towns, was concentrated in an area adjacent to the mills and the rivers that supplied their power. Streets with

---

University óf Wisconsin, 1968), p. 125, found that as early as 1860 there were already thousands of ex-Maine residents living in other states. By 1880, 182,257 Maine-born residents had left the state. The figure represented a fourth of Maine's population. Albert Faucher, "L'Émigration des Canadiens français aux États-Unis au XIXe siècle: position du problème et perspectives," *Recherches sociographiques* 5 (septembre-décembre 1964): 286; *The Union and Journal*, 1870-1880; Roy Fairfield, *Sand, Spindles and Steeples* (Portland, Maine: House of Falmouth, 1956), pp. 217, 243, 423; James P. Allen, "Catholics in Maine: A Social Geography," (Ph.D. dissertation, Syracuse University, 1970), p. 176; *Biddeford Record*, May 4, 1899; *Biddeford Weekly Journal*, November 16, 1900.

[4]   [According to the 1990 Census, Biddeford, with 35%, is one of five cities in which 20-40% of the local population reports *speaking French*. The others are Berlin, N.H. (40%), Lewiston, Maine (34%), Woonsocket, R.I. (21%), and Sanford, Maine (20%). See Madeleine Giguère "New England's Francophone Population" in this volume for additional information on French-speakers in New England.—Editor]

names like River, Water, and Bridge were usually located in the heart of the *Petits Canadas* of New England. According to the city directories, most Francos in Biddeford lived in an area bounded by the Saco River and River Street, the Boston and Maine Railroad, and the mills—that is, on the west side of the city. The 1870 Census also indicated that the French Canadians tended to cluster together. Although there were no addresses listed on the census sheets, families were numbered in order of visitation. Two large clusters of French names, and several small ones, were evident. By 1877, this area of the city was referred to as the "French Patch."[5]

The 1880 Census, which was taken by wards, indicates an extremely high level of concentration: Ward V included the River Street area and had such a high concentration of French Canadians—75%—that a Franco was hired to take the census there that year. After 1880, this area was referred to as "Little Canada." On the other hand, Ward I with a 1% Franco population and Ward VII with 12%, were located on the edge of town, in the upper-class neighborhoods. In 1880, few Francos lived near the ocean at Biddeford Pool or in the rural community of Dayton.

By 1907, Ward V was still being referred to as "Little Canada." The Franco population, however, was shifting without becoming less concentrated. By 1900, the mills were expanding into the center of "Little Canada." They soon swallowed up much of the Smith, River, Thornton, Gooch, and Laconia Streets area. By the turn of the century, Ward II—the Water Streets area—had become the leading area of Franco concentration. As early as 1896, Francos living in the Ward II area petitioned the bishop to form a French parish, on the east side of the city. Founded in 1899, the new parish, called St. André's, had, by 1907, almost as many faithful as St. Joseph's parish, which had been founded in 1870.[6]

---

5.   This information is gathered from the 1870 *Biddeford-Saco Directory* which listed addresses of French-Canadian residents. Almost half of the migrants lived on Gooch, Laconia, Maple, Spruce, Smith, Hooper, Thornton, and River Streets, all near the river, the railroad, and the mills. Almost all the others lived in areas adjacent to the mills. *Biddeford-Saco Directory* 1877, pp. 16, 23. I am not certain which area earned the nickname "French Patch," but it was most probably the River Street area.

6   *Biddeford-Saco Directory*, 1907, p. 37; 1910, 1912; *La Justice*, July 13, 1899 and January 30, 1902.

This Franco-American concentration in the city led to a Franco-American concentration in local textile mills that, by 1910, employed 78% of the city's blue-collar workers. In fact, by 1910, one out of every four residents in Biddeford was employed in the mills, hence Biddeford's nickname, the "Mill City." The percentage of Franco-American workers in Biddeford's mills increased steadily in the nineteenth century. In 1849, according to the Biddeford-Saco *Directory*, there were no Francos listed among the hundreds of young female mill hands at the Pepperell or at neighboring Saco, Maine's York Mill. According to the Pepperell Manufacturing Company's payroll records, only a handful of Francos worked in the mills in the early 1850s. By 1870, 15% of the Pepperell's workers were of French-Canadian origin. By 1880, the figure had grown to over 30%. By 1890, the figure stood at 55%. The percentage of Francos working in these mills continued to increase until, by 1950, 70% of the Pepperell's work force was Franco.[7]

What was the effect of such concentration in the mills? One of my interviewees showed me a picture of herself and her co-workers taken c. 1918. The only non-Frenchman in the photo was the foreman, Charles McCarthy. I asked, "Did you mind having an Irish boss?" She answered, "Not really, since McCarthy spoke French like an *habitant*." Another interviewee mentioned that her boss, a Mr. Donahue, spoke French also.

While Francos in Lawrence and Lowell, Massachusetts, were, by 1910, laboring side by side with Polish, Italian, and Greek-Americans, Francos in Biddeford were insulated from contact with foreign cultures and were better able to maintain their own identity. Immigrants from southern and eastern Europe did come to Biddeford, but not in large numbers because Francos, fearing for their jobs, resented the newer groups and formed an organization that appointed a committee to ask Pepperell Agent Robert McArthur not to import Greek and Italian workers. It was not uncommon to read in *La Justice*, Biddeford's French

7   Vicero, "Immigration of French Canadians," pp. 298, 313, 332-334, 345; Maine, Bureau of Industrial and Labor Statistics, *Twenty-Fourth Annual Report* 1910; *Biddeford-Saco Directory* 1849 shows no French girls among the Pepperell's employees or among the Bates Manufacturing Company's 665 workers; Pepperell Manufacturing Company, Payroll Books, 1849-1854, June 1870, June 1880, and 1885-1891; Knowlton, *Pepperell's Progress* (Cambridge, MA: Harvard University Press, 1948), p. 163; Fairfield, *Sand, Spindles and Steeples*, p. 191.

newspaper, published from 1896 to 1950, about confrontations between angry French Canadians and frightened Greeks weakly trying to defend themselves by saying, "I didn't come here to take jobs away from Canadians. Only Syrians and Armenians do that." Alfred Bonneau, the editor of *La Justice* until his death in 1920, warned about the influx of Greek and Italian workers into Biddeford and probably expressed the sentiments of his readers when he advocated restriction on European immigration at the turn of the century. At the York Mill, where Agent Page hired fifty Armenians and Syrians in 1899 during a local strike, Francos complained bitterly and were told by mill agents to write to their relatives in Quebec and urge them to immigrate to the "Mill City." Consequently, not many European immigrants came to Biddeford after the Francos arrived, except for a fairly sizeable number of Greeks, who became self-employed not long after their arrival rather than compete with the Francos in the mills.[8]

The size of the group was as important as their concentration in preventing Franco assimilation in Biddeford. James Paul Allen, in his Ph.D. dissertation on Maine's Catholics, found an inverse relationship between the size of the Franco community and the rate of intermarriage, regardless of the Franco percentage in the population. Allen also found that the smaller the Franco-American population, the weaker its compartmentalization and the less exclusive the interaction within the ethnic group milieu.[9]

Franco-Americans in Biddeford have ranked either first or second in Maine in terms of numbers. By as early as 1890, over eight thousand Francos lived in Biddeford. In 1970, Biddeford's Franco-American population ranked twelfth in New England with over twelve thousand Francos out of a population of 19,900. Thus, Biddeford Francos were able to support their churches, schools, societies, and a press of their own, thereby increasing their compartmentalization and interaction within the group.

Because of the size and concentration of the Franco-American community in Biddeford, Francos in the city could go about their

---

8   *La Justice*, April 30; June 18, 25; July 2, 30, 1903; *Biddeford Record*, June 24, 1903; Fairfield, *Sand, Spindle and Steeples*, p. 220; Gibb, *The Saco-Lowell Shops* (Cambridge, MA: Harvard University Press, 1950), p. 500. Allen, "Catholics in Maine," p. 217, maintains that Francos feared eastern Europeans because they were "new and uncertain peoples."

9   Allen, "Catholics in Maine," pp. 70, 211, 222, 338, 343.

daily routine without speaking or hearing English. Even in the mills, other ethnics learned to speak French in order to get along. It is not surprising then to discover from U.S. Immigration and Naturalization Records that dozens of Biddeford Francos spoke no English even after living in the city for decades.[10]

The immigration pattern of French Canadians into Biddeford also contributed to *la survivance*—that is, the preservation of the Catholic faith, the French language, and French-Canadian culture. The influx was not steady, but was characterized by spurts followed by periods of almost no immigration. Periods of rapid Franco-American immigration to Biddeford included 1865-1873, 1877-1881, and 1890-1893. The periods of no growth corresponded to years of financial panics and depressions. Dr. George F. Theriault, who wrote his Harvard doctoral dissertation on Francos in Nashua, New Hampshire, commenting on the ebb and flow characteristic of Franco migration, concluded that:

> The wave-like pattern of migration . . . had much to do with the successful establishment and maintenance of *la Franco-Américanie* in New England. The simultaneous arrival in New England's cities of large numbers of like-minded French Canadians, sharing a strong tradition, similar status as poor, unskilled, uneducated wage workers . . . created the necessary conditions for the prompt establishment of a minority sub-society. [11]

Any discussion of Franco-American immigration patterns and how they facilitated *la survivance* would not be complete without highlighting two characteristics that distinguished

---

[10]   The Immigration and Naturalization Act of 1952 provided that those permanent residents, fifty years of age or older, who had lived in the United States for at least twenty years, could become citizens without any knowledge of English. Twenty-four Biddeford Francos, whose records indicated they spoke only French, became citizens soon thereafter. They had lived in Biddeford an average of forty-seven years. My father, who came to Biddeford in 1919, still speaks no English. See U. S. Department of Justice, Immigration and Naturalization Service, *Naturalization Requirements and General Information* 1972, p. 15 and *Record of Declaration of Intention*, vols. 50-58, at the U. S. District Court, Portland.

[11]   Theriault, "The Franco-Americans of New England," *Canadian Dualism. Studies of French-English Relations*. Edited by Mason Wade. (Toronto: University of Toronto Press, 1960), p. 399.

French-Canadian immigration from the European phenomenon: 1) the proximity of the Quebec homeland and 2) continued French-Canadian migration into the United States after the 1924 Immigration Restriction Acts went into effect.

Because of the proximity to Quebec, the French Canadian, in travelling south across the border to find work, was making no firm commitment to remain in the United States. To quote Dr. Theriault once again:

> However nostalgic the Polish immigrant might feel about his childhood in a peasant village, he had made and knew he had made an irrevocable commitment in coming to a new . . . land. He had turned his face on the past, made a clean and definite break with it . . . Not so the Franco-American.[12]

Hence, the French Canadian sometimes hesitated to put down roots in New England. Rather than take an active interest in the community and learn English, he yearned for the day when he could return to *la belle province.* An examination of Biddeford City Directories shows that between 1870 and 1890 the turnover of the Franco population was almost 50% every three years. According to Stephan Thernstrom, in his book *Poverty and Progress,* Biddeford led New England, along with two other mill towns, in the transiency of its population.[13]

Because of this high rate of transiency, few French Canadians in New England became naturalized or took an active role in politics and civic affairs. For example, according to T.-A. Chandonnet, only 3% of Worcester's French Canadians were citizens in 1871, even though half the French-Canadian population in the Bay State had been residents for over ten years.[14] In many other Little Canadas of New England, the figures were similar. It is thus not surprising that Francos ranked second only to the Chinese in the number of years of United States

---

[12]   Ibid., p. 399.

[13]   Thernstrom, *Poverty and Progress* (Cambridge, MA: Harvard University Press, 1964), p. 199.

[14]   T.-A. Chandonnet, *Notre-Dame-des-Canadiens* (Montreal: Desbarats, 1872), p. 137.

residence prior to naturalization—sixteen and a half years. [15] The rate of naturalization among Francos in Biddeford did not vary greatly from those of the rest of New England. The manuscript figures for 1850, 1860 and 1870 all show that fewer than 13% of the Franco males over twenty-one years of age were citizens. Israel Shevenell claimed to be Biddeford's first Franco voter, but failed to mention that he became naturalized only fifteen years after his arrival. Ferdinand Gagnon, the noted editor of Worcester's famous French-language newspaper *Le Travailleur*, reported in 1881 that only 7% of the French Canadians in Biddeford were citizens. By 1891, although Francos comprised over 50% of Biddeford's population, only 14% of the city's voters were French. In 1898, William McDonald, a professor at Bowdoin College, estimated the number of Franco voters in Biddeford to be only six hundred out of a French ethnic population of nine thousand. [16]

The several political organizations which were established to encourage naturalization among local Francos apparently had only limited success. From 1945 to 1957, those French Canadians residing in Biddeford who became naturalized had lived in the city for an average of twenty-seven years. Five of them had lived in Biddeford for over sixty years before becoming citizens. Two-thirds of the Canadian-born spouses of Biddeford Francos, who became citizens between 1945 and 1973, were aliens themselves.

Because of Quebec's proximity, Franco-Americans in Biddeford frequently sojourned in the land of their ancestors. The pages of *La Justice* are full of notices of locally sponsored religious pilgrimages to Quebec. In addition to pilgrimages, Biddeford Francos, according to *La Justice*'s local news columns, often visited friends and relatives in Canada or simply vacationed there.

Railroads, of course, encouraged this travel. Ralph Vicero estimates that by 1900 there were eighty-seven Francos in New

---

[15]   N. Carpenter, *Immigrants and Their Children* (Washington, D.C.: Census Monograph, U.S. Printing Office, 1927), p. 264.

[16]   In 1850, none of the eight Franco males over twenty-one were citizens. In 1860, only seventeen of the 101 adults had been naturalized. In 1870, only forty-five of 299 were citizens. Massachusetts, Bureau of Statistics of Labor, *Thirteenth Annual Report* (1882), p. 17. *Weekly Standard*, December 2 and 30, 1891; McDonald, "The French-Canadians in New England," *The Quarterly Journal of Economics*, p. 270.

England who served as railroad agents. Often they were
professionals who sold tickets in their pharmacies, offices, and
publishing rooms. Both Alfred Bonneau and his successor, Joseph
Bolduc, were agents of the Grand Trunk Railroad, which may
explain the preponderance of ads in *La Justice* for this railroad as
compared with its competitor, the Maine Central. The
competition between the two lines prevented a steady increase in
fares, enabling even indigent Francos to visit Quebec. From 1896
to 1910, prices for a trip from Biddeford to Montreal, Quebec City,
and St. Anne de Beaupré remained the same. Both companies also
offered special group rates to encourage pilgrimages.

Consequently, at the turn of the century, travel to Quebec was
so common in Biddeford that local textile mills often closed their
plants in June, July, and August when French-Canadian
operatives returned to Canada for the summer, to visit friends or
farm the old homestead. Extended vacations in Canada were also
common because of the propensity of Franco-Americans to leave
the United States during slack business periods. *La Justice* cited a
number of Biddeford Francos who journeyed to Canada for several
months at a time. Almost 20% of those Biddeford French
Canadians, naturalized between 1945 and 1973, had spent at least
one period of six months or more in Canada since their arrival in
the "Mill City."

Because of the proximity of their homeland, Francos could
also regularly entertain friends from Canada. The *curés* in
Biddeford often invited priests from Quebec to say Mass, give
sermons, and perform other religious duties during their
sometimes lengthy stays in Biddeford. The annual retreats
sponsored by Franco parishes were usually preached by Canadian
priests, even in the 1960s. *La Justice*'s social pages mentioned
news of Canadians visiting among local Francos on a regular
basis. The *Biddeford Record* once reported that 450 excursionists
had come from Canada to Biddeford on a special express train to
visit friends and relatives in the city.[17]

---

[17]   *Biddeford Record*, June 24, 1902. It was not uncommon for as many
as three hundred club members to make a pilgrimage together in Canada.
Often these pilgrims were led by priests. Ads called attention to trips to
Lourdes and Rome. Another issue mentions the death of a young Franco
girl from Biddeford on a train bound for Canada carrying two hundred
Biddeford Francos. *La Justice*, June 23, 1897; June 18, 1903; June 9, 1904;
July 25, 1907.

The closeness of Quebec to New England thus helped the Franco in Biddeford to remain in constant contact with his or her homeland. Frequent trips there served to reinforce old ties and facilitate the retention of language and culture. This repeated interaction between the Franco and the French Canadian surely had an effect in helping the former resist Americanization.

Another extremely important effect of Quebec's proximity to Biddeford was the number of Biddeford Franco students who attended school in that province. Between 1900 and 1930, *La Justice* carried numerous articles about local sons and daughters studying in Quebec. As early as 1905, thirteen young women from Biddeford were attending a convent in Stanstead, Quebec. In 1910, twenty Francos from Biddeford were attending the *Collège de Beauceville* and other local students were studying in more than ten other Quebec cities. Attendance at Canadian schools by Biddeford students reached its peak in the 1920s as Quebec schools sent recruiters to entice Biddeford Francos to Quebec. As enrollment increased, notable Biddeford Francos were invited to Canadian school graduation ceremonies to award prizes to local students. The fact that so many youngsters from Biddeford received a Canadian education also played an important role in the maintenance of the French language and French-Canadian culture in Biddeford.[18]

Quebec's proximity to Biddeford was also important because it no doubt contributed to the success of Canadian repatriation efforts, which in turn increased the transiency of French-Canadian immigrants. Between 1870 and 1920, Biddeford was fertile soil for repatriation agents. Father P.-E. Gendreau, one of the more successful agents from Quebec, visited the city in 1873 and found a number of its French residents ready to return to Canada. During the 1873 St. Jean-Baptiste Convention in Biddeford, the delegates, 15% of whom were from the "Mill City," passed a resolution asking Quebec to initiate a repatriation program. One of the convention's delegates, Worcester's own Ferdinand Gagnon, reported that there were dozens of families in Biddeford willing to repatriate, but who lacked the funds to do so. In his capacity as a repatriation agent, he arranged rebates on the railroads for would-be Biddeford repatriates and found them land

---

18   *La Justice*, September 4, 1902; June 18, 1903; June 29, September 7 and 27, 1905; January 2 and September 24, 1908; September 8, 1910; February 22 and September 6, 1917; June 6, 1918; December 8, 1922; August 23, 1929; and June 13. 1930.

near Sherbrooke. Articles in *La Justice* lauded Gagnon's efforts. When he died, those in Biddeford who remembered his repatriation work had a special Mass celebrated for him. Bonneau praised the man and his work.[19]

In the 1880s, *Curé* Labelle visited Biddeford and other New England cities in an effort to repatriate French Canadians. "Noted for his zeal in the cause of immigration and colonization," Labelle, carrying maps and enticing literature, was very effective in his appeals. In the 1890s, repatriation efforts achieved even greater success in the "Mill City." Biddeford Francos, like those in other mill towns, were especially open to Canadian repatriation efforts in this decade. The textile competition from southern mills, the depression of 1893, and the especially bitter strikes which followed, in 1898, served as catalysts for repatriation from Biddeford. During the depression of 1893, whole families were repatriated to Canada. In fact, the city of Biddeford subsidized the repatriation of indigent Francos to Quebec. Hundreds of Franco-American mill employees left Biddeford permanently after 1897 as several colonization agents descended upon the area. In early 1898, another priest named *Curé* Fèvre succeeded in repatriating one hundred Francos from Biddeford, many of whom had been without work for months. By 1899, two other repatriation agents were working in Biddeford. Roger Carufel arrived in August of 1899 and, in November, was joined by René Dupont. Working for the Canadian government, they encouraged colonization in the Lake St. John area of the Province of Quebec.[20]

Ottawa was aided in its efforts by the clever choice of René Dupont. A native of Biddeford, Dupont was the nephew of *Curé* Pierre Dupont, pastor of St. Joseph's parish. During his sixteen years in Biddeford, the younger Dupont was probably helped by his uncle, who much preferred that the *habitants* worship in Quebec than in protestant New England. Because he was born and raised in Biddeford, Dupont was easily able to establish contact with the local Franco-American population, thus facilitating his work. Dupont's greatest ally, however, was Alfred Bonneau, the

---

[19]   "Report of P.-E. Gendreau," p. 68. Gatineau, *Conventions générales* (Woonsocket, R.I.: L'Union St-Jean-Baptiste d'Amérique, 1927), p. 39; *La Justice*, June 14, 1900, and June 2, 1904.

[20]   Fairfield, *Sand, Spindles and Steeples,* pp. 218-219; *Biddeford Weekly Journal*, February 9, and April 15, 1898; *La Justice,* August 31 and November 29, 1899; May 20, 1909; Vicero, p. 237.

editor of *La Justice*. He strongly backed the repatriation movement and constantly highlighted its efforts in his newspaper. Between 1907 and 1909, *La Justice* carried weekly ads of repatriation societies. These continued to appear monthly until 1922 with a four-year hiatus during World War I. The same issue often carried ads from both provincial and federal agencies. The Société de colonisation de Montréal probably paid little for its ads since its agent was none other than Alfred Bonneau himself. Bonneau understandably stressed the free land offered by the Province of Quebec, but he also carried numerous and extensive ads from the government of Ottawa. Offering 160 acres of free land, these ads invariably emphasized the healthful climate, the fertile soil, the plentiful harvests, the rich grazing land, the free wood for fences and homes, the good neighbors, the just laws, the low taxes, the cheap prices, the good transportation system, and the churches and schools in Canada. The ads urged readers to contact the local repatriation agent or write the parent organization in Canada for more information.

Bonneau printed dozens of speeches and articles by repatriation agents and others who favored the colonization of new regions in Canada. In April 1910, Bonneau described the visit of a *curé* to the "Mill City" who was quoted as saying:

> I have seen the Canadians in Biddeford, especially those of the working-class, who love their homeland and want to come home to die in peace. Poverty is ruining their health. Inflation has taken its toll too. Those who continue leaving Canada will have a difficult time making a living. we must show the Franco how happy and prosperous he would be if he returned to Canada.[21]

In June 1910, Bonneau featured an article on a Canadian *curé* and repatriation agent named Albert Bérubé who addressed local Francos this way:

> You are tired of life in the mills. You have told me so. Many among you have written me to that effect and I have seen it with my own eyes. Your financial status is not what it should be. For a long time you have served masters without hearts. For too long you have built fortunes for rich Americans. It is time to think about yourself and your children. Your fifteen to twenty-year

---

[21]   *La Justice*, April 21, 1910.

experience in the United States shows you that there is
nothing but the life of a mercenary there. Do you want
to be truly free? . . . Do you want your independence? Do
you want to be your own boss once again? Come to
Canada and we will provide you and your sons over the
age of seventeen with very good and plentiful land.[22]

Repatriation agents used nationalist and ethnic arguments, as
well as economic and sentimental approaches. One expressed his
strong doubts that the *habitants* could maintain *la survivance* if
they made the United States their permanent home. Another
urged his compatriots to come back to Quebec, saying that the only
way the province could maintain its identity within the dominion
was to persuade its brothers living in the United States to return
home. Bonneau himself wrote an article entitled "Return to Our
Homeland," whose theme was that French blood transcended all
other considerations.[23]

Bonneau continually referred to the success of the
repatriation drives in Biddeford, often citing the prosperity of ex-
Biddeford families who were now living in Canada and describing
in detail the departure of Francos for residence there. In one 1910
article, for example, Bonneau devoted several columns to a group
of 118 Biddeford Franco repatriates, led by Father Bérubé, who
were headed for western Canada. Bonneau made special mention
of the fact that they were travelling in luxurious railroad cars
provided especially for them.[24]

One Franco businessman-pharmacist Linière Doyon, head of
an informal Franco-American Chamber of Commerce, became so
alarmed by the growing number of local French Canadians
returning to Canada to settle, that he set up a committee to try to
stem the flow of repatriates. As an aside, the pharmacy started by
druggist Doyon is one of the few Franco-owned businesses,
founded at the turn of the century, still in existence today. The
pages of *La Justice,* during its fifty-five years of publication,
featured ads from dozens of French businesses on Main Street. All
have disappeared.

---

[22]   *La Justice*, June 9, 1910.

[23]   *La Justice*, July 28, 1910; August 31,1911; September 26 and
December 12, 1912; September 2, 1915; November 3, 1933.

[24]   *La Justice*, April 14, 1910.

The obvious effect of the repatriation movement, of course, was the number of French-Canadian migrants it induced to return to Canada. Even for those repatriates who eventually returned to Biddeford, their absences from their adopted country served to insulate them from assimilationist forces. For those who remained in New England, the "movement with its permanent and closely woven ties to the old country, together with the . . . stimulated desire to return through the repatriation agencies . . . no doubt contributed" to their resolve to resist American-ization.[25]

If repatriation agents did not entice French Canadians to return to their homeland, they delayed naturalization by weakening the immigrants' commitment to Biddeford. Repatriation appeals reminded the *habitants* that they were Canadian immigrants whose roots were in Quebec. Those who did not succumb to the recolonization appeal resented the implication of the movement's leaders that only French Canadians living in Canada could maintain their ethnic identity. This resentment led them to a more tenacious effort in favor of *la survivance.*

The success of Canadian resettlement efforts was also one of the reasons French-Canadian migrants were pegged as the "Chinese of the Eastern States." The report that carried this charge contains a description of the repatriation effort and its contribution to the transiency of Francos. "Indeed," maintains Ralph Vicero, "the major result of the [repatriation] movement may have been its effect in alienating a large segment of public opinion in New England against the French-Canadian element."[26]

In Biddeford, there was ample evidence of nativism against the French Canadians. Local historian Roy Fairfield has written that without a doubt Francos were second-class citizens in the Biddeford-Saco area. Local Francos I interviewed spoke of sections of the city they feared entering as children. Although most citizens had no opportunity to express an opinion about immigration in general, many seemed skeptical about its value. Speeches, sermons, and letters to the editor often expressed opposition to immigration. At the 1893 Biddeford High

25   Dexter, "*Habitant* Transplanted," p. 153.

26   Vicero, "Immigration. . .1840-1900," pp. 236, 357.

graduation, graduate John Flood lectured on the trouble occasioned by the lack of restrictive immigration laws: "The immigrant with no knowledge of self-government, of the constitution or of the language should not be allowed to colonize upon our shores." He urged Congress to find a remedy "for the present menacing condition of affairs."

Another local nativist voiced his opinion in an April 27,1907 letter to the editor of the *Biddeford Record*:

> There is a certain class of people in Biddeford that you must admit are the ruination of one of the fairest cities in Maine, that is the French-speaking people as you style them, who are a curse to any city wherein they reside and you know where Biddeford is today with them. But they can't have a kitchen dance but what your paper will come out the next day and tell what a great time they had and rattle off a lot of French names that nobody can read or else wants to read. [. . .] Now I have gotten sick and disgusted with it and so have all the neighborhood where I live that read your paper, and we have made up our minds to stop it. We are not French, neither Irish. We are true-born Americans and we don't want to read any more about the exploits of the French in Biddeford, nor of the Irish neither, for one is no better than the other. I helped to build the Pepperell and Laconia Mills and we didn't have any use for the French or Irish then and I haven't any now.

Biddeford's Francos were also blamed for smallpox epidemics by the city's Yankees. The city's Overseer of the Poor complained that local immigrants who couldn't find jobs immediately went on welfare, using deception and deceit to get aid. "Unlike most of our native poor, the foreigners seem to have no manly pride about them in regard to becoming paupers," continued the official.[27]

The hostility engendered against French-Canadian

---

[27]   The local official is quoted in Fairfield, p. 219. See also *Ibid.*, pp. 215-217, 292; *Biddeford Standard*, June 27, 1893; *Biddeford Record*, October 28, 1902 and April 27, 1907; *La Justice*, June 13, 1901. Nativist fears of disease-bearing French migrants in other cities are cited in Gustav Schwab, "A Practical Remedy for Evils of Immigration," *Forum* 14 (February 1893): 805-814 and U. S. Department of State, Consular Report, Montreal, Wendell Anderson to James Porter, August 28, 1885.

newcomers because of the repatriation movement, as well as their religion, their language, and their seemingly strange customs, served to increase Franco group solidarity and helped Francos resist assimilation.

Because the French Canadians were considered sedulous and docile workers, local mill agents continued to recruit them well into the twentieth century in spite of nativist sentiment, and urged their workers to entice their relatives to settle in "Mill City." It is difficult to estimate just how many French Canadians have come to Biddeford since 1920. Between 1920 and 1930, however, the Franco population in Biddeford increased by over two thousand as French Canadians and Acadians from northern Maine came to the "Mill City." An examination of Franco obituaries in the local newspaper reveals that a significant number of French-Canadian migrants came to Biddeford after 1920. A perusal of Immigration and Naturalization Service records also confirms that hundreds of French Canadians continued to arrive in Biddeford after the flow of southern and eastern European immigration had been slowed to a trickle by post-World War I immigration restriction laws.

The Pepperell Manufacturing Company continued to recruit hundreds of French Canadians until the mid-1960s. Personnel Manager, Maurice Roux, and his successor, Paul LaRose, used their French-language skills to the fullest. One possible reason making recruitment in Canada a necessity was that local young Francos tried to avoid working in the mills. We remembered what our teachers in the city's parochial schools used to say when exhorting us to study harder, "*Veux-tu travailler à la Pepperell pour le reste de tes jours?*" ["Do you want to work at the Pepperell for the rest of your life?"]

While interviewing recent immigrants from Quebec to the "Mill City" in the early 1970s, I noticed that few remained in the mills very long, unlike many French Canadians who had come to Biddeford before them. Social mobility appeared much more rapid for these newcomers than it had been for their predecessors in the nineteenth century. Almost every one of the recent arrivals whom I interviewed mentioned that a critical factor in their decision to come to Biddeford was their feeling that they could adjust to a city in which the French language was still spoken extensively on the street, in churches, parochial schools, and many clubs and organizations.

Thus the relationship between the city and recent migrants has been a symbiotic one. The city has afforded a place for the *Québécois* to feel at home and adapt very gradually to American ways. In turn, these migrants have provided the city with a steady stream of new French blood that has served to keep old ties alive and reinvigorate its Franco element. These new migrants sought membership in French societies, attended the French-language Masses at St. Joseph's and St. André's parishes and sent their children to parochial schools. In short, they bolstered Biddeford's ethnic institutions.[28]

Since the mid-1960s, however, few *Québécois* have immigrated to Biddeford. The Pepperell transferred some of its operations from Biddeford and ceased recruiting in Canada. A new immigration law that went into effect in January 1969 placed a numerical limitation of twenty thousand on Canadian immigration to the United States and by the end of 1969 had cut Canadian immigration to the U.S. in half. Other changes increased the waiting time for Canadian non-preference applicants, the category which included prospective mill workers, to two and one half years.

The flow of French Canadians to Biddeford, permanently curtailed by the Immigration Act of 1965, and the closing of St. Louis High School in 1970, signaled the end for other Franco institutions in the city and dealt a death blow to the quest for *la survivance.*

Twenty-five years later, assimilation and acculturation continue unabated in Biddeford. The two Franco-American parochial elementary schools, St. Joseph and St. André, have merged with the Irish-American school. The new shool is called St. James—a name difficult to pronounce in French. The school's enrollment is below 300. When I attended St. Joseph's grammar school in the early 1950s, there were almost 1000 students—more

---

28   Prior, "French-Canadians in New England" (Master's thesis, Brown University, 1932), pp. 151-152; Allen, "Catholics in Maine," p. 115; Foley, "French-Canadian to Franco-American" (Ph.D. dissertation, Harvard University, 1939), p. 389; and Theriault, "The Franco-Americans of New England," p. 399, all cite the importance of continued migration after 1924 in helping the Franco resist assimilation. In 1924, Dexter in "*Habitant Transplanted*" (Ph.D. dissertation, Clark University, 1929), p. 2, warned that the new immigration laws did not bar French Canadians and worried that this continued influx would prevent the Francos from assimilating.

than the entire public school enrollment in the city.

The 1990 Census for Biddeford showed a total of 6,730 people, out of 20,710, who answered "French" when asked "What language do you speak in your home?" That only a third of the "Mill City's" residents say they speak French at home, when more than 60% of its residents have French surnames, is another indication of increasing assimilation.

Although Franco-Americans are the state's largest ethnic group, Maine has never had a Franco governor, senator, or congressman. In November 1994, there was an excellent opportunity to elect one in the person of Dennis Dutremble, State Senator from Biddeford and President of the Maine State Senate. As the Democratic nominee for the open Congressional seat in Maine's First Congressional District, Mr. Dutremble was running against a political novice. Born and raised in Biddeford, Mr. Dutremble was educated at St. Joseph's Grammar School and St. Louis High School. He speaks French fluently, having attended St. Joseph's when instruction there was still in French for half the day.

Mr. Dutremble lost in a tight race—52% to 48%. At first I surmised that racism against Franco-Americans among Maine's non-Franco voters probably tipped the scales. Yet, when I inquired if Mr. Dutremble had carried 90% of Biddeford's Franco votes as was traditional among French native-son candidates, I was told that he had barely received 70% of the vote. I was dumbfounded by the realization that Mr. Dutremble had probably done worse in Biddeford than the Democratic candidate for Congress in 1992, Tom Andrews. Sure enough, Andrews polled 72.6% of Biddeford's votes that year. To add salt to the wound, Andrews received 2,000 more votes in 1992 than Dutremble received in 1994 in the "Mill City."

That a native son had done so poorly against someone named Longley, from the posh town of Falmouth, shows the sad state of *la survivance* in Biddeford today.

[This article first appeared as "Geographic and Demographic Forces Facilitating Ethnic Survival in a New England Mill Town: The Franco-Americans of Biddeford, Maine," in the French Institute's publication entitled *The Little Canadas of New England*. It has been reviewed by the author and up-dated for inclusion in this volume.]

APPENDIX A

Biddeford's Franco-American Population
1840-1970

Year	Biddeford's population	Biddeford's Franco population	Percentage of Franco population
1840	2,574	?	-
1850	6,095	28	.004
1860	9,350	432	.046
1870	10,282	1,680	16.4
1880	12,652	4,283	33.8
1890	14,443	8,155	56.4
1900	16,145	9,650	59.7
1910	17,079	9,641	56.4
1920	18,008	10,740 (1922)	59.8
1930	17,633	13,150 (1931)	74.5
1940	19,790	?	-
1950	20,836	?	-
1960	19,255	?	-
1970	19,983	14,961 (1969)	75.0
1980	19,638	12,570	64.0
1990	20,710	12,314	59.5

The figures for Biddeford's population are cited in the *Maine Register,* 1971. The figures for Biddeford's Franco-American population from 1850 to 1880 were taken from the manuscript census. They are disputed by Vicero, "Immigration," pp. 171 and 289, who found forty-four Francos in the city in 1850 and 587 in 1860, and Allen, "Catholics in Maine," p. 176, who argues that 31% of Biddeford's population was French in 1880. Vicero's claim that there were 4,301 Francos in Biddeford-Saco in 1880 is consistent with my findings if there were only eighteen Francos in Saco.

The 1890 Franco-American population is taken from Hamon, *Les Canadiens français de la Nouvelle-Angleterre,* p. 402. The figures for 1900 and 1910 are taken from Vicero, "Immigration," pp. 288-289, 343 and Allen, "Catholics in Maine," pp. 150, 164 and 175.

Vicero gathered his figures from Ambroise Choquet's estimate of the Franco population in Biddeford in *Reports of the Commissioner of Agriculture and Colonization of the Province of Quebec.* Allen arrived at his figure for 1900 by taking Vicero's estimate for that year for both Biddeford and Saco and subtracting the number of Francos which McDonald, in "French Canadians in New England," p. 254, found in Saco in 1898—one thousand.

Allen took his 1910 figure from the U. S. Department of Commerce, Bureau of the Census, *Thirteenth Census of the United States Population* II, p. 18, and Odule LaPlante's 1908 census of parishes in Maine cited in *Le Messager* of Lewiston.

The figures for 1922 and 1931 come from Albert Bélanger, *Guide officiel des Franco-Américains* (Fall River, Massachusetts: n.p., 1922) and Ibid., 1931.

The 1969 figure was supplied to the author by the pastors at St. Joseph's and St. André's parishes.

The figures on the foreign-born and foreign-stock in Biddeford are taken from U. S. Department of Commerce, Bureau of the Census, *Thirteenth Census of the United States Population,* III, p. 818; *Fourteenth Census of the United States Population,* III, p. 541; *Fifteenth Census of the United States Population,* III, p. 1031; *Sixteenth Census of the United States Population,* II, p. 477, and Truesdell, *The Canadian-Born in the United States,* p. 89.

Although by 1890 Biddeford had the highest concentration of Francos in New England among cities of over fourteen thousand population, it was not unique in this respect. Vicero, "Immigration," p. 295, found a high degree of concentration among Francos all over New England. By 1880, in the top twenty Franco-American cities, Francos comprised 36% of the population in those communities. By 1900, the figure was 43%. In 1900, in the top ten Franco communities, an average of 31% of the population was French. This geographic concentration was unknown among other groups, according to Vicero who attributed this high level to the fact that Francos did not gravitate to the largest towns in New England or the Middle Atlantic States. Moreoever, comparatively few Francos settled in rural farm and rural non-farm areas. See U. S. Department of Commerce, Bureau of the Census, *Fifteenth Census of the United States Population*, II, p. 527. Truesdell, *The Canadian-Born in the United States*, p. 44, and Walker, *Politics and Ethnocentrism*, p. 3, also comment on the geographic concentration of Francos, as compared with other groups.

The 1970 census figure is taken from U. S. Department of Commerce, Bureau of the Census, 1970 Census of the Population, *General Social and Economic Characteristics*, Maine, Tables 49, 81, and 102. The concentration found by Vicero was still common in Maine in 1970. In the top ten Franco-American communities in Maine, Francos comprised an average of 45% of the population twenty-five years ago.

[The 1980 and 1990 figures are based upon the research of Madeleine Giguère who also provided the following figures on French-speakers in Biddeford for the same periods: 1980—7,856; 1990—6,728. See her article "New England's Francophone Population" in this volume.—Editor]

Other estimates of Biddeford's French population include:

1867	1,250	1886	7,500
1873	2,500	1887	7,562
1877	2,537	1891	8,731
1881	6,500	1897	9,000

Sources: 1867— *Pepperell Sheet*, June, 1942, p. 12 and the *Maine Democrat*, a Saco newspaper, January 28, 1868.
1873— "Report of P.-E. Gendreau," p. 68.
1877— Ponsardin, *Curé* Jean. "Documents," Chancery Library, Diocese of Portland, Maine, p. 94
1881— Massachusetts Bureau of the Statistics of Labor . . . *Report* 1882, p. 17.
1886— Rumilly, pp. 119, 133.
1887— Avila Bourbonnière, *Le Guide français des Etats-Unis*. Lowell, Massachusetts, La Société de Publications françaises des États-Unis, 1887.
1891— Bourbonnière, 3rd edition, 1891.
1897— McDonald, "French Canadians in New England," p. 254.

Bibliography

Allen, James Paul. "Catholics in Maine: A Social Geography." Ph.D. dissertation, Syracuse University, 1970.

Carpenter, Niles. *Immigrants and Their Children*. Washington, D.C.: Census Monograph, U. S. Printing Office, 1927.

Chandonnet, *Abbé* Thomas-Aimé. *Notre-Dame-des-Canadiens et les Canadiens aux États-Unis*. Montreal: Desbarats, 1872.

Dexter, Robert Cloutman. "The French-Canadian Immigrant or the *Habitant* Transplanted." Ph.D. dissertation, Clark University, 1923.

Fairfield, Roy. *Sand, Spindles and Steeples*. Portland, Maine: House of Falmouth, 1956.

Faucher, Albert. "L'Émigration des Canadiens français aux États-Unis au XIXe siècle: position du problème et perspectives." *Recherches Sociograpiques*. 5 (septembre-décembre, 1964).

Foley, Richard Allen. "From French-Canadian to Franco-American 1650-1935." Ph.D. dissertation, Harvard University, 1939.

Gatineau, Félix. *Historique des conventions générales des Canadiens français aux États-Unis, 1865-1901*. Woonsocket, R.I.: L'Union Saint-Jean-Baptiste d'Amérique, 1927.

Gendreau, *Abbé* P.-E. "Report of P.-E. Gendreau, Special Agent, on his visit to French-Canadians in the United States to Minister of Agriculture, 1873." Canada, House of Commons: *Sessional Papers*, 1874, No. 9.

Gibb, George. *The Saco-Lowell Shops*. Cambridge, MA: Harvard University Press, 1950.

Holbrook, Stewart. *The Yankee Exodus*. New York: Macmillan and Co., 1950.

Knowlton, Evelyn. *Pepperell's Progress*. Cambridge, MA: Harvard University Press, 1948.

McDonald, William. "French-Canadians in New England." *Quarterly Journal of Economics* 12: 245-279, 1898.

Prior, Granville Torrey. "The French-Canadians in New England." Master's thesis, Brown University, 1932.

Rumilly, Robert. *Histoire des Franco-Américains.* Woonsocket, R.I.: Union Saint-Jean-Baptiste d'Amérique, 1958.

Sorrell, Richard. "The *Sentinelle* Affair 1924-1929 and Militant *Survivance*: The Franco-American Experience in Woonsocket, Rhode Island." Ph.D. dissertation, State University of New York at Buffalo, 1975.

Theriault, George F. "The Franco-Americans of New England." in *Canadian Dualism. Studies of French-English Relations.* Edited by Mason Wade. Toronto: University of Toronto Press, 1960.

Thernstrom, Stephan. *Poverty and Progress.* Cambridge, MA: Harvard University Press, 1964.

Vicero, Ralph D. "Immigration of French Canadians to New England, 1840-1900: A Geographical Analysis." Ph.D. dissertation, University of Wisconsin, 1968.

Neighbors From the North: French-Canadian Immigrants vs. Trade Unionism in Fall River, Massachusetts

Philip T. Silvia, Jr.

Of all Fall River's ethnic bloc arrivals, the French-Canadian immigrants—the *habitants*—were destined to have the greatest numerical impact upon the so-called Spindle City. As the only nineteenth-century nationality of any appreciable size in Fall River that faced a language barrier, these newcomers were originally welcomed by Spindle City management primarily because they were viewed as docile pawns to be manipulated in its struggle with trade unionism. A cultural minority, the Canadians sought desperately to preserve their ethnic identity as a shield against a multitude of unsympathetic critics disturbed by, among other things, their apparent acceptance of injustices associated with cotton mill employment.

In their Canadian homeland, the economic problems of the nineteenth century had mushroomed into a picture of despair by the late 1860s. Crop blight and crop failures added to the woes of a people whose traditional farming methods, combined with soil exhaustion and antiquated farm implements, resulted in a strained economy made further intolerable by a burgeoning birth rate. These isolated Canadian farmers were also hurt by factors over which they had no control. Tariff barriers and an increasingly complex international economy had led to a world market grain surplus, thereby reducing the selling price of wheat, their foremost crop. Factory work might serve as a safety valve, providing jobs for the surplus populace. It seemed an answer for people now confronted by land subdivision, lack of capital, and limited opportunity.

Quebec, however, had no industry to speak of and, consequently, farmers had to look elsewhere. Fortunately for them, and perhaps more so for Yankee mill owners, New England was close by.[1] The exodus from lower Quebec rural areas intensified in the immediate post-Civil War years, coinciding with the aggressive building program launched by these American entrepreneurs. Only an inadequate labor supply, now that the native-born were turning from mill employment,[2] had discouraged the construction of new cotton textile factories. By attracting an English and Irish immigrant work force that included skilled operatives capable of operating spinning mules, repairing looms, and overseeing department production, half of the manufacturers' problem had been solved. But the majority of jobs were in the unskilled or semi-skilled classifications and could be performed after limited training. For them Quebec's farmers were tapped.[3]

A steady stream of French Canadians was thus encouraged to move southward, penetrating northern New England from 1865 to 1869. Although they only trickled into Fall River before 1870, because of its geographical location in southern New England, these newcomers were in the van of a later flood that, by 1900,

---

[1]   Ralph Dominic Vicero, "Immigration of French Canadians to New England, 1840-1900: A Geographical Analysis" (Ph.D. dissertation, University of Wisconsin, 1968), Chaps. 1-2. For another informative account of the causes of emigration, see Granville Torrey Prior, "The French Canadians in New England," 2 vols., Master's thesis, Brown University, 1932, 1, Chap 1.

[2]   As early as 1860, a wholesale displacement of Fall River's American-born mill employees had occurred. The census of that year, for example, recorded 191 spinners and mule spinners, ninety-eight of whom were born in England and another seventy-one in Ireland. Calculated from: U.S. Bureau of the Census, *Eighth Census of the United States: 1860*. Manuscript, Bristol County, vol. 4, pp. 633-986.

[3]   Local French-Canadian authorities have written about the pre-industrial agrarian heritage of *habitants* arriving in Fall River during the quarter century following the end of the Civil War. A meticulously constructed census of 3,921 French-Canadian adults resident in Fall River in 1888 demonstrated that a substantial proportion of these people came from rural parishes. Only 281 immigrants had come from the cities of Quebec and Montreal, and, of these, a mere 104 were working in Fall River textile manufacturing. Compiled from *Le Guide Français de Fall River et Notes Historiques sur les Canadiens de Fall River*, ed. Edward F. Lamoureux (Fall River: n.p., 1888), pp. 1-104. See also *Le Guide Français de Fall River, Mass.* (Fall River, 1909), pp. 27-28, and D. M. A. Magnan, *Notre-Dame-de-Lourdes de Fall River, Massachusetts* (Quebec City: *Le Soleil*, 1925), p. 23.

would convert Spindle City into the largest French-Canadian community in New England.[4]

One local authority reported that Fall River's French Canadians numbered 3,000 by 1870, but the federal census for that year registered a more plausible 1,129, up from the 107 for 1865.[5] As the Fall River directories of 1869-71 indicate, the occupational listing of fifty-nine French-Canadian male heads of families in 1869 included a sprinkling of carpenters, painters, and masons.[6] However, this work force was predominantly unskilled; half of it was composed of laborers, while over one-quarter were mill employees, none of them holding a position above that of weaver. Thirty-eight of these names were missing from the following year's directory. The holdovers from 1869 included ten laborers and only three mill operatives. This outward migration had been more than compensated for by a replacement force of seventy-six male French-Canadian arrivals who fell into three major vocational categories—laborer (34), carpenter (13), and mill worker (13).[7] The last figure is significant, for it suggests that Spindle City mills were still not attracting substantial numbers of adult French-Canadian males.

The composition of the factory work force during the turbulent, strike-marred 1870s continues this early pattern. To be sure, 943 French-Canadian males had moved into Fall River cotton mills by 1878, but this was only 7.6 percent of the total Spindle City textile labor force, and only 234 or a mere 1.9 percent

4   Vicero, *op. cit.*, pp. 289, 293. By 1900, Fall River, the largest textile-producing city in the Western Hemisphere, contained 31,725 people of French-Canadian stock out of a total population of 104,863. Philip T. Silvia, Jr., "The Spindle City: Labor, Politics, and Religion in Fall River, Massachusetts, 1870 to 1905" (Ph.D. dissertation, Fordham University, 1973), p. 860. The earliest effort to recruit a contingent of French Canadians was undertaken by the American Linen Company in 1865, whose housing area was soon dubbed "Little Canada." *Le Guide Français de Fall River, Mass., op. cit.*, p. 20; *Fall River Daily Herald*, June 24, 1899.

5   *Le Guide Français de Fall River, Mass.*, op. cit., p. 30; U. S. Bureau of the Census, *Ninth Census of the United States: 1870. Population*, I, p. 386.

6   Fall River, *City Directory* (1869), pp. 17-161.

7   Ibid., (1870-1871), pp. 17-176.

were at least twenty-one years of age.[8] The female French-Canadian operatives outnumbered their male counterparts by 273. French-Canadian ethnics thus totalled 2,159 in 1878, which was approximately one-sixth of all Spindle City cotton employees. Among foreign-born textile employees, they were entrenched in third place behind the 4,237 English-born and the 2,591 natives of Ireland. But, while about 40 percent of Irish and English workers were under twenty-one years old, 77 percent of the French Canadians fell into this age group.[9]

These statistics demonstrate that the Fall River mills attracted labor that was unskilled, female, and young. Such employees were sought out for a number of reasons. First, as even a French-Canadian spokesman admitted in 1881, they could be paid wages low enough to assure the cotton textile industry that it would be competitive on a worldwide basis.[10] Second, French Canadians immediately established their mark as industrious workers who quickly adapted to their mechanical tasks. Moreover, they had a reputation for reliability, particularly on the day following payday. Their reputed sobriety, which vividly contrasted with the stereotyped drinking habits of the Irish immigrants, was appreciated by mill owners and substantiated by the disproportionately low arrest rate of Fall River's French Canadians during the 1870s.[11] Management also regarded them as providing corrective balance to the labor "agitator" sector of the mill force arriving from Lancashire.[12] Understandably, then, Fall River corporations sometimes incurred the expense of hiring an agent, paying the travel costs of poverty-stricken Canadian families, and performing the bothersome tasks of providing tenements and provisions for them. One French-Canadian agent, who had arrived at Fall River in 1872, procured French-Canadian help not only for Spindle City employers, but also for mills

---

8   Commonwealth of Massachusetts, Bureau of Statistics of Labor, *Ninth Annual Report* (1878), p. 215. Hereinafter referred to as M.B.S.L.

9   Ibid.

10   Ibid., *Thirteenth Annual Report* (1882), p. 22.

11   Ibid., pp. 64, 380; Sylvia Chase Lintner, "A Social History of Fall River, 1859-1879" (Ph.D. dissertation, Radcliffe College, 1945), p. 564.

12   M. B. S. L., *Thirteenth Annual Report* (1882), 64.

throughout New England and New York State.[13]

After the mid-1870s, however, the persuasiveness of agents sent out by mills seems to have become unnecessary in enticing this labor supply. If a mill were commencing operations and large numbers of operatives were immediately required, or if a strike created a labor demand, a selling campaign might be needed.[14] Otherwise the law of survival could be depended upon to drive thousands across the Canadian border toward a new life, one that held out the promise of more satisfactory material rewards, or simply the assurance of more food.[15] Voluntary migration emptied entire Canadian villages of inhabitants. Those already in Fall River and elsewhere in New England wasted little time encouraging relatives and friends at home to share the opportunities afforded by America's manufacturing communities.[16]

This depletion of the Canadian countryside was deplored by Quebec authorities, particularly the clergy. Those who left became the target of diatribes. They were charged with a lack of moral fiber for forsaking their beloved motherland in favor of New England, the home of the ancient Puritan and Protestant enemy, a region that was part of a secular and even anti-Christian nation.[17] Such weaklings, it was implied, would one day know the wrath of an angry God.

---

[13] Ibid., pp. 62-63.

[14] Ibid., p. 62; *Fall River Daily Evening News*, October 24, November 8, 1881; Vicero, op. cit., p. 259.

[15] Magnan, op. cit., pp. 22-23; Vicero, op. cit., pp. 330-331; U.S. Congress, Senate, *Report of the Committee of the Senate Upon the Relations Between Labor and Capital*, 4 vols., S. Rept. 1262, 48th Cong., 2nd Sess., vol. 3, 1885, pp. 669-670. Hereinafter referred to as U.S. Senate, *Labor and Capital.*

[16] Magnan, op. cit., p. 39; *Le Guide Français de Fall River, Mass.* op. cit., p. 20.

[17] Jacques Ducharme, *The Shadows of the Trees: The Story of French-Canadians in New England* (New York: Harper and Brothers, 1943), p. 24; Robert D. Cross, *The Emergence of Liberal Catholicism in America* (Cambridge: Harvard University Press, 1958), p. 76.

But a counter-propaganda campaign, to support the decision of the émigrés was also set in motion. It was fitting that their most effective early defender was a resident of Fall River, the New England mecca for French Canadians. In 1878, Honoré Beaugrand, who four years earlier had been co-founder of Fall River's first French-language newspaper, *L'Echo du Canada*, published a 300-page work. Thinly disguised as a romantic novel, it was heavily weighted with comments on life in New England, especially in the Spindle City, and on the wage opportunities afforded by mill work. Beaugrand's effort was inspired by a desire to refute calumnies directed against New England that were appearing in Quebec Province.[18]

Manufacturers were attracted by the work habits of the French-Canadian newcomers. But contemporary labor reformers and Fall River craft unionists, particularly class-conscious male mule spinners of Irish and English heritage, weaned on the Lancashire labor movement, experienced difficulty finding anything positive to say about these immigrants. The grievances of organized labor, stated time and again, were that these Canadians were too submissive toward employers, unsympathetic or actively opposed to strikes, and ready to accept any wages, thereby dragging down the pay of other operatives. Additionally, they violated both child labor and maximum-hour laws and were not interested in trade unionism.[19]

Two of these criticisms, submissiveness and anti-strike sentiment, might profitably be seen from a French-Canadian rather than a trade-union perspective. Ethnic leaders insisted that their people were proud of these qualities which, after all, were appreciated by most citizens and would hasten their social acceptance by the larger community.

Part one of the *Thirteenth Annual Report* of the Massachusetts Bureau of Statistics of Labor, devoted to "the Canadian French in New England," had publicized such traits. It

18   *Fall River Daily Evening News,* July 19,1873, March 19,1878.

19   One Fall River craft union officer supplied an example of this outlook when he wrote in 1884 that "Canada supplies most of our mills with cheap unskilled labor [French Canadians]. They work for very low wages, as a rule, and seem to have no desire to help to alleviate the condition of factory work." *John Swinton's Paper* (New York), January 6, 1884.

contained comments by prominent French Canadians and by a few sympathetic manufacturers about the virtues, philosophy, growth, and accomplishments of this ethnic group. This testimony, delivered at a hearing before Bureau Commissioner Carroll B. Wright on October 25, 1881, was in response to a segment of the previous *Twelfth Annual Report* which had been critical of the French-Canadian influx:

> These people have one good trait [stated the earlier report in its most complimentary passage]. They are indefatigable workers, and docile. All they ask is to be set to work, and they care little who rules them or how they are ruled. To earn all they can no matter how many hours of toil. . . .[20]

The disparaging *Twelfth Annual Report* found that manufacturers could depend upon the passivity of French Canadians because they did "not believe in strikes or in revolutions."[21] Their attitude toward the Fall River textile strikes of 1870, 1875, and 1879 validated such assertions. To be sure, French-Canadian behavior in 1870 could be explained by fear of what must have been incomprehensible incidents of strike-associated violence witnessed for the first time by these farmer immigrants.

But, with the exception of a small body of weavers, they again responded unsympathetically by refusing to participate in the 1875 strike.[22] Nor was it merely coincidence that the French-Canadian community bestowed its first public award of honor, a portrait of Charles Sumner,[23] on controversial James Davenport, a belligerently anti-labor mayor who had ordered city police to use force in subduing demonstrators.

When the third major labor dispute erupted in 1879 as the climactic event of the most class-conscious and socially discordant decade in city history, management's agents returned

---

[20]   M. B. S. L., *Twelfth Annual Report* (1881), p. 470.

[21]   Ibid., *Thirteenth Annual Report* ((1882), p. 59.

[22]   *Fall River Daily Evening News*, February 22, March 1, 1875.

[23]   Ibid., February 9, September 27, 1875; *Le Guide Français de Fall River, Mass.*, op. cit., p. 35.

from other New England textile communities accompanied by French Canadians willing to work in Fall River mills.

The resulting animosity was most clearly demonstrated as the strike was drawing to an end, when eighty French-Canadian immigrants arrived by train from Boston. While wending their way toward two mills where they were to serve as strikebreakers, these newcomers were subjected to an attack which included stonings and kickings inflicted by an angry crowd estimated at 150 strong.[24]

Shortly thereafter, the strike ended in failure for the workers, who were forced to accept management's terms of employment. The demoralized members of the mule spinners' union, who had spearheaded the resistance, were embittered to learn that certain mill superintendents were determined to retain inexperienced French Canadians hired to operate mule frames during the strike, thereby further punishing the unionized malcontents.[25]

By that time, it was generally recognized that the anti-strike disposition of these staunchly Catholic French Canadians had been fortified by the insistence of Rev. Pierre J. B. Bedard, their priest and ethnic community leader, that they not participate in labor walkouts. His dictates were followed, for French-Canadian mill operatives had an abiding faith in clerical judgments,[26] particularly those of this priest who had been pastor of Notre-Dame-de-Lourdes Church in the city's east end since arriving from Canada in 1874.

While the 1879 strike had been in progress, however, Irish and English mule spinners had become aroused over reports that Bedard was in communication with Canadian officials in an attempt to procure strikebreakers. Such allegations compounded trade union hostility toward the Canadian immigrants. Previous indifference to labor's cause had been bad enough; now their priest had linked arms with management.

A delegation of spinners reportedly traveled to Providence,

24   *Fall River Daily Evening News*, September 18, 1879.

25   *Labor Standard* (Fall River), December 13, 1879.

26   M. B. S. L., *Thirteenth Annual Report* (1882), p. 53.

R.I., to beseech the intervention of Bishop Thomas Hendricken, urging him to prohibit Bedard from soliciting "knobstick" (strikebreaker) help for the factories.[27] Hendricken had delivered an anti-strike sermon two years earlier, but now, whatever the inconsistency, he was sufficiently persuaded by the supplicants to write to Bedard, threatening him with ecclesiastical penalties unless the priest retracted his position.[28]

Concerned with the economic impact of a strike upon the proverbially large French-Canadian families, most of whom had not been in Fall River long enough to have a financial cushion against unemployment, Bedard politely refused. If strikers possessed the right to leave work, he declared, then they must respect the rights of others and not interfere when the needy accepted positions offered to them.[29]

Bedard's intransigency, easily identifiable and exasperating to friends of organized labor, led to anonymous threats upon his life, followed by forced entry into the sacristy and mutilation of the Notre-Dame birth and marriage registers.[30] During the 1880 municipal election contest, placards scoring Father Bedard and condemning one French-Canadian aspirant for office as being the sycophant of the "knobstick" priest were affixed to several fire stations where voting was conducted.[31]

Bedard was presumably undeterred. In 1882, when labor-capital relations were again deteriorating, and manufacturers were preparing for a potential strike by encouraging an influx by French Canadians, the priest reportedly sent for twenty-three families in Canada, thus further arousing

[27]   *Weekly Visitor* (Providence, R.I.), July 20, 1879; *Fall River Daily Evening News*, July 31, 1877.

[28]   *Weekly Visitor*, July 20, 1879; *Le Guide Français de Fall River, Mass.*, op. cit., p. 22.

[29]   *Weekly Visitor*, July 20, 1879.

[30]   P. U. Vaillant, *Notes Biographiques sur Messire P. J. Bedard* (Fall River, 1886), pp. 19-20.

[31]   *Le Guide Français de Fall River, Mass.*, op. cit., 23; Prior, op. cit., 2, p. 271.

labor union ire.[32] At least partly because of anger over Bedard's anti-strike bias, the Irish Catholic minority separated from Notre-Dame Church and with the bishop's sanction organized a new parish.

A division of opinion between worker rights' advocates and French Canadians, highlighted by the strikebreaking controversy, extended to other facets of employment. On one major issue, however, French-Canadian spokesmen were undisturbed by and did not attempt to contradict organized labor's contention that their ethnic group had failed to campaign for or abide by a ten-hour maximum workday for women and children under eighteen employed in factories. Their lack of support for a statute limiting working hours, which labor advocates had sought for a generation before it became State law in 1874, was in part prompted by the perception that unacceptable, evil means had been used in behalf of a presumably good end. According to a French-Canadian lawyer's later recollection, the lobbying drive to secure this law's adoption had created an atmosphere dominated by "intimidation, violations of laws, rows, [and] public demonstrations, which were converting the whole city into a state of rebellion."[33]

Though this statement distorted historical fact by exaggerating the degree of disorder, it was offered to explain why French-Canadian mill workers were "not miserly of an hour if it was necessary to benefit their employer." The unacceptable alternative of worker militancy to gain supposed rights inevitably led to violations of "law and order."

The French-Canadian ethnic leaders constantly stressed that their people were orderly and peace-loving. Who, they asked, could find fault with this? Only labor leaders – men who were painting a negative picture of French Canadians.[34] Rebutting such critics,

32   *The New York Times*, March 26, 1882.

33   *Labor Standard*, September 11, 1880; *Fall River Daily Herald*, May 29, 1882, October 8, 1883, April 1, 1899. For the religiously divisive ramifications of this labor controversy among Irish and French Catholics, see Philip T. Silvia, Jr. "The 'Flint Affair': French-Canadian Struggle for *Survivance*," *The Catholic Historical Review*, LXV (July, 1979), pp. 414-435.

34   M. B. S. L., *Thirteenth Annual Report* (1882), pp. 23-26, 64.

Fall River attorney Hugo A. Dubuque[35] and Bedard, among others, reiterated their belief that Canadian immigrants were acting responsibly in their new home. The French-Canadian concept of an orderly society and good citizenship, they claimed, paralleled the attitude of the most respectable native-born elements in Fall River, such as its ministers, who had reacted similarly to labor turmoil.

In effect, there was an alliance, a shared conservatism, between the established Yankee and the Canadian newcomer, each assisting manufacturers in preventing any Old World-style "revolutions."[36] Minority sentiment, the alien concept of aggressive labor warfare, they charged, belonged to the European-born trade unionists who truly deserved censure for acting in an un-American manner.

French-Canadian spokesmen were more sensitive when organized labor equated child labor with the arrival of their ethnic group. To a certain degree they need not have been so uneasy, for Fall River history was on their side. The penchant among parents for sending children into the mills at a very tender age had been manifest since the first mills were constructed during the War of 1812.

The related problem of educational deprivation had persisted since that time. Thus, in 1860, the pupil absenteeism rate from Fall River public schools was an astounding 60 percent. Five years later, a statute prohibiting the employment of children under ten was being flagrantly violated, while at the same time, nearly twenty percent of all ten to fourteen-year-old minors were not spending a single day in the classroom. Two-thirds of the city's minors were classified as mill workers, and only thirty-seven

---

[35]   Recognized for his intelligence and as an accomplished bilingual orator, the Canadian-born Dubuque, who had been practicing law in Fall River since receiving an LL.B. degree from Boston University in 1877, headed the French-Canadian delegation that confronted Commissioner Wright at the State House in 1881.

[36]   French Canadians had felt this way for a century, from the time they had soured on the French Revolution because of its religious consequences. In 1880, two Frenchmen who were guests of Father Bedard delivered speeches at Notre-Dame Church condemning a recent law that expelled Jesuits from their republican homeland. *Fall River Daily Evening News*, July 17, 1880.

percent of this group could read and write English! When Fall River's first superintendent of schools spoke out against these abuses, he was apparently eased out of office for his effort. In 1872 the twenty-one percent illiteracy rate for the total Fall River populace was the highest of any city in the Commonwealth and provided further evidence of extensive indifference to formal education prior to any substantial influx of French Canadians.[37]

By the 1880s, organized labor, ignoring the historical connection, had succeeded in isolating the French Canadians as the solitary ethnic entity responsible for child labor problems. When spinner secretary Robert Howard, the city's best-known and most influential labor official, spoke of manufacturers importing mill hands from Canada at fifty and seventy-five cents per day, he must have been referring to children's wages.[38] Howard chose not to focus upon the role of management in this issue, but instead berated uneducated émigré parents for encouraging their children to violate compulsory school laws and conspiring with their offspring who falsified ages so that they might gain mill employment before turning the minimum legal age of ten.[39]

Statistics do support Howard's criticism, for, by the late 1870s, the problem of illiteracy was primarily related to the Canadians. In the 1878 tabulation of Fall River mill workers by ethnic origin, 1,009 of the 2,159 French-Canadian employees were classified as illiterate, while illiteracy among all other ethnic groups had been substantially reduced since the 1860s, the average rate having dropped to fourteen percent. Furthermore, the French-Canadian census guide, published in 1888, listed 3,921 adults, recording that 1,821 were illiterate and only 946 could read English.[40]

---

37   Lintner, op. cit., pp. 252-253, 257, 259, 263.

38   U.S. Senate, *Labor and Capital*, I, p. 655.

39   Ibid. I, p. 648.

40   M. B. S. L., *Ninth Annual Report* (1878), pp. 215-216; *Le Guide Canadien-Français de Fall River*, op. cit., p. 256. There were only 138 schools in the entire Province of Quebec in 1838, and the *habitants* were reluctant to recognize their value. Inroads against a "widespread illiteracy," dominant during the first half of the nineteenth century, came slowly after 1850. Vicero, op. cit., pp. 33-34.

French-Canadian leaders, who opposed repatriation to Canada and were committed to their new existence in Fall River, were perplexed over this issue of education because they themselves were critical of a certain element within their ethnic group. These were the "rolling stones" to whom Fall River residency was but an interim period of their lives. Their primary purpose, which demanded total family involvement, was to save money before returning to Canada. Schooling in America seemed superfluous and nonsensical.[41] Labor union efforts to raise the legal working age were to be objected to vociferously, for they would interfere with maximizing family income. One statute, in effect since 1880, was particularly galling and interpreted by these French Canadians as discriminatory against themselves.

This law, which prohibited illiterates between ten and thirteen years of age from working in the mills, was, in fact, vaguely written, particularly because it did not specify whether or not one had to be able to read and write in the English language. Even worse, the law was revised by 1887 to mean precisely this form of literacy, which would apparently deprive many French-Canadian youngsters of employment, even though they could read and write in their native tongue.[42]

Even for French-Canadian parents intending to remain in the United States and appreciative of the value of education, economic conditions mandated that children participate in "family system" mill employment. Howard and other critics overlooked the tribulations encountered by French Canadians, particularly men, which contributed to this practice. Coming from the farm to the factory, *habitants* could not offer their services as skilled loom fixers or overseers without first acquiring

---

[41]   M. B. S. L., *First Annual Report* (1869-1870), p. 248.

[42]   Commonwealth of Massachusetts, *Acts and Resolves* (1878), c. 257, sec. 4; *Public Statutes* (1882), c. 48, sec. 7; *Fall River Daily Herald,* September 27, 1887. Joining in the protest against this further revision was an Irish-American physician, John W. Coughlin, future mayor of Fall River and brother-in-law of Hugo Dubuque, who insisted that "the French, in matters of education, are not the gigantic lump of ignorance they have been reported, as Carrol [sic] D. Wright found out to his entire satisfaction when confronted by them." The protestors had their way when the English language stipulation was repealed in 1888. Commonwealth of Massachusetts, *Acts and Resolves* (1887) c. 433 sec. 3; (1888), c. 348, sec. 12; *Fall River Daily Herald,* September 27, 1887; *Fall River Weekly News,* October 6, November 10, 1887.

on-the-job training. Nor is it likely that these workers, even when experienced, were welcomed into the skilled high-paying positions which had been the traditional domain of the English and Irish operatives, and would basically remain so until the end of the nineteenth century.

It was not until 1909 that French-Canadian unhappiness over their first years of mill life was set down in written form. Readers were then reminded of a time when, "if there arrived a friend from England, Ireland, or elsewhere, the Canadian worker would be obliged to give up his place to the newcomer."[43] It had been useless to remonstrate against this type of ethnic job discrimination, as arguments usually degenerated into mutually incomprehensible shouting matches between English-speaking overseers and French-speaking operatives.

These overseers also resorted to less direct but equally effective discriminatory practices, such as increasing the work load of French Canadians or withholding credit commensurate with full productive output. This kind of injustice drove Canadian men from the mills, and, presumably, contributed to family decisions to let French-Canadian children work at those least remunerative mill tasks not vigorously competed for by English-speaking labor.

Ultimately, then, while it was not possible to deny that some French-Canadian parents were ignoring the long-term best interests of their children by sending them into the mills, ethnic defenders insisted that hardship most frequently governed this practice. Being poor and friendless, living in an alien and seemingly hostile land, these adults often depended upon supplemental wages. Who deserved greater censure, asked French-Canadian leaders, the parents or the avaricious manufacturers who were none too careful about checking the ages of job applicants?[44] Why was it that the mills did not "refuse employment to these poor little ones, pay a little more to adult

---

43   *Le Guide Français de Fall River, Mass.*, op. cit., 1909, p. 21.

44   *Fall River Daily Evening News*, March 9, 1882; M. B. S. L., *Thirteenth Annual Report* (1882), pp. 20-21.

members of these families, and give the children a chance to have an education?"[45]

By the early 1880s there were conflicting reports about whether the French Canadians of Fall River and other New England mill towns were driving down the wages of all workers, a charge commonly attributed to all immigrants. Robert Howard and the other Fall River mule spinners believed as much.[46] Newly-arrived French Canadians, organized labor declared, accepted work without bargaining or understanding their wage compensation. Manufacturers, one Lowell resident feared, would come to appreciate ignorance of this sort to such an extent that they would next turn to importing Chinese workers.[47]

Even the French-Canadian community leaders agreed that first-generation Canadians came hat-in-hand, that is, seeking work in an overtly "beggar" approach.[48] But there is no proof that they caused lower wages for other workers. They certainly could not be held accountable for mule spinner and loom fixer wage reductions, which were approximately 40 percent in the 1870s. Their job mobility, which took them to various New England localities, and back to Canada, suggests that they soon became

---

[45]   M. B. S. L., *Thirteenth Annual Report* (1882), p. 21.

[46]   Their attitude was shared by Howard's friend Frank K. Foster, typographer by trade and a prominent figure associated with the founding of the American Federation of Labor. His virulent, total denunciation of the French Canadians compared with Dennis Kearney's condemnation of the Chinese on the West Coast. In the course of offering sensational, exaggerated testimony during 1883, Foster contended that other nationalities, sometimes forced by circumstances beyond their control to live in worker-tenement dwellings with French Canadians, suffered the consequences of being exposed to unsanitary domestic habits. U.S. Senate, *Labor and Capital*, 1, pp. 66-67. Hugo Dubuque defended his fellow nationals by dispatching a letter to the United States Senate labor committee which was intended to refute this "vile slander" given before that body by Foster. *Fall River Daily Herald*, February 12, 1883.

[47]   U.S. Senate, *Labor and Capital*, 1, pp. 66, 68; M. B. S. L., *Thirteenth Annual Report* (1882), p. 376.

[48]   M. B. S. L., *Thirteenth Annual Report* (1882), p. 59, Hugo A. Dubuque, *Les Canadiens Français de Fall River, Mass.*, ed. by H. Boisseau (Fall River: *Le Castor*, 1883), p. 20.

dissatisfied with wage reductions.[49] To be sure, women and children accepted the lowest-paying jobs. But their wages had been standardized before the French Canadians arrived in New England. By accepting employer "magnanimity" and displacing other workers as unskilled mill labor, the Canadians mostly hurt themselves. Their children, besides receiving pitiful wages, were often exploited in other ways.[50] Witness, for example, the weeks of labor as "apprentices" in which children received no income at all.[51]

Nevertheless, Fall River workers regarded the French Canadians as being opposed to trade-union interests, and in early 1884 petitioned Congress to prohibit direct importation of foreign labor by manufacturers in the hope of discouraging the use of French Canadians as strikebreakers. The mule spinners' union instructed Howard to urge that Senators George F. Hoar and Henry L. Dawes vote in favor of the Foran Act which prohibited the importation of contract labor.[52]

Organized labor thought it had legitimate grievances against the French Canadians, who seemed to be employer pawns,[53] but the editor of Fall River's *Labor Standard* warned against believing that their faults were inherent in their ethnic background. He insisted that people did not leave home, live in miserable quarters, and accept low wages because they were Irish, French, or English. They did so because of poverty. Wage increases, not

---

[49]   M. B. S. L., *Thirteenth Annual Report* (1882), p. 17.

[50]   *Fall River Daily Herald*, September 23, 1877.

[51]   A young boy named Eugène Lebeau, having arrived four or five months earlier from Canada, was working without monetary compensation when he was accidentally killed in the mule room of the Granite Mill during 1872. *Fall River Daily Evening News*, June 6, 1872.

[52]   Ibid., December 10, 1884; *Fall River Daily Herald*, January 14, 1884. It was ironic that the Foran Act, which became law in early 1885, contained no provision excluding Canadian immigration. Organized labor's attitude toward contract labor has been thoroughly analyzed by Charlotte Erickson in *American Industry and the European Immigrant, 1860-1885* (Cambridge, 1957).

[53]   Vicero, op. cit., pp. 349-352.

chauvinism, were the ultimate remedy.[54] But Fall River trade unionists found it difficult to be as objective. It was more convenient to make scapegoats of French-Canadian mill hands, to hold them responsible for miserable working conditions and a depressed wage scale.

Only the passage of time and a large-scale influx of "new" immigrants would soften this trade-union animus. When Canadian migration shriveled at century's end, after flourishing for a generation, fresh recruits drawn by the thousands from Poland, and particularly from Portuguese territory, mainly the Azores, were welcomed as unskilled replacements by Spindle City industrialists.

These aliens were soon regarded as the major menace undermining organized labor's struggle for work amenities and a wage scale commensurate with a decent living standard. "Old" immigrant trade unionists harbored little compassion for and no sense of class solidarity with these cultural strangers. Whether as willing allies or as dupes of management, these most recent arrivals now represented *the* enemy below. Benefiting from the testing process of negative comparison, the Canadian textile worker's status rose—if only to a limited extent. Trade unionist hostility was transformed into condescending indifference.

[This article first appeared in the French Institute's publication entitled *The Little Canadas of New England.* It has been reviewed by the author for inclusion in this volume.]

---

54   *Labor Standard*, October 8, 1881.

Bibliography

Commonwealth of Massachusetts. *Acts and Resolves.* 1878, 1887.

____. *Public Statutes.* 1883.

____, Bureau of Statistics of Labor. *First Annual Report.* 1869-1870.

____. *Ninth Annual Report.* 1878.

____. *Twelfth Annual Report.* 1887.

____.*Thirteenth Annual Report.* 1882.

Cross, Robert D. *The Emergence of Liberal Catholicism in America.* Cambridge: Harvard University Press, 1958.

Dubuque, Hugo A. *Les Canadiens Français de Fall River, Massachusetts.* Edited by H. Boisseau. Fall River: *Le Castor* 1883.

Ducharme, Jacques. *The Shadows of the Trees: The Story of French-Canadians in New England.* New York: Harper and Brothers, 1943.

Erickson, Charlotte. *American Industry and the European Immigrant, 1860-1885.* Cambridge: Harvard University Press, 1957.

Fall River. *City Directory* 1869-1871.

Fall River Daily Evening News. Fall River, 6 June 1872, 19 July 1873, 22 February 1875, 1 March 1875, 31 July 1877, 19 March 1878, 18 September 1879, 17 July 1880, 24 October 1881, 8 November 1881, 9 March 1882.

Fall River Daily Herald. Fall River, 23 September 1877, 29 May 1882, 12 February 1883, 8 October 1883, 14 January 1884, 27 September 1887, 1 April 1899, 24 June 1899.

Fall River Weekly News. Fall River, 6 October 1887, 10 November 1887.

John Swinton's Paper. New York, 6 January 1884.

Labor Standard. Fall River, 13 December 1879.

Lamoureux, Edward F., ed. *Le Guide canadien-français de Fall River et Notes historiques sur les Canadiens de Fall River.* Fall River, 1888.

_____, ed. *Le Guide français de Fall River, Massachusetts.* Fall River, 1888.

Lintner, Sylvia Chase. "A Social History of Fall River, 1859-1879." Ph.D. dissertation, Radcliffe College, 1945.

Magnan, D. M. A. *Notre-Dame-de-Lourdes de Fall River, Massachusetts.* Quebec City: *Le Soleil,* 1925.

The New York Times, New York, 26 March 1882.

Prior, Granville T. "The French Canadians in New England." 2 vols. Master's thesis, Brown University, 1932.

Silvia, Philip T. Jr. "The 'Flint Affair': French-Canadian Struggle for *Survivance.*" *The Catholic Historical Review.* LXV: 414-435.

_____. "The Spindle City: Labor, Politics, and Religion in Fall River, Massachusetts, 1870-1905." Ph.D. dissertation, Fordham University, 1973.

United States Bureau of the Census. *Eighth Census of the United States: 1860.* Vol. IV.

_____. *Ninth Census of the United States: 1870. Population.* Vol. 1.

United States Congress, Senate. *Report of the Committee of the Senate Upon the Relations Between Labor and Capital.* 4 vols. Senate Report 1262,48th Congress, 2d Session. 1885.

Vaillant, P. U. *Notes biographiques sur Messire P. J. Bedard.* Fall River: 1886.

Vicero, Ralph D. "Immigration of French Canadians to New England, 1840-1900: A Geographical Analysis." Ph.D. dissertation, University of Wisconsin, 1968.

Weekly Visitor. Providence, 20 July 1879.

Beyond Textiles: Industrial Diversity and the Franco-American Experience in Worcester, Massachusetts

Charles W. Estus and Kenneth J. Moynihan

Industrial Diversity in Worcester

Students of immigration history tend to generalize about the experiences of cultural groups in the United States and attribute differences in acculturation to differences in cultural backgrounds. However, the attempt to apply such generalizations to the lives of immigrants in specific settings suggests that very important differences in the experiences of the same immigrant group occur as a result of differences among the communities into which they settle. The interaction between the host community and the immigrant group must be examined in detail if we are to understand the rich and creative variety in the experiences of any immigrant people.[1]

So it is with the Franco-American experience in New England. While there are important and major differences between that experience and those of other immigrant peoples to the region, there are also very instructive differences between the Franco-American experience in a Fall River and a Providence or a Worcester. Worcester, in particular, appears to offer a major variation of the Franco-American story in New England. Unlike the many French-Canadian "colonies" in the mill towns of the Merrimack, Blackstone, Connecticut, and Quinebaug Valleys, the immigrants to Worcester did not have the opportunity to create a single "little Canada." To find the

---

[1]   For an excellent example of this approach to the study of immigration history see Josef J. Barton, "Religion and Cultural Change in Czech Immigrant Communities, 1850-1920," in Randall M. Miller and Thomas D. Marzik, eds., *Immigrants and Religion in Urban America.* (Philadelphia: Temple University Press, 1977), pp. 3-24.

reasons for this, we must first examine the character of Worcester itself as their host community.

During the 1860s, when the French-Canadian population in Worcester grew from 386 persons to 2,805,[2] the city was fast becoming the leading manufacturing center of New England. Like many of the region's communities, it had depended upon agriculture for its first century of development.[3] But the poor quality of its topsoil, continuously washed down the sides of its many hills into a series of relatively narrow valleys extending north and south, prevented much more than subsistence farming except in those valleys.

Attempts to develop manufacturing industries using water power were made at the turn of the nineteenth century but failed to produce substantial manufacturing for want of sufficient quantity and continuity in that source of energy. A southeasterly tilt in the earth's crust on which Worcester rests does allow several streams in their southerly courses to join and form the Middle River and the headwaters of the Blackstone in the south of the city. Here, with extensive damming and carefully controlled water privileges, water was stored in sufficient quantities throughout the year. A few textile mills were developed along this strong current at such sites as Valley Falls, New Worcester, Jamesville, Trowbridgeville, Hopeville, and South Worcester. As an economic base, however, such mills could support only a very limited working population.

Trade, with its dependence upon animal-drawn conveyances, had always been a part of Worcester's economic life, but, in this activity, other central Massachusetts communities such as Mendon, Boylston, and Lancaster had been more successful before 1830.

---

2   Ralph D. Vicero, "Immigration of French Canadians to New England, 1840-1900: A Geographical Analysis," Ph.D. dissertation, University of Wisconsin, 1968, p. 173; Rev. T. A. Chandonnet, *Notre-Dame-des-Canadiens et les Canadiens aux États-Unis* (Montreal: Desbarats, 1872), p. 64.

3   The following brief summary of Worcester's industrial development to 1870 is taken from Kevin L. Hickey, "Geography and Leadership: An Interdisciplinary Evaluation of Worcester's Industrial Development," a paper presented at the Joint Conference of the Victorian Society in America and the National Archives, Washington, D.C., March 1979.

Although it was midway between Boston and the Connecticut Valley and at the center of crude roadways leading north and south as well, Worcester remained relatively isolated for the aspiring industrialist. Fifty dollars a ton bought transportation for goods to and from Boston or Springfield or Providence along these dirt roads, but no manufacturer could afford to bring raw materials in and ship finished products out at those rates. In 1806 Isaiah Thomas and others tried to end this frustration by surveying a direct line from Worcester to Brookline and, hills be damned, cut the Boston Turnpike straight through wood and glen. Rates, however, did not improve, and the floating bridge over Lake Quinsigamond, made necessary by Thomas' straight line, always sinking and in need of constant care, symbolized Worcester's problems of transport. In still another effort to find access to the world's materials and markets, Worcester's leaders joined with those of Providence and, using Irish labor, cut the Blackstone Canal to the sea in the 1820s. But long and hard New England winters closed the canal with ice, and frost heaves drove down its stone sides each year so that maintenance costs cut deeply into profits. And it did not help matters when angry mill owners along the river, distressed at the loss of power to the water-greedy canal, occasionally filled the shallow waterway with stones. In spite of its promise, the canal venture did not succeed. Worcester's industrial development, then, had to be created with other sources of energy, alternatives to the use of the land, water power, and animal transport.

The town's entrepreneurs and craftsmen found that source in steam. As early as 1825, the steam engine was used in Worcester, and in 1835 those tortuous dirt roadways that linked all New England to Worcester began to be replaced by the iron rail for commercial transport. By 1850, Worcester lay at the center of iron roads connecting it to Fitchburg, Nashua, Portland, Boston, Providence, New London, Hartford, Springfield, and Albany. By then, steam power was also used extensively throughout the city's manufacturing industries. Worcester's water, filtered through the sand and gravel of its hills, was relatively free of minerals. Steam engines and boilers, using that water, were free of mineral deposits and required little maintenance.

Heavy industry on a large scale was, therefore, possible; problems of both transport and local energy were solved by the steam engine. Worcester's craftsmen-industrialists brought materials into the city, worked them and shipped them out in bulk. We cannot here detail that industrial development, but suffice it to say that the mills along waterways gave way to heavy industry along those rail lines. Bulk transport gave rise to a metal industry that produced every variety of goods, from heavy iron-rolling mills to watch springs. Never an important agricultural center herself, Worcester now furnished the barbed wire fence that enclosed the ranges of the Far West. Removed from the rivers on which the textile industry grew, Worcester now built the carding machines and looms for textile development elsewhere. Sister industries grew which provided leather belting, rolling stock, machine tools, grinding wheels, and metal-working machines; and a dazzling array of small metal-based industries produced such items as hand tools, roller skates, razor blades, metal reed organs, corsets, and lunch wagons.

In the post Civil War years, this industrial expansion beckoned to the French Canadian, and easy passage to the city was available over the Nashua and Worcester Railroad, the rail link to Montreal. What these French Canadians found when they arrived, however, was not a single-industry mill town but a booming city which needed and rewarded construction workers, metal craftsmen, tool and die makers, pattern makers, machinists, and other skilled workers. If there was to be a place for the French Canadians in Worcester, they would have to discover their opportunities in the midst of this diversity.

Table I[4] suggests the early results of this search for opportunity among French Canadians in three neighborhoods in Worcester in 1870. Several important observations may be made about the diversity of occupations described in Table I. First, no single industry invited the gathering of a large French-speaking work force under one roof. The boot and shoe industry, which provided one-fifth of the jobs in our sample, was dominated by Yankee supervisors and Irish

---

4   Sources for this table include the Federal Decennial Manuscript Census for Worcester, 1870; F. W. Beers, *Atlas of the City of Worcester*, 1870, (republished by Charles E. Tuttle, Rutland, Vt., 1971); "Worcester Street Guide for the Federal Decennial Census, 1870," Community Studies Program, Assumption College, 1982.

laborers. Of 374 workers in Worcester's three largest boot and shoe industries: C. C. Houghton and Co., D. G. Rawson and Co., and Bay State Shoe Co.—only fourteen were French-Canadian. In smaller boot and shoe shops scattered throughout Worcester's center, French Canadians were a minority of the work force in each instance.[5] With the possible exception of the brickyards, which provided jobs for 18% of the workers in our sample, English was no doubt the language of the work place for French-Canadian labor in Worcester.

Secondly, the metal industries, Worcester's largest employer, provided less than 10% of the work for French Canadians in these neighborhoods. Yet hauling and lifting and moving had to be done in Worcester's many shops and factories, so that laborers made up over 20% of our neighborhoods' work force. On the other hand, French Canadians found that crude skills developed on the farm could be turned to employment in construction-related trades. If we assume that a good proportion of work done by day laborers was construction-related, it well may be that almost two-fifth's of the work opportunities were in construction-related occupations.

Finally, the limited opportunity for work in textile for French Canadians in Worcester in 1870 stands in sharp contrast to other communities in New England. Only 4% of the workers in our three-neighborhood sample were employed in textiles. In that same year, twenty-five miles west of Worcester, 76% of the labor force in Ware, Massachusetts, was in textiles; to the southwest that proportion was 64% in Southbridge and to the south 57% in Oxford.[6]

The uneven distribution of occupations between these three neighborhoods also reminds us that we are looking at a population that walked to work. Their work reflected different employment opportunities in different areas of the city. The fact that 34% of Green Island's workers were in boots and shoes suggests a walk north from

5   "Worcester House Directory, 1872." Unpublished manuscript, compiler and date unknown, based on the Worcester City Directory, 1872. Because the City Directory provided information on place of occupation as well as place of residence, the compiler was able to reconstruct places of business with their work force.

6   Vicero, "Immigration," p. 313.

the Island into the city's center where that industry was concentrated. The brickyards on French Hill and the woolen mills and heavy industry of South Worcester reflect this same regional diversity of opportunity within the city.

While we have had the opportunity to examine three neighborhoods in Worcester and their French-Canadian residents, other evidence points to the conclusion that many families resided, as well, in the center of the city in 1870. A parish census taken in October 1871, tells us that 228 persons from a total of 562 French-Canadian families in Worcester, worked in boots and shoes.[7] Our three neighborhoods account for only one-fourth that number of families and one-fifth of that number of boot and shoe workers, suggesting a concentration of French-Canadian families within walking distance of the boot and shoe shops around Worcester's Common.

The emerging picture of the French-Canadian settlement in Worcester in 1870, then, is not of a concentrated French-speaking colony. Given the possibilities for work and settlement in a rapidly growing city of diverse manufacturing, French Canadians settled throughout the city's center and in areas to the east and south. With fifty-two families on French Hill, forty-four on the Island, thirty-nine in South Worcester and perhaps as many as three hundred families scattered among the Irish and Yankees just south and east of Worcester's Common, the building of a French-Canadian community would require the linking of separate neighborhoods and of scattered families. Industrial diversity in Worcester and the determination of the French Canadians to take advantage of opportunities where they found them made that task more difficult.

Charles W. Estus

---

[7] Chandonnet, *Notre-Dame*, p. 64.

TABLE I
Occupational Distribution among French Canadians in Three Worcester Neighborhoods, 1870

	French Hill		The Island		South Worcester		Total	
	%	(No.)	%	(No.)	%	(No.)	%	(No.)
Construction Related								
Bricks	29.9	(23)	20.5	(18)	0.0	(0)	18.2	(41)
Brick and Stone Work	2.6	(2)	8.0	(7)	1.7	(1)	4.4	(10)
Carpenters	16.9	(13)	8.0	(7)	8.3	(5)	11.1	(25)
Painter	1.3	(1)	0.0	(0)	0.0	(0)	0.4	(1)
sub total	50.6	(39)	36.4	(32)	10.0	(6)	34.2	(77)
Laborers								
Day	14.3	(11)	10.2	(9)	33.3	(20)	17.8	(40)
Farm	1.3	(1)	0.0	(0)	10.0	(6)	3.1	(7)
Wood Cutter	1.3	(1)	0.0	(0)	0.0	(0)	0.4	(1)
sub total	16.9	(13)	10.2	(9)	43.3	(26)	21.3	(48)
Boots and Shoes	2.6	(2)	34.1	(30)	18.3	(11)	19.1	(43)
Metals								
Blacksmith	2.6	(2)	1.1	(1)	6.7	(4)	3.1	(7)
Gunsmith	2.6	(2)	0.0	(0)	0.0	(0)	0.9	(2)
Heavy Machine Mfg.	0.0	(0)	3.4	(3)	1.7	(1)	1.8	(4)
Moulder	1.3	(1)	1.1	(1)	0.0	(0)	0.9	(2)
Tool Maker	0.0	(0)	1.1	(1)	5.0	(3)	1.8	(4)
Wire Worker	0.0	(0)	1.1	(1)	0.0	(0)	0.4	(1)
sub total	6.5	(5)	8.0	(7)	13.3	(8)	8.9	(20)
Transportation								
Car Shop	2.6	(2)	0.0	(0)	0.0	(0)	0.9	(2)
Carriage Shop	3.9	(3)	0.0	(0)	0.0	(0)	1.3	(3)
Railroad Worker	5.2	(4)	0.0	(0)	0.0	(0)	1.8	(4)
Teamster	2.6	(2)	0.0	(0)	0.0	(0)	0.9	(2)
sub total	14.3	(11)	0.0	(0)	0.0	(0)	4.9	(11)
Textiles								
Dye House	0.0	(0)	0.0	(0)	1.7	(1)	0.4	(1)
Silk Mfg.	1.3	(1)	0.0	(0)	0.0	(0)	0.4	(1)
Woolen Mill	0.0	(0)	2.3	(2)	8.3	(5)	3.1	(7)
sub total	1.3	(1)	2.3	(2)	10.0	(6)	4.0	(9)
Independent								
Barber	0.0	(0)	1.1	(1)	0.0	(0)	0.4	(1)
Dress and Millinery	0.0	(0)	3.4	(3)	0.0	(0)	1.3	(3)
Grocer	0.0	(0)	1.1	(1)	0.0	(0)	0.4	(1)
Pedler/Huckster	2.6	(2)	1.1	(1)	0.0	(0)	1.3	(3)
Saloon Keeper	1.3	(1)	0.0	(0)	0.0	(0)	0.4	(1)
sub total	3.9	(3)	6.8	(6)	0.0	(0)	4.0	(9)
Light Industry								
Reed Organ Mfg.	0.0	(0)	0.0	(0)	1.7	(1)	0.4	(1)
Sausage Mfg.	1.3	(1)	0.0	(0)	0.0	(0)	0.4	(1)
Sash and Blind Mfg.	0.0	(0)	0.0	(0)	1.7	(1)	0.4	(1)
sub total	1.3	(1)	0.0	(0)	3.3	(2)	1.3	(3)
Domestic Service	1.3	(1)	2.3	(2)	0.0	(0)	1.3	(3)
Retail Clerks	1.3	(1)	0.0	(0)	1.7	(1)	0.9	(2)
TOTAL	100.0	(77)	100.0	(88)	100.0	(60)	100.0	(225)

The Franco-American Experience

The first efforts at community-building among Worcester's French Canadians were focused, not surprisingly, on rallying together as Catholics. For six months in 1846, a Canadian priest said Mass in a rented hall on Main Street, but he left due to ill health. There were around 150 French Canadians then in a city which, during that decade of the 1840s, grew—or should we say exploded—in population, from around 7,000 to over 17,000.[8]

In 1852, when the Canadians still numbered only around forty families, a more ambitious undertaking began, this time with the clear goal of establishing a permanent base in Worcester, as Canadians and as Catholics. The migrants pooled their resources, bought a piece of land, and installed the foundations of a church building they had already named for St. Anne. To further solidify their bonds, they organized a St. Jean-Baptiste Society in July of 1853, but both the building project and the society were dissolved in 1854, apparently because some of the original members had moved on in search of opportunities elsewhere. The land and the foundation were turned over to the only Catholic parish in the city, the Irish St. John's.[9]

In 1869, when by their own count the French-Canadian population had reached 1,743, the community would finally succeed in permanently establishing the parish of Notre-Dame-des-Canadiens with the indispensable resident French-Canadian pastor.[10] But before we reach that point, it is worth pausing to notice two organizations founded in 1868. In January, the St. Jean-Baptiste Society was revived, and in May a most interesting organization called the St. Hyacinthe Society was founded.[11] French-Canadian

---

[8]   Chandonnet, *Notre-Dame*, p. 1; Vicero, "Immigration," p. 156.

[9]   Chandonnet, *Notre-Dame*, p. 1.

[10]   J. Arthur Roy, ed., *Le Worcester Canadien* (Worcester, 1886-1907), 10 (1896), p. 127.

[11]   Chandonnet, *Notre-Dame*, pp. 96, 98.

communities routinely formed St. Jean-Baptiste societies, of course, but the St. Hyacinthe Society seems to have been unique to Worcester. Its name symbolizes the pre-existing bonds French Canadians brought with them to Worcester, and its purpose tells us something important about the fears Worcester provoked in them.

First, the name. As Ralph Vicero has pointed out, a very large population of the migrants to Worcester came from the valley of the Richelieu River, to the east of Montreal, and from Montreal itself. In one of his samples, 89% of the Worcester French Canadians applying for American citizenship listed as their points of origin Montreal, St. Hyacinthe, St. Ours, Sorel, or other communities in the Richelieu Valley.[12] My colleague, Charles Estus, has determined that 42% of the working adults among the Canadians of the French Hill area in 1891 had been born within a twenty-five mile radius of St. Hyacinthe.

So the choice of the new society's name in 1868 probably reflected the Worcester migrants' recognition of the ancient bonds of kinship and community they could draw upon for strength in the alien environment of Worcester. On the other hand, the society's statement of purpose reveals very forcefully the fear that brought them together in Worcester, the fear of losing their Catholic identity in this largely Protestant environment, and thus inevitably, in their minds, their identity as *Canadiens*.

The society's preamble noted the threat to "the faith and morals of Catholics in the United States" posed by the disdain toward their faith that was constantly being communicated by their Protestant neighbors. The society's one purpose was to help its members resist the snares of "*le respect humain*," an inordinate concern over the opinions of others. The slide began, they warned, with "a simple accommodation," perhaps a "smile at a statement against religion." But before long such concessions led to anti-religious—by which they meant anti-Catholic—sentiments being expressed by the Canadians themselves, and the fatal links in the chain were forged. "The gravity

---

12   Ralph D. Vicero, "L'Exode vers le sud—Survol de la migration canadienne-française vers la Nouvelle-Angleterre au XIXe siècle," Premier colloque de l'Institut français du Collège de l'Assomption, Worcester, MA. (Quebec City: *Vie française*, 1980), p. 7.

of a danger that threatens so many persons simultaneously struck us," the members wrote, and the society was formed to "act as a stimulant for all Catholics by encouraging them to be honestly what they should be: that is, Catholics and Canadians at heart."[13]

We may pass over the notion that all Catholics were called also to be Canadians, but it is worth emphasizing the defensive nature of the society's mission. The combined Catholic-Canadian identity was not secure in the Worcester environment, and preserving it demanded an act of will. A few months after the parish of Notre-Dame-des-Canadiens was established in 1869, the St. Hyacinthe Society went out of existence.[14] The parish had replaced it as the repository of the community's hopes for defending their identity as Catholics and as *Canadiens*.

Although they spurned excessive concern over public opinion in Worcester, the members of the St. Hyacinthe Society joined in the first St. Jean-Baptiste Day festivities organized in Worcester by the St. Jean-Baptiste Society in 1869.[15] It was a day to march in the streets behind their banners, to show the flag, to demonstrate their growing strength of numbers. But the fear of assimilation pervaded that day, too. The emotional ambivalence of the occasion was captured by a twenty-year-old native of St. Hyacinthe who attended as editor of *La Voix du Peuple* of Manchester, N.H. Ferdinand Gagnon was impressed with what he saw in Worcester that June day of 1869. By October he would take a Worcester bride, and by November he would be publishing Worcester's French-Canadian newspaper, *L'Étendard National*, the precursor of *Le Travailleur*, the renowned publication that would be Gagnon's voice from Worcester from 1874 until his premature death in 1886.[16]

---

13   Chandonnet, *Notre-Dame*, pp. 98-99.

14   Ibid., p. 98.

15   An account of this event, written by Ferdinand Gagnon for *La Voix du Peuple* of Manchester, N.H., is included in Alexandre Bélisle, *Histoire de la Presse Franco-Américaine* (Worcester, 1911), pp. 82-87.

16   Belisle, *Histoire de la Presse Franco-Américaine*, p. 73.

His report on the June celebration of 1869 bubbled over with enthusiasm because of its promise for "*la religion, la patrie et l'honneur.*" He claimed to have triumphed over a haunting doubt and, in making the claim, confessed the nature of the doubt. He returned to Manchester, he said, "with a heart full of joy, with a soul full of hope for the future, and with the conviction, ever more firm, ever more unshakeable, that the French-Canadian race cannot die out."[17]

A priest from St. Hyacinthe was also in Worcester during that spring of 1869, preaching a retreat. He carried back to Canada the insistent plea of the Worcester colony for a priest of their own. Fr. Jean-Baptiste Primeau, a graduate of the *Séminaire de St-Hyacinthe*, departed on September 8 for an interview with the bishop of Boston, and on September 10 he arrived in Worcester in time to celebrate a High Mass at St. Anne's the next morning, on the feast of St. Hyacinthe.[18]

What Primeau found in Worcester was hardly a community of strangers. Louis Allen, Sr., who greeted him as president of the St. Hyacinthe Society, was, like Primeau, a native of Chateauguay, born three years later than the man who was about to become his new pastor.[19] An older man, in his sixties, rushed to the rectory after Primeau's first Mass, to be sure a Canadian priest had really come to stay. "Don't you know me?" Primeau asked.

"No, Father."

"Well, you used to know me, anyway, at Chateauguay . . . . When you were a school commissioner and I was in school, . . . with Louis."
"Then who are you, if you please?"

"Jean-Baptiste Primeau."

---

17   Ibid., p. 83.

18   Chandonnet, *Notre-Dame*, pp. 2-6.

19   Roy, ed., *Le Worcester Canadien*, 5 (1891), p. 17; Belisle, *Histoire de la Presse Franco-Américaine*, p. 83.

"Father Primeau! *Our* priest?"

"Your priest."

"At that word," the account goes "the good old man could no longer control his emotions. He became pale, his hands trembled in spite of himself. He couldn't say a word, and large tears flowed down his cheeks."[20]

Just what the emotions were that produced those tears, we cannot know. But from the evidence we have, it is not unreasonable to suppose that they were to a significant extent tears of relief, of consolation. The French Canadians of Worcester in those years spoke of themselves as a people in exile, surrounded by hostile forces intent on their cultural annihilation. It was a feeling deeply rooted in the memories of the people of French Canada. To have, at last, a Canadian priest, meant that survival, if not assured, was possible in Worcester.

On September 26, 1869, the French Canadians worshipped together for the first time as the separate parish of Notre-Dame-des-Canadiens. A community determined to preserve its identity had at last the rallying point it had dreamed about, and through the parish it began to form new organizations for young men, for young women, for adult women, and for the adult men already organized in the St. Jean-Baptiste Society, a new Temperance Society.[21]

For the next twenty-two years, as the French-speaking populations of French Hill and South Worcester continued to grow, Notre-Dame in the center of the city remained the only French-Catholic church. By 1891, when St. Joseph's on French Hill became the second parish, the French-speaking population had grown to over 10,000 in a city of over 85,000.[22] The process that led to the separation of St. Joseph's parish indicates that a new generation, more

---

20   Chandonnet, *Notre-Dame*, pp. 7-8.

21   Ibid., pp. 17, 94-101.

22   Roy, ed., *Le Worcester Canadien*, 5 (1891), p. 205.

confident, more aggressive, less alienated from the American milieu, was coming into its own.

In the years since the founding of Notre-Dame, the Canadians of Worcester had at an accelerating pace founded organizations not directly focused on the preservation of their national and religious identity. In addition to a variety of social, literary, and musical societies, one could find the Lacrosse Club; the Businessmen's Society, the National Naturalization Club of the Canadians of Worcester, naturalization clubs in Wards Three, Five, and Six, the Canadian Republican Club, the Canadian Democratic Club, the Batallion and Club of the Rochambeau Grenadiers, the Casino Club, and a variety of others.[23] Although clearly Canadian and Catholic in tone, these organizations provided organized involvement, not directly sponsored by the parish, in a variety of economic, social, and political activities. Where the emphasis a generation earlier had been on cultural defense, by 1891 there was the stir of collective and organized entry into the secular life of a booming American city.

The founders of the second parish illustrate another dimension of the difference. The community leaders Gagnon had met on his visit to Worcester in 1869 had included one independent businessman (a saloon operator), a teamster, and an assortment of skilled craftsmen: a bricklayer, three carpenters, five blacksmiths, a woodworker, an armorer, and a bootmaker.[24] When the French Hill residents in 1886 organized their first committee to launch the process of setting up a separate parish, they chose Napoléon Huot, a former wholesale merchant, in 1886 a real estate developer, founder and first president of the Ward Three Naturalization Club, active Republican, and later the first French-Canadian alderman elected in Worcester; Samuel Pilet, a grocer on Wall Street, where St. Joseph's chapel and later the church would be located; J. Arthur Roy, born in Illinois, owner of a printing business on Wall Street, publisher of the annual local directory, *Le Worcester Canadien*, vigorous promoter of

---

23   Ibid., 10 (1896), pp. 127-134.

24   The identities of the leaders are based on Gagnon's account in Belisle, *Histoire de la Presse Franco-Américaine*, pp. 82-87. Their occupations are listed in the Worcester city directories for 1868, 1869, 1870, and 1871.

naturalization and voting, and active Republican; and Narcisse E. Lavigne, then a lastmaker, soon to be a dry goods and clothing merchant on Wall Street.[25] As committee succeeded committee, leading members were almost invariably businessmen, many of them grocers, most established on or near Wall Street. St. Joseph's was brought to French Hill by something resembling a chamber of commerce. The establishment of the parish attracted new residents to the area and promoted the construction of new housing.

The creation of the new parish—and the same might be said of the creation two years later of Holy Name of Jesus Parish in South Worcester—recognized not a new community, but a community with a sense of its separate identity prior to the parish separation. What the French Hill community now had at its disposal was the most effective community-building institution French Canadians—now frequently referring to themselves as Franco-Americans—knew how to use. The new parishes fostered the development of community, but now of communities based on neighborhoods as well as on religious and ethnic identity.

In 1911, a writer who knew the situation well reflected upon the relationship between the geographic concentration of Franco-American residential districts in some cities and the preservation of the use of the French language among them. "In the centers in which our people make up a compact population," he wrote, "the French character is better maintained. Being less mixed in with the English-speaking population, people have less occasion to deal with them, and their habitual language is French. There is every indication that in these centers the dominant language among our people will be French for several more generations." Those centers, he wrote, were "the hope of the nationality in this country," and he listed Fall River, New Bedford, Woonsocket, Lowell, and Manchester. Since Worcester was not on the list, and since the author was the editor of *L'Opinion Publique* in Worcester, we can safely conclude that his own city was

---

25   The names of the committee members are from Roy, ed., *Le Worcester Canadien* 5 (1891), p. 181. Biographical details on Huot are from *Le Worcester Canadien*, 11 (1897), p. 111; 15 (1901), p. 195; on Pilet, from ibid., 5 (1891), p. 55; on Roy, from ibid., 14 (1900), p. 7; 19 (1906), pp. 14-16; 8 (1894), p. 126; on Lavigne, from Charles Nutt, *History of Worcester and Its People* (New York, 1919), 4, p. 670; *Le Worcester Canadien*, 5 (1891), pp. 46, 194.

among those the writer declined to name as places where "the French-Canadian groups . . . show a general marked tendency toward the loss of the French tongue."[26]

Worcester's French Canadians never reached in their city a numerical proportion comparable to that found in some of the textile towns and cities. In addition, they were not compactly settled. Responding to economic opportunities French Canadians in a highly diversified and rapidly-expanding manufacturing city, they were, in the 1860s and 1870s, residentially dispersed but still drawn together by the memory of their ties in the homeland, by fears of cultural annihilation in the American environment, and by a determination to establish themselves permanently in Worcester while remaining *Canadiens*. Notre-Dame-des-Canadiens is their monument.

A generation later, still French-speaking, still devotedly Catholic, they had the confidence to separate, to build their futures as three communities of Franco-Americans, taking on that hyphenated dual identity that has been the essence of ethnicity for all American immigrant groups. No longer *Canadiens* in the old sense, they were not yet prepared to relinquish the language which linked them to the old culture, but it was a culture from which they were increasingly distant as they entered the mainstream of American life.

Kenneth J. Moynihan

[These two companion articles were first published in the French Institute's publication entitled *The Little Canadas of New England*. They have been reviewed by the authors for inclusion in this volume.]

---

26   J. G. LeBoutillier, Preface to Belisle, *Histoire de la Presse Franco-Américaine*, p. [v].

From Farm to Factory: Acadians in Fitchburg, Massachusetts (1880-1910)

Paul D. LeBlanc

Over the past twenty years or so, Tamara Hareven, Frances Early, Philip Silvia, Gerald Blazon, and others have studied the community, family, and work life of French Canadians who emigrated from Quebec to New England in the latter half of the nineteenth century.[1] This research, while important in helping to place Franco-American history in its proper perspective in the literature of American immigration history, has lacked any solid documentation on the Acadians who emigrated south from the Maritime Provinces of Canada to the region in the same period. While work on Old Town, Fitchburg, and Waltham has begun, more research needs to be done on Sanford, Gardner, Leominster, and other cities and towns where Acadians settled.[2]

---

[1]   Frances Early, "French-American Beginnings in an American Community: Lowell, Massachusetts, 1868-1886" (Ph.D. dissertation, Concordia University, 1979). Gerald Blazon, "A Social History of the French-Canadian Community of Suncook, New Hampshire, 1870-1920" (M.A. thesis, University of New Hampshire, 1977). Tamara Hareven and Randolph Langenbach, *Amoskeag: Life and Work in an American Factory City* (New York: Pantheon, 1978). Tamara Hareven, *Family-Time and Industrial-Time: The Relationship between the Family and Work in a New England Industrial Community* (New York: Cambridge University Press, 1982). Philip Silvia, "The Spindle City: Labor, Politics and Religion in Fall River, Massachusetts, 1870-1905" (Ph.D. dissertation, Fordham University, 1973). See also Kenneth J. Moynihan and Charles Estus, "Beyond Textiles: Industrial Diversity and the Franco-American Experience in Worcester, Massachusetts," in this volume.

[2]   Béatrice Chevalier Craig, "Économie, société et migrations: le cas de la vallée du Saint-Jean au 19e siècle," Marcella Harnish Sorg, "La formation d'une communauté à Old Town, Maine, 1835-1930: endogamie et origines natales parmi les Acadiens," and C. Stewart Doty, "Perspectives sur Old Town, Maine, dans les années 30: témoignages tirés des récits de vie d'Acadiens et de Franco-Américains, recueillis dans le cadre du *Federal Writers' Project*," in *L'Émigrant acadien vers les États-Unis: 1842-1950* (Worcester: French Institute, 1984). Barbara LeBlanc

Acadians often emigrated to mill towns where French Canadians were already residing. The question has often been raised as to whether the Acadian experience was similar or different from that of the immigrants from Quebec. This article examines the social and cultural positions of both groups between 1880 and 1910 in the "Little Canada" of Fitchburg, Massachusetts, known as Cleghorn. Our research suggests that French Canadians and Acadians did not live in cultural isolation from each other, that they, in fact, often had similar interests and frequently pooled their common resources to create the basis for the formation of a new identity as Franco-Americans.

Like French Canadians, Acadians brought with them from Canada traditions of language, religion, and folk culture which they sought to reinforce in Fitchburg by establishing social, religious, and political institutions to represent their interests. Because of industry's pressing need for labor, Acadians, like their Quebec cousins, found many jobs open to them in the city's textile and other manufacturing concerns.

By 1880, Fitchburg, a small textile town in 1800, had grown into a burgeoning manufacturing center. The harnessing of water power along the Nashua River and the introduction of the railroad at mid-century had led local and outside investors to pour capital into the city's economic development.[3] By 1900, there were three hundred different industries valued at three million dollars producing a variety of finished goods for foreign and domestic markets.[4] Industrialization and urbanization, especially between 1880 and 1900, led to a massive influx of immigrants from Europe and Canada into Fitchburg to work in the city's many mills. Textile manufacturers especially welcomed French Canadians and Acadians to the city with open arms.

The Cleghorn District developed as a planned neighborhood in the period of renewed industrialization after 1880, following the recession caused by the Panic of 1873. The opening of two large

---

and Laura Sadowsky have studied Waltham's Acadian population from a musical standpoint. *Le Patrimoine folklorique des Franco-Américains* (Worcester: French Institute, 1986).

3   Jeffrey Robbins, "The French Canadians of Fitchburg: *Survivance* and Industry" (Honors thesis, Middlebury College, 1980), p. 3.

4   U.S. Census 13, Census of Manufacturers 8 (1900), p. 382.

textile mills in Fitchburg, in 1882, by cotton manufacturer John Parkhill, gave a tremendous boost to the city's economic development and created much enthusiasm among the Board of Trade there for further industrial expansion. By 1886, Parkhill and his brother-in-law, Andrew Cleghorn, with the Board's help, opened a third mill in an unsettled section of town in Ward 2. The new mill, eventually called the "Cleghorn Mill" after one of the founders, served with five other smaller woolen and worsted mills as the economic base for the new sub-community which would include house and road building, and streetcar development, connecting the area to the city's business district. In the first year of the Cleghorn Mill's operation, French speakers made up three-quarters of the two hundred employees.[5]

By 1888, John Daniels of the Board of Trade and Andrew Pratt, owner of land in the area, were selling lots to French families to build two-family houses. Later, with increased immigration, larger tenements were necessary to house the many new workers.[6] By 1890, numerous grocery stores, barber shops, and other business concerns dotted the neighborhood's new streets and, by 1891, St. Joseph's parish had been founded. It was in this neighborhood that the largest number of French Canadians and Acadians would settle.[7]

What brought members of these two groups to Fitchburg? It seems that migration to New England in the latter half of the nineteenth century was the result of both pull factors, related to an increased industrialization, especially after 1880, and to the push factors of persistent depression and severe economic

---

[5]   Doris Kirkpatrick, *Around the World in Fitchburg* (Fitchburg: Fitchburg Historical Society, 1975), pp. 172-175.

[6]   From the general studies on Fitchburg, it would seem that French Canadians and Acadians in Cleghorn lived in factory-owned housing only in the earlier years, as in Manchester, Lowell, and other cities, before building their own dwellings, often renting to other immigrants. It would be necessary to check the city, state or federal primary records to determine home ownership status in this period.

[7]   Kirkpatrick, pp. 176, 190.

dislocation in Quebec and the Maritime Provinces.[8] Zoël Richard, a Cleghorn native and local historian of Fitchburg, whose Acadian parents emigrated from New Brunswick in the 1890s describes these factors in a telling way:

> My parents talked about how little they received in Canada for a barrel of potatoes or fish. When they would come to sell it they were paid so little that it was hardly worth selling, so they put it on the ground to use as fertilizer on their farms. They never made much of a living there because they were always working for nothing. . . they couldn't get enough money to prosper, so they came to Fitchburg where they could make a better life. Everyone could work. It would be a different way of life, but it was what they wanted.[9]

Before 1880, French speakers from Canada constituted a very small part of the city's total population. In 1872, the first city directory listed one hundred sixty-four people with French-Canadian names, a very small percentage of the city's population of 11,000. By 1880, that number had increased to four hundred, including some Acadian names, when the city population numbered 12,500.[10] It was not until 1882, when the first two Parkhill mills opened, that the French population began to increase at a faster rate. Between that year and 1886, French Canadians were more prevalent in the city than Acadians. By 1900, well over one thousand families lived in Fitchburg. The

---

8   Mason Wade, "The French and French Canadians in the U.S.," in Madeline Giguère, ed., *Franco-American Overview* 3 (Cambridge, Mass.: Evaluation, Dissemination and Assessment Center, 1981), pp. 37-39; Alan A. Brookes, "Out-Migration from the Maritime Provinces, 1860-1900. Some Preliminary Considerations," *Acadiensis* (Spring 1976); Iris Saunders Podea, "Quebec to 'Little Canada': The Coming of the French Canadians to New England in the Nineteenth Century," in *Franco-American Overview*, pp. 114-115.

9   Zoël Richard, oral interview, Fitchburg, December 12, 1983, typewritten catalog, pp. 8-9.

10   Robbins, "*Survivance* and Industry," Chap. 1, pp. 9-10.

city's population had doubled since 1880. It now numbered over 25,000.[11]

In 1900, in the Ward 2 area of Cleghorn, four hundred twenty-eight French-Canadian and one hundred sixteen Acadian heads-of-households were listed in the federal manuscript census for that year. Ninety percent of each group had come to the United States as immigrants. Quebecers outnumbered Acadians four-to-one. About half the French Canadians had immigrated before 1886 with thirty percent of them arriving before 1880, and twenty percent coming between 1880 and 1886. The remaining half came between 1886 and 1900, with immigration peaking between 1886 and 1890 and then receding in the next decade. On the other hand, only ten percent of the Acadians came before 1886 with the remaining ninety percent arriving after that date. Looking at male and female boarders in Cleghorn in 1900, one discovers a similar pattern of Acadians arriving later with over ninety-two percent of the total number immigrating between 1880 and 1900. Out of eighty-two Acadian boarders, fifty (over seventy percent) arrived in the year 1900. French-Canadian boarders, fewer in number, were more evenly divided over these two decades.[12]

The earlier migration of French Canadians to New England and to Fitchburg can be attributed to two factors. First, textile manufacturers sent agents only to Quebec to recruit prospective workers for their mills. In the secondary literature on Fitchburg's history, reference is made only to the recruitment of French Canadians and not Acadians. It seems that this system did not apply to the Maritimes. With such a setup in place, French Canadians would have been attracted to mill towns at a much earlier date. [13] Second, since out-migration from Quebec, as Ralph Vicero has so clearly pointed out, began in the 1840s, the communication network between immigrants already in the States and their relatives and friends in Quebec would have had a

---

[11]   U.S. Bureau of the Census. Federal Manuscript Census, Fitchburg, Massachusetts, 1900.

[12]   Ibid.

[13]   Kirkpatrick, p. 176.

better chance to develop.[14] Many of Fitchburg's French Canadians could easily have learned about job opportunities from family and friends in other New England cities or from those trickling into Fitchburg before 1880.

Acadians did not begin emigrating from Canada until the late 1870s. Yet, despite their late start, by the 1880s, because out-migration from the Maritimes was achieving massive proportions, they were developing a system of their own.[15] Alida Thibodeau, an Acadian immigrant to Cleghorn, described her parents' experience in the 1890s:

> My oldest brother Philippe had left Canada and found work in Fitchburg. He wrote my father in New Brunswick and told him that if he wanted to come he would find him some work. My mother, my three other brothers, and I stayed behind for one month.[16]

Alphée Légère, also of Cleghorn, described his father's experience as being the last in his family to leave New Brunswick:

> It got harder to live down there, so my father, who had kept in touch with all his brothers who had gone to Fitchburg, said, "Let's sell the farm and get over there and work where we can make a good life. Let's go to Fitchburg, we'll do well there."[17]

The earlier migration of French Canadians to Cleghorn was confirmed by Zoël Richard who claimed that the group was the first to reside in the neighborhood:

---

[14]   Ralph Vicero, "Immigration of French Canadians to New England, 1840-1900: A Geographical Analysis" (Ph.D. dissertation, University of Wisconsin, 1968).

[15]   Rev. Clarence d'Entremont, "Acadians in New England," in *The French in New England, Acadia and Quebec*, (Orono: New England-Atlantic Provinces-Quebec Center, 1972), p. 30.

[16]   Alida Thibodeau, oral interview, Fitchburg, Massachusetts, Dec. 12, 1983, typewritten catalog, p. 2.

[17]   Alphée Légère, oral interview No. 1, Fitchburg, Massachusetts, December 12, 1983, typewritten catalog, pp. 1-2.

When the Cleghorn section was first developed, the area around Beech St. was settled by French people from Quebec and was called *Petit Québec*. Then later, when the Acadians and other French Canadians came to the area, both groups lived anywhere they could rent, buy, or build a home.[18]

After 1888, three and four-decker houses were built on streets closer to the mills, in Cleghorn Square, where French-Canadian and Acadian families found housing, often in the same tenements, near their work. Mr. Richard again remembered his father's stories:

The people from Quebec and the Maritimes didn't necessarily live separately from each other, but usually lived where there was lodging. They often moved next to someone they might know in a tenement, and sometimes grouped together, but not against each other. Most of the lower part of Cleghorn was all people who worked in the mills.[19]

Alphée Légère confirmed Zoël's comments:

People from Quebec and Acadia lived in the same buildings and used to get along pretty well.[20]

By 1900, the majority of French Canadians and Acadians lived in the lower section of Cleghorn where many commercial enterprises were also located. Over half of the families of both groups listed in the census for that year lived either on Fairmount, Clarendon, Plymouth, Daniels, or Madison Streets, with one-quarter of each group residing on Fairmount St., the "Main Street" of Cleghorn. The other half of each group resided in housing on Rockland, Federal, Woodland, and other streets adjacent to Cleghorn Square, near the mills. Some French-Canadian families remained in the *Petit Québec* area while others settled on nearby Pratt St., but their numbers in 1900 were

---

18   Zoël Richard, p. 16.

19   Ibid., p. 4.

20   Alphée Légère, oral interview No. 2, Fitchburg, Massachusetts, Dec. 12, 1983, typewritten catalog, p. 6.

negligible. Boarders, too, found lodging near the mills, with more than one-half of both ethnic groups living in houses on Fairmount St.[21]

Occupationally, French Canadians and Acadians in Cleghorn worked mostly in unskilled jobs with many operating machines in textile production. About eighty percent of the people who worked in the mills were French-speakers. In the Cleghorn area, there were six mills (four cotton, one worsted woolen, and one paper) within a half-mile. The Cleghorn Mill, owned by Parkhill, and managed by Andrew Cleghorn, was the biggest employer.

In 1900, over half the French Canadians and Acadians worked in unskilled jobs with one-half of each of these being in textiles. French Canadians held a wider variety of occupations and were more prominent in service-oriented positions, mostly as proprietors and sales clerks. Having arrived earlier, immigrants from Quebec would have wanted their commercial establishments to be located where the neighborhood was developing, so as to be able to serve the consumer needs of their ethnic group. About one-quarter of each ethnic group worked in skilled jobs. Many of these had probably come to the States with certain manual skills since most of them had previously worked on farms and would have worked with their hands. The majority of the boarders for each group (seventy percent for males and eighty-five percent for females) held unskilled jobs with about half of each group working in textiles.[22]

Jobs seemed quite plentiful in Fitchburg in 1900 and French-Canadian and Acadian immigrants often worked side by side in the mills. Whole families were frequently seen working in the same factories. Alida Thibodeau gave a good description of her situation in some of the mills in Cleghorn:

> Most of the workers were French-speaking women where I worked in the cotton mill. Some came from New Brunswick and others were Canadians. Children began work in the shops at fourteen. The work didn't pay much. I went to work at the Parkhill Mill. It was the best shop. My first pay

---

[21]   Federal Manuscript Census.

[22]   Ibid.

there was $29.00 and a bit more for a week's work
and that was quite a lot for those days. After six
months there I went to the Orswell Mill which was
also in Cleghorn. I liked it there because it was
piece work. Later, I went to Nockege where I worked
a long time . . . People were able to get jobs quite
easily from one mill to the other. Getting jobs was
not reliant on kinship ties. My brother left one job
one day and the next day had another one . . . On the
job we were paid weekly. We worked 7:00 A.M. to
5:00 P.M. and often worked Saturday mornings,
averaging forty-five hours a week.[23]

Mrs. Thibodeau also stated that often women worked very hard to
keep a family going while at the same time holding a job in the
factory:

Women with families also worked. My sister-in-
law had twelve children alive and four dead and
she always worked. When a baby was old enough
for her to leave him, she went back to the mill. The
oldest would take care of the younger ones. The
poor woman struggled and worked in her lifetime.
At home she did everything and also worked.[24]

In examining the social and demographic characteristics of
French Canadians and Acadians in Cleghorn, between 1880 and
1900, it is evident that despite some differences in the year of
immigration, both groups shared housing in close proximity to
each other and worked in similar occupations. There were also
similarities in the age of the people examined on the 1900 census.
The majority of the heads-of-households of both ethnic groups
were between twenty-five and thirty, and forty-five and fifty years
old. It seems that most of the immigrants came to America at
these two ages because of convenience. The younger group would
have been newly married and just beginning a family, so
migration and settlement would have been easier. The older group
would perhaps have waited until their small children had grown
old enough so that they too could work in the mills.

---

23   Alida Thibodeau, p. 2.

24   Ibid., p. 8.

Despite these similarities, evidence indicates that cultural distinctions existed between the French Canadians and the Acadians. Wondering whether these differences might lead to ethnic separation in Cleghorn, I was reminded of Rev. Clarence d'Entremont's analysis of the question. He maintains that Acadians in New England, as in Canada, maintained a separateness from French Canadians:

> An Acadian from the Maritime Provinces, in his stubbornness, will never admit that he is a French Canadian. In fact, his history, his traditions, his manners and even his language have always been different than those of the *Québécois*, and Acadia has never been a part of Quebec. So, in New England, he might well have lost his identity, not only on account of his contact with New Englanders, but also with French Canadians. In other words, did the Acadians in coming to New England throw themselves into a "double melting-pot?"25

Initially, I thought that this was the case for Acadians in Cleghorn since some of my findings pointed to some definite cultural differences between them and French Canadians. I discovered that in the neighborhood the two groups established separate fraternal organizations and spoke a different French. For example, Acadians in Cleghorn were among the founding members of the Assumption Society which had its organizational meeting at St. Joseph's Church. French Canadians in the neighborhood, on the other hand, formed chapters of the St. Jean-Baptiste Society and the Association Canado-Américaine. In the early days of each of these societies, membership in the Acadian association was restricted to Acadians, and membership in French-Canadian associations was generally open only to French Canadians.26

Acadians were also often targets of French-Canadian prejudice over language issues and other cultural elements. Alida Thibodeau remembered times when she was put down for the way she spoke:

---

25   d'Entremont, p. 29.

26   Zoël Richard, p. 6.

> Some of the French Canadians from Quebec
> sometimes criticized us because we talked
> different. They evidently thought that their
> language was better than ours. This made us a bit
> timid.[27]

On one level, the situation in Fitchburg seems to support Rev. d'Entremont's statement that differences did exist in New England between the two groups. The above evidence would suggest that the Acadians were under a certain amount of pressure from the other French-speaking group who saw themselves in some ways as being superior. However, other evidence suggests that the two groups, more often than not, cooperated in many areas of cultural activity, and as a result transcended their cultural differences because their situation as neighbors in Cleghorn demanded it. In this ethnic neighborhood, faced with a brand new experience as immigrants residing, working, and socializing together, traditions eventually had to be adjusted and adapted to the new situation. As a result, the need to be ethnically separate was overcome and a new identity of being Franco-American was forged. Indications of this are seen in the fact that, by 1910, the St. Jean-Baptiste and Assumption Societies had opened their membership to both French Canadians and Acadians.[28] Also, as early as 1900, the St. Camille Society had been instituted in Cleghorn to give financial assistance to poor families from both groups faced with misfortunes and emergencies. While the majority of the founding members were Acadians, the society was clearly designed to meet the needs of both groups. Over the years many French Canadians joined the association.[29]

Another indication of cooperation between French Canadians and Acadians can be seen in the weddings that took place between young people from both groups. Intermarriage, which might not have been expected between the groups if they had been determined to remain separate, was common. According to Mrs. Clara Rousseau, an immigrant to Cleghorn from Quebec at

---

[27]   Alida Thibodeau, p. 20.

[28]   Zoël Richard, p. 6.

[29]   Ibid., p. 5. "Final Report of St. Camille Society," St. Joseph's Parish, Fitchburg, Massachusetts, 1904-1974.

the turn of the century, some opposition to such marriages existed in the early days, but receded after a while:

> There were some older Acadian women who didn't want their girls to marry *Canadiens* from Quebec, but eventually attitudes about this changed.[30]

Alida Thibodeau remembered her brother's marriage:

> Acadians didn't necessarily marry with other Acadians. Many married *Canadiens*. My brother married a Nadeau girl. The situation here allowed for that.[31]

Alphée Légère saw it as a good thing:

> Pretty soon they started marrying each other and that was the best thing that ever happened. There was no opposition to *Québécois* and Acadians marrying each other.[32]

Socially, both groups intermingled freely in Cleghorn and for the most part enjoyed each other's company. Délima Bourgault, a Cleghorn French Canadian, often enjoyed her interaction with Acadian women:

> I don't think that either group had too many bad words for each other. I knew some Acadian women and we would often see each other on the street and enjoy very good conversation.[33]

Zoël Richard remembered that:

> Many people would come down to Cleghorn Square

---

[30]   Mrs. Clara Rousseau, oral interview No. 2, Dec. 15, 1983.

[31]   Alida Thibodeau, p. 9.

[32]   Alphée Légère, p. 8.

[33]   Délima Bourgault, oral interview, Dec. 13, 1983.

and socialize. It didn't matter whether you were
Acadian or *Québécois*.[34]

Some people developed close relationships in the workplace.
Alida Thibodeau talked about her friends with whom she worked
in the woolen mill:

I chummed with French Canadians I worked with.
I had two best friends who were like sisters to me.
They didn't smoke or drink like me and when we
went out somewhere we were really close.[35]

In conclusion, it seems that the French Canadians and
Acadians in Fitchburg's "Little Canada" were well on their way to
becoming Franco-Americans by 1910. The cultural legacy, which
each group brought with it from its respective region of Canada,
helped it to become established in Cleghorn. However, in the long
term, social and cultural factors in the new country required
adaptation and accommodation, both of which led to the
emergence of a new identity which could be shared equally by both
groups—that of being Franco-American.

[This article first appeared in a French translation as "De la ferme à
l'usine: les Acadiens à Fitchburg, Massachusetts (1880-1910)" in the
French Institute's publication entitled, *L'Émigrant acadien vers les États-
Unis: 1842-1950*. It has been reviewed by the author for inclusion in this
volume.]

---

34   Zoël Richard, p. 5.

35   Alida Thibodeau, p. 21.

III

RELIGION

The Corporation Sole Controversy

Michael J. Guignard

When one discusses the influence of religion on Franco-Americans, one usually focuses on the Franco-American parish. The themes are similar—the founding of national parishes, with their bilingual schools staffed by religious orders from Canada and France, parish societies for men, women, boys, and girls, retreats, the fostering of vocations, in a word, the parish as the center of social as well as religious life in the "Little Canadas" of New England.

Notwithstanding the revisionist works which have been published in recent years, the evidence is persuasive that our forebears in New England had a strong attachment to their religion. Even during the most vitriolic controversies between the Franco-Americans and the Irish-American catholic hierarchy in New England, such as Maine's Corporation Sole Controversy and the Sentinelle Affair in Rhode Island, our ancestors maintained that they were loyal Catholics who believed that the assimilationist policies of the Irish hierarchy would lead to the loss of faith among French-Canadian migrants to New England.

"*Qui perd sa langue perd sa foi*" (He who loses his language loses his faith) was a conviction which the *Québécois* brought with them from *la belle province*. This belief was difficult for the Irish clergy to understand since, although the use of Gaelic had disappeared among Irish-American Catholics, their faith had nevertheless remained strong. Irish-American bishops, such as William O'Connell and Louis Walsh of the diocese of Portland, soon became aware of the tenacious attachment of the Franco-American faithful to their mother tongue and to the concept of the national parish which they felt would preserve that mother tongue. The national parish ministered to one ethnic group only while the territorial parish encompassed all the Catholics living in a certain geographic area, with English as the primary language of worship.

American church leaders accepted the national parish concept, but viewed it as a temporary accommodation to the various ethnic immigrant groups who did not speak English upon their arrival in the United States. Once parishioners in a national parish learned English and acculturated themselves to American ways, national parishes would be transformed into territorial ones, according to their way of thinking. Franco-Americans were staunchly opposed to any decision on the part of the hierarchy which seemed to be trying to accelerate the process of phasing out national parishes.

Early conflict between the Irish-American hierarchy and Franco-Americans had centered around the refusal by the local bishop to establish a national parish or the appointment of Irish priests to already-established Franco national parishes. The Fall River[1] and North Brookfield[2] incidents in Massachusetts, and the Danielson Affair[3] in Connecticut, all engendered vigorous opposition among Franco-Americans to the Irish-American hierarchy's denial of what they perceived to be a God-given right, i.e., to worship God in their mother tongue, in a church they were willing to pay for.

Given this distrust of the Irish-American hierarchy, it is not surprising that Franco-Americans soon questioned the way parishes were administered in the United States. Franco-

---

[1]   [See Yves Roby "Franco-Americans and the Catholic Hierarchy" in this volume, for a description and analysis of the conflict.—Editor]

[2]   [The North Brookfield Affair (1897-1904) was a dispute between the Franco-Americans of this Central Massachusetts town and the Bishop of Springfield, Mass. who refused to grant them a parish of their own where they could worship in French. Their appeal to the pope was rejected. Some Franco-American parishioners formed *L'Association religieuse canadienne-française*, built a chapel, and brought in a French priest, Jean Berger, to minister to them in French. In 1900, the dissidents were excommunicated, the chapel padlocked, litigation was undertaken, and threats were made to establish a French-language Protestant church. No resolution of the conflict was ever reached.—Editor]

[3]   [The Danielson Affair (1888-1896) was the result, initially, of the refusal of Bishop McMahon, and later Bishop Tierney, of Hartford to name a French-Canadian priest to minister to the parishioners of Saint James which numbered 1800 French Canadians and only 300 Irish. An attempt was made by the French Canadians to organize a separate French-speaking parish to no avail. In spite of appeals to Rome through the apostolic delegate and Bishop Gravel of Nicolet (QC), the dissidents were unsuccessful in their efforts.—Editor]

Americans wanted more lay involvement, and less diocesan control, in the running of parish financial affairs as they were accustomed to having in Quebec.

Yet, the underlying point of contention was always the question of language. Had the Church hierarchy been of French-Canadian descent, and sympathetic to appointing French-speaking clergy to minister to Francos, there would have been no Sentinelle Affair or Corporation Sole Controversy. Both of these conflicts arose as a result of the belief among Franco-Americans that an Irish-American bishop was draining their parishes of money through diocesan fund drives to finance institutions where only English would be spoken or where French would clearly not be the dominant language.

By tracing the events in Maine between 1906 and 1913, which became known as the Corporation Sole Controversy, one can better understand the dynamics of the conflict. When Louis Walsh was appointed Bishop of Portland in 1906, Franco-Americans were bitterly disappointed for they had hoped that one of their own would be appointed. Walsh soon angered Maine's Francos by deciding to implement a plan to separate the national parish of St. Francis de Sales in Waterville into a smaller French parish and a territorial one called Sacred Heart. Although a large majority of the new Sacred Heart parish was French-Canadian, the newly-appointed pastor was Irish. When *curé* Narcisse Charland tried to explain to the new bishop the reluctance of his parishioners to worship at Sacred Heart, the bishop told him emphatically to force his recalcitrant flock to join the new parish. When Charland demurred, Walsh accused Charland of acting like the bishop of Waterville. Walsh's impatience with his opposition can be seen in his letters. Charland, he wrote, "does not think straight, see straight, talk straight, walk straight or act straight." Walsh's attitude toward those in Waterville, unhappy with his decision, can be summed up in another letter in which he tartly observed, ". . . in the Catholic Church, the people are not to think and say and do as they like but they are to follow and obey the Church Authorities."

Soon after this unpopular decision, the *Comité Permanent de la Cause Nationale du Maine* was formed by Franco-Americans concerned about preserving the ethnic identity of national parishes and insuring that French would be the dominant language in their churches and schools. This battle against Bishop Walsh became known as *La Cause Nationale*.

Walsh would brook no interference in diocesan matters, however. In his first meeting with the *Comité* in June 1907, acrimony reigned as Walsh warned that he would not tolerate any insubordination within his bishopric. He refused to recognize the group as having any official standing and criticized its members for what he considered to be their impudence.

That same month, Franco-Americans held a second state convention. Frustrated by their inability to get a Franco bishop for their diocese, and faced with Walsh's adamant position, the delegates grew increasingly radical. This convention, which was appropriately held in Waterville, dismayed the Franco-American clergy by its hostility to diocesan authorities. It marked the end of clerical participation in *Comité*-sponsored conventions. Two years later, Franco-Americans met again, this time in Brunswick, and mounted the first systemic attack on the Corporation Sole, the system under which a bishop legally owns all diocesan and parish property. The delegates were convinced that Bishop Walsh was draining French national parishes of funds to establish more territorial parishes and other diocesan institutions for the Irish-American Catholics of Maine who comprised only twenty percent of the Pine Tree State's Catholics. Particularly galling were the bishop's efforts to meet diocesan collection quotas by ordering Franco *curés* to draw money from parish operating expenses and turn it over to the diocese. Feelings ran particularly high in Biddeford, where the bishop forced *Curé* Dupont of St. Joseph's parish to close an orphanage and his attempt to transfer the children to an orphanage run by English-speaking nuns. Dupont instead sent the children to orphanages in Quebec.

The delegates to the Brunswick Convention believed that by changing the method of property ownership from Corporation Sole to the parish corporation under which individual parishes had more financial autonomy, Francos could better resist an assimilationist bishop. Thus, they passed a resolution for the introduction in the legislature of a bill to repeal an 1887 Maine law which made the Bishop of Portland the sole owner of all parish property.

The controversy was covered extensively by Maine's two French-language journals—*Le Messager* of Lewiston and *La Justice* of Biddeford. The editors of both newspapers, Jean-Baptiste Couture and Alfred Bonneau, were eventually interdicted by Bishop Walsh for their role in the conflict. During this period, charges were hurled at Bishop Walsh by the editors with each new issue. Epithets such as "Francophobe," "barbarous assimilator," and "an enemy trying to saxonize little French children" were hurled at Walsh. The exhortation *Fermez vos Bourses* (Close your Wallets) to diocesan collections became a rallying cry of the editors.

Walsh, not surprisingly, reciprocated the disdain, but never publicly. When, as Bishop of Portland, he interdicted the leaders of the fight against the Corporation Sole, it was because they had caused what he considered to be a public scandal. Less than twenty years later, the Bishop of Providence was to use the same rationale for his excommunications.[4]

The unity of Catholics in fighting nativism was seriously undermined during this period. During the Corporation Sole Controversy, relations between the Irish of Biddeford and local Francos were badly strained. One can well imagine the Yankee reaction at seeing two groups of Catholics, whose loyalty to America was already suspect, behaving in what they considered to be a most un-American manner. Yankees in Biddeford-Saco most probably concurred when, in 1910, Albert Beland, soon to be interdicted by Bishop Walsh, urged local Francos to avoid membership in the Knights of Columbus because he deemed that organization to be a tool of the Catholic hierarchy in Maine. It is not surprising that attacks against the Irish and Francos increased during the Corporation Sole Controversy.

In Biddeford, *La Cause Nationale* appeared to have the support of a good majority of the city's Franco inhabitants, as measured by subscriptions to *La Justice,* money donated to *Le Comité Permanent,* and the lack of support for diocesan fund drives locally. But there was division among Francos statewide, especially after the Waterville Convention of 1907 when *La Cause Nationale* took a decidedly radical turn and the active participation of the Franco-American clergy ended. This division was highlighted by the positions taken by the two *curés* in Biddeford during the Corporation Sole Controversy. *Curé* Dupont was sympathetic to the agitators while *Curé* Louis Bergeron supported the bishop.

---

[4]   Those doing research on religious controversy in Maine can easily find Bishop Walsh's diary and correspondence at the Chancery Library in Portland.   These sorts of primary source documents are not available from the Diocese of Providence, much to the chagrin of historians doing research on the Sentinelle Affair.

It is doubtful that many Francos supported the more radical attacks on the Church voiced by Godfroi Dupré, one of Biddeford's five interdicted Francos. His anti-clerical diatribes were more likely approved by nativist Protestants who shared his deep suspicion of the Catholic clergy as anti-democratic and un-American.

Ironically, the movement, dedicated to the survival of the French language and customs, especially religious ones, probably did little for the cause of *la survivance*. The money and energy expended to fight Corporation Sole in the legislature, where the battle was lost, could well have been used to finance more positive programs for the promotion of *la survivance*. Furthermore, the division between radicals and moderates in Maine delayed any statewide and regional efforts on behalf of that cause.

But, perhaps the most damaging result of the Corporation Sole Controversy was its effect on non-Catholics. In the nineteenth century the Know-Nothings and the American Protective Association had hurled diatribes at Catholics, especially the clergy and the Church hierarchy. When the more radical members of *La Cause Nationale* attacked the Catholic Church hierarchy, they were playing into the hands of the nativists. Less than a decade after the agitation against Corporation Sole ended, the Ku Klux Klan helped elect a governor in Maine. The Catholic Church and its schools were the special targets of the Klan. The Church, which had been growing rapidly in Maine, was put on the defensive. Yet Bonneau's successor as editor of *La Justice* continued to see Irish-Americans as the primary antagonists of *la survivance*, claiming that they belonged to the KKK and were behind legislative efforts to ban French from Maine parish schools. That preoccupation with *les Irlandais* caused a schism among Catholics in Maine which was exploited by Yankee nativists, who were the true enemies of *la survivance* and *La Cause Nationale*.

[This article first appeared in the French Institute's publication entitled *Franco-Americans and Religion: Impact and Influence*. It has been reviewed by the author, and up-dated where necessary, for inclusion in this volume.]

Franco-Americans and the Catholic Hierarchy

Yves Roby

At the beginning of their presence in the United States, French-Canadian immigrants experienced great difficulty in practicing their religion. Some groups, isolated and small in number, were deprived of priests. The best they could expect was the visit, two or three times a year, of missionaries sent by the bishops of Quebec. Others, in more important communities, had to attend the churches of their co-religionaries of Irish origin who had arrived earlier. They were often poorly received in these churches and felt ill at ease in them.

French Canadians did not like the way Irish-Americans practiced their religion. They complained that the Irish services were too simple and plain and that the Irish cared little for the solemnity and pomp which so pleased French Canadians. Furthermore, French-Canadian emigrants discovered that ". . . it's expensive to practice one's religion in the States." However, the question of language was the main problem. The French Canadians felt estranged in parishes where the pastor preached and made public announcements in a language which they did not know. They suffered from their inability to be understood in the confessional and deplored the fact that the pastor could not be their privileged counselor and guide as he had been in Quebec.

The solution: create national parishes directed by French-Canadian priests. Such requests had to be presented to bishops, the majority of whom were of Irish descent. The problem facing French Canadians was: Could they claim this as a right or was it simply to be regarded as a favor to be granted? In other words, did the bishops have to encourage the emergence of national churches, i.e., French-Canadian, German, Polish, etc? Or, on the contrary, should they be working toward the rapid assimilation of all Catholic immigrants by eliminating differences in language, traditions, and customs, in order to facilitate the emergence of a united Church, strong, influential, and able to compel the respect and admiration of the country at large?

An incident at Notre-Dame-de-Lourdes of Fall River posed the problem clearly. Rome's decision in this case was to have a significant impact on relations between Franco-Americans and their Irish-American bishops. Let us examine the affair.

In August 1884, Father P.-J.-B. Bédard, pastor of Notre-Dame-de-Lourdes in Fall River, passed away. In October 1884, his replacement, Father Nobert, left for health reasons. Mgr. Hendricken, Bishop of Providence, then appointed Father McGee, an "Irish" pastor, to replace him. Six years earlier, he had named Father Briscoe to Sainte-Anne of Fall River to replace the pastor, a Breton, Father Montaubricq. The parishioners were furious. They could not understand why in Fall River, French-Canadian parishes were now being served only by priests of Irish ancestry. What was the use of making sacrifices to build churches, rectories, and schools only to have them taken away? Parishioners thereupon demanded the recall of pastor McGee and that he be replaced by a French Canadian.

The bishop refused. According to him, Pastors Briscoe and McGee were excellent priests and McGee spoke better French than his parishioners. Moreover, he countered to a group of parishioners who met with him: Why would you want a French priest? In ten years, everyone will be speaking English in the parishes. Disappointed and insulted by the bishop's attitude, the parishioners decided to make life unbearable for Pastor McGee. On February 7, 1885, Father McGee, unable to improve relations with his parishioners, asked to be replaced. When parishioners greeted McGee's successor, Owen Clarke, also of Irish ancestry, as they had Pastor McGee, Father Clarke also resigned. This was too much for Bishop Hendricken who had the Blessed Sacrament removed from the tabernacle and closed the church.

Immediately thereafter, the parishioners decided to appeal to Rome. Narcisse-Rodolphe Martineau, their representative, met with Pope Leo XIII on two occasions and was in constant contact with Cardinal Simeoni, Prefect of the Office of Propaganda. To the pope and to the cardinal, Mr. Martineau pointed out that what French Canadians needed were priests of their own nationality, for they were the only ones capable of keeping them within the bosom of the Church. They were estranged from the faith by priests who did not speak French well, knew little or nothing of their customs, and treated them with disdain. Mr. Martineau went on to explain that parishioners were not taking issue with episcopal authority as such, but noted the bishop's lack of understanding and good will on their behalf. Mgr. Williams, archbishop of Boston, and Mgr. Hendricken responded to Mr. Martineau's charges by affirming that the behavior of the parishioners had been violent and scandalous, reflecting the fact that they were led by impious and lying leaders to whom some French-Canadian priests had been repeating for years that Francos should have no other priests but those of their own nationality. Were one to give in to the demands of these persons, it would make it impossible to control French Canadians in the future and would have grievous consequences everywhere in New England, concluded Bishop Hendricken.

Without blaming anyone, Rome secretly recommended to the bishop to be very flexible and also suggested that he call upon religious orders, either French or Canadian, to minister to the parishioners of Notre-Dame-de-Lourdes. Bishop Hendricken offered the parish to the Oblates who refused. While waiting for a solution to his problem, he sent Father Cassidy and a French-Canadian priest to attempt to reopen the church. Parishioners successfully opposed the move because the priest in charge was "Irish." They argued that to accept that an Irish priest be placed in charge would have resulted in the negation of their most sacred rights. Noting the fact that the parishioners now insisted that the nomination of a French-Canadian priest be recognized as a matter of right, Archbishop Williams of Boston found this to be a dangerous widening of the conflict. He argued that "if this decision is considered as a recognition of the *right* of French Canadians *always* to have a *French Canadian* as a pastor, all of the French-Canadian congregations of Canadians in the United States will want the same privilege even if their priests are French or Belgian." A few malcontents in a parish would suffice for trouble to start anew. It would no longer be possible to administer a diocese. That was the crux of the matter: Was it a right or a favor to have a French-Canadian pastor? Rome settled the question on October 23, 1885. Its decision was of fundamental importance for the future of Franco-Americans as a group.

Officially, the Office of Propaganda did not grant French Canadians the right in strict justice to be served only by priests of their own nationality. It thus affirmed that Mgr. Hendricken had acted within his rights. However, in the interest of peace and for the welfare of souls, Rome invited the bishop to recognize the value of the reasons cited and to grant to the people of Notre-Dame-de-Lourdes a priest of their own nationality. Five months later, Mgr. Hendricken appointed Father Joseph Laflamme as pastor. French Canadians exulted and claimed victory.

"The Flint Affair"[1] had an enormous impact on the relations between Franco-Americans and the Catholic hierarchy. Let us examine why. Mgr. Hendricken, who had authorized the creation of Sainte-Anne and Notre-Dame-de-Lourdes parishes, was of the opinion that French Canadians had now had sufficient time to adapt to their new surroundings, and that he could thus accelerate their assimilation by naming English-speaking priests to lead them. During the struggle which followed, French Canadians became aware of the need to have priests of their own nationality as heads of their national parishes to ensure the promotion and survival of the French presence in America. Rome reminded them, however, that this was to be construed as a favor and not as a right. Events also taught them that, with Rome's help, a relentless and resolute struggle could allow them to avoid setbacks, even to gain ground. Had not the people of Fall River compelled the Bishop of Providence to give ground? Such is the explanation of the continuous battles which punctuate the history of French-Canadian immigrants and that of their children. Up to 1930, the struggle to ensure the integrity of national parishes and of their institutions would take diverse shapes.

1 — In Ware, Massachusetts, Brunswick, Maine, Danielson, Connecticut, and North Brookfield, Massachusetts, battles analogous to those of "the Flint" in Fall River were waged by Franco-Americans. In Ware and Brunswick, parishioners attempted unsuccessfully to replace Irish pastors with French-Canadian priests. In Danielson, they succeeded in having Pastor Preston replaced by a French priest, Father Socquet, of the La Salette Order. The parishioners were disappointed, however, because for them, there was no difference between a French priest and an Irish priest. In North Brookfield, attempts were made in vain to be granted a national parish directed by a priest of their own nationality. Each time, they appealed to Rome to achieve what they wanted. There is reason to believe that these confrontations had beneficial results, despite the fact that they ended in failure. Indeed, without the constant menace of contention and rebellion, bishops would have been more reticent

1   [*L'affaire de la Flint*" or "The Flint Affair," thus named for one of the "Little Canadas" of Fall River, located in the East End of the city where John D. Flint had built the Flint and the Wampanoag Mills in the early 1870s. Along with the mills, the parish church of Notre-Dame-de-Lourdes was the focal point of this French-Canadian neighborhood.—Editor]

in authorizing the creation of national parishes and more inclined to name Irish pastors.

2 — In order to avoid these sorts of conflicts, Canadian immigrants came to recognize the need for them to have understanding bishops, sympathetic to their cause. That is why each time a bishop passed away, as in the case of Mgr. Hendricken in 1886, they fought doggedly against the candidacy of priests known to be hostile to their cause. However, since all the Irish bishops dreamt of having a united and influential Church, they were in favor of the earliest possible assimilation of Catholic immigrants. In the long run, the strategy of the French-Canadian immigrants proved unsuccessful.

3 — Thus, Franco-Americans came to believe that all the problems which brought them into conflict with the religious authorities would be solved if they had bishops of their own nationality. Indeed, how could anyone imagine that a Franco-American bishop would refuse to create national parishes where these were deemed to be necessary, or would hesitate to assign French-Canadian priests wherever there lived a sufficient number of his compatriots, or would dare to replace one of their pastors with an Irish priest! That is why, beginning in 1901, they made every effort possible to obtain Franco-American bishops. Toward this end, they carried on active press campaigns, made appeals to the apostolic delegate in Washington and even to the Pope himself and to the cardinals concerned with these matters. From 1901 to 1930, eleven such appeals were made. Only one of these was successful: it came in 1906, with the nomination of Mgr. George A. Guertin of Manchester, New Hampshire, and was due to the express intervention of the apostolic delegate, Mgr. Diomene Falconio. Certain members of the community, like J.-L.-K. Laflamme of the *Revue franco-américaine*, saw in this poor record of achievement the proof of an Irish plot, according to which a well-defined plan existed to limit French-Canadian influence to the Province of Quebec.

4 — As sole proprietors of parish property and funds, bishops could dispose of them as they wished. They could go so far as to sell or mortgage parish assets without even informing those who had paid for them; they could even change a national parish into a mixed one where English would be spoken and then transfer it to the Irish, thus transforming Franco-American schools into instruments of assimilation. This threat appeared much more serious by the twentieth century, given the desire of bishops to

exercise a more direct control over parishes as a means either of improving their finances or of ensuring a better distribution of resources among the various ethnic groups, or even of financing the development of a diocesan system of secondary education. To Franco-Americans who viewed the national parish as their bulwark against assimilation, this effort at centralizing seemed to be a deadly menace to their survival as a distinct national group. It became necessary therefore to limit episcopal powers. How? In Maine, at the time of the Corporation Sole controversy,[2] Franco-Americans endeavored, without much success, to obtain recognition of parish *fabriques*[3] from the legislature. In Rhode Island, during the *Sentinelle* crisis,[4] Franco-Americans would institute judicial proceedings against twelve parish corporations headed by the bishop *ex-officio* in order to prevent the possibility of drawing upon parish funds for diocesan purposes. None of this proved to be of any avail.

All of these actions were directed at ensuring the survival of the Franco-American group by maintaining the national parish intact, as their "fortress" in the battle for *survivance*. This was an impossible mission. The adversaries of the *Sentinellistes* noted this by recognizing, in 1929, the primacy of the diocese over the parish. In religious life, they stated, the diocese was the vital cell. The parish structure comes after that of the diocese; it cannot exist without it.

Translated by †Raymond J. Marion

[This article first appeared as "Les Franco-Américains et les évêques 'irlandais'," in the French Institute's publication entitled *Franco-Americans and Religion: Impact and Influence*. It has been reviewed by the author, and up-dated where necessary, for inclusion in this volume.]

---

2   [See Michael J. Guignard, "Maine's Corporation Sole Controversy," in this volume, for a detailed account of this question.—Editor]

3   [The *fabrique* is a committee made up of parishioners and the pastor of a given parish. It controls all the property and finances of a parish in the Province of Quebec.—Editor]

4   [See Richard S. Sorrell, "*La Sentinelle* and *La Tribune*—The Role of Woonsocket's French Language Newspapers in the Sentinelle Affair of the 1920s," in this volume, for more information on this crisis.—Editor]

The Foundation of the Little Franciscans of Mary in Worcester, Massachusetts

Jacquelyn Alix, P.F.M.

This is the story of eleven valiant women who responded to God's call to serve Him in the poor and the abandoned. By the late nineteenth century, Worcester, located in Central Massachusetts, had become one of the principal commercial and industrial centers of New England. So many French-Canadian immigrants had come to find work in this city that, by 1888, this ethnic group numbered some seven thousand persons.

At the cost of much financial sacrifice, these immigrants founded and built their own French-Canadian church which they named Notre-Dame-des-Canadiens thereby proudly affirming the country of their birth. Father Joseph Brouillet, who became their pastor in 1883, was a man of energy, enthusiasm, and generosity. *Curé* Brouillet had opened two temporary chapels—one in South Worcester, Saint Anne's, later to become Saint-Nom-de-Jésus parish, and Saint Joseph's on "French Hill," so that his parishioners, who lived in these neighborhoods, could fulfill their religious obligations more easily. A few classes were taught at each of these locations by the Sisters of Saint Anne, a religious community founded near Montreal in 1850.

One group, however, was not being cared for—the orphans. No Catholic institution existed to care for these French-speaking children and Father Brouillet realized the necessity to found a home for them so as to give them the Christian education and the love they needed. In 1888, having gone to Manchaug, a small town some fifteen miles south of Worcester, for the Forty Hours devotion, Father Brouillet shared his plan with his friend, Father Alexis Delphos. The latter approved his friend's project to the point of offering him two Franciscan tertiaries, who were teaching in his parish, to assist him with the task of opening an orphanage. These two women were granted permission to wear the Franciscan habit and to pronounce simple vows for one year. The two "Sisters" readily agreed to this move, seeing this as an opportunity to immerse themselves more fully in religious life.

They had chosen as their religious names Sister Saint-François-d'Assise and Sister Sainte-Claire-d'Assise.

As news of the proposed orphanage spread, Father Brouillet realized that these two Sisters would never be able to assume the full operation of such an undertaking. An entire religious community would be needed to ensure its success. He thus decided to found just such a community, seeking candidates among the French-American women of Worcester. Establishing an apostolate in the midst of his own people, he would recruit and train his own parishioners to meet the special needs of his orphans. And, in order to do so, he knew just where to begin—at 80 Wall Street on "French Hill," the home of Rémi Rondeau.

There, Father Brouillet spoke of his dream of founding a religious community under the leadership of the two professed Franciscan Sisters for the purpose of caring for orphans and even the elderly, as well as for teaching in parochial schools. He explained that the novitiate would last one year, after which the novices would be allowed to pronounce religious vows. He then asked Mr. and Mrs. Rondeau to permit their eighteen-year-old daughter, Marie-Louise, who was studying with the Sisters of the Presentation of Mary in Canada, to be his first novice.

There were many reasons Marie-Louise's parents could think of to object to this proposal, but *Monsieur le Curé* had spoken, so they agreed to speak with their daughter. The following day, Marie-Louise herself went to see her pastor who argued convincingly that surely she would be proud to see a French-American congregation, under the patronage of Saint Francis of Assisi, the holy patriarch of the poor, take root in the soil in which she had been born. After a few days of reflection, Marie-Louise Rondeau returned to the rectory to agree to his proposal. She would enter as the first postulant of a yet-to-be founded community at a still non-existent orphanage.

Father Brouillet had decided to locate the orphanage in South Worcester, in the same building that housed one of the temporary chapels. It was a three-story building on the corner of Southgate and Grand Streets. The second floor was to be the home of the Franciscan tertiaries, their postulant, and the orphans.

On August 13, 1889, the two Franciscan tertiaries and their first orphan, Amanda Narreau, crossed the threshold of this empty and comfortless home. Father Brouillet was there to welcome them. Father Zotique Durocher, his assistant, who had been assigned to perform religious services at the chapel, was also present. That same evening, Marie-Louise Rondeau, the first postulant, arrived.

Father Brouillet was constantly on the lookout for other Franciscan vocations from among his parishioners and, almost immediately, other women came to join the three "Sisters." The two professed sisters initiated the postulants in the Rule of the Third Order Regular of Saint Francis. Father Durocher, as chaplain of the orphanage and spiritual director of the community, celebrated Mass daily and administered the sacraments to all those who frequented the mission chapel. He gave lectures and direction to the Franciscans and taught them that "the Cross is the fundamental cornerstone of God's work. Ask for it so that your institution may be strong and firm."

The first investiture ceremony took place on September 22, 1889. The celebrant blessed and gave each novice the holy habit and a religious name. Marie-Louise Rondeau, from this day forward, was to be known as Sister Marie-Joseph. The homily was preached by Father Durocher who appealed for imitators of those who had already heard the divine call. He also pleaded for charity to feed and clothe the orphans. His entreaties did not go unheeded.

The first to answer the Lord's call was Cordélie Robillard, the housekeeper of the parish in East Douglas. She brought with her another postulant, Marie Bibeau, a dressmaker from Manchaug, Father Delphos' parish. Father Brouillet thought it to be in the interest of the Institute to make its growth known to the whole city, so he scheduled a second investiture ceremony for November 24 of the same year. The new novices received the names of Sister Marie-Alexis (Cordélie Robillard) and Sister Marie-Anne-de-Jésus (Marie Bibeau).

As the number of religious increased, so did the number of orphans and elderly. Daily begging of alms was needed since this was the principal source of income of the Institute. Parishioners and non-parishioners alike were generous in their support.

In the fall of 1889, a two-story annex was built to enlarge the orphanage. By Christmas, the new wing was completed and Midnight Mass was celebrated in the new Chapel. The New Year (1890) brought with it a new postulant Étudienne Blais. Father Brouillet immediately arranged for another investiture to be held on January 5. The holy habit was bestowed on Étudienne as well as the name Sister Marie-Zotique. The joy of this solemn occasion was not to last. On the morning of January 9, the Superior, Sister Sainte-Claire-d'Assise, did not attend Mass. Later, when she still had not appeared, the novices went to her room only to find her religious habit lying on her bed. Father Durocher explained that, since the bishop had not permitted a renewal of their vows after the year had expired, the two tertiaries were no longer bound by them. Sister Marie-Joseph was now named as Superior and Sister Marie-Anne-de-Jésus as her assistant.

Other women were being accepted by Father Brouillet to enter the community and another investiture took place on February 24. This time the Franciscan habit was given to Albertine Riopel along with the name Sister Alphonse-Marie-de-Liguori. Yet another investiture took place on May 15. The brown habit was given on that day to Emma Decelles along with the name Sister Marie-des-Sept-Douleurs and to Lumina Bolduc with the name Sister Marie-Dominique.

These arrivals, succeeding one another in joyful rhythm, corresponded to departures, which also took place in rapid succession. Nevertheless, happiness reigned among the sisters as they worked and prayed and looked forward to the day they would in fact become "real" religious.

Their year of probation nearing its end, they were about to become eligible to pronounce their vows, as Father Brouillet had promised. However, by May 1890, whenever the sisters alluded to their desire to take vows, Father Brouillet changed the subject. When asked when the ceremony would take place, he became hostile. His manner toward the sisters changed completely from this time forward.

Father Brouillet was not in close daily contact with the Franciscans at this time because of the many other demands made on him by his large parish. Father Durocher, who was, argued with his pastor over the fate of the sisters. A rift developed between the two men which, unfortunately, became public knowledge.

Despite the shadows gathering around the Institute, women still came to the orphanage asking to be admitted. One such was Rosanna Marcil who received the habit on July 27 and the name Sister Marie-Egide-d'Assise. A few days later, two sisters, Zelia and Agnes Perron, crossed the border from Montreal to Worcester to become, on August 21, Sister Marie-Frédéric (Zelia) and Sister Marie-de-Bon-Secours (Agnes). No sooner had these two received the habit than another postulant presented herself—Elzire Roy who, on October 5, became Sister Marie-Thérèse-de-Jésus.

The summer of 1890 saw a marked decrease in the amount of alms received and the sisters were forced to borrow, simply to make ends meet. This caused them considerable alarm as they realized that they, or their parents—for some were still minors in the eyes of the law—were responsible for the debt, should the fledgling Institute be dissolved. Friends suggested the forming of a corporation to ensure the protection of the law. What were they to do? Creating a corporation with Father Brouillet would be impossible, and creating one without him could be disastrous. The sisters wanted to meet with Patrick Thomas O'Reilly, Bishop of Springfield, then the diocesan see, but he was in Rome. Having prayed and consulted, they reached the decision to incorporate without Father Brouillet. Father Durocher was asked and accepted to be their agent, despite the fact that he knew it would spell disaster for himself.

And so, on August 27, 1890, the sisters and Father Durocher met with a lawyer to draw up by-laws and elect officers. The name of the Society was to be Oblate Sisters of Saint Francis of Assisi, and the aim was "to found, maintain, and support a home for orphans and for the aged who are in need, and to provide for the education of poor and destitute children." The legislature approved the corporation on September 13, 1890.

On September 3, learning that the bishop had returned, Sister Marie-Joseph and a companion set out for Springfield to explain their situation to him. When the two entered the bishop's office, he confronted them, asking brusquely: "Who are you? Where do you come from?" Imagine their dismay as they tried to explain to him their understanding that he had given his permission for the foundation of their community. He in turn indicated that he had only given permission to two Franciscan tertiaries to wear the habit and pronounce simple vows for one year. He added that he did not want the responsibility of a new religious community in his diocese and that he saw only three possibilities for them: they could go back into the world, they could join an already-existing Franciscan congregation, or they could establish their Mother House in Canada. If they chose one or the other of the last two alternatives, he would approve the Oblates in his diocese. He also added his approbation of the incorporation. Since they were not religious, he could not deprive them of their civil rights! They were not religious! Now what? The bishop suggested that they return to Worcester. "I will see Father Brouillet myself," he added.

When they returned to the orphanage, Father Brouillet was there to greet them. He did not approve of their having formed a corporation, nor of their visit to the bishop without his authorization.

During this period, frail vocations were shaken and departures were numerous, but those who remained drew closer together. The sisters lived agonizing days. Father Brouillet was obsessed with the idea of removing Sister Marie-Joseph from her position as superior, for he was convinced that she was responsible for initiating the corporation. On December 7, 1890, he insisted that elections be held, though he had already decided their outcome. He also dismissed Father Durocher as chaplain.

On January 9, 1891, deciding that the bishop should be made aware of these developments, Sister Marie-Joseph, Sister Marie-Anne-de-Jésus, and Sister Marie-Zotique boarded a train headed once again for Springfield. The bishop encouraged them not to give up their civil rights if they wished to continue living together as a society. He suggested that they separate themselves from Father Brouillet and encouraged them to see him whenever they felt the need to do so.

With the bishop's encouragement, the sisters secretly began preparations for moving, and on January 12, vans arrived at the back door to transfer the meager belongings of the orphanage and the seventy-five children to their new quarters—a large rented room in a building on Southgate Street.

Only a few trips had been made when Father Brouillet arrived on the scene with the deputy sheriff who locked the house in the name of the law. The sisters were now split into two groups—some were inside the orphanage, and some were outside. Father Brouillet insisted that they remove their religious habits before he would allow them to leave. This they refused to do. Some sisters managed to "escape," as did some children. They sought refuge with Mrs. Durocher, the mother of their chaplain. The sheriff, called to the scene, ordered all doors unlocked and declared the sisters free to leave. In all, fifteen of the then seventeen sisters left the orphanage to find refuge at the home of Mrs. Durocher. One of the two who remained at the orphanage was Sister Saint-François-d'Assise. For the next several days, some of the sisters remained at the Durocher home while others stayed with relatives or friends. The Rondeau residence became their gathering place, and here meetings and elections were held. Once again, Sister Marie-Joseph was unanimously elected superior. The sisters begged Father Durocher to take up again the task of directing the Institute. Since Father Brouillet had dismissed him as chaplain, he had not returned to the orphanage, and his presence was sorely missed. He knew what accepting this task would mean for him—yet he accepted the sacrifice to ensure the life of the Franciscan community.

Lodgings had to be found as soon as possible and an old dilapidated house up on a hill was located. Though it had been vacant for a long time, and was seemingly uninhabitable, the sisters declared it to be the answer of Divine Providence. The house was rented for $10 a month. The most urgent repairs were made and on January 22, fifteen sisters and four orphans moved into their new home at 98 Orient Street. Referred to by the sisters as the "House of Misery," this was to be their home for the next three months.

One evening, the two assistants from Notre-Dame-des-Canadiens arrived to read them Bishop O'Reilly's letter to Father Brouillet in which he ordered the Franciscans to remove their religious habit. And so it was that Sister Marie-Joseph and Sister Marie-Anne-de-Jésus, dressed as laywomen, went again to Springfield to assure the bishop of their submission. The bishop, impressed by their will to continue staying together, allowed them to wear a modified habit for the time being.

Two incidents which took place at this time are particularly noteworthy. One was Father Brouillet's refusal to give them communion at High Mass one Sunday morning at Notre-Dame-des-Canadiens. This led Bishop O'Reilly to advise them to seek a confessor from among the Jesuits at Holy Cross College. Father Darveni Hugues Langlois, S.J., willingly accepted to give spiritual direction to the sisters and to administer the sacraments to them. The sisters made this weekly journey on foot. Father Langlois was a great source of encouragement, support, and strength during this period of trial and anguish.

In June, 1891, Father Durocher, recognizing that his mission in Worcester had come to an end, solicited Bishop Ludden of

Syracuse, New York, for a position in his diocese. On June 12, 1891, Father Durocher went into "exile" with his aged mother, to Pulaski, New York, where he died on May 3, 1899.

For their part, the sisters left the "House of Misery" in April 1891, to take up residence at 51 and 53 Benefit Street. Orphans arrived in quick succession, and soon the sisters had to rent the whole house in order to accommodate both the orphans and the elderly who sought refuge there. In October 1891, they moved again to larger quarters, this time to 10 Bleeker Street in Saint Joseph's parish.

During these same years, Father Ambroise Martial Fafard, pastor of Baie-Saint-Paul, located in Charlevoix County in the Province of Quebec, Canada, was struggling to help the poor and abandoned elderly in his parish. With the assistance of some kind and generous women, he had opened a home for elderly parishioners, naming it Saint Anne's Home. He was looking for ways to fund this house when he was made aware that the provincial government was paying $50 a year to persons caring for idiots, the senile feeble-minded, and all who suffered from an incurable disease. Father Fafard signed a contract with the government for the care of fifty feeble-minded patients. This, he calculated, would cover the major expenses of the Home while charitable donations would cover the board and care of the aged. His current staff not being large enough to care for all these patients, he began seeking the services of a religious congregation.

As fate would have it, the link to Worcester was to be made once again by Father Delphos through his cousin, Dr. de Martigny, Inspector of the Provincial Insane Asylums. Sister Marie-Joseph and Sister Marie-Anne-de-Jésus were invited to Baie-Saint-Paul, where they arrived on July 17. They spent several hours discussing their own situation with Father Fafard. He was satisfied that these women were sincere in their desire to follow the Lord in the footprints of Francis of Assisi, and he sent them to meet Bishop Bégin in Chicoutimi who agreed to accept them in his diocese. And so it was that on November 13, 1891, four Franciscan sisters entered Saint Anne's Home in Baie-Saint-Paul. The fragile shoot, which had germinated in Worcester, was being transplanted hundreds of miles away to the homeland where the ancestors of the sisters had lived for generations. The four foundresses of the novitiate in Baie-Saint-Paul were: Sister Marie-Anne-de-Jésus, Sister Marie-Dominique, Sister Marie-Égide-d'Assise, and Sister Marie-Frédéric. The latter was making a double sacrifice, not only leaving the sisters she loved in Worcester, but her own blood sister, Sister Marie-de-Bon-Secours, who was ill and who subsequently died on March 7, 1892. She was the only foundress who did not see her dream of religious profession realized.

Though the sisters in Canada had their share of trials and insecurities, these were nothing compared with the miseries they had encountered in Worcester. After almost three years of desiring religious profession, eight of the foundresses did receive this privilege on August 12, 1892. The other two, Sister Marie-des-Sept-Douleurs and Sister Marie-Thérèse-de-Jésus, had to remain in Worcester for the time being, but their turn would come in January 1893. It was at this time that the congregation became known as *Les Petites Franciscaines de Marie*.

The time had come to begin formalizing a structure for this new congregation. The motherhouse would be located in Baie-Saint-Paul. A Rule of Life was established, and Sister Marie-Anne-de-Jésus was elected as superior general. Sister Marie-Joseph was to remain as the superior in Worcester where her talents at solving American problems could best be utilized, for all was not well for the Franciscans in Worcester. The struggle for survival would continue for the next five years.

At Bishop O'Reilly's death, he was succeeded by Bishop Thomas D. Beaven who was not as favorably disposed toward the Franciscans as his predecessor had been. Father Brouillet, in the meantime, had called upon the Grey Nuns to administer the orphanage in South Worcester after the departure of the Franciscans to Canada. The new bishop did not feel the need for two orphanages in Worcester, despite the fact that both were filled with children needing care. The sisters pleaded their case, but to no avail. As a last resort, they sought the intervention of the apostolic delegate in Washington to settle their fate once and for all. After much communication and negotiation, the matter was finally resolved, and the Little Franciscans of Mary were officially recognized in the Diocese of Springfield on July 28, 1897. This was accomplished at the cost of a great sacrifice, however. The Little Franciscans of Mary would have to turn over the care of orphans to the Grey Nuns and accept the care of the aged. God had spoken! The foundresses bowed in submission. After several months of working out the details, Father Brouillet mounted the pulpit in the church of Notre-Dame-des-Canadiens, in December 1897 and announced to the gathered congregation that the Little Franciscans of Mary had been officially recognized as religious in the Diocese of Springfield.

Father Jules Graton, then pastor of Saint Joseph's parish, had shown great kindness to the sisters whose home was located in the parish. All of his successors up to the present time have demonstrated that same kind generosity. Father Graton had already told the aged of his parish that a warm welcome awaited them at Saint Francis Home. By January 19, 1898, the separation had been completed and Sister Marie-Joseph now resolutely turned to her new mission in which she was to find much peace and joy.

In the early days of the congregation's existence in Canada, Father Fafard had stated that, if some day the congregation could number one hundred sisters, it would be considered successful. The community has been blessed with ten times that many sisters and over one hundred years of service to the poor and the elderly.[1]

[This article first appeared as "'God gave me some Sisters': The Foundation of the Little Franciscans of Mary in Worcester, Massachusetts (1889)" in the French Institute's publication entitled *Franco-Americans and Religion: Impact and Influence.*]

---

[1]   [For those seeking a more detailed account of this Franco-American foundation, the history of the congregation entitled *Par ce signe tu vivras,* by Sister Marie-Michel-Archange, P.F.M., is recommended. The title of the English translation is *By this Sign You Will Live: History of the Congregation of the Little Franciscans of Mary—1889-1955.*—Editor]

The Congregation of the Sisters of Saint Joan of Arc
A Franco-American Foundation

Yves Garon, A.A.

The aim of this essay is to describe the role played by Franco-American women in the foundation and development of the Sisters of Saint Joan of Arc.

The congregation was founded in December of 1914, in Worcester, Massachusetts, at Assumption College—then located in the Greendale area of the city, on West Boylston Street—by the Assumptionist Father Marie-Clément Staub. The purpose of the foundation of this community was to render spiritual and temporal assistance to priests. The sisters work principally in rectories, almost exclusively in New England and in Quebec. Their maximum numerical expansion was reached around 1965 when the congregation numbered some three hundred sisters. On January 1, 1989, the year of their seventy-fifth anniversary, there were just over two hundred sisters and, since one hundred and twenty-seven sisters had died, there were altogether three hundred and twenty-eight sisters during the congregation's first seventy-five years.

With very few exceptions, these religious were Franco-Americans or French Canadians. For the purpose of this essay, are considered as Franco-Americans not only those who were born in the United States and lived there at the time of their entering the community—that is seventy-five religious—but also those who, though born in Canada, were living in the United States when they entered—namely twenty-nine religious. Are also considered to be Franco-Americans, three religious who, though born in the United States, lived in Canada at the time of their joining the congregation.

The founder of this congregation, an Assumptionist, Father Marie Clément Staub, born in Alsace on July 2, 1876, had been ordained to the priesthood in Rome on March 19, 1904. Before he was sent to Worcester, arriving in December 1909, he had been assistant master of novices, then master of novices in Belgium and had been a preacher in England. Father Marie Clément was a great apostle of the Sacred Heart who labored intensely to make known the Archconfraternity of Prayer and Penance centered in Paris at the shrine of Montmartre. He was exceptionally successful in this apostolate, getting the faithful to enroll in the Archconfraternity by the tens of thousands.

In February 1913, while preaching a mission to the young women of the Franco-American parish of St. Joseph in Fitchburg, Massachusetts,[1] Father Marie Clément was approached by Alice Caron, the housekeeper of the rectory. She declared to him that what the Sacred Heart expected from him was a congregation of "women religious, victims for priests."

Father Marie Clément had never thought of founding a religious congregation, but he did have such a great consideration for the priesthood and such solicitude for priests, that he listened very attentively to the words of Alice Caron. He questioned, he examined, he consulted, above all he prayed. After two years had passed, his superiors authorized him to undertake the founding of the proposed congregation and, during Christmas night of 1914, in the chapel of Worcester's Saint Francis Home,[2] the foundation was laid for what was to become the Congregation of the Sisters of Saint Joan of Arc.

It was on December 31st, 1914, that the small group of foundresses gathered in a house, which no longer stands,[3] on the original campus of Assumption College. There were seven of them, all Franco-Americans and, until June 1918, the young institute was to be comprised only of Franco-Americans.

---

1   [See the article in this volume by Paul LeBlanc entitled "From Farm to Factory: Acadians in Fitchburg, Mass. (1880-1910)," for further information on this particular community of immigrants.—Editor]

2   [Then called *Hospice St-François*. See article in this volume by Jacquelyn Alix, P.F.M. entitled "The Foundation of the Little Franciscans of Mary in Worcester, Mass."—Editor]

3   [The house was levelled in the 1953 tornado which struck the city of Worcester and Assumption College with devastating consequences.—Editor]

But, from that date on, things changed. In September 1917, the motherhouse had been transferred from Worcester to Canada and, after a brief stay in Quebec City, the congregation settled in Sillery, a suburb of Quebec, during the summer of 1918. It remains there to this day.[4]

With the arrival of the institute in Canada, Canadian candidates began to apply and, up to the present day, there have always been both Franco-Americans and Canadians among the candidates. The proportions have varied, however. Here are some figures for the first seventy-five years of the congregation, divided into three twenty-five-year periods.

First third: for the first twenty-five years, from January 1, 1915, to December 31, 1939, out of 211 admitted, there were eighty Franco-Americans, i.e. thirty-eight percent.

Second third: for the next twenty-five years, from January 1, 1940, to December 31, 1964, there were seventeen Franco-Americans among the 123 candidates admitted, i.e. thirteen percent.

Third third: from January 1, 1965, to 1989, there were two Franco-Americans, but in a total of only three candidates. This represents sixty-six percent of the total, but given the small number involved, there is little meaning in such a high percentage.

It should be noted that, apart from the Franco-Americans and the Canadians, the only other women to join the Order were French. They were few in number, in fact only six in all. It must also be pointed out that the Congregation of the Sisters of Saint Joan of Arc, like other congregations, has experienced a radical drop in the number of vocations in the last twenty-five years.

As stated at the beginning of this essay, during the first seventy-five years of its history, the Congregation of the Sisters of Saint Joan of Arc had reached a total of three hundred and twenty-eight religious. Of these 328, 103 are Franco-Americans, i.e. thirty-two percent of the total.

---

4   [For a more detailed account of the life of Father Marie Clément Staub, A.A., and the history of the Sisters of St. Joan of Arc, see Claire Quintal, *Herald of Love* (Quebec City: SSJA, 1984). The French edition is entitled *Héraut de l'Amour* (Quebec City: Anne Sigier, 1989).—Editor]

In the entire history of the congregation, therefore, the Franco-American sisters constituted about one third of its membership. More recent statistics indicate that this percentage has fallen to about one quarter. As of January 1, 1989, of the 201 religious living on that date, forty-six or twenty-three percent were Franco-Americans.[5]

Let us now go on to another aspect.

Rectories are the most frequent place of service for the sisters. Since Saint Joan of Arc came from the province of Lorraine the group of religious working in a rectory, as well as the place where they live, are called a "Lorraine."

If, in accounting for the number of Lorraines established during the first seventy-five years of the order's existence, one proceeds by looking separately at each of the three successive twenty-five year spans, as we did for the statistics of the sisters, here is what we come up with:

First third: from January 1, 1915, to December 31, 1939, forty-two Lorraines were established during the first twenty-five years:

> 29 in the United States (69%)
> 8 in the Province of Quebec (19%)
> 5 in France (12%)

By December 31, 1939, there remained:

> 29 Lorraines in the U.S. (74%)
> 5 in Canada (13%)
> 5 in France (13%)

The Lorraines in France were as numerous as those in Canada. There were almost six Lorraines in the United States for one in Canada; three-fourths of the Lorraines were thus in the United States while Franco-American religious then constituted

---

5   [In December 1993, the numbers were as follows: 187 living religious—forty-nine working in Canada, twenty-five in the United States, and three in Rome. Of these, twenty-eight were Franco-Americans. An additional 110 were at the motherhouse because of illness or old age. As of December 1995, there were 179 living religious—forty-six working in Canada, twenty-four in the United States and three in Rome. A total of 152 religious had passed away since the foundation of the community, four of them in 1995.—Editor]

only 38% of the members of the congregation. It thus becomes evident that at that time, the congregation was mainly serving Franco-American as well as American communities.

Second third: from January 1, 1940, to December 31, 1964, i.e. the next quarter century, while thirteen Lorraines were established in the United States, thirty-six were established in Canada.

By December 31, 1964, there were, in the entire Congregation, twenty-four Lorraines in the United States and thirty-one in Canada. The Lorraines in France had been closed during that period.

The following remark can be made at this point: during that twenty-five year period, the congregation experienced a total reversal of trends as regards its foundations. During the first third or quarter century, there had been twenty-nine foundations in the United States as compared to five in Canada (74 percent and 13 percent); during the second period, whereas there were only thirteen foundations in the United States, there were thirty-six in Canada (26 percent and 74 percent).

Third third: from January 1, 1965 to 1989, no founding of a new Lorraine took place in the United States, except for the opening of a novitiate; whereas there were seventeen foundations in Canada. Add to this a foundation in Rome and another in Zaire—therefore seventeen foundations in Canada out of a total of nineteen about 90 percent. Nine of the seventeen foundations were already closed by 1989.

By January 1, 1989, there were thirteen Lorraines in the United States, twenty-six in Canada, one in Rome and one in Zaire.[6] Therefore 33 percent of the Lorraines were still in the United States, staffed by forty-five religious, whereas sixty-four religious staffed the Lorraines of Canada. It is evident that, in 1989, the Franco-American portion of the Congregation remained quite significant.

---

6   [As of December 1995, there were six Lorraines in the United States, twenty-two in Canada, and one in Rome. The Zaire foundation closed in 1990.—Editor]

I will conclude by emphasizing a very important aspect of the Franco-American contribution to the life of the Congregation of the Sisters of Saint Joan of Arc. The first two superiors general were Franco-Americans—Sister Jeanne, from New Bedford, Massachusetts, and Sister Josephine, born in Chicago, Illinois, and brought up in Holyoke, Massachusetts, who governed the congregation during its first thirty-three years. The first, Sister Jeanne, was superior general for thirteen years—the second, Sister Josephine, for twenty years. Sister Josephine was superior general when the founder died rather suddenly, at the age of sixty. This left her with a particularly difficult and delicate mandate which she assumed with courage.

Similarly, the first two general treasurers of the order were Franco-Americans: Sister Marguerite and Sister Rosario. They bore that responsibility for more than fifty years, from 1920 to 1971—the first, Sister Marguerite for twenty-six years, the second, Sister Rosario for twenty-five years. Many other Franco-American sisters played an important role, but the limits of this essay preclude mention of them.

Conclusion

Few religious congregations have been founded in New England by or with the collaboration of Franco-Americans: there are the Sisters of Saint Joan of Arc, the Little Franciscan Sisters of Mary, and the secular institute, of Pius X.[7] I know of no other. All three of these institutes, founded in New England, have this unique feature that, not long after their foundation, they transferred their headquarters to the Province of Quebec.

Although the motherhouse of the Sisters of Saint Joan of Arc migrated to Quebec, the bonds with New England remained nonetheless firm, constant, and harmonious, creating a veritable osmosis. Of the forty-five sisters stationed in the United States in 1989, twenty-three were Canadian.

---

7   [This institute, for priests and laymen, originated in Manchester, N.H., in 1940. It was approved as a secular institute in 1959, the first secular institute of diocesan right founded in the United States to be approved by the Holy See. The institute also admits married couples and unmarried men as associate members. Source: *Catholic Almanac*—Editor]

In North America, the congregation did not expand beyond New England and Quebec, but the Sisters accomplished beautiful work, that was and is highly appreciated. The Sisters of Saint Joan of Arc have but one regret: the fact that they never could and still cannot respond to all the requests addressed to them, soliciting their collaboration.

Translated by Gary Crosby Brasor

[This article first appeared as "Religieuses franco-américaines: les Soeurs de Sainte-Jeanne d'Arc" in the French Institute's publication entitled *Religion catholique et appartenance franco-américaine/Franco-Americans and Religion: Impact and Influence*. It has been up-dated, where deemed necessary, in notes by the Editor.]

Saint Anne's Shrine, Fall River, Massachusetts

Pierre E. Lachance, O.P.

Had it not been for the Shrine of Sainte-Anne-de-Beaupré in Canada, there would probably never have been a shrine to Saint Anne in Fall River.

The devotion to Saint Anne in her Fall River shrine goes back to the very foundation of the parish, in 1869, and to the fact that it was placed by its founder, Rev. Adrien de Montaubricq, under the patronage of Saint Anne.

The *Canadiens* of Fall River—they still called themselves Canadians at that time, not Franco-Americans—had brought with them from Quebec a great devotion to Saint Anne, a devotion that had been nurtured for two centuries by the famous shrine at Beaupré, to which they were deeply attached. A church dedicated to Saint Anne in Fall River was in a way predestined to become, for these expatriate Canadians, a new center of devotion to *la bonne Sainte Anne* (good Saint Anne).

We know that under the aegis of the second pastor, the Rev. Thomas Briscoe (1878-1887), an annual novena was instituted that culminated on July 26, Saint Anne's feast day, which was also that of the parish.

The French Dominicans, who arrived in Fall River in November of 1887, were to become the great promoters of the devotion to Saint Anne in New England. Under their spiritual influence, the parish church would be transformed into a highly-frequented shrine, eventually attracting thousands of pilgrims and exercising a wide influence.

A study of the devotions practiced at Saint Anne's Shrine will give us some insight into the matter of how the deep faith of Franco-American Catholics was expressed.

Pilgrimages

Pilgrimages quickly became very popular among the Franco-Americans of Fall River. In July 1888, only eight months after the arrival of the Dominicans, these Friars organized, with their colleagues of Lewiston, Maine, an imposing pilgrimage to Sainte-Anne-de-Beaupré. Some six to seven hundred pilgrims took part, according to accounts. Of these, nearly two hundred were from Fall River. Three years later, the same experience was repeated. These pilgrimages on a massive scale manifest the intense devotion of Franco-Americans to Saint Anne and their deep-seated affection for the shrine of Beaupré which was considered by them to be their national shrine.

But soon, Fall River would have its own shrine, due to the untiring efforts of *curé* Sauval, a holy man of broad vision. As early as January 1892, he laid out before his parishioners a grand project: to build a new church that would be so spacious that it could welcome large groups of pilgrims. We must keep in mind that, at the time, there had not yet been any pilgrimage to Saint Anne in Fall River. Father Sauval, dreaming of the future, envisioned multitudes of pilgrims who would come some day. In his mind, this new shrine in honor of Saint Anne would become as famous in the United States as that of Beaupré in Canada. That is how and why the Dominican Fathers, with the money collected from their parishioners, built the magnificent church dedicated to Saint Anne, which is admirably situated, facing Kennedy Park.

Father Sauval began to organize pilgrimages in 1892. I use the word "organized" advisedly. Pilgrimages just don't happen. They must be arranged and promoted. And that is what Father Sauval did, starting with his own parishioners. The entire month of July 1892 was proclaimed a "month of pilgrimages." The parishioners came in groups to pay homage to their holy patroness. They came by neighborhood; then it was the turn of each of the religious societies of the parish. On July 26 of that year, the Fathers were also pleased to welcome the first group of pilgrims coming from outside the city: the Ladies of Saint Anne, from Taunton, Massachusetts, accompanied by a few Children of Mary.

Thereafter, a growing stream of pilgrims came every year from the French-Canadian parishes of Fall River and neighboring New Bedford, as well as from all of Rhode Island. They came in large numbers: 300, 500, 1000, 1500, and more. They came as entire parishes, accompanied by their pastor and even possibly his assistant to lead them. They came by train and by bus (horse-drawn in those days); they also came by trolley and even, for many years, by steamboat from Providence and Pawtucket, and Central Falls, Rhode Island. During the journey, these devout people prayed and sang religious hymns. It is even recorded that on one occasion one of the priests leading a group delivered a sermon to the pilgrims on the boat. During the era of large "parish pilgrimages," the Dominican Fathers often went to these parishes to preach a *triduum*[1] to prepare the parishioners for their pilgrimage. A pilgrimage was not an excursion for pleasure. Although the voyage was no doubt enjoyable, it was a spiritual exercise of faith and devotion. The pilgrimage was an event in the life of French Canadians. With what faith and confidence they came to pray to *"la bonne Sainte Anne"* for all their needs!

Upon arriving at Saint Anne's Church, the pilgrims usually attended a mass in the forenoon, then, in the afternoon, the pilgrimage devotions were held at the shrine. These consisted of hymns, prayers, including the rosary, a homily, benediction of the Blessed Sacrament, and concluded with the veneration of Saint Anne's relic. It was at his time that healings often occurred, either during or after the veneration of the holy relic.

Relics

Relics have pride of place in popular piety. Father Sauval acquired a relic of Saint Anne as early as 1892. With the help of a colleague, Father Knapp, he even obtained a very special relic in 1901—the forearm of Saint Anne, from the Shrine of Saint Anne of Apt, in southern France. The arrival of this relic was celebrated in a grandiose manner. A huge throng of pious and reverent people, including Bishop Matthew Harkins of Providence, attended these ceremonies.

Popular devotion finds support in visible realities: relics, statues, pictures and icons, stacks of crutches, songs, processions, incense, etc. The Fall River shrine offers all of this. Human beings have a need to see, to touch. That is why devout people place their hand on a statue while they pray to the saint in silence. Sacraments too, are visible signs of spiritual realities we cannot see; that is the reason for all of our liturgical rites: the Mass, Benediction, Forty-Hours Devotions, processions, etc. For the

---

[1]   A three-day period of prayer.

same reason, the faithful venerate the relic of Saint Anne by kissing it devoutly. They even ask the Fathers to apply the relic to the part of their body that is suffering or infirm: eyes, ears, head, heart, wherever it can be applied within the rules of decency. They desire to touch the relic of the saint, imitating that woman in the Gospel who fought through the crowd to be able to touch only the hem of Jesus' garment and . . . she was cured.

More of the Visible and the Concrete

Among the many other objects to be seen at Saint Anne's Shrine which offer visible support to the devotion of the faithful, there is the beautiful wooden statue of Saint Anne carved in a Belgian studio which has been at the shrine since 1893. At the request of the Dominican Fathers, this statue was made in the likeness of the one which can be admired at Saint Anne de Beaupré.

The Fathers not only wanted to have a statue that would remind the French-Canadian immigrants of their beloved shrine in Canada, they also wanted to have the body of a martyr. And so, laid out in a glass case, which originally rested under an altar, is the statue of Saint Concordia who, as a young girl employed as a children's nurse by a Christian family of Rome in the third century, was put to death with the entire family, in 258 A.D., and her body buried in the Catacombs of Priscilla in Rome. The Dominican Fathers, having obtained relics of the saint, celebrated the arrival of these objects at the shrine with a *triduum*. For many years, the feast of Saint Concordia was celebrated on August 13th, her feast day in the Roman martyrology. The wax image of the young martyr, showing abundant blood stains, speaks in a moving way to the piety of the faithful.

We also have at Saint Anne Shrine a stone from the house of Saint Anne in Jerusalem, also obtained in 1893, with the help of our Dominican Fathers at the *École biblique*[2] in Jerusalem. This stone is enshrined in a block of artistically wrought white marble which bears the inscription: *"Pierre de Ste Anne—Jérusalem"* (Stone from St. Anne—Jerusalem). This is yet another visible and even tangible object which evokes the memory of Saint Anne.

---

2   [A highly regarded institution for the study of Sacred Scripture.—Editor]

Another form of popular devotion introduced by Father Sauval in 1893 was the ceremony of the descent of the cross on Good Fridays. I have never seen anything like it elsewhere. The large crucifix at the front of the church has a corpus that is easily detachable, and the arms of Christ can be brought down alongside his body. On Good Friday evenings, in former times, a sermon on the passion would be preached. Later on, Dubois' famous oratorio "The Seven Last Words of Christ" was played and sung. All of this was followed by a meditation. In more recent years, a meditation on the stations of the cross takes place. At the thirteenth station, the body of Christ is taken down, placed on a stretcher, and carried in procession around the church, accompanied by children who carry the instruments of the passion: the crown of thorns, the nails and the hammer, etc. There is much to see and hear, in accord with the desires of the human heart. The body of Christ, reverently carried in procession, is laid in a chapel behind the main altar. There, the faithful come to kiss the feet of Jesus. Appropriate songs, executed by the choir, move the faithful to the depths of their soul. In particular, the famous *"Jerusalem, Jerusalem, convertere ad Dominum"* ("Jerusalem, Jerusalem, come back to the Lord"). Every year the main church fills up with the faithful who come from all around to assist at a form of devotion accessible to the people and capable of touching the hearts of all.

Novenas

Among devotional practices that enjoy great popularity, novenas must be mentioned. An annual novena marking the feast of Saint Anne, regularly preached by a guest homilist, and held since the very beginning of the parish, took on an even greater solemnity with the coming of the Dominicans.

In 1928, Father Marchildon, the great apostle of Saint Anne at the Fall River shrine, introduced the perpetual Tuesday novenas in honor of Saint Anne. These have enjoyed great popularity. Finally, in January of 1960, the perpetual novenas to Saint Jude were added on Thursdays, responding to the popularity in this country of the apostle of so-called difficult and hopeless cases.

Healings and Miracles

The faithful take part in pilgrimages to pray for all sorts of needs, but more often to obtain healings. And God rewards their faith with amazing supernatural interventions. The shrine has a collection of many hundreds of testimonies of healings, going back to 1895, healings attributed to the intercession of "la bonne Sainte Anne."

Since 1978, the shrine has renewed its link with this age-old tradition by introducing "Healing Services" in the contemporary style of the Charismatic Movement. And the Lord, faithful to his promises, continues to multiply healings of all sorts.

A Place of Peace and Prayer

Saint Anne's Shrine is for many an oasis of peace and prayer. Quite apart from the devotional services, the faithful come each day to pray quietly. During this silent time, many assure us that they find great inner peace in such close contact with the Lord. Others come to seek peace and comfort in the Sacrament of Reconciliation or in the spiritual direction provided by the Fathers.

Saint Anne's Shrine is truly a place of outstanding faith and devotion; it is also a place of peace and grace where the faithful can speak to God in all simplicity and beg Saint Anne to intercede on their behalf.

Translated by the author

[This article first appeared as "Les dévotions populaires chez les Francos: le Sanctuaire de Sainte-Anne de Fall River, Massachusetts" in the French Institute's publication entitled *Franco-Americans and Religion: Impact and Influence*. It has been reviewed by the author, and up-dated where necessary, for inclusion in this volume.]

IV

EDUCATION

The Spiritual and Intellectual Foundations of the Schooling of Franco-Americans

Armand Chartier

> To the Sisters of the Holy Cross, as an expression of faithful remembrance as well as filial gratitude.

This article attempts to define the circumstances under which the Franco-American school system took shape more than a century ago. It is neither a history of teaching nor of Franco-American schools. Neither is it a study of the pedagogy or the curriculum, or the books then in use, although all of these subjects are in need of lengthy and substantial study before the facts disappear with the last generation of Franco-Americans to have known the system of bilingual parochial schools.

We have also put aside a study of the mores, customs, and traditions of the school children while recognizing that the folklore of our schools in itself provides a vast field for research. The article will focus on conceptual sources in order to identify those foundation stones on which our forebears built an edifice that has profoundly affected the lives of hundreds of thousands of Franco-Americans. Schools being a part of our roots, we have tried to trace the furthest ends of those roots, limiting our inquiry to the spiritual and intellectual aspects of the topic, less so for specialists than as a primer for those who never experienced this system of teaching.

Having established in a first section some points of reference relative to French and Quebec antecedents, we will then consider the importance of the schools during the period of immigration in order to feature, in a final section, the contributions of religious communities.[1]

---

[1] Since some documentation is not easily accessible, we were unable to include all the teaching communities, and we have regretfully had to limit our focus to some twelve of the thirty or forty who worked among us.

French and Quebec Roots

The roots of schooling among Franco-Americans, which go back to the Catholicism of the Middle Ages, were strongly shaped by three great ages of renewal in the life of the Church: the Counter Reformation, the religious restoration following the French Revolution, and the Catholic resurgence which began in Quebec about 1840. Additionally, the expulsion of the religious communities from France at the beginning of the twentieth century provided a certain number of religious teachers. Franco-American life has, therefore, been influenced, much more than has been stated up to now, by some of the great currents of history.

From the Counter Reformation came forth what is sometimes called the heroic epoch of the history of Canada, where the foundations of French Catholic America are to be found. This is so true that Georges Goyau was able to formulate this definition of New France: "A good work, a prayer in action: it is in this light that the Canadian undertaking appears between 1610 and 1660..."[2] This statement is amplified by Canon Lionel Groulx:

> French Catholicism having emerged victorious from the Renaissance and from that period's troubled currents. . ., it was then able to link up with the healthiest sources of the medieval period. As such, truly the finest of Catholicism came to Canada with the founders of its Church: a Catholicism of ancient lineage, reformed, enriched by trials and by a generous asceticism. Here, as there, religious life would thrive under the triple aspect of a force at once intellectual, social, and mystical.[3]

One of the ways in which this "prayer in action" became concrete was the establishment of religious communities in New France. Two of these communities, the Ursulines and the Congregation of Notre Dame, are of particular interest, and we will be discussing them further on.

Closer to us is the religious renewal seen in Quebec beginning in the 1840s after decades of uncertainty following the Conquest

---

2   Georges Goyau, *Les origines religieuses du Canada* (Paris: Grasset, 1924), p. 236.

3   Chanoine Lionel Groulx, *Histoire du Canada français depuis la découverte* (Montreal: Fides, 1960), vol. 1, p. 74.

(1760). This renewal was due in some measure to the circumstances of the time, but also in part to a key person, His Excellency Ignace Bourget (1799-1885), Bishop of Montreal from 1840 to 1876. Bishop Bourget was a key person from the point of view of the education of Franco-Americans, first and foremost because of his resistance to laicism, then by his recruitment of French religious communities (about ten came to establish themselves in Canada during his episcopacy, including the Sisters of the Holy Cross and the Sisters of Jesus-Marie), and also, by his prodigious encouragement of the founding of Canadian orders, which gave us, among others, the Sisters of Saint Anne. The historian Gérard Parizeau sums up as follows the importance of the Bishop of Montreal in the area that interests us here: "We cannot overemphasize the role of Bishop Bourget in the creation and direction of education in Lower Canada, whatever may later have been its merits, its weaknesses or its faults."[4]

Since the education of Franco-Americans, from its beginnings in the nineteenth century to its full flowering in the 1950s, bears the indelible stamp of the Church of Quebec of which it was, in large measure, the product, we think it useful to indicate here the principal characteristics of Catholicism in Quebec in the nineteenth century.

In full flood of expansion after 1840, as witnessed by the multiplication of parishes, communities, and foundations of every sort, the Church in Quebec was at that time oriented toward action much more than contemplation. The activity of the Church is evident in two critical areas, education and charity, and the Church succeeded in "clericalizing" these areas all the more easily because the government had little interest in them and because the numbers of religious men and women continued to grow.

In less than half a century, beginning in 1840, the Catholic Church in Quebec ventured into practically every area of human activity. This omnipresence must be attributed not only to a need for expansion, to the desire to serve society, or to an apostolic zeal, but also to the urgency of the message propagated by the Church—that the goal of human life, the only one which matters, is eternal salvation. The urgent spreading of this message, a message believed by the majority of the population, explains in large measure why the presence of the Church was so well received

---

4   Gérard Parizeau, *La société canadienne-française au XIXe siècle: essais sur le milieu* (Montreal: Fides, 1975), p. 197.

in the different sectors of society.

And certainly society needed the hospitals and educational services offered by the Church. But, prior to working in these sectors, the Church had engaged the people's collective spirit, since the bulk of the population were already believers, that is, they believed *dur comme fer* [5] that the ultimate goal of life was to avoid damnation and save one's soul. In that sense, the Church was a pervasive presence, for it was to be found everywhere in the *interior* as well as in the *exterior* life of the community.

At the heart of the message, there was a moral rigor that attempted to govern each thought and each act of the people. This intransigent morality, which tolerated no laxity, was founded on a quasi-Manichean vision, which calls to mind the Middle Ages. Historians of Catholicism in Quebec are all of this opinion; Nive Voisine affirms that Quebec society is "a medieval-type Christianity,"[6] and Benoît Lacroix reminds us that by mindset, the founders of Canada "were men and women of the Middle Ages."[7]

From this point of view, one and all were urged to strive for spiritual perfection, and liturgical ceremonies for the purpose of stimulating piety among the people flourished. There was also the desire that this piety be an active one, and soon Brother André would be there to embody "the ideal of this practical mysticism."[8] We must emphasize also the deep-seated pessimism of this Catholicism, strongly eschatological in character. From this insistence on the afterlife of the individual and of humanity no doubt came a great deal of the underlying motivation for each person's conduct.

---

5   [To have a cast-iron belief.—Editor]

6   Nive Voisine, *Histoire de l'Église catholique au Québec (1608-1970)* (Montreal: Fides, 1971), p.66.

7   Benoît Lacroix and Madeleine Grammond, *Religion populaire au Québec: Typologie des sources, bibliographie sélective (1900-1980)* (Quebec City: Institut québécois de recherche sur la culture, 1985), p. 19.

8   Jean Hamelin and Nicole Gagnon, *Le XXe siècle*, vol. 1, 1889-1940, in Nive Voisine (dir.), *Histoire du catholicisme québécois* (Montreal: Boréal Express, 1984), p. 172.

Under the direction of Bishop Bourget and of Bishop Laflèche, the Church of Quebec went through a period of militant, conquering, and triumphant ultraconservatism. This caused the regretted Mason Wade to write: "In 1870, Quebec was more French and more Catholic than it had ever been since the best days of New France."9

This conservatism was felt by the faithful, since bishops and priests constantly urged them to conformity of the most rigid kind, and to the strictest orthodoxy. That conservatism was also expressed by a "clerical-nationalistic" ideology, also called the ideology of *survivance*, which endured for more than a century. *Survivance* was based upon a French-Canadian tradition that was Catholic, family-oriented, and agricultural.10

As a consequence of all this, the Church in Quebec entered a triumphant phase which lasted for several decades, and manifestations of this triumphalism were everywhere. There was, first of all, the prodigious influence of the Church on the public and social life of Quebec, although to speak of a theocracy would be an exaggeration. As to public events, there were, during the course of each year, and over time, innumerable processions, pilgrimages, and ceremonies, the high point of which was undoubtedly the Eucharistic Congress of Montreal in 1910. The most permanent legacy of this era is probably the huge collection of cathedral churches, monastic and parochial buildings (monasteries, convents, colleges, seminaries, academies), and huge sanctuaries, concrete witnesses of a power that was almost governmental.

To these traits must be added the idealism inherent in the Church's teaching. This idealism meant many things, beginning with the totality of those pressures imposed upon the individual so that he or she would tend always toward altruism, nobility of soul, and perfection. That is to say also that highly intense moral climate that gives to each thought, word, and act a spiritual or supernatural dimension, urging the individual to bank on spiritual rather than material values.

---

9   Mason Wade, *Les Canadiens français de 1760 à nos jours* (Ottawa: Le Cercle du livre de France, 1963), 2d ed., rev. vol. 1, p. 386.

10   According to Paul-André Linteau (et al.), *Histoire du Québec contemporain: de la Confédération à la crise (1867-1929)* (Montreal: Boréal Express, 1979), pp. 608-609.

Here then, described in very summary fashion, is the ambiance in which the people of Quebec lived, including, of course, the approximately 900,000 souls who emigrated to the United States between 1840 and 1930, including also those who came to serve these immigrants, as well as the hundreds of men and women religious who came to New England to shape the minds of four generations of Franco-Americans.

Before exploring education in the context of immigration, it is important to highlight two fundamental truths: in the Quebec of the nineteenth century and the first half of the twentieth century, it was the Church and the Church alone that controlled the system of education. Secondly, the primary goal of that educational system was to preserve the faith of the rising generations, in order to ensure the eternal salvation of each one. And the enormous resources of society were mobilized in that direction, following the dogmatic will of the hierarchy, according to which the child should come out of the Catholic school with "the Gospel in his blood." Or, as summarized by Professor George Theriault:

> Hence its (French Canada's) sedulous twin-pronged program of action designed to, on the one hand, hold at bay through segregation the forces of evil and corruption, while, on the other hand, it clings and nurtures ideals and institutions inherited from seventeenth century France, which in the ancient religious nationalism of "Gesta Dei per Francos" embody for them the "City of God" in which all right-thinking, Christian, French men and women should seek a good, if humble home.[11]

For the student, this mentality was translated daily, in a very precise way, in the classroom and in textbooks, as was verified by the American sociologist Horace Miner in his study of Saint-Denis-de-Kamouraska. Moral and religious lessons, values, and concepts appear in the teaching of all subjects.[12]

---

[11]   George French Theriault, *The Franco-Americans in a New England Community: An Experiment in Survival* (New York: Arno Press, 1980), p. 399.

[12]   Horace Miner, *St. Denis, A French-Canadian Parish* (Chicago: University of Chicago Press (© 1939), 1967), p. 184.

That way of thinking crossed the American border, especially between 1870 and 1930.

Immigration and Implantation

Sad from the point of view of Canada, because Quebec and Acadia lost almost a million people, the era of immigration is a heroic one in Franco-American history. First, because it was the age of pioneers, of people who, in emigrating and remaining emigrants, succeeded in practicing in many cases an altruism that has been praised too little. Also, because those immigrants made a decision which would decisively affect the lives of their descendants for generations upon generations.

That age was made the more heroic by the quantity and the quality of the institutions created by people who, not having a penny to their name, somehow found the money to create and maintain an incredible number of institutions. This is not the place to list the hundreds of parishes, societies, newspapers founded by the immigrants, but we must at least recall in what a dynamic way the immigrants mobilized their resources to develop a network of institutions which remains imposing even today.

Without minimizing the role of the people in the development of those many institutions, it is necessary nonetheless to recognize the determining role played in all this by the elite, that is, the clergy and those in the professions, including certain key people who conceived the idea of these institutions and who persuaded their colleagues and the people themselves to go forward with them. One such was Bishop Louis Joseph de Goësbriand (1816-1899), Bishop of Burlington, who, around 1870, managed to convince some colleagues within the Canadian episcopate to send priests to serve the immigrant population and to found parishes.

In the Catholic world of the end of the nineteenth century, any one who spoke of a parish spoke also of a school for all practical purposes, since the Vatican had condemned attendance at public schools in 1875, and Pope Leo XIII addressed this question in his Encyclical to the Bishops of France in 1884. In the United States, the Third Plenary Council of Baltimore (1884) directed all parishes to build a school within two years. This indicates to what extent the situation demanded the establishment of Catholic schools, although unilingual, of course.

Ferdinand Gagnon (1849-1886), a journalist, patriot, and leader within the immigrant community in the 1870s and 1880s, was one of the first to advocate a new nationalism founded on bilingualism and biculturalism. The school obviously formed an integral part of that doctrine, though it soon became the object of controversy, for, in a speech given at Cohoes (New York) in 1882, Ferdinand Gagnon castigated those "would-be Canadians" who "denounce our schools as being disloyal."[13]

In other respects, benefit societies were being formed in the various immigrant centers, which were not only solicitous of widows and orphans, but also constituted pressure groups to demand from the bishops the establishment of "Canadian" parishes. Thus, among the priorities of the immigrants, the church and the school came close behind their most pressing economic needs.

These priorities were also reflected at the General Conventions, of which some twenty were held between 1865 and 1901. At these gatherings, representatives of the benefit societies, members of the clergy, and other leaders discussed the problems of the immigrants. These members of the group's "general staff" often returned to the question of the schools, a question always tied to *survivance*, that is, to upholding the faith and maintaining the language. In 1886, at the Convention held in Rutland, Vermont, for example, Father Notebaert dedicated a long speech to the subject, in which he declared that "the issue of the schools is an issue of life or death."[14]

Thus the idea of the Franco-American parochial school makes its way, quickly followed by the reality, as these schools multiplied throughout New England and New York State. This idea did not exist in a vacuum; it came out of a very precise context in which we find one of the aspects of the intellectual foundations of education among the Franco-Americans—that of strife.

The immigrants were being assailed from all sides. In Canada, they were treated as deserters; in the United States, the

13   *Ferdinand Gagnon: Biographie, éloge funèbre, pages choisies* (Manchester, N.H.:, L'Avenir National, 1940), p. 181.

14   Quoted by Félix Gatineau, *Historique des Conventions générales des Canadiens-Français aux États-Unis 1865-1901*, Woonsocket, R.I., L'Union Saint-Jean-Baptiste d'Amérique, 1927, p. 187.

Anglo-Americans perceived them as lacking culture, and the Irish hated them because they monopolized the jobs in the factories and because they insisted on developing a separate network of churches and schools. That insistence, to which the Irish-American episcopate had to yield, since the Canadian immigrants did not speak English, rendered more complex the task of having Catholicism accepted by Protestant Yankees.

In the face of so many assaults, reaction was necessary, and there is ample documentary evidence of the period to support the proposition that a counteroffensive was mounted from the beginning of Franco-American history, a broad and incessant campaign of counterpropaganda, directed sometimes toward Canada and sometimes toward the English-speaking milieu of United States. At the same time, it was necessary to spur the people on, to obtain their support in the elaboration of the national *oeuvre* and in the effort deployed to ameliorate the opinion held by the other groups concerning Franco-Americans.

In that controversy, the school was a weapon of choice, since it could serve to show the Anglos that, because education was a priority for the immigrants, they were not the ignoramuses that they had been made out to be. And, by insisting that the teaching be Catholic, they met the requirements of Rome and the American episcopate. Finally, by insisting that religion, the French language, and the history of Canada be taught in these Franco-American schools, they were proving their loyalty to their country of origin.

Thus was the intelligentsia among the immigrants forced to wage an ideological war on many fronts, which would result, after many decades, in a partial victory for the supporters of *survivance*. Throughout that long war, the parish, that is to say, the churches and their parochial schools, would be key elements.

That is how the school question was understood by the founding pastors of Franco-American parishes. Father Joseph Augustin Chevalier, the first Canadian pastor in the Diocese of Manchester, established the first Franco-American school in New Hampshire in 1881 in the parish of Saint Augustin (Manchester), a parish that he had himself founded in 1871. According to his biographer, Monsignor Adrien Verrette:

> The person we celebrate had understood, from the time of his arrival in Manchester, the urgency of founding

parochial schools that were clearly bilingual in character. His faith in the *survivance* of the race—which remained firm despite the storms of a tempestuous past—in protecting its religious faith with the shield of the French language, inspired him, shortly after construction of the church, to begin the project of opening a school where his children would be able to acquire an education in conformity with the ideals of their race. [15]

In that same biography, the author quotes an article from the *Canado-Américain* which speaks to the importance of teaching, for Father Chevalier himself and for posterity, since the article is dated 1917, and Msgr. Verrette's work which quotes it is dated 1927. Here is an excerpt from that article which informs us regarding the qualities that were highlighted in eulogizing a jubilarian pastor:

> There is also in the life of this respected jubilarian a less well-known page, but one which we hope will be written some day. He experienced, about forty years ago, the anguish of a pastor obliged to defend, alone and without weapons, the weakest and youngest of his flock. It happened at the time of the founding of the first French-Canadian parish school in Manchester. Arrayed against Father Chevalier was the power of numbers, of politics, and of money. But he found in his priestly soul, in his patriotism, and in that love he had always shown to the young, the strength and the means necessary to assert the principle of religious education and to command respect for it from his fanatical opponents. Of all the good works which he accomplished, this one is probably the most obscure. It is nonetheless the most meritorious because of the influence it has had on the destinies of the French Canadians of Manchester. [16]

This text also brings to mind another dimension of the ideological war mentioned above since the author is careful to

---

15   [Msgr. Adrien Verrette], *Messire Joseph-Augustin Chevalier: Jubilé de diamant sacerdotal 1867-1927* (Manchester, N.H.: L'Avenir National, 1927), p. 49.

16   Ibid., p. 102.

point out that Father Chevalier had to struggle to have the principle of religious education accepted by a hostile group. This points to another aspect of the origins of the Franco-American educational system that we are here trying to define, that is, the accurate understanding that this pastor-founder, and others like him everywhere in New England, had of the situation of immigrants to American territory. On the one hand, there were the spiritual needs of the immigrants and their children; on the other, there was in the United States, in matters of religion, a freedom capable of serving the immigrants, but, as in the case of Manchester and in so many others, a struggle was needed so that the immigrants could enjoy that freedom. Thus, at the beginning of the Franco-American educational system, one finds the strong convictions of the early pastors.

We would like to know more about these first pastors whose influence on the lives of their flocks seems to have been enormous. Some of them cut an original figure. Such a one is Father Louis Onésime Triganne (1860-1931), who built the magnificent Notre Dame Church in Southbridge, Mass. Pastor of Notre-Dame-des-Sept-Douleurs Church in Adams, Mass., from 1890 to 1904, he tried to give his parishioners both religious and "patriotic" motives for building a Franco-American parochial school. What makes one smile, a century later, is the method chosen by the good pastor, preaching from the height of the pulpit, exhorting his parishioners to join in the work of building the school, telling them first of all that they did not, of course, want to see their children become "renegades," "strangers," "degenerate sons." He would then outline for them what their own thought process should be:

> On the contrary, what you wish is that your children should be proud of you as you are proud of your ancestors; that they be made in your image and your resemblance, with the same mentality that you have, thinking like you, speaking like you, acting like you; you wish to continue to live through them, you wish them to be an extension of your own life.[17]

Having lauded such a noble ambition, Father Triganne then formulated a question as inevitable as its answer:

---

[17]   Rev. Hormisdas Hamelin, *Notre-Dame-des-Sept-Douleurs ou une paroisse franco-américaine* (Montreal: Arbour et Dupont, 1916).

But how are your children going to become what you'd wish them to be, Canadians like you in their very souls? How will they be worthy to carry your honorable name? How will you realize your most noble ambition? How?. . . There is only one way and that is the Canadian school. It alone is capable of molding your children in your image and resemblance; it alone is capable of making them love what you love and of adoring what you adore.[18]

His biographer, Father Hormisdas Hamelin, asserts that he pressed that idea again and again with a rare stubbornness, with the goal of winning his people to the cause of the parochial school. Father Triganne's argument, original and picturesque, was also effective, for he succeeded in establishing a school.

What role did religious motivation play in the establishment of so many schools? What part was played by nationalistic motives, first with the leadership that, during more than half a century, succeeded in persuading the faithful to support the founding of schools, and then with the people? The available texts strongly suggest that there was a range of opinion during the period of immigration, at times emphasizing one or the other aspect.

For certain members of the clergy, the schools were to be "a small part of Canada transported into the parish."[19] Others were less categorical. In his history of Saint Anne's parish in Fall River, Mass., written about 1919, Father Jean-Dominique Brosseau, O.P., stated that the first task of a Catholic parish was to assure its children of a Christian education. But he was quick to add, "Here, the Catholic school has, in addition, the mission of safeguarding nationality, family customs, domestic virtues."[20]

For his part, Rev. Denis Magnan seems to be stating a paradox by claiming that a "parish without a church is better than a parish without a Catholic school, for the very good reason that

---

18   Ibid., p. 270.

19   Ibid., p. 273.

20   (Rev. Jean-Dominique Brosseau, O.P.,) *Cinquante années d'activité paroissiale: Sainte-Anne de Fall River, Mass. 1869-1919*, s.l, s.e., s.d., p. 79.

where the second is missing the first often becomes useless."[21]

Thus summed up are some of the most significant aspects of the spiritual and intellectual foundations of the schooling of Franco-Americans, at least insofar as concerns the leadership of those generations of immigrants. Before discussing the contribution of the religious communities within the framework of these spiritual and intellectual bases, we believe it useful to cast a quick glance at the decade of the 1930s because it marks both the end of immigration and the end of what we might call the "the golden age" of Franco-Americanism.

During the decade of the 30s, a new generation began to express itself, a generation of observers and continuators, of men of action and men of letters. In the first rank can be placed the ideologues of *survivance*, and especially the imposing figure of Monsignor Adrien Verrette, in whom the pastor-builders found a kindred spirit, even at a generation's distance. In his numerous parish monographs and in his biographies of the early pastors, Msgr. Verrette never missed an opportunity to commend their efforts on behalf of bilingual parish schools.

Josaphat Benoit, also an ideologue of *survivance*, dedicated a chapter to schools in his key work, *L'âme franco-américaine* (1935). That chapter is at once an apologia for the Franco-American school and an assessment of the American educational system, perceived as "essentially Protestant."[22] By putting his compatriots on guard against the alleged neutrality of the American public schools, Josaphat Benoit echoed Rev. Edouard Hamon, a Jesuit preacher who came frequently from Canada to preach retreats to Franco-Americans at the end of the nineteenth century. In his study entitled *Les Canadiens-Français de la Nouvelle-Angleterre* (1891), Rev. Hamon identified the hostility of the public schools toward the religion of the French-Canadian immigrants as one of the reasons for the immigrant community's need for parish schools:

Everything came together to make this idea enter deeply into the head and the heart of the Canadian: public

---

[21]   Rev. D.-M.-A. Magnan, *Notre-Dame-de-Lourdes de Fall River, Mass.: Notice historique* (Quebec City: Imprimerie Le Soleil, 1925), p. 82.

[22]   Josaphat Benoit, *L'âme franco-américaine* (Montreal: Éditions Albert-Lévesque, 1935), p. 117.

schools that were hostile to his faith and to his nationality, the efforts made by Americans to take his children and to Anglicize them, open hostility against them from certain quarters, all of that resulted in inscribing at the head of the national agenda, the creation of convents or schools in the French parishes.[23]

And so, at a half-century's distance, the perception of the American public school had evolved little, and one can say that the public school, or at least the perception that was held of it, was also a factor in the founding of Franco-American parish schools.

Having stated that "the primary reason for the existence of the parochial schools" was to provide "a religious and moral formation," Josaphat Benoit added that Franco-Americans had "another urgent reason for founding schools everywhere: so that their children could be taught the French language and national history, rightly considered as the foundation stone of their ethnic *survivance* and the necessary condition for their complete development."[24]

Since immigration had scarcely begun to come to an end—Josaphat Benoit wrote his work in the mid-thirties—there were schools yet to be built in order to serve the needs of those immigrants who were still arriving, and the educational needs brought on by the natural increase in the population. The argument developed by Josaphat Benoit was about the same as that of the Franco-American leaders who had gathered together at the general Conventions as early as the 1860s. This constitutes further written proof that a clerical-nationalist French-Canadian ideology prevailed regarding the origins of the education of Franco-Americans and that it dominated everyone's thinking from the beginning to the end of the period of immigration.

However, the nationalist aspect of this ideology was received in a variety of ways by the Franco-American community. Again in the 1930s, Father—and later Monsignor—Georges Duplessis argued that "national education" was lacking in certain

---

23   Rev. Édouard Hamon, S.J., *Les Canadiens-Français de la Nouvelle-Angleterre* (Montreal: Éditions du 45e Parallèle Nord, 1982), (Reprint of the 1891 edition, Hardy, Quebec), p. 107.

24   Benoit, *L'âme franco-américaine*, pp. 118-119.

Franco-American schools.[25] And he recalled the point of view of Cardinal Bégin of Quebec, according to whom teaching in a Franco-American milieu included "a patriotic as well as a religious mission."[26] According to Father Duplessis, "the formation of the Franco-American soul was to be achieved" especially by teaching history, that of Canada and that of the United States, in order to instill pride in the young.[27]

Our purpose is not to stir up old quarrels that pitted a given pastor against one or the other teaching community, nor is it a question of defending one party against another, but rather to achieve a more subtle understanding of a collective past. The supporters of *survivance* and certain religious communities developed two different concepts of the duty of teachers toward the minority group. It is not impossible that this type of disagreement had also existed from the first decades of immigration and that it had affected both the origin and the evolution of the education of Franco-Americans. Certainly it is difficult, from the hindsight of a half-century, to quarrel with Father Duplessis when he exhorts his readers to inspire in the child "first of all an immense love for his race, for his ancestors, for his language, and for what he is."[28]

In conclusion, we would like to share this text of Professor George Theriault on the ideological context within which we can situate the rise of Franco-American schools:

The great importance which Franco-Americans attach to "their own" parochial schools is rooted in other than religious motives, as important as these are to them. Religion, the French language, a French-language press, separate and distinct institutions and associations are all so intimately conjoined in the thought of Franco-Americans that the attribution of motives to the influence of particular segments of their culture is extremely difficult. Each is related to and dependent upon

---

[25]   Rev. Georges-H. Duplessis, "Les communautés enseignantes," in *Les Franco-Américains peints par eux-mêmes* (Montreal: Éditions Albert-Lévesque, 1936), p. 175 *and passim.*

[26]   Ibid., p. 169

[27]   Ibid., pp. 170 and 172.

[28]   Ibid., p. 172.

the others, since, taken collectively, as an integrated culture, they all compose the ramparts upon which the Franco-Americans take their stand and look out upon the world. The Roman Catholic faith and view of life suffuses them all, but serves to enhance rather than to diminish the importance which the Franco-American attaches to French, his Franco-American organizations and associations, his institutions and, among them, his schools.[29]

This overview seems to us correct, conclusive even; and, added to all that has preceded, it explains how, at the Second Congress of the French Language held at Quebec in 1937, Msgr. J. Alfred Laliberté, pastor of St. Mathieu Parish in Central Falls, R.I., could make the following comprehensive judgment:

All the same, the parish school remains the cornerstone of our national *survivance* in the United States. We can have parishes, societies, newspapers, and efforts of all kinds, but if our children do not attend parochial schools we lose all that; it will all become useless because within two generations no one would speak French.[30]

The Contribution of the Religious Communities

Observers of Franco-American culture almost always agree concerning the positive impact that the religious communities had on the life of the group. Father Hormisdas Hamelin, for example, tells us of the arrival of the Sisters of the Holy Cross to establish a school in Adams, Mass. in 1899. Awaited "with impatience," the Sisters arrived on August 23, 1899 "and the good news traveled as quick as a flash. Everybody repeated the good news with delight, 'The Sisters have arrived.' Souls thrilled with

---

[29]   Theriault, p. 378. In the same work, pp. 490-493, we find a useful comparison between the divergent views of the public school teachers and those of the Catholic schools.

[30]   Msgr. J.-Alfred Laliberté, "L'école paroissiale," in [Rev. Adrien Verrette] *La Croisade franco-américaine* (Manchester, N.H.: L'Avenir National, 1938), p. 256.

joy, parents were reassured, and hearts relieved."[31]

At the Second Congress of the French Language at Quebec in 1937, Rev. Louis Bachand, O.M.I., spoke of the religious communities without which "the Franco-American schools could not even have begun to exist."[32] During the decade of the 30s, Rev. Georges Duplessis confirmed that judgment: "We recognize that without our teaching communities, without their missionary spirit, our parishes could not have built and maintained schools due to the lack of financial resources."[33]

In our opinion, these religious communities constitute both an unrecognized aspect of the Franco-American heritage as well as one of the great pillars of *survivance*, quite as much as the parishes, the societies, and the newspapers. Let us hasten to add, however, that a religious community goes well beyond the boundaries of *survivance* both in its goals and in its evolution. But because we are dealing here with the foundations of schooling for Franco-Americans, we will glance at the origins of these communities and examine succinctly their spirituality and their spirit before describing the principal features of an educational effort which left its mark on several generations of Franco-Americans.

To go back to the origins is of necessity to learn or relearn about those exceptional people who were the founders and foundresses of communities.

First and foremost, according to the seniority of our French and French-Canadian communities, is the imposing figure of Marguerite Bourgeoys (1620-1700), foundress of the Congregation of Notre Dame. She was a "true Champenoise" [i.e. from the province of Champagne], "a builder and a woman of prayer," according to her biographer, Sister Thérèse Lambert, C.N.D.[34] Traveling across the Atlantic, in imitation and in honor of "the

---

[31]   Hamelin, pp. 278-279.

[32]   Rev. Louis Bachand, O.M.I., in *La croisade franco-américaine*, p. 199.

[33]   *Les Franco-Américains peints par eux-mêmes*, p.168.

[34]   "Champenoise de race"; "bâtisseuse et orante," in Sr. Thérèse Lambert, C.N.D., *Marguerite Bourgeoys éducatrice (1620-1700) Mère d'un pays et d'une Église* (Montreal: Éditions Bellarmin, 1978), p. 53.

travelling life of Our Lady," she remained faithful to the guiding star of her life, the Holy Virgin who had promised her: "Go, I will not abandon you."[35] And we cannot resist the temptation of quoting once again from Sister Lambert who summarizes the achievements of that "vagabond" of the Absolute as follows:

> She who had taken part in the Great Adventure of the Associates of Montreal, who had created schooling in the apostolic enterprise of Ville Marie, was leaving to the newborn colony examples of courage, of apostolate, of help to the colonists, and, to the Congregation, words to live by which span the centuries: meekness, simplicity, poverty. In the Church of time and space, Marguerite Bourgeoys had followed the Christ of history: a community of secular daughters, without wimple or veil, that is to say without cloister, now existed in New France.[36]

Marie Rivier (1768-1838), foundress of the Sisters of the Presentation of Mary, the "Woman-Apostle" who died "in the hunger of her zeal,"[37] also remains an attractive personality, despite the upbraiding remarks that she inserts in her letters to her Sisters. She, who, at the age of five, had already decided to devote her life to teaching the children of the poor, declared, upon being refused entry into a community at the age of eighteen: "since they won't let me enter the convent, I will make one myself."[38]

Rev. Basile Moreau (1799-1873), founder of the Sisters of the Holy Cross, and Esther Blondin (Mother Mary Anne, 1809-1890), foundress of the Sisters of St. Anne, would both have to live "a mysterious Way of the Cross that would last throughout their

---

[35]   "La vie voyagère de Notre-Dame"; "Va, je ne te délaisserai pas," in Ibid., p. 92.

[36]   Ibid., p. 112

[37]   Msgr. André-M. Cimichella, S.S.M., *La Bienheureuse Marie Rivier, fondatrice des Soeurs de la Présentation de Marie* (Montreal: Les Éditions Jésus-Marie et Notre Temps, 1982), p. 80.

[38]   Ibid., p. 13.

lifetime."[39] For reasons that remain obscure to those not specialized in these matters, both would be removed from office, subjected to "personal heartbreak" and to conflicts over rights and authority. What Sister Marie-Jean-de-Pathmos, S.S.A., says of Mother Mary Anne is just as true of Father Moreau: "Immersed in the Divine Will, Mother Mary Anne builds the future of her institution with her own sufferings. She disappears so that her work will grow and bear the fruits of eternity."[40]

In short, reading the biographies of the founders and foundresses, one quickly understands that they all possessed creativity, dynamism, tenacity, and strength of character which seem prodigious. That fact becomes even more obvious if one considers the circumstances in which the communities came into being.

As stated by Msgr. Cristiani, biographer of Claudine Thévenet, foundress of the Religious of Jesus and Mary (R.J.M.): "There were heroic beginnings in most of the institutions. All of them began in a small way, with great effort, with daily sacrifice. The virtues of the founders made up for the lack of resources."[41]

The age of faith that was the seventeenth century certainly favored the flowering of the work of Marguerite Bourgeoys on Canadian soil—and yet, her first school was a stable. From the human point of view this could not have been very encouraging. Marie Rivier founded her Institute during the French Revolution, an era during which the mass, forbidden by the state, had to be celebrated in an attic or a barn in the middle of the night. The strict diet the foundress and her first Sisters were compelled to follow, says a great deal about the atmosphere of these arduous beginnings:

> We ate only rye bread in the house; wheat flour was used
> for the bread of the boarding students, and bran was put
> into that of the teachers, who waited to eat their meal

[39]   Sr. Marie-Jean-de-Pathmos, S.S.A., *Les Soeurs de Sainte-Anne: un siècle d'histoire—1850-1900* (Lachine, Quebec: Les Soeurs de Sainte-Anne, 1950), t, I, pp. 450-451.

[40]   Ibid., p. 115.

[41]   Msgr. Cristiani, *Au service de l'enfance: Claudine Thévenet* (Paris: Éditions France-Empire, 1961), p. 182.

until the students had had enough; they lived on the students' leavings, so that very often they must have suffered pangs of hunger.[42]

And Sister Alice Migneault, writing the history of the Sisters of the Assumption of the Blessed Virgin, describes for us "in what an atmosphere of material poverty, work, and abnegation the Congregation developed."[43]

If we now examine the sources of the Rules and Constitutions which govern these communities, we find some of the greatest saints of the Church: Saint Augustine (354-430), Saint Benedict (480-547), Saint Ignatius (1491-1556), and Saint Francis de Sales (1567-1622), to whom we must add the name of Jean-Jacques Olier (1608-1657), founder of the Sulpician Fathers. In the case of the Ursulines, the influence of the *Ratio Studiorum*, the plan of studies of the Jesuits, is so direct that Mother Marie-de-Saint-Jean-Martin, O.S.U., was able to draw a parallel between it and the Rules of the Ursulines.[44] Marie Rivier chose three saints of the Society of Jesus as protectors and models for her religious: Saint Francis Regis, Saint Louis of Gonzaga, and Saint Stanislas Kostka.

Such sources already indicate what goals they would pursue. In fact, of the twelve or so communities studied, the first goal was always the same: the personal sanctification of each member. To this goal was intimately tied the sanctification of others by educating the young and, frequently, by caring for the needy. In certain communities, the original goal would be extended. The Daughters of the Holy Spirit, for example, initially concentrated their efforts on teaching the children of poor fishermen in the French province of Brittany and then later went forth to many countries. As for the Sisters of the Assumption, their historian, Rev. Germain Lesage, states explicitly: "All of the rules were clearly organized around the principal goal of the Community,

[42]   Cimichella, p. 40.

[43]   Sr. Alice Migneault, S.A.S.V., *Vingts ans d'expansion chez les Soeurs de l'Assomption de la Sainte Vierge, 1874-1894* (Nicolet, Quebec: Éditions S.A.S.V., 1985), p. 13.

[44]   Sr. Marie-de-Saint-Jean-Martin, O.S.U., *Ursuline Method of Education* (Rahway, N.J.: Quinn and Boden, 1946), pp. 291-320.

which is education."[45] The same can be said for the Sisters of Saint Anne, the Sisters of Saint Chrétienne, the Sisters of Saint Joseph (of Le Puy), etc.

Sanctification being the primary goal, it was logical that prayer would become the cornerstone of a spirituality which permeated the entire existence of each member. Even as we assert that this spirituality was Christocentric and Marian, the variations are numerous, for, as we know, there are many ways of living the faith. Marguerite Bourgeoys, for example, urged her Sisters to renew "the true spirit of cordiality and love which constituted the glory as well as the joy of early Christendom."[46]

These communities of necessity bore the stamp of the spirituality of the age in which they were founded. What Rev. Germain Lesage states concerning the spirituality of the Sisters of the Assumption applies just as well to other institutions established in the nineteenth century. This spirituality, he writes, "expresses a general insistence on asceticism, on the strong virtues of obedience, mortification, humility, and flight from the world."[47]

As a general rule, the spiritual life of these teaching communities, while remaining grounded in prayer, was much more oriented towards action than towards contemplation. In addition to this pragmatism, one can also discern what might be called the absolutism of this type of spirituality. There is, in the regulations of the Daughters of the Holy Spirit, a formula that expresses this attitude well: "Heart empty of all except of God in order to be entirely for God."[48] Or again, according to an idea of Rev. Louis Lallemant transmitted to the Daughters of the Holy Spirit, "To want to belong only and supremely to God, to want

---

45   Rev. Germain Lesage, O.M.I., *Le Transfert à Nicolet des Soeurs de l'Assomption de la Sainte Vierge* (Nicolet, Quebec: Éditions S.A.S.V., 1965), p. 82.

46   Hélène Bernier, *Marguerite Bourgeoys* (Montreal: Fides, Collection "Classiques canadiens", 1974), no. 3, p. 64.

47   Lesage, p. 69. See also pp. 79-81 and Migneault, pp. 39-40 and 68.

48   Sr. Anita Dion, "The Spirituality of the Daughters of the Holy Spirit" (Putnam, Conn.: 1975), p. 4.

nothing but that, but to want it to the full extent of my strength."[49]

This all-embracing spirituality, which encompasses the entire life of the religious, was expressed by Claudine Thévenet as follows:

All of these minor points, these minute practices are of little import in themselves: people of the world view them as puerile activities and tend to laugh at them. But, in the eyes of God, what a grand and beautiful thing it is to accomplish all these little nothings with loyalty and perseverance.[50]

Let us note finally that this spirituality is actuated by a profound spirit of faith, manifest in the attitude of Mother Mary Anne, who received her pupils, as she herself said, "at the expense of Providence, for we lean on its help for this as for all else."[51]

And now, how can we best define the *spirit* that animated the communities of women religious teachers, both French and French-Canadian, in New England? That spirit contained several traits of which, unquestionably, the most important was love. Love, or charity, upholds this whole educational enterprise and constitutes the dominant theme of the literature relating to this subject. Here is how Marguerite Bourgeoys defines it, after having evoked different kinds of love:

But it is only the love of lovers which penetrates the heart of God, and to which nothing is refused; that love is rarely found and it is the true love, for it knows no self-interest, not even its own needs; it is indifferent to sickness or to health; prosperity or adversity, consolation or coldness, are all the same to it; and it gives its life with pleasure for the loved one.[52]

In the vast corpus of works treating this question, not one text contradicts this statement of Marguerite Bourgeoys—to the

49   Ibid., p. 8.

50   Quoted by Cristiani, p. 168.

51   Sr. Marie-Jean-de-Pathmos, S.S.A., p. 102.

52   Bernier, p. 73.

contrary, they all support it.

According to the wish of the founders and foundresses, this same spirit of love is destined to govern the relationships between each Sister and the other religious members of the community. Representative of this view, as it is on many points, the Directory of the Sisters of St. Joseph, in a chapter entitled "Charity of the Sisters Among Themselves," is explicit in this regard:

> They [the Sisters] should zealously seek the advancement of one another, and should experience great joy in seeing each other grow in virtue, and [they should take] particular care to help each in becoming more perfect, whether it be by their examples, by their good advice, or by the prayers they will say for one another.[53]

As for relationships with the students, Claudine Thévenet sums up an attitude that was very prevalent when she declares, "We must be Mothers for our children, yes, true Mothers, as much for the soul as for the body."[54] In this she joins in the thinking of Rev. Basile Moreau, who asserts in the Directory of the Sisters of the Holy Cross, "As love is acquired by loving, the teacher will show that she loves her pupils. . . ."[55]

That spirit of love would often have to be expressed in concrete terms by sacrifice and service. Once again, the declarations, the precepts of the founders and foundresses are explicit in this regard. They all share the opinion of Claudine Thévenet that "Jesus Christ came on earth to serve and not to be served . . ."[56] Marie Rivier wrote, "I find no greater joy on earth than that of working to do good for and to be useful to one's

---

[53] *Constitutions de la Congrégation des Soeurs de Saint-Joseph du Puy-en-Velay*, Le Puy-en-Velay, France, Imprimerie "Jeanne d'Arc," 1932, p. 204.

[54] Quoted by Cristiani, p. 162.

[55] Quoted by Sr. Marie-Madeleine, C.S.C., *Mère d'éducatrices* (Saint Laurent, Quebec: Sisters of the Holy Cross, 1962), p. 26.

[56] Quoted by Cristiani, p. 157.

neighbor!"[57] All of which amounts to saying that in service to others one finds happiness. In all of the communities studied, this sacrifice of self and this lifelong service was offered in preference to the poor and the needy. This was a deliberate choice. In an open letter, Mother Marie-des-Sept-Douleurs, C.S.C. reminds her young religious of a basic truth that other superiors also called to the minds of their adherents, that is to say, that "compassion for the afflicted is, among all of the Christian virtues, the one that is most dear to the heart of Our Lord. . ."[58]

That perpetual gift of self, by means of sacrifice and service, could never be either lukewarm or cold. On the contrary, it had to be driven by that zeal of which Marie Rivier often speaks, as indicated by Sister Isabelle Bouchard, who compiled her correspondence: "But what is it then to love the children? The Mother whose love and zeal are as one knows the answer well and she explained to young Sister Isaac: 'If you have zeal, you will always feel a fire burning inside you.' "[59] Further on, Sister Bouchard states categorically, "she [Marie Rivier] eagerly wished her teachers to be daughters of fire . . . 'How I love the Sisters who are fervent, who enjoy their vocation, their state in life, and who breathe only zeal and ardor for their work. Those are my true daughters.' "[60] She even affirmed, "one can do anything one wishes when one is fervent and zealous."[61]

. . . All that one wishes. The first religious of all the communities studied knew what it was like for having survived the difficult and often painful beginnings of their institutions. Being resigned to trials thus constitutes a common element in the histories of these various communities. The anonymous writer of the annals of the Sisters of Saint Anne recounts with elegance the time when these Sisters established themselves at Lachine, "someone had come along with them: Dame Poverty! For years on

---

57   Isabelle Bouchard, P.M., *Marie Rivier, son coeur et sa main: son ardente vie apostolique d'après sa correspondance* (Rome: Imprimeria Sped. Im-Monte Compatri, 1985), p. 36.

58   Sr. Marie-Madeleine, C.S.C., p. 56.

59   Bouchard, p. 37.

60   Ibid., p. 100.

61   Ibid., p. 102.

end, she would remain the assiduous hostess, austere but respected by those courageous pioneers . . ."[62]

An additional element needs to be highlighted in the description of the spirit common to these religious: joyousness. It is part and parcel of the common ethic, equal in importance to devotion and solidarity. So much so that Marie Rivier inscribes it in an "agreement" made in 1826 between herself as superior and "the young lady boarders," who specifically pledge "to maintain, and at all times to show joy and good humor; in accordance with the aforesaid article, each shall contribute to the best of her ability to the recreation and amusement of all."[63] In a letter to one of her dear daughters, she even counsels the following, "laugh sometimes even when you are 'up to your neck' in misery . . ."[64]

Finally, we should highlight the missionary spirit of these religious women who accepted to leave their native country, going to foreign lands to consecrate their lives to being witnesses of Christ to unknown youths and people. This aspect of their vocation deserves greater development in a detailed study about the contributions of these communities in New England.

*   *   *

Having reviewed the principal characteristics of the religious foundations of these communities, it now remains for us to see upon what values, upon which concepts rests the education offered by these communities for over a century.

Let us note at the outset that the entirety of the texts consulted reveals high professional standards and great regard for perfection. Among other things, these texts unanimously recommend that firmness united to goodness should govern the relationship between teachers and students. They seek to practice "the pedagogy of love," according to the designation given to the

---

62   Sr. Marie-Jean-de-Pathmos, p. 205.

63   Bouchard, p. 47.

64   Ibid., p. 222.

system of Don Bosco by Sister Marie-Aimée-de-Jésus.[65] That is what Marie Rivier meant when she repeated to her disciples: "Be magnets."[66]

Everywhere there is an attempt, as with the Ursulines, to give a complete course of study, including the formation of the spirit, of the will and the heart, without neglecting physical development. Everywhere there is an effort to maintain a wise balance between tradition and progress, that is to say, that from the start, the founders and foundresses were open to change, to modifying their teaching according to the discoveries of science, pedagogical or otherwise, and according to the new needs created by changing circumstances.

In each case, priority is given to religion, not only as a subject matter, but also as an atmosphere to be created and nurtured. For the goal is to "engrave Christ into the heart of the child," according to the forceful expression of Marie Rivier.[67]

In all of the communities, there is an active effort to see to the formation of those within them who will be responsible for the training of future Sisters, knowing full well that the completion of that formation was the work of a lifetime. From this sustained reflection on education have come a number of texts whose reading is still useful even for the lay teachers of today. The reader can readily find them in our bibliography.

Conclusion

Whoever attempts to study the education of Franco-Americans will quickly realize to what extent this field has been left fallow. For example, we are lacking empirical studies concerning the effects on the life experience of the concepts set forth here in some detail. Having sought to define the spirit present at the founding of the communities, we would like to know how that spirit evolved and how it influenced its subjects.

---

[65]   Sr. Marie-Aimée-de-Jésus, *L'enseignement à l'Institut de la Présentation de Marie* (Saint Hyacinthe, Quebec: Présentation de Marie, 1939), pp. 157-158.

[66]   Bouchard, p 81.

[67]   Sr. Marie-Aimée-de-Jesus, p. 257.

Moreover, next to the conceptual aspect, there is the factual history, which we were unable to take up in such a restricted setting. But, it is clear that circumstances also form a part of the foundations of schooling among Franco-Americans and that they deserve careful attention. One example among many is the fervent appeal written by the "Canadians" of Worcester to the Sisters of Saint-Anne.[68]

It would also be useful to understand more regarding the governing of these schools, about the division of responsibility between the pastors and the religious communities, and about the role of parents in the development of these schools. Similarly, what degree of truth and objectivity is there in the famous comparisons, made by everyone over a century, between the parochial and the public schools? To what extent were the leaders and the people in agreement on this subject?

The school question also has an emotional side not well known by most of us. We know, for example, that the clergy of Quebec in the nineteenth century maintained a definite mistrust of the French Revolution and of Republican France. What impact did that mistrust have, eventually, on the French-Canadian religious communities in New England and, as a result, on the Franco-Americans themselves?

In order to define with precision the diverse facets of the matrix in which the education of Franco-Americans evolved, e.g. Are there beliefs other than those discussed here which deserve an analysis? Would there be considerations of a religious or ecclesiastical nature to be studied, in this same context, such as ultramontanism? Or political considerations perhaps? I am thinking, for example, of the atmosphere of conflict, of struggle, in which *survivance* was maintained: did that atmosphere have some results, other than those already known, on the development of the Franco-American system of education?

In a word, this system was formed *also* by forces other than those we have scrutinized in this essay on its intellectual and spiritual foundations—forces that are different, but perhaps no less important.

Finally, we lack in-depth studies of the intellectual and spiritual sources which nourished many generations of our

---

68   Sr. Marie-Jean-de-Pathmos, pp. 580 - 581.

women religious teachers. In addition to the sources already named, there are many others including periodicals such as *L'Écho de la France*, as well as the works of the great masters such as St. Jerome, St. John Baptist de La Salle, Madame de Maintenon, Fénelon, Msgr. Félix Dupanloup, and countless others.

In short, having completed the present study, we have the clear impression of having only broached a subject that remains rich in possibility. Hopefully, others will share this view and will pursue the research begun in this essay.

Translated by the Hon. André A. Gélinas

[This article first appeared as "L'enseignement chez les Franco-Américains: ses assises spirituelles et intellectuelles" in the French Institute's publication entitled *Les Franco-Américains et leurs institutions scolaires*. It has been reviewed by the author, and up-dated where necessary, for inclusion in this volume.]

Bibliography

French and Quebec Antecedents

Falardeau, Jean-Charles. "The Role and Importance of the Church in French Canada," in Marcel Rioux & Yves Martin. *French-Canadian Society*. Toronto: McClelland & Stewart, 1964. Vol. I, pp. 342-57.

Goyau, Georges. *Les origines religieuses du Canada*. Paris: Grasset, 1924. xlvii, 285 p.

Groulx, chanoine Lionel. *Histoire du Canada français depuis la découverte*. Montreal: Fides, 1960. 2 vol.

Hamelin, Jean, ed. *Histoire du Québec*. Toulouse, Privat and Saint-Hyacinthe, Quebec: EDISEM, 1976. 538 p.

Hamelin, Jean and Nicole Gagnon. *Le XXe siècle*. Tome I, 1898-1940, in Nive Voisine (dir.), *Histoire du catholicisme québécois*. Montreal: Boréal Express, 1984. 507 p.

Jean, Marguerite, s.c.i.m. *Evolution des communautés religieuses de femmes au Canada, de 1639 à nos jours*. Montreal: Fides, 1977, x. 324 p.

Lacroix, Benoît and Madeleine Grammond. *Religion populaire au Québec: Typologie des sources, bibliographie sélective (1900-1980)*. Quebec City: Institut québécois de recherche sur la culture, 1985. Collection "Instruments de travail," no 10. 175 p.

Linteau, Paul-André (et al.). *Histoire du Québec contemporain: De la Confédération à la Crise (1867-1969)*. Montreal: Éditions du Boréal Express, 1979. 658 p.

Miner, Horace. *St. Denis, A French-Canadian Parish*. Chicago: University of Chicago Press, c1939, 1967, xix. 299 p.

Parizeau, Gérard. *La société canadienne-française au XIXe siècle: Essais sur le milieu*. Montreal: Fides, 1975. 550 p.

Voisine, Nive. *Histoire de l'Eglise catholique au Québec (1608-1970)*. Montreal: Fides, 1971. 112 p.

Wade, Mason. *The French Canadians 1760-1945*, New York: The Macmillan Co., 1955. *Les Canadiens français de 1760 à nos jours*. 2d ed., rev. Ottawa: Le Cercle du Livre de France, 1963, 1966. 2 vol.

Immigration and Settlement

Benoit, Josaphat. *L'âme franco-américaine*. Montreal: Éditions Albert-Lévesque, 1935. 247 p.

[Brosseau, Jean-Dominique, o.p.]. *Cinquante années d'activité paroissiale: Sainte-Anne de Fall River, Mass., 1869-1919*. n.p., n. pub., n.d., 312 p.

Ferdinand Gagnon: Biographie, éloge funèbre, pages choisies. Manchester, N.H.: L'Avenir national, 1940. 279 p.

Les Franco-Américains peints par eux-mêmes. Montreal: Éditions Albert-Lévesque, 1936. 287 p.

Gatineau, Félix. *Historique des Conventions générales des Canadiens-Français aux États-Unis 1865-1901*. Woonsocket, R.I.: L'Union Saint-Jean-Baptiste d'Amérique, 1927. 500 p.

Hamelin, Hormisdas (Rev.). *Notre-Dame-des-Sept-Douleurs, ou Une paroisse franco-américaine*. Montreal: Arbour et Dupont, 1916. 362 p.

Hamon, Edouard, S.J. *Les Canadiens-Français de la Nouvelle-Angleterre*. Montreal: Éditions du 45e Parallèle Nord, 1982, xv. 484 p. (Reprint of the 1891 edition, Hardy, Quebec.)

Magnan, D.-M.-A. (Rev.). *Histoire de la race française aux États-Unis*. 2e édition revue et corrigée. Paris: Charles Amat Editor, 1913, XVI. 386 p.

_____ *Notre-Dame-de-Lourdes de Fall River, Mass.: Notice historique*. Quebec City: Imprimerie Le Soleil, 1925. 248 p.

Theriault, George French. *The Franco-Americans in a New England Community: An Experiment in Survival.* New York: Arno Press, 1980, vi. 569 p.

[Verrette, Adrien (Rev.)]. *La Croisade franco-américaine.* Manchester, N.H.: L'Avenir National, 1938. 500 p.

_____ *Messire Joseph-Augustin Chevalier: Jubilé de diamant sacerdotal 1867-1927.* Manchester, N.H.: L'Avenir National, 1927. 118 p.

_____ *Messire Joseph-Augustin Chevalier (1843-1929) Curé fondateur de la paroisse Saint-Augustin, Manchester, New Hampshire.* n.p., n. pub., n.d., 54 p.

_____ *Paroisse Sainte-Marie, Manchester, New Hampshire: Cinquantenaire 1880-1930.* Manchester, N.H.: Imprimerie Lafayette, 1931. 402 p.

Contributions of Religious Communities

General

Bachand, Rev. Louis (O.M.I.). "L'ecole paroissiale franco-américaine," in Rev. Adrien Verrette, *La Croisade franco-américaine.* Manchester, N.H.: L'Avenir National, 1938. pp. 198-202.

Duplessis, Georges-H. (Rev.). "Les communautés enseignantes," in *Les Franco-Américains peints par eux-mêmes.* Montreal: Éditions Albert-Lévesque, 1936. pp. 167-77.

See also the works referred to in Part II of this bibliography.

Daughters of the Holy Spirit

"Congrégation des Filles du Saint-Esprit: Notes sommaires sur ses origines, son oeuvre et son esprit," tiré à part, *Revue de l'Archiconfrérie du Saint-Esprit,* [1916?]. 15 p.

Dion, Sister Anita, D.H.S. (Trans.). *Gleanings from Our Early Days: Daughters of the Holy Spirit,* Plerin - Saint-Brieuc. Brittany, n. pub., n.d., 100 p.

_____ (D.H.S.). *"Since They Must Be Filled With Love. . .":*
Daughters of the Holy Spirit - Our Mission in the Church.
n.p., n. pub., 1979. 111 p.

_____ *The Spirituality of the Daughters of the Holy Spirit.*
Putnam (Conn.), n. pub., 1975. 74 p.

Presentation of Mary

Bouchard, Isabelle (P.M.). *Marie Rivier, son coeur et sa main: son*
ardente vie apostolique d'après sa correspondance. Rome:
Imprimeria Sped. Im - Monte Compatri, 1985. 367 p.

Cimichella, Msgr. André-M. (O.S.M.). *La bienheureuse Marie*
Rivier, fondatrice des Soeurs de la Présentation de Marie.
Montreal: Les Éditions Jésus-Marie et Notre Temps, 1982.
96 p.

Marie-Aimée-de-Jésus (Soeur, P.M.). *L'enseignement à l'Institut de*
la Présentation de Marie. Saint-Hyacinthe, Quebec:
Présentation de Marie, 1939, iii. 265 p.

Religious of Jesus Mary

Cristiani, Monsignor. *Au service de l'enfance: Claudine Thévenet.*
Paris: Éditions France-Empire, 1961. 222 p.

Directory of Education of the Congregation of Jesus and Mary.
Rome: Maison généralice, 1961. 187 p.

Viatte, Auguste. *Histoire de la congrégation de Jésus-Marie*
1818-1950. Sillery, Quebec: Collège Jésus-Marie, 1952.
309 p.

Servants of the Immaculate Heart of Mary

Jean, Marguerite (S.C.I.M.). *Marie Fitzbach: In the Footsteps of the*
Good Shepherd. Strasbourg, France: Éditions SADIFA,
1985, xvi. 31 p.

Sisters of the Assumption of the Blessed Virgin Mary

Lesage, Germain (O.M.I.). *Les origines des Soeurs de l'Assomption*
de la Sainte Vierge. Nicolet, Quebec: Éditions S.A.S.V.,
1957. 342 p.

_____ *Le transfert à Nicolet des Soeurs de l'Assomption de la Sainte Vierge.* Nicolet, Quebec: Éditions S.A.S.V., 1965. 323 p.

Mignault, Alice (S.A.S.V.). *Vingt ans d'expansion chez les Soeurs de l'Assomption de la Sainte Vierge, 1874-1894.* Nicolet, Quebec: Éditions S.A.S.V., 1985. 430 p.

Saint-Jean-Baptiste (Soeur, S.A.S.V.). *La religieuse enseignante,* Nicolet, Quebec: Éditions S.A.S.V., 1965, xxii. 198 p.

Sisters of the Holy Cross
Bergeron, Henri-Paul. *Basile Moreau.* Rome: Congrégation de Sainte-Croix, 1979. 200 p.

_____ *Léocadie Gascoin 1818-1900.* Saint-Laurent, Quebec: Soeurs de Sainte-Croix, 1980. 181 p.

Marie-Madeleine (C.S.C.). *Mère d'éducatrices.* Saint-Laurent, Quebec: Soeurs de Sainte-Croix, 1962. 131 p.

Parent, Louise (C.S.C.). *A Mosaic to the Glory of God: The History of the Sisters of Holy Cross and of the Seven Dolors in the New England States 1881-1980.* n.p., n. publ., n.d. 214 p.

Sisters of the Holy Union of the Sacred Hearts
A Sister of La Sainte Union. *By Their Fruits You Shall Know Them: A Short Sketch of the Life of Jean Baptiste Debrabant. . . Founder of La Sainte Union des Sacré-Coeurs 1801-1880.* Dublin: Irish Messenger Office, [1956?]. 43 p.

Sisters of Notre Dame
Bernier, Hélène. *Marguerite Bourgeoys.* Montreal, Fides, 1974. 94 p., Collection "Classiques canadiens" no. 3, 2nd edition.

Lambert, Thérèse (C.N.D.). *Marguerite Bourgeoys éducatrice (1620-1700) Mère d'un pays et d'une Eglise.* Montreal: Éditions Bellarmin, 1978. 137 p.

Sisters of Saint Anne
Marie-Jean-de-Pathmos (S.S.A). *Les Soeurs de Sainte-Anne: Un siècle d'histoire.* volume I, 1850-1900. Lachine, Quebec: The Sisters of Saint Anne, 1950. 641 p.

Sisters of Saint Joseph
Aherne, Consuelo Maria (S.S.J.). *Joyous Service: The History of the Sisters of Saint Joseph of Springfield.* Holyoke, Mass.: Sisters of Saint Joseph. 1983.

Constitutions de la Congrégation des Soeurs de Saint-Joseph du Puy-en-Velay. Le Puy-en-Velay, France: Imprimerie "Jeanne d'Arc", 1932. 408 p.

Ursulines
Martin, Marie-de-Saint-Jean (O.S.U.). *Ursuline Method of Education.* Rahway, N.J.: Quinn & Boden, 1946, x. 342 p.

The Achievement of the Teaching Orders in New England: The Franco-American Parochial Schools

Gerard J. Brault

I dedicate this work to the Sisters of the Assumption of the Blessed Virgin and especially to those who were my teachers at St. George's School in Chicopee Falls, Massachusetts, from 1934 to 1942. I take great pride in noting that Sister Jeanne Béliveau made a special trip from Nicolet, Quebec, to hear this paper delivered at the colloquium on Franco-American Schools by her former student.

Everyone agrees that parochial schools played a very important role in Franco-American history. Thus, this educational system was always, to borrow an expression from Josaphat Benoit, "one of the pillars of our ethnic group."[1] It is surprising then to see how little research has been done on these institutions as a whole. What I shall endeavor to do here is to provide a broad outline of the history of Franco-American parochial schools and show also the close connection that exists between what happened in the case of Franco-Americans and what was occurring at the same time in a general way in Catholic primary education in the United States.

Two basic facts emerge from any study, however superficial, of Franco-American parochial schools:

1. In an overwhelming majority of cases, the teaching responsibilities were entrusted to religious congregations of women. In the beginning, and for a long time afterward, it was considered wise to separate boys from girls and the ideal was to have a boys school operated by brothers and a girls school under the direction of sisters. This is what was accomplished in a few large parishes, for example, in Fall River, Lawrence, Lowell, Massachusetts; Manchester, New Hampshire; Waterville, Maine; Central Falls and Woonsocket, Rhode Island. However, the small

---

[1]   Josaphat T. Benoit, *L'âme franco-américaine* (Montreal: Éditions Albert Lévesque, 1935), p. 74. In the present study, parochial school means primary school: Franco-American secondary schools were not considered here.

number of congregations of men associated with these schools as opposed to the congregations of women, shows that in most cases parishes proceeded otherwise due to circumstances beyond their control.

Most French-Canadian emigrants to New England had not known this kind of school. Until World War II and even, in a great number of places, until the establishment of the Ministry of Education in 1964, children in the rural areas of Quebec attended *écoles de rang*, or one-room schoolhouses, that were almost always under the supervision of lay female schoolteachers.[2] Academies or convents, that is, boarding schools for girls administered by nuns, were attended by a small minority.[3]

It is worth noting that what has generally been called, since Father Édouard Hamon in 1891,[4] the earliest Franco-American parochial school, namely the Rutland Academy in Vermont, was a boarding school for girls. It is widely claimed that this school, which bore the lovely name Our Lady of Vermont, was founded in 1869; in fact, the Sisters of the Holy Names of Jesus and Mary only arrived in Rutland in January 1870.[5] It is true that this academy affiliated itself with Sacred Heart of Mary Parish but it is also a fact that the pastors who succeeded one another rapidly in this parish did very little to minister to the sisters' needs.[6]

A goodly number of the early convents established in Franco-American communities, for example, those of the Sisters of the Holy Cross in Nashua, New Hampshire, New Bedford, Massachusetts, North Grosvenordale, Connecticut and Rochester,

---

2   Jacques Dorion, *Les Écoles de rang au Québec* (Montreal: Éditions de l'Homme, 1979), p. 309.

3   Horace Miner, *St. Denis: A French-Canadian Parish*, 1939; rpt. (Chicago: University of Chicago Press, 1963), p. 83.

4   Edouard Hamon, S.J., *Les Canadiens-Français de la Nouvelle-Angleterre* (Quebec City: N.S. Hardy, 1891), p. 206.

5   Hélène Chaput, S.N.J.M., *Histoire de la Congrégation des Sœurs des SS.NN. de Jésus et de Marie: Mère Marie-du-Rosaire* (St. Boniface, Manitoba: Éditions du Blé, 1982), p. 39.

6   Chaput, pp. 39-44.

New Hampshire,[7] took in boarders or gave music lessons in order to increase somewhat the paltry wages the pastors accorded them.

2. Franco-American parochial schools were staffed by some forty congregations of men and women—there were already more than thirty in 1891[8]—but some of them distinguished themselves by the scope and duration of their ministry. They include, in alphabetical order:

> Daughters of the Holy Spirit;
> Religious of Jesus and Mary;
> Religious of the Holy Union of the Sacred Hearts;
> Sisters of St. Anne;
> Sisters of St. Chretienne;
> Sisters of St. Joseph;
> Sisters of the Assumption of the Blessed Virgin;
> Sisters of the Holy Cross and the Seven Dolors;
> Sisters of the Presentation of Mary;
> Ursuline Nuns.

On the male side:

> Brothers of Christian Instruction;
> Brothers of the Sacred Heart;
> Marist Brothers.

A Canadian missionary, Father Joseph Quévillon, founded the first Franco-American parish, St. Joseph's at Burlington, in 1851.[9] Responding to an appeal from the Most Reverend Louis de Goësbriand, bishop of Burlington, a small group of Breton missionary priests followed Father Quévillon to Vermont, in 1869. Shortly afterward, other Canadian and French missionaries established contact with numerous immigrant groups who, having assembled, requested permission from their bishops to found ethnic parishes.

Promptly after moving into his rectory, a founding pastor set

---

7   Louise Parent, C.S.C., *A Mosaic to the Glory of God: The History of the Sisters of the Holy Cross and the Seven Dolors in the New England States, 1881-1980*, n.p., n.d., pp. 25, 54-55.

8   Hamon, pp. 467, 468-71.

9   Hamon, pp. 184-88.

about giving an impetus to parish activity. Quite frequently and, almost always in large cities, the pastor considered that he would be derelict in his duty if he did not immediately found a parish school. In the early years, he would sometimes commit schoolchildren to the charge of laypersons.[10] This happened, for instance, at Notre Dame School in Southbridge, Massachusetts, from 1871 to 1879, and at St. Joseph's School of Biddeford, Maine, from 1875 to 1882.[11] As a rule, however, pastors routinely invited members of a religious community to assume all teaching responsibilities.

What prompted a pastor to contact one religious congregation rather than another? At times, it was the bishop of Montreal who suggested that a particular community be approached or it was a fellow priest who imparted this information to the pastor.[12] After Franco-American parishes began to mushroom, the sisters often agreed to help out a neighboring parish temporarily, then eventually managed to staff it on a permanent basis.

The history of Franco-American schools can be divided into two phases. There were many other turning points, but none were so critical as the watershed of the 1960s.[13] A tabulation of the number of schools founded over the years shows rapid growth corresponding more or less to the increase in Franco-American parishes before and after World War I.[14] There were two peaks, the first reached in the 1900s, the second in the 1920s, when more

---

[10]   Gerard J. Brault, *The French-Canadian Heritage in New England* (Hanover, New Hampshire, and London: University Press of New England; and Montreal, Quebec, and Kingston, Ontario: McGill-Queen's University Press, 1986), pp. 73-74.

[11]   Alice Mignault, S.A.S.V., *Vingt ans d'expansion chez les Sœurs de l'Assomption de la Sainte Vierge, 1874-1894* (Nicolet, Quebec: Éditions S.A.S.V., 1985), p. 326; Michael J. Guignard, *La Foi, la langue, la culture: The Franco-Americans of Biddeford, Maine*, n.p., 1982, p. 58.

[12]   Parent, pp. 24, 40.

[13]   Brault, pp. 155, 171-72.

[14]   See the list of Franco-American parishes (with dates) in Paul P. Chassé, "Church," Franco-American Ethnic Heritage Studies Program, Title IX (ESEA) Grant, Worcester, Massachusetts, Assumption College, 1976, Appendix.

than thirty schools were established in each decade.

The Robert-Landry Report provides statistical tables referring to 427 Franco-American parishes and 264 schools—that is, at the primary, secondary, and college levels—in 1949, but it does not name them. [15] Even with a little more than two hundred primary schools—that is my own calculation, at any rate—it appears likely that 1949 was about the time Franco-American parochial schools reached their apogee insofar as numbers are concerned.

But a sea change was in the offing, or rather had already been under way for some time. I shall return below to this crisis, but it should be borne in mind that the growth and the decline in the number of Franco-American schools corresponds exactly to the ebb and flow of Catholic parochial schools in the United States. Let us return for the moment, however, to the early years of these schools.

For a long time, a very great number of Franco-Americans took for gospel truth the *programme patriotique*, or ethnic agenda, spelled out in detail by their priests, doctors, lawyers, and businessmen, and they left no stone unturned in order to remain a distinct group, by retaining their Catholic faith, their French mother tongue, and their traditional way of life. It is clear that this sustained effort lasted until World War II and even, in certain places, somewhat longer. [16]

---

[15]   Adolphe Robert and Thomas M. Landry, O.P., *Notre Vie franco-américaine* (Manchester, N.H.: L'Avenir National, 1949), p. 19. At the 2nd *Congrès de la langue française,* held in Quebec in 1937, two papers on this topic were delivered by Rev. Louis Bachand, O.M.I., of Lowell, Massachusetts and the Rev. Fathers Wilfrid J. Dufault, A.A., and Armand Desautels, A.A., of Assumption College in Worcester, Massachusetts. Rev. Bachand stated in his paper, entitled "L'école paroissiale franco-américaine," that, by 1912, 123 schools had been built and that 57,743 students were enrolled in them. By 1937, the number had risen to 189 schools—66 more than in 1912—and that 89,957 students were enrolled, that is to say 32,214 more than in 1912. Rev. Fathers Wilfrid Dufault and Armand Desautels, for their part, count 197 schools with a total enrollment of 104,074. Of the 197, 16 were in Connecticut, 32 in Maine, 31 in New Hampshire, 20 in Rhode Island, 10 in Vermont, and 88 in Massachusetts.

[16]   Hamon, p. 48; Brault, pp. 65-66, 86-87, 159-60.

Parochial schools were among the most significant achievements of this campaign. It should be underscored that Franco-American leaders, and especially their clergy, succeeded in making the most of certain decisions arrived at by the American hierarchy in the 1880s.[17]

Seeking to put new life into the faith of Catholic immigrants who were reaching these shores by the millions, the American, that is to say the Irish bishops, made an all-out effort to establish a primary school in each parish. The American episcopacy had often called for the establishment of parochial schools, but the Third Baltimore Plenary Council in 1884 marked a new era.

Organized and presided over by Archbishop James Gibbon— he would be named cardinal two years later—this Council conducted a lengthy study of educational issues and reached several decisions in this regard, including a resolution requiring each pastor to establish a parochial school as soon as possible and, in any event, in no more than two years.[18] The reason was that immigrants were often abandoning their religion after arriving in America. It is estimated that between 1840 and 1920, three-fourths of Catholic immigrants lost their faith.[19]

This resolution of the Baltimore Council did not, however, electrify the American pastorate. A quarter of a century after the Council, nearly sixty-five percent of parishes were still without a school.[20] The fact of the matter is that the great rise in parochial

[17]   Robert Rumilly, *Histoire des Franco-Américains* (Montreal: Robert Rumilly [Under the auspices of L'Union Saint-Jean-Baptiste d'Amérique], 1958), p. 113; however, Rumilly, pp. 127-30, following Hamon (pp. 86-87, 121-24, 384-85), writes, above all, of the reaction of the Franco-American leaders at the first Congress of Catholic laymen in the United States held in Baltimore in 1889.

[18]   Martin A. Larson, *When Parochial Schools Close: A Study in Educational Financing* (Washington and New York: Robert B. Luce, 1972), pp. 219, 281.

[19]   Larson, p. 184.

[20]   Ibid.

school enrollments occurred after World War II, between 1946 and 1965.[21]

The American hierarchy urged pastors to establish parochial schools, but they had no intention, in 1884 and later, of fostering various ethnic groups. Quite the contrary. Having themselves been victims of cruel persecutions, they considered that the most effective way of combating nativism was to adopt an assimilationist policy.[22] French Canadians took a different view of the matter. By founding parochial schools in New England, they were, instead, counting on reliving the successful struggle that had enabled them to survive the Conquest of Canada in 1760.

The original idea was to build *citadelles* in New England. Father Hamon, a French Jesuit, but one of the principal spokesmen of the Franco-American elite in 1891, was among the first to use this expression to characterize Franco-American parishes, institutions, and even cities. "They are," he wrote, speaking of boarding school for girls, "after the parish church or, better still, together with the parish church, the *citadelle* that will preserve the faith and the language of the emigrants." He reiterates the same idea a little farther: "The French-Canadian boarding schools for girls will therefore be, with the parish church, the mighty *citadelle* that will preserve the emigrants' faith and language." Father Hamon uses the same metaphor a third time:

> Let us assume, for a moment, that a tyrannical rule suppresses the use of the French language in boarding and parochial schools; Canadians will still have the principal citadel of their nationality: "the parish church," where services are conducted entirely in French. There, at the very least, they will be at home, a tyrant will never dare cross the threshold of this fortress.

Finally, there is a fourth attestation of the same expression in Father Hamon, and this time the quote has relevance to the city where Assumption College is located: "Situated in the center of numerous Canadian parishes in Rhode Island and Massachusetts,

---

[21]   Larson, pp. 184, 285, 288.

[22]   Richard B. Sorrell, "The Sentinelle Affair (1924-1929) and Militant *Survivance*: The Franco-American Experience in Woonsocket, Rhode Island" (Ph.D. dissertation, State University of New York at Buffalo, 1975), pp. 69-70.

Worcester seems destined be one of the strongest *citadelles* of the Canadian cause in New England."23

To place such thinking in its proper context, it is important to understand that some French Canadians of the day secretly hoped that the divided segments of the Canadian nation, that is, *Québécois* and Franco-Americans, would some day be reunited through annexation. This pipe dream persisted for years, it would appear.24

Early on, however, other Franco-American leaders drummed up support for a more balanced agenda. In 1949, the *Comité d'Orientation Franco-Américaine* summed up this doctrine by urging members of the ethnic group "to integrate our French with our Catholic and American life" rather than isolate ourselves.25

At first, there were all sorts of schools. Teachers often set up shop in the basement of a church under construction, as, for example, at St. Aloysius in Nashua in 1883; or in the parish convent, as at Our Lady of Lourdes in Fall River in 1877. Sometimes parishioners constructed a separate building near the church, as at St. Joseph's in Springfield in 1898.26

The most unusual arrangements were perhaps the church-schools.27 Old St. Joachim's in Chicopee Falls, my home town, was that kind of building: a large, three-story, wooden structure erected in 1894. The ground floor was for worship and the second floor was intended for classrooms. These plans fell through, however, and it was only in 1928, after the construction

---

23   Hamon, pp. 106, 108, 118, 249. Cf. Brault, pp. 66 and 214, n. 65.

24   Robert G. LeBlanc, "The Francophone 'Conquest' of New England: Geopolitical Conceptions and Imperial Ambition of French-Canadian Nationalists in the Nineteenth Century," *American Review of Canadian Studies*, 15 (1985), 288-310.

25   Robert and Landry, p. 12.

26   Parent, p. 31; Hamon, p. 316; *Springfield's Ethnic Heritage: The French and French-Canadian Community* (Springfield, Massachusetts: U.S.A. Bicentennial Committee of Springfield, 1976), p. 30.

27   Hamon, pp. 297 (Our Lady of the Holy Rosary in Gardner), 346 (St. Anne's in Woonsocket), 409 (St. Peter's in Lewiston).

of a new church (now called St. George's), a convent, and a new building designed exclusively for instruction that, 35 years after its foundation, my parish had its first school.[28]

I have no intention of dwelling upon the sometimes very humble and often difficult beginnings of the earliest Franco-American parochial schools. It would be unforgiveable for me, however, to gloss over the fact that for thirteen years the sisters at Rutland, like so many others, lived in abject poverty, were obliged to move several times, to put up with the hostile actions of the pastor of the neighboring Irish parish, and to weather several attacks from local newspapers,[29] and that at Notre Dame in Southbridge, in 1891, the Sisters of the Assumption were often forced to use drastic measures to maintain discipline, or even to be heard over the din. The following is an extract from the chronicles of the latter mission:

> It's Friday, which means that we have finished the second week of class . . . The little boys still haven't learned how to hold their books, nor how to open them at the right place; while four or five are busy with their lessons, 45 are playing and fighting, breaking inkwells, making a mess all around them. We've never seen anything like this in all our lives.[30]

What proportion of Franco-Americans sent their children to parochial schools? We do not know, but the percentage seems to have varied from one parish to another. In 1901, a concerned Father Jean-Edmond Marcoux, pastor of Immaculate Conception in Fitchburg, where the school was limping along, enrolling a mere 200 children on average, asked his parishioners from the pulpit:

> Why are you lagging behind where school is concerned? Why aren't you enrolling your children? Why aren't you doing as in

---

[28]   *Jubilé paroissial, Saint-Georges, 1893-1943* (Chicopee Falls, Massachusetts: 1943), pp. 13, 15, 17, 19.

[29]   Chaput, pp. 39-44, 55, n. 10; Patrick T. Hannon, *Immaculate Heart of Mary Parish: A History* (Rutland, Vermont: 1977), pp. 52-56.

[30]   Mignault, p. 330.

St. Joseph's Parish where there are 750 children in school?[31]

According to Peter Haebler, an average of only thirty-five to forty percent of Franco-American children registered at Precious Blood School in Holyoke from 1881 to 1891, but as soon as Our Lady of Perpetual Help School opened its doors in the latter year, school attendance immediately rose to more than fifty percent until 1904. Curiously, when the third Franco-American educational establishment in Holyoke, Immaculate Conception School, was inaugurated in 1904, the percentage of children enrolled remained unchanged.[32] On the other hand, in Woonsocket in 1926, three-fourths of the Franco-American children attended parochial schools.[33]

It is widely felt that the years from 1920 to 1940 were the golden age of Franco-American parochial schools, and this popular perception is accurate. One should not forget, however, that this was also a troubled period. The Sentinelle Affair pitted a large number of Franco-Americans in Rhode Island against their bishop, and the consequence was that two factions of Franco-Americans tore each other to pieces for five years.[34] Then came the Wall Street Crash of 1929 and the Great Depression of the 1930s.[35]

It is a well-known fact that the birth rate in the United States plunged immediately in 1930, which meant that five years later and then, for about ten years, there was a marked drop in the number of parochial and public school enrollments. The sudden rise in births, the famous baby boom, which began after World

---

31   Guillaume J. Morin, La Paroisse de l'Immaculée-Conception de Fitchburg, Massachusetts: Un Cinquantenaire, 1886-1936 (Fitchburg, Massachusetts: Imprimerie de La Liberté, 1936), p. 52.

32   Peter Haebler, "Habitants in Holyoke: The Development of the French-Canadian Community in a Massachusetts City, 1865-1910" (Ph.D. dissertation, University of New Hampshire, 1976), pp. 223-26.

33   Bessie Bloom Wessel, An Ethnic Survey of Woonsocket, Rhode Island (Chicago: University of Chicago Press, 1931), p. 12.

34   Sorrell, "The Sentinelle Affair."

35   Brault, pp. 90-91.

War II and lasted until 1961, filled Franco-American schools to overflowing from 1950 to 1965.[36]

Yet, in the 1960s, at least thirty-eight Franco-American parochial schools shut down and, in the ten years that followed, at least seventy more. In 1986, eighty-five schools remained, including consolidated schools, which means that more than half (56 percent) of Franco-American institutions went out of existence during this twenty-five year period.

Two reasons are generally adduced to explain the closings of these parochial schools: 1) the rise in costs due to inflation in the 1960s and 1970s; and 2) the sudden shortage of nuns. One often neglects to mention also the fall in the birth rate that followed the baby boom whose effect began to be noticed in the schools about 1969.[37]

These three reasons may suffice but there is another, and that is the decline of Catholicism in the United States (and in Quebec) in the 1960s.[38]

The launching of Sputnik in October 1957 had already occasioned heated debate about the quality of education in the United States, when suddenly Vatican II and certain other changes in the mores of contemporary society caused even deeper concern for many American Catholics. A large number found that the parochial school curriculum and ambiance no longer met the requirements of modern life.[39]

It is difficult to compare the case of Franco-Americans with that of other ethnic groups, but I would venture to say that the present-day situation is relatively good. The bilingual program from which so many reaped such great benefits and the instruction received in Canadian history have gone by the board. However, contrary to what is often stated, a few Franco-American

---

[36]   Larson, p. 169.

[37]   Ibid.

[38]   Larson, pp. 184-86. For the decline in church attendance in Quebec, see Henry Milner, *La Réforme scolaire au Québec*, trans. Jean-Pierre Fournier (Montreal: Québec/Amérique, 1984), p. 62.

[39]   Larson, pp. 184-86.

parochial schools still cling to the teaching of French. To be sure, this usually amounts to no more than two, three, or four hours per week—at times only in the last two years—but in a partial survey I conducted in 1986, French was still part of the curriculum in the majority of parochial schools. Teachers rarely, however, discuss at any length the Canadian origins of the group or its Franco-American heritage. I expect that what has been substituted is matter relating to French civilization and culture since the pedagogical material that is most readily available understandably emphasizes France.

In conclusion, I would say that, when all is said and done, the teaching orders who staffed Franco-American parochial schools were entirely successful in New England. Things are no longer the way they used to be, of course, but, when we look back on the magnitude of their century-old achievement and when we take into consideration all the meetings, all the publications, and colloquia that are, in a real sense, the product of the education they dispensed, we have every reason to rejoice and to be proud of what they accomplished.

Translated by the author

[This article first appeared as "L'oeuvre des communautés enseignantes en Nouvelle-Angleterre 1869-1986—les écoles paroissiales franco-américaines" in the French Institute's publication entitled *Les Franco-Américains et leurs institutions scolaires*. It has been reviewed by the author, and up-dated where necessary, for inclusion in this volume.]

Franco-American Parochial Schools

[The list of schools which follows has been up-dated for this publication.—Editor]

*   The school was still in existence in 1995
**   Consolidated schools

Connecticut

*Baltic, Immaculate Conception
    SCMM, 1873-1970; SCMC, 1970-
Bridgeport, St. Anthony
    DHS, 1936-80
Bristol, St. Anne
    SASV, 1918-82
*Danielson, St. James
    CSJ
*Hartford, St. Anne
    1892; DHS, 1911-1987
*Jewett City, St. Mary
    DHS, 1911-1985
*Meriden, St. Laurent
    SASV, 1893-   (Lay teachers now)
*Moosup, All Hallows
    DHS, 1905-1993** (Regional school with Plainfield)
New Haven, St. Louis
    DHS, 1906-75
*North Grosvenordale, St. Joseph
    CSC, 1882-1981; SCMC, 1981-
*Plainfield, St. John
    DHS, 1929-1992** (Regional school with Moosup)
*Putnam, St. Mary
    DHS, 1913-
*Taftville, Sacred Heart
    SCMM, 1887-1970; SCMC, 1970-
*Waterbury, St. Anne
    CND, 1894-1906; DHS, 1906-
Wauregan, Sacred Heart
    DHS, 1905-69
**Willimantic, St. Mary
    SCMM, 1907-71; SCMC, 1971- (**1968)

Maine

Auburn, St. Louis
   PFM, 1904-70
*Augusta, St. Augustine
   OSU, 1982-1902; PM, 1904-
*Biddeford, St. Joseph
   SCIM, 1882- ; FIC, 1929-70** (St. James Regional school)
*Biddeford, St. André
   SCIM, 1901-04; PM, 1904- ; SC, 1930-69
*Brunswick, St. John the Baptist
   1887; OSU, 1915-
Caribou, Holy Rosary (see also North Caribou)
   OSU, 1928-45; PM, 1945-73
Chisholm, St. Rose of Lima
   OSU, 1923-45
Daigle, Holy Family
   1916-31
Eagle Lake, St. Mary
   PFM, 1918-?
Fairfield, Immaculate Heart of Mary
   1910; OSU, 1911-34
Fort Kent, St. Louis
   PFM, 1906-75
Grand Isle, St. Gerard
   SCIM, 1933-83 (S.A.D. 24, 1965-83)
Hamlin, St. Joseph
   SCIM, 1944-65 (S.A.D. 24, 1965)
Jackman, St. Anthony
   1914; CSJ, 1920-65
*Lewiston, SS. Peter and Paul (originally St. Peter)
   SCSH, 1878-92; FMS, 1886-93; NDS, 1892-1904; OP,
   1923-   (Lay teachers)
Lewiston, St. Mary
   OSU, 1916-68
Lewiston, Holy Family
   CSJ, 1926-71
*Lewiston, Holy Cross
   PM, 1927-
Lille, Notre Dame
   DW, 1905-62
Lisbon, St. Anne
   PM, 1931-74
Madawaska, St. Thomas Aquinas
   DW, 1930-67

Mexico, St. Theresa
    SSCh, 1926-72; PM, 1975-
North Caribou (North Lyndon), Sacred Heart
    SCIM, 1944-58 (Public school); 1946-63 (Sacred Heart
    School)
Old Town, St. Joseph
    SCIM, 1938-69
*Rumford, St. Athanasius and St. John
    1912; SSCh, 1914-   (Lay teachers)
*Sabattus, Our Lady of the Rosary
    OP, 1929-
*Saco, Notre Dame
    PM, 1929-
St. Agatha, St. Agatha
    DW, 1904-66
**Sanford, Holy Family
    OSU, 1922-72
**Sanford, St. Ignatius
    1895; RSMN, 1904; OSU, 1919-72; FIC, 1940-63
Skowhegan, Notre Dame
    1897, Ursuline Nuns (from France); 1902, Franciscan
    Sisters; OSU, 1913-54
South Berwick, St. Michael
    1909 (St. Rose's School); CSJ, 1920-66 (St. Michael's
    School)
**Springvale, Notre Dame
    OSU, 1919-56; SSA, 1956-67; PM, 1967-73
Van Buren, St. Bruno
    SCIM, 1891-1965 (Sacred Heart School; 1965-76, S.A.D.
    24); 1919-65 (Champlain School)
Van Buren (Keegan), St. Remy
    SCIM, 1906-76
Wallagrass, St. Joseph
    PFM, 1898-1965
Waterville, St. Francis de Sales
    OSU, 1888-1969; FIC, 1928-57
Waterville, Notre Dame
    Ursuline Nuns (from France), 1911-20; OSU, 1920-69;
    FIC, 1938-61
Waterville, Sacred Heart
    1953; OSU, 1954-69
Westbrook, St. Hyacinth
    PM, 1894-1974
*Winslow, St. John the Baptist
    OSU, 1937-59; CSJ, 1959-   (Lay teachers)

Massachusetts

*Acushnet, St. Francis Xavier
    OP, 1925-
Adams, Notre Dame
    CSC, 1899-1977
Agawam (Mittineague), St. Theresa (originally St. William)
    DHS, 1905-21
Amesbury, Sacred Heart
    1903; SSCh, 1904-76
Attleboro, St. Joseph
    RCE, 1909-13; CSC, 1913-72
Beverly, St. Alphonse
    SSA, 1927-1928
*Brockton, Sacred Heart
    SASV, 1902-
Cambridge, Our Lady of Pity
    1898; SUSC, 1901-73
*Chelsea, Our Lady of the Assumption
    SUSC, 1912-
*Chicopee, Assumption
    DHS, 1903-1993 (Lay teachers)
Chicopee (Aldenville), St. Rose of Lima
    PM, 1914- (St. Joan of Arc School)
*Chicopee (Willimansett), Nativity of the Blessed
    Virgin Mary
    PM, 1922-74 (Lay personnel since 1974)
*Chicopee (Chicopee Falls), St. George
    SASV, 1928-1995** [Consolidated with St. Joan of Arc
    School, Aldenville]
Dracut, St. Theresa
    SASV, 1954-78
East Blackstone, St. Theresa
    PM, 1929-74
**Easthampton, Our Lady of Good Counsel
    SSA, 1908-81
Everett, St. Joseph
    SASV, 1927-68
Fairhaven, Sacred Heart
    SHJM, 1908-68
*Fall River, St. Anne
    CSC, 1883-95; FSC, 1895-1930; OP, 1895-
Fall River, St. Matthew
    1885; SCQ, 1896-1905; CSJ, 1905-73

Fall River, Blessed Sacrament
      OP, 1891-93; SCQ, 1897-1905; CSJ, 1905-71
      (originally St. Dominic's School)
*Fall River, St. John the Baptist
      1898; CSJ, 1903-
Fall River, St. Roch
      CSJ, 1903-71
*Fitchburg, St. Joseph
      1890; FCJ, 1894-1982
Fitchburg, Immaculate Conception
      CSC, 1895-1902; FCJ, 1902-08; DHS, 1908-70
Fitchburg, St. Francis of Assisi
      DHS, 1904-76
*Gardner, Our Lady of the Holy Rosary
      PM, 1903-
Gilbertville, St. Aloysius
      SSA, 1895-1908
*Haverhill, St. Joseph
      SCO, 1888- ; FSC, 1894-1902; FMS, 1904-47
Holyoke, Precious Blood
      SCSH, 1881-87; SSA, 1888-1971
Holyoke, Our Lady of Perpetual Help
      PM, 1891-1979
Holyoke, Immaculate Conception
      PM, 1907-71
Hudson, Christ the King
      SSA, 1928-33
Indian Orchard. See Springfield
Ipswich, St. Stanislaus
      1910; SSCh, 1925-77
Lawrence, St. Anne
      SCIM, 1886- ; FMS, 1892-1950
*Lawrence, Sacred Heart
      1899; SUSC, 1905-
Leominster, St. Cecilia
      DHS, 1903-77
Linwood, Good Shepherd
      PM, 1921-72
*Lowell, St. John the Baptist (originally St. Joseph)
      SCO, 1883-1980; FMS, 1892-1968
Lowell, St. Mary
      1906; SASV, 1944-61
*Lowell, St. Louis de France
      SASV, 1907-

Lowell, Our Lady of Lourdes
    SCO, 1908-75
*Lowell, St. Joan of Arc
    SCO, 1929- ; FMS, 1936-46
*Ludlow, St. John the Baptist
    1913-18; SSA, 1925-
Lynn, St. John the Baptist
    SSA, 1900-78
Manchaug, St. Anne
    DHS, 1906-24
Marlboro, St. Mary (originally St. Anthony School)
    SSA, 1887-1970
Methuen, St. Theresa
    SCIM, 1926-71 (originally St. John the Baptist School)
*Millbury, Our Lady of the Assumption
    SASV, 1925-
Mittineague. See Agawam
New Bedford, Sacred Heart
    CSC, 1886-1972
New Bedford, St. Hyacinth
    CSC, 1892-1967
*New Bedford, St. Anthony of Padua
    CSC, 1896-
New Bedford, St. Anne
    1905; CSC, 1911-75 (Catholic Alternate
    School, 1972-75)
New Bedford, Our Lady of the Holy Rosary
    CSC, 1908-62
* New Bedford, St. Joseph
    CSJ, 1913-84
New Bedford, St. Theresa
    CSJ, 1927-73
Newburyport, St. Aloysius
    SSCh, 1907-22; IJA, 1920-65
Newton, St. John the Evangelist
    SSA, 1925-79
North Adams, Holy Family
    SSA, 1927-66
North Adams, Notre Dame
    SSA, 1890-1969
Northampton, Sacred Heart
    1886; CSJ, 1891-1930; PM, 1930-68
**North Attleboro, Sacred Heart
    SUSC, 1923 (**1972)

**Northbridge, St. Peter
    SASV, 1928-72
**Pittsfield, Notre Dame
    DHS, 1937-71 (**1971-76, 1978-1992)
    (Now a regional school)
Salem, St. Anne
    1890; SSCh, 1907-76
*Salem, St. Joseph
    SGM, 1893-1903; SSCh, 1903-25; SASV, 1925-
Shirley, St. Anthony of Padua
    SSCh, 1907-21; IJA, 1921-48; SUSC, 1948-69
Southbridge, Notre Dame
    SSA, 1881-89; SASV, 1891-1972
Southbridge, Sacred Heart
    SASV, 1910-67; 1971-75
Spencer, St. Mary
    SASV, 1892-1973
**Springfield, St. Joseph
    CSJ, 1884-98; CSC, 1898- (**1977)
Springfield (Indian Orchard), St. Aloysius
    SASV, 1895-1972
**Springfield, St. Thomas Aquinas
    CSC, 1919-77 (**1977)
Swansea, St. Louis de France
    CSJ, 1931-71
Swansea (Ocean Grove), St. Michael
    CSJ, 1931-75
Taunton, St. James
    SUSC, 1908-78
Three Rivers, St. Anne
    PM, 1901-71
Turners Falls, St. Anne
    SSA, 1896-1968
Waltham, St. Joseph
    1895; FJ, 1903-10; RCE, 1910-70
Ware, Our Lady of Mount Carmel
    SSA, 1889-1969
*Webster, Sacred Heart
    SSA, 1885-
*Westport, St. George
    CSC, 1956-
West Warren, St. Thomas Aquinas
    DHS, 1904-69
Worcester, Notre Dame des Canadiens (Holy Family School)
    SSA, 1881-1957

Worcester, Holy Name of Jesus
    SSA, 1883-1977
Worcester, St. Joseph
    1886; SSA, 1893-1969
Worcester, St. Anthony
    SSA, 1906-51

New Hampshire

Berlin, St. Anne
    PM, 1889-1973 (St. Regis Academy; (**1971-73)
Berlin, Guardian Angel
    PM, 1918-81 (**1971-81)
Cascade, St. Benedict
    1926; PM, 1928-69
*Claremont, St. Mary
    RJM, 1890-96; RSM, 1896-   ; PM, 1991-1995
Concord, Sacred Heart
    PM, 1903-67
Dover, St. Charles Borromeo
    PM, 1903-73 (**1973-78)
Epping, St. Joseph
    1906-17
Gonic, St. Leo
    CSC, 1921-71
Greenville, Sacred Heart
    SASV, 1905-69
Hooksett, Holy Rosary
    1891; CSC, 1903-04
Hudson, St. John the Evangelist
    PM, 1957-75
Laconia, Sacred Heart
    SASV, 1906-73
Lebanon, Sacred Heart
    RSM, 1913-71
Manchester, St. Augustine
    RJM, 1881-1936; SC, 1889-1936; CSC, 1936-74
**Manchester, St. Mary
    SCSH, 1885-95; FMS, 1890-1941; PM, 1895-
    (Guardian Angels, St. Mary, Hévey Schools)
Manchester, St. George
    CSC, 1899-1970
**Manchester, St. Anthony of Padua
    1900; CSC, 1904- (**1970)

Manchester, Sacred Heart
    PM, 1912-73
Manchester (Pinardville), St. Edmund
    PM, 1912-73
Manchester, St. John the Baptist
    PM, 1916-74 (**1973-74)
Manchester, St. Theresa
    RJM, 1927-36; CSC, 1936-74 (**1972-74)
**Nashua, St. Aloysius
    CSC, 1883- (**1977); SC, 1891-1965
Nashua, St. Francis Xavier
    CSC, 1886-1973
**Nashua, Holy Infant Jesus
    1910; CSC, 1914- (**1977; first four years since 1973);
    PM, 1993-
Newmarket, Saint Marie
    CSC,
**Rochester, Holy Rosary
    1888; CSC, 1893- (**1974)
Rollinsford (Salmon Falls), St. Mary
    CSJ, 1926-40; CSC, 1940-67 (St. Joseph's School)
Somersworth, St. Martin of Tours
    1888; CSC, 1902-75
Suncook, St. John the Baptist
    1886; CSC, 1888-1974
*West Stewartstown (Beecher Falls, Vermont), St. Albert
    PM, 1927-

Rhode Island

Albion, St. Ambrose
    PM, 1930-68
**Central Falls, Notre Dame (Our Lady of the Sacred Heart)
    SSA, 1892-1977
**Central Falls, St. Matthew
    SSA, 1908-1995 [Now a regional school renamed Saint
    Elizabeth Ann Seton Academy]
*Coventry (Anthony), St. Vincent de Paul
    PM, 1933-1993
Manville, St. James
    SSA, 1893-1972
Mapleville (Oakland), Our Lady of Good Help
    CDP
Marieville. See North Providence

Nasonville, St. Theresa
    SASV, 1926-67
*Natick (West Warwick), St. Joseph
    CDP, 1923-?   (Lay teachers)
North Providence (Marieville), Presentation of the Blessed
    Virgin Mary
    PM, 1929-73
**Pawtucket, St. John the Baptist
    SUSC, 1896-1972 (**1972)
*Pawtucket, Our Lady of Consolation
    SSA, 1902-05; SSCh, 1905-
Pawtucket, St. Cecilia
    SUSC, 1912-
Providence, St. Charles Borromeo
    RJM, 1887-1972
Providence, Our Lady of Lourdes
    RJM, 1912-68
Warren, St. John the Baptist
    CDP
West Warwick (Arctic), St. John the Baptist
    RJM, 1889-99; PM, 1900 (Mgr. Vincent
    School beginning in 1950)
West Warwick (Arctic), Christ the King
    PM, 1933-73
West Warick (Natick). See Natick
**West Warwick (Phenix), Our Lady of Good Counsel
    PM, 1908- (**1971)
Woonsocket, Precious Blood
    RJM, 1884-1973; SC, 1898-?
Woonsocket, St. Anne
    RJM, 1891-93; PM, 1893-1972
Woonsocket, St. Aloysius
    PM, 1910-70
Woonsocket, Holy Family
    RJM, 1912-72
**Woonsocket, Our Lady of Victories
    PM, 1920 (originally St. Joan of Arc School; **1972)
    Our Lady of Victories Regional School 1984-1994
**Woonsocket (Chapman's Corners), St. Joseph
    PM, 1930- (**1972) Regional School 1972-1994
**Woonsocket, Our Lady Queen of Martyrs
    PM, 1960- (**1972)

Vermont

Alburg, St. Amadeus
*Barton, Conversion of St. Paul
    SASV, 1907-   (Lay teachers)
**Bennington, Sacred Heart
    SSJ, 1892-   (Lay teachers only since 1994)
*Burlington, St. Joseph
    DHM, 1870-1943 (Nazareth School);
    DHS, 1943-85; FCSCJ, 1985-
*Burlington, St. Anthony
    PM, 1931-71
Graniteville, St. Sylvester
    DHS, 1903-67
Island Pond, St. James
    1872; PM, 1886-1969
*Newport, St. Mary Star of the Sea
    FCSCJ, 1905-83
Riverside. See West Stewartstown, New Hampshire
Rutland, Immaculate Heart of Mary (originally Sacred Heart
    of Mary)
    SNJM, 1870-83 (Our Lady of Vermont Academy); SSND,
    1948-69 (Sacred Heart of Mary School)
St. Albans, Guardian Angels
    CSC, 1889-1976
St. Johnsbury, Our Lady of Victories
    SCSH, 1877-79; CND, 1879-1961; FSG, 1890-96,
    1903-28; SP, 1928-?
Swanton, Nativity of the Blessed Virgin Mary
    DHM, 1873-1903; DHS, 1903-75
Vergennes, St. Peter
    CSC, 1886-1907
*Winooski, St. Francis Xavier
    SP, 1878-

Index of Order Abbreviations

Congregations of Women

CDP	Sisters of Divine Providence
CND	Sisters of the Congregation of Notre Dame
CSC	Sisters of the Holy Cross and the Seven Dolors
CSJ	Sisters of St. Joseph
DHM	Daughters of the Heart of Mary
DHS	Daughters of the Holy Spirit
DW	Daughters of Wisdom
FCJ	Society of the Sisters, Faithful Companions of Jesus
FCSCJ	Daughters of the Charity of the Sacred Heart of Jesus
FJ	Daughters of Jesus
IJA	Sisters of the Joan of Arc Institute of Ottawa
NDS	Congregation of Notre Dame de Sion
OP	Roman Congregation of St. Dominic
OSU	Ursuline Nuns (Roman Union)
PFM	Little Franciscan Sisters of Mary
PM	Sisters of the Presentation of Mary
RCE	Religious of Christian Education
RJM	Religious of Jesus and Mary
RSM	Sisters of Mercy
RSR	Congregation of Our Lady of the Holy Rosary
SASV	Sisters of the Assumption of the Blessed Virgin
SCIM	Good Shepherd Sisters (Servants of the Immaculate Heart of Mary)
SCMC	Sisters of Charity of Our Lady, Mother of the Church
SCMM	Sisters of Charity of Our Lady, Mother of Mercy
SCO	Sisters of Charity of Ottawa (Grey Nuns of the Cross)
SCQ	Sisters of Charity of Quebec (Grey Nuns)
SCSH	Sisters of Charity of St. Hyacinthe (Grey Nuns)
SGM	Sisters of Charity (Grey Nuns of Montreal)
SHJM	Sisters of the Sacred Hearts of Jesus and Mary
SNJM	Sisters of the Holy Names of Jesus and Mary
SP	Sisters of Providence
SSA	Sisters of St. Anne
SSCh	Sisters of St. Chretienne
SSND	School Sisters of Notre Dame
SUSC	Religious of the Holy Union of the Sacred Hearts

Congregations of Men

FIC	Brothers of Christian Instruction
FMS	Marist Brothers (Little Brothers of Mary)
FSC	Brothers of the Christian Schools
FSG	Brothers of St. Gabriel
SC	Brothers of the Sacred Heart

V

LITERATURE, JOURNALISM, AND FOLKLORE

Toward a History of Franco-American Literature: Some Considerations

Armand Chartier

In memory of Rev. Polyeucte Guissard, A.A.
and Rev. Denys Gonthier, A.A.

To return to the sources of Franco-American literature is to reconnect with a pre-history, with an oral tradition dating back, in some instances, to the Middle Ages. There one finds tales, legends, and songs which passed from Old France to New France when the first colonists arrived in the seventeenth century. Fortunately, much of this folklore has been transmitted from mother to daughter and from father to son, with the result that some of it remains alive in the towns and villages of New England. This is a pre-literary heritage, which everything incites us to collect, for otherwise it is at high risk of disappearing with us.

To this oral culture, was added, in the nineteenth century, a journalistic tradition marked from the very start by controversy, polemics, and patriotism. Franco-American journalism had promising beginnings to which the Alexandre Bélisles, the Wilfrid Beaulieus, the Antoine Cléments, the Philippe-Armand Lajoies, among so many others, provided fitting continuity.

Given the impossibility of speaking of literary generations in the strict sense (since they do not exist) and also hoping to avoid the monotony which a simple enumeration would entail, I propose, for the twenty or so poets worthy of retaining our attention, a grouping based upon the prevalence in their work of lyric, didactic, or "ethnic" elements. These, of course, are not mutually exclusive, there is some overlapping, but, in most cases, one element does dominate over the others.

The first three collections, in chronological order, can be situated in the wake of the first wave of French Romanticism, that of Lamartine. For the same current circulates throughout *Fleurs du printemps* by Anna-Marie Duval-Thibault (1892), *Voix étranges* by Joseph-Hormidas Roy (1908) and *Au fil de la vie* by Joseph-Amédée Girouard (1909), a current made up of nostalgia, desolation, and melancholy, of the waking dream maintained as an end it itself. If Franco-Americans can claim these early lyric voices as their own—even though they transmit feelings more universal than ethnic—Louis Dantin presents a different case.

Of Quebec origin, Dantin lived half of his long life in exile in Boston, where, during the 20s and 30s, he succeeded in becoming one of the great literary critics of Quebec. In fact, he managed several careers at once—as a critic, a poet, and even as a humble typographer, since literature rarely provides the writer with the wherewithal to earn a living. In spite of an existence which may seem dreary, Dantin produced a corpus of some five thousand lines. It is personal poetry, full of allusions to a private drama—the loss of faith—and it reveals Dantin's soul, but not that of the Franco-American people. This is true, moreover, of all the poets that one can categorize as "lyric." Each speaks in his or her own name only, and rarely does the word "Franco-American" appear in their writings. One may wonder to what extent one can consider as "Franco-Americans" poets who nowhere express their sense of belonging to the ethnic group, any more than they describe an aspect, however minute, of this group. The question is particularly thorny in the case of Dantin who did not live in a Franco-American center, and whose (known) contacts with Franco-Americans were restricted to a limited number of writers.

The problem of belonging is less complex in the case of Henri d'Arles, to the extent that he participated in Franco-American life through several organizations, including the newspaper *L'Avenir national* of Manchester, the Société historique franco-américaine, the Association Canado-Américaine, to name but a few. Poet though he was, he expressed his lyricism for the most part in prose, that was in no way prosaic, since he was a master of elegance and refinement, in addition to being a consummate word painter of landscapes. But, like any lyric poet, he wrote mainly about himself, paying scant attention to the dreams, the aspirations, the memories, the impulses of the Franco-American collective soul.

As for Georges Boucher, he is most definitely Franco-American, if only because of his nostalgia for Quebec, his soul's homeland. His poetry is permeated with memories of a happy boyhood spent in Quebec and melancholy reminders focused on his native village; one also finds in it explicit allusions to "the race"—that of French Canadians in North America. In my opinion, he surpassed himself in his *"Ode à Québec,"* a moving tribute to the ancestral homeland where he chose to be buried, according to an *"Ultime volonté"* which touches us still. It is because he defines himself thus, in terms of this absent homeland, and because he is conscious of being a Franco-American that we can consider Georges Boucher as truly a Franco-American writer.

Rosaire Dion-Lévesque, who has been called the "national poet" of Franco-Americans, was Franco-American, first of all by his Catholicism. *Oasis*, his first important collection, is in great part a poetry of stained glass windows, solitary churches, and tributes to the Virgin Mary. Quite different is *Vita* with its tribute to Walt Whitman, whom he dares to call his "new Christ." What merits our attention here is the sight of a Franco-American "appropriating" an Anglo-American author, to the point of making him the model for his thinking—a new phenomenon in this literature. That Whitman influenced the poetry of Dion-Lévesque, is clearly indicated by the numerous pieces on sensual love; that *Leaves of Grass* profoundly affected Dion-Lévesque can scarcely be doubted, since he translated what he considered to be its "most beautiful pages." He was also Franco-American by his deliberate decision to sing of *his* town, *his* woods, *his* river, all of them undeniably situated in the New England Franco-Americans call home.

Closer to us in time, poets such as Rodolphe-Louis Hébert or Paul-P. Chassé are not Franco-American poets in quite the same manner as their predecessors. They are Franco-American especially perhaps by the preponderant influence that certain French poets have had on them. Of Hébert, let us recall "*Soir d'automne à Salem*" and "*Vitrail IX,*" that sumptuous evocation of a stained glass window which itself evokes that tragic pair, John the Baptist and Salome. The density of these poems, their hermeticism, as well as their solemnity of tone, are reminiscent of Mallarmé. Elsewhere, it is his native Rhode Island that he celebrates, in "*Reverdie pawtuxetoise,*" or again Quebec, the Old Capital, in a beautiful poem titled "*Rue des Remparts,*" which in some measure reminds us of Monet.

As for Paul Chassé, the play of literary influence alone, in his poetic work, could justify our designating him a Franco-American poet. There is, indeed, in the work of Hébert and Chassé, an exceptional attraction for the French poets, exactly as though the reading of these masters—going as far back as Villon—awakened in the very depths of their soul, a very acute awareness of an ethnic affinity,—an affinity of race and blood. In spite of these influences, one can recognize in the two collections of Paul Chassé's verse, a personal voice, especially in poems like the long lament on the assassination of President Kennedy. The very fact of reacting in French to a national American tragedy constitutes precisely yet another aspect by which one can classify as Franco-American this poet whose numerous prose writings also give strong evidence of an ethnic consciousness.

The poetry of Normand Dubé is one of spontaneity and abundance which flows easily. The poet sings of nature in its most diverse manifestations, he sings of love, but he also sings of the child and the couple, to which he grants a special significance. Someone will someday enumerate the various characters which populate his work, to give it an in-depth, nuanced interpretation and will surely not fail to point out, among others, the figure of an immigrant widow in 1854; of Théophile, the old Acadian storyteller, at once wise and comical; and of an Eskimo who speaks of himself with an eloquent reserve.

Much poorer, in Franco-American poetry, is the *didactic* vein. It does not seem to date back beyond Rémi Tremblay, but here again, it is impossible to be sure of this before having thoroughly examined all Franco-American newspapers. Of Tremblay's works, we will single out especially "*Le chant de l'ouvrier*," which denounces the exploitation of workers, and the "*Lettre d'un abonné*," which gives a dressing-down to all those troublesome individuals who, with their excessive demands, waste the time of the Franco-American newspaper editor.

Known as the defender of our cultural heritage, Rev. Louis A. Nolin has left us several plainly moralizing poems, such as "*Le désenchantement*," "*Sous les cyprès*," and "*Fugitives années*," all of which carry the most austere of messages, which can be summed up thus: pleasure, ambition, loathing, regret, all is vanity, except eternal life; moreover, this present life has no other goal than to prepare us for the afterlife; one must see beyond the illusory attractions of existence to seize what is essential. In the same way, Father Aristide D. M. Magnan also had concerns which went beyond the framework of Franco-America, since he scoffs at the arrogance and the fanciful visions of President Wilson, or the stupidity, in his opinion, of the gullible people who accept Darwinism. Finally, for memory's sake, Doctor Philippe Sainte-Marie should be mentioned, if only for his poem "*Le Franco-Américain d'origine, son nom, sa langue*," in which he denounces the apostates and the renegades, that is to say the dupes who give in to assimilation by anglicizing their names.

By *"ethnic"* poets, I mean those whose principal subject matter consists in bringing to life one or another aspect of the Franco-American experience; this can take the form of a moment in our history or a reflection on the Franco-American experience. Here are some examples: *"Premier anniversaire,"* by Charles-Roger Daoust, recalls the heroic feat of arms of Georges Charrette (of Lowell, Mass.) during the Spanish-American War. *"La Sentinelle"* —by the same author—expresses wishes for the success of the new newspaper of the same name. *"Les Silhouettes,"* by Joseph Lussier, evokes Franco-American journalists in a good-natured spirit of solidarity and friendship. It is hard to see how one could classify this type of poetry, if not in a genre by itself, which one might call "ethnic," since there is in all of these cases an element of complicity, a sense of belonging to a group, which the expression "occasional poetry" does not encompass. And it would be tempting to place in this category poems like those of Joseph Thériault which recount, in French, several pages of the history of New England, or those which describe, also in French, various geographical aspects of New Hampshire. Such an original way of capturing and expressing the surrounding reality justifies, it seems to me, the creation of a special category in some future history of Franco-American literature.

As for fiction, it seems opportune to classify the works according to traditional categories, that is: the novel of manners, the historical novel, the novel of ideas, the autobiographical novel. The first, chronologically, is *Jeanne la fileuse*, by Honoré Beaugrand which contains elements proper to the historical novel, but deals more with manners; with manners and with the *défense et illustration* of the life of French-Canadian immigrants. The work of Beaugrand is easy to tear apart on literary grounds, but critics have not sufficiently stressed the distinctive features that make it a precious contribution to Franco-American literature. Rare, for example, are Franco-American works so well anchored in the history and folklore of Quebec. Thus, Beaugrand evokes a family conflict which dates back to the "Troubles of 1837-38"; in other words, four decades after the Insurrection, animosity persisted, according to whether one had been for or against the activity of the *Patriotes*. Here, as elsewhere, the author makes room for tales and legends, one of which is *"Le fantôme de l'avare"*; he also takes us through the fabled *pays d'en haut* around 1825 and includes the words of the folk song, *"Canot d'écorce qui va voler.*" Judged from this perspective, the historical or anthropological interest alone would justify a re-evaluation of *Jeanne la fileuse.*

Les deux testaments, by Anna-Marie Duval-Thibault, is considerably less appealing, for the work has too many features of the serialized novel. And yet it contains the only known evocation of the "Little Canada," of New York City. More successful, with regard to the description of immigrant customs, *Canuck,* by Camille Lessard, gives a good idea of the problems experienced after leaving a beloved country for the unknown, the difficulty of moving from a rural life to an existence in an urban and industrial setting, as well as the unforeseen cultural conflicts which can arise.

All this subject matter is taken up again, with many variations, by Jacques Ducharme in *The Delusson Family,* one of the first Franco-American novels in the English language. This work makes us realize, once again, the importance of the parish in the lives of the immigrants, but also the importance of material progress. Drawing on local history, Jacques Ducharme makes the reader relive the first decades of immigration. His novel merits consideration for that reason alone, as well as for its insights into the Franco-American soul as, for example, the difficulty experienced by Holyoke Franco-Americans in getting along with one another and in uniting in a common effort,—a difficulty which is one of the principal reasons for the group's ethnic disintegration and which the novelist rightly attributes to French individualism.

However little his reading public realized it, Jack Kerouac too has expressed a fragment of Franco-American reality, but seen in a rather unflattering light. For some time now, because of a rather unforeseen swinging of the pendulum, people have been priding themselves on the "Franco-Americanism" of Kerouac, concerning themselves little about the image of our universe projected in his work. Seen thus, he will remain a "case" not easy to come to terms with; for if, on the one hand, one readily applauds his successes, the (re-) reading of works like *The Town and the City, Dr. Sax* or *Visions of Gerard* remains painful, depressing, sometimes heartbreaking. One cannot help thinking that we deserve better, that it is necessary, in order to express *all* of Franco-American life, to get beyond this *misérabilisme,* and one wonders (in vain, of course) whether a Jack Kerouac integrated within the ethnic community would have been willing to tell its story in other than a maudlin and nightmarish fashion.

Grace Metalious, in *No Adam in Eden*, makes us penetrate into an even deeper darkness wherein all Franco-American traditional values find themselves subverted, to the point of becoming unrecognizable. Hence, there are grounds for deploring once again that a well-known author has projected such a vexatious image of Franco-Americans.

The atmosphere is decidedly different in the works of Gérard Robichaud, who has given us *Papa Martel* and *The Apple of his Eye*. Both novels, especially the first, deserve to be designated as novels of "integration." The characters of Louis and Cécile Martel, for example, succeed in uniting different values—a French and Catholic heritage with adaptation to a new country, to a new socio-cultural milieu. In brief, they live fully and deeply the philosophy of acculturation such as Rev. Thomas M. Landry, O.P. would later formulate it. In addition to this, the Martels have the rare merit of applying their French critical sense to their religious life, so much so that, for once, Jansenism, one of our national scourges, is held in check. In fact, it would require much more space to account fully for this extraordinary little novel. Finally, what touches us perhaps most here, beyond the perfect bilingualism and biculturalism of the characters, is the grace, the harmony, the joy of living of this family, an uncommon phenomenon in Franco-American literature, and all the more precious for it.

David Plante has given us, in *The Family*, a Franco-American novel in which one may well discern Kerouac's influence, for in both there is the same gloomy, even lugubrious atmosphere. Although confined to the Little Canada of Providence, Rhode Island, this family is not even "ghettoized," it is curled up on itself to the point of suffocation.

Unfortunately, the harvest is rather meager when it comes to the *historical* novel: *Un revenant*, by Rémi Tremblay, is partly spoiled by its melodramatic aspects, but more successful in its evocation of the American Civil War. *Bélanger*, by Georges Crépeau, using local history, recounts a crime of passion; but it has not been emphasized that Georges Crépeau, unknown though he may be, demonstrates a profound knowledge of the mentality of Franco-Americans, of their most plausible reactions, of the rhythm of their speech; thus, it is an undervalued novel, and one which needs to be reconsidered. *Mirbah*, by Emma Port-Joli, describes the beginnings of the Franco-American colony of Holyoke (Mass.) and especially the tragic fire that destroyed the Church of the Precious Blood in 1875. Here, as in *Un revenant*, melodrama reduces the readership that the work might otherwise have had. The same judgment applies to *Under Canadian Skies*, by Joseph Choquet; as it is, since he deals with the "Troubles of 1837," the author deserves to be rescued from oblivion.

In this category of the historical novel, however, the truly unknown little masterpiece is certainly *La Fille du Roy*, by Gabriel Nadeau. Inspired by the history of New France, this "humorous tale" relates the adventures of a certain François Barnabé, *dit* Barnabé, who refuses to marry the King's ward for whom he is destined, for the excellent reason that she is unimaginably ugly. The hilarious results of this refusal are narrated with verve, in a wonderfully archaic language.

The works that one can call *propaganda* novels are even less numerous; as a matter of fact, only three have surfaced to date, beginning with *La jeune Franco-Américaine*, by Alberte Gastonguay. To place it in this category is simply to recognize that this work conveys the ideology current during the Franco-American golden age of the 1930s. It is the story of Jeanne Lacombe, supremely faithful to her cultural heritage, too clever in surmounting obstacles, virtuous to an unrealistic degree; she would have been a worthy heiress of her people, if only the author had been able to breathe a little life into her.

More convincing, in some respects, is the thesis that Adélard Lambert defends in *L'innocente victime*. More convincing for certain readers that is, but, in a general sense, less "popular." It deals with the superiority of Quebec over the United States, not such a laughable idea as that may seem, since Lambert places above the din and the materialism of the United States, the glorious ancestral past and the serenity of the Quebec countryside. Let us add, for a better understanding of his novel, his fear of seeing French heritage crushed by the American steam-roller and his conviction that the demographic bloodletting from Quebec southward [i.e. to the United States] had to come to an end.

Even if Reine Malouin was not a Franco-American, it would be regrettable not to mention her novel *Où chante la vie*, given that it was written with Franco-Americans in mind. At the level of the plot, it is about a young Franco-American who discovers his origins, makes them an object of worship and—unforeseen recompense?—receives as his share a pretty Quebec girl . . . Reine Malouin's great error was to subordinate the plot and the characters to the thesis, stated a hundred times over, from beginning to end, *i.e.* the absolute necessity of resisting assimilation. In spite of the sermonizing, rather irritating in the long run, we must not shelve this novel, for it raises pertinent questions (at least they were so at the time) concerning the interaction between success and ambition, and between self-realization and faithfulness to one's origins. Moreover, this work is a reflection of the ideology of *survivance* which required a quasi-spiritual loyalty to the French-Canadian cultural heritage. It was an ideology advocated by the Franco-American "elites" for more than a century. For this reason alone, the book possesses an unquestionable historic interest.

As for the *autobiographical* novel, the first, chronologically, is by Louis Dantin. *Les enfances de Fanny* narrates, rather faithfully it would seem, the details of his liaison with a black woman during his exile in Boston. On the whole, the scenes of life in the ghetto are more convincing that the rather clumsy evocation of a liaison one has trouble believing, so deep is the cultural gulf between the two lovers. But the work remains precious to the extent that Dantin, as a member of a minority group, gives us a glimpse of the mentality of people who are made to feel inferior, and who are marginalized as he is himself.

There is no other title to place in this subdivision except, of course, the entire novelistic production of Jack Kerouac, which was eventually to form a long autobiographical cycle—a project ended by a premature death.

The *theater*, at least those works which the authors bothered to publish, is assuredly the poorest genre. So poor, that it is difficult to generalize about it. We know that there existed a theatrical activity worthy of interest in the various Franco-American centers, that melodrama was preferred by the audiences, but even these meager assertions will remain poorly documented until we have undertaken a thorough inventory of Franco-American newspapers.

Of the few printed texts, let us cite at least *Reflets de vie conjugale*, by Rev. Louis A. Nolin, which leaves us wondering if the moralizing tendency we find in it is typical of Franco-American theater. However that may be, much as Father Nolin's playlet is simple so, by contrast, does *Un Jacques Cartier errant*, by Grégoire Chabot, seem complex. Not at the level of the plot, but at that of the meanings which can be drawn from it. It is, first of all, a caustic satire of Franco-American society as seen by a "young Franco-American" in 1976. As a matter of fact, the list of grievances drawn up by the author is so long that one can wonder whether the play is not an attempt at scuttling the whole question of *survivance*. But that is simply a false trail since the author insists in several ways on the fact that the Franco-American seeks desperately to endure as a Franco-American. *Un Jacques Cartier errant* is thus a plea for the development of an indigenous culture which would have a soul, and be attractive to the younger generations. It is even, in and of itself, a move in that direction. As such, the play deserves to be reread and pondered.

Before finishing this discussion of the theater, we must point out the historical drama of Guy Dubay, *With Justice for All,* which brings to life the effort of a large Anglo-American firm to evict the Acadian farmers from their land in the Saint John Valley of northern Maine. Were it but the echo of the Acadian Deportation of 1755, this drama would deserve to endure, as a testimonial to a people who do not appear enough in Franco-American literature.

It could seem bizarre, at first glance, to suggest that one should attribute a great deal of importance in a future literary history, to that agreed-upon term, *oratory*. And yet, it is quite probably, of all the literary genres, one of the most abundant; it is especially the one which, of all the genres, has most touched the people, if only through the Sunday homily. Every Franco-American assembly, moreover, favored oratorical jousts, and valued the entry into the lists of orators of regional or national fame. Thus, the "General Conventions," the first of which took place in New York, in 1865, brought together the leaders of the first rank, many of whom had been educated in the "classical" colleges of Quebec. From this education comes the probable influence of Demosthenes, Cicero, and Bossuet. From this also derives the possibility that Franco-American orators had heard the great voices of Quebec: Chauveau, Mercier, Laurier, Bruchési, and Laflèche, among others.

What astonishes us somewhat in rereading these speeches— of which several were fortunately collected by Félix Gatineau in his *Historique des Conventions générales des Canadiens-Français aux États-Unis*—is to see cultural heritage discussed with a gravity, a solemnity normally reserved for sacred subjects. So much so, that the line of demarcation between sacred and profane oratory disappears (or nearly so). It is true that the Catholic religion itself is one of those ethnic values which are sometimes defended with vehemence; but whether the topic is religion, the French language, or the history of Canada, the tone does not change. In part because French had always been the language in which one prayed, and because the past was perceived as a reservoir of examples, of virtually sacred models of conduct suitable for guiding the young.

In the nineteenth century, Ferdinand Gagnon serves as a good illustration of what one could call "ethnic oratory." By turns lecturer, litigant, "professor," he always remained a "patriot," *i.e.*, always anxious to remind his people of their origins and the pride they ought to derive from them. Closer to us in time, Rev. Thomas M. Landry is the embodiment of the Dominican ideal placed at the disposal of "the cause," in this very precise sense that he will have spent his life "transmitting to others the fruits of contemplation," according to the Dominican motto. His life and his writings bear witness to his role as a Franco-American pastor, preoccupied, as he always was, with the spiritual but also with the ethnic well-being of his people.

Before we can truly study the *essay* as a genre, it will be necessary to undertake an inventory of the newspapers, without which any generalization will remain rash and conjectural. It is impossible, for example, to nuance our discussion, impossible to make a comparative study of the different regions of New England. For the time being, we must be content to study the essays published in book form, assuming them to be representative of several hundred others buried in newspapers. And yet, it would be difficult to overestimate the importance of the essay, of the genre which, above all, lends itself to sustained and searching reflection on ethnic questions, whether they be of a theoretical or practical nature.

We know, nonetheless, of a good number of essays which have served the ideology of *survivance*. They are impregnated with idealism, their authors do not hesitate to distinguish between what is desirable and what is not, and the tone is not always conciliatory. An example of the genre, *Les Franco-Américains peints par eux-mêmes*, gathers together texts by different authors and seems to give a good summary of the salient facts regarding Franco-American society in the 1930s. Some of these essays surely deserve to emerge from the shadows, either for their originality, their vigor, their penetrating thought or for the quality of the writing itself. To be convinced, one has only to reread a text by Elphège Daignault or Philippe-Armand Lajoie. Another excellent collection, grouping sermons, speeches, and essays, is the work of Rev. Thomas M. Landry. In *Mission catholique et française en Nouvelle-Angleterre*, the central question is the integration of the diverse components which make up the collective Franco-American soul. These essays are suffused with a sense of urgency, sometimes even of anguish, for the author is fully conscious of being engaged in a battle which rarely justifies optimism.

To the extent that one would wish to be complete, we would welcome, in our literary history, the writings which arose out of the most resounding of our controversies, the one which people have taken care not to talk about too much until the present time, undoubtedly to avoid shaking the columns of the temple. We refer, of course, to the commotion surrounding "*la Sentinelle.*" To continue to hush it up would be aberrant and unjust, for this ideological quarrel seems destined to remain one of the culminating points in the evolution of the collective mind. Let the historian of ideas refrain from passing judgment if necessary, but let us at least give an account of the two arguments facing each other, by relying on the books and the newspapers they gave birth to, even if each side denounced the other in rather discourteous terms. It is essential also to attempt to specify the influence and contribution of French and French-Canadian thought on the one and the other camp; let this be done at the level of the writings if not that of the individuals.

The project of including *history* in a discussion of Franco-American literature is less paradoxical than it seems, especially if one keeps in mind the particular character of Franco-American historiography. In a word, history as it was practiced by our predecessors was very overtly a combat weapon in the struggle for *survivance*, a way of serving the cause, of accomplishing a patriotic act. In this domain, the determining influence is certainly that of Quebec, land of François-Xavier Garneau and of Lionel Groulx, two intellectual masters to several generations of French Canadians and Franco-Americans.

It is impossible, in such a brief account, to review this abundant historical literature . . . abundant and diverse, since it includes major syntheses (as early as 1891, with the work of Rev. Édouard Hamon), local histories, and especially parish histories.

The latter offer a special interest, since they often include oratorical pieces. We should also point out works like the *Mémorial des Actes de l'Association Canado-Américaine*, by Adolphe Robert, and *La Saint Jean-Baptiste, Manchester, New Hampshire*, by Msgr. Adrien Verrette. That is to say that there exists a fascinating amount of documentation on the Franco-American past which includes the accomplishments of one of the group's great institutions, the *Association Canado-Américaine*, and the history of one of its principal traditions, the group's national holiday.

Even an account which seeks to be as brief as possible—such as the present essay—has to stress the prodigious contribution of Msgr. Verrette, the priest-patriot who never ceased either pleading for the cause or defending it. The historian of today or tomorrow will be grateful to him, in particular, for having been, for forty years, the chronicler of Franco-American life, in publications indispensable to any serious researcher, like the series entitled *La Vie franco-américaine* or the *Bulletin de la Société Historique Franco-Américaine*. It is hard to see how one could, in the future, write Franco-American literary, social or cultural history without taking these basic works into account.

The name Adolphe Robert was mentioned above. His writings, scattered in various newspapers and magazines, would be worth collecting and circulating widely. For the moment, we have to be content with rereading *Souvenirs et portraits*, one of whose great lessons is the capacity of the past to enrich the present. Let us underline the use of the term "enriching" rather than "replacing," for, in spite of the historical richness that one senses in this collection, to accuse it of attachment only to the past would be unjust. Quite the contrary, it involves a life lived in a present and often placed in the service of the future, but enlarged by being conscious of the past. It involves too the full realization of self in, first, a Quebec framework, and then a Franco-American one.

Here now, in a few words, are the generalizations justified by the preceding rapid survey. Franco-American literature in French was conditioned, to a great degree, by a definite ideology, that of *survivance*. It was a fertile ideology, if we judge solely by the number of newspapers which have appeared since the arrival of the first immigrants. It was an ideology which tended to favor the utilitarian text rather than gratuitous aesthetic creation; to favor committed writing, sometimes idealistic, sometimes pragmatic, rather than "artistic" writing. Often, the texts respond to the danger of assimilation, perceived as a threat of collective extinction. The need to stave off these threats of ethnocide result in numerous defenses and celebrations of the group, especially in speeches and essays, sometimes in novels. It is, therefore, a literature based upon events, action, and combat, but also on dreams; it is a literature steeped in ideals.

The texts in English—and often those in French—are the achievement of isolated authors. Each one is forced to create his/her own tradition, for there exists no literary tradition in the ordinary sense of the term. If Kerouac read Beaugrand, he speaks of it nowhere, and one finds no trace of such a reading in his works. Consequently, a significant number of these authors speak for themselves only, not voicing the concerns of the group (from which some of them probably felt alienated), which leaves us without a Balzacian "human comedy," that is without a unifying literary expression. Rare indeed are the authors in whom one can see what Albert Thibaudet caught a glimpse of in Maurice Barrès, namely "a collectivity encountered through the expression of an individual self."

All that has preceded is really only the preface to our true subject: the reconstruction of Franco-American literary history, the questions which must be asked, those to which one must bring at least a provisional response, with this reservation, nevertheless, that the provisional in this field has a good chance of becoming permanent. First and foremost, there are terms to define, aesthetic criteria to specify, and, in all of this, some pitfalls to point out. Moreover, the expression "Franco-American literary history" already contains three terms rich in possible misunderstandings.

As we have indicated at the outset of this article, it is indispensable, in order to be comprehensive, to return to the sources of our literature, that is to say to an oral tradition hundreds of years old. Tales, legends, and songs constitute a pre-literary domain that we ought not to disregard. But if we were absolutely forced to date the beginnings of Franco-American "literature" properly called, thus of our "literary history," it seems to me that 1839, the year of the founding of the *Patriote Canadien* by Ludger Duvernay in Burlington, would be the obvious date.

The word "literary" raises more problems. As early as 1946,

Dr. Gabriel Nadeau wondered about the existence of a Franco-American literature and gave a nuanced answer: "If one understands by literature the artistic expression of thought, one must not try to find any worthy of the name. But literature also means the totality of the writings which give an account of the movement of ideas within a people. For this reason, Franco-Americans certainly do have a literature; this book [*La littérature française de Nouvelle-Angleterre*] demonstrates the fact by making that literature known." (Therriault, p. 9) This assertion seems to me to be still valid today, even taking into account what has appeared since the 1940s. And, Gilles Marcotte (*Anthologie*, I, xi), referring to Quebec's early literature, made similar remarks: "The fact remains that the Quebec literary corpus . . . appeals to other interests, to other sentiments than those of the lover of literature. We cannot exclude the great speeches of an Étienne Parent, a Louis-Joseph Papineau, an Henri Bourassa . . ."

There is, finally, the conception of literary history of Professor Robert E. Spiller, head of the team that has given us the prestigious *Literary History of the United States*: "History as it is written in this book will be a history of literature within the margins of art but crossing them to follow our writers into the actualities of American life. It will be a history of the books of the great and the near-great writers in *a literature which is most revealing when studied as a by-product of American experience.* [1]

If one adds that the Franco-American press has very often taken the form of the newspaper of ideas having a combative approach, one will understand, starting from the establishment of this very fact, starting also from some ideas expressed by our predecessors in the Franco-American, Quebec, and Anglo-American fields, that it is necessary to enlarge our framework. To restrict our literary history to the traditional genres (novel, poetry, theater) would, in the long run, distort reality. That would be no more justifiable than in the case of eighteenth-century French literature.

Thus, could one consider as "literary," any text in which the author commits himself, any text revealing subjectivity and an aesthetic preoccupation; but the text must, at the very least, be subjective. For this reason, and for what they are able to convey of the Franco-American soul, we could claim for our project the chronicles, the travel accounts, the works of propaganda or

---

[1]   p. xxi; the italics are mine.

morality. We would certainly discard them at our peril. Let us therefore exclude, deliberately, only scientific texts . . . taking pains, however, to reread them carefully *before* excluding them.

It remains for us to state precisely what one understands by "Franco-American." Without reviving the old quarrel underlying the definition elaborated by Sister Mary Carmel Therriault, S.M.,[2] without even accepting this definition, there are still grounds for wondering about the exact significance of the term. More precisely, does it cover writers who identify themselves as Franco-Americans of the third and fourth generation, who write in English about subjects which are not explicitly Franco-American? One could cite, for example, Harding Lemay, Paul Théroux, Robert Cormier, and John Dufresne. It is clearly not an easy issue to settle. Especially if one takes into account the rather persuasive arguments formulated by thinkers such as Michael Novak. According to the latter, four or five generations must pass before one has completely immigrated, that is, before one is wholly assimilated. For his part, Irving Howe affirms: "Tradition broken and crippled still displays enormous power over those most ready to shake it off. And tradition seemingly discarded can survive underground for a generation and then, through channels hard to locate, surface in the work of writers who may not even be aware of what is affecting their consciousness."[3] Perhaps a sociologist or a specialist in social psychology could help us discern the Franco-American qualities in the aforementioned authors. Lacking such a transdisciplinary process, the literary historian could, if need be, be content to include authors like these in his work—even if it entails backing up his choice by nothing more than the laudable intention of being complete—even also if it entails displeasing the authors in question, who would derive from it, however, the benefit of unexpected publicity—even, finally, if it entails bringing about a long overdue collaboration between literary critics and sociologists.

Without claiming to have drawn up a complete list of the problems—far from it—but conscious of having pointed out the principal ones, we would like to share some ideas concerning possible, or at the very least desirable, research initiatives. Let us

---

2   "*Nous avons constaté qu'il existe ici trois sortes d'écrivains: a) les Franco-Américains de naissance, b) les Franco-Américains de séjour, c) les Franco-Américains de passage.*" pp. 13-14.

3   *Jewish-American Stories*, p. 13.

stress first the absence of any synthesis since the work of Sister Mary Carmel which appeared in 1946. Doubtless prudence is the reason why Sister Mary Carmel scarcely dealt with polemical writings which already constitutes a first lacuna. In addition, by applying to our novelistic or poetic works solely aesthetic criteria, she cut the discussion short in a rather unfortunate manner. For these reasons, there is work here which needs to be looked at again. There have been, since that time, studies by Professors Paul Chassé and Richard Santerre on poetry and the novel respectively; but, apart from some theses and articles, there is nothing in the area of the history of ideas.

Once can further adduce the statement made by Professor Spiller in the 1940s to justify his own audacious endeavor: "Each generation should produce at least one literary history of the United States, for each generation must define the past in its own terms."[4] Thus, why not consider a new history of our literature? Better yet, why not set for ourselves the goal of passing on to the Franco-Americans of tomorrow a cultural history in which a new literary history would be integrated, a cultural history which would strive to answer these questions: what is the Franco-American soul, what has it been, how has it evolved, how has it manifested itself?

For we have a very faulty knowledge of Franco-American folklore, of our oral tradition, and the popular origins of our literature, that is to say, the first manifestations of the ancestral soul. Sister Mary Carmel Therriault tries to reassure us, claiming that Franco-American folklore is *approximately* Canadian folklore.[5] We do not accept her claim at face value, for we insist that one specify what this "approximately" represents. Along the same lines, we know very little of the popular literature, what people used to read—and still read. We certainly do not know it as well as Victor-Lévy Beaulieu knows his, he who was able to put together a *Manuel de la petite littérature du Québec,*—a possible model, and one not to be overlooked.

Furthermore, we would need to have certain tools at our disposal, such as a "Romancero" like that of Marius Barbeau or even a *Répertoire national* similar to the one James Huston published in Quebec over a century ago. Indeed, it has not been said

---

4   p. xii.

5   p. 199.

enough to what extent a project like Huston's could be of interest to Franco-Americans. Here is how Georges-André Vachon sums up Huston's effort: "Courageously, the compiler of the *Répertoire national* took pains to collect, from the newspapers of the eighteenth and nineteenth centuries, a certain number of works in verse and in prose, whose sole merit was to have been written by Canadians."[6] Even if the *Répertoire* contains many decidedly mediocre pieces, it is quite clear that it can still serve as a model. And even if the examination of the newspapers that such a work presupposes gave only a descriptive inventory of the essays of all types buried in these dusty old collections, threatened with being swallowed up forever in the gulf of time, it would be worth the trouble to undertake it, for with or without dust, we are dealing here with expressions of individual Franco-Americans, and—perhaps—of certain aspects of the collective soul. It is literally a whole section of our cultural property which is in the process of crumbling in these yellowing newspapers. Without this "archaeological" exercise, nothing serious is possible.

Once this enormous work on source documents has been accomplished, the historian, pursuing the research, could settle on the goal of offering the reading public a synthesis which would be, at one and the same time, a descriptive rather than a critical work, a reference tool, exhaustive to the truest extent possible. Once again, a special place would be set aside for historical, polemical, ideological, and oratorical writings without which one would deform Franco-American literary reality to the point of rendering it unrecognizable. In such a work, the prose of ideas would be highlighted as has always been done in the history of French literature.

The importance of properly situating Franco-American literary history in its socio-historic context can never be repeated enough if one does not want to run the risk of falling into abstraction, and to avoid this, one needs to stress the importance of specifying the spiritual atmosphere, the circumstances, the intellectual, personal, and social factors which could have influenced the composition of a work, affected the form or the content; the importance, throughout this effort, of tending toward a history of Franco-American culture that would itself be exhaustive; to attempt to go to "to the heart of things;" to try, in short, to define the Franco-American *ethos*, *ethos* meaning an ensemble of characteristics which distinguishes Franco-

---

6   *Littérature canadienne-française*, p. 272.

Americans from other groups. It would be necessary to go to the very limits of social history, recalling these words of Robert Escarpit: "The outdated borders between science and art having been abolished, we will no longer write the history of literature but something which could be the history of man in society from the point of view of his esthetico-imaginative dialogue with his contemporaries and with posterity."

So much for the essential points. Later—or concurrently, if human resources allow—there would be an entire work to be undertaken on the confluence of circumstances which conditioned this corpus, quite as much on the part of the French as on the part of Quebec. In other words, there is a great need to make up for lost time, there is a pressing need for traditional studies on the sources of Franco-American literature. It is of little importance that this type of study, undertaken with the sole aim of arriving at a better knowledge of ourselves as Franco-Americans, may seem old-fashioned to the avant-garde. We must study the sources, the influences, the antecedents, the affinities, regardless of what people may say.

If we allow ourselves to dream of these questions, we imagine affinities, we perceive, for example, plausible connections with the old French store of knowledge from the Middle Ages. Thus, in thinking about the theme of fidelity and the preponderant place it occupies in our literature, how can we avoid recalling the importance of this theme in epic literature as much as in courtly literature? We are also entitled to ask ourselves to what extent we are heirs of the great French intellectual tradition. Or if our literature bears, more than other ethnic literatures, that imprint of intellectuality which, for centuries, made France the most intellectual nation in Europe? Or again, to what extent is our polemical literature tributary to that of France? to that of Quebec?

On the other hand, it is at the very least strange, that even the themes of Franco-American literature have never been studied to their fullest extent. Yet, there are such obvious themes,—those of alienation and integration (as in Gérard Robichaud's *Papa Martel*) or even what one could call the dialectic of fidelity and assimilation. This type of study could well lead us to examine, in our literature and, by extension, in our collective subconscious, the presence of the country of origin, its conception, as evinced in the writings, and the evolution of this phenomenon. One could also wish that someone might establish a typology of our literary characters.

And, finally, let us wish that authors so unjustly neglected such as Hugo Dubuque, Yvonne Lemaître ("the Cerberus of Franco-American letters," according to the picturesque image of Adolphe Robert), Adélard Lambert and so many others might soon be rehabilitated. Let us especially hope for a greater dissemination of Franco-American literature and a growth in the studies devoted to it. Let us work toward this end, even if only in order not to fail in our duty to our ancestors and to guard against accusations of indifference.

Translated by Gary Crosby Brasor

[A slightly different version of this essay first appeared as "Pour une problématique de l'histoire littéraire franco-américaine" in the French Institute's publication entitled *La situation de la recherche sur les Franco-Américains*. It has been reviewed by the author for inclusion in this volume.]

The Franco-American Press: An Historical Overview

Robert B. Perreault

As its title suggests, this essay will attempt to recount, in general terms, the history of French-language journalism in the United States. What follows is meant to recall the extent of this effort in addition to serving as a reminder of what this institution once was.

Long before the founding and eventual rise of a New England-based Franco-American press, a significant number of French newspapers, some ephemeral, others lasting for many years, were to be found throughout the United States, especially where strong clusters of immigrants from France, Acadia, or Quebec had settled.

In fact, this press dates as far back as the American Revolution. By all indications, the country's first French-language newspaper, *La Gazette française*, appeared during the winter of 1780-1781 and was printed on the presses of the French fleet at Newport, Rhode Island.[1] From the late eighteenth century to the beginning of the nineteenth century, no fewer than ten publications were born, including *Le Courrier de l'Amérique* (1784) in Philadelphia, *Le Courrier de Boston* (1789), *La Gazette française et américaine* (1794-1795) in New York City and, the most successful one of this era, *Le Moniteur de la Louisiane* (1784-1814) in New Orleans.[2] As a matter of fact, between 1794 and 1870, Louisiana gave birth to the greatest number of French-language newspapers, at least sixty, including the daily *L'Abeille* of New Orleans, which lasted for nearly a century from 1827 to 1916.[3] Fifteen or so French

---

[1]   Jacques Habert, "Histoire de la presse française aux Etats-Unis" in the *Bulletin de la Société historique franco-américaine 1966*, new series, vol. 12 (Manchester, N.H.: Imprimerie Ballard Frères, 1967), pp. 127-129.

[2]   Ibid., pp. 129-131; see also Josaphat Benoit, *L'Ame franco-américaine* (Montreal: Éditions Albert Lévesque, 1935), pp. 133-135.

[3]   Alexandre Belisle, *Histoire de la presse franco-américaine* (Worcester: Ateliers de *L'Opinion publique*, 1911), pp. 380-383; André Lafargue, "Le français en Louisiane" in *Deuxième congrès de la langue*

newspapers were published in New York City during the nineteenth century, including the country's oldest, *Le Courrier des Etats-Unis*. Founded in 1828, the newspaper today goes by the name of *France-Amérique*. French residents of California gave that state approximately a dozen newspapers, the only survivor today being *Le Journal français d'Amérique*. Founded in 1852 as *L'Echo du Pacifique*, this newspaper changed titles at least seven times during the 143 years of its existence.[4] In short, the French press made its mark throughout this country, from East to West.

In the region of the Great Lakes, although Father Gabriel Richard wrote an article in French for the *Michigan Essay or Impartial Observer*, a Detroit newspaper that published only a single issue in 1809, the French-language press or, more precisely, the "French-Canadian" press in the United States, did not truly make its debut until 1817 when, for a period of four months, the *Detroit Gazette* published a French-language column by a contributor who wrote under the byline of "Vieux Philippe." It was also in Detroit, in 1825, that an American, Ebeneezer Reed, founded the region's first French-language newspaper, *La Gazette française*, only four issues of which came off the presses. In this same city, Edouard N. Lacroix's two ventures, *L'Ami de la jeunesse* (1843) and *Le Citoyen* (1850), met a similar fate, one after four months, the other after six months. Between 1850 and 1912, the Great Lakes' region served as a breeding ground for about forty French-Canadian or Franco-American newspapers whose numbers were nearly equally divided among the states of Michigan, Illinois, and Minnesota, with only one newspaper appearing in Wisconsin, *La Tribune* of Marinette (1889).[5]

---

française au Canada—Mémoires, vol. 2 (Quebec City: Imprimerie du *Soleil* Limitée, 1938), pp. 119-120.

[4]   With regard to the *Courrier des Etats-Unis*, see Belisle, *op. cit.*, pp. 358-368; information on the *Journal français d'Amérique* comes from two sources: Anonymous, "Centenaire français en Californie" in *La Vie franco-américaine 1950*, published under the auspices of the Comité permanent de la survivance française en Amérique (Manchester, N.H.: Imprimerie Ballard Frères, 1951), pp. 316-317; Interview with Marie Galanti, editor of the *Journal français d'Amérique*.

[5]   Belisle, *op. cit.*, pp. 27-41, 116-126; Maximilienne Tétrault, *Le rôle de la presse dans l'évolution du peuple franco-américain de la Nouvelle-Angleterre* (Marseille: Imprimerie Ferran et Cie, 1935), pp. 15-45, 58-59; "Gabriel Richard" in Rosaire Dion-Lévesque, *Silhouettes franco-américaines*, Publications de l'Association Canado-Américaine (Manchester, N.H.: Imprimerie Ballard Frères, 1957), pp. 764-765.

Despite the ephemeral nature of the majority of these newspapers, it is nevertheless important to mention at least the largest and most interesting ones. In 1857, in Kankakee, Alexandre Grandpré and Claude Petit founded *Le Courrier de l'Illinois*, that state's first French-language newspaper, which they moved to Chicago for a few months, after which they brought it back to Kankakee, where it ceased publication in 1863. In 1875, J.B.A. Paradis resurrected it in Chicago where, in 1903, it became part of a merger of several newspapers, thus creating a new publication, *Le Courrier franco-américain*, which was printed, not in Chicago, but on the presses of *L'Indépendant* in Fall River, Massachusetts. This merger swallowed up another newspaper that had existed for quite some time, *Le Canadien* of St. Paul, Minnesota, founded in 1877 by Désiré A. Michaud. Success appears to have come only to the two newspapers in the region that made their mark in the twentieth rather than in the nineteenth century. The first, *L'Echo de l'Ouest*, founded in 1883 in Minneapolis, Minnesota, by Zéphirin Desmeules, lasted for forty-six years, before folding in 1929 after the death of Augustin Desmeules who had succeeded his father. *Le Courrier du Michigan*, which existed for approximately the same length of time as *L'Echo de l'Ouest*, was, from beginning to end, the product of one individual, Pierre-Eudore Mayrand. Founded in Lake Linden in 1912, and subsequently transferred to Detroit, *Le Courrier du Michigan* became, after 1929, the only French-language newspaper in the region of the Great Lakes. It maintained this distinction until 1959, the year in which its founder died, at the age of eighty-four.[6]

Mention should be made of at least a few of the ephemeral newspapers. *L'Observateur* and *L'Amérique* both appeared in Chicago in 1868. These publications had the distinction of having been founded by the Québécois poet Louis Fréchette who, for political reasons, was at that time living in the United States. Meanwhile *Le Devoir* of Muskegon, Michigan, was founded in 1890 by Elie Vézina who was destined one day to become secretary-general of l'Union Saint-Jean-Baptiste d'Amérique, an important mutual benefit society for Franco-Americans, founded in 1900.

---

[6]   Belisle, *op. cit.*, pp. 27, 30, 46-47, 52-53, 206-207, 216-217; Tétrault, *op. cit.*, p. 11, 16-17, 24, 28-29, 42-43; Anonymous, *Le Courrier du Michigan* —Trentenaire 1912-1942" in *La Vie franco-américaine 1942* (Manchester: *L'Avenir national*, 1943), p. 256; "Pierre-Eudore Mayrand" in Lévesque, *op. cit.*, pp. 637-640; Anonymous; "Pierre-Eudore Mayrand" (obituary) in the *Bulletin de la Société historique franco-américaine 1959*, new series, vol. 5 (Manchester, N.H.: Imprimerie Ballard Frères, 1960), p. 269.

Vézina also served as a contributing writer for *Le Courrier de l'Illinois* in 1891 after the failure of his *Devoir*.[7]

In New England, a few newspapers of a distinctly French-Canadian nature were founded in the wake of the Insurrection of 1837-1838 in Lower Canada. The failure of their rebellion obliged those among the *patriotes* who had escaped deportation, imprisonment, or the gallows, to seek refuge across the border in the United States. Several were reunited in northern Vermont where, in Burlington, the *patriote* leader Ludger Duvernay continued the struggle by founding *Le Patriote canadien*, the first issue of which appeared on 7 August 1839. Duvernay published articles, sometimes in English, but mostly in French, from correspondents from here and there in the United States. Among these contributors were five political refugees like himself. The newspaper's primary goal being the advancement of the French-Canadian people through the creation of an independent Canadian republic, Duvernay received the moral support of his exiled colleagues, the majority of whom were living in straitened circumstances. In light of his own precarious financial state, not to mention the fact that Canada had banned *Le Patriote canadien*, Duvernay was obliged to cease publication after six months with the 5 February 1840 issue. In 1842, Duvernay was granted amnesty, thereby allowing him to return home to resume the editorship of his Montreal newspaper, *La Minerve*.[8]

Although the majority of studies on the Franco-American press make mention only of *Le Patriote canadien*, Maximilienne Tétrault maintains that other independence-oriented newspapers also appeared in Vermont during this era.[9] First of all, there was a bilingual newspaper, *Le Patriote canadien*, founded in Derby in 1837 by a Mr. Blanchard and "some [French] Canadians," to which the Québécois historian Gérard Filteau refers as the *Canadian*

[7]   Belisle, *op. cit.*, pp. 28, 34, 54-60, 302-303; Tétrault, *op. cit.*, pp. 17-18, 35.

[8]   Belisle, *op. cit.*, pp. 16-20; "Ludger Duvernay" in Lévesque, *op. cit.*, pp. 287-290; Robert Rumilly, *Histoire des Franco-Américains*, published under the auspices of the Union Saint-Jean-Baptiste d'Amérique (Montreal: Robert Rumilly, 1958), pp. 17-25; L. O. David, *Les Patriotes de 1837-1838* (Montreal: Eusèbe Senécal et Fils, imprimeurs-éditeurs, 1884), pp. 72-73.

[9]   Tétrault, *op. cit.*, p. 16, from an article by Maxime O. Frenière in *La Justice* of Holyoke, Massachusetts, 9 November 1933.

Patriot.[10] Next, Tétrault writes about another *Patriote*, founded in Burlington in 1838 by Ludger Duvernay, but it is evident that she erred by stating the incomplete title and the wrong date of founding of *Le Patriote canadien* of 1839. There was also *La Révolution canadienne*, founded in Burlington in 1838 by Duvernay and the *patriote* leader Georges-Etienne Cartier. Finally, Tétrault mentions another newspaper published "half in French and half in English," *The North American*, founded in Swanton in 1839 by the physician and *patriote*, Dr. Wolfred Nelson. However, Robert Rumilly classifies this publication as being among "a few American newspapers [that] accepted articles favorable to Canadian 'republicans.' "[11]

In spite of their brief existence, it goes without saying that the influence of these newspapers continued to be felt even after their demise. In 1867, the year of the establishment of the Canadian Confederation, J.B.A. Paradis and his colleagues of L'Ordre des Dix, a French-Canadian independence-oriented society in New York City, founded *Le Public canadien* in this same city. It lasted for ten months, during which it spread ideas favoring French-Canadian independence. According to Alexandre Belisle, "the nationalist tone was so pronounced within its columns that the United States was listed among foreign countries in reports of the daily news..."[12] In 1869, after having founded French-Canadian independence-oriented societies the previous year in Manchester, New Hampshire, and in Lowell, Massachusetts, Médéric Lanctôt, a French-Canadian politician and advocate of French-Canadian independence through peaceful means, went to Burlington, where he founded *L'Idée nouvelle*. Not long afterwards, he transported his newspaper to Worcester, Massachusetts. As such, *L'Idée nouvelle* became that city's first French-language newspaper despite its having published only two issues. Subsequently, Lanctôt made another attempt, this time with *L'Impartial*, which he moved from Worcester to Detroit after having published only a single issue.[13]

---

[10]   Gérard Filteau, *Histoire des patriotes*, vol. 3 (Montreal: Éditions Modèles, 1942, p. 146.

[11]   Rumilly, *op. cit.*, p. 22.

[12]   Belisle, *op. cit.*, p. 44.

[13]   Ibid., pp. 21-22; Tétrault, *op. cit.*, pp. 18, 60.

From the beginning to the middle of the nineteenth century, emigrants from Lower Canada tended to head toward the fertile lands and urban centers around the Great Lakes, more so than toward the manufacturing cities and towns of New England which, during that era, were barely developed. Eventually, however, the rise of the textile industry created a need for an increased work force in the mills, while to the north of the forty-fifth parallel, the political, economic, and social situation, still unfavorable for French Canadians, drove a significant number of *habitants* to seek a better life elsewhere. Consequently, with the end of the Civil War (1861-1865) commenced the great wave of migration from Quebec toward New England. At this moment in time, in conjunction with other institutions that were authentically Franco-American, came the birth of a press that was aimed directly at the immigrants from Quebec, one that dealt with their difficulties as well as with their aspirations in order to aid them in preserving their ethnic culture while adapting to their new environment.

Two factors led to the founding of New England's first Franco-American newspaper. To begin with, Antoine Moussette, a merchant in St. Albans, Vermont, had promised in 1867 that, prior to the next convention of French Canadians, to be held in Springfield, Massachusetts, the following year, they would have a newspaper devoted to their interests. On the other hand, Mgr. Louis de Goësbriand, Bishop of the Diocese of Burlington, who recognized a need for French-speaking priests to establish Franco-American parishes throughout New England, also championed the idea.[14] Therefore, with the encouragement of the latter and with the financial backing of Antoine Moussette, Father Zéphirin Druon, vicar-general of the Diocese of Burlington and pastor of Sainte Marie's parish in St. Albans, founded *Le Protecteur canadien*. During its three years of existence, from 1868 to 1871, this weekly exerted considerable influence, having subscribers as far away as the American West. Belisle considers *Le Protecteur canadien* to have been "in reality the first successful French journalistic endeavor in New England."[15] However, *Le Protecteur canadien* ceased publication in the wake of a fire which destroyed the building that had housed the newspaper's presses.

---

[14]   Belisle, *op. cit.*, pp. 61-67; Tétrault, *op. cit.*, pp. 18, 60; Edouard Hamon, s.j., *Les Canadiens-français de la Nouvelle-Angleterre* (Quebec City: N.S. Hardy, libraire-éditeur, 1891), pp. 169-177.

[15]   Belisle, *op. cit.*, p. 61.

Although Father Druon's *Protecteur canadien* was a successful endeavor, it was Ferdinand Gagnon's *Le Travailleur* which gave the Franco-American press the needed impetus to achieve genuine success. But, in order to arrive at that stage, Gagnon, as had been the case with his predecessors, went through a period of trial and error. It must be remembered that Gagnon entered the field of journalism during a period of uncertainty. No one knew at that time if the migration from Quebec was a temporary or a permanent phenomenon, nor if this population had the means or even the desire to support a journalistic undertaking on foreign soil.

Having left his hometown of Saint-Hyacinthe, Quebec, in 1868 at the age of nineteen, Gagnon first went to Concord, New Hamphire, and the following year to Manchester where, in collaboration with Dr. Adolphe L. Tremblay, he founded that city's as well as New Hampshire's first French-language newspaper, *La Voix du peuple*. After seven months, *La Voix du peuple* ceased publication and Gagnon moved to Worcester, where he became editor of *L'Etendard national* which he founded in the fall of 1869 with a group of investors and which, after one year, began to be published as the American edition of *L'Opinion publique* of Montreal. This newspaper lasted until 1874. Gagnon remained editor of *L'Etendard national* up to the moment when he founded *Le Foyer canadien* of Worcester with Frédéric Houde in 1873. Gagnon and Houde also published an edition of *Le Foyer canadien* in Woonsocket, Rhode Island, called *Le Courrier du Rhode Island* (1873-1874). However, *Le Foyer canadien* was more Houde's project and so, in 1874, Gagnon sold him his shares in the newspaper. Houde transferred *Le Foyer canadien* to St. Albans, where he had already worked as a journalist, at *Le Protecteur canadien* and at *L'Avenir national*.

Finally, Gagnon was ready to create his journalistic *magnum opus* which, one day, would earn him the title of "father of the Franco-American press in New England." Published weekly beginning on October 16, 1874, *Le Travailleur* of Worcester became a bi-weekly in 1879. All seemed to be going well for the newspaper and its founder when, on April 15, 1886, not yet having attained his thirty-seventh birthday, Gagnon succumbed to Bright's disease, an illness which had struck him only seven months earlier. Gagnon left *Le Travailleur* in the hands of his brother-in-law, Charles Lalime, who continued to publish it until he sold it to Benjamin Lenthier in 1892. The latter transformed it into a political sheet similar to the fifteen or so other newspapers that he'd purchased in order to run a campaign favorable to the presidential candidacy of

Grover Cleveland. Not long after the elections of November 1892, on 31 December, *Le Travailleur* died along with most of Lenthier's other newspapers.[16]

Deprived of *Le Travailleur* and of its founder, Franco-Americans nevertheless reaped the benefits of Ferdinand Gagnon's dream of creating for his compatriots a press that would assist them in establishing a collective and distinct identity on American soil, while also serving as a mouthpiece for their religious, linguistic, cultural, and political interests. Aware of the enormous power of the press, Gagnon did not hesitate to employ it as a means of expressing his ideas and offering suggestions to his readers. In his capacity as a repatriation agent for the government of Quebec, he recommended a return to the homeland to those émigrés who were not satisfied with their situation in the United States. This controversial question gave rise to the first of many polemics among newspapers, quarrels destined to leave their imprint on the history of the Franco-American press.[17] As an advocate of American citizenship for those who intended to remain in New England on a permanent basis, Gagnon was responsible for the founding of several naturalization clubs.[18] He employed his pen to rectify the false impression, harbored by certain Québécois with regard to the United States, that the émigrés were rapidly losing their Catholic faith and their ability to speak French. Moreover, in the face of whatever challenge, for example, "the Chinese of the Eastern States" incident,[19] Gagnon never backed off, always attacking his adversaries with vigor.

During his brief but fruitful career, Ferdinand Gagnon was able to establish a solid base for a press that would serve Franco-Americans for more than a century. Undoubtedly, Gagnon's success

---

[16]   Ibid., pp. 68-92; Tétrault, *op. cit.*, pp. 19-21, 61; "Ferdinand Gagnon" in Lévesque, *op. cit.*, pp. 336-340; Benjamin Sulte, ed., *Ferdinand Gagnon: sa vie et ses œuvres* (Worcester: C.F. Lawrence et Cie, imprimeurs, 1886), pp. 7-24; Josaphat Benoit, ed., *Ferdinand Gagnon: biographie, éloge funèbre, pages choisies* (Manchester, N.H.: *L'Avenir national*, 1940), pp. 11-45.

[17]   Belisle, *op. cit.*, pp. 93-107; Tétrault, *op. cit.*, pp. 69-74.

[18]   Tétrault, *op. cit.*, pp. 75-82.

[19]   Jean-Georges LeBoutillier, "Une page d'histoire franco-américaine: un rapport de M. Carroll D. Wright sur l'uniformité des heures de travail en 1881" in *La Revue franco-américaine*, vol. 2, no. 6, 1 April 1909, pp. 423-433. This text also appears in Belisle, *op. cit.*, pp. 321-330.

encouraged many other journalists to follow suit in spite of the risks involved, and always to start over again, without regard to their past failures. In his lifetime, Gagnon himself witnessed the birth of approximately sixty Franco-American newspapers in New England and New York State, not counting his own. And from 1869, the year in which Gagnon first entered the field of journalism, to today, some 330 Franco-American newspapers were born in all. If, to this number, one adds the French newspapers published during the eighteenth century, the French and Acadian newspapers of Louisiana, those of the Great Lakes' region and elsewhere, this number would reach almost 500.[20]

Due to the impossibility of relating the history of each one of these newspapers, especially taking into consideration that most were ephemeral publications and that copies of a good many of these can no longer be found today, the most remarkable among them nevertheless warrant mention.

To begin with, the following is a list of the titles, locations, and dates of founding of the first *truly* Franco-American newspapers, that is to say, those published for and about Franco-Americans, in each of the six New England states: *Le Protecteur canadien* of Burlington, Vermont (1868); *La Voix du peuple* of Manchester, New Hampshire (1869); *L'Etendard national* of Worcester, Massachusetts (1869); *L'Emigré canadien* of Biddeford, Maine (1870); *L'Etoile* of Woonsocket, Rhode Island (1873); and *Le Connecticut* of Waterbury (1897).[21]

---

[20]   In addition to the lists of newspapers in Belisle, *op. cit.*, pp. 27-38, 216-217, 380-384, and in Tétrault, *op. cit.*, 5-50, it is possible to calculate, at least in round figures, the total number of newspapers by using the following sources: Joseph Lussier, "Les Journaux de langue française aux Etats-Unis depuis 1912" in *Deuxième Congrès de la langue française au Canada—Mémoires*, vol. 1, *op. cit.*, pp. 367-369; also, the series *La Vie franco-américaine* (1939-1952) and the new series of the *Bulletin de la Société historique franco-américaine*, vols. 1-19 (1955-1973) both keep up with the founding and the disappearance of newspapers on a year-to-year basis.

[21]   Belisle, *op. cit.*, pp. 27-28, 35-36; Tétrault, *op. cit.*, pp. 18-20, 37, 40. Although *Le Courrier du Connecticut* appeared in 1892, five years prior to the founding of *Le Connecticut* of Waterbury, it was merely one of Benjamin Lenthier's many political sheets that were printed at *Le National* in Lowell, and therefore it was not a Connecticut newspaper in the true sense since it did not come from any city in that state.

Of all the newspapers founded before 1880, only *Le Jean-Baptiste* of Northampton, Massachusetts (1875-1933) had a relatively long and interesting existence, having changed hands and cities several times before becoming the property of Jean-Baptiste Brazeau of Pawtucket, Rhode Island, in 1894, and of his daughter Henriette in 1930. Among its other proprietors were Ferdinand Gagnon (1883-1886) and Benjamin Lenthier (1892). When Lenthier's political sheets ceased publication on 31 December 1892, *Le Jean-Baptiste* was one of only two that survived.

Over the years, many different types of newspapers were created for a variety of reasons and to serve a number of causes. In 1875, Virginie Authier founded *Le Journal des dames* in Cohoes, New York. Along with *Le Bulletin* of the Fédération féminine franco-américaine—founded in 1953 to serve the interests of Franco-American women throughout New England—these are the only two publications devoted entirely to women. However, this did not in any way prevent numerous other newspapers from including women's columns or pages, serial novels, poetry, memoirs, and literary criticism, much of which was published under the byline of a woman: Anna Duval-Thibault at *L'Indépendant* of Fall River, Albini Boulay-Belisle at *L'Opinion publique* of Worcester, "Rosine Caudert," pen name of Victoria Langlois at *L'Avenir national* of Manchester, "Liane," pen name of Camille Lessard-Bissonnette at *Le Messager* of Lewiston, Alberte Gastonguay-Sasseville, also at *Le Messager*, Yvonne Le Maître at *L'Etoile* of Lowell and at Wilfrid Beaulieu's *Le Travailleur* of Worcester, Corinne Rocheleau-Rouleau at *L'Opinion publique* and at Beaulieu's *Le Travailleur*, Hélène Thivierge at a whole host of newspapers, including that of her hometown, *La Justice* of Biddeford, Ninette Fortin at *L'Action* of Manchester, and finally, Charlotte Michaud at *L'Unité* of Lewiston.

Although the majority of Franco-American newspapers were published in French, each era saw the birth of at least a few bilingual French-English papers, for example *Le Charivari* of Champlain, New York (1869), *Le Bulletin et Charivari* of Fall River, Massachusetts (1874), and *Le Tricolore* of Lynn, Massachusetts (1896). There also existed newspapers that were essentially French-language publications but which, from time to time, accepted articles written in English. *Le Clairon* of Lowell (1905-ca.1942) and *Le Citoyen* of Haverhill (1906-1939), both published by Joseph E. Lambert, figured among these. Today, *L'Union* of Woonsocket (1901) is totally bilingual, while within the pages of *Le Canado-Américain* (1900) and *InformACTION* (1982), both of Manchester, as well as in those of *Le F.A.R.O.G. Forum* of Orono, Maine (1973), a certain percentage of English exists.

During the final decades of the nineteenth century, a French-language Protestant missionary movement with origins in both Quebec and Europe surfaced in several Franco-American centers. In addition to the already well-known sermons of the apostate Charles Chiniquy of Illinois, who visited Lowell, Manchester, and elsewhere to preach, in the hope of converting Franco-Americans to Protestantism, there was a French-language press devoted to this same cause. Among these few Protestant papers were *L'Artisan canadien* of Lowell (1880), *Le Républicain* of Boston (1884), founded by the minister Narcisse Cyr, *Le Franco-Américain* of Fall River (1888), founded by the ministers Benoit, Aubin and Co., *Le Fidèle messager* (1891-1892) and *Le Réveil* (1894-1895), both of Manchester and founded by the minister Thomas A. Dorion.[22]

If Franco-Americans, who were fervent Catholics for the most part, had difficulty keeping their Catholic-oriented newspapers alive, it almost goes without saying that they lent far less support to the Protestant French-language press. Only *Le Citoyen franco-américain* of Springfield, Massachusetts, founded in 1891 by the Collège français-américain,[23] a Protestant educational institution that recruited its students among Yankees who desired to learn French, enjoyed relative success, since it lasted until the time of World War I.[24]

Among the 330 or more Franco-American newspapers that have appeared in New England since *Le Protecteur canadien* in 1868, roughly 190 of these, far more than half, were founded

---

[22]   Since neither Belisle nor Tétrault mentions the two Manchester publications, their dates are approximate. It is certain that, according to the date of publication of certain books that came off the presses of *Le Fidèle messager*, this newspaper appeared at least during the years 1891-1892. See Marc Ami, pastor, *Le Naufrage de l'Annie Jane* (Manchester, N.H.: *Le Fidèle messager*, éditeur, 1891); Louis Martin, ex-priest, *Mon Voyage à Tracadie* (Manchester, N.H.: *Le Fidèle messager* and Montreal: Librairie L.E. Rivard, 1891); Joseph Provost, pastor, *Portrait et biographie de Jean Vernier* (Manchester: *Le Fidèle messager*, éditeur, 1892). With regard to the monthly periodical *Le Reveil*, a copy of a single issue can be found in the archives of the Association Canado-Américaine, that of vol. 2, no. 2, July 1895, which indicates that the periodical could have been founded during the previous year.

[23]   This institution eventually became American International College, which still exists, but with no particular religious identification.

[24]   Belisle, *op. cit.*, pp. 128-129, 208; Tétrault, *op. cit.*, p. 36.

between 1880 and 1900. Despite the failure of most of these newspapers, this period nevertheless offered the best conditions under which to launch and maintain such an undertaking. The flow of immigrants from Quebec was constant, life in the Little Canadas was carried on almost entirely in French, and the need for a good newspaper in this language made itself felt everywhere. With few exceptions, all of the large dailies and weeklies had their humble, modest beginnings at this moment in history, before maturing and reaching their peak during the course of the first two or three decades of the twentieth century, the most successful period of the Franco-American press.

In 1881, *L'Abeille* of Lowell, founded the preceding year, became the first Franco-American daily, although *La Tribune* of Woonsocket (1895-1934) was the first Franco-American newspaper to be published as a daily from its very first issue. Undoubtedly, one of the most important dailies of this era was *Le National*, which Benjamin Lenthier founded with Léon Bossue dit Lyonnais at Plattsburgh, New York, in 1883, only to move it in 1890 to Lowell where, the following year, it became a daily. It was the leading newspaper among Lenthier's sixteen political sheets and the only one, besides *Le Jean-Baptiste*, to escape the fate of the others in 1892.

The following is a list of the best-known newspapers published in the various Franco-American centers during the most active period in the history of the press, along with the names of their principals throughout the years:[25]

—*Le Messager*, Lewiston, Maine (1880-1968), Jean-Baptiste Couture, Louis-Philippe Gagné, Roméo Boisvert.
— *L'Indépendant*, Fall River, Mass. (1885-1962), Onésime Thibault, Godfroi de Tonnancour, Louis Clapin, Philippe-Armand Lajoie.

---

[25]   Belisle, *op. cit.*, pp. 214, 217, and Tétrault, *op. cit.*, p. 10, give 1904 as the year of founding of *La Justice* of Holyoke, while in *La Vie franco-américaine 1942*, op. cit., p. 253, there is mention of the "Quarantenaire 1902-1942" of *La Justice*, and in the volumes that follow, this date, 1902, is reaffirmed. With regard to *La Liberté* of Fitchburg, the annual report of the Alliance des Journaux franco-américains for 1959, published in the *Bulletin de la Société historique franco-américaine 1959*, *op. cit.*, p. 213, indicates that *La Liberté* had changed manager after the death of Léonard Rémy. Sold for the sum of $6,000 to Gerard Rand in 1959, it was transformed into a largely English-language newspaper by the latter, while keeping the name of *La Liberté*. The newspaper succumbed in 1965.

— *L'Etoile*, Lowell, Mass. (1886-1957), Louis A. Biron, Antoine Clément.

— *L'Opinion publique*, Worcester, Mass. (1893-1931), Alexandre Belisle and Brothers, Levi Bousquet, Wilfrid Beaulieu.

— *L'Avenir national*, Manchester, N.H. (1894-1949), Joseph E. Bernier, Jean-Georges LeBoutillier, Ernest Bournival, Josaphat T. Benoit.

— *La Tribune*, Woonsocket, R.I. (1895-1934), Philippe Boucher.

— *La Justice*, Biddeford, Maine (1896-1950), Alfred Bonneau, Joseph C. Bolduc.

— *L'Impartial*, Nashua, N.H. (1898-1964), Louis A. Biron, Armand J. Biron.

— *Le Courrier*, Lawrence, Mass. (1899-1981), Edouard Fecteau, Rodolphe Janson-Lapalme; ceased to exist with the aging of Janson-Lapalme who published it four times a year starting in the mid-fifties.[26]

— *Le Courrier*, Salem, Mass. (1902-1950), Paul N. Chaput, Albertine Vanasse.

— *La Justice*, Holyoke, Mass. (1902 or 1904-1964), Joseph Lussier, Roméo D. Raymond.

— *Le Citoyen*, Haverhill, Mass. (1906-1939), Joseph E. Lambert.

— *La Liberté*, Fitchburg, Mass. (1908-1965), J.E. Venne, Josaphat T. Benoit, Léonard Rémy, G. Rand.

— *Le Lynnois*, Lynn, Mass. (1910-1935), Paul N. Chaput, Orphée and René Gingras, Aimé Chassé.

There were, of course, other lesser-known newspapers, such as *Le Clairon* of Lowell (1905-ca. 1942), a weekly that had to live in the shadow of a large daily, *L'Etoile*, or *Le Progrès* of Nashua (1912-1930), which was eclipsed by the semi-weekly and later tri-weekly, *L'Impartial*, before being moved to Manchester in 1930, after which it merged with Wilfrid Beaulieu's *Le Travailleur* of Worcester in 1932. Certain newspapers that were published in cities and towns far removed from the large Franco-American centers did not reach beyond their locality. *Le Journal de Madawaska* (1902-1906), founded in Van Buren, Maine, in the St. John River Valley and *Le Canado-Américain* of Norwich, Connecticut (1898-1902) belong to this category.

Given this favorable climate for journalistic undertakings, many monthly, bi-monthly, and quarterly periodicals, most of them having a religious orientation, appeared one after the other just before, during, and after World War I. In 1910, the Oblate Fathers of Lowell founded *Le Bulletin paroissial* and later *L'Apostolat*. The same year, the Marists of Lawrence started their own *Bulletin paroissial* and the following year, Father Alphonse Graton of Pawtucket launched a periodical by the same title. The

---

[26]   [He died in early January 1994, at the age of 97.—Editor]

Dominicans at Sainte Anne's parish in Fall River followed their example with their periodical, *La Semaine paroissiale* (1911-1929) which subsequently became the official organ of all of that city's Franco-American parishes. The Assumptionists of Worcester published several periodicals, including *Vers l'idéal* (1912-1923), *L'Assomption* (1924-1957), and *L'Apôtre du Sacré-Cœur* (1930-1933).[27] In 1922, Irène Farley, a lay missionary, founded the "Rosiers missionnaires de Sainte-Thérèse de l'Enfant-Jésus," as well as their periodical, *La Rose effeuillée* of Manchester. Today, more than thirty years after the death of Irène Farley, her work continues, thanks to the Sisters of the Precious Blood in Manchester. In fact, the majority of these periodicals had an enormous success that, without a doubt, inspired the founding of new periodicals of the same type, even up to the time of World War II. *Celle qui pleure* (1940), the organ of the La Salette Fathers of Attleboro, Massachusetts, is one example. It was also at this time that *Le Réveil*, a temperance journal, appeared as a successor to the *Revue anti-alcoolique* (1926), organ of the *Cercles Lacordaire*, founded by the Dominicans of Fall River, especially Father Amédée Jacquemet, who preached in favor of temperance.

Besides these periodicals, whose purpose was the edification of their readers, there existed a few literary journals, among them *Cœurs français* of Manchester (1907-1908), the creation of Joseph Dumais. Aimed at Franco-Americans, especially those of the working class, its purpose lay in trying to correct their spoken French, which was denigrated in a column entitled "Le langage des 'States.' " This periodical failed after only one year. *Le Foyer littéraire* of Providence (1911) and *L'Heure agréable* of Attleboro (1911), the latter being both literary and musical in nature, met the same fate as *Cœurs français*, as did Joseph Laferrière's attempt, *Le Beau parler* of Boston (1914).

As ardent defenders of the Catholic faith and of the French language—not necessarily always in that order—Franco-American newspapers did not hesitate to involve themselves in the numerous quarrels that erupted between the members of the Irish-American clergy on one side and those of the Franco-American clergy and their flocks on the other. These battles centered around questions such as the teaching of French in the schools, the administration of

---

[27]   The dates of the Assumptionist periodicals given by Tétrault, *op. cit.*, pp. 11, 48, 50, are erroneous as are those given by Lussier, *op. cit.*, p. 369. The dates above have been established by Rev. Donat Lamothe, A.A., Archivist of Assumption College.

parish finances, and clerical appointments. With the firm belief that the mother tongue, the one in which they had learned at a tender age to pray to God, was the sole guardian of the faith of Franco-Americans, the press fearlessly attacked those among Irish bishops and priests whom they labelled as "assimilators." Without going into all of the details, it can be said that the crises or "affairs" such as those of Fall River and North Brookfield, Mass., Danielson, Conn., that of the Corporation Sole in Maine, and that of Sainte Anne's parish in Woonsocket, R.I., caused much ink to flow.

In the wake of World War I, anti-German sentiments evolved into anti-ethnic feelings that culminated in a full-fledged patriotic Americanization movement. The Irish joined in with the hope of "denationalizing" once and for all the country's Catholic "hyphenated-Americans." The ethnic explosion that resulted from this—for the situation had finally come to a head after years of discrimination—became the *raison d'être* of a counteroffensive and its mouthpiece. It included the founding of *les Croisés* [the Crusaders] and their newspaper, *La Sentinelle* of Woonsocket (1924-1928). The insults that *La Sentinelle* hurled at the Irish clergy and, in particular, at Bishop William A. Hickey of Providence, gave rise to a polemic not only between the *Sentinellistes* and the Irish, but also between the Sentinellistes and more moderate Franco-Americans. Never had such a heinous war been witnessed among Franco-American newspapers representing two ideologies. When, in 1928, the *Sentinellistes* and their leader, Elphège J. Daignault, publisher and editor-in-chief of the newspaper, were excommunicated from the Roman Catholic Church and their newspaper placed on the Church's *Index*, they attempted to make a comeback with a succession of new publications that were destined to fail: *La Vérité* (1928), *La Bataille* (1928), and *La Défense* (1928-1929), of Woonsocket, as well as *Le Cahier* (1929) and *L'Intransigeant* (1929), both of Central Falls, Rhode Island.

Ultimately, no one won this battle. *La Tribune* tottered for a few more years and finally fell in 1934. In 1935, *L'Indépendant* of Woonsocket, which was nothing more than a local edition of Fall River's large daily, replaced *La Tribune*. By 1942, *L'Indépendant* of Woonsocket had gone out of existence. Without a doubt, the *Sentinelliste* movement proved to be the turning point in the history of the Franco-Americans and their press.[28]

28   J. Albert Foisy, *Histoire de l'agitation sentinelliste dans la Nouvelle-Angleterre 1925-1928* (Woonsocket: La Tribune Publishing Co., 1928); Elphège J. Daignault, *Le vrai mouvement sentinelliste en Nouvelle-Angleterre 1923-1929 et l'affaire du Rhode Island* (Montreal: Les Editions

Having lived since the end of the Civil War in New England's Little Canadas, where French was the everyday language at home, at church, at school, in the press, in the social organizations, in business establishments, and sometimes even at work, Franco-Americans could, if they so desired, maintain their "Franco" character easily enough. Early immigrants had brought with them a spirit of *survivance*—French linguistic and cultural survival—which they tried, as much as possible, to inculcate into their children. Moreover, the frequent visits that these families paid to their relatives in Quebec and vice versa, as well as the continuous influx of new émigrés from the mother country, aided Franco-Americans in remaining French and resisting American and Irish assimilative forces. However, as is the case with most ethnic groups, those generations born in the United States became, with each passing year, more and more attached to the American way of life and less and less in touch with their ancestral culture. After World War I, the partial success of the Americanization movement, coupled with the failure of the *Sentinelliste* movement, accelerated the evolution of Franco-Americans toward a more American and less French-Canadian identity.

Although the elderly continued to live in French out of habit, for the young, the preservation of the language and culture of their forebears had by now become a question of will. Having familiarized themselves sufficiently with the English language and with American mores, they were not obliged to speak French, read French-language books and newspapers, or belong to any Franco-American societies in order to feel at home or to get ahead. And, if they did, it was, for many, simply out of respect for their parents.

The period of growth for Franco-American institutions, including the press, had passed, and the era of decline was already setting in. The stock-market crash of 1929 and the Great Depression that ensued, not to mention the closing of the American borders to immigration, added to the difficulties encountered by the press. Having always found it difficult to survive, the situation only worsened for the press from the 1930s onwards. Nevertheless, Franco-American journalists did not give up. As always, despite

---

du Zodiaque, 1936); Rumilly, *op. cit.*, pp. 364-503; Richard S. Sorrell, "The Sentinelle Affair (1924-1929) and Militant Survivance: The Franco-American Experience in Woonsocket, R.I." (Doctoral dissertation, State University of New York, Buffalo, 1976); Robert B. Perreault, *Elphège J. Daignault et le mouvement sentinelliste à Manchester, New Hampshire* (Bedford, N.H.: National Materials Development Center for French and Creole, 1981).

numerous failures, they continued to found new papers, a few of which would achieve remarkable success, given the circumstances under which they started. To name a few: *La Justice* of Sanford, Maine (1925-1945), founded by Joseph C. Bolduc, proprietor of *La Justice* of Biddeford; *Le Messager* of New Bedford (1927-1953), founded by J. Arthur Desaulniers; *Le Journal* of Haverhill, Massachusetts (1927-1956), founded by Joseph-Arthur Smith; and finally, *Le Franco-Américain* of Waterville, Maine (1929-1947), founded by Jules Savarin.

Accustomed to seeing only small weeklies die out, after only a few years of existence, Franco-Americans must have taken for granted a large daily that was approaching its fortieth anniversary. In light of this, shock waves were felt throughout New England when, in 1931, *L'Opinion publique*, Worcester's daily, bade farewell to its readers. It was the first toll of a bell that, in later years, would often be heard. However, Wilfrid Beaulieu, a staunch *patriote*, veteran of *Le Devoir* of Montreal, *L'Etoile* of Lowell, and *La Sentinelle* of Woonsocket (he was one of those excommunicated during that fratricidal era) as well as of *L'Opinion publique*, wasted no time in filling the gap by founding *Le Travailleur* of Worcester (1931-1979), which he named thus to honor the memory of Ferdinand Gagnon. Of all the newspapers born during the Depression, *Le Travailleur* lasted the longest, forty-eight years. In time, it would bury all of its predecessors, with the exception of *Le Courrier* of Lawrence and *Le Canado-Américain*, a publication of the Association Canado-Américaine—the oldest of the mutual benefit societies for Franco-Americans, having been founded in 1896—and *L'Union*, published by the Union Saint-Jean-Baptiste.

In 1911, Alexandre Belisle had published a list of the thirty-six newspapers in existence at that time. In 1935, Maximilienne Tétrault asserted that there were twenty-eight of these left.[29] They were disappearing more rapidly than others could be founded, and most new attempts, in spite of the efforts and good will of their creators, were doomed to die out. Nevertheless, a certain number of attempts were made, *Le Canadien* of Waterbury, Connecticut (1934), *L'Etendard* of Hartford (1935), and so on.

Ever since the era of the region-wide Conventions of the French Canadians of the United States in the nineteenth century, some had dreamed of forming an association of newspapers to try

---

[29]   Belisle, *op. cit.*, pp. 216-217; Tétrault, *op. cit.*, pp. 5-14.

to reinforce the foundations of the Franco-American press.[30] The realization of that project would have to wait until a time when the life of the newspapers would truly be at risk. Therefore, in Woonsocket, on 4 April 1937, the eve of the Deuxième Congrès de la Langue française [Second French-Language Convention] which was to be held in Quebec City, the Alliance des Journaux franco-américains [Alliance of Franco-American Newspapers] came into being. Louis Clapin, Ernest Bournival, Arthur Milot, Philippe-Armand Lajoie, and Louis A. Biron were the major players. Its purpose was to "encourage solidarity among publishers, proprietors, editors, and friends of [Franco-American] newspapers."[31] In addition to gathering together most of the Franco-American journalists, this society organized an annual "Press Week," the best known of which was that of 1949 in Manchester where, in Lafayette Park, Franco-Americans unveiled a statue of Ferdinand Gagnon in honor of the centennial of the birth of the "father of the Franco-American press."[32]

During this period of decline, there were, nonetheless, a few positive happenings. In 1934, *Le Messager* of Lewiston, one of New England's most important Franco-American newspapers, began to appear daily. Beginning in 1935, the *Société historique franco-américaine* published its *Bulletin* on a regular basis, a practice that ceased only in 1973. Meanwhile, the Comité permanent de la survivance française en Amérique, known today as the Conseil de la Vie française en Amérique, began to publish a detailed annual report of Franco-American activities from 1939 to 1952. Entitled *La Vie franco-américaine*, these volumes, which were edited by the Rev. Adrien Verrette, a Franco-American priest and pastor, have become an indispensable resource for all historians. During the

---

[30]   See "La presse," article no. 5 of the report of the sixteenth national convention of French Canadians, held in Rutland, Vermont in 1886, published in Félix Gatineau, *Historique des conventions générales des Canadiens-Français aux Etats-Unis 1865-1901* (Woonsocket: L'Union Saint-Jean-Baptiste d'Amérique, 1927), p. 161.

[31]   Anonymous, "Alliance des Journaux franco-américains" in the *Bulletin de la Société historique franco-américaine 1957*, new series, vol. 3 (Manchester, N.H.: Imprimerie Ballard Frères, 1958), p. 362; Adrien Verrette, *La Croisade franco-américaine* (Manchester, N.H.: L'Avenir national, éditeur, 1938), p. 447.

[32]   Anonymous, "Monument Ferdinand Gagnon" and "Semaine de la presse" in *La Vie franco-américaine: centenaire franco-américain 1849-1949* (Manchester, N.H.: Ballard Frères., 1950), pp. 484-520.

years 1942-1943, three papers were born in New Hampshire: in Berlin, in Greenville, and in Suncook, all bearing the title of *Le Journal*.[33] However, only *Le Journal* of Berlin succeeded, lasting into the 1950s. The annual report of l'Alliance des Journaux franco-américains for 1948, published in *La Vie franco-américaine*, indicates that at the time, there were only nineteen French-language newspapers left in New England, which amounted to a net loss of nine newspapers since 1935 and seventeen since 1911.

During World War II, the U.S. government which, in the past, had wanted to eradicate every trace of ethnicity in the country, changed its attitude when it recognized the advantages that a multi-ethnic American society had to offer. On two occasions, at the conventions of the New England Foreign Language Newspaper Association of 1942 and 1943, held in Boston, members of the Alliance des Journaux franco-américains heard the chief of the division of foreign languages at the Information Office in Washington, Alan Cranston, praise the 1,402 newspapers published in thirty-five languages in the United States at that time.[34] However, for the Franco-American press, the period of decline was already too far advanced, since the assimilation that occurs naturally from one generation to the next, and which had been accelerated by the Americanization movement, had already greatly eroded the readership base. People read Franco-American newspapers to a far lesser degree than previously, preferring the large English-language dailies that were easier to read, had a more attractive appearance, and offered a wider variety of news and other material.

In order to give readers the variety that they sought, or at least a French-language publication of an altogether different sort, Lucien and Thérèse SanSouci of Woonsocket launched their "magazine des Franco-Américains," *Le Phare,* in 1948. While the husband saw mainly to the administrative side of the periodical, his wife and their daughter, Paulette, the two editors, travelled throughout the United States to gather information on

---

[33]   Anonymous, "*Le Journal* de Berlin," "*Le Journal* de Greenville," and "*Le Journal* de Suncook" in *La Vie franco-américaine 1943* (Manchester, N.H.: Ateliers de *L'Avenir national*, 1944), pp. 413-417.

[34]   Anonymous, "La presse" in *La Vie franco-américaine 1942, op. cit.*, pp. 243-244; Anonymous, "Alliance des Journaux franco-américains" in *La Vie franco-américaine 1943, op. cit.*, pp. 399-400.

contemporary and historical figures and events that related to the French presence in this country. In addition, they included the writings of contributors from coast to coast, as well as those of correspondents from Canada and from Europe's Francophone nations. Due to its nature as an expensive undertaking, *Le Phare* lasted only until 1952.

In 1949, when Franco-Americans gathered in Manchester to celebrate the centennial of the birth of Ferdinand Gagnon, founder of the city's first Franco-American newspaper, they could not foresee that by the end of that same year the city would have lost *L'Avenir national*, once the area's large daily. Six months later, a new weekly, *L'Action*, replaced it, with Josaphat T. Benoit, mayor of the city, as editor. The next year, the Franco-Americans of Biddeford and those of Salem witnessed the disappearance of their newspapers, *La Justice* and *Le Courrier*. *Le Messager* of New Bedford and *Le Journal* of Haverhill met the same fate in 1953 and 1956 respectively. And, in 1957, *L'Etoile* of Lowell published its last issue.

During that same year, for the first time ever in New England, the Association des hebdomadaires de langue française au Canada [Association of French-Language Weeklies of Canada] held its convention in Manchester. On that occasion, the Franco-American press became affiliated with this organization.[35] The following year, 1958, the Association Canado-Américaine transformed its house organ, *Le Canado-Américain*, up to then a monthly newspaper, into a bimonthly periodical. It would subsequently become a quarterly. *Le Canado-Américain*, edited by Adolphe Robert for nearly sixty years, distinguished itself by the high quality of its graphic appearance, in addition to the intellectual, historic, and literary character for which it had been recognized over the years.

With 1962 came the end of yet another newspaper of great importance, *L'Indépendant* of Fall River. Not long afterwards, having lost a majority of its members, the Alliance des Journaux franco-américains succumbed. Faced with this painful situation, all the while maintaining some hope, many members and officers of the Comité de Vie franco-américaine decided to attack the problem head-on by organizing the Septième Congrès des Franco-

---

[35]   Anonymous, "Association des Hebdomadaires de Langue française" in the *Bulletin de la Société historique franco-américaine 1958*, new series, vol. 4 (Manchester, N.H.: Imprimerie Ballard Frères, 1959), pp. 207-208.

Américains [Seventh Convention of Franco-Americans] in Holyoke, Mass. Its theme would be "The Fate of Our Press." Participants offered several proposals, among them the founding of a new association that would come to the aid of the remaining newspapers, the transformation of an existing newspaper into a weekly with widespread appeal, and the proclamation of the following year, 1964, as "The Year of the Franco-American Press."[36] By an ironic twist of fate, during this "Year of the Franco-American Press," *La Justice* of Holyoke, the very city where the convention had taken place, as well as *L'Impartial* of Nashua, both closed up shop. Finally, not far behind, came the demise of *Le Messager* of Lewiston in 1968 and that of *L'Action* in 1971.

For any Franco-American journalist, the early 1970s must have been one of the darkest moments in the history of the Franco-American press. It was a time when, regardless of their ancestral origins, most Americans preferred going to the cinema to reading a book, or watching television to reading a newspaper. It seemed as if the press in general, and not simply the ethnic press, was suffering from indifference toward newspapers. However, during the 1960s, along with other changes in society, there occurred an "ethnic liberation movement" which is still in a state of evolution to this day. This evolution created among all groups, Franco-Americans included, the possibility of a cultural renaissance, a means for renewal after so many years of losses and disappointments.

From this ethnic "renaissance," which finally arrived in the early 1970s, a new generation of Franco-American newspapers was born. The first of these was *Observations* of Lewiston (1972). According to its French-language editor (it was a bilingual publication), Paul Paré, it lasted only six months due to its tone, which was somewhat too radical.[37] Next came *Le F.A.R.O.G. Forum* (1973), a student newspaper from the University of Maine at Orono. With its militant leftist tone and its penchant for sociopolitical questions, *Le F.A.R.O.G. Forum* has become, under the guidance of Yvon Labbé, not only the mouthpiece of students, but also the voice

---

36   Anonymous, "Comité de Vie franco-américaine" in the *Bulletin de la Société historique franco-américaine 1963*, new series, vol. 9 (Manchester, N.H.: Imprimerie Ballard Frères, 1964), pp. 75-82.

37   Paul Paré, "A History of Franco-American Journalism" in Renaud S. Albert, ed., *A Franco-American Overview*, vol. 1 (Cambridge: National Assessment and Dissemination Center for Bilingual/Bicultural Education, 1979), pp. 258-259.

of anyone who wishes to express an opinion without reservation on any topic of concern to the Franco-American population.

In the domain of community newspapers, there were *Le Journal de Lowell* (1974-1995), published by Albert Côté, and *L'Unité* of Lewiston (1976-1984), whose publisher-editors were Paul Paré, Donat Boisvert, Jr., Robert Couture, and Roger Lacerte. More than simple sources of local and regional news, these papers offered substantive articles, especially *L'Unité*, which Roger Lacerte purchased in order to safeguard French life in Lewiston.[38] Elsewhere, the *Union Leader* of Manchester published until recently a weekly column in French, "En bref," begun in 1974 by Marcelle Savard-Martel and continued by Julien Olivier from 1982 to 1995. In 1975, the directors of the American-Canadian Genealogical Society, located in Manchester, New Hampshire, started a semi-annual periodical entitled *The Genealogist*; the American-French Genealogical Society of Pawtucket and Woonsocket, Rhode Island began publishing a Summer and a Winter issue of *Je me souviens* in 1978.

Outside of New England, the ethnic revival of the 1970s inspired the founding of new French-language publications (or, at the very least, bilingual ones) elsewhere in the United States. The *Revue de Louisiane / Louisiana Review*, the journal of the Center for Louisiana Studies of the University of Southwestern Louisiana at Lafayette, published from 1972 to 1982, was replaced by the *Revue francophone de Louisiane* in 1986. This periodical has since become the organ of the Conseil international d'études francophones. *Feux Follets*, a literary journal, has been published at the same university since 1991. The growing francophone population in South Florida, made up for the most part of retirees from New England and Quebec, gave rise to the *Journal de la Floride*. After the demise of this paper, *Le Soleil de la Floride* appeared in 1983 and is still published in that state by Denise Chartrand and Jean Laurac.

At a time when the majority of Franco-Americans either barely spoke and read English, or not at all, French-language newspapers were essential to their lives, first of all as sources for local, regional, national, and world news. Moreover, these newspapers kept their readers informed about events of major importance affecting French life in the United States, Canada, France, and elsewhere, thus reinforcing the ties that already existed

---

[38]   Interview with Roger Lacerte, Manchester, N.H., March 1983.

among members of all of these Francophone communities. In addition, the press, in conjunction with the family, the church, the school, and social organizations, worked toward the preservation, promotion, and defense of the French language, the Catholic faith, and ethnic traditions among Franco-Americans. Newspapers also aided new immigrants in adapting more easily to an anglophone, Protestant, urban, and industrial ambiance, a strange environment compared to the rural life most of them had experienced in their mother country. Like their French ancestors, Franco-Americans are a people with varied ideas and opinions, and their press has always reflected their passion for discussions, clashes, and polemics. Time and again, newspapers championed such causes as the civil rights and political advancement of the Franco-American population. Finally, in keeping with their desire to encourage artistic and creative expression, while at the same time offering their readers entertaining and stimulating material, Franco-American newspapers did not hesitate to open their pages to novelists, poets, and playwrights.

It is evident that the press played a fundamental role in the development of the Franco-American population. If present-day Franco-American newspapers no longer play a central role as did their predecessors, they nonetheless have their *raison d'être*. In conclusion, one might borrow the title of Ferdinand Gagnon's first newspaper, *La Voix du Peuple*—for as long as there will be a Franco-American population, there will be a Franco-American voice, and this "voice of the people" that was the Franco-American press, spoke long, loud, and clear for and to an emigrant people seeking to adjust to a new reality in their adopted country.

Translated by the author

[This article first appeared as "Survol de la presse franco-américaine" in the French Institute's publication entitled *Le Journalisme de langue française aux États-Unis*. It has been reviewed by the author, and up-dated where necessary, for inclusion in this volume.]

Bibliography

Albert, Renaud S., ed. *La presse chez les Franco-Américains.* Cambridge: National Assessment and Dissemination Center for Bilingual/Bicultural Education, 1979, 91 p.

Ami, Marc. *Le Naufrage de l'Annie Jane.* Manchester: *Le Fidèle messager,* éditeur, 1891, 112 p.

Bealieu, Wilfrid. "La langue française et sa conservation par la presse" in Adolphe Robert, ed., *Les Franco-Américains peints par eux-mêmes.* Montreal: Éditions Albert Lévesque, 1936, pp. 129-137.

Belisle, Alexandre. *Histoire de la presse franco-américaine.* Worcester: Ateliers typographiques de *L'Opinion publique,* 1911, 434 p.

Benoit, Josaphat. *L'Ame franco-américaine.* Montreal: Éditions Albert Lévesque, 1935, 245 p.

_____. *Ferdinand Gagnon: biographie, éloge funèbre, pages choisies.* Manchester: *L'Avenir national,* 1940, 277 p.

Bulletin de la Société historique franco-américaine. New series, Vols. I-XIX, 1955-1973. (Various anonymous reports on the press).

Clement, Antoine. "Notre presse et nous" in the *Bulletin de la Société historique franco-américaine 1956.* New series, vol. 2. Manchester: Imprimerie Ballard Frères, 1957, pp. 110-115.

Daignault, Elphège J. *Le vrai mouvement sentinelliste en Nouvelle-Angleterre 1923-1929 et l'affaire du Rhode Island.* Montreal: Éditions du Zodiaque, 1936, 246 p.

David, L. O. *Les Patriotes de 1837-1838.* Montreal: Eusèbe Senécal et Fils, imprimeurs-éditeurs, 1884, 297 p.

Filteau, Gérard. *Histoire des patriotes,* vol. 3. Montreal: Éditions Modèles, 1942, 286 p.

Foisy, J. Albert. *Histoire de l'agitation sentinelliste dans la Nouvelle-Angleterre 1925-1928.* Woonsocket: *La Tribune* Publishing Co., 1928, 427 p.

Gatineau, Félix. *Histoire des conventions générales des Canadiens-Français aux Etats-Unis 1865-1901.* Woonsocket: L'Union Saint-Jean-Baptiste d'Amérique, 1927, 500 p.

Guillet, Ernest B. *Essai de journalisme.* Bedford: National Materials Development Center for French and Creole, 1981, 78 p.

Habert, Jacques. "Histoire de la presse française aux Etats-Unis" in the *Bulletin de la Société historique franco-américaine 1966.* New series, vol. 12. Manchester: Imprimerie Ballard Frères, 1967, pp. 127-131.

Hamon, Edouard, s.j. *Les Canadiens-français de la Nouvelle-Angleterre.* Quebec City: N.S. Hardy, libraire-éditeur, 1891, 483 p.

Lacasse, Amédée. "Nos journaux français" in *Le Phare*, vol. 1, no. 9, October 1948, pp. 21-23.

Lacerte, Roger V. "Une thèse artificielle . . . celle de M. Elphège Roy" in *Le Travailleur*, Worcester, Mass., in two parts, vol. 39, nos. 24 and 25, 14 and 21 June 1969, pp. 1-4.

Lafargue, André. "Le français en Louisiane" in *Deuxième congrès de la langue française au Canada—Mémoires*, vol. 2. Quebec City: Imprimerie du *Soleil* Limitée, 1938, pp. 118-126.

Lajoie, Philippe-Armand. "Les organismes vitaux: les journaux" in Adolphe Robert, ed., *Les Franco-Américains peints par eux-mêmes.* Montreal: Éditions Albert Lévesque, 1936, pp. 53-59.

Leboutillier, Jean-Georges. "Une page d'histoire franco-américaine: un rapport de M. Carroll D. Wright sur l'uniformité des heures de travail en 1881" in *La Revue franco-américaine*, vol. 2, no. 6, 1 April 1909, pp. 423-433.

Lévesque, Rosaire Dion-. *Silhouettes franco-américaines.* Publications de l'Association Canado-Américaine. Manchester: Imprimerie Ballard Frères, 1957, 933 p.

Lussier, Joseph. "Les journaux de langue française aux Etats-Unis depuis 1912" in *Deuxième congrès de la langue française au Canada—Mémoires*, vol. 1. Quebec City: Imprimerie du Soleil Limitée, 1938, pp. 363-369.

Martin, Louis, ex-priest. *Mon voyage à Tracadie*. Manchester: *Le Fidèle messager* and Montreal: Librairie L.E. Rivard, 1891, 76 p.

Paré, Paul. "A History of Franco-American Journalism" in Renaud S. Albert, ed., *A Franco-American Overview*, vol. 1. Cambridge: National Assessment and Dissemination Center for Bilingual/Bicultural Education, 1979, pp. 237-260.

Perreault, Robert B. *Elphège J. Daignault et le mouvement sentinelliste à Manchester, New Hampshire*. Bedford: National Materials Development Center for French and Creole, 1981, 243 p.

_____. *La presse franco-américaine et la politique: l'œuvre de Charles-Roger Daoust*. Bedford: National Materials Development Center for French and Creole, 1981, 102 p.

_____. "The Franco-American Press" in Sally M. Miller, *The Ethnic Press in the United States: A Historical Analysis and Handbook*. Westport, Conn.: Greenwood Press, 1987, pp. 115-130.

Provost, Joseph. *Portrait et biographie de Jean Vernier*. Manchester: *Le Fidèle messager*, éditeur, 1892, 19 p.

Robert, Adolphe (pseud. "Le Mohican"). "La presse . . . ça presse" within the column "Le carquois du Mohican" in *Le Canado-Américain*, vol. 3, no. 6, April-May 1963, pp. 5-6.

Roy, Elphège E. *Les causes du déclin de la presse franco-américaine*. Master's thesis, Rivier College, Nashua, N.H. Manchester: Elphège Roy, 1965, 48 p.

Rumilly, Robert. *Histoire des Franco-Américains*. Under the auspices of l'Union Saint-Jean-Baptiste d'Amérique. Montreal: Robert Rumilly, 1958, 552 p.

Sorrell, Richard S. "The Sentinelle Affair (1924-1929) and Militant Survivance: The Franco-American Experience in Woonsocket, R.I." Doctoral dissertation, State University of New York, Buffalo, 1976, 484 p.

Sulte, Benjamin, ed. *Ferdinand Gagnon: sa vie et ses œuvres.* Worcester: C.F. Lawrence et Cie, imprimeurs, 1886, 249 p.

Tetrault, Maximilienne. *Le rôle de la presse dans l'évolution du peuple franco-américain de la Nouvelle-Angleterre.* Marseille: Imprimerie Ferran et Cie, 1935, 143 p.

Therriault, Sœur Mary-Carmel. *La littérature française de Nouvelle-Angleterre.* Montreal: Éditions Fides, 1946, 324 p.

Verrette, Adrien, Rev. *La Croisade franco-américaine.* Manchester: *L'Avenir national,* éditeur, 1938, 500 p.

[Verrette, Adrien, Rev.] *Vie franco-américaine, La.* 14 volumes, 1939-1952. (Various reports on the press).

La Sentinelle and La Tribune:
The Role of Woonsocket's French-Language Newspapers in the Sentinelle Affair of the 1920s

Richard S. Sorrell

Those involved in historical research are well aware that newspapers play a dual historical role, participating in events as well as recording them. This truism is exemplified by the Sentinelle Affair. *La Sentinelle* and *La Tribune* did far more than report the cataclysmic events which proved to be the Armageddon of fifty years of struggle for *la survivance* in New England; the editors were also actively involved in Sentinellism itself as protagonists of the opposing viewpoints: militant *survivance* (*La Sentinelle*) versus moderate *survivance* (*La Tribune*). This article examines how the opposing journals both reported and shaped the course of events, as well as how the internecine struggle eventually consumed not only the newspapers themselves, but also, ironically, the cause of *la survivance* to which each paper was devoted.

Since the diocese of Providence has not yet opened its voluminous archival holdings on Sentinellism, New England's French and English language newspapers of the 1920s have, of necessity, become the major available source on the conflict. Thus, in a sense, the history of the Sentinelle Affair is primarily based upon the records of *La Sentinelle*, *La Tribune*, and the other journals which covered the events. This article does not intend to cover the whole of Sentinellism,[1] but will focus on an examination of the direct relationship between the two major

---

[1]   Richard S. Sorrell, "The Sentinelle Affair (1924-1929) and Militant *Survivance*: The Franco-American Experience in Woonsocket, Rhode Island" (Ph.D. dissertation, State University of New York at Buffalo, 1975). Two additional works should also be consulted: Robert B. Perreault, *Elphège-J. Daignault et le Mouvement Sentinelliste à Manchester, New Hampshire* (Bedford, N.H.: National Materials Development Center, 1981); Pierre Anctil, "Aspects of Class Ideology in a New England Ethnic Minority: The Franco-Americans of Woonsocket, Rhode Island (1865-1929)" (Ph.D. dissertation, New School for Social Research, 1980), pp. 148-278.

French-language newspapers of Woonsocket in the 1920s, and the affair in which they were so intricately enmeshed.

First, a brief chronology will provide the setting. In the years following World War I, a group of Franco-Americans in New England, most notably in Woonsocket, became increasingly militant concerning the state of their ethnic and religious survival in the United States. They felt that *la survivance*, which their ancestors in Quebec had fought so long to maintain, was being threatened. Led by Elphège Daignault of Woonsocket, these militant Francos identified the principal "Americanizing" threat as the Irish hierarchy of the Catholic Church. They felt that the Irish took advantage of their dominant position within the Church by attempting to force Catholic immigrant groups who arrived later than most Irish, and unlike them did not speak English, to quickly assimilate themselves. Daignault et al. also distrusted increasing centralization of diocesan activities which, they felt, threatened the autonomy of individual Franco-American parishes. Sentinellists viewed both of these policies as related to a long-standing desire on the part of the hierarchy to eliminate all vestiges of "national" parishes from American Catholicism.

By 1924, the battle had begun in earnest, as Daignault and his followers established a newspaper, *La Sentinelle*, in Woonsocket and began to gather support in other Franco-American centers in New England. They refused to contribute to the diocesan fund drives of Bishop William Hickey of Providence, particularly for the new Catholic high school in Woonsocket, Mount St. Charles. Although this high school had been built primarily for the use of Franco youths, Sentinellists claimed that it was being used by Bishop Hickey to further his assimilationist goals. In addition, they argued that the diocese should discontinue its practice of assessing each parish for an obligatory quota in fund drives, and they demanded that the French language have at least equal footing with English in all Franco parish schools.

The tactics of the Sentinellists became increasingly aggressive from 1924-27. They petitioned Rome in an attempt to halt the accepted practice by which each diocese took a percentage of the funds of its local parishes. When the Pope backed Bishop Hickey, the Sentinellists instituted a civil suit and began a boycott of all contributions to the Church, including pew rent. The struggle in Woonsocket reached its apex in 1927-28, when Holy Family parish refused to permit anyone who would not pay pew rent to attend Mass, and when the pastor of St. Louis parish was suspended and then dismissed by the bishop, for supposed *sentinelliste* leanings. These and other incidents resulted in a series of large public gatherings called by the Sentinellists, involving acrimonious name-calling and occasional physical violence. The culmination came in April 1928 when the Pope excommunicated all the Sentinellists who had signed the civil suit. This dramatic event chimed the death knell of the movement, for within a year all had repented and the excommunications had been lifted.

This five-year battle (1924-29) greatly agitated Franco-Americans in Woonsocket, as well as throughout New England. Indeed, it caused a split within Woonsocket's Franco community. Moderates, including almost all parish priests and most lay community leaders, such as those involved in the direction of *La Tribune*, insisted that loyalty to the Church overrode ethnic concerns. Consequently, they opposed both the tactics and the goals of the *Sentinellists*. During the most troubled time (1927-28), the conflict became fratricidal, heightening its drama and emotional impact.

*   *   *

From the 1830s until well into the first half of the twentieth century, many French-language newspapers were founded in New England. They provided important news of Quebec and local happenings in the Franco-American community, as well as a positive attitude towards Francos and *la survivance*, not available in English language newspapers. However, most were short-lived. The elders read them, but young Francos of the second generation and beyond often preferred American newspapers. Franco-American newspapers fought a long and usually losing financial battle, particularly since they were in competition with more established French-language newspapers, readily available from nearby Quebec, and many Franco-Americans simply did not read any papers.

From 1873 to 1925, more than twenty French-language newspapers were founded in Woonsocket, a figure topped only by Manchester, Lowell, Fall River, and Worcester. However, all failed after a relatively short life with the notable exception of *La Tribune*. Founded in 1895, it published a daily edition until 1934, when it was succeeded by *L'Indépendant* of Woonsocket, a local edition of the Fall River paper of the same name. This failed in

1942, leaving Woonsocket and all of Rhode Island without a daily French-language newspaper.[2] The only serious competition *La Tribune* faced from a French-language counterpart during its long life is the focus of this article.

One final stage setting is required before turning to the Sentinelle Affair itself: the story of how *La Tribune* was transformed from a champion of militant *survivance* into an advocate of moderate *survivance* in the decades before Sentinellism. One of the ironies of the affair is that if it had occurred twenty years earlier, *La Tribune* would, in all probability, have been a champion of Elphège Daignault's cause.

The French Canadian who contributed most to militant *survivance* in Woonsocket before the Sentinellists was J.-K.-L. Laflamme. The peak of this Quebec-born journalist's career was achieved during 1901-07 when he, as editor of *La Tribune*, made it a leading defender of Franco-American rights. He filled the pages of the journal with news and editorials about the harassment of Francos throughout New England at the hands of the Irish and the Protestants, exemplified by incidents such as the North Brookfield[3] and Corporation Sole disputes.[4] Laflamme urged all Francos to maintain their heritage, and pledged *La Tribune*'s support for this with slogans on page one: "*La Tribune* is always ready to defend its own" and to "protect the rights of Franco-Americans."[5] His militancy was most evident in his denunciations of Franco-Americans who became *déracinés*, and

---

2   Robert Rumilly, *Histoire des Franco-Américains* (Montréal: L'Union Saint-Jean-Baptiste d'Amérique, 1958), pp. 497 and 525; Alexandre Belisle, *Histoire de la Presse Franco-Américaine et des Canadiens-Français aux États-Unis* (Worcester: L'Opinion Publique, 1911), pp. 27-38; Rev. André Houle, "A Preliminary Checklist of Franco-American Imprints in New England, 1780-1925" (Ph.D. dissertation, Catholic University of America, 1955), pp. 8-9 and 163-164; *La Tribune* (Woonsocket) 23 Dec. 1914.

3   [See Michael Guignard "The Corporation Sole Controversy," note 2 in this volume, for information on the North Brookfield Affair and for an analysis of the Corporation Sole dispute.—Editor]

4   [Corporation Sole—the system of church property ownership in the American Catholic Church under which the bishop and his successors hold absolute title to all diocesan and parish property.—Editor]

5   Author's translation.

of Irish church "fanatics" who were lurking, ready to quicken the process. There could be no mingling with assimilators and no compromise.

In 1906, Laflamme became involved in an altercation with Bishop Matthew Harkins of Providence, over the issue of more national parishes, priests, schools, and bishops for Francos. He left *La Tribune* within a year, dissatisfied with what he considered to be Franco-American apathy concerning *la survivance*. The effects of Laflamme's presence remained, providing an example for the Sentinellists who would later claim him as their predecessor in militant *survivance*. However, there is evidence that he might have disapproved of their extreme tactics. Although he advocated fierce resistance to assimilation, his editorials stopped short of open rebellion, which he felt would hurt the cause by adding fuel to the assimilators' fire, and which, in the final analysis, would run against the need to respect Church authority. Thus, even Laflamme took a contradictory and ambiguous stand on the distinction between militancy and open rebellion.[6]

One of Laflamme's successors as editor of *La Tribune*, J.-Adélard Caron, was also involved in militant *survivance* during his brief tenure at the paper in 1911-12. Caron was removed from this post, as well as from his previous position as an officer of the Union St-Jean-Baptiste and editor of its organ, *L'Union*, partially because of his extremist views on *la survivance*. The result of Caron's dismissals,[7] when added to Laflamme's departure, was

---

[6]   Rosaire Dion Lévesque, *Silhouettes Franco-Américaines* (Manchester, N.H.: Publications de l'Association Canado-Américaine, 1957) pp. 450-52; Rumilly, pp. 208, 220-24 and 262-69; Belisle, pp. 314-20; "Fête St-Jean-Baptiste, 24 juin 1924, Woonsocket, R.I." (Woonsocket, 1924); *La Sentinelle* (Woonsocket), 17 Sept. and 15 Oct. 1925, 26 April 1928. Examples of Laflamme's militant writings on *la survivance* while in Woonsocket can be found in: *Le Progrès* (Woonsocket), 12 Oct. 1906; *La Tribune*, 1900-1907, especially 6 Nov., 13 and 18 Dec. 1900, 25 Jan., 22-30 July, August and 6 Dec. 1901, 2 Jan. and 7 May 1902, 21 March 1903, 20 Feb., 1 Nov. and 24 Dec. 1904, 6-15 April, 31 July, 15 August, 22-23 Sept. and 26-30 Dec. 1905, 26 May, 28-29 August, 5, 14 and 25-29 Sept., and 31 Dec. 1906, and 5 July 1907; and Laflamme's "Les Canadiens aux États-Unis" in *La Revue Canadienne*, especially 40, pp. 153-159 and 232-39, and 41, pp. 57-64 and 137-42.

[7]   Rumilly, pp. 220-24, 235, 239, 242-52, 258 and 271; Belisle, pp. 193-202 and 233-34; Rev. D.M.A. Magnan, *Histoire de la Race Française aux États-Unis* (Paris: Librairie Vic et Amat, 1913), pp. 291-94; Walter B.

the discrediting of militancy within both *L'Union* and *La Tribune*. These institutions, under the leadership of men like Eugène Jalbert, Philippe Boucher, and Élie Vézina, became advocates of the moderate brand of *la survivance* from this time on. Those who opposed their viewpoint, like Daignault and Phydime Hémond, would henceforth have to create their own newspaper and organizations.

By April of 1924 they had done just that, with the founding of *La Sentinelle* (The Sentry) as the journalistic organ of their *survivance* organization, established a few years earlier as *les Croisés* (the Crusaders), and now renamed *"les Sentinellistes."* *La Sentinelle*'s original statement of purpose showed little evidence of militancy, however, since it professed to be a Catholic journal, dedicated to the defense of the Church, working for *la survivance,* but only nationalistic in the broadest sense.[8] For the next few months, *La Sentinelle*'s nationalism did not seem unlike that of its competitor, the moderate *La Tribune,* since there were only a few radical articles concerning the role of Francos in America, and the language of the paper was seldom abusive towards diocesan officials and other supposed assimilators. During the early months, the newspaper featured national news and other features drawn from wire services, unlike the following years, when its pages were filled mainly with local sentinellist activities, complaints, and propaganda. The only hint of opposition appeared in the form of omission: there was no mention of the 1924 diocesan fund drive.

All of this changed in November when Daignault personally took over the direction of *La Sentinelle.* Until this time, the editor had been J.-Albert Foisy, a Franco-American journalist who had been working in Canada until he was hired by Daignault. Whether Foisy set the moderate tone of the paper during his editorship, or whether he was at first following orders from Daignault, is unclear. However, by November, he and Daignault were obviously

---

Chafee, Commissioner, "John B. Brindamour vs. L'Union St-Jean-Baptiste d'Amérique (Equity No. 2163)", State of Rhode Island, Providence Superior Court; *La Tribune,* 5 Feb., 8 Sept., 2 and 5 Nov. 1910; *Le Progrès,* 18 and 25 Nov. 1910; *The Evening Call* (Woonsocket), 10, 15 and 23 Nov. 1910, 17 Jan., 26 June, 14 July, 14 and 20 Dec. 1911; *La Sentinelle,* 17 March 1927; *The Call* (Woonsocket), 1 March 1929; *The Rhode Islander* (Providence), 13 July 1928.

8   *La Sentinelle,* 4 April 1924.

at odds, so Foisy resigned and became editor of *La Tribune*.[9] From this time on *La Sentinelle* became more militant in content and aggressive in tone. The transition from daily to weekly publication in November, just before Foisy's resignation, may have been due to the stated reasons of poor business conditions and a desire for easier regional circulation, but this also signalled the change from a daily "news" paper to a weekly propaganda sheet. Daignault was assisted by another local leading *Sentinellist*, Phydime Hémond, in the running of the paper. In mid-1925, they were joined by Henri Perdriau, a recent immigrant from France, who surpassed even Daignault in aggressive vitriol.[10]

During Foisy's tenure as editor of *La Sentinelle*, the rival *La Tribune* made few references to its competitor, other than an occasional complaint that Franco-Americans should not divide on petty or personal issues, or that some were failing to work hard enough in support of Mount St. Charles and were indulging instead in useless criticism. However, in late 1924 and early 1925, just before and after Foisy made his switch from *La Sentinelle* to *La Tribune*, the latter journal published a series of letters by Eugène Jalbert. These featured strongly worded attacks against Daignault and *La Sentinelle* for their recent criticisms of Jalbert and his moderate *survivance* organization, the Fédération Catholique Franco-Américaine. Jalbert defended himself as a true patriot who worked hard for his race, and labeled Daignault a do-nothing.[11]

By the summer of 1925, the dispute between the two

---

9   Foisy became a prominent anti-*Sentinellist* and wrote a tract, *The Sentinellist Agitation in New England, 1925-1928* (Providence: 1930), which was a strident condemnation of the movement. Daignault, in *Le Vrai Mouvement Sentinelliste en Nouvelle Angleterre, 1923-1929, et l'Affaire du Rhode Island* (Montreal: Les Éditions du Zodiaque, 1936), attacked Foisy as an opportunist who put the paper into debt, refused to edit it according to sentinellist wishes, and publicly revealed confidences after leaving. See pp. 15-30.

10   Daignault used the pen name of "Blaise Juillet," and Perdriau wrote as "Etienne Le Moyne." This description of the early months of *La Sentinelle* is drawn from an examination of its issues during 1924-25, as well as from Rumilly, pp. 359-63.

11   *La Tribune*, 6 May, 30 Oct., and 24 Dec. 1924, and 6 Jan. 1925.

newspapers was out in the open. *La Tribune* reprinted an article from another French-language newspaper, *La Justice* of Holyoke, in which Sentinellists were compared to the Ku Klux Klan. *La Tribune* said that it had maintained silence concerning the affair, but now that the dispute had spread outside Woonsocket it was necessary to answer the Sentinellists' false charges. By the fall, the newspaper admitted that one of its reporters was barred from covering a sentinellist banquet because he showed himself to be openly hostile.[12]

Nevertheless, *La Tribune* continued in large part to ignore the Sentinellists, or limited itself to mild statements against their general goals and methods, until early 1927. In March of that year, *La Tribune* announced that it had remained quiet during 1926 in hopes that the affair would be settled when the pope responded to Daignault's appeals to Rome. But now it was obvious that the Sentinellists were continuing their agitation even after the pope had rejected their appeals for a second time, in February 1927. Since they would not even listen to the pontiff, *La Tribune* declared that henceforth it would discard its policy of no direct comments, and would give its version of events.

As part of this new tactic, *La Tribune* reprinted articles from the diocesan newspaper, *The Providence Visitor*, which were critical of Sentinellism. The editors hastened to add that this did not mean that they were slaves of diocesan authorities, or Judases to their race, as militants claimed. They, the editors, were firm in their belief in *la survivance*, but were opposed to sentinellist means and ends. *La Tribune* then launched into a two-year period of vituperative attacks against Sentinellists, and refused to carry any reports of their activities. Objective journalism was disregarded as *La Tribune* felt its goal was to discredit and destroy the militants. Readers of the newspaper saw Sentinellists labeled as "Bolsheviks," "Satanic," and "Sacco-Vanzetti anarchists" whose main purpose was to destroy the Catholic Church and who, if they succeeded would destroy Franco-American unity. Their attempt to put patriotism over religion was "disastrous" and their "intemperate language" could lead only to "suicidal division." In

---

[12]   Ibid., 6 July 1925; "Éphémérides," (collection of 33 volumes of newspaper clippings in the Union St. Jean-Baptiste d'Amérique library, Woonsocket—collection hereafter referred to as Éph.), 30, p. 29 (*La Tribune*, 15 Oct. 1925).

short, the Sentinellists were not martyrs, since there was "no honor in their cause."[13]

The mudslinging was not one-sided. In general, La Tribune's tone was less vitriolic than that of its rival, particularly by 1928. By this time the cause was on the decline and La Sentinelle's editors may have been getting desperate. La Tribune often chose to ignore sentinellist meetings and accusations, particularly after the excommunications when the paper may have felt that "benign neglect" would work more effectively than angry retorts. La Sentinelle had begun heaping acerbic abuse upon moderate Francos as soon as Daignault and Hémond took over the direction of the paper from Foisy, labeling Philippe Boucher (publisher of La Tribune) as an assimilator as early as May 1925. After 1924 any reader was sorely disappointed who looked for news of activities not concerned with Sentinellism, or for balanced reports of the affair. There was no pretense of objectivity, as the newspaper consisted mostly of denunciations of Bishop Hickey and of any Francos who dared support him or oppose the cause. The most egregious example of this was the banner headline: Judas n'est pas mort, et il a des frères! (Judas is not dead and he has brothers!) The rival La Tribune was consistently charged with carrying false accounts of sentinellist activities. La Sentinelle accused its French-language compatriot of "gloating" over any setback which the cause suffered, even taking pleasure in the dismissal of Franco-American priests.[14]

Both newspapers were so inextricably involved in and violently divided over the affair, that it was impossible for either to give an objective account. The same is true for a third basic Franco-American primary source dealing with the dispute. Employees of the Union St. Jean-Baptiste—whose headquarters are in Woonsocket—kept an invaluable multi-volumed scrapbook of newspaper clippings on varied aspects of Franco life from 1900 to the 1930s, entitled Éphémérides. Volumes 14-17 deal with La Controverse du Rhode Island, and contain a vast number of clippings from newspapers of the time, in both French and English, on the Sentinelle Affair. The reader of these scrapbooks

---

13   La Tribune, 8 and 9 March, 5, 9 and 23 April, 31 May and 25 Oct., 1927, and passim, 1927-28; Éph., vol. 15, pp. 128 and 192 (La Tribune, 13 August and 20 Sept. 1927), and vol. 16, p. 34 (La Tribune, 29 Nov. 1927).

14   La Sentinelle, 14 and 28 May 1925, 20 May 1926, 4 August and 8, 15 and 22 Sept. 1927, and passim 1927-28.

soon realizes that they are biased against the sentinellist cause. Except for a few entries in the first volume, there are no articles from *La Sentinelle*, although *La Tribune* is well represented throughout. The sentinellist point of view is presented by occasional clippings from French-language newspapers outside of Woonsocket—particularly *L'Opinion Publique* of Worcester—but these are far outweighed by excerpts from French and English language journals outside Woonsocket which were unsympathetic to the militants, notably *The Rhode Islander* of Providence and *The Providence Visitor*. When one remembers that these scrapbooks were compiled by Élie Vézina, secretary-general of the Union, who was violently opposed to the sentinellist cause and had borne the brunt of many attacks by its advocates, the reason for such bias in the *Éphémérides* becomes clear.[15]

All of this demonstrates that the fratricidal nature of the Sentinelle Affair had a strong impact upon Woonsocket's Franco-American journalistic life. *La Sentinelle*, *La Tribune*, and *Éphémérides* all show evidence of severe and opposing biases. For a relatively unslanted account of the dispute, one must turn to the city's English-language newspaper, *The Call*. During the 1920s, this journal showed little trace of nativism towards Francos. It betrayed faint hostility towards the *Sentinelles*, primarily by giving more space to the activities of Franco-American moderates than to those of their opponents. However, *The Call*'s coverage of the affair was far more objective and factual than that of either of its Franco counterparts. This demonstrates the degree to which the Sentinelle Affair in Woonsocket was characterized by familial feuding within the confines of the Franco-American community.[16]

In April of 1928, at the same time that the leading Sentinellists were excommunicated, *La Sentinelle* was put on the Church Index of forbidden works.[17] In an attempt to circumvent this ban, *La Sentinelle* changed its name to *La Vérité* in May. There was no longer any listing of the editorial board, and all

---

15   *Éph.*, vols. 14-17, passim. See Edward B. Ham, "The Library of the Union St. Jean-Baptiste d'Amérique," *The Franco-American Review* 1 (1936-37), pp. 273-74, for a description of the various volumes of *Éphémérides*.

16   See the files of *The Call*, 1927-28.

17   *The Call*, 7 April 1928.

articles were unsigned. This attempt to protect the directors through anonymity was futile, since Daignault and company were obviously still editing the paper. [18] The Church was not deceived, and *La Vérité* was soon condemned, necessitating a further name change in November to *La Bataille*, and a final metamorphosis in December to *La Défense*. All was in vain, as circulation and the number of advertisements declined. The newspaper became less aggressive in tone, except for a flurry of excitement during the 1928 Presidential election, and it died a quiet death in February of 1929. [19]

The end of *La Sentinelle* coincided with the formal end of the movement, since in the same month Daignault, and all but a handful of the others who had been excommunicated, signed repentance forms. But it did not take too sharp an eye to see that Daignault had not completely given up the fight. The final issue of *La Défense* stated that although it was necessary to cease active resistance, this did not mean that the Sentinellists were in the wrong: their original grievances had been just and the excommunications too severe a punishment. [20]

Throughout the following year, Daignault, at a series of public meetings, proclaimed that a new newspaper would be founded if there were sufficient interest, since "the fight is dead only for those who are dead!" [21] In 1931, a weekly newspaper, *Le Travailleur*, was established in Worcester, and promised to carry on the tradition of *La Sentinelle*. Wilfrid Beaulieu, the editor, had been a leading militant on the staff of *La Sentinelle*. He was one of those excommunicated for signing the civil suit against Bishop

---

[18]   Daignault was assisted by Perdriau as editor, Hémond as financial administrator, and Emile Brunelle as publicity director.

[19]   *Éph.*, 16, p. 258 (*L'Opinion Publique* [Worcester], 2 June 1928); *La Sentinelle, La Vérité, La Bataille*, and *La Défense*, May 1928-Feb. 1929.

[20]   Rumilly, pp. 442-52 and 455-56; Daignault, pp. 202-14; *Éph.* 17, pp. 15, 16, 18, 21-22, 27 and 35 (*La Tribune* and *L'Étoile* [Lowell], 11 Feb., *The Providence Journal*, 11, 14 and 15 Feb., *The Call*, 11 Feb. and 20 May, *The Rhode Islander* [Providence], 1 March and 5 April, *L'Impartial* [Nashua], 16 Feb., and *La Tribune*, 17-18 and 20 May and 4 June, all 1929).

[21]   *Éph.*, 17, pp. 27 and 37-40 (*The Rhode Islander*, 5 April, 21 June and 15 Nov. 1929, *The Providence Journal*, 24 June and 11 Nov. 1929, *The Call*, 24 June and 11 Nov. 1929, and 23 June 1930); Rumilly, p. 458.

Hickey, and soon afterwards he moved to Worcester.[22] As editor of *Le Travailleur*, he announced that Daignault would be an occasional contributor to the journal, which would be combative and militant in tone, fighting assimilation and the Irish. The irascible Beaulieu maintained the Sentinellist spirit of this newspaper for decades thereafter. However, one should not overestimate the influence of *Le Travailleur* as a transmitter of sentinellist heritage. It generated only a fraction of the notoriety and attention which *La Sentinelle* had attracted in the 1920s. By the 1960s and 70s its influence was diminished, as French-language newspapers were less often read, and Beaulieu further lost readers by his feuding with those Francos who did not agree with his view of *la survivance*. [23]

To return to the Sentinelle Affair itself, how did *La Sentinelle* fare in its attempt to supplant *La Tribune* as *the* French-language newspaper of Woonsocket? Circulation figures for *La Sentinelle* are one way to determine how much support Daignault and his cause had. Although the offices of the newspaper were located in Woonsocket and one may assume that most of the copies were sold there, the journal was circulated widely throughout New England. After Foisy was dismissed as editor and the paper became sensationally propagandistic, the new editors claimed phenomenal sales, ranging from 8,000 to 10,000 weekly in 1925-26, to 15,000 to 20,000 in 1927 at the peak of the affair. *La Sentinelle* boasted that it was walloping *La Tribune* in sales, since the latter only had a circulation list of 1600 in 1926 and was experiencing further difficulties in 1927. According to its rival, *La Tribune* was being bailed out by the Union St-Jean-Baptiste which was buying hundreds of copies and giving them free to its members.

All of this should be taken with a grain of salt. There is no doubt that *La Sentinelle* cut into the circulation of *La Tribune*, especially during the summer of 1927 when militant agitation was

22 Beaulieu was living in Worcester by June 1928. At that time, he was editor of *L'Opinion Publique*, another journal which was strongly pro-sentinellist. *Éph.* 16, p. 260 (*The Rhode Islander*, 8 June 1928); Hélène Forget, "L'Agitation Sentinelliste au Rhode Island (1924-1929)" (M.A. thesis, University of Montreal, 1953), p. 81.

23 Rumilly, pp. 475 and 488; Lévesque, p. 42; Elphège E. Roy, "Les causes du déclin de la presse franco-américaine" (M.A. thesis, Rivier College, 1965), pp. 17, 41 and 43.

strongest.[24] What seems uncertain is whether *La Sentinelle* ever actually reached such astronomical sales levels. Josaphat Benoit, admittedly no friend of the militants, states that *La Sentinelle*'s circulation never surpassed 8,000. Its editors sometimes contradicted themselves. If circulation was over 8,000 by late 1925, why did Hémond say, in May 1927, that it had shot up in a short time from 2,000? Also, the charge of free distribution leveled against *La Tribune* may more accurately reflect the situation of *La Sentinelle*. Since the militants' cause depended upon wide dissemination of their point of view, would it not make sense to give it away, especially since the price was low and it came out only once a week? Because of the low price, free distribution, and lack of advertising after 1925, *La Sentinelle* never produced much revenue for the cause.[25]

The lack of advertisements in sentinellist publications seems to belie their claim of a large following. In 1924 and 1925, during the early stages of the agitation, the *Sentinellists* sponsored celebrations in Woonsocket on St. Jean-Baptiste Day. *La Sentinelle* published souvenir booklets to commemorate the event and help defray expenses. There were a substantial number of ads in each booklet, most taken by Franco businessmen and professionals in the city, which may signify a measure of support by prominent local Franco-Americans during the early years of the movement. In addition, there were some ads representing out-of-town Francos, most notably from Manchester, New Hampshire. However, even at this time there were bad omens: none of the large textile industries in Woonsocket took out ad

---

[24]   In 1922, *La Tribune* reported a circulation of 3400. During the Sentinelle Affair, the paper omitted any circulation figures, which may indicate that sales had declined. *La Tribune*, 7 Oct. 1922.

[25]   *La Sentinelle*, 10 and 24 Dec. 1925, 8 April 1926, 17 Feb., 28 July, and 22 Sept. 1927; *Éph.*, 14, pp. 35 and 287 (*The Providence Journal*, 14 Feb., and *The Lowell Courrier Citizen*, 16 May 1927); Rumilly, p. 421; Josaphat Benoit, *L'âme franco-américaine* (Montreal: Éditions Albert Lévesque, 1935), pp. 215-28.

space,[26] and in 1925 there were an increasing number of anonymous ("a friend") ads.[27]

When *La Sentinelle* began publishing in April 1924, it also had a considerable number of advertisements. But by the fall, when Foisy had departed and the paper had definitely become militant, advertising space diminished. Although some large ads remained, the majority by this time were confined to a classified section. By early 1928, even this classified section had shrunk. The few ads outside the classifieds were syndicated and thus originated far outside the geographical confines of the sentinellist dispute. *La Sentinelle* had some loyal supporters throughout who gave their business to the newspaper, but most Franco-American businessmen were either unwilling or afraid to be identified publicly as a supporter of the militants' journal.[28]

In retrospect, it seems obvious that the Sentinelle Affair damaged many of the institutional props of *la survivance*, such as French-language newspapers. In the short run, the crisis may have helped militant journals like *La Sentinelle, L'Opinion Publique,* and *Le Progrès de Nashua,* which could attract readers with their tales of dramatic events and their subjective, overblown style. However, the fortunes of such single-interest journals were mercurial and, when the drama flagged, they fell as fast as they had risen. Likewise, more established Franco newspapers, like *La Tribune,* often lost readers when they opposed

---

[26]   This may show wariness on the part of industrialists, both Franco-American and otherwise, since they usually rented space in such booklets.

[27]   While this is often done in commemorative booklets, in this case it may indicate the fear of being identified as a sentinellist supporter. "Fête St-Jean-Baptiste, Woonsocket, R.I.," 1924 and Ibid., 24 June 1925 (Woonsocket, 1925).

[28]   Eugène Jalbert had a classified ad for his law firm in some 1924 issues, demonstrating the less militant stand of the paper at that time. By January 1925 this leading opponent of Sentinellism had withdrawn his notice. Twenty-five Woonsocket Franco-American professionals and businessmen had classifieds in a January 1926 issue. In April of 1927 the number was twenty-six, which fell to eighteen by January 1928 and fourteen by December of that year. Most of the Franco classifieds from outside of Woonsocket were now from Pawtucket and Central Falls, also sentinellist strongholds. *La Sentinelle,* 8 Sept. 1924, 2 Jan 1925, 21 Jan. 1926, 21 April 1927, and 12 Jan. 1928; *La Défense,* 27 Dec. 1928.

the Sentinellists. In the long run, Sentinellism only served to increase the tradition of feuding which had long hindered French-language newspapers. Although *La Tribune* was on what was supposedly the winning side in the affair, that of the moderate Franco-Americans, one must remember that it survived its militant counterpart by only five years.[29]

The influence of the 1920s in all this should not be overlooked. This was a decade in which the mass media, such as newspapers, played a large role in publicizing melodramatic and sensational events. The excitement and drama of the *Sentinelle* crisis, which were magnified by extensive New England newspaper coverage, mark this affair as symptomatic of the 1920s. But the hoopla could not obscure the fact that time was running out for both *La Sentinelle* and *La Tribune*, as well as for the cause of *la survivance*, both militant and moderate.

The strife and tension of the 1920s, evident in events such as the Red Scare, the resurgence of the Ku Klux Klan, the Sacco-Vanzetti and Scopes "monkey" trials, as well as the Sentinelle Affair, were often the result of a cultural lag which promoted a clash between traditional ways of living and new technological developments. Thus, in the 1920s, as full of "future shock" as the times in which we live, those Franco-Americans involved in publishing *La Tribune* and *La Sentinelle* may have reacted by trying to retreat into a past in which *la survivance* dominated all. However, their readers were ultimately more interested in a future which promised the automobile, the radio, and the movies. If *La Sentinelle* and *La Tribune* would not provide them with enough articles and advertisements about such phenomena, they would turn to English-language newspapers which would do so.

[This article first appeared, in a French translation, as "*La Sentinelle* et *La Tribune*: Le rôle joué par ces journaux de Woonsocket dans 'la Sentinelle',"* in the French Institute's publication entitled *Le Journalisme de langue française aux États-Unis.* It has been reviewed by the author, and updated where necessary, for inclusion in this volume.]

---

29   Rumilly, pp. 408-22; Roy, pp. 41-43.

"History as a Novel, the Novel as History": Ethnicity and the Franco-American English-Language Novel

Richard S. Sorrell

Norman Mailer subtitled *The Armies of the Night,* "History as a Novel, the Novel as History." This apt phrase indicates my approach in examining Franco-American ethnic English-language novels, that is, novels whose common features are that the authors wrote in other than their mother tongue and that all deal, at least in part, with how Franco-Americans have been affected by their nationality. My intent is not literary analysis or criticism, but historical understanding of what views these novels put forth concerning the question of ethnic identity and its many variables, such as *survivance,* acculturation, assimilation, disorganization, ambivalence, marginality, rebellion, cultural duality, and conflict. As indicated by the preceding terms, I shall consider both positive and negative aspects of Franco-American ethnic identity, as they are reflected in this fiction.

A fictional approach to history is fraught with difficulties if one's concern is primarily factual accuracy. But when it comes to evoking the *ambiance* of a historical situation, novelists surpass professional historians. This is particularly the case with immigration or ethnic history, where the subject is usually the everyday lives of "ordinary" people. Few would argue with the contention that one should read, for example, the novels of Pietro DiDonato, Mario Puzo, Abraham Cahan, Michael Gold, and Philip Roth to understand the Italian and Jewish-American experiences.

Franco-Americans have no novelists specifically identified as chroniclers of their ethnic experience with the fame of a Puzo or the stature of a Gold or a Roth. There has been a long tradition of fiction dealing with French-Canadian life in the Quebec homeland, represented by such novels as *Maria Chapdelaine, Bonheur d'occasion* [*The Tin Flute*], *Trente Arpents* [*Thirty Acres*], *Au pied de la pente douce* [*The Town Below*], *La Guerre, yes Sir!,* and *Une saison dans la vie d'Emmanuel* [*A Season in the Life of*

Emmanuel]. The production of Franco-American ethnic novels in the United States has been neither as extensive nor as illustrious, partially because of the lack of the ready-made audience available in Quebec. Nevertheless, the thesis of this article is that one can achieve valuable perspectives on Franco-American ethnicity through a reading of the fiction which does exist.

From 1878, when the first Franco-American novel appeared, until 1939, all Franco ethnic novelists wrote in their mother tongue, a tribute to the degree of ethnic preservation attained by French-Canadian emigrants and their American-born children during these years. I shall not analyze this large body of French-language novels. Their picture of immigrant life is circumscribed by a narrow concern with French-Canadian *survivance.* Because they were written in French, their readership was limited primarily to those within the Franco-American and French-Canadian communities.

The first Franco-Americans to write ethnic novels in English, three in number, did so during 1939-43. Writing in English may be taken as a basic indicator of acculturation, since it denotes facility with a language other than the mother tongue and a desire to reach an audience beyond the native language speakers of one's ethnic group. The 1930s and 1940s were decades of rapid acculturation within immigrant communities. Immigration declined drastically as a result of the 1920s quota laws and the Great Depression. During the depression, ethnicity seemed less important than class. World War II gave most Americans a common purpose, and members of all nationalities who served in the war gained new horizons beyond their ethnic neighborhoods.

In order of appearance of their novels, the first Franco-American English-language authors were Jacques Ducharme (*The Delusson Family: A Novel*), Vivian Lajeunesse Parsons (*Not Without Honor*), and Alberic A. Archambault (*Mill Village: A Novel*). Two 1950s novelists, whose names are seldom linked, shared Franco-American roots: Jack Kerouac and Grace Metalious. In the 1960s, as a neo-ethnic revival began in America, Gerard Robichaud's *Papa Martel: A Novel in Ten Parts* was published, along with three novels by Robert Cormier. The most recent contributor to the field is David Plante, whose *The Family* (1978) was the first volume in the saga of the Francoeur family [*The Country* (1981), *The Woods* (1982), *The Native* (1988)].[1]

Ducharme and Robichaud offer slightly different variations on a common theme: acculturation without disorganization. They present multi-generational views of Franco life in, respectively, a Massachusetts mill town (Holyoke) during the late nineteenth and twentieth centuries, and a small Maine mill town near Lewiston during the 1910s-1930s. Each focuses on a particular Franco family, tracing its emigration from Quebec and eventual adaptation to life in the United States, which occurs without grievously disabling or causing a disorganizing loss of prior French-Canadian traditions. The result is a positive and traditional view of Francos who emigrate from Quebec to find a better life across the border. They encounter economic and social problems, such as low wages and long hours in the mills, some (but not much) nativism, and different values among young Francos born and raised in New England. In the end, the family perseveres. The members learn English and adopt American attitudes towards politics and social mobility, yet maintain a core of customary French-Canadian values, such as the French language and a reliance on the stabilizing forces of Catholicism and a large family.

Papa Martel is the more appealing of the two. This is not an ethnic novel, *per se*, since Robichaud's central concerns are not immigration and *survivance*. However, his portrait of a large, happy, closely-knit Franco family does give many glimpses of traditional Franco values. Robichaud's lively style and engaging

---

[1]   For complete citations, see the bibliography. I cite here only those sources which do not appear in the bibliography. There were many other novelists in addition to those here mentioned such as Gertrude Côté, *As I Live and Dream* (Manchester, N.H.: Dirigo Edition, 1953), and Robert Fontaine, *The Happy Time* (New York: 1945), which talks about French-Canadian life in Ottawa rather than New England. Archambault, Parsons, Cormier, Plante, Paul Théroux also wrote other novels which usually do not deal with Franco-American subjects. [Since this essay was written, Paul Théroux has published *My Secret History* (1989), E. Annie Proulx won the National Book Award (1993) and the Pulitzer Prize (1994) for *The Shipping News*, John Dufresne has published *The Way That Water Enters Stone* (1991) and *Louisiana Power and Light* (1994), and Richard Belair has written *The Fathers* (1991)—Editor]

story (really a chronological linking of short stories) make *Papa Martel* the best "read" of the Franco novels. *The Delusson Family* is more tightly organized, in both the novelistic and historical-sociological senses. Three generations of Francos gradually acculturate to the host society, with love of rural life, *survivance*, and upward mobility dominating countervailing urban disorganization and nativism.

Archambault's *Mill Village*, set in a Connecticut mill town during the same years as *The Delusson Family*, offers a grimmer picture. Unlike the Martels and the Delussons, the central family returns permanently to Quebec. They have encountered hostility from both Yankees and Irish-Americans. Poor working conditions in the mills are ignored by unsympathetic mill owners and political bosses. The father decides to repatriate after a second disabling mill injury, overruling his younger children who wish to stay. Archambault's low view of human nature (encompassing employers, workers, and politicians) is superficial, however, and seldom rises above stereotypical portraits. Although fashioned in an explicitly ethnic format, *Mill Village* yields surprisingly few insights into specific aspects of Franco-American *survivance* and acculturation.[2]

Ducharme and Robichaud do provide such information. Yet, after reading their novels, I wondered about the traditional, nostalgic, and romantic hue. Did matters always turn out this well? Weren't there more battles within the Franco community? Weren't there those who refused to accept *survivance*, or acculturation, or wavered between the two poles? In his 1949 survey of Franco-American literature, Adolphe Robert commented favorably on the unvarying patriotism and good citizenship of the authors. Although they maintained *survivance*, they were never subversive and never attacked the American

---

[2]   Archambault was not a professional writer, which may explain his somewhat superficial and stereotypical style. The son of immigrants, he became a political figure and a well-known judge who held a state Senate seat in Rhode Island for fourteen years and twice made unsuccessful bids for the Governor's seat. Gabriel Nadeau, "Chronique franco-américaine."*Culture* 3, no. 2 (June 1942), p. 237. Nadeau's *Chronique* of June 1945 (6, no. 2) pp. 215-218 contains extracts from *Mill Village*.

government or way of life, manifesting a *civisme pur*. In short, *pas de moutons noirs* [no black sheep].[3]

It is precisely this lack of black sheep which is troubling. Not that disorganization or rebellion are lacking in these novels. The negative aspects of *Mill Village* have already been mentioned. The eldest son of the Delusson family is a wandering spirit, a remnant of New France's *coureurs de bois*, who leaves home to wander through big cities, drinking, brawling, and going to jail.[4] The father and mother in *Papa Martel* are no idealized saints: they frequently disagree with each other and do not always accept traditional Franco values. Neither mindlessly follows the advice of the Church, particularly Cécile Martel, who disagrees with the lack of academics and English language instruction in the Franco parochial school. Papa Martel complains about the fear which the Catholic Church instills in its followers and compares himself (like the eldest Delusson son) to adventurous *voyageurs* rather than the opposing French-Canadian strain of docile *habitants*. One of their daughters takes a markedly rebellious attitude towards Franco-American conventions. She doesn't want to marry, especially not a fellow Franco, since they are too timid to leave the mill town of their birth. She doesn't want to have a large family, since raising many children in poverty will eventually cause her to hate them and her whole life.[5]

These novels do show rebellion against customary Franco values, and disorganization resulting from contact with an urban-industrial way of life in New England mill towns. Yet this rebellion and disorganization seem aberrant, actions of *moutons noirs* who will eventually return to the fold. Conflict is the exception rather than the norm. Consequently, such novels do not adopt the cultural conflict approach recommended for Franco literature by Burton Ledoux—people seeking a liberated life but

---

3   Adolphe Robert, "Essai bibliographique sur l'apport franco-américain à la littérature des États-Unis." *Revue d'Histoire de l'Amérique Française* 2 (1949), p. 555 et seq.

4   He does go home eventually, nonetheless, to work on the farm which his family finally acquires. Kerouac's Joe Martin, in *The Town and the City*, recalls the Delusson's eldest son.

5   These attitudes are similar to those of Monique, one of the Franco-Americans who rebels in Grace Metalious' *No Adam in Eden*, published one year after *Papa Martel*.

restrained by their French-Canadian Catholic heritage, with resulting ambivalent behavior and psychological frustration.[6]

It is to Vivian Parson's *Not Without Honor* that one must turn to find a full-blown picture of Franco cultural conflict and rebellion. Set in the late nineteenth century, in a Michigan mining town rather than in the mill towns of New England, the hero is the eldest son of a Quebec farm family, who hates everything that his family and traditional French-Canadian values represent. He abhors the poverty and restrictions of life with his parents. Given the chance of going temporarily to Michigan to earn money to bring back home, he has no intention of ever returning. He leaves, not for money, but for freedom and tells the Franco community in the Michigan mining town that he left Quebec because his parents had total control over his life. Here he will be free, not silently obedient, and no Franco will tell him what to do. He further decides that Franco-Americans are incapable of adapting to life in the United States, so he will totally reject their way of life. However, circumstances cause him to decide to become the leader of the Franco community, in order to convince them to reject their old ways and accept life in America, and to mix and intermarry with other nationalities. After a long struggle, he triumphs, forcing the accepted Franco leader (his mother-in-law) to return to Quebec. The hero explains that

> Hers was a life of the past. Only those loving freedom . . .
> found refuge here . . . We can't bring Canada here. Down
> inside us we don't even want to. If we'd loved Canada
> enough, we'd never have left it.[7]

This is a perceptive statement. Much of the French-Canadian cult of *survivance* in Quebec was based on an explicit rejection of supposedly egotistical and materialistic "Protestant" values and on the glorification of poverty, submission, resignation, and sacrifice. Might not a Franco who left Quebec for economic

---

6   *Culture* 6 (1945), pp. 210-212. Ledoux cites the example of Émile Gauvreau, the son of French-Canadian immigrants, who became the famous editor of a New York tabloid. Oscar Handlin cites passages from Gauvreau's autobiography in *Children of the Uprooted* (New York: Universal Library, 1966), chapter 16, as examples of the marginal existence of the second generation.

7   Vivian Lajeunesse Parsons, *Not Without Honor*. (New York: Dodd Mead, 1941), pp. 342 and 285.

reasons feel guilty about placing   material concerns over *survivance*, hence not "lov[ing] Canada enough?" However, contrary to the hero's admonition, many resolved this precisely by "bring[ing] Canada here," *i.e.*, their valiant if ultimately unsuccessful attempt to transplant Quebec to New England.

Not Without Honor stresses negative aspects of the French-Canadian heritage and rebellious disputes within the Franco-American community. Parsons pictures Francos as the hardest immigrant group to win over to "American" ways of living and emphasizes that such adaptation is not an easy task, but nevertheless she advocates total assimilation for Franco-Americans.

A comment is called for here on some historical, geographical, and sociological implications of the novel. Written in 1941, it reflects a wartime desire for Americanization of immigrants more typical of World War I than World War II, when the ethnic ideal seemed closer to cultural pluralism (Japanese excepted, of course). Parsons' atavistic militance on this subject may have reflected a fear that Franco-Americans, unlike European immigrants, were not following the acculturation trend of post-World War I America.

The Michigan setting is significant. Although French Canadians have been in Michigan since the days of New France, their demographic concentration has never been as high as in the mill cities of New England. [8] Did Parsons realize that her theme of rebellion against the ethnic group's values would have been unconvincing if set in a New England milieu (as are the novels of Archambault, Ducharme, and Robichaud), where *survivance* dominated Franco-American communities?

---

[8]   Leon T. Truesdell, *The Canadian Born in the United States.* (New Haven: Yale University Press, 1943), pp. 54, 60, 72-73 and 86-89. Since the beginning of the century, three-quarters of Franco-Americans live in New England. In industrial cities like Woonsocket, Lewiston, and Manchester they have, for some time, been the largest ethnic group, often comprising more than half the total population. In Michigan, the Franco-American population is smaller and made up of the descendants of fur-traders and foresters.

Parsons' fictional hero, the rebel who rejects his ethnic heritage, corresponds to the conflict theories of Irvin Child and Marcus Hansen. They saw such rebellion among second-generation immigrants, which featured the conscious discarding of much of their foreign heritage, as an attempt to escape "marginal" status, that is, being considered "outsiders" in both the American world and in their immigrant communities.[9] *Not Without Honor*, with its emphasis on conflict and rebellion, is also the precursor of the Franco vision which one finds in the works of Jack Kerouac and Grace Metalious.

I am not implying that Parsons' story is more representative of the actual historical experience of Franco-Americans than are the tales of Archambault, Ducharme, and Robichaud. If anything, the contrary may be true. There is no doubt that the latter novels correspond more closely to the dominant view which the Franco-American elite—particularly the clergy—historically espoused: gradual but patriotic acculturation, combined with *survivance* resting on the traditional French-Canadian triad of devotion to Family, Church, and Land.[10]

Robert Cormier's *Now and at the Hour* also presents this traditional and positive view of Franco life, even though its hero is dying of cancer. The dying man's family has seen hard times, having lived in a tenement for many years and never having had much money; but husband, wife, and their six children have persevered, managed to buy a bungalow, and maintained a warm family atmosphere. The grown children have achieved some

---

9   Child's theoretic formulation is not as simplistic as that of Hansen, who would have one believe that most second-generation Franco-Americans were discontented and rebellious. Child, in a study of the social psychology of the male children of Italian immigrants in New Haven, Connecticut, identifies three equally likely reactions: rebellion, attachment to the ethnic group (identification with a national origin), and apathy (refusal to be drawn into rivalries). Irvin I. Child. *Italian or American? The Second Generation in Conflict* (New Haven: Yale University Press, 1943). Marcus L. Hansen, "The Problem of the Third Generation Immigrant" in Handlin, *Children of the Uprooted*, chap. 18. Handlin's classic book, *The Uprooted* (New York: Universal Library, 1951) is a questionable attempt to apply this theory of conflict-rebellion-marginality-disorganization to the entire American ethnic experience.

10   Josaphat Benoit, *L'Âme franco-américaine* (Montreal: Éditions Albert Lévesque, 1935) gives the most complete explanation of the attitudes of the Franco elite.

upward mobility. The moribund father has doubts and fears, yet in the end, his simple but deep Franco-Catholic faith bolsters him and he dies as he has lived, with quiet dignity and grace.

Cormier's next two novels are set in the same Massachusetts mill town, patterned after Leominster, where he was born in 1925, and where he still lives today. *A Little Raw on Monday Mornings* is similar in moral tone to *Now and at the Hour*. Its heroine is a Franco widow in her late thirties with three surviving children. She has become a perfunctory Catholic as a result of the murder of her eldest daughter and the subsequent suicide of her husband. The dramatic action of the novel revolves around her becoming pregnant after a one-night fling and her decision to have an abortion when the man responsible leaves town. The moral resolution of this dilemma is much the same as in Cormier's preceding novel. The heroine overcomes her doubts and fears by regaining a sense of sin.

> To feel a joy at sin, a sweetness: did that make sense? . . .
> Despite the doom of her sins hanging over her, she was
> swept with happiness . . . for she had faced all her sins,
> absorbing the guilt but crying out for forgiveness . . . . [11]

After refusing the abortion, she is reunited with the man responsible for the pregnancy and, although he is timid and unprepossessing, they are prepared to try to make a go of it. Grace, the heroine, regains her honor as well as an inner sense of grace in the religion which is her "gift from God." *A Little Raw* is in many ways not a traditional Franco ethnic novel, since no French is spoken. Both Grace and her mother have married outside of their nationality, and Grace's lifestyle for most of the book comes nowhere near the ideal put forth by the Franco-American elite. But the ending, featuring a return to religion, which hinges on the regaining of a sense of sin, is quintessentially Franco-Catholic. Cormier, despite all of his concern with negative doubts, fears, and questioning, is in the final analysis a Franco novelist with much the same outlook as Ducharme and Robichaud.

Take Me Where the Good Times Are has even less of an ethnic quality than *A Little Raw on Monday Mornings*. The central character is an elderly Franco-American widower, who has no children and is living in an infirmary (poor house). Another

---

[11]   Robert Cormier, *A Little Raw on Monday Mornings* (New York: Sheed and Ward, 1963), pp. 162 and 164.

major Franco figure in the book is an old bachelor who also has no family, lives alone in a rooming house, and eventually commits suicide. *Good Times* thus raises one interesting question concerning Franco ethnicity: if the elite emphasized the central role of a large family in preserving *survivance* and French Canadian values, what about those who failed to produce such a family? Their lonely old age differs conspicuously from the stereotype of revered patriarchs and matriarchs cared for by an extended household.

David Plante's *The Family* focuses on a large household—seven sons—in Providence, Rhode Island, during the 1950s. As with all other Franco novels, life centers around family and religion. Besides providing insights into the ethnic culture of Franco-Americans, Plante has an intriguing perspective concerning familial relationships. Although mother, father, and children cling to an almost desperate belief in "family" as an abstract ideal, tensions mount until, by the end of the novel, all lies in ruin. The aloof and inflexible father has lost his job, the mother is mentally ill, and the two have become alienated from each other as well as from their children. Plante challenges the validity of the model of a warm and cohesive ethnic family, put forth by the Franco-American elite. This challenge takes on added impact when compared with the family life of Jack Kerouac and Grace Metalious.

Kerouac and Metalious—*On the Road* and *Peyton Place*—are names and novels seldom put in tandem by students of literature. What possible connection could there be between the hip spokesman of the counterculture of his time, the "beat" generation, and the crass purveyor of smutty best-selling pap, other than the coincidence that both entered the public eye during 1956-1957? What if the common thread were something which does not mesh with the popular image of either figure?—the fact that both were Franco-Americans whose ancestral roots lay in a French-Canadian heritage steeped in maintenance of traditional nationality and religion, and famous for militant defense of conservatism, Catholicism, and the family.

Neither Jack Kerouac nor Grace Metalious was primarily concerned with writing ethnic fiction, and most of their readers have not approached their books with the goal of learning about Franco-American life. Nevertheless, they provide fascinating case studies of how ethnicity can pervade the vision of novelists whose output is not ordinarily considered as dealing with such matters.

Seeing him as a "crazy Catholic mystic"[12] and her as a rebel against her national origins provides new insights into writers usually pigeonholed into the respective niches described above.

Kerouac's Franco-Catholic upbringing explains much of the contradiction between public image and real life. The so-called "King of the Beats" was indeed a rebel, but an unsuccessful one. The tragedy of his life and the genius of his literature find their origins in the ambivalent tensions he felt towards his ethnic-religious background.

Jean-Louis Lebris de Kérouac was born in Lowell in 1922, to Francos whose families had emigrated from Quebec to New Hampshire around the turn of the century. His parents raised him in a totally French-speaking family environment. "Ti Jean" spoke no other language until he entered school, and French continued to be his primary means of communication throughout childhood because of its dominance in his Franco neighborhoods, national parishes, and parochial schools. Although he left Lowell and the Franco-Catholic atmosphere of his youth at age seventeen and became the spokesman of a movement and a liberated lifestyle which seem antithetical to traditional Franco-American culture, Jack never forgot his Franco origins. He was not able to transcend his ethnicity; indeed, he seemed unsure about whether he wanted to. As a hyphenated American, he found himself cast in a role typical of many children of immigrants, that of "marginal outsider." "In" two worlds, Franco and American, he could be truly "of" neither. This identity crisis haunted him throughout his life and may have been responsible for his early death.

The marginal ambivalence he felt towards his confining ethnic past and the broader possibilities available in America produced an almost dual personality in Kerouac. Beat versus Lowellite, Rebel versus Good Boy, Jack was and was not more than his Franco, Catholic, mill town origins. Like his mother, who was profoundly Franco, but had a desire for upward mobility, he wanted something more than Lowell could offer. He spent most of his years searching for this, but always returned to his simpler roots. Such antithetical, contradictory duality was due in large part to conflicting feelings towards the three major components of his ethnicity, *foi*, *langue*, and *moeurs* [faith, language, and mores] which correspond to the Quebec *survivance* triads of Church,

---

12   Jack Kerouac, *Lonesome Traveller* (New York: McGraw-Hill, 1950), p. vi describes himself thus.

Family, and Land. Kerouac's components were Catholicism, Family (particularly his relationship with his mother), and Franco Lowell, which furnished the broader ethnic environment of his childhood.

Reading his five "Lowell" novels (*The Town and the City, Doctor Sax, Maggie Cassidy, Visions of Gerard*, and *Vanity of Duluoz*), which describe his life in the Franco sections of the town before he left for New York City at age seventeen, is perhaps the best way to pursue an analysis of Kerouac's ethnicity.The most revealing of these, for ethnic-religious purposes, are *Visions* and *Sax. Satori in Paris* is also valuable, as an account of a search in France for his ancestral origins. Although his major biographers have never fully understood the extent to which Jack was influenced by his Franco heritage, Ann Charters, Dennis McNally, and Gerald Nicosia provide much data which can be used to demonstrate this influence. Victor Lévy Beaulieu's *Essai poulet* [Chicken essay] on Kerouac and Professor Armand Chartier's overview of Franco-American literature (which briefly covers both Kerouac and Metalious) are exceptions, in that they do make ethnicity their central focus. Nevertheless, Jack Kerouac, Franco-American, remains far less well-known than Jack Kerouac, rebellious beat.

In 1924, when *Ti Jean* Kerouac was two, a girl was born a few miles up the Merrimack River from Lowell, in Manchester. Her parents, of mixed French-Canadian and French ancestry, named her Grace Marie Antoinette Jeanne d'Arc de Repentigny, but she later became known to the world as Grace Metalious, author of the scandalous best-seller *Peyton Place*. There is no evidence that Kerouac and Metalious ever met, or that either knew that the other was a Franco, or that Grace even knew who Jack Kerouac was. However, there are superficial similarities in their lives and careers. Both were Francos of nearly the same age, born and raised a few miles apart in two of the major Franco-American centers of New England. Each became a famous novelist but had a short and unhappy life. Neither managed to make it through the 1960s— Grace died in 1964 at age thirty-nine, five years before Jack died.

Differences between the two seem more significant than similarities. Many of his readers are aware of Kerouac's French-Canadian ancestry, since this is duly noted on the back page of his novels, although most readers are unaware of the importance this ancestry played in shaping his life and writing. But few people, even her avid readers, had any idea that Metalious was a Franco-

American or that she wrote a novel (*No Adam in Eden*) about French Canadians in Quebec and New England.

A more serious difference for someone who wishes to analyze Grace's ethnicity is the paucity of available materials. Kerouac wrote voluminously and autobiographically and a wealth of biographical and critical studies exist. Such is not the case with Metalious. She wrote only four novels, all of which bear some relation to her life, but in which she veiled or repressed her own circumstances far more than did Jack. Only *No Adam in Eden* has much bearing upon her Franco childhood and upbringing. There was no reliable account of Grace's life until the publication of Emily Toth's biography in 1981.

Compounding the lack of sources is an analytical difficulty. The role of ethnicity in Metalious' life is not as clearly defined as it is in Kerouac's. Her upbringing was not as heavily Franco as was Jack's, and her rebellion against whatever ethnic heritage she possessed was more complete and more traumatic in its consequences than was Kerouac's. Veritably she may be seen as the ultimate iconoclast of French-Canadian institutions and ideas.

Outwardly, she rebelled totally against the triads of traditional French-Canadian *survivance*. Yet, like Kerouac, she continued to be bound inwardly by some of their strictures; the resulting feelings of guilt meant she could achieve no lasting beatitude. However, I feel that her problems, unlike Jack's, stem more from the lack of a traditional Franco upbringing than from rebellion against such. Grace had no close family environment, no meaningful religious training, and no network of relationships with other Francos. This was made worse by status and sexual dilemmas, such as dissonance between her supposedly aristocratic background and the actual poverty of most of her life, and discontent with her traditional female role. Thus Grace was left with nothing to believe in, no motivating principle, be it Franco, spiritual, or otherwise. No wonder she had such a low view of human nature and believed there were far more ugly people in the world than beautiful. Both her fiction and real life have an utterly negative, bleak, and repellent quality; her ambivalence towards her ethnic background is an important aspect of this. *Peyton Place, The Tight White Collar,* and particularly *No Adam in Eden*, Grace's only novel which gives any direct evidence of her Franco heritage, all say there's no hope within one's nationality but it's equally hopeless to try to rise outside of it. The life which

Grace led showed that such advice was no more useful in reality than in fiction. Francos may take heart, at least, from the fact that her unhappiness seemed more a function of deficiencies in her ethnic rearing than the inevitable result of trying to maintain *survivance* in New England.

My purpose has been neither to present ethnicity in a negative light nor to imply the opposite: that Kerouac and Metalious would have been happier if they had remained wholly within the world of Franco *survivance*. If they had been either assimilated or primarily *survivance*-oriented, one can postulate that neither would have had the urge or ability to produce the fiction which was a creative result, after all, of the marginality they experienced by being both Franco and American.

It is fashionable today to emphasize adaptive aspects of what has been called neo-ethnicity, that is, the re-creation of an ethnic identity in the 1970s by descendants (usually the third generation or beyond) of those immigrants who arrived in the United States before the 1920s. Such a theory stresses the possibilities for situational manipulation of ethnicity through the creation of multiple identities: in one context one can play the role of the ethnic (family life, reunions, weddings, social gatherings) while in other contexts one takes on the identity of the Anglo host society (school, the workplace, the larger world).[13]

----

[13]   For a discussion of the rise of neo-ethnicity, see Michael Novak. *The Rise of the Unmeltable Ethnics* (New York: Macmillan, 1971); Nathan Glazer and Daniel P. Moynihan, eds. *Ethnicity: Theory and Experience* (Cambridge: Harvard University Press, 1975); Judith A. Nagata. "What is a Malay? Situational Selection of Ethnic Identity in a Plural Society." *American Ethnologist* 1 (1974), pp. 331-350; Sydelle Brooks Levy, "Shifting Patterns of Ethnic Identification Among the Hassidim," in John Bennett, ed. *The New Ethnicity: Perspectives from Ethnology* (St. Paul: West Publishing Co., 1975), pp. 25-50.

The author is very grateful to Professor Paul J. Bohannan, director of the "Dual Cultural Heritages in the United States" seminar at the University of California at Santa Barbara, which provided him with new insights into the ethnic phenomenon. The year-long seminar was part of the National Endowment for the Humanities Fellowship in Residence Program for College Teachers. This seminar allowed the time needed to study Kerouac, Metalious, and the other Franco-American novelists discussed in this article.

I don't question the validity of this view, but such situational neo-ethnicity should not be romantically overemphasized and extended backwards to include the generations raised before World War II. For people like Kerouac and Metalious, bred in an environment far different from that in which the neo-ethnics were reared, one must recognize the confining and often disruptive quality of traditional ethnic identity.

[This essay first appeared in a French translation as "L'histoire comme roman, le roman comme histoire" in the French Institute's publication entitled *La situation de la recherche sur la Franco-Américanie*. It has been reviewed by the author, and up-dated where necessary, for inclusion in this volume.]

Select Bibliography

Franco English-Language Novelists and Novels

Archambault, Alberic A. *Mill Village: a Novel.* Boston: Bruce Humphries, 1943.

Cormier, Robert. *Now and at the Hour.* New York: Coward-McCann, 1960.

_____*A Little Raw on Monday Mornings.* New York: Sheed and Ward, 1963.

_____*Take Me Where the Good Times Are.* New York: Macmillan, 1965.

Ducharme, Jacques. *The Delusson Family: a Novel.* New York: Funk and Wagnalls, 1939.

Kerouac, Jack. *The Town and the City.* New York: Universal Library edition, 1959; origianlly published 1950.

_____*Doctor Sax: Faust Part Three.* New York: Grove Press, 1959.

_____*Maggie Cassidy.* New York: Avon, 1959.

_____*Visions of Gerard.* New York: Farrar, Straus, 1963.

_____*Vanity of Duluoz: an Adventurous Education.* New York: Coward-McCann, 1968).

_____*Satori in Paris.* New York: Grove Press, 1966.

_____*Book of Dreams.* San Francisco: City Lights Books, 1961.

_____*Desolation Angels.* New York: Coward-McCann, 1965.

_____*Lonesome Traveler.* New York: McGraw-Hill, 1960.

Metalious, Grace. *Peyton Place.* New York: Julian Messner, 1956.

_____*The Tight White Collar.* New York: Julian Messner, 1960.

_____No Adam in Eden. New York: Trident Press, 1963.

Parsons, Vivian Lajeunesse. Not Without Honor. New York: Dodd, Mead, 1941.

Plante, David. The Family. New York: Farrar, Straus, Giroux, 1978.

Robichaud, Gerard. Papa Martel: A Novel in Ten Parts. Garden City: Doubleday, 1961.

Critical, Bibliographical, Biographical Studies

Chartier, Armand. "The Franco-American Literature of New England: A Brief Overview." In Ethnic Literatures Since 1776: The Many Voices of America, pp. 193-215. Lubbock: Texas Tech Press, 1978.

Chassé, Paul. "La littérature franco-américaine sur nos campus?" Le Canado-Américain 5 (1969): 26-31.

Daziel, Bradford. "Franco-American Fiction: Isolation Versus Assimilation." Presentation at the Association for Canadian Studies in the United States conference, 7-8 October 1977, Burlington, Vermont.

Robert, Adolphe. "Essai Bibliographique sur l'apport franco-américain à la littérature des États-Unis." Revue d'Histoire de l'Amérique Française 2 (1949): 540-556.

On Kerouac and Metalious

Beaulieu, Victor-Lévy. Jack Kerouac: A Chicken-Essay. Translated by Sheila Fischman. Toronto: Coach House Quebec Translations, 1975.

Charters, Ann. Kerouac. A Biography. San Francisco: Straight Arrow, 1973.

Chassé, Paul. "Jack Kérouac, 1922-1969." Le Canado-Américain 6 (1970): 16-20.

Duberman, Martin. *Visions of Kerouac*. Boston: Little Brown, 1977.

Gifford, Barry and Lee, Lawrence. *Jack's Book: An Oral Biography of Jack Kerouac*. New York: St. Martin's, 1978.

Hipkiss, Robert A. *Jack Kerouac, Prophet of the New Romanticism*. Lawrence: Regents Press of Kansas, 1976.

Jarvis, Charles E. *Visions of Kerouac: The Life of Jack Kerouac*. Lowell: Ithaca Press, 1974.

McNally, Dennis. *Desolate Angel: Jack Kerouac, the Beat Generation, and America*. New York: Random House, 1979.

Metalious, George and O'Shea, June. *The Girl from "Peyton Place": a Biography of Grace Metalious*. New York: Dell, 1965.

Nicosia, Gerald. *Memory Babe: A Critical Biography of Jack Kerouac*. New York: Grove Press, 1983.

Toth, Emily. *Inside Peyton Place: The Life of Grace Metalious*. Garden City: Doubleday, 1981.

Tytell, John. *Naked Angels: the Lives and Literature of the Beat Generation*. New York: McGraw-Hill, 1976.

Corinne Rocheleau-Rouleau:
Advocate for the Handicapped
(1881-1963)

Béatrice Belisle MacQueen

Corinne Rocheleau-Rouleau was a true Franco-American. The third of six children, she was born in Worcester, Massachusetts, in the late nineteenth century, of parents who had migrated there a generation earlier. She lived in the midst of a happy, united, and cultured middle-class family. Her mother was the organist at Notre-Dame Church, and her father owned and managed a retail business in men's clothing and accessories. Her parents were dedicated to the education of all their children, watching over their religious training as well as their intellectual and artistic development.

But the ideal milieu in which this privileged child was growing up was suddenly and overwhelmingly upset by tragedy. At the age of nine, Corinne, who was in boarding school in Fall River at the time, became progressively deaf over a period of four years. Her ear drums had completely atrophied. None of the specialists consulted in Boston and Worcester were able to pinpoint the cause or correct the problem. Since she no longer heard herself or others, her speech became unintelligible. Her parents kept her in boarding school so that she might receive individual attention and have lessons adapted to her handicap. The aim was to help this child develop as normally as possible.

Unfortunately, each time Corinne's father came to visit, the child rushed into his arms, begging to be brought home. She thus shuttled back and forth between home and boarding schools in Massachusetts and in the Province of Quebec. Everywhere, even at table, she sought refuge in books. She hid when guests came to visit. She was at ease only with her family or with babies and toddlers whom she could hug and cuddle and who looked to her only for a smile.

After years of praying, Corinne's mother resigned herself to this ordeal, which she came to accept as God's will. But Mr.

Rocheleau did not accept the situation so easily. He insisted that Corinne participate as much as possible in family life, that she be neither coddled nor pitied. Like the rest of the family, she had to greet visitors as well as go out with her family. When they gathered in the living room for an evening of music, she had to be there with the others. However, they did allow her a privilege—she always had a place next to her father.

Corinne's parents took her regularly to appointments with doctors, at times in Worcester, at others in Boston. When she went to Boston with her father, she occasionally had to return home alone by train. Her father hoped that this would help her gain some self-assurance.

In the long run, her parents realized that the medical treatments that Corinne was receiving were ineffective. Having heard of a school in Montreal where the deaf learned to speak, Mr. Rocheleau suggested to Corinne that she might go there if she promised to stay for a full school year. The school was called the Institution des Sourdes-Muettes, a school for deaf-mute girls and women. Because she loved and respected her parents, who had showered her with loving care and attention, and also because she had an innate need to express herself, she agreed to go.[1]

What courage and docility were needed by the young girl to reactivate her vocal chords and to acquire clear and easily-understood speech! What patience was needed by the Sister of Charity of Providence who taught her once again to speak and to make herself understood! All this took a full year. Corinne learned to speak and to lip-read both French and English. She spent summers at home but went back for three more school years. In fact, her whole life through, she would return again and again to the Sisters for more and more lessons and practice.

Unfortunately, by the time Corinne reached the age of eighteen, both of her parents had died. Once her younger sisters had found their niche, Corinne registered as a student in a business school. Upon completing her courses and passing the Civil Service examination with flying colors, she accepted a position in the Census Bureau in Washington, D.C. She worked there for two years and loved that beautiful city. However, the climate affected her health, and she had to return to Worcester,

---

[1]   "My Education in a Convent School for the Deaf," *The Catholic Educational Review*, May 1931.

where she became her brother's partner in managing the business established by their father.

During the following seventeen years, even though she was still active in the family enterprise, Corinne studied constantly. She joined civic and cultural groups in Worcester and published a large number of articles on literary and historical subjects. She also wrote tales for children, short stories, playlets, poems, and some two thousand letters.[2]

In 1913, Corinne composed a series of tableaux under the title "Françaises d'Amérique"[3] for the Cercle Jeanne-Mance of Worcester, a social and cultural club for Franco-American women, founded on October 12, 1913. Abridged elementary books on the history of Canada available to Franco-Americans did not go into much detail. Few of them mentioned that Marie Rollet, the widow of Louis Hebert, had adopted orphaned Indian children, or that Mère Marie de l'Incarnation had learned the Algonquian language to serve as an interpreter and to translate Sacred Scripture into that tongue. "Françaises d'Amérique" had a highly successful debut at the Cercle Jeanne-Mance.

In May 1913, Corinne Rocheleau was invited to write the first "Woman's Page" in *L'Union*, a periodical published by the Union Saint-Jean-Baptiste d'Amérique for its members. In these articles, Corinne set forth her values: a strong faith, an unswerving optimism, and a heartfelt patriotism for three countries: the United States, Canada, and France, which shared her loyalty without dividing it. Her first "Woman's Page" ended with the words *Gesta Dei per Francos*.

In the columns of *L'Union*, Corinne Rocheleau also expressed her opinions concerning the traditional role of women as mothers of a family and teachers of their children, as well as on the less traditional roles of those she called "workers outside the walls," among whom she placed herself.[4] She also shared slightly ironic comments on the eternal patience of women who sought and fully

---

2 [These can be consulted in the Archives of Rivier College, Nashua, New Hampshire, founded by the Sisters of the Presentation of Mary in 1933.—Editor]

3 Published by the Belisle Press, Worcester.

4 *L'Union*, November 1913.

deserved the elusive right to vote.[5] In 1938, in an article entitled, "Les femmes bien réussies," written for the first Rivier College yearbook, she praised the formation given by this Catholic college to students privileged to study there.[6]

The author had other and more general interests as well. In 1914, when France and Germany declared war, Corinne Rocheleau's article in *L'Opinion Publique* was a rallying cry. Many young men with names like Rocheleau, Tougas, Granger, Daudelin, and others belonging to well-known Franco-American families in Worcester, went off to serve in France.

In 1921, Corinne, who had always felt attracted to France, made a long sojourn in Europe. Besides France, she visited Italy, Belgium, and England. She wrote of her travels in articles titled "Lettres de Corinne," which she sent to *L'Opinion Publique*. On her return, she was invited to speak in Worcester to the Alliance Française, to a group called La Quinzaine,[7] to the Cercle Jeanne-Mance, and to Les Dames du Dispensaire.[8] During the "Great War," the members of those societies had not only provided medical supplies to the Allies, but had furnished monetary help to French and Belgian families who had lost a mother or a father, a son or a daughter.

In her "Lettres de Corinne," the author tells of visiting several survivors who welcomed her as a member of the family. She describes the monuments, the ceremonies, and the heroes who touched her deeply. She composed a beautiful tribute to

---

5   "Du calme, cher auteur, du calme!" *L'Opinion Publique*, September 25, 1915.

6   "Accomplished Women." Printed by the Lakeview Press, Framingham, Mass., May 1938, and reprinted in *Le Devoir*, Montreal, September 14, 1938.

7   [La Quinzaine was, and still is, a group of fifteen francophile women who meet at one another's home every fifteen days to discuss cultural topics and issues in French.—Editor]

8   [This last group was the Ladies' Auxiliary of a clinic, the Dispensaire Franco-Américain, founded in 1915 by a group of Franco-American doctors in Worcester for the treatment of Franco-Americans. Its services were free to indigent Franco-Americans.—Editor]

Guynemer,[9] a pilot who died for France during World War I and whose deeds had become legendary.

If we can say that Corinne Rocheleau found history enthralling, especially the history of the French in America, we must also note that describing the education of deaf-mutes resulted in her most important writings; she wrote *Hors de sa prison*,[10] the medical and social history of Ludivine Lachance, an unfortunate among unfortunates. This biography is a wonderful tribute to the persevering faith and unflagging devotion of the Sisters of Charity of Divine Providence.

Ludivine Lachance arrived at the Institution des Sourdes-Muettes in Montreal at the age of sixteen. A forlorn wretch, she had become blind, deaf, and mute about the age of two after a serious illness. The parents, wanting to protect their unfortunate child while they were at work in the fields, sometimes at some distance from the house, kept her locked up in a tiny room next to the kitchen of the cabin they lived in. Because they were ignorant, they distrusted their pastor and the village doctor, fearing that both men wanted to take their daughter from them.

Still, the Lachance family despaired of their child's future. After endless discussions over many long months with the pastor, the doctor, and the chaplain of the Institution des Sourdes-Muettes, they finally agreed to let her go. The Sisters promised to bring her back if the family was not satisfied with the care she received. The father, who made the first trip alone to check on his daughter, found that not only was she clean and neatly dressed, she had already learned to find her way through the hallways to her classroom and to her own room. She was able to recognize by

---

9   Lecture to the Cercle Jeanne-Mance of Worcester.

10   [*Hors de sa prison: Extraordinaire histoire de Ludivine Lachance, l'infirme des infirmes, sourde, muette et aveugle* was published by Arbour and Dupont Press, Montreal, in 1927. The book attracted great interest on the part of the English-reading public. In 1932, the Royal Institute for the Blind in London sought publication rights for their English translation. In 1934, the Xavier Publishing Company for the Blind sought permission for a translation in Braille. These never appeared in print because the Sisters of Providence wanted the author's own translation to be published. This typescript translation is at the Rocheleau-Rouleau Archives of Rivier College in Nashua, N.H., under the title "Freed of Her Chains." Persons interested in consulting these archives should contact Sister Arlene Callahan, Director of the Regina Library at Rivier.—Editor]

touch the Sisters who had been entrusted with her care. Filled with wonder and gratitude, he returned later with Ludivine's mother and younger brother. They were overwhelmed by the total transformation of the poor child who had for so long been considered an idiot.

This biography contains many references to other cases of deafness, muteness, and blindness in France and Belgium, as well as to that of Helen Keller in the United States. Corinne Rocheleau thus became known for the influence her book exerted on the pedagogy of educating the handicapped.

In 1928, the Académie française singled out this book by awarding the author its Médaille d'Or and its Prix de la langue française. In granting the French-language prize to Corinne Rocheleau for this work, the Académie française cited the author's clear style, her accurate vocabulary, the careful research, the pure idiomatic flow of the language, qualities all the more remarkable "because they are found in an author whose background is more American than French."[11]

She wrote *Hors de sa prison* while still working in the business office of the family store. Then came the Crash of 1929. Corinne suddenly found herself obliged to make a fresh start elsewhere. She was already working on a new book, so she left for Cincinnati to join Rebecca Mack who was her collaborator in this new work entitled *Those in the Dark Silence*.

Upon her return to Worcester, she was feted by the Cercle Jeanne-Mance which honored her as a new laureate of the Académie française. A few days later, she accepted an invitation from the Sisters of Charity of Providence who suggested that she come to them in Montreal for a rest before facing an unknown and uncertain future. The following spring, she was back in Cincinnati to finish *Those in the Dark Silence*. The Volta Bureau, which was publishing the book, invited her to Washington, D.C.[12]

It was during this trip to the capital that Corinne Rocheleau renewed her acquaintance with Mr. Wilfrid Rouleau, a longtime

---

[11]   Author's translation.

[12]   [The Volta Bureau was an organization established for the education and well-being of the deaf-mute, the deaf-blind and the hard-of-hearing.—Editor]

family friend. In August 1930, they were married in the private chapel of the Cathedral of Montreal by the auxiliary bishop of that city, the Most Reverend Alphonse Deschamps, former chaplain of the Institution des Sourdes-Muettes, who had remained the spiritual advisor and friend of Corinne.

Mr. and Mrs. Rouleau lived in Washington for three years, both busy with historical research and enjoying the cultural atmosphere of Pierre L'Enfant's [13] city. At that time, Mrs. Rouleau was asked to serve on two committees at the Volta Bureau, committees whose members were not handicapped. What is striking is the fact that for two years in a row, Mrs. Rouleau was elected secretary of both committees, whose duty it was to gather statistics on the number of deaf-mutes, to study and publish the most recent and most effective methods for their education and treatment, and to develop courses for the teachers of these handicapped citizens.

During her Washington years (1930-1932), Corinne Rocheleau-Rouleau wrote a brochure entitled "The National Guard of the United States," published by the Department of the Interior and sent by the American government to Paris for the International Commercial Overseas Exhibition. [14] She lectured at the Catholic University in Washington and was invited to speak before the International Federation of Workers for the Blind. She also published another brochure entitled "Normality for the Handicapped," which included the lecture she had given at a National Catholic Education Association conference. [15]

Unfortunately, the Rouleaus' busy life in Washington had to end because Mr. Rouleau could no longer bear the intense summer heat of the Capital. They settled in Worcester, where Corinne continued her historical research and literary critiques. Wilfrid

---

[13]   [Pierre L'Enfant (1754-1825), a French architect and engineer, was asked by George Washington to submit a design for the city. It was later used in laying out the city's center.—Editor]

[14]   1931.

[15]   "Normality, the Goal of all Handicapped Children," published in "Normality for the Handicapped," Philadelphia, 1932.

took charge of the library of Major Edmond Mallet.[16]

In 1936, Mr. and Mrs. Rouleau moved to Laprairie, a beautiful town near Montreal, where they planned to spend their summers, going back to Washington for the winter months. But that proved to be wishful thinking.

The administration of the Institution des Sourdes-Muettes asked Mrs. Rouleau to prepare a series of lectures for the teachers of the deaf-mute. These courses required a great deal of research, since they had to include the history of the instruction given to deaf-mutes as well as the methods used in special schools for them in Europe and both of the Americas. This work lasted for three years.

To spare Mrs. Rouleau the almost daily trip from Laprairie, where she lived, to Montreal, when she lectured, the Sisters invited Mr. and Mrs. Rouleau to spend the winter of 1939-1940 at the Institution. Mr. Rouleau died there, quite suddenly, in March 1940. This was a huge loss for Mrs. Rouleau, now deprived of the caring and supportive company of her husband. Six months went by before she felt able to return to teaching and research. The tasks she had undertaken were to last until 1941.

After that, she kept an apartment at the Institution in Montreal. But she did not stop working. She read, she studied, and continued to write, even adding to her daily routine by doing social work among the deaf-mute.

In 1947, Corinne Rocheleau-Rouleau was awarded the Grande Médaille of the Société Historique Franco-Américaine in recognition of her literary contributions and her historical research.

In 1953, Mrs. Rouleau received a literary award from the

---

16   [This priceless collection, comprising "some 2000 volumes, as well as a large number of unpublished manuscripts," centers on Native Americans as well as on the contributions of the French in North America. It was bought in 1908 from Major Edmond Mallet (1842-1907), a friend of Wilfrid Rouleau. Major Mallet, a Civil War veteran, later served his country with distinction in Indian Affairs and as head of the Bureau of Land Management until his death. The Union Saint-Jean-Baptiste d'Amérique of Woonsocket, R.I. purchased the collection for the sum of $1,975.50 thanks to the efforts of Wilfrid Rouleau.—Editor]

Association Canado-Américaine for her book *Laurentian Heritage*, a novel based on the memoirs of her husband Wilfrid Rouleau. Written in English, the book was intended for English-Canadian pupils, to sensitize them to the history of their French-speaking compatriots and to increase their awareness of the role played by French Canadians in the development of all of Canada.

In the foreword to this book, professor W.F. Langford of the Sir Adam Beck Collegiate of London, Ontario, recommends it as an ideal introduction to the rural way of life in Quebec during the 1870s and 80s. He further states that unless English-Canadian students spent some time visiting in the "belle Province," they would never fully know "the real Quebec."

Laurentian Heritage is the first of two volumes which Mrs. Rouleau entitled The Heritage Series. The second volume, *Heritage of Peace*, tells the story of its hero Justin Rivier, who, at the age of fifteen, left his home in Quebec for New England because his share of the family legacy was not sufficient to provide the wherewithal to earn a decent living. Having studied with the pastor of his parish, he was looking forward to an intellectually challenging life.

Unfortunately, for a newcomer who knew no English, there were few opportunities outside of factory jobs. He worked hard to earn his living, taking night classes. Little by little, he made his way to larger and larger cities in New England to better his life. In the end, he learned four foreign languages, English, first of all, and became a printer and then a newspaper editor. He finally succeeded in obtaining a job at the U.S. Printing Office. The phases of Justin's life are based on Wilfrid Rouleau's diaries. It is the odyssey of a young man who reached his goal by dint of enormous physical, intellectual, and moral effort. [17]

We should also consider an article written in 1954 for the *Bulletin* of the Fédération Féminine Franco-Américaine on the importance of reading French-language publications. Corinne Rocheleau-Rouleau gives several reasons for this:

---

[17] [Some forty years after having been written, *Heritage of Peace* will finally be published in the near future thanks to the efforts of Cdr. Charles Rocheleau, USN, Ret., the author's nephew, and the expertise of Louise Lind, her cousin.—Editor]

The more foreign languages we master, the more we expand the horizons of our thought and of our understanding.

It is more convenient and more intelligent to know several languages than to know only one.

English is, practically speaking, the language of the whole of North America. Hence, the need for Franco-Americans as well as for their French-Canadian cousins to seek the means of maintaining their French roots.

In this article, she recommends the reading of modern as well as classical authors, but especially of those that are good and great, the only ones worth seeking out, in her opinion. She wanted the French schools and colleges, as well as the French newspapers, to list books for all ages in order to help Franco-Americans retain their moral and ethnic character.[18]

In another article, published in *Le Travailleur* of Worcester, *L'Etoile* of Lowell, and *L'Impartial* of Nashua, in 1955, Corinne Rocheleau-Rouleau congratulated the Société Historique Franco-Américaine for having placed a marker commemorating the discovery of the port of Boston by Champlain in 1605. She expressed the hope that all Franco-American societies, whether devoted to historical pursuits or not, would follow this fine example. She argued that although nineteen-year-old Lafayette captured the popular fancy, Americans should not forget that Rochambeau was the general, in command of both land and sea forces sent by France to help the United States win its War of Independence. "How few Americans today are aware of his vital importance for our country, or of the extent of the aid sent by France," she added. "Well-informed analysts estimate that some 40,000 French troops came to help the decimated, exhausted, ill-equipped American forces," she concluded.[19]

Mrs. Rouleau's work brought her continued gratification and new honors. She was invited to speak before the Société Historique de Montréal by its president, Msgr. Olivier Maurault,

---

[18]   "Prends et lis," *Bulletin*, Fédération Féminine Franco-Américaine, April 1954.

[19]   "Mobilisons notre histoire", *Le Travailleur*, July-August 1955.

who later became Chancellor of the University of Montreal. Her book *Laurentian Heritage* was adopted for the high school curriculum of several cities in the English-speaking provinces of Canada. She was also elected a life member of the Gallery of Living Catholic Authors.

Corinne Rocheleau-Rouleau said of herself that her infirmity had given her a better life than would have been hers without her deafness. Evidently she would not have been able to understand so clearly the difficult life of the handicapped, nor could she have developed such successful teaching methods, aimed at improving their lives, had she not herself been hearing-impaired. She was especially grateful to her father for having fostered her independence and self-confidence. True to his example, as well as that of the Sisters of Charity of Providence, she left the clear message in both her writings and her teaching that the focus of teaching the handicapped must always be to help them lead as normal a life as possible.

Translated by the author

[This article first appeared as "Corinne Rocheleau-Rouleau—femme hors pair, femme de chez nous" in the French Institute's publication entitled *The Franco-American Woman.* It has been reviewed by the author, and up-dated where necessary, for inclusion in this volume.]

Bibliography

The source of the following references is: Sister Mary-Carmel Therriault, S.M., *La Littérature française de Nouvelle-Angleterre*. Montreal: FIDES, 1946, pp. 306, 310.

Perreault, Antonio, "Edmond de Nevers." In *l'Action Française*, 1919, pp. 193 et seq.

Port-Joli, Emma, *Mirbah*. Holyoke: La Justice. Published in 10 installments from May 1910 to March 1912.

Tétrault, Maximilienne, *Le rôle de la presse dans l'évolution du peuple franco-américain de la Nouvelle-Angleterre*. Marseille: Imprimerie Ferran & Cie, 1935, 143 pp.

Camille Lessard-Bissonnette (1883-1970)
Immigrant Author and Itinerant Journalist

Janet L. Shideler

Camille Lessard-Bissonnette's life, quite as much as her work, provides us with multiple insights into the migrant experience, especially that of women.

Born in 1883, in Sainte-Julie-de-Mégantic, in the asbestos-mine region of Quebec, Camille Lessard was the eldest of seven children. She attended elementary school in the village of Laurierville and, at the age of sixteen, obtained her teaching certificate. This diploma testified to the remarkable ambition of young Camille Lessard, especially given the fact that her parents were illiterate. After working for three years as a rural schoolteacher, she emigrated with her family to Lewiston, Maine, in 1904, where she spent four years in the textile mills of that city. It was during this period, more precisely in 1906, when she was twenty-three years of age, that Lessard began to write short stories and chronicles for Lewiston's Franco-American newspaper, *Le Messager*. She spent two years torn between the need to ensure her own financial stability while contributing to the family income, and her increasingly fervent desire to write. By 1908, she was able to devote her energies more seriously to journalism, even becoming a member of *Le Messager*'s editorial team. Due to her efforts, the newspaper would henceforth boast a woman's page.

Nonetheless, in the year 1912, she left Lewiston, this time for Alberta, where her family had recently settled, apparently caught up in the wave of colonization of the Canadian West. A succession of other jobs and other moves within Canada and the United States were to follow, a factor that both interrupted and, at the same time, enhanced her career in journalism. For example, during the 1930s, while working as a colonization agent for a railroad, she took advantage of her nomadic lifestyle to prepare chronicles and travel stories which she subsequently submitted to *Le Messager*. Moreover, it was *Le Messager* which published her serial novel, *Canuck*, in 1936. In 1938, she was appointed editor of the women's page of Montreal's *La Patrie* newspaper, a post that ill health would force her to abandon after only two months. In 1943, at the age of sixty, she married N.P. Bissonnette, a former member of the Connecticut legislature. From her home in California, she continued to contribute articles to *Le Messager* as well as to *La Patrie*. Her husband died in 1951, and she spent her last days in Long Beach, California, where she passed away in 1970.[1] Her life is all the more exceptional if one bears in mind that she was an immigrant woman born into an *habitant* family. Her work, like her life, reflects an extraordinary mix of traditionalism—the result of her rural roots—and of feminism, due largely to her urban experience.

A summary of her novel *Canuck* is probably called for before undertaking an analysis of the work. The novel is the story of a fifteen-year-old young woman, Victoria Labranche, who leaves the Quebec countryside in 1900, destined for Lowell, Massachusetts. The family, whom she accompanies, includes: her father, Vital Labranche; her mother, who remains unnamed in the novel; and her younger brothers, Maurice and Besson, ten-year-old twins. Victoria—or Vic, as she is nicknamed—is the story's main character. Like the overwhelming majority of Quebec families of this period, the Labranche family has come to the United States with the precise purpose of earning a living in the textile mills. In this sense, *Canuck* opens on a note of authenticity as the novel seeks to relate the social history of the Franco-American experience. The intent of the Labranche family is to return to the Quebec homeland once accumulated debts on the land there have been paid. However, in order to realize this dream, which borders on obsession, each member of the family must work in the mills. The only exception is sickly Besson. On the surface, all appears relatively calm within this family in their adopted home . . . until the moment when Vic rebels against her tyrannical father. She leaves home but continues, nonetheless, to contribute to the family budget and, without saying a word to anyone, to put aside enough money to ensure the education of her brother Maurice. The separation between Victoria and her family becomes more pronounced, however, following the death of Besson. The other members of the family then return to Canada, leaving the young woman behind.

Vic meets Raymond Fénélon, a mining engineer, who comes to her rescue when she is assaulted by other young girls, French Canadians like herself, who call her "Canuck" because of her

---

[1]   Richard Santerre, Compiler, *Anthologie de la littérature franco-américaine de la Nouvelle-Angleterre*, volume 8 (Manchester, New Hampshire: National Materials Development Center for French and Creole, 1981), pp. 164a-164b.

peasant apparel. Raymond is her hero, but it is to Jean Guay that she gives her heart. At the moment when she finally resolves to see Jean no longer, she receives a telegram informing her of the imminent death of her father. She leaves immediately for Quebec and remains there after his passing to look after the needs of the entire family. Her assistance is particularly crucial to her mother, who would otherwise have been incapable of managing the family farm by herself. Moreover, if Vic had stayed in the United States, Maurice would have had to abandon his studies at the seminary. After many years of rigorous work, Vic discovers what she believes to be a mineral deposit in a far-flung corner of the family farm. Her friend, Raymond, comes to Quebec in order to confirm the good fortune of the Labranche family. The minerals, however, are not the only discovery Vic makes: she also learns that she loves Raymond and that he loves her. At the novel's closing, the two marry and head off for an adventurous life together in Central America.

First, let us examine Lessard's description, in Chapter One, of the members of the Labranche family. It is not surprising that even their physiognomies announce the conflict that exists between father and daughter, a first clue to the eventual overturning of patriarchal power:

> In one corner five members of a family clung to one another, frightened, nervous. The father, Vital Labranche, was a tall brown-haired man with sharp eyes whose lips, like the blades of a knife, let it be known that it would be unwise to step on his toes. He might have been about 40 years of age.[2]

The reader senses immediately that this man, whose lips resemble "the blades of a knife," is already the adversary. Even the color of his hair—brown rather than blond—suggests his nefarious, "dark" nature according to traditional imagery. Moreover, the fact that his description appears first among the descriptions of all of the members of the Labranche family underscores his role as patriarch and *chef.*

Next we have the description of Madame Labranche:

> The mother, a petite, frail blonde with large, soft, dreamy eyes, had the fearful look of an animal who expects its throat to be slit

---

[2]   Camille Lessard-Bissonnette, *Canuck* (Lewiston, Maine: *Le Messager,* 1936; new edition, Durham, New Hampshire: National Materials Development Center for French and Creole, 1980), p. 2.

at any moment. She was undoubtedly the same age as her husband, but she appeared to be about 50.3

She is described as a victim, aged by adversities, defenseless, and without recourse.

Next the author offers a description of the eldest and only girl, the novel's heroine:

Victoria (who was called Vic) was a young girl of 15, long and thin as a flute, with eyes as deep as night. Her long braided hair was as black as the wings of a crow. She had the tapered fingers of an artist which seemed out of place attached to this body of a little unpolished country girl.4

It is noteworthy that Vic distinguishes herself from the stereotypical heroine: she is neither blonde nor frail, synonymous with femininity according to traditional imagery. The emphasis here is on a deep, artistic soul, not on gender. Lessard is neither unique nor is she first in refusing to confine her character within circumscribed notions of femininity, but rather she mirrors the efforts of Charlotte Brontë, Florence Nightingale, and Louisa May Alcott, among others, in their creations of Jane Eyre, Cassandra, and Christie and Jo respectively. Although the author adds, "she would have been pretty had she been dressed differently," she also states, "But underneath a dress, which announced her poverty and poor taste due to lack of money, was a young, well-formed body that stood tall in defiance of life."5

The omniscient narrator concludes her portrait of the heroine by stating, "A careful observer would have been able to make out the bravado on her lips and the revolt in her eyes, indicating that it would be difficult to lead this one to slaughter."6 This last image underscores the fact that the author, like the majority of French-Canadian immigrants, came from an agricultural family. In this way, the description of Vic links her to a collectivity while also giving her an individual personality.

---

3   Ibid.

4   Ibid., p. 3.

5   Ibid.

6   Ibid.

Finally, we move on to the twins: "Maurice, 10 years of age, was a fine-looking, young, blond-haired boy with his mother's dreaming eyes, with delicate features and an alert expression. He clung to Vic as if he felt that from her would come the surest protection and understanding."7 And, finally, there is the description of the last member of the Labranche family:

> Besson, Maurice's twin, suffered from a poorly-treated pleurisy which had attacked his bones and lungs to such an extent that now his poor body was twisted and hunchbacked. He sat huddled on the bench, his pale, thin head resting on his mother's knees. His large devouring eyes—which seemed to devour his tiny angelic face, pale as wax—were open, indicating that he was not asleep but exhausted.8

This last description completes the portraits of the novel's principal characters. The narrator has divided her players into three camps: the father, who is the enemy, the mother and sons, who are the victims, and Vic, the protector of her mother and brothers.

Besson is not a crucial character in the novel, his death occurring shortly after the story opens. Nonetheless, two justifications for his presence, however brief, must be noted. First, his death having brought about the transformation of Vital Labranche, leads to a reconciliation of sorts between father and daughter. Second, the presence of this young, weak creature amidst others who are quite healthy represents a reminder of the misery that haunts this people, even when living in a different land. Despite the glorification of agricultural life, an important leitmotif in traditional Quebec literature,—Lessard herself will also offer readers a joyous depiction of the Quebec countryside—a significant social reality is present in these opening pages. It is poverty, not love of luxury or thirst for adventure, which had forced the departure of thousands of French Canadians for the United States. In this sense, all immigrants—the Labranches as well as all the others who arrived in Lowell, Woonsocket, Manchester, Lewiston, or elsewhere—were victims of the same material conditions. Lessard, while noting differences in roles based on gender, sees no distinctions amongst men, women, and children when it comes to the penury that caused their exodus. A common misery unites this people whom she describes thus:

---

7   Ibid.

8   Ibid.

Men with large bags under their arms, packs on their backs, overstuffed suitcases in their hands, young girls dragging children by the wrist, women carrying whimpering babies in their arms, all of these people,—like a herd moving toward the same goal . . .9

For these French Canadians—and herein again lies the authenticity of the story—this goal is a better life in Uncle Sam's country. These persons, who share a common past, part from one another at the train station, just as this scene was played out at train stations throughout the Province of Quebec, in search of an unknown future. It is toward another type of solidarity that Lessard now turns her attention by speaking more precisely of the Lessard family.

We have already seen the establishment in the text of a tension: numerous victims versus a single oppressor. That oppressor is the father, who represents the patriarchal structure of Quebec society. Exploitation of the most defenseless, a cruelty endured by the mother, by Maurice, and by Vic herself, is denounced by the heroine in a succeeding episode that takes place three years after the family's arrival in Lowell. Labranche becomes furious when he learns that Maurice has changed his workplace, thus losing a half-day's worth of pay. The moment is not only dramatic, it is also decisive, both in the story's plot and in Vic's life. Fearing that her brother will be physically punished, she intervenes to protect him against her enraged father: "Dare to touch Maurice tonight, and my room will be empty tomorrow,"10 she cries out. Labranche responds in the same defiant tone: "even if you are 18, I still have rights over you!"11 Vic, no longer able to hold back, retorts:

> Yes, you have rights over me, replied Vic, losing all reserve and all respect, but I dare you to exercise those rights! Make the police bring me back home and for my part, I'll see to it that you take my warm place in the patrol car! Don't forget that you committed a crime when you forced Maurice to work in the mills when you should have sent him to school. You passed him off as a 15-year old in order to exploit his health and the sweat of this child for your own profit!12

9   Ibid., p. 1.

10   Ibid., p. 25.

11   Ibid.

To underscore the way in which Vital symbolizes the oppression and subservience imposed upon many immigrant wives and children by their husbands and fathers, Vic goes on:

> You can ruin Maurice's future and his health . . . you can kill Besson more quickly by forcing us to live in a hovel where he is deprived of fresh air and sunlight, just so that your bankbook will be heavier! . . . you can continue to make my mother's life a martyrdom![13]

It is thus that Vic begins a revealing and painful story of her life and that of her mother, of the lives they led in Quebec. It is a story where exploitation and brutality prevail, rather than being a nostalgic glorification of rural life:

> The work in the fields and in the stables, it was Mama who did it, and me, once I was big enough, and I wasn't very old! . . . In the meantime, you went for rides in your buggy or your carriage, you played cards, you lived it up!
> . . . When you got back to the house, if we hadn't managed to get the heavy work done, there was hell to pay! . . . One time, you even dared to hit Mama because a gate couldn't be repaired, and the animals had wandered onto the neighbor's land! . . . Hit Mama! who has more worth in her little finger than you in your entire body![14]

Since we will later examine the mother-daughter relationship, let us, for the moment, consider instead the relationship between Maurice and his older sister. It is Vic, by dint of her hard work, who will make possible Maurice's education for the priesthood, for it is Maurice's dream to become a priest. Moreover, in a very concrete fashion, it is Vic and her mother who assume responsibility for Maurice's early instruction at home, Vital having deprived him of the opportunity to go to school by sending him to work instead. With this in mind, it could be stated that Vital Labranche also poses an obstacle to the faith while the two women serve as its guardians, the fulfillment of another traditional role for women. What is also traditional is the sacrifice made by a sister in order to help a male sibling realize his goals, in this case, a priestly vocation. So that Maurice can prepare for the priesthood, Victoria will use her own money and abandon any hope of furthering her own education.

---

12   Ibid.

13   Ibid., pp. 25-26.

14   Ibid., p. 26.

The two women, mother and daughter, thus find the means to circumvent paternal authority for a traditional end, just as women have done from time immemorial. Can we see here a nascent form of feminism? For, it should be noted that while rejecting the father figure and refusing a cruel form of patriarchy, Vic nevertheless makes enormous sacrifices so that her brother might one day belong to this same patriarchal structure of Quebec society and the Catholic Church. As children, Maurice and Vic both suffer from the situation, but, inasmuch as he is a man, Maurice has the possibility of climbing the social ladder and becoming part of this powerful group of male leaders, even though it is a woman, Vic, who will ensure his ascent to such heights.

When Monsieur Labranche dies, Maurice abandons his studies and decides to remain at home in order to assist his mother in farming the land. Vic refuses to allow her brother to sacrifice his future in this way. According to the narrator, it is she who "puts her neck to the yoke with the same courage she had shown during other difficult circumstances in her life."[15] Maurice is deeply moved by his sister's act of selfless devotion. The author/narrator then relates what transpires between them:

> Maurice, doing what he used to do when he was very young and broken-hearted, went to kneel at Vic's feet and placed his forehead upon her knees, crying all the while. Impulsively, the young woman, as in an unconscious benediction, placed her hand on his blonde head, lowered at her side. Then, overcoming her emotion, she raised his face and teased: "That's a fine example you just set for me! One day I will be the one to kneel at your feet, Father!"[16]

A woman thus makes possible, not only the maintenance of the faith, but its continuation and advancement by ensuring that yet another generation of priests will be present to minister to the faithful. In noting the generosity traditionally associated with women, the author/narrator also underscores the impossibility for that same woman to climb the social ladder. She, nonetheless, softens her statement by concealing it in a moving passage of touching affection and mutual respect between brother and sister.

Turning now to Mother Labranche and the mother-daughter relationship, it should be noted that Vic's mother is identified only

---

15   Ibid., p. 69.

16   Ibid.

by her relationship to someone else. She is called Mme Labranche or "her mother," "his mother," "my mother," "his wife," etc. What do we know about this woman? We learn that she was once a rural schoolteacher, and, since Maurice studies from the books his mother had used, we know that she has kept these reminders of her past and of a career abandoned in order to marry Vital Labranche. She is, therefore, an educated woman whose only hope now is that her children can better their own lives through a love of learning: "You see, Mama having been a country schoolteacher, she communicated to us her love of books. If I had the means, I would spend all my free time studying. That's all that interests me."17 However involuntary Vic's introduction to the work force may have been, once there she refuses to remain a victim of circumstance or of the will of others. Rather, she uses the serious nature that is a legacy from her mother to become a productive, respected, and more self-directed individual. The qualities that Mrs. Labranche has passed on to her daughter result, not for herself, but for her daughter, in promotions at work: "she threw herself into her work and into her studies with more drive than ever. She left her position as drawing-in girl to go to work in a shoe factory where, thanks to her ability, her salary doubled in a short time."18

It should be said, however, that the most striking feature in the character of the mother is her almost total silence. A quiet sigh, for example, constitutes one of the rare noises to come from her mouth: "Her father was definitely gone, and she heard her mother sigh."19 And also: "As soon as he [Vital] had gone, mother and daughter, without looking at each other, breathed a sigh of relief: they were sure of a few hours of peace."20 We should be aware that during these moments of silence, the two women—mother and daughter—are together. These sighs speak eloquently of the masculine tyranny that victimizes both women, resulting in their solidarity. However, their response to the misery of their condition is quite different. The silence, sighs, and tears of the mother testify to the impossibility of her breaking away. By contrast, Vic, faced with her lamentable life, both speaks out and acts decisively, leaving the paternal home in order to distance herself from her father's tyranny. It should not be forgotten, however, that from her new home—where, in her own

17   Ibid., p. 37.

18   Ibid., p. 36.

19   Ibid., pp. 26-27.

20   Ibid., p. 11.

words, "there are no men in the house to . . . make life miserable!"21—she continues to help her mother. Even distance cannot prevent communication between these two women. Indeed, neither man nor distance can hinder the solidarity that binds mother and daughter. In one of the rare moments in which the mother does utter a few words, these take the form of a prayer in which she states—neither angrily nor reproachfully, but resigned to her lot in life—that her cross is heavy and that the road stretching before her will not be an easy hill to climb: "My God, how high your Calvary is for me!"22 Her regret is also compounded by the recognition of the burden of masculine tyranny that she has passed on to her daughter.

Louise Bernikow, in her book *Among Women,* expresses what might very well have been the unconscious objective of Lessard in this novel when she states:

> The daughters have taken it upon themselves to tell the story of mothers and daughters, partly to break the silence of the mothers and partly to stand against the primacy of the father in our lives, in culture and in history. In becoming archaeologists of the world of our mothers, we are trying to retrieve the female past and to invent a future.23

This retrieval of the past and invention of the future are necessary, even when the father is reduced to silence. As Vital lies suffering and ultimately losing his battle to stay alive, the narrator comments, "he cannot speak."24 But his eyes fill with tears at seeing the daughter who had defied him many years before. Here is the true moment of emancipation for Vic: paternal authority is no longer able to tyrannize the family. However, the reader knows that this liberation is relevant only for Vic. Despite a clearly established solidarity between mother and daughter, distance still exists between them, due to generational differences certainly, but also attributable to the fact that Vic has succeeded in earning her own living because of emigration to the United States.

---

21   Ibid., p. 27.

22   Ibid.

23   Louise Bernikow, *Among Women,* (New York: Harper & Row, 1980), p. 46.

24   *Canuck*, p. 67.

One might suggest that had Vic remained on the family farm in Quebec, her emancipation would probably never have taken place. Agricultural life in that province, which represents Vic's beginnings as it does those of the majority of French-Canadian women who emigrated to the United States, was a hard way of life and one that required the contribution of women and girls to field labor. At the same time, motherhood was the almost inevitable destiny of women. The Church required it; the community expected it. Without it, how could the survival of a people without power be assured?

Although Franco-Americans took Quebec's parish structure with them in order to "transplant" it in New England's "Little Canadas"—thus reconstituting, to a certain extent, within the adopted society, the one they had left behind—they succeeded somewhat in distancing themselves from the demands and the duties imposed upon them as members of a minority community. To use a literary and very French-Canadian allusion, if Vic does not at all resemble Maria Chapdelaine, the heroine of the novel by that name, it is because she has moved far enough away no longer to hear the "voices" of her native Quebec: the call of the land; the desire to live in a French-speaking society to which one belongs by birth and which has been defended from all encroachments by succeeding generations; and, finally, the need to ensure the continuation of all that! Once established on the other side of the border, immigrants adapted to new values, a new reality. For instance, the very foundation of the manufacturing centers of New England was not the community but rather the individual. Their example reinforced the belief that, as an individual, one could achieve anything. To succeed in this new home, one needed only to work hard, and the Quebec woman, as we have just commented, was no stranger to work. Indeed, it should be added here that in no way did her work at the factory liberate her from household chores. As she recounts a day in the lives of Vic and her mother, Lessard is also describing the typical day of a *Franco-Américaine*:

> Labranche and his wife each had a "set" of looms in the same section, so that Vital could push his wife to do her work more perfectly, in such a way that the pay envelopes would be fatter! She did not rebel because her life was the life of the rural women of her country. She went along like an animal beneath the yoke, feeling sharply the whip of its master, but making no effort to escape the blows.25

25   Ibid., pp. 6-7.

Then the narration continues, showing that the workday of Vic and her mother is not finished upon leaving the factory. "While Labranche and Maurice took turns washing up in a basin placed in the sink, Vic and her mother took out the pots of meats, stews, fricassees, or soups cooked the previous evening."26 Then, "The meal finished, while Vic and her mother cleared the table, Labranche took off his shoes to rest his feet . . ."27 And a last detail: "Maurice, his dinner eaten, buried his nose in his books . . . Sometimes his mother, at other times Vic would make him recite lessons and solve problems."28

What was the advantage, then, for the French-Canadian woman who emigrated to the United States? At least part of her daily work was salaried labor. Moreover, this remuneration meant that young women like Vic could help their parents to make both ends meet, but also pursue their own lives, less controlled by family constraints.

It is necessary to note, nonetheless, that a female work force existed in the urban centers of Quebec at this time, more precisely in Montreal. Between 1901 and 1915, the years that comprise the beginnings of the early literary efforts of Lessard, women constituted 58% of all textile employees in Montreal. Most of them were young, unmarried women, the work of married women outside the household still being frowned upon, although more and more necessary.29 But although the urbanization and proletarization of Quebec women were already facts, propagandists throughout the province continued to advocate a particular and increasingly anachronistic image of *la femme québécoise*: that of a creature destined to become wife and mother, devoted heart and soul to her husband, her children, and her household duties. In politics as in the trade union movement—the two being intrinsically linked to the Church in Quebec—the effort to perpetuate this image is underscored in a quote from 1935. That year, one year before the

---

26   Ibid., p. 10.

27   Ibid., p. 11.

28   Ibid.

29   Marie Lavigne and Jennifer Stoddart, "Ouvrières et travailleuses montréalaises, 1900-1940," in *Travailleuses et féministes.*   Eds. Marie Lavigne and Yolande Pinard (Montreal: Boréal Express, 1983), p. 103.

publication of *Canuck*, the *Confédération des travailleurs catholiques* declared:

> Given that one of the principal causes of unemployment is the exaggerated growth of female labor, the convention asks the provincial legislature to restrict to fair proportions the use of female workers . . . and especially by beginning with the laying off of married women.30

In rural Quebec, wives of farmers also did their part to live up to the myth of the perfect woman, as wife and mother. Even at the time of the publication of *Canuck*, the *Cercles de fermières*, founded to bring together rural women, worked tirelessly to realize the objective they had established some years earlier: "To attach [the choice of verb is revealing] the woman to the home by making her duties as spouse, educator, and housekeeper agreeable and easy to accomplish."31 The image that makes of the accomplishment of these duties a sacred act—and thus of the woman who carries them out a veritable saint—is the image that Vic leaves behind her, at the age of thirty-four, when she moves to Central America with her new husband and with—significantly—no allusion to motherhood as her eventual destiny.

The fact that tens of thousands of Quebec women left that province, as did Lessard herself, in order to work in the mills and factories of New England—while it caused a demographic crisis—made possible the creation of a new woman, the *Franco-Américaine*, who felt quite at home in the "Little Canadas" of the northeastern United States.

Translated by the author

[This article first appeared as "Camille Lessard-Bissonnette: A la recherche d'un féminisme franco-américain," in the French Institute's publication entitled *Franco-American Literature: Writers and Their Writings*. It has been reviewed by the author, and up-dated where necessary, for inclusion in this volume.]

---

30   Ibid., p. 111. [It should be noted that the Catholic Church in the United States was preaching along the same lines. See *supra* Y. Roby, "A Portrait of the Female Franco-American Worker (1865-1930)."—Editor]

31   Ghislaine Desjardins, "Les Cercles de fermières et l'action féminine en milieu rural, 1915-1944," in *Travailleuses et féministes*. Eds. Marie Lavigne and Yolande Pinard (Montreal: Boréal Express, 1983), p. 225.

Bibliography

Bernikow, Louise. *Among Women.* New York: Harper & Row, 1980.

Desjardins, Ghislaine. "Les Cercles de fermières et l'action féminine en milieu rural, 1915-1944," *Travailleuses et féministes.* Montreal: Boréal Express, 1983.

Lavigne, Marie and Stoddart, Jennifer. "Ouvrières et travailleuses montréalaises, 1900-1940," *Travailleuses et féministes.* Montreal: Boréal Express, 1983.

Lessard-Bissonnette, Camille. *Canuck.* Lewiston, Maine: *Le Messager*, 1936; Durham, New Hampshire: National Materials Development Center for French and Creole, 1980.

Santerre, Richard, comp. *Anthologie de la littérature franco-américaine de la Nouvelle-Angleterre.* Volume 8. Manchester, New Hampshire: National Materials Development Center for French and Creole, 1981.

Rosaire Dion-Lévesque
(1900-1974)
Poet and Translator of Walt Whitman

Michel Lapierre

I - Born and Died in Nashua, N.H.

Léo-Albert Lévesque was born in Nashua, New Hampshire, on November 26th, 1900, the son of Edmond Lévesque and Rosanna Dionne, both of French-Canadian origin. In 1925, when he began publishing poems in *Le Progrès*, the weekly newspaper for French-speaking citizens of Nashua, he adopted Rosaire Dion as a pen name. He would later change it to Rosaire Dion-Lévesque. Baptized in the Franco-American parish church of St. Louis-de-Gonzague, he grew up, with his five sisters, in a milieu where the ancestral language was still spoken. In 1918, he received a diploma from the Nashua Business College and thenceforth worked at modest jobs in both private enterprise and the civil service until his retirement in 1968.

It was during his adolescence that he developed "un goût violent" for poetry. In 1950, he confided to Lucien-C. San Souci:

> I read all the books of poetry that I could obtain
> with raging intensity . . . Old Hugo and Lamartine,
> Vigny, and then Verlaine and Rodenbach, and
> Rollinat whom I intermingled with Keats and
> Shelley (no Shakespeare), and Oscar Wilde, and,
> closer to home, Nelligan, Lozeau, Paul Morin, René
> Chopin . . .[1]

On August 20th, 1927, he even visited Emile Nelligan, an inmate of the psychiatric hospital of Saint-Jean-de-Dieu in a Montreal suburb, to let him know of his admiration for Nelligan's own *oeuvre*. During the same period, another Canadian-born writer, Henri d'Arles (pseudonym of Rev. Henri Beaudet, a

---

[1]   Lucien C. SanSouci, "Le poète Rosaire Dion-Lévesque," in *Le Phare*, Woonsocket, Rhode Island, vol. 3, no. 2, March 1950, p. 2.

Canadian-born priest of the Manchester, N.H. Diocese, encouraged him to continue writing verse. For the sum of twenty-five dollars,[2] this haughty aesthete even accepted to write the preface of *En égrenant le chapelet des jours*, Rosaire Dion's first book of poetry, published in Montreal in 1928.

Following Nelligan's advice, the poet also went to meet Louis Dantin, a Canadian critic living in exile in Cambridge, Massachusetts. For sixteen years, from 1928 to 1944, the two men maintained a regular correspondence. In addition to this, every Friday evening, Dion-Lévesque visited his older friend to submit some poems which he was constantly reworking.[3]

In 1931, he began collaborating with Wilfrid Beaulieu who had just founded the newspaper *Le Travailleur* in Worcester, Massachusetts. This title for the newspaper had been borrowed by Beaulieu from the well-known paper, published in Worcester in the nineteenth century by Ferdinand Gagnon, considered to be "the father of Franco-American journalism." That same year, Rosaire Dion-Lévesque met a few writers in Paris which he was visiting for the first time: Fernand Gregh, Jehan Rictus, Pierre l'Ermite, before traveling to the South of France, Italy, Switzerland, Belgium, and England. Although he was joyful at finding there certain aspects of the old France of his dreams, he was a harsh judge of contemporary France. In a letter to Wilfrid Beaulieu, he wrote: "All of these artists or so-called artists, disciples of the Dadaist, Realist and Cubist movements, seem to me to be the last displays of a civilization which, by dint of refinement, labors each day at its own destruction."[4]

Four years later, he married the French-Canadian writer Alice Lemieux (1906-1983), who had been awarded the "Prix David" in 1929 for a book entitled *Poèmes*. In 1941, he began to collaborate with a professor at the University of Houston, in Texas, who was publishing *Bayou*, a small French-language magazine. From 1946 to 1951, he was editor-in-chief of the weekly

---

2   cf. Manuscript account of the visit of Dr. Gabriel Nadeau to Rosaire Dion-Lévesque on March 16, 1946, p. 3. Gabriel Nadeau Collection, National Library of Quebec (Montreal).

3   cf. Lucien-C. SanSouci, *op. cit.*, p. 6.

4   Letter to Wilfrid Beaulieu, 23 November, 1931. Wilfrid Beaulieu Collection, Boston Public Library.

L'Impartial of Nashua, and for a year he edited the monthly *Le Phare* of Woonsocket, Rhode Island. During the same period, he published in *Le Haut-Parleur*, a Montreal newspaper directed by T.-D. Bouchard, a series of translations of American poets. From 1952 to 1957, the Montreal daily *La Patrie*, published each week his biographical articles on outstanding persons of French descent living in the United States. These numerous texts were later compiled and published in 1957 in a book entitled *Silhouettes franco-américaines*. Two years later, the author received the "Prix Champlain" for this work, awarded by the Conseil de la vie française en Amérique.[5] At the outset of the following decade, that of the 1960s, Dion-Lévesque wrote for the periodical *Rythmes et couleurs*, directed in Paris by the French-Canadian writer François Hertel. He also published poems and some articles in *L'information médicale et paramédicale* of Montreal.

Dion-Lévesque died in Nashua on January 6, 1974. In 1957, the *Académie française* had awarded him the Auguste-Capdeville Prize for his poetry; in 1963, the Royal Society of Canada had granted him the Chauveau Medal for his collected works. Most of the documents concerning Dion-Lévesque are to be found in the Archives of the Bibliothèque nationale of Quebec in Montreal and at the Boston Public Library.

An American *Oeuvre*

From the Thirties to the Fifties, Dion-Lévesque acquired a certain notoriety in French Canada and of course, in Franco-American cultural circles. However, since what has come to be called the "Quiet Revolution"[6] in Quebec, his name is rarely mentioned there. *Quête*, his last collection of poetry, published by Garneau in 1963 was hardly noticed. Yet, this solitary writer, like

---

5   The CVFA was founded in 1947 for the support of francophone communities throughout North America.

6   [The Quiet Revolution (*la Révolution tranquille*) is the name given to a profound upheaval in the ideology and lifestyle of Quebecers that occurred in the years 1960-1966. The period was characterized by a lessening of the power of the Church, the coming of age of a new intellectual leadership, and the desire on the part of Quebecers to become players in their own right on the national as well as on the international scene.—Editor]

Walt Whitman, felt things as a North American and bared his soul as very few French-Canadian poets of his time had done.

For Auguste Viatte, Dion-Lévesque:

> . . . is the best "Franco-American" poet and the most authentic of these writers since he was born in the United States, whereas Henri d'Arles or Louis Dantin only settled there later in life. Dion-Lévesque was influenced by Dantin: like him, he rebelled against "conformity" as had Walt Whitman, whose works he translated. Like Whitman, he reacted against the industrialism of his environment and extolled Life with pagan fervor. His first collections of verse suffer from a somewhat affected symbolism, but his style matured resulting in both passionate verse and quasi-perfect classical stanzas in *Vita* (1939) *Solitudes* (1949) and *Jouets* (1952).[7]

Although Dion-Lévesque is unquestionably the only New England francophone poet worthy of the name, if we consider the prose *genre*, Yvonne LeMaître, who arrived in New England at the age of 10, and Corinne Rocheleau Rouleau, born in Worcester, Massachusetts, clearly surpass him. The style of *Silhouettes franco-américaines* is tainted by the author's daily use of English. Though it is true that the poet's last works are much less inspired by the "somewhat mawkish symbolism" which characterized his early writings, they are nonetheless marred by artifice and banality.

The musicality of Dion-Lévesque's classical prosody is what confers value upon it. Certain sonnets, like "Ma rivière" in *Quête* are stunning melodic successes. In addition, his Whitmanesque

---

[7]   Auguste Viatte, *Anthologie littéraire de l'Amérique francophone* (Sherbrooke, Quebec: C.E.L.E.F., 1971), pp. 161-162. Dion-Lévesque is the only Franco-American writer of New England mentioned by Viatte in *Histoire des littératures* of the *Encyclopédie de la Pléiade* (1958 edition): "In the United States, among Franco-Americans," he writes in the chapter devoted to French Canada, "Rosaire Dion-Lévesque translates Whitman and sings of life following his example" (Paris: Gallimard, 1958, vol. 3, p. 1389). However, the 1978 edition of the same work mentions no francophone writer of the American Northeast.

lines[8] and the free verse which he used from the 1930s on, without altogether abandoning the use of traditional prosody, conferred upon his work a direct confidential tone which perfectly fits his vocation as a *poète intimiste*.

Yet, a slavish imitation of the Romantics often deprives Dion-Lévesque's verse of the vivid rhythm and secret strength which characterize the best of his output. For example, the following stanza from *Solitudes* is too reminiscent of Lamartine:

> Les choses ont-elles une âme?
> Plus vibrantes que nous, vivent-elles davantage?
> Nous aimons, nous nous détachons.
> Les choses demeurent. [9]

The author's belated romanticism has often been underscored by critics.

> His inspiration, like his talent, situate him at mid-point between Pamphile Le May and Nelligan. More complex than LeMay, less of an artist than Nelligan, the sonneteer of *Les Oasis* does not differ essentially from the Canadian Romantics of the 19th century. That the poet was able to situate himself at such an antiquated poetic level can, no doubt, be explained by the setting of Nashua, a small New Hampshire city where *Les Oasis* was written. In the United States, how can one protect oneself against the all-powerful American language . . . What is astounding is that Rosaire Dion-Lévesque, since his beginnings in poetry, has continued to grow . . .[10]

Even in his last collections of poems, Dion-Lévesque

---

8   *Hymne à l'Amérique* (1932) certainly constitutes the best example of this.

9   Do objects have a soul?
     More vibrant than we, do they live more [intensely]?
     We love, we become detached
     Objects remain.
     "Les choses ont-elles une âme?", in *Solitudes*, p. 17.

10   Gérard Tougas, *Histoire de la littérature canadienne-française*, 3rd ed. (Paris: Presses universitaires de France, 1966), p. 216.

remains a Romantic in his own way. But his pagan impulses, his sensual tones, a certain tendency towards agnosticism, his deep solitude, his powerlessness in the face of life, his conviction of the futility of things, increasingly distinguish him from French-Canadian poets of the last century.

The essentially North American character of his inspiration confers upon his work an undoubted originality, an undeniable authenticity. In 1936, Alfred DesRochers was correct in classifying him, among the eight French-Canadian poets who attempted, in his opinion, to lay "the groundwork of a local tradition"[11] instead of keeping their eyes riveted on Europe. DesRochers wrote:

> . . . at the risk of losing those friends I still have, I will give you the names of those eight, in alphabetical order: William Chapman, René Chopin, Robert Choquette, Octave Crémazie, Rosaire Dion-Lévesque, Eudore Evanturel (whom neither Mgr. Roy nor *Abbé* Dandurand mention in their textbooks), Jean Narrache, and Simone Routier.[12]

He greatly admired the informality of the North American sensitivity of Dion-Lévesque which he also found in the distinctive style of Simone Routier and Robert Choquette:

> In Rosaire Dion . . ., he writes, are combined in diverse degrees the qualities of Mlle Routier and Robert Choquette. Like the former, he possesses an intimacy which I dare to characterize as intense, but which expresses itself much more richly. I am thinking here, especially, of a certain "Petite Suite Marine" and of some unpublished poems which I have had the good fortune to read. Like Choquette, he possesses a talent for the evocative word, for the image which has a limitless resonance, for the line which can often be in turn both compact and vague, the verse which makes one dream much more than it comments upon or describes.

---

[11]   Alfred DesRochers, "L'Avenir de la poésie en Canada français" (2nd part), in *Les Idées* (Montréal), 2nd year, vol. 4, no. 1, July 1936, p. 110.

[12]   Ibid.

In addition, there is in Rosaire Dion-Lévesque, especially in "Salut à Whitman," with which he opens his translation of selected works by this master, a fraternal sentiment which goes far beyond the snob allegiance to socialism which was in vogue among writers a few years ago. By the number and the richness of the literary qualities with which he is endowed, Rosaire Dion is the contemporary replica of [René] Chopin before 1911, but he belongs to the last generation of Franco-Canadian francophones. Around him, French is spoken less and less. The generation which will follow him will know French the way we know Latin.[13]

Aware of the extremely precarious situation of the French language in New England, DesRochers hints that only the everyday use of the ancestral language distinguishes the French Canadians from their Franco-American brothers. He even speaks of the "Anglo-Saxon" character of Robert Choquette's poetic works, daring to assert: "If we are destined to survive, Choquette will be a literary ancestor, for his style matches what we already are in our acts: French-speaking Americans."[14]

Whether or not one accepts this opinion about francophones still living in the Saint Lawrence River Valley, we cannot deny that the works of the Franco-American Rosaire Dion-Lévesque obviously express this identity as defined by DesRochers. But the cultural isolation of the poet cannot but make us think of the inevitable assimilation. As far back as 1936, DesRochers was writing:

Unless an American culture expressed in French can be constructed, unless the situation of some South American republics—minus the revolutions, I hope—can be repeated, we are fast moving towards the abyss of absorption into the vast North American anglophone mass.[15]

Emphasizing the unusual nature of a poetic *oeuvre* written in

13 Ibid., pp. 118-119.

14 Ibid., p. 117.

15 Ibid., p. 126.

French in the United States,[16] Dion-Lévesque quoted the following remarks of Louis Dantin, in his acceptance speech, delivered in 1964, at the award ceremony for the Chauveau Medal, thereby adhering to the premise set forth by Dantin:

> Two or three writers, a few poets are desperately trying to produce books in the midst of a population which does not hear them and is incapable of comprehending them. Their works belong to the corpus of French-Canadian literature, and for this reason they will not have labored in vain.[17]

In spite of deploring this cultural decline, the Nashua poet attempted to maintain the culture of his forebears by integrating it into his American identity. Throughout his life, he maintained bonds with Canada without for a moment contemplating leaving his dear New Hampshire to live on the banks of the Saint Lawrence, for he felt rooted there.

"Hymne à l'Amérique,"[18] a poem written in Paris in 1931, best expresses the writer's feelings for his native land. Charmed

---

[16]   Only Louisiana had already produced poets writing in French. Among the American-born were: Alexandre Latil (1816-1851), the Rouquette brothers—Dominique (1810-1890), and Adrien (1813-1887), Oscar Dugué (1821-1872), and especially Georges Dessommes (1855-1929), who was, undoubtedly, the most talented of the group. Among writers of Creole stock, some good novelists are to found: Alfred Mercier (1816-1894), who also wrote poems, and Sidonie de La Houssaye (1820-1894). On the question of Louisiana French literature, see Auguste Viatte, *Histoire littéraire de l'Amérique française des origines à 1950* (Quebec-Paris: Presses de l'Université Laval and Presses Universitaires de France, 1954), pp. 219-300; and Reginald Hamel, *La Louisiane créole littéraire, politique et sociale (1762-1900)*, (Montreal: Leméac, 1984), 2 volumes.

[17]   Quoted by Gabriel Nadeau in *Louis Dantin, sa vie et son oeuvre*, Manchester, New Hampshire, Editions Lafayette, 1948, p. 234; "Discours de M. Rosaire Dion-Lévesque," from *Mémoires de la Société royale du Canada*, vol. 2, 4th series, June 1964, first section, p. 46.

[18]   "Hymne à l'Amérique," in *Revue de l'Amérique latine*, (Paris) 11th year, vol. 23, no. 121, January-February-March 1932, pp. 44-47. Reprinted in *Le Travailleur* (Worcester, Mass.), vol. 1, no. 32, April 17, 1932, p. 2; and in Richard Santerre, *Anthologie de la littérature franco-américaine de la Nouvelle-Angleterre* (Manchester, New Hampshire: National Materials Development Center for French and Creole, 1981, vol. 9), pp. 140-143.

by Europe, the continent of ancient civilization, the mother of arts and letters, moved by France in particular, the ancestral land, the cradle of his mother tongue, he, nonetheless, prefers the United States, his true homeland. Many American intellectuals, of diverse ethnic origins, having made a pilgrimage to the Old World, arrive at the same conclusion: as young, as untamed as it may be, America remains their mental universe and the continent of the future. Europe can give them a great deal, but they need not become Europeans to think and to write; it is enough for them to be Americans. Henry Miller in *Tropic of Cancer* and Thomas Wolfe in *Of Time and the River* touched upon this disillusion. The splendors of the past led them, at a distance, to an inner re-discovery of their own country. Before them, Melville, in an essay entitled "Hawthorne and his Mosses" (1850); and Whitman in his Preface to *Leaves of Grass* had proudly claimed an authentic American culture. One senses the influence of Whitman in these verses of Dion-Lévesque:

> *Amérique! Amérique!*
> Titan dont les mains sinueuses et puissantes
> Sont capables de tenir toutes les rênes du vieux monde!
> [. . .]
> Je t'aime pour la force immarcescible
> Qui circule en tes veines généreuses et gonflées.[19]

And the tone becomes prophetic. It is no longer aging Europe that has become artificial, transformed as it is into a museum, but the haughty and vigorous America which will save civilization:

> Une race qui monte à l'assaut des temps futurs,
> Sur les ailes du Progrès, franchit
> Les bornes trop étroites des âges révolus.
> Et tu t'avères, de jour en jour, Amérique,

---

[19]   America! America!
      Titan whose sinuous and powerful hands
      Are capable of holding all the reins of the Old World!
      [. . .]
      I love you for the irrepressible strength
      Which flows in your generous bulging veins.
Santerre, pp. 140-141.

Comme le Messie de l'humanité chancelante.[20]

Under this spell of the birth of a new culture, Dion-Lévesque, in 1933, published a translation of excerpts of *Leaves of Grass* and, in an introductory "Hommage," saluted in Whitman the liberator of the human body, going so far as to consider him as "a new Christ."[21] In fact, throughout his work, he continued to celebrate the flesh, evoking its pleasures and its torments.

In spite of this obsession, the poet, from time to time, knows how to sing of that tenderness which comes straight from the heart. The following lines taken from *Solitudes* are proof of this:

> Quand on est deux,
> On n'entend pas le bruit de la pluie.
> Le battement d'un pouls
> Au creux d'un bras replié
> Oblitère
> Tous les bruits de la terre.[22]

Translated by Henry L. Messier

[This article first appeared as "Rosaire Dion-Lévesque, fils d'expatriés" in the French Institute's publication entitled *Franco-American Literature: Writers and Their Writings*. It has been reviewed by the author, and updated where necessary, for inclusion in this volume.]

---

[20]   A race which arises to storm the future
On the wings of Progress, it overcomes
The confining limits of bygone days
And, little by little, America, you prove to be
Like the Messiah of a faltering humanity.
Ibid., p. 142.

[21]   *Walt Whitman, ses meilleures pages traduites de l'anglais*, Montréal: Les Elzévirs, 1933, p. 21.

[22]   When there are two of us
We do not hear the sound of the rain.
The beating of a pulse
In the hollow of a folded arm
Obliterates
All the sounds of the earth.
"Pluie de janvier," in *Solitudes*, p. 52.

Principal Works of Rosaire Dion-Lévesque

En égrenant le chapelet des jours. Montreal-New York: Éditions du Mercure, 1928, 168p.

Les Oasis. Rome: Desclée, 1930, 132 p.

Walt Whitman, ses meilleures pages traduites de l'anglais. Montreal: Les Elzévirs, 1933, 240 p. Reprinted in Quebec by the University of Laval Press in 1971.

Vita. Montreal: Valiquette and Action canadienne-française, 1939, 127 p.

Solitudes. Montreal: Chantecler, 1949, 94 p.

Jouets. Montreal: Chantecler, 1952, 72 p.

Silhouettes franco-américaines. Manchester, New Hampshire: Association Canado-Américaine, 1957, 933 p. Supplement, 6 p.

Quête. Quebec City: Garneau, 1963, 50 p.

Selected passages in Richard Santerre, *Anthologie de la littérature franco-américaine de la Nouvelle-Angleterre.* Bedford-Manchester, New Hampshire: National Materials Development Center for French and Creole, 1981, vol. 9, pp. 128-362.

Three Major Witnesses of Franco-American Folklore In New England: Honoré Beaugrand, Adélard Lambert, and Roméo Berthiaume

Brigitte Lane

"Franco-American folklore, born of Canadian and French blood, derives its vigor and its vitality from Canada and from France."
Mary Carmel Therriault, R.S.M.
La littérature française de Nouvelle-Angleterre

The story of Franco-American folklore has yet to be written. Still, it is possible even now to give an overview of the work of three men who contributed in very different ways to the life and the study of this folklore in New England. These men are Honoré Beaugrand (1848-1906), Adélard Lambert (1867-1946), and Roméo Berthiaume (1907-1980). Although they lived in somewhat different times, these three authors have enabled us (by their lives and their work, exemplary from this point of view) to arrive at an extremely important historical awareness: to realize that there existed in New England in their lifetime—and that there exists even today—a traditional culture of French-Canadian origin expressed in French, a still rich and vigorous culture which constitutes the body of what we can today call "Franco-American folklore."[1]

What have these authors left us as regards folklore: at both the documentary level as well as at that of "evidence?" What place does their work occupy in the large puzzle of Franco-American culture? And finally, what is the extent of their historical significance? It is with these questions in mind that their lives and their work will be examined in turn to arrive at a conclusion

---

[1]   The three authors studied here would, no doubt, have preferred to this expression that of "Canadian traditions," but the historical perspective at our disposal (a perspective that they could not have had) obliges us to use the term "folklore" as well as the adjective "Franco-American."

regarding the impact of their folkloric contribution within the current framework of research on francophone ethnic folklore in North America.[2]

HONORÉ BEAUGRAND (1848-1906)

"Hey! Hervieux! Why don't you sing us one of your old rowing songs: we'll help out with the chorus and the trip will not seem so long."

Jeanne la Fileuse (1878)

The Man

Great traveler, adventurer, journalist, a writer and a politician, Honoré Beaugrand was born in 1848 in Lanoraie, Quebec. At the age of 17, having completed his education, he enlisted in the French army and left for Mexico to fight for Napoleon III.

Upon his return from Mexico, having become a journalist, he practiced this profession in France, in New Orleans, and then in New England, where he settled in 1871. After a difficult period of adjustment, during which he had to work as a house painter, Beaugrand married, in 1873, Eliza Walker, a young woman from Fall River, and founded the city's first Franco-American newspaper, *L'Echo du Canada*. During the years which followed, Beaugrand was very active in New England, as well as in Quebec and the South (notably Louisiana and the State of Missouri). In 1875, he left New England to settle in St. Louis, Missouri, where he founded another weekly newspaper: *La République*. Less than a year later, however, he had returned to Fall River where he continued to publish *La République* until February of 1878, when he returned to Quebec for good.[3] His Canadian career was to be illustrious: founder of the great Montreal daily, *La Patrie*, he was elected mayor of Montreal and died in 1906 in possession of a large fortune.

While we are quite familiar with the political and religious

---

2   For a general study of research in the area of ethnic folklore in the U.S.A., see my doctoral dissertation: "Franco-American Traditions and Popular Culture in a Former Mill Town: Aspects of Ethnic Urban Folklore in Lowell, Massachusetts," Harvard University, 1983 (Chapter 3).

3   See Roger LeMoine, "Honoré Beaugrand: Chronologie" in *Jeanne la fileuse* (Montreal: FIDES, Coll. Nénuphar, 1980), pp. 53-71.

ideas of Honoré Beaugrand (his desire to annex Quebec to the United States, his strong anti-clerical opinions, his association with Freemasonry), we know much less about his role as a folklorist.

However, his name is associated with the foundation of the first Canadian branch of the American Folklore Society, in Montreal, where he presided at the first meeting in 1892. The minutes of that meeting, held on April 25, 1892, indicate that he presented (to an audience of about 40 persons) a paper on goblins: "Those tiny creatures, sometimes diabolic, sometimes beneficent, which still subsist in many Canadian parishes."[4] This presentation was followed by his own reading of one of his tales: "La Chasse-Galerie," a narration based upon a tradition attached to the camps of the lumberjacks, a superstition which Beaugrand defined as follows, in the introduction to his collection of tales of the same name:

> A popular belief which goes back to the era of the *coureurs de bois/voyageurs* of the Northwest. The men of the lumber camps have continued the tradition, and it is especially in the parishes bordering the St. Lawrence that the legends of the *chasse-galerie* are known.

And he added:

> I encountered more than one old *voyageur* who alleged having seen, travelling in mid-air, birch bark canoes filled with the possessed going to see their girlfriends under the aegis of Beelzebub.[5]

It is also as a folklorist—as president of the *Société des traditions populaires du Canada*—that Beaugrand would attend, in 1900, the International Congress of Popular Traditions held in Paris, where he was elected its vice president. For this occasion, he

---

4   John Reade, "Local Meetings and Other Notices," in *Journal of American Folk-lore*, 5, 1928, pp. 155-158.

5   Introduction to *La Chasse-Galerie: Légendes canadiennes* (Montreal: FIDES, 1973), p. 17.

had prepared a *"Journal de voyage des Peaux Rouges"* ["Redskin Travel Diary"] which, in the end, was not read but published.[6]

His Folkloristic Work

Like all the people of his time, folklore came to Beaugrand through literature. Thus it is that in the first part of his novel *Jeanne la fileuse* (entitled "The Canadian Countryside"), he presents to us, in a romantic, nostalgic and perhaps idealistic manner, the traditional life of the Canadian *habitants* (farmers) of the St. Lawrence region in 1872, a time when he himself was still in New England.[7]

The book is rich in folkloristic details. In it can be found, helter-skelter:
- fragments of traditional songs such as: *Mon père n'avait fille que moi* ("My father had no other daughter but me"; *Canot d'écorce qui va voler* ("Birch bark canoe which will fly"—an allusion to the motif of the *chasse-galerie, À Bytown il y a une jolie place* ("In Bytown there is a lovely place.").[8]
- proverbs originating in traditional French-Canadian wisdom: *"Qui ne dit mot consent,"* ("Silence is consent") or *"Sois joyeux à dix-huit ans, sérieux à vingt-cinq ans, sage à trente ans et tu seras riche à quarante ans"* ("Be joyous at eighteen, serious at twenty-five, wise at thirty, and you will be rich at forty").
- an old legend: *"La légende du fantôme de l'avare,"* ("The Legend of the Miser's Ghost") a legend which is attached to the

---

6   See note 3, p. 66. Honoré Beaugrand's published output is quite extensive. His writings referring to folklore include: *Jeanne la fileuse*, first serialized in the Fall River newspaper *La République*, during the years 1875-1876, then published in book form in Montreal in 1878. This work is generally considered as being the first Franco-American novel. Then came the small collection of Canadian legends *La Chasse-Galerie*, consisting of a series of traditional tales and stories which had first been published individually—in 1892—in the newspaper *La Patrie*. Finally, in 1904, he published a short work in English: *New Studies of French-Canadian Folklore* which consists of a study of the sprites of French Canada, a reprise of the story of "Macloune" (presented this time not as being a legend but a true story) and a study of the graphic symbolism of the American Indians: "Indian Picture and Symbol Writing."

7   We can ask ourselves to what extent the element of idealization of Canadian rural life is not due precisely to distance and exile.

8   Bytown was the original name of Ottawa.

custom of waiting for an unknown guest on New Year's Eve. It appears again in the collection *La Chasse-Galerie.*[9]

But the most interesting part of the novel is that which recalls and describes the seasonal chores and activities of rural French Canadians in the nineteenth century: haying (during the first two weeks of July); the departure of the men for the lumber camps (about mid-September); then, their return in the spring— "their purses well-lined and their arms filled with gifts they had purchased."[10] Beaugrand also describes the old holidays of Canadian villages, festivities during which the farm people gathered together in the evening to dance the "cotillion" to the music of the local fiddler called *violoneux* or *ménétrier* (referred to here as *Crin-Crin*).

If the second part of the book (which takes place in Fall River) does not deal with the cultural continuity of these traditions in New England, Beaugrand has nonetheless (consciously or unconsciously) already made his point by showing us beforehand where the real base, the origin, the deep cultural roots of the French-Canadian immigrants to the United States were to be found.

When the novel came out in Montreal in 1878, Joseph Desrosiers (critic for *La Revue canadienne*) wrote sarcastically:

> He (Beaugrand) has his country folk speak in a solemn and theatrical fashion far removed from the simplicity, both dignified and naive at the same time, which distinguishes the language of our farmers. These lumberjack *voyageurs* arriving by canoe at Lavaltrie in 1872, constitute a veritable anachronism and their clothing could at that time have been taken for a carnival costume.[11]

It is quite possible that Beaugrand, in his folkloric tales, sought out the picturesque and otherwise aimed at describing stereotypical images. Whatever the case may be, this approach is evident in his *Légendes canadiennes,* especially so in his stories

---

9   See Chapter 5, *Jeanne la fileuse.*

10   Ibid., Chapter 1.

11   See Introduction to *Jeanne la fileuse,* p. 47.

entitled *Macloune* and *Le Père Brindamour* which (more so than
the tales or the legends) are, in fact, literary portraits whose
utilization seems to be to establish some "village types"—as is
proven by the subtitles of the illustrations of the 1904 edition with
captions such as *Le docteur de village* (The Village Doctor), *Deux
fermiers aisés* (Two Rich Farmers), *Un vieux patriote de 1837* (An
Old "Patriot"[12] of 1837). It is purely and simply a matter of
stereotypical vignettes, based upon the generalization of the
picturesque traits of an individual person applied to a social
category.

From this point of view, Beaugrand is once again very much
of his time, and the authenticity of a certain part of the folkloric
material he presents could be questioned. Nevertheless, he tries in
his three tales (*La chasse-galerie*, *Le loup-garou* [The Werewolf]
and *La bête à grand' queue* [The Long-Tailed Beast]) not only to
depict authentic popular beliefs, but also to re-create the
traditional form of the tales of the people with a set form for the
introduction, the narrative, and the ending. Thus, seeking to
imitate the style of a traditional narrator, he begins the story of
La chasse-galerie in the following manner:

> And now, I am going to tell you a complicated story, in
> all its details, but there are among you daring fellows
> who would like to 'run' the *chasse-galerie*. I warn you it
> would be better for them to look outside to scc if the
> screech owls are holding their midnight revels because
> I shall begin my story by making a big sign of the cross
> to chase away the devil and his imps. I had enough of
> those damned creatures in my youth.[13]

As a transient Franco-American, Honoré Beaugrand
prepared the way for the history of Franco-American folklore by
revitalizing an entire pre-literary patrimony.[14] Precursor and

---

12   [Name given to the farmers and villagers of the Richelieu Valley who
rebelled against British rule.—Editor]

13   *La Chasse-Galerie*, p. 17.

14   Sister Mary Carmel Therriault defines "transient Franco-
Americans" ["Franco-Américains de passage"] as being Canadians who
had lived in New England for ten or more years and who composed works
during their stay in the country—and often because of this sojourn—and
then returned to Canada. See *La littérature française de Nouvelle-
Angleterre*, Montreal, FIDES, 1946, p. 14.

ancestor of all the historians of Franco-American folklore, he introduced into Franco-American literature the tradition of the "folkloristic-portrait," a certain idea of the Canadian past and traditional life as lived in the countryside of Canada—an exoticism which would be revisited in the 1930s by the Franco-American author, Camille Lessard-Bissonnette, in her serial novel *Canuck*.[15] The folkloristic work of Honoré Beaugrand, which bears the stamp of his time—and, for this reason, seems to have certain limitations from the point of view of authenticity—is no less precious. For it allows us, among other things, to appreciate how far the science of folklore has come. It is perhaps not a coincidence that Beaugrand was born only two years after the term "folklore" itself had been coined.[16]

Adélard LAMBERT (1867-1946)

"I set about gathering and classifying many facts and behaviors that I had picked up about the first Canadian immigrants to the United States. There was a little of everything there: old songs, legends, etc. My aim was to pass on to others these notes on the way Canadians in exile acted and thought . . . After this bold stroke, I threw myself with reckless abandon into Folklore."

Adélard Lambert

The Man

Adélard Lambert was born on March 14, 1867, in Saint-Cuthbert-de-Berthier-en-Haut in Quebec to a family of thirteen children. His family immigrated to Woonsocket, Rhode Island, when he was only two years old. During his childhood he lived, in

---

15   The author of *Canuck* (1936) establishes a contrast between the traditional Canadian way of life (embodied by *Père l'Allumette*, an old beggar and healer) and the American (Franco-American) way of life of the Canadian immigrants in the mills of Lowell.

16   It was in a letter published in the *Atheneum* (August 22, 1846) that the Englishman John William Thoms, after having used the word "folklore," claimed the honor of having invented it. This new term was meant to replace the expression "popular antiquities" which had been used up to that time.

succession, in Woonsocket and Albion, Rhode Island, and in Putnam, Connecticut.[17]

In the many personal notes he has left us, and which are today in the Lambert Collection of the library of the Association Canado-Américaine (ACA) in Manchester, New Hampshire, he recalls his work experience in a factory at the age of ten as well as an even older memory, the Saint John the Baptist parade in Woonsocket in 1872 when he was only five years of age.[18]

Adélard Lambert studied in French-speaking schools up to the age of 17, but, in 1884, his parents had him quit school and he began to work in a grocery store. It was at this time that he discovered his vocation as a bibliophile-collector. Among the first books he obtained were *Jeanne la fileuse* of Honoré Beaugrand and the works of Louis Fréchette. In 1878, however, he was obliged to return to Canada where he spent three years clearing his parents' land—"work (he tells us himself in his personal notes) which left little time for reading."

In 1890, he returned to New England, having married Philomène Vigneault, a young Canadian girl he had met in Quebec. He settled in Manchester where he would live for many years. An impassioned collector of books, he had, by 1912, acquired 1,500 works related to Canada, a collection which would number more than 4,000 works by 1919—when he sold his entire library to the ACA before returning to Quebec to settle for good.

Coming from a traditional French-Canadian family, Adélard Lambert was exposed at a very early age to the oral traditions (tales, legends, songs, etc.) of his native culture. Gustave Lanctôt describes the family evenings of the Lamberts in Woonsocket as follows:

> During those long evenings in the lamplight, once all
> the homework was finished, Madame Lambert occupied
> and distracted her large family by singing songs for

---

[17]   Lambert having been born nineteen years after Beaugrand, the two men thus belong to clearly distinct generations.

[18]   See *Notes personnelles*. Lambert Collection, ACA, Manchester. I wish here to thank most warmly the *Association Canado-Américaine* and in particular Dr. Robert Beaudoin who generously allowed me access to their collection of documents relating to Adélard Lambert, documents which, for the most part, remain unpublished.

them and teaching them round dances. She had a lovely voice as well as a remarkable memory. In her youth, over the course of many gatherings which make the long Canadian winters in the countryside more enjoyable and break their monotony, she had heard tales aplenty and especially a great many songs. [19]

His Folkloristic Work

Adélard Lambert tells us that his career as a folklorist really began in 1916. He recounts in his personal notes that, having become aware of the existence of the *Journal of American Folklore,* which contained popular Canadian tales in the French language, he noticed that certain ones were in fact songs and that, having become interested in the question, he then sent these songs, "as they should be sung," to the Quebec chapter of the *American Folklore Society.*[20] He was then invited to Montreal to meet the members of the Society. About the meeting, he wrote: "I had brought along a large number of old tales and old songs and they congratulated me for having gathered and preserved so many of the old things of a time gone by."[21]

Thus began the long collaboration between Adélard Lambert, "the literate illiterate"—as Adolphe Robert, president of the *Association Canado-Américaine*, from 1936 to 1956, called him— and the great French-Canadian folklorists of his era: Marius Barbeau, Gustave Lanctôt, and E.-Z. Massicotte.

This collaboration was at times a bitter one as the following anecdote illustrates.

In his *Romancero du Canada* (1937), Marius Barbeau, quoting Gustave Lanctôt, writes on the subject of Adélart Lambert:

For a few years, Mr. Lambert was for me a very useful collaborator. His collection of tales and popular songs in our files numbers several hundred. An old man with little education, but enamored of the books and the traditions of his milieu, he came to live in Arthabaska

---

[19]   Cited in Marius Barbeau, *Romancero du Canada*, p. 201.

[20]   See *Echos de France*, Lambert Collection, ACA.

[21]   *Notes personnelles*, ACA.

after having spent the better part of his life in New England. He then set about writing his memoirs and those of his family and he sent them on to me a little at a time by mail between 1919 and 1928. His manuscripts now form part of our national collection.[22]

For his part, Adélard Lambert "rectified" this declaration with annotated comments in his personal copy of the Romancero. He replaced the expression "hundreds of works" by writing in "thousands," he crossed out the word "Arthabaska" and he added, at the end of the volume, a page of "Remarks and Corrections," the contents of which seem to indicate that he felt strongly that his collaboration had not been sufficiently appreciated by his masters in Canadian folklore.

What then has he left us in the realm of folklore? First of all, several published works: Rencontres et entretiens (1918), Les contes de ma Tante Rose (1923), and several small brochures grouped under the title Propos d'un castor (1933), as well as a series of tales published over the course of many years, in the Journal of American Folk-lore, but, most especially, a series of unpublished, badly typed collections, bound by himself.[23]

Among these are collections of songs such as: Les premiers échos de la Nouvelle-France, a work in three volumes, the first of which (1914) is divided into "Légendes et complaintes" ["Legends and Laments"], the second (1920) into "Ballades et complaintes" ["Ballads and Laments"], and the third (1921) into "Chants du voyageur" ["Songs of the Voyageur"] and "Chants à boire" ["Drinking Songs"].

At the beginning of Volume I, Lambert writes: "Paroles et musique reconstituées par Adélard Lambert" (Words and music reconstituted by Adélard Lambert, Manchester, N.H., 1919).

We can obviously ask ourselves what the term "reconstituted" means here, all the more so because Lambert does not give us any information as to his sources or the dates on which he would have collected these songs.

---

22   Marius Barbeau, Romancero du Canada, p. 201.

23   His serialized novel L'Innocente victime (1936) has no connection to folklore.

It is the same with his other collection of songs, *Echos de la Nouvelle-France* (a collection divided this time into *"Chants de nos mères"* ["Songs of our mothers"], and *"Chants de nos pères"* ["Songs of our Fathers"], as well as in the collection of stories *Dans le jardin d'autrui [In the Other's Garden]*, and even in *"Les enfants disent"* (1922), a collection of rhymes, riddles, and other childish *formulettes.*[24]

The Lambert Collection is a gold mine, for in it can be found all kinds of treasures with regard to folklore: songs, tales, riddles, as well as notes on popular beliefs or customs which have now disappeared. Lambert also tells us of sorcerers, hobgoblins, and "Petit Albert,"[25] of a saying according to which if the sun shines on the 22nd of February we must expect forty days of bad weather, and of a thousand other things.

The folkloristic work of Adélard Lambert remains, nonetheless, difficult to evaluate: at the quantitative level, first of all, for it is difficult for us to measure the totality of his output given the fact that a complete inventory of his American and Canadian collections has never been made; but also at the qualitative level, for his sources remain vague, and it is even difficult at times to know if the traditions were collected in Canada or in New England. In addition, the texts which he transmits to us were generally transcribed in standard French— which is obviously damaging to their authenticity. What should we make of all this? First of all, the work of Adélard Lambert shows us how permeable the cultural barriers between French Canada and New England were in his time. From the point of view of folkloristic documentation, his most precious contribution (and perhaps the most authentic) remains, however, the collection of sixty-nine tales published for him by Gustave Lanctôt in the *Journal of American Folk-lore* over the course of the years 1920, 1923, 1931, and 1940.

Concerning the transfer of traditional French-Canadian customs to the United States, Lambert leaves us a precious

---

24   According to Lambert, this collection was supposed to be the continuation of an identical one published in 1920 by the Canadian folklorist Edouard Massicotte in the *Journal of American Folk-Lore* and would even surpass it. For a more complete inventory of the Lambert Collection see my doctoral dissertation, pp. 140-145.

25   A classic country compendium of home recipes based upon witchcraft.

testimony: a little story entitled *"Une fête Saint-Jean-Baptiste dans un village américain."* In it, he recounts how, around 1892, a small group of French-Canadian immigrants of the Manchester region gathered together to organize—for the first time since their arrival in the States—a celebration of the feast of St. John the Baptist.

Although the result obtained was only an approximate adaptation of the original custom, the group found great satisfaction in having renewed with the tradition, and the story concludes as follows:

> We parted, delighted, promising to come again to celebrate the Feast of St. John the Baptist at Central Village among these good people who had accompanied us to the station. But, we said to each other: "Next year we will do even better because we will have a young St. John with a lamb."[26]

Adélard Lambert, a man of the people, died feeling that his contribution to the study of folklore expressed in French (in New England as well as in Canada) had never really been appreciated at its true value by the French-Canadian university folklorists with whom he had worked for so many years. He would, no doubt, have been pleased to hear the tribute given to him by the great Canadian folklorist, Luc Lacourcière, at the meeting of the Canadian chapter of the American Folklore Society, in 1947, one year after his death:

> What treasures he saved for us from ruin and oblivion. What respect and what recognition this man of the people deserves, trustee of a family tradition and pious gatherer of a collective patrimony. Without him, we would know little of these traditions brought from Canada to New England. More so by his behavior than by his writings, does he symbolize the faithful guardian of the unadulterated patrimony, common to us all.[27]

---

26   Adélard Lambert, *Rencontres et entretiens* (1918), p. 50.

27   In a similar vein, Armand Capistran, his biographer, writes in the introduction to his thesis, "Adélard Lambert, collectionneur et folkloriste": "A man of the people, [Adélard Lambert] set down in writing, a personal and family treasure of oral traditions which, without him, would have been irretrievably lost."

Roméo BERTHIAUME (1907-1980)

"Santa Claus, although not as popular as he is today, made his rounds then, but for us French Canadians, it was not on Christmas but on New Year's Day."

Roméo Berthiaume, *Memoirs*

The Man

Born in 1907, in Southbridge, Massachusetts, forty years after Adélard Lambert, Roméo Berthiaume thus represents a third generation in the historical continuity of oral French-Canadian tradition in New England. It is a generation still quite close to our own. Although he was a Franco-American by birth, Roméo Berthiaume went to live in Quebec with his parents when he was still very young. There, the family settled in the region of Saint-Ours, near the shores of the Richelieu River, the region from which they had originated.

It was not until he was thirteen years old that Roméo Berthiaume returned to the United States, where he worked in factories, as had Adélard Lambert as a youth. Around the age of twenty, he returned to Canada to work on the family farm. But during the Depression, he came back to the United States, where he found employment for several months on a farm in Pennsylvania, before returning anew to Quebec until 1941, at which time he settled in Woonsocket, Rhode Island. Married in 1944, it is in Woonsocket that he would spend the rest of his life with his wife and his five children.

Roméo Berthiaume held many different types of jobs over the course of his lifetime, but when the factories moved South, he became a landscape gardener—a profession which brought him close to nature which he loved so much and which allowed him to fulfill what he himself called his *"vocation de la terre"* ["dedication to the earth"].

His Folkloristic Contribution

It is not so much as a critic or as a literary author that Roméo Berthiaume contributed above all to the history and life of Franco-American folklore, but especially as a "tradition bearer." Although he had spent just a few years in school, which he always regretted, Roméo Berthiaume had a profound knowledge of French-Canadian traditions. All his life he devoted himself to translating or composing tales, poems, or songs attached to that tradition. He also wrote, for the *Soirées franco-américaines* of Woonsocket, a short, humorous play with two characters entitled *"D'la visite originale"* [An Unusual Visitor]. This play was first performed in 1975.

In 1979, the Rhode Island Folklife Project, directed by the folklorist Jerry Johnson, asked him to participate in the establishment of Franco-American folklore archives for the Library of Congress. This resulted in his recording a series of tapes which today form part of the archives of the National Collection in Washington, D.C.

According to Roméo Berthiaume, Jr.—who estimates that his father's repertory consisted of about 300 songs—these archives essentially contained songs and photographs, although Roméo Berthiaume, Sr., also had a repertory of tales, comic stories, and other folkloric traditions, which, still according to his son, did not interest him as much as the songs.[28]

At the end of his life, Roméo Berthiaume wrote six volumes (six large school notebooks) of *Memoirs*, in English, for his family. His aim was "to perpetuate the culture [that is the French-Canadian culture of his birth] so that the young people will not forget it." This historic document is unequalled as a testimony on the history of Franco-American immigration.[29]

Although his repertory of tales and songs is more representative of Franco-American culture as a culture of immigration rather than as an ethnic culture, because of the time in which he lived, Roméo Berthiaume very early on became preoccupied with the problem of cultural continuity between his generation and that of his children. That is how he came to realize—well ahead of his time—that this continuity itself depended upon a linguistic continuity and, for this reason, that

---

[28] Not having known Roméo Berthiaume, personally, I wish here to thank his son Roméo Berthiaume, Jr., who allowed me, in a sense, to come to know his father through the family documents which he communicated to me. Other researchers, such as Deborah Waldman and Pierre Anctil, who had the privilege of knowing Roméo Berthiaume, Sr. during his lifetime, have described him as a man deeply imbued with French-Canadian traditions and having a profound understanding of them.

[29] These notebooks are, as of this writing, in the hands of the Berthiaume family.

the language problem risked being an insuperable obstacle to the realization of his wishes.

Through his life and his contribution to Franco-American folklore, by his position as a precursor, Roméo Berthiaume, embodies for us today the final phase of a first historic period of Franco-American folklore: that is to say, the phase of affirmation and public recognition of this folklore. Having become ethnic, Franco-American culture, and consequently its folklore, asserts itself as such. We no longer speak of "Canadian traditions" or of "Canadian folklore," except to refer to the cultural origins of the group. The concept of accepting the existence of a Franco-American folklore has not only come into being but is affirmed as such. In this matter, Roméo Berthiaume, although unique, remains the symbol of all the elderly Franco-Americans who continue to be attached to the traditions learned from their parents, traditions which they keep alive, while at the same time familiarizing us with them, and, in so doing, making them both dear to us and indispensable.

Historically, Honoré Beaugrand, Adélard Lambert, and Roméo Berthiaume thus represent for us, three distinct but complementary periods of a cultural awareness which is public as well as historic. Their work is the undeniable affirmation of the fact that a Franco-American folklore does exist (at least three generations of Franco-American traditions), but also that this folklore is—in great part—symbolic of a way of life, a manner of being, and perhaps even a way of thinking, which form the essential nucleus of Franco-American culture, for as the proverb says: " Folklore is everywhere and nowhere."[30]

Translated by Jeanne Gagnon McCann

[This article first appeared as "Trois témoins du folklore franco-américain: Honoré Beaugrand, Adélard Lambert, Roméo Berthiaume" in the French Institute's publication entitled *Le patrimoine folklorique des Franco-Américains*. It has been reviewed by the author, and up-dated where necessary, for inclusion in this volume.]

---

[30]   The work of these three men is today continued by a new generation of Franco-American folklorists, among them Julien Olivier and Roger Paradis.

Bibliography

Bance, Pierre. "Beaugrand et son temps." Doctoral dissertation. University of Ottawa, 1964.

Barbeau, Marius. "Contes populaires canadiens." (1st series). *Journal of American Folk-lore*, 29, 111 (1916), pp. 1-151.

_____. "Contes populaires canadiens." (2nd series). *Journal of American Folk-lore*, 30, 115 (1917).

_____. "The Field of European Folklore in America." *Journal of American Folk-lore*, 32, 124 (1919), pp. 185-197.

_____. "Le folklore canadien-français." *Mémoires de la Société du Canada, IX, Series III* (March 1916), pp. 449-481.

_____. "The Folklore Movement in Canada." *Journal of American Folk-lore*, 56 (1943), pp. 166-168.

_____. "Jeux d'enfants." *Journal of American Folk-lore*, 53, 208-209 (1940), pp. 163-181.

_____. *Romancero du Canada*. Toronto: The Macmillan Company, 1937. 251 p.

Beaugrand, Honoré. *La Chasse-galerie et autres légendes*. Montreal, 1900,123 p.

_____. *Jeanne la fileuse*, ed. Roger Le Moine. Montreal: FIDES, 1980.

_____. *New Studies of Canadian Folklore*. Montreal: E.M. Renouf-Roy, 1904. 130 p.

Berthiaume, Roméo. "D'la visite originale." Unpublished play. 1975. 15 p.

_____, translator, "The First Windmill" of Théodore Botrel. p. 2 Unpublished.

_____. *Memoirs*. Unpublished. Berthiaume Family Collection.

Boivin, Aurélien. *Le conte littéraire québécois au XIXe siècle.* Montreal: FIDES, 1975.

Brûlé, Dorilla. "Le folklore français à Central Falls, Rhode Island." Master's thesis, Boston College, 1951, 138 p. bibl.

Capistran, Armand. "Adélard Lambert (1867-1946) folkloriste-bibliophile." *Bulletin de la Société historique franco-américaine* (1954), pp. 70-75.

_____. "Bio-bibliographie d'Adélard Lambert." Master's thesis, Laval University, 1951.

Carrière, Joseph-Médard. "The Present State of French Folklore in North America." *Southern Folklore Quarterly*, 10 (1946) pp. 219-226.

Danielson, Larry. "Introduction to Ethnic Folklore and the Folklore of Ethnicity." *Western Folklore*, 36, 1 (January 1977) pp. 1-7.

Daviault, Pierre. Editor. "Contes populaires canadiens." *Journal of American Folklore*, 53, 208-209 (1940), pp. 91-190.

Degh, Linda. "Approaches to Folklore Research Among Immigrant Groups." *Journal of American Folklore*, 79 (1966), pp. 551-556.

Dupont, Jean-Claude. *L'art populaire du Canada français.* Quebec City: Presses de l'Université Laval, 1975.

_____. "Culture populaire de l'émigrant québécois, 1850-1920," *Vie française.* Ed. Claire Quintal. Quebec City: Conseil de la vie française, 1981. Second Colloquium of the French Institute, Assumption College, Worcester, Mass., 14 March 1981, pp. 47-60. bibl.

Klymasz, Robert. "From Immigrant to Ethnic Folklore," *Journal of the Folklore Institute*, 10 (1973), pp. 133-137.

Lacourcière, Luc. "The French in New England, Acadia and Quebec." University of Maine at Orono: NEAPQ Center, 1973. (Proceedings of the May 1 & 2, 1972 Conference) pp. 93-113.

Lambert, Adélard. *Chansons populaires du vieux Québec.* Manchester, N.H.: Collection Lambert, ACA, Unpublished, 277 p.

———. *Contes de ma Tante Rose, ou Contes du Bon Vieux Temps pour les enfants.* Montreal: Ed. Edouard Garaud, 1927.

———. *Dans le jardin d'autrui: Recueil de contes, légendes et récits.* Manchester, N.H.: Lambert Collection, ACA, 1919, 111 p.

———. *Echos de la Nouvelle-France.* Manchester, N.H.: Lambert Collection, ACA.

———. *Les enfants disent.* Manchester, N.H.: Lambert Collection, ACA. 1919.

———. *Grand-mère raconte le lever de la Reine.* Montreal: Beauchemin 1935.

———. *Il était une fois.* Manchester, N.H.: Lambert Collection, ACA.

———. *Journal d'un bibliophile.* Drummondville, Quebec: Imprimerie La Parole, 1927.

———. *Lettres de France.* Manchester, N.H.: Lambert Collection, ACA.

———. *Premiers échos de la Nouvelle-France.* Manchester, N.H.: Lambert Collection, ACA, 1919.

———. *Propos d'un Castor ou Entretiens du Père Jean Nault.* Drummondville, Qué.: Imprimerie La Parole, 1934, 32 p.

———. *Rencontres et entretiens.* Montreal: Le Devoir, 1918, 159 p.

Lessard-Bissonnette, Camille. *Canuck.* Lewiston, Maine: Éditions du Messager, 1936. 131 p.

Massicotte, E.W. et Marius Barbeau. "Chants populaires du Canada." (1st series) *Journal of American Folk-lore,* 32, 123 (1919).

_____. "Diverses sortes de chasse-galerie." *Bulletin de Recherches historiques*, XLIV, 6 (June 1938), pp. 163-166.

_____. "Formulettes, rimettes et devinettes du Canada." *Journal of American Folk-lore*, 33, 130 (1920), pp. 299-319.

Olivier, Julien. *D'la boucane: Introduction au folklore franco-américain de la Nouvelle-Angleterre*. Cambridge, Mass.: NADC, 1971, 141 p. bibl.

Paradis, Roger. "Franco-American Folklore: A Cornucopia of Culture." In *Vers l'évolution d'une culture*. Ed. Céleste Roberge, Orono, Maine: FAROG, 1973, pp. 43-87.

Robert, Adolphe. *Un lettré illettré: Étude sur Adélard Lambert, collectionneur et folkloriste*. Manchester, N.H.: Lambert Collection, ACA, 1944, 11 p.

Société historique de Montréal et Société de folklore d'Amérique. *Veillées du Bon Vieux Temps à la Bibliothèque Saint-Sulpice à Montréal, le 18 mars et le 24 avril 1919*. Montreal: G. Ducharme, 1920, 92 p.

Stern, Stephen. "Ethnic Folklore and the Folklore of Ethnicity." *Western Folklore* 36, 1 (January 1977), pp. 7-33.

Therriault, Soeur Mary-Carmel. *La littérature française de Nouvelle-Angleterre*. Montreal: FIDES. Publications de l'Université Laval, 1946, 324 p.

Waldman, Deborah. "Transcultural Song Survival: Active and Passive Tradition-Bearers of the French-Canadian Folk Song Tradition in Woonsocket, R.I. and Adjacent Towns." Master's thesis. Brown University, 1976, 267 p. bibl.

The Dream of a Better Life
in the Songs
of Departure for the United States

Donald Deschênes

French-Canadian folklorists began some years ago to study popular songs of so-called "local composition" (native songs), a distinct repertoire composed on the North American continent itself. While the native song is modeled on the form and structure of the traditional French song, its subject matter deals with the lives and preoccupations of the people of French North America.

From the beginnings of French-Canadian history, a repertoire developed which included lumber camp songs, shanteys, songs of social protest and political satire, etc. This article will focus on songs of departure for the United States, or those having the United States as their subject matter. The twenty-seven songs that comprise our corpus were all collected in Canada, primarily in Acadian regions and Quebec, but also in Ontario and Alberta.[1]

These songs teach us a great deal about the working and living conditions experienced by French-Canadian emigrants in the nineteenth century and at the beginning of the twentieth. They help us to grasp more clearly how this region to the south, this land of exile, but also of prosperity, was perceived at the time.

Albeit on another scale, and at a different level, these traditional songs contain the same preoccupations that French-Canadian literature grappled with up to the 1930s:

> aspirations, hopes, frustrations, resentments, adventurous lives . . . analyzed and defined, which translate the age-old desire of the French Canadian, tortured by the anguish of his Laurentian existence, to

---

[1] See Anthology at the end of this article for the music and words of these songs.

turn his gaze toward the image of American reality.[2]

These songs can thus be considered as sources of information as conclusive as oral testimonies and as valuable as historical documents.

A.   Making One's Living in the United States

1. Departure for a Better Life

Songs of departure, in English as well as French, occupy an important place in traditional repertoires because of their quantity as much as for their quality. The subjects are varied: someone leaves to seek his fortune or go into exile whether it be as a colonist—leaving behind parents, loved ones, friends, and country—as a lumberjack taking part in a log drive, as a sailor going to sea, or as a soldier or draftee going off to war.

Emigrants did not really have much of a choice as to leaving or staying. The demands of having to earn a living created the push factor. Exile, even though voluntary, was, more often than not, inevitable. In the nineteenth century, apart from college for the more fortunate, a young man had no other choice but to become a lumberjack, a farmer or a fisherman, occupations in which the wages earned were both meager and seasonal. The lack of land suitable for tilling, usually too rocky for cultivation as farmland, coupled with chronic poverty, created a situation hardly likely to persuade or even enable young people to remain in their homeland.

What emerges, first of all, from these sung testimonies is the importance accorded to departure with all that it implies of hopes and dreams, but also the sadness of separation and the foreboding of trouble. The emigrant goes off with very little, while leaving behind family and friends for an often uncertain destination. Here are some examples:

Quand j'ai parti du Canada	*When I left Canada*
Pour m'en aller dans les États	*To go to the States*
Je n'avais qu'une valise	*I had only one suitcase*
Tout mon butin était dedans	*All my belongings were inside*

---

[2]   Guildo Rousseau, *L'Image des États-Unis dans la littérature québécoise (1775-1930)* (Sherbrooke, Quebec: Naaman, 1981), p. 12.

Je n'avais qu'une valise	I had only one suitcase
Mais de l'argent, j'n'en avais pas.	But as for money, I had none.

(I-1)³

J'ai parti [de] chez mon père	I left my father's home
À l'âge de dix-neuf ans,	At the age of nineteen
Craignant point de misère	Not afraid of poverty at all
En quittant mes parents.	In leaving my parents.
Je pars pour l'Amérique	I am leaving for America
Pour y gagner de l'argent. (III-1)	To earn money there.

The good-byes are poignant, the emigrant realizing that he is leaving his country behind and that he will be lonely:

Or, adieu donc, mes chers amis,	So! good-bye then, my dear friends,
Je m'en vas quitter le pays.	I am leaving the country.
Or, adieu / y a pour m'en aller	So, good-bye! For I am going away
dans l'Amérique,	to America,
Bien éloigné de mon pays.	Far away from my country.
Beau Canada, faut donc je te quitte	Beautiful Canada, I must leave you
Pour m'en aller vivr' dans l'ennui.	To go live a life of loneliness.

(V-1)

Often scarcely a good-bye, or none at all, is uttered:

Nous somm's partis, ces jeunes voyageurs,
Nous somm's partis pour les États-Unis,
Sans dire adieu à nos pères, à nos mères,
Sans dire adieu aux parents, aux amis.
(. . .)
Or, adieu donc, beau villag' de Lamèque!
Or, adieu donc, notre joli pays.   (XVI-1)

We have gone, young travelers,
We have gone to the United States
Without saying good-bye to our fathers, to our mothers,
Without saying good-bye to relatives, to friends.
(...)
Now, good-bye then, beautiful village of Lamèque!
Now, good-bye then, our pretty country.

These departures are heartrending.

Quand je partis du Canada,	When I left Canada,
C'était pour monter aux États.	It was to go to the States.
Je n'avais pas cinq lieues de faits	I hadn't gone five leagues

---

³   The roman numerals throughout the text refer to the songs in the Appendix while the arabic numerals indicate the stanzas of these songs.

Que j'avais déjà les larmes aux yeux.   *That I already had tears in my eyes*
                    (IV-1)

The prospect of an easier lifesyle, however, buoyed the spirit of the
emigrants:

Quand j'ai parti du Canada   *When I left Canada*
Pour m'en aller dans les États,   *To go to the States,*
J'avais le coeur tout à mon aise,   *My heart was at ease*
J'avais le coeur tout réjoui,   *My heart was joyous*
Qu'on me disait qu'on travaillait   *They told me that one didn't*
                    point fort   *work hard at all*
Dans les moulins, dans les *fact'ries*.   *In the mills, in the factories.*
                    (II-1)

                    *   *   *

Un jeun' garçon d'une honnête famille   *A young man from an honest family*
Pensait toujours de gagner sa vie facile, *Was always thinking about*
                                                  earning an easy living,
S'en a 'té dans les États-Unis,   *He went to the United States,*
Pensait toujours de revenir au pays.   *Thinking always of returning to*
                                                  his country.
                    (XIX-2)

The dream of an easy life included the lure of finding gold in
California:

Ils m'ont offrit de l'or-e,   *They offered me gold,*
De l'or-e florissant;   *Bright, shiny gold*
Moi qui est encore jeune,   *I, who am still young,*
J'aimais encore l'argent.   *I still loved money.*
On est que dans ce monde   *We are in this world*
Pour chercher des trésors.   (XI-3)   *Only to seek some treasures.*

Je suis avide de ma pauvre patrie.   *I am longing for my poor homeland*
Pour un peu d'or, j'ai quitté mon pays.   *For a bit of gold, I left my country.*
                    (XII-1)

These trips were not without their pitfalls. They entailed long
hours on the train and the discovery of a very different and most
often inhospitable country:

Les chars nous mèn'nt quarant'-cinq milles à l'heure,
Quarant'-cinq mill's sans jamais modérer.
Pendant vingt heur's, nous marchons sans relâche
Pour arriver à notre destinée. (XVI-2)

The trains carry us at forty-five miles an hour,
Forty-five miles an hour without ever slowing down.
For twenty hours we travel without a break
To arrive at our destination.

Going to California was even more wrenching. This was pioneer country, totally lacking in comfort and services, and reached only after a very long and exhausting journey:

Dans un pays sauvage,	*Into a wild country,*
I[l] a fallu s'en aller,	*We had to go.*
Faire un si long voyage	*To make a trip so long*
Qu'on ne puisse en parler. (XI-2)	*That it can't be talked about.*

The myriad problems to be faced there result in the advice not to go so far away:

Mes chers amis, je vous conseille pas	*My dear friends, I do not recommend*
D'aller si loin dans ces pays-là.	*That you go so far away to those*
(XV-2)	*countries.*

Having arrived at one's destination, whatever it might be, the main objective was to find work:

En arrivant à cett' ville étrangère,	*Arriving in this strange city,*
Tout aussitôt nous nous somm's t-engagés	*We hired ourselves out right away*
À un monsieur d'au nom d'René Springer,	*To a man by the name of René Springer,*
Pour les chantiers où nous devons bûcher.	*To work in the camps as lumberjacks.*
(XVI-2)	

*   *   *

Je vas partir pour les États-Unis	*I'm going to leave for the States.*
Tout' personne qui s'engage pour	*Every person hired must work*
y passer une année. (XV-1)	*there for a whole year.*

Throughout the journey, in the most difficult moments, the traveler knew, however, that he or she could count on religion as a constant and reliable support. God would protect the travelers from accidents and sorrow and would come to their assistance in time of need:

"Nous poursuivrons notre route,	*"We will continue on our way,*
Dieu nous protèg'ra d'accident." (I-3)	*God will protect us from harm."*

Je pars pour l'Amérique	*I am leaving for America*
Pour y gagner de l'argent,	*To earn my living there,*

Si le bon Dieu m'y conserve		If the good Lord keeps me
De peine et d'accident.	(III-1)	From harm or trouble.

Si Dieu vient à mon aide,		If God comes to my aid,
J'espèr' que dans deux ans,		I hope that in two years,
Au retour du voyage		Upon my return from the trip
Y voir mes bons parents.	(XI-2)	To see my dear parents there.

2. Working Conditions

The French Canadians who arrived in the United States were most often unskilled farmers. The men became workers in the lumber camps or the mills, while the women and children found themselves toiling for meager salaries in the factories. Among the principal employers in New England, the first to come to mind are the textile manufacturers:

Et aussitôt qu'nous fûm's arrivés,	And as soon as we arrived,
L'on a commencé à weaver. (XVII-1)	We started to weave.

Another version of the same song states:

La première semaine qu'on est arrivé,	The first week that she arrived
A bien fallu apprendre à weaver.	She had no choice but to learn to weave.

The songs rarely describe working conditions or the jobs themselves. Rather, they tend to describe the emotions felt in coping with them. However, one song does offer us a realistic description of conditions in the factories. We collected this song—incomplete unfortunately—from Mrs. Angélina Paradis-Fraser of Cap-Chat, on the Gaspé Peninsula, who lived with her parents in Salem, Massachusetts, from 1905 to 1911. That was where she learned this song:[4]

Dans les manufactures,	In the factories,
Je vous assur' que c'est dur.	I tell you it's tough.
Ils sont là renfermés,	They are shut in there,
C'est pour tout' la journée.	For the whole day.
Quand ils sortent le soir,	When they come out at night,
Oh! que c'est triste de les voir.	Oh! how sad it is to see them.
Il[s] ont la figur' blême,	Their faces are pale,
De la peine à marcher. (XVIII-2)	They have trouble walking.

---

4   Donald Deschênes, *C'était la plus jolie des filles*, p. 13.

Questions of money are also frequent themes—the fortune one is seeking, or quite simply the minimum necessary to live on, which seems almost impossible to attain in spite of backbreaking work:

Il y a sept ans et quelques mois | It has been seven years and a few months
Que nous étions dans les États. | That we have been in the States.
J'n'ai pas ramassé fortune, | I didn't pick up a fortune,
Pourtant j'ai beaucoup travaillé. | Yet I worked a lot.
Le soir au clair de lune, | At night by the light of the moon,
Le matin avant soleil levé.   (I-4) | In the morning before sunrise.

* * *

Voilà deux ans et quelques mois | It was two years and some months ago
Que je suis arrivé ici aux États. | That I arrived here in the States.
J'ai travaillé toute la semaine | I worked all week
Pour une piastre et demie. | For a dollar and a half.
Je vous assure qu'on travaille pour la peine, | I tell you that we work very hard
Dans les moulins, dans les *fact'ries*. | In the mills, in the factories.
(II-4)

* * *

Mais à la fin de la semaine, | But at the end of the week,
On r'tir' pas un' maudit' cenne! | We don't take home a damned cent!
(...) | (...)
Ah! la bonn' femm' veut mettr' la chicane: | Ah! the old lady wants to start a fight:
Va t'assir, viens pas m'bâdrer! | Go sit down, don't bother me!
Tu sais bien qu'j'ai pas 'té payé! | You know very well that I haven't been paid!
(XVII-4, 6)

Obsession with the factory clock is present in more than one song:

Ils sont au son d'la cloche, | They are there at the sounding of the bell,
Cherch' quand ils en sortiront! | Who knows when they'll come out of there!
(XVIII-1)

* * *

J'entends plus sonner les cloches | I don't hear the bells ringing anymore
De tous bords et de tous côtés, | From every direction, from everywhere

J'entends plus sonner la cloche | I don't hear the bell ringing anymore
Le matin pour nous appeler.   (I-7) | Calling us every morning.

Monotony and the demands of the job are also mentioned in these songs:

Et tous les jours, c'est à recommencer,	And every day it starts all over again,
C'est son ouvrage qu'il faut cleaner.	It's his work that he has to clean.
Mais il cleane la machine,	But he cleans the machine,
Car aussi la débourrer,	Removing the lint,
Car il faut changer de routine. (II-5)	For one needs to change the routine.

3. Living Conditions

It is obvious that the emigrants' life was a far cry from the dream that prompted them to leave. These unqualified laborers, at the mercy of big business, led precarious lives. "At first, young men, especially, emigrated and later entire families left Quebec and New Brunswick to settle in New England and in the Midwest."[5]

The theme of poverty and its ensuing problems, is often repeated. This leads Michel Oriano to state, "The song constitutes not only the privileged means of expression of oppressed peoples, but also that of the people in societies wherein all the media and all the institutions are monopolized by the ruling class."[6] One sings of what rankles; often one sings of what might be difficult to say outright. As with the Afro-Americans, music, and most especially song, is a release, a necessary outlet. Thus, these songs are full of warnings about poverty and trouble:

Où allez-vous? - Dans les États.	Where are you going? - To the States.
- Vous courez après la misère.	- You are headed for poverty
Virez de bord, n'y allez donc pas!	Turn around, don't go there!
(I-2)	

Ne fait's pas comm' ces gens	Don't do like those folks
Qui vont dans les États,	Who go to the States,
Plongés dans la misère	And are plunged in poverty
Et aussi dans l'embarras. (XVIII-1)	As well as trouble.

---

5   For a statistical analysis of this phenomenon, see Yolande Lavoie, *L'Émigration des Canadiens aux États-Unis avant 1930* (Montreal: Presses de l'Université de Montréal, 1972), and *L'Émigration des Québécois aux États-Unis de 1840 à 1930* (Documentation du Conseil de la langue française, 1981).

6   Oriano, *Les travailleurs de la frontière*, p. 7.

Longing for the homeland is a recurring theme:

J'entreprends le voyage	*I am setting out on the journey*
De soucis et d'ennui. (XI-1)	*Of worries and loneliness.*

En vous parlant d'Californie,	*Telling you about California,*
Triste pays que de l'ennui	*Sad country of loneliness only.*
(...)	*(...)*
Regardant vers nos campagnes,	*Looking toward our countryside,*
Souvent on ne fait que pleurer.	*Often all we can do is cry.*
(XIV-1,2)	

Oui, j'ai pleuré loin de ma pauvre mère.	*Yes, I cried far from my poor mother.*
Loin de sa mère, on s'ennuie pour mourir.	*Far from one's mother, one feels lonely enough to die.*
(XII-refrain)	

C'est dans un' maison de pension	*It's in the boarding house*
Là où l'on trouv' le temps bien long,	*That one is bored to tears*
Là où l'on pleure et l'on s'ennuie	*That is where we cry and suffer*
D'être éloigné de ses parents,	*At being separated from our parents*
De son amie, de son pays	*Our girlfriend, our country*
Et ceux qu'on aim' bien tendrement.	*And those we love so tenderly.*

When a man falls ill in the lumber camps and must return home, everyone is eager to have him carry messages to their loved ones:

Chacun de nous on lui donne un message	*Each of us gives him a message*
Et tous chagrins de se voir séparés:	*And all of us are sad at being apart*
"F'ras des respects à ceux de ma famille,	*"Pay my respects to my family,*
Tu iras voir ma très chèr' bien-aimée.	*Go see my dear beloved.*
Tu lui diras après cet dur hiver-e	*Tell her that after this tough winter*
Que j'espèr' que je la reverrai." (XVI-5)	*I hope to see her again."*

4. Drinking

Under these living conditions, the main diversion is drink. A weaving song contains this refrain:

Et buvons donc nous autr's, nos gens,	*And let's drink too then, us folks,*
Et buvons donc nous autres.	*And let's drink then too.*
(XVII-refrain)	

In the song, "La Vie de chercheur d'or en Californie"/"The Life of the Gold Seeker in California," regret is expressed that card games and drinking are taking the place of religion:

Quand l'heur' d'la grand' messe arrive,	*When the time for high mass arrives*
Dans les *saloons* nous les voyons	*You see them in the saloons*
Aux jeux de cartes, à boire, à rire	*Playing cards, drinking, laughing*
Comm' du mond' sans religion. (XIV-5)	*Like people without religion.*

As can be expected, drunken brawls occur, with inevitable results:

Alors, on se mit à boire	*Then, we began to drink*
Avec tous mes amis.	*With all my friends.*
À boire comme de raison,	*Drinking of course,*
On vient hors d'espoir.	*We go mad.*
J'entendis lorsqu'on buvait:	*While drinking I heard:*
"Henri, viens à mon secours	*"Henri, come help me*
Car ils vont me tuer,	*For they are going to kill me,*
Car ils vont me tuer."	*For they are going to kill me."*
Alors, il lève la planche	*Then, he raises the plank*
Et puis le frappa.	*And hit him with it.*
Vous voyez ce pauvre jeune homme,	*See this poor young man,*
Mort, en bas il tomba. (XXV-2 to 4)	*Who fell down dead.*

5. Holiday Celebrations

However, when community life begins to function, entertainment centers around the celebration of holidays such as New Year's Day. The following is but one example:

Sur le sol d'Amérique,	*On American soil,*
Là tous nos Canadiens	*All our Canadians there*
Ont la manière logique	*Have a logical way*
De fêter l'jour de l'An.	*Of celebrating New Year's Day.*
Mais quand qu'l'année commence,	*But when the year begins,*
On aime à visiter	*We like to visit*
Nos vieilles amies d'enfance	*Our old childhood girlfriends*
Pour se faire embrasser.	*In order to get kissed.*
Refrain:	Refrain:
Aux États-Unis,	*In the United States,*
On n's'embrass' pas avant minuit;	*They don't kiss before midnight;*
On s'occup' pas de d'ça	*We don't worry about that*
Dans notre Canada.	*In our Canada.*
C'est dans la New Hampshire	*It is in New Hampshire*
Qu'on se plaît pas pour rire,	*That we really enjoy ourselves,*
Mais surtout à Queenville	*But especially in Queenville*

Qu'on a tout's nos belles filles.   *That we have all our pretty girls.*
          (XXIII-1 and refrain)

6. Love and Separation

Most often, however, love is associated with separation and distance. One song, discovered recently, tells of the separation of two lovers. He returns to Canada while she remains in the United States to continue her work in the factory. She expresses some envy over his departure:

Oh! quel bonheur que c'est pour lui   *Oh! what joy it is for him*
De s'en aller dans son pays   *To go home to his country*
Et moi qui reste dans les *fact'ries*,   *And me, I stay behind in the factory,*
À mon ouvrage pensant à lui.   *At my work, thinking of him.*
          (XXIV-2)

À mon ouvrage de chaque jour,   *At my work each day,*
Penseras-tu à nos amours?   *Will you think of our love?*
Et toi, l'ouvrage que tu feras,   *And at the work that you do,*
Penseras-tu à Rosanna?   *Will you think of Rosanna?*
          (XXIV-3)

B.   Contrasts between Canada and the United States

In spite of difficult living conditions, backbreaking work, and long hours of toil for low wages, the songs still point to the advantages of living in the United States. The songs reiterate that life is better there than in Canada:

N'allez pas au Canada   *Don't go to Canada*
Car la misère est par là.   *Because there's poverty up there.*
À la mod' du Canada,   *The Canadian way*
On mang' d' la soupe aux pois,   *Is to eat pea soup,*
Pis à la mod' des Canadiens,   *And the Canadian way*
On mang' du sarrasin.   (XXI-1)   *Is to eat buckwheat.*

In a song from Alberta, Mathilda Gauthier-Plamondon, a Franco-American native of Michigan, shares her feelings about being torn at having to leave her country and children to settle with her husband in Alberta:

Pour moi, j'aim' mieux les États qu'l'Alberta
Parc' qu'on récolt' plus de fruits par ici,

Mais il faut bien suivr' son mari.
Pour moi j'aim' bien suivr' mon mari.

Refrain:
Je vas retourner au Canada
Parc' que les enfants sont tous placés là.
Je vas retourner au Canada
Parc' que les enfants veul'nt tous rester par là. (VIII-1 and refrain)

As for me, I like the States better than Alberta
Because we harvest more fruit here,
But a woman has to go where her husband goes.
As for me, I really like to follow my husband.

Refrain:
I'll go back to Canada
Because all the children have found a place there.
I'll go back to Canada
Because the children all want to stay there.

It is easier also to have fun in the United States, where even the priests are more modern than the *curés* of Canada:

Les curés du Canada,	*The pastors of Canada,*
Ils sav'nt pas nous conduire:	*They don't know how to lead us:*
Ils nous défend'nt les danses	*They forbid dances*
Et les veillées d'plaisir.	*And evening parties.*
Les curés des États,	*The priests in the States,*
Ils nous conduis'nt mieux qu'ça:	*They lead us better than that:*
Ils nous font des veillées,	*They hold parties for us*
C'est pour nous fair' danser.	*Where we can dance.*

(XXII-3 and 4)

For many, as we have seen time and again, life in the United States represents poverty and loneliness in a strange land far from one's childhood home and living apart from the values one holds dear: Catholicism, French language and culture. . .[7]

The thought of returning to the peace and quiet of one's childhood home and of settling down on a farm is a recurring theme:

Il faut nous embarquer d'abord	*We have to get on board first*
Pour nous rendre à Saint-Léonard.	*To go back to St. Leonard.*

---

[7]   Guildo Rousseau, p. 225.

C'est là l'endroit d' ma naissance,	*That's where I was born,*
Là où que j' suis toujours resté.	*It is there that I always lived.*
Nous achèt'rons une terre	*We'll buy a farm*
Qui nous sera parfaite en beauté. (I-6)	*That will be perfectly beautiful.*

Emigrants return to their homeland because poverty on a farm is still better than the sweat and toil of factory work:

Mais puisque c'est comme ça,	*But since it's like that,*
On va r'descendre en Canada	*We're going to go back to Canada*
J'vous assure qu'on vit mieux qu'ça.	*I tell you that they live better than that.*

*   *   *

Je n'accroch'rai plus mon châle dans ces tristes moulins
Je m'en retourne au Canada où l'on y vit très bien. (IX-1)

I won't hang up my shawl any more in these sad mills.
I'm going back to Canada where one lives very well.

These returns were sometimes only temporary, for a vacation, as in this song by Catherine Poirier from Chéticamp on Cape Breton:

En vacances nous sommes partis,	*We are leaving for our vacation,*
Nous venons des États-Unis	*We come from the United States*
En passant par Ottawa	*Passing through Ottawa*
La capitale du Canada.[8]	*The capital of Canada*

The song then lists all of the places visited along the road to Cape Breton.

But returns could also be definitive. Having saved some money, the emigrants could go back to their homeland and live out their days in comfort. A couplet of recent composition describes this state of affairs:[9]

Quand j'm'en r'tournais au Canada,	*When I returned to Canada,*

---

8   Barbara LeBlanc et Laura Sadowski, "La Survivance de la chanson et de la danse: Chéticamp, Nouvelle-Écosse et Waltham, Massachusetts," *Le patrimoine folklorique des Franco-Américains* (Quebec City: Le Conseil de la vie française en Amérique, 1984), p. 139.

9   Ibid.

J'm'avais ach'té un nouveau Impala,   *I had bought myself a brand*
                                                    new Impala,
Un beau *trailer*, je vous assure,   *A beautiful trailer, I assure you.*
Trois ou quatr' *rooms* de *furniture*.   *Furniture for three or four rooms.*
J'avais quelqu' piasses dans ma poche,   *I had some dollars in my pocket,*
Mais dans la têt', j'avais des roches. (X)   *But in my head, I had stones*

1. Dying in a Foreign Land

For those who did not return, dying in exile in a foreign land, was to be avoided at all costs:

C'est point le dégoût du pays   *It isn't dislike of the country*
J' vous assure qui me fait partir-e.   *That makes me leave, I tell you.*
Oh! que ma joie serait profonde   *Oh! how deep my joy would be*
D'aller mourir-e au Canada,   *To go back to die in Canada,*
Et au berceau de ma naissance   *To the cradle of my birth*
Où je dois aller finir-e mes jours.   *Where I must go to end my days.*
                        (V-3)

Georges Arsenault, in his work *Complaintes acadiennes de l'Île-du-Prince-Édouard*, has gathered five laments about accidents that occurred en route to or in the United States. Perhaps because they speak only of the accident itself, as in *Pierre Arsenault* (XIX), we do not find in these songs the fear of dying far from home expressed in the preceding example. Instead one hears the laments of the family the victim has left behind and the deep faith that consoles them.

Il s'est noyé le saint temps   *He drowned during the holy time*
            du carême   *of Lent*
Où Jésus-Christ a souffert tant   *When Jesus Christ suffered so*
            de peine,   *much agony,*
Où Jésus-Christ a versé tout   *When Jesus Christ shed all of*
            son sang   *his blood*
Pour le salut de tous ses chers enfants.   *For the salvation of all his*
                                                    dear children.

C.   Historical Songs

During the eighteenth and nineteenth centuries, Canadians sometimes enlisted in the American army. Historical songs were the result, although oral tradition has rarely focused on them. "Le Sergent mort à la bataille"/"The Sergeant Killed in Battle" (XXVI), which, by strict definition, is not a historic song, recounts the adventures of a young man who preferred enlisting in the American army over being mistreated by his father. The fact that he joins up with the "Bostonians to fight against the British" suggests that the conflict described could be the American Revolution or the War 1812. Many French Canadians also fought in the Civil War.

D.   Literary Aspects

As mentioned at the start of this article, the songs of departure, with two exceptions, were collected in eastern Canada, in the very places where they would have been composed; however, some seem to have been written in New England, for example, "Dans les manufactures"/"In the Factories" (XVIII) and probably "Le Jour de l'An aux États-Unis"/"New Year's Day in the United States" (XXIII). The writing style is rudimentary. Only one song, "Sous le climat de la Californie"/"In California Climes" (XIII), composed in the nineteenth century, could suggest a literary origin.

The texts of the American songs are comprised of simple verse structures: stanzas of four, six, or eight lines of equal length; and of structures that conform to this type of song. As for rhyme, it is simple, nothing more: "Canada" will necessarily rhyme with "États" [States]; "misère" [poverty] with "terre étrangère" [foreign land]; "Californie [California] with "patrie" [homeland]; "souci" [worry], with "ennui" [loneliness] or "folie" [madness]; and "manufacture" [factory] with "dure" [hard].

As in all other songs of local composition, the usual formulaic openings are utilized:

Écoutez, j'vas vous chanter Une chanson de vérité. (XIV-1)	*Listen, I will sing for you* *A song of truth.*
Écoutez, j'vas vous chanter Une histoir' qui m'est arrivée. (IV)	*Listen, I will sing for you* *A story that happened to me*
Venez tous si vous voulez entendre Une complaint' qui vous fera comprendre. (XIX)	*Come one come all if you want to hear* *A lament that will make you understand*

Others, from the outset, inform the audience that the song is one of departure:

Quand j'ai parti du Canada   *When I left Canada*
                    (I, II and XVII)

Quand j'ai parti de Caraquet (XXV)   *When I left Caraquet*

In the very formulation of these verses, there is a constant drawing upon a common tradition, resulting in sameness from one song to another. For example, a prayer to the Blessed Virgin begs her not to abandon the supplicant:

Sainte Vierge Marie,   *Holy Virgin Mary,*
Ne m'abandonnez pas.   *Do not abandon me.*
J'espère un jour à venir   *I hope some coming day*
Mourir entre vos bras. (III-3) *To die in your arms.*

Another invokes her protection and influence over her Son:

"Bonn' Sainte Vierg', ne l'abandonnez pas!
Priez Jésus de lui tendre les bras." (XIX-6)

"Good, Holy Virgin, do not abandon him!
Pray Jesus to stretch out His arms to him."

In addition, it is commonplace to find in these songs of local composition entire stanzas borrowed from the French tradition, as, for example, in the song "Quand je partis du Canada"/"When I Left Canada" (IV). The third stanza comes from the French tradition and is to be found also in "Le Retour des chantiers - la Blonde mariée" (II-L-58).[10]

Petit oiseau, tu es bien chanceux   *Little bird, you are very lucky*
De voltiger là où tu veux.   *To fly wherever you want.*
Ah! si j'avais tes avantages,   *Ah! if I had your advantages*
Ah! oui, j'irais prendre ma volée   *Ah! yes, I would take flight*
Sur les genoux de ma bien-aimée   *On the knees of my beloved*
Ah! oui, j'irais m'y reposer. (IV-3) *Ah! yes, there would I rest.*

It is also interesting to note that in the numerous Canadian songs of French tradition, one finds some borrowing from Canada's neighbor to the south. In "La fille tombée à l'eau et sauvée"/"The Girl Fallen in the Water and Saved," the first verse, "On London Bridge," becomes "In the City of Boston" in several Acadian versions. The same thing happens in the song "Elle a ravi

---

10   Madeleine Béland, *Chansons de voyageurs, coureurs de bois et forestiers*, p. 306.

le coeur du marinier"/"She Stole the Heart of the Bargeman." In the French versions, the song begins "Within Paris" or "In Gennevilliers." In the Gaspé Peninsula, it becomes "In Illinois,"[11] and in an Acadian version from the Magdalen Islands, "In Canada, there are pretty girls."[12]

E.   Musical Aspects

The vast majority of the songs in this corpus are composed "to the tune of" other songs that originate, for the most part, in the French tradition. Some examples include "Le Jardinier du couvent"/"The Convent Gardener," "Le Départ pour les îles"/"Departure for the Islands," "Envoyons d'l'avant, nos gens"/"Let's Go Forward, Folks." One also finds a melody based upon a hymn: "Loué soit à tout moment"/"Praised Be At All Times." To this tune was written "La Vie de chercheur d'or en Californie"/"The Life of the Gold Seeker in California" (XIV). There are also melodies drawn from American folklore such as "Sweet Betsy from Pike," which are used a great deal in songs of local composition, and which served notably in the composition of "Le Voyage à Boston"/ "The Trip to Boston" (XXVII), a humorous song that is half-French, half-English—a "macaronic song" to use the expression of Ontario's folklorist, Edith Fowke.[13]

Finally, let us emphasize that even though some of these songs, such as "Le Départ pour les États-Unis"/"Departure for the United States" (I) and "Le Départ pour la Californie"/ "Departure for California" (XI), were fairly widely known, most of them had a limited audience that was often restricted to a single region. This is the situation, for example, of "Beau Canada, je te quitte"/"Beautiful Canada, I Am Leaving You" (V) or "Je pars, c'est

---

11   Marguerite and Raoul d'Harcourt, *Chansons folkloriques françaises au Canada*, p. 194.

12   Rev. Anselme Chiasson, *Tout le long de ces côtes*, p. 30. For more information on this topic, cf. "La Chanson locale acadienne: une expression artistique folklorique," in *Francophonies d'Amérique*, no. 5, 1995, p. 11-22.

13   Edith Fowke, *Canadian Folk Music Bulletin*, vol. 18, no. 4, p. 21. Charlotte Cormier's article entitled "Acadian Native Songs," *The Proceedings of the Colloquium on the Art and Music of New Brunswick*, pp. 53-74, provides additional information on this topic.

dans ce jour"/"I'm Leaving On This Day"(VI). Moreover, eight songs appear in a single version, and four have only two versions.

Conclusion

This brief overview has focused only on traditional songs of local composition. No attempt has been made here to assess the impact of poems that were set to music by composers and widely disseminated. This has been done elsewhere. It is worthwhile, however, to mention the very popular "Un Canadien errant" by Antoine Gérin-Lajoie, which relates the exile of the defeated "Patriots" of the Rebellion of 1837. At the end of the nineteenth century, Rev. F.-W. Burque turned it into a lament that could have "promoted the return of thousands of French Canadians scattered throughout the urban centers of New England."[14] He hoped thereby to express "the love of country, the loneliness of exile, the hope of returning, and the joys of coming home."[15]

We hope to have shared the richness and the interest of this repertoire. Its significance is historical quite as much as it is ethnological, for these songs bring to light certain human reactions rarely found in historical documents.

More numerous searches for songs among Franco-Americans would, perhaps lead to the discovery of a large number of other songs and would make it possible to learn more about their origin, their authors, and the context in which they were written. Popular songs are, it bears repeating, a valuable source of information that is vital to our knowledge about cultures and societies.

Translated by Janet L. Shideler

[A shorter French version of this essay, entitled "Le rêve d'une vie meilleure dans les chansons acadiennes de départ vers les États-Unis," appeared in the French Institute's publication *Le patrimoine folklorique des Franco-Américains*. It has been reviewed and considerably expanded by the author for publication in this volume.]

---

14   Rousseau, pp. 209-211, 225.

15   F.-X. Burque. «Correspondance», dans *Le Monde illustré*, vol. 8, 9 janvier 1892, p. 586. Cité par Rousseau, p. 209.

ANTHOLOGY

Since most of these thirty-one songs have not been published and are only available as recordings in various archival and folklore centers in French Canada, we thought it best to include them here, both lyrics and music. For each of these songs, we offer only one representative example, even if, in certain cases, it would be necessary to present two, indeed three versions, in order to illustrate fully the diversity that tradition brought to these songs.

I.   LE DÉPART POUR LES ÉTATS-UNIS/
DEPARTURE FOR THE UNITED STATES

II.   LE TRAVAIL AUX ÉTATS/WORKING IN THE STATES

III.   LE DÉPART POUR L'AMÉRIQUE/
DEPARTURE FOR AMERICA

IV.   QUAND JE PARTIS DU CANADA/WHEN I LEFT CANADA

V.   BEAU CANADA, JE TE QUITTE/
BEAUTIFUL CANADA, I AM LEAVING YOU

VI.   JE PARS, C'EST DANS CE JOUR/
I'M LEAVING ON THIS DAY

VII.   ADIEU, JE PARS POUR L'AMÉRIQUE/
GOOD-BYE, I'M LEAVING FOR AMERICA

VIII.   J'AIME MIEUX LES ÉTATS QUE L'ALBERTA/
I LIKE THE STATES BETTER THAN ALBERTA

IX.   LE RETOUR AU CANADA/RETURN TO CANADA

X.   QUAND JE M'EN RETOURNAIS AU CANADA/
WHEN I WAS RETURNING TO CANADA

XI.   LE DÉPART POUR LA CALIFORNIE/
DEPARTURE FOR CALIFORNIA

XII.   LOIN DE MA MÈRE/FAR AWAY FROM MY MOTHER

XIII.   SOUS LE CLIMAT DE LA CALIFORNIE/
IN CALIFORNIA CLIMES

XIV.   LA VIE DE CHERCHEUR D'OR EN CALIFORNIE/
THE LIFE OF THE GOLD SEEKER IN CALIFORNIA

XV.   L'ENGAGEMENT POUR UN AN/
THE ONE-YEAR COMMITMENT

ACRONYMS

AFCEA Folklore Archives, Centre d'études acadiennes, Université de Moncton, Moncton, New Brunswick

AFUL   Folklore Archives, Université Laval, Sainte-Foy, Quebec

CFOF   Centre franco-ontarien de folklore, Sudbury, Ontario

DFUS   Folklore Department, University of Sudbury, Sudbury, Ontario

MN   National Museum of Man, Ottawa, Ontario

Coll. Collection

ms   Manuscript

I.   LE DÉPART POUR LES ÉTATS-UNIS/ DEPARTURE FOR THE UNITED STATES

Deschênes-Cormier Collection, AFCEA, reel 16, recording 208. Sung March 10, 1985, by Mrs. Hélène Léger-Myers, age 64, of Cocagne, New Brunswick. More than 20 versions collected in the Maritime Provinces, Quebec, and Ontario. In the 1980s, the group Garolou popularized it among the young. This song is composed to the French-Canadian traditional tune, "Le Jardinier du couvent"[16]. "Le Départ pour les États-Unis"/"Departure for the United States," VI-B-140[17]).[18]

Quand j'ai parti du Canada
Pour m'en aller dans les États,
Je n'avais qu'une valise,
Tout mon butin était dedans,
Je n'avais qu'une valise
Mais de l'argent, j'n'en avais pas.

Dans mon chemin j'ai rencontré
Un homm' que je ne connaissais bien.
Il m'a dit: "Mon camarade,

---

16   Rev. Anselme Chiasson and Rev. Daniel Boudreau, *Chansons d'Acadie*, 4th series, p. 54.

17   The title and the number refer to the *Catalogue de la chanson folklorique française* of Conrad Laforte.

18   Unless otherwise indicated, the musical notations are by the author. The musical calligraphy is by Jean Cormier.

Où allez-vous? - Dans les États.
- Vous courez après la misère.
Virez de bord, n'y allez donc pas!"

 Moi, je m'ai trouvé bien surpris,
J'en avais le coeur-e bien saisi.
Là, j'ai dit à ma femme,
Aussi à mes petits enfants:
"Nous poursuivrons notre route,
Dieu nous protèg'ra d'accident."

Il y a sept ans et quelques mois
Que nous étions dans les États.
J'n'ai pas ramassé fortune,
Pourtant j'ai beaucoup travaillé,
Le soir au clair de lune,
Le matin avant soleil levé.

Pour être un bon habitant,
Il faut être un bon travaillant.
Il faut point que l'endormitoire
Vienn' nous surprendre sur le champ.
Si vous en perdiez mémoire,
Vous péririez en peu de temps.

Il faut nous embarquer d'abord
Pour nous rendre à Saint-Léonard.
C'est là l'endroit d'ma naissance,
Là où que j'suis toujours resté.
Nous achèt'rons une terre
Qui nous sera parfaite en beauté.

Quand nous serons au Canada,
Les enfants nous diront: "Papa!"
J'entends plus sonner les cloches
De tous bords et de tous côtés,
J'entends plus sonner la cloche
Le matin pour nous appeler.

II.   LE TRAVAIL AUX ÉTATS/WORKING IN THE STATES

Rev. Archange Godbout Collection, MN, ms nº 108. Sung by Mr. Wilbrod Papillon, 28, Des-Écureuils, Portneuf County, Province of Quebec. One and only version, probably sung to the same tune as the preceding song, *Le Jardinier du couvent.* "Le Départ pour les États-Unis" (les moulins)/"Departure for the United States" (The Mills).

Quand j'ai parti du Canada
Pour m'en aller dans les États,
J'avais le coeur tout à mon aise,
J'avais le coeur tout réjoui,
Qu'on me disait qu'on travaillait point fort
Dans les moulins, dans les *fact'ries*.

Le premier jour que j'ai travaillé,
Je vous assure que j'étais fatigué.
Mais le matin, à mon réveil,
Je ne pouvais point manger,
Quand je pensais que dans une demi-heure
C'est au moulin qu'il faut s'en aller.

Voilà le midi arrivé,
Là, c'est chez nous qu'il faut s'en aller.
On a seulement que une heure
Pour y prendre son dîner.
Une heure dans dix qui va sonner,
C'est au moulin qu'il faut s'en aller.

Voilà deux ans et quelques mois
Que je suis arrivé ici aux États.
J'ai travaillé toute la semaine
Pour une piastre et demie.
Je vous assure qu'on travaille pour la peine,
Dans les moulins, dans les *fact'ries*.

Et tous les jours, c'est à recommencer.
C'est son ouvrage qu'il faut *cleaner*.
Mais il *cleane* la machine,
Car aussi la débourrer,
Car il faut changer de routine.
Vivons, vivons au Canada.

III.   LE DÉPART POUR L'AMÉRIQUE/
DEPARTURE FOR AMERICA

Charles-Marius Barbeau et Marie-Rose Turcot Collection MN, ms n⁰ 1698. Recorded in Laurierville, Mégantic County, Québec, sung by Mrs. William Saint-Pierre, née Alméda Larochelle. One and only version "Départ pour l'Amérique"/"Departure for America," II-H-36).

J'ai parti [de] chez mon père
À l'âge de dix-neuf ans,
Craignant point de misère
En quittant mes parents.
Je pars pour l'Amérique
Pour y gagner de l'argent,
Si le bon Dieu m'y conserve
De peine et d'accident.

Étant dans ces prairies,
Regardant de tous côtés,
Un oiseau de campagne
Qui vient me faire ennuyer.
Ce n'est point là l'ennui,
C'est d'être abandonné,
Car c'est ma très chère mère
Dont je vais être si éloigné.

Si le bon Dieu me conserve
Que j'aille en Canada,
Je prie la Sainte Vierge
Qu'elle m'abandonne pas.
Sainte Vierge Marie,
Ne m'abandonnez pas.
J'espère un jour à venir
Mourir entre vos bras.

IV. QUAND JE PARTIS DU CANADA/ WHEN I LEFT CANADA

Taken from the Donald Deschênes Collection, CFOF, recording 56, sung September 7, 1995, by Ange-Émile Maheu Des Hazards, 64, from Azilda, Ontario. He sang the song in the lumber camps of Maine at the end of the 1940s. He learned it from his father Édouard, who was from Saint-Joseph-de-Beauce. It is sung to the tune of "Le Départ du marin pour l'Amérique."[19]

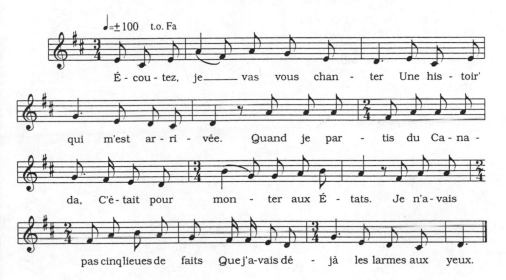

Écoutez, j'vas vous chanter
Une histoir' qui m'est arrivée.

Quand je partis du Canada,
C'était pour monter aux États.
Je n'avais pas cinq lieues de faits
Que j'avais déjà les larmes aux yeux.

C'est dans un' maison de pension[20]
Là où l'on trouv' le temps bien long,
Là où l'on pleure et l'on s'ennuie

---

[19]   Rev. Anselme Chiasson and Rev. Daniel Boudreau, *Chansons d'Acadie*, 3rd series, p. 6.

[20]   The singer also sings: "C'est dans un camp de bûcheron"/"It was in a lumber camp."

D'être éloigné de ses parents,
De son amie, de son pays
Et ceux qu'on aim' bien tendrement.

Petit oiseau, tu es bien chanceux
De voltiger là où tu veux.
Ah! si j'avais tes avantages,
Ah! oui, j'irais prendre ma volée
Sur les genoux de ma bien-aimée
Ah! oui, j'irais m'y reposer.

Cett' p'tit' chanson fut composée
Par un garçon sur le chantier
Et qui partit du Canada,
C'est pour aller travailler;
Dans les États il est allé,
Mais il voudrait s'en retourner.

V. BEAU CANADA, JE TE QUITTE/ BEAUTIFUL CANADA, I AM LEAVING YOU

Five versions of this lament of departure have been listed, all of them collected in southeastern New Brunswick. The musical transcription is by the Frenh folklorist Alfred Pouinard, who recorded this song (AFCEA, reel 4, recording 77) in June, 1952 with Mrs. Éloi Boudreau of La Hêtrière, Memramcook, New Brunswick. The text is taken from the manuscript collection of Joseph-Thomas LeBlanc, MN, ms 9924, version collected in the *Voix d'Évangéline* by Miss Marie-Anne Richard of Grande-Digue, New Brunswick. This song is composed on the French traditional tune of "Le Départ du marin pour l'Amérique."[21]

Or, adieu donc, mes chers amis,
Je m'en vas quitter le pays.
Or, adieu/ ya pour m'en aller dans l'Amérique,
Bien éloigné de mon pays.
Beau Canada, faut donc qu'j'te quitte
Pour m'en aller vivr' dans l'ennui.

Je suis un enfant délaissé,
Bien affligé de la pauvreté.

---

[21] Chiasson and Boudreau, *Chansons d'Acadie*, 3rd series, p. 6.

Oh! je ne vois ni père, ni mère,
Aucun support d'aucun côté.
Hélas! mon Dieu, soyez mon aide,
Ayez toujours pitié de moi.

C'est point le dégoût du pays
J'vous assure qui me fait partir-e.
Oh! que ma joie serait profonde
D'aller mourir-e au Canada,
Et au berceau de ma naissance
Où je dois aller finir-e mes jours.

La belle a pris ses beaux atours
Pour écouter ces beaux discours.
Que feras-tu donc de ma couronne,
Qui s'ra toujours pour me louer?
Oh! c'est l'écho qui m'environne
Sera toujours mon cher ami.

Qui a composé la chanson?
C'est le garçon de grand renom.
Un jour, il était dans l'Amérique,
Bien éloigné de son pays.
A composé la chansonnette,
C'est pour dissiper son ennui.

VI. JE PARS, C'EST DANS CE JOUR/ I'M LEAVING ON THIS DAY

Allain-Doucet Collection, AFCEA, reel 10, recording 133. Sung June 20, 1973 by Mrs. Exelda Cormier, 74, Sainte-Marie-de-Kent, New Brunswick. Another version comes from Bouctouche, New Brunswick. "Départ du marin pour l'Amérique (les cloches)"/"Departure of the Sailor for America (The Bells)."

Je pars,— c'est dans ce jour,— A - dieu mon coeur, mes a-
mours.— Je pars,— c'est dans ce jour. Ma pe - ti - te mi -
gnon - ne, Oh! re - t'nez donc vos pleurs;— J'entends les cloch's qui son - nent Et je pars a - vec dou-leur.—

Je pars, c'est dans ce jour,
Adieu mon coeur, mes amours.
Je pars, c'est dans ce jour.
Ma petite mignonne,
Oh! ret'nez donc vos pleurs;
J'entends les cloch's qui sonnent
Et je pars avec douleur.

Je pars, c'est pour deux ans,
Voyez mon embarquement
Pour profiter du temps.
Voyez mon équipage,
Mon butin préparé,
Les voiles et les cordages
Et les ancres ils sont levés.

- Si tu pars mon cher amant,
Tu vas donc me délaisser.
Tâch' donc de retarder.

Peut-êtr' tu f'ras naufrage
Par quelques méchants vents.
Que ton départ m'occupe
Et me reste dans l'esprit.

Quand tu seras par là,
Quelqu's Américain's t'aim'ront,
Quand tu seras par là.
Oh! quelqu's Américaines
Te deviendront z-amoureux.
Que je regrett' ma peine
Et que mon sort est affreux.

- Non, j't'abandonn'rai pas,
J'suis garçon fidèle et brave.
Non, j't'abandonn'rai pas.
Aucun' belle ou jolie fille
N'aura de mes amitiés.
Et toi, belle Acadienne,
Et quand je reviend-e-rai."

VII. ADIEU, JE PARS POUR L'AMÉRIQUE/ GOOD-BYE, I'M LEAVING FOR AMERICA

Collected and presented by Donald Deschênes, this song, from Angélina Paradis-Fraser's repertoire, is taken from "C'était la plus jolie des filles," p. 109. About fifteen versions listed in Quebec, Ontario, Acadia, and France. ("Voyage à faire"/"A Trip to Be Taken," II-H-23). This song, as well as the following one, belong to the French tradition and give us a more European view of America.

♩= 66 t.o. Do   4e couplet

—Quand je se - rai dans l'A-mé - ri - que, Ton blanc por -
trait, je le vou - drais. Je le met - trai de-dans ma cham - bre bien en-fer -
mé.___ Cinq ou six fois dans la se - mai - ne l'em-bras-se - rai.

"Adieu, je pars pour l'Amérique,
Ma bien-aimée, y viendrez-vous?"
Ell' me répond: "Non, non, dit-elle, je n'irai pas,
Car tous garçons qui vont dans l'Amérique en revienn'nt pas.

- J'ai de l'argent dans mon gousset-te,
Ma bien-aimée en voulez-vous?"
Ell' me répond: "Non, non, dit-elle, je n'en veux pas.
Tous garçons qui vont dans l'Amérique en ont besoin.

Quand tu seras dans l'Amérique,
Bien loin de moi, tu m'oublieras.
Tu voiras un', tu voiras l'autre, tu m'oublieras.
En attendant de tes nouvelles, je languirai.

- Quand je serai dans l'Amérique,
Ton blanc portrait, je le voudrais.
Je le mettrai dedans ma chambre bien enfermé.
Cinq ou six fois dans la semaine l'embrasserai."

**VIII.   J'AIME MIEUX LES ÉTATS QUE L'ALBERTA/
I LIKE THE STATES BETTER THAN ALBERTA**

C25/18 (RAM 3.1), band B 78. Collected in 1981 by Raymond
Ménard from Mrs. Éloise Plamondon-Ulliac. This song was
composed around 1907-1910 by Mathilda Gauthier, wife of Joseph
Plamondon, at the time of the founding and colonization of
Plamondon, Alberta. Mathilda Plamondon was a native of Lake
Leelanau, Michigan, where she met her husband. Mr. and Mrs.
Plamondon were sought out by Catholic missionaries to found a
Francophone parish in Alberta. One and only version collected
and composed on a popular American melody[22].

Pour moi, j'aim' mieux les États qu'l'Alberta
Parc' qu'on récolt' plus de fruits par ici,   *bis*
Mais il faut bien suivr' son mari.
Pour moi j'aim' bien suivr' mon mari.

---

22   This song was published by Gilles Cadrin and Paul Dubé in an
article entitled "Traditions orales de Plamondon, un village franco-
albertain,"*Francophonies d'Amériques*, no. 5 (Ottawa: Les Presses de
l'Université d'Ottawa, 1995), p. 98.

Refrain:
Je vas retourner au Canada
Parc' que les enfants sont tous placés là.
Je vas retourner au Canda
Parc' que les enfants veul'nt tous rester par là.

Il faut laisser notre fill' par ici,
Car son mari aime trop son pays.
Parlez-lui pas du Canada.
Il faut laisser notre fill' par ici
Car son mari aime trop son pays,
Et elle aussi suit son mari.

J'ai rien à dir' contre mon mari,
Car quand je m'ennuie,
Il m'emmène par ici,
Mais c'est sa bours' qui en pâtit.
J'ai rien à dir' contre mon mari
Je m'en retourne avec lui.

IX.   LE RETOUR AU CANADA/RETURN TO CANADA

Adélard Lambert Collection, MN, recording 3652. Sung January 22, 1925. The name of the singer has been lost. Lambert left these comments: "I heard this song sung in about 1876 by an Irishman who was born in Canada and had emigrated to the United States. After two years of working in the factories, disgusted, he had decided to return to a farm in Canada. The evening before his departure, he sang this refrain for us." (*Le Retour au Canada/Return to Canada*, I-Q-12).

Je n'accroch'rai plus mon châle dans ces tristes moulins.
Je m'en retourne au Canada où l'on y vit très bien.

Refrain:
Rin-gue-de-doo-dle-ding-don-dai-ne,
Rin-gue-de-doo-dle-ding-don-dé.

Je travaille au grand air, au soleil du matin.
Le soir on se couche, on repose jusqu'au lendemain.

X.   QUAND JE M'EN RETOURNAIS AU CANADA/ WHEN I WAS RETURNING TO CANADA

Taken from Barbara LeBlanc and Laura Sadowski, "La survivance par la chanson et la danse: Chéticamp, Nouvelle-Écosse et Waltham, Massachusetts," *Le patrimoine folklorique des Franco-Américains*, p. 150. Song composed by Milton Aucoin, Waltham, MA, on the tune *Le Jardinier du couvent*,[23] with as a pattern *Le Départ pour les États*.

Quand j'm'en r'tournais au Canada,
J'm'avais ach'té un nouveau Impala,
Un beau *trailer*, je vous assure,
Trois ou quatr' *rooms* de *furniture*.
J'avais quelqu's piasses dans ma poche,
Mais dans la têt', j'avais des roches.

---

[23]   Chiasson and Boudreau, *Chansons d'Acadie*, 4th series, p. 54.

**XI.   LE DÉPART POUR LA CALIFORNIE/
DEPARTURE FOR CALIFORNIA**

Donald Deschênes Collection, AFUL, recording 318. Collected in the fall of 1971, by Gérald Gaul from his uncle Walter Gaul of Cap-des-Rosiers, Gaspé Peninsula, Quebec, who had learned it from his mother. Reprinted in the magazine *Gaspésie*, March 1985, Vol. XXIII, No 1 (No 89), p. 32. About 20 versions have been listed in Acadia, Quebec, and Ontario. ("Départ pour la Californie"/ "Departure for California," II-H-33).

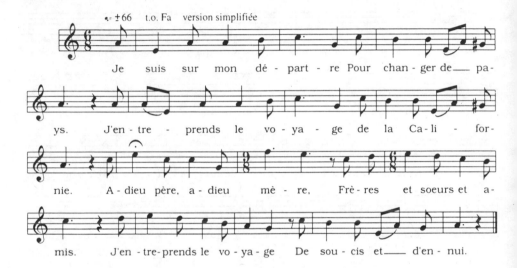

Je suis sur mon départ-re
Pour changer de pays.
J'entreprends le voyage
De la Californie.
Adieu père, adieu mère,
Frères et soeurs et amis.
J'entreprends le voyage
De soucis et d'ennui.

Dans un pays sauvage,
I[l] a fallu s'en aller.
Faire un si long voyage
Qu'on ne puisse en parler.
Si Dieu vient à mon aide,
J'espèr' que dans deux ans,
Au retour du voyage
Y voir mes bons parents.

Ils m'ont offrit de l'or-e,
De l'or-e florissant;
Moi qui est encore jeune,
J'aimais encore l'argent.
On est que dans ce monde
Pour chercher des trésors;
Souvent dans des voyages,
On n'y trouv' que la mort.

Dans un vaisseau de guerre,
Y a fallu s'embarquer.
Surpris par la tempête,
Y a fallu s'y noyer.
Ç'a bien causé d'la peine
À tous mes bons parents,
Mais bien plus de misère
À tous mes bons enfants.

XII.   LOIN DE MA MÈRE/
FAR AWAY FROM MY MOTHER

Reprinted in the song book of Alice Michaud-Latrimouille, *Chansons de Grand'mère*, p. 121. This song was collected in the Eastern Provinces and in New England. It was published twice by Fathers Chiasson and Boudreau[24]. The text varies greatly from one version to another. However, this version deals eloquently with the theme of departure for America ("Loin de sa mère"/"Far Away From His Mother" II-H-47).

Je suis avide de ma pauvre patrie.
Pour un peu d'or, j'ai quitté mon pays.   ] *bis*

Refrain:
Secours en secours, priant notre mère,
Faut prier Dieu, c'est pour nous secourir.
Oui, j'ai pleuré loin de ma pauvre mère.
Loin de sa mère, on s'ennuie pour mourir.

Faut embarquer dans un vaisseau de mer
Pour y braver tous les plus gros dangers.
Les flots de l'eau et l'éclat de la mer
Sont toujours prêts à vous faire renverser.

Faut faire la guerre à ces pauvres sauvages,
Tous comme nous connaissant le danger.
Ils nous envoient des flèches à la tête,
Tous comme nous connaissant le danger.

A fallu prendre le bâton de voyage
Pour m'en aller dans mon triste pays.
Le sort était sur mon visage,
Ma mère est morte en appelant son fils.

Refrain:
Oh! rendez-moi mes habits, ma patrie!
Gardez votre or et laissez-moi partir.
Oui, j'ai pleuré loin de ma pauvre mère,
Loin de sa mère, on s'ennuie pour mourir.

---

24   Chiasson and Boudreau, *Chansons d'Acadie*, 3rd series, p. 23, and 4th series, p. 15.

XIII. SOUS LE CLIMAT DE LA CALIFORNIE/ IN CALIFORNIA CLIMES

Rev. Anselme Chiasson Collection, AFCEA, reel 2, recording 46. Sung in 1957 by Miss Joséphine Roach of Chéticamp, Nova Scotia. More than ten versions listed in Québec, the North of Ontario, and Acadia. "La Californie, le Climat de"/"In California Climes," II-H-34).

Je vais quitter ma belle patrie,
Quitter la cell' que mon coeur aime tant.
Sous le climat de la Californie,
Je vais trahir la foi de mes serments.

Tu ne veux pas que je te dis' ces mots.
Tu veux me suivre; hélas! tu n'as pas d'ailes.
Permets-moi donc que je te dise adieu.

Me permets-tu que je dise encore
Ce que mon coeur te disait autrefois?
Ange du ciel, toi bell' que j'adore,
Je te regard' pour la dernière fois.

Viens dans mes bras, la bell', que je t'embrasse,
Viens recevoir ce doux baiser d'adieu.
Viens recevoir de mon âme attendrie.
Le souvenir de nos derniers adieux.

Si tu m'aimais d'une amour qui t'enflamme,
Tu m'aimerais avec bien plus d'ardeur.
Si la blessur' ne blesse pas ton âme,
Prends ce poignard et déchire mon coeur.

**XIV.   LA VIE DE CHERCHEUR D'OR EN CALIFORNIE/
THE LIFE OF THE GOLD SEEKER IN CALIFORNIA**

É.-Z. Massicotte Collection, MN, recording 843. Collected in 1917 from Mr. Vincent Perrier of Repentigny, Quebec. He learned it from Charles Hamelin of Muskegon, Michigan, around 1878.[25] One and only version. This song is composed on the melody of the hymn *Loué soit à tous moments.*[26] ("Vie de chercheur d'or en Californie"/"Life of the Gold Seeker in California," VI-B-122).

Écoutez, j'vas vous chanter
Une chanson de vérité
En vous parlant d'Californie
Triste pays que de l'ennui.

---

25   É.-Z. Massicotte, "Nos chansons historiques: la recherche de l'or en Californie", *Bulletin de recherches historiques*, vol. 30, 1924, p. 29.

26   Louis Bouhier, *300 cantiques*, p. 137.

Refrain:
Ah! faut-il donc pour de l'argent
Quitter sa femme et ses enfants!
Pour une si triste vie,
Hélas! quelle folie!

Quand nous somm's sur ces montagnes
À travailler sans s'y lasser,
Regardant vers nos campagnes,
Souvent on ne fait que pleurer.

Refrain:
I[l] faut-il donc pour un peu d'or
Subir un si malheureux sort!
Pour une si courte vie,
Hélas, quelle folie!

Les fêtes et les dimanches,
On ne fait que travailler.
Le soir, ils nous mett'nt dehors;
Sur le champ, il faut s'coucher.

Premier refrain

Quand nous somm's dans ces cabines,
Nous pensons à notre maison;
Et souvent on se chagrine
De se voir parmi ces nations.

Second refrain

Quand l'heur' d'la grand' messe arrive,
Dans les *saloons* nous les voyons
Aux jeux de cartes, à boire, à rire
Comm' du mond' sans religion.

Premier refrain

XV. L'ENGAGEMENT POUR UN AN/ THE ONE-YEAR COMMITMENT

Coll. Babin-Fortin, AFCEA, reel 10, recording 117. Sung on July 16, 1975 by Mrs. Zelda Joseph Roy, 84 years old, of Moncton, New Brunswick. Partial and only version.

Je vas partir pour les États-Unis. } bis
Tout' personne qui s'engage pour y passer une année.
Voilà la peine qui me tourmente.
Soit de la peine ou de l'ennui.

Mes chers amis, je vous conseille pas
D'aller si loin dans ces pays-là.   } bis
Tout' personne qui s'engage pour y passer une année.
Voilà la peine qui me tourmente.
Soit de la peine ou de l'ennui.

XVI.   LES CHANTIERS AUX ÉTATS-UNIS/ LUMBER CAMPS IN THE UNITED STATES

Cyrille Mallet Collection, AFCEA, reel 1, recording 6. Sung in 1974 by Mrs. Hélène Noël, 74, of Petite-Lamèque, New Brunswick. The composition is attributed to Lazare Duguay. Three versions have been collected in the northeastern part of New Brunswick. ("Les Chantiers aux États-Unis"/"The Lumber Camps in the United States," II-L-25).

Nous somm's par - tis,_____ ces jeu - nes vo - ya-
geurs, Nous somm's par - tis pour les É-tats_ U - nis._____ Sans dire a -
dieu_____ à nos pères, à nos mères, Sans dire a - dieu   aux
pa - rents, aux_____ a - mis.   Nous somm's al - lés_____ ren -
con - trer la mi - sè - re,   Dans les chan - tiers_____ des
pa - ys é - tran - gers.   Or, a - dieu   donc,_____ beau
vil - lag' de La mèque! Or, a - dieu donc, no - tre jo - li pa - ys.

Nous somm's partis, ces jeunes voyageurs,
Nous somm's partis pour les États-Unis,
Sans dire adieu à nos pères, à nos mères,
Sans dire adieu aux parents, aux amis.
Nous somm's allés rencontrer la misère
Dans les chantiers des pays étrangers.
Or, adieu donc, beau villag' de Lamèque!
Or, adieu donc, notre joli pays.

Les chars nous mèn'nt quarant'-cinq milles à l'heure,
Quarant'-cinq mill's sans jamais modérer.
Pendant vingt heur's, nous marchons sans relâche
Pour arriver à notre destinée.
En arrivant à cett' ville étrangère,
Tout aussitôt nous nous somm's t-engagés
À un monsieur d'au nom d'René Springer,
Pour les chantiers où nous devons bûcher.

En arrivant à cett' triste cabane,
En arrivant à ce triste chantier,
Thomas Corbett, le *boss*, [souffl' la *wingagne*][27]
Et il nous donn' des haches à amancher
En nous disant: "Après cet ouvrag' fait-e,
Vous irez dans ces ch'mins-là travailler."
Là, il s'en va trouver ses autres hommes
Sans nous offert un' bouchée r-à manger.

Jour après jour, nous allions t-à l'ouvrage,
À tous les jours sans jamais nous lasser.
Et après quelque temps de dur ouvrage
Nous commencions à être fatigués.
Voilà bientôt les jours de fêt' qu'arrivent,
Il faut passer ces beaux jours au chantier.
Grand Dieu! qu' c'est trist' quand on pense à l'église.
À nos parents qui y vont pour prier.

Par un beau jour, un de notre brav' gang
Tomba malade. Il lui faut s'en aller.
Chacun de nous on lui donne un message
Et tous chagrins de se voir séparés:
"F'ras des respects à ceux de ma famille,
Tu iras voir ma très chèr' bien-aimée,
Tu lui diras après cet dur hiver-e
Que j'espèr' que je la reverrai."

---

[27]   In another version, the words "rouvre la waguine" [opens the wagon]
are sung, thus clarifying the meaning.

Bientôt hélas! finira le *skidage*,
Il nous faudra encor' recommencer.
Nous somm's pas las-se de notre esclavage,
Il nous faudra que nous. chargions les *sleighs*.
Il nous faudra remuer le *cant-hook*-e
Lever bien fort sur ces pesants billots;
Il nous faudra travailler dans la neige
Et dans la pluie comm' quand qu'il fera beau.

Bientôt hélas! finira le mois d'mars
Et le printemps, bientôt z-il fera beau.
Le beau soleil consommera la neige
Et nous aurons fini nos durs travaux.
Nous retourn'rons au villag' de Lamèque
Voir nos parents, aussi nos bien-aimées.
Nous retourn'rons à notre beau village
Et tous ensembl', nous passerons l'été.

XVII.   WEAVER AUX ÉTATS-UNIS/
WEAVING IN THE UNITED STATES

This song is known in Ontario, Quebec, and New Brunswick, although there are only four listed versions. The text comes from the Germain Lemieux, S.J. Collection, CFOF, recording 936, sung in 1958 by Mr. John Armstrong, 61, of Warren, Ontario. For the melody, we reproduce below the one that was sung to us on May 5, 1985 by Mr. Sylvain Roussel, 58, of Lavillette, New Brunswick, Deschênes-Cormier Collection, reel 16, recording 212. Even though Mr. Roussel sings "To go away to Lac St-Jean," it would appear that "To go away to the States" was also sung in the region. "Départ pour les États-Unis" (Buvons donc)/"Departure for the United States" (Let's drink then), VI-B-141). This song is composed on the French-Canadian tune "Envoyons d'l'avant, nos gens."[28]

Quand j'ai parti du Canada,
C'était pour monter aux États; } *bis*
Et aussitôt qu' nous fûm's arrivés,
L'on a commencé à *weaver*.

Refrain:
Et buvons donc, nous autr's, nos gens!
Et buvons donc, nous autres.   } *bis*

Et aussitôt. . .
Mais on a joué d'la rissonnette
Pour l'enfiler c'saudit' navette!

Mais c'qu'i[l] [y] a de plus d'valeur,
C'est d'voir mon frèr' contr' les *boileurs.*
Le lundi, l' mardi se passe,
Et on voit de second *boss*!

Le lundi. . .
Mais à la fin de la semaine,
On r'tir' pas un' maudit' cenne!

Mais à la fin. . .
Mais on arrive au p'tit logis
Pour payer tout' notr' *groc'rie.*

Mais on . . .
Ah! la bonn' femm' veut mettr' la chicane:

---

28   Marius Barbeau, *Alouette!* p. 88.

Va t'assir, viens pas m' bâdrer!
Tu sais bien qu'j'ai pas 'té payé!

Va t'assir . . .
Mais on arriv', les Canadiens.
Comment ça va, les Américains?

Mais on . . .
À Woonsocket, ç'a bien été,
Mais on a sacrement *weavé*!

Qui est-c'qu'i[l] y a qui nous fait tort,
C'est d's'en v'nir dans les p'tits chars,
Car vous savez tous comm' moi
Qu'les p'tits chars donn'nt mal dans l'corps.

XVIII.   DANS LES MANUFACTURES/IN THE FACTORIES

Donald Deschênes Collection, AFUL, recording 530. Sung July 16, 1982 by Mrs. Angélina Paradis-Fraser, 88, of Cap-Chat, Gaspé Peninsula, Quebec, and reprinted in *Gaspésie*, March 1985, Vol. XXIII, Nº 1 (Nº 89), p. 31. Mrs. Fraser learned this song in Salem, Massachusetts, at the very beginning of the century (when she was a child). One incomplete version, composed to the French traditional tune "Le Départ pour les îles."[29]

Ne fait's pas comm' ces gens Qui vont dans les É - tats.

Plon - gés dans la mi - sère Et aus - si dans l'em - bar - ras.

Ils sont au son d'la clo- che, Cherch' quand ils en sor - ti - ront!

Vo - yez donc ces pau-vres gens-ses Com-ment qu'ils sont par là!

Ne fait's pas comm' ces gens
Qui vont dans les États,
Plongés dans la misère
Et aussi dans l'embarras.
Ils sont au son d'la cloche,
Cherch' quand ils en sortiront!
Voyez donc ces pauvres gens-ses
Comment qu'ils sont par là!

Dans les manufactures,
Je vous assur' que c'est dur.
Ils sont là renfermés,
C'est pour tout' la journée.
Quand ils sortent le soir,
Oh! que c'est triste de les voir.
Il[s] ont la figur' blême,
De la peine à marcher.

---

29   Chiasson and Boudreau, *Chansons d'Acadie*, 3rd series, p. 17.

XIX.   PIERRE ARSENAULT

Deschênes-Cormier Collection, AFCEA, reel 15, recording 192. Sung February 16, 1985, by Mrs. Hélène Léger-Myers, 64, of Cocagne, New Brunswick. The song, composed on the traditional tune "Petit rocher de la haute montagne,"[30] relates the story of the accident and death of Pierre Arsenault, from Egmont Bay, Prince Edward Island, which took place around 1890. The composition of this lament is attributed to Émilie Bernard. Approximately ten versions have been collected in Prince Edward Island and New Brunswick. ("Noyade d'Edgar ou Pierre Arsenault"/"Drowning of Edgar or Pierre Arsenault," VI-C-3.2).

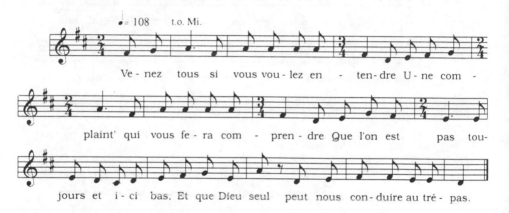

Venez tous si vous voulez entendre
Une complaint' qui vous fera comprendre
Que l'on est pas toujours et ici-bas,
Et que Dieu seul peut nous conduire au trépas.

Un jeun' garçon d'une honnête famille
Pensait toujours de gagner sa vie facile.
S'en a 'té dans les États-Unis,
Pensait toujours de revenir au pays.

Par un beau jour, il s'en va-t-à la pêche;
Le temps n'avait aucun' min' de tempête.
Après avoir bien passé la journée,
En s'en r'venant, son vaisseau a viré.

Un' de ses soeurs qui a appris la première;

---

30   Ernest Gagnon, *Chansons populaires du Canada*, p. 164.

Sur les journaux, ce fut un' triste nouvelle.
Ell' fut aussitôt s'informer
De la nouvell', si c'était la vérité.

Elle a-t-appris la nouvelle à son père
Lui demandant de pas trop s'fair' de peine,
Lui demandant de pas trop s'attrister:
Son très cher frèr' venait de se noyer.

Elle a-t-appris la nouvelle à sa mère.
C'est donc au ciel qu'elle adressait ses prières:
"Bonn' Sainte Vierg', ne l'abandonnez pas!
Priez Jésus de lui tendre les bras."

Consolez-vous et séchez tous vos larmes;
Priez Jésus et ayez confiance!
Car dans cett' vie tout doit se r'consoler
Puisque Jésus est mort pour nous sauver.

Il s'est noyé le saint temps du carême
Où Jésus-Christ a souffert tant de peine,
Où Jésus-Christ a versé tout son sang
Pour le salut de tous ses chers enfants.

En regardant dans le fond de la tombe,
Bon Saint Joseph, on a trouvé l'image.
Bon Saint Joseph, patron de la bonn' mort,
Assurément prend-e-ra soin de son sort.

XX.   LE BÛCHERON ÉCRASÉ PAR UN ARBRE/
THE LUMBERJACK CRUSHED BY A TREE

According to Georges Arsenault, in *Complaintes acadiennes de l'Île-du-Prince-Édouard*, p. 204, «Jérôme Maillet was born in the parish of Palmer Road on 16 March 1870, son of Anselme Maillet and Françoise Arsenault. He died in Bethel, Maine, on 5 June 1892 at the age of 21. The lament was written by Laurent Doucette . . . and sung to the tune of the folksong "Les Amants séparés par le père et la mère."[31] This version was collected by Gérald Aucoin and Alain Doucet, AFCEA, recording 22, sung July 1991 by Mrs. Marie Martin-Doucet of Saint-Antoine-de-Kent, New Brunswick. More than twenty versions have been collected in the Maritimes Provinces and the Magdalen Islands ("Le Bûcheron écrasé par un arbre"/"The Lumberman Crushed by a Tree," II-L-47).

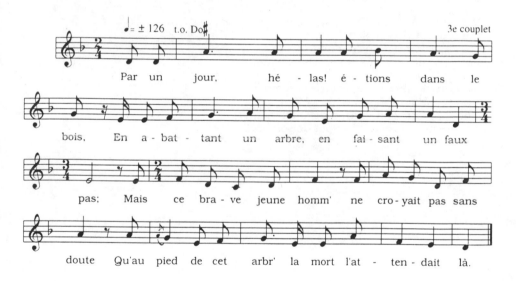

Par un jour, hé - las! é - tions dans le bois, En a - bat - tant un arbre, en fai - sant un faux pas; Mais ce bra - ve jeune homm' ne cro - yait pas sans doute Qu'au pied de cet arbr' la mort l'at - ten - dait là.

Écoutez mes chers amis c'triste récit
D'un brave bûcheron qui, en quittant sa patrie,
Laissant bien jeune encor' ses parents attristés
Pour s'en aller au loin d'[ans] pays étranger.

---

31   Marguerite and Raoul d'Harcourt, *Chansons folkloriques françaises au Canada*, p. 266.

Parti de chez lui, c'est pour s'en aller
Dans les États-Unis pensant y travailler.
Mais ce brave jeune homme ne croyait pas sans doute
Que la mort lui était destinée.

Par un jour, hélas! étions dans le bois,
En abattant un arbre, en faisant un faux pas;
Mais ce brave jeune homm' ne croyait pas sans doute
Qu'au pied de cet arbr' la mort l'attendait là.

Son cousin Joseph s'en est animé,
Il s'est hâté, [sans aide], c'est pour le dégager.
Mais, hélas! quel spectacle de le voir ensanglanté,
Il est tout difforme, c'est tout meurtrié. [32]

Il l'a pris dans ses bras, il l'a t-emmené
Dans un petit camp qui était peu éloigné.
Il est sans connaissanc', mais il y reste ainsi
Pendant trois jours entiers, sans aucun signe de vie.

Il faut aller chercher le docteur le plus proche et d'l'emmener ici.
Le docteur, il dit: "J'ne crois pas que cet homme va mourir de cela!"
Mais de . . ., l'homme de science s'est bien trompé,
Car deux mois, au plus tard, l'homme est décédé.

Au pied de son lit, son frère est assis.
Il dit: "Jérôme, tu dois bien mourir.
- Je voudrais, très cher frère, c'est avant de mourir,
Voir mon père et ma mère qui m'avont tant chéri.

- Jérôme, consoles-toi car tu ne peux pas voir
Ceux que tu désires; enfin, résignes-toi,
Car les ceux qu'tu veux voir sont trop éloignés d'ici.
Espèr' de les voir un jour en paradis.

- Puisqu'il faut, [ce] cher frère, se soumettre à la mort,
Vous voirez mon corps, c'est dans notre pays,
Aussi dans la terr' sainte où le faire enterrer
Avec tous mes amis qui m'avont tant chéri."

Enfin, ses désirs s'en all'nt accomplis,
À la suit' de son frère transporté chez-lui.
Que la journée de larmes pour des parents jolis
Voir ce corps agréable qui est mort enseveli!

Sa mère tombe à genoux: "Vierg', secourez-nous!
Prenez part à mes peines car je m'adresse à vous!
Prenez part à mes peines et priez votre Fils,
Que mon enfant jouiss' de son saint paradis!"

---

[32] Meurtri; the "é" is required for the rhyme.

XXI. N'ALLEZ PAS AU CANADA/DON'T GO TO CANADA

Donald Deschênes Collection, AFUL, recording 645. Sung April 17, 1983 by Mrs. Angélina Paradis-Fraser, 89, Cap-Chat, Quebec and reprinted in *Gaspésie*, March 1985, Vol. XXIII, Nº 1 (Nº 89), p. 33. Four versions listed in Quebec and northern Ontario. ("Les Gens du petit village"/"The Folks of the Little Village," II-D-22).

N'allez pas au Canada
Car la misère est par là.] *bis*
À la mod' du Canada,
On mang' d'la soupe aux pois,
Pis à la mod' des Canadiens,
On mang' du sarrasin.

Tous les gens du bord de l'eau
Ils n'ont pas tout c'qu'il leur faut.
Ils pêch'nt des barbottes,
Pis se font des gib'lottes,
Pis aussi de l'esturgeon,
Ils dis'nt que c'est bien bon.

Et les gens du p'tit village,
Ils ne vivent qu'aux herbages.
Vous voyez les créatures
Encarcannées sur la clôture,
Ramassant les cotonniers
Pour se faire à déjeuner.

Quand vient le mois de mai,
V'là les puces en quantité.
Vous voyez les demoiselles
Le soir à la chandelle
Se poussant de tous côtés
D'un air bien tourmenté.

Et parmi nos jeunes garçons,
Il y en a qui sont pas bien bons.
Vous les voyez à la veillée,
Le soir-e rassemblés
Autour-e du flacon
Qui sucent le bouchon.

XXII.   LES CURÉS DU CANADA/THE PASTORS OF CANADA

Rev. Médard Daigle, AFCEA, reel 2, recording 16. Sung in 1955 by Mrs. Arthur Roy, 60, Moncton, New Brunswick. Four versions collected. This song is sung to the French-Canadian traditional tune "Avance mon âge."[33]

Revenant du Canada,
Regardant de tous côtés,
Les clôtur's débordées,
Ça m'y fait ennuyer.

Refrain:
Sainte Vierge Marie,
Ne m'abandonnez pas.
Je pens' dans quelque temps
De m'en retourner aux États.

Le villag' de Saint-Laurent
Ce villag' renommé,
Ce villag' renommé,
C'est pour la pauvreté.

---

33   Deschênes, *C'était la plus jolie des filles*, p. 115.

Les curés du Canada,
Ils sav'nt pas nous conduire:
Ils nous défend'nt les danses
Et les veillées d'plaisir.

Les curés de États,
Ils nous conduis'nt mieux qu'ça:
Ils nous font des veillées,
C'est pour nous fair' danser.

C'est la vill' de New Bedford,
Cett' ville renommée,
L'argent en quantité
Pour ceux qui veulent en gagner.

Le dimanche arrivé,
Le curé monte en chaire,
C'est pour nous annoncer
Sam'di, i[l] a-t-un' veillée.

C't'à vous autr's, mes jeun's garçons,
C't'à vous autr's d'emm'ner les filles.
C'est vingt-cinq cenn's d'entrée,
Dansez tant qu'à veiller.

XXIII.   LE JOUR DE L'AN AUX ÉTATS-UNIS/
NEW YEAR'S DAY IN THE UNITED STATES

Laurent Comeau Collection, AFCEA, reel 17, recording 507. Sung March 6, 1976, by Mr. Lazare Hébert, Allainville, New Brunswick. This is the only collected version, but, according to some accounts, it was known in southeastern New Brunswick.

Sur le sol d'Amérique,
Là tous nos Canadiens
Ont la manièr' logique
De fêter l'jour de l'An.
Mais quand qu'l'année commence,
On aime à visiter
Nos vieilles amies d'enfance
Pour se faire embrasser.

Refrain:
Aux États-Unis,
On n's'embrass' pas avant minuit;
On s'occup' pas de d'ça
Dans notre Canada.
C'est dans la New Hampshire
Qu'on se plaît pas pour rire,
Mais surtout à Queenville
Qu'on a tout's nos belles filles.

Voyez ces vieill's grand-mères,
La figur' tout' plissée,
Essuyant leur vieux bec-que
Avec leur tablier.
Mais quand ça voit un homme,
Vite ell' lui saute au cou:
"Écout', mon vieux bonhomme,
Embrass'-moi, fais pas l'fou!"

Mais toujours les jeun's filles
I[ls] avont le bec sucré,
I[ls] se font un' bell' mine
Pour se faire embrasser.
Les garçons sont timides,
Ils n'os'nt pas s'approcher.
En arrière, ils fortillent
Pour se faire embrasser.

XXIV.   LA FILLE BIEN CHAGRINÉE/THE VERY SAD GIRL

This is the story of two lovers who separate: he returns to Canada while she continues her work in the factory in the United States. The text comes from the *Cahier de chansons* by Mrs. Marc Nowlan (née Maillet) of Upper Bouctouche, New Brunswick, edited around 1906. A photocopy of it is kept in the AFCEA. Mrs. Hélène Léger-Myers, 64, of Cocagne, New Brunswick, provided the melody for a single couplet only. (Deschênes-Cormier Collection, AFCEA, reel 16, recording 216, May 28, 1985).

Je suis la fille bien chagrinée
D'avoir perdu mon bien-aimé.
Il part, il change de pays.
Pour moi j'en n'aime pas d'autre que lui.

Oh! quel bonheur que c'est pour lui
De s'en aller dans son pays.
Et moi qui reste dans les *fact'ries*,
À mon ouvrage pensant à lui.

À mon ouvrage de chaque jour,
Penseras-tu à nos amours?
Et toi, l'ouvrage que tu feras,
Penseras-tu à Rosanna?

Auparavant de nous séparer,
Viens dans mes bras t'y reposer.
Tu entendras tous mes soupirs
Et tu voiras mon coeur mourir.

XXV. QUAND J'AI PARTI DE CARAQUET/ WHEN I LEFT CARAQUET

Coll. Jean-Claude Dupont, AFUL, manuscript provided by Mr. Alfred Richard, Pointe-Sapin, New Brunswick. Only version.

Quand j'ai parti de Caraquet
Pour monter dans les États,
Je marchais si joyeux
Avec tous les amis.

Alors, on se mit à boire
Avec tous mes amis.
À boire comme de raison,
On vient hors d'espoir.

J'entendis lorsqu'on buvait:
"Henri, viens à mon secours
Car ils vont me tuer,
Car ils vont me tuer."

Alors, il lève la planche
Et puis le frappa.
Vous voyez ce pauvre jeune homme,
Mort, en bas il tomba.

Ç'a bien été décidé
Qu'il ne serait pas pendu,
Mais qu'il aurait vingt-cinq ans,
Vingt-cinq ans de captivité.

XXVI.   LE SERGENT MORT À LA BATAILLE/
THE SERGEANT KILLED IN BATTLE

Taken from *Chansons d'Acadie*, 2nd series, collected by Chiasson and Boudreau, p. 22. The first stanza is taken from the only other version collected by Marius Barbeau (MN, ms 2609) in Saint-Joachim-de-Tourelle on the Gaspé Peninsula and sung by Charles Samson.

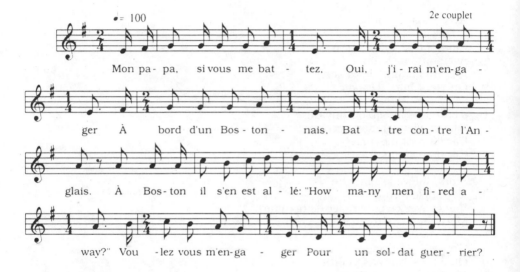

La fille de notre voisin,
Son compère va la voir.
I[l] la trouve à son gré,
Mais i[l] lui demande
Quand ell' veut se marier.
À son père en a parlé.
I[l] a pris le manche à balais,
I[l] a manqué l'éreinter.

"Mon papa, si vous me battez,
Oui, j'irai m'engager
À bord d'un Bostonnais
Battre contre l'Anglais."
À Boston il s'en est allé:
"How many men fired away?"
Voulez-vous m'engager
Pour un soldat guerrier?

- Oui, nous t'engagerons
Si tu veux fair' le bon garçon,
Nous irons t'y mener
À la têt' de l'armée."
Le sabre à son côté
Et le pistolet à la main,
François marchait devant
Comme un vaillant sergent.

Dès la première volée.
Les mâchoir's lui ont fêlé.
François tomba en bas;
On s'écria: "Hourra!"
Mais il s'est relevé:
Il faut pas s'arrêter
Pour un sergent blessé."

François se lamenta
À son cher et bon papa
Qu'il avait été blessé
Par un coup d'grenadier.
"Je n'te l'avais-t'y pas bien dit
Qu'tu périrais par le fusil!
À présent t'y voilà,
Ramass'-toi comm' tu pourras!"

XXVII.   LE VOYAGE À BOSTON/THE TRIP TO BOSTON

Even though this song was not collected in many locations, it is quite well known in Quebec, Ontario, and Acadia as interpreted by the Acadian folklorist Charlotte Cormier. This song is among the most interesting on the very popular traditional American tune, "Sweet Betsy from Pike."[34]

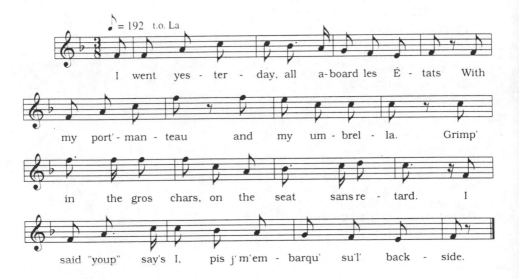

I went yesterday, all a-board les É - tats With my port' - man - teau and my um - brel - la. Grimp' in the gros chars, on the seat sans re - tard. I said "youp" say's I, pis j' m'em - barqu' su'l' back - side.

I went yesterday, all aboard les États
With my port'-manteau *and my umbrella.*
Grimp' in the gros chars, *on the seat* sans retard.
I said "Youp" *say's I,* pis j' m'embarqu' su' l' *backside*.

À travers le *window,* j'ai voulu embrasser
My cavalier but the train run away.
The train go so fast que *very* plus loin;
J'embrass' un' gross' vach' qui r'gardait passer l'train.

The conductor came and he said: "Your ticket!"
I said: "Her' it is. You gros *big* feluette!"
He giv's me un clin d'oeil *and I said: "You,* bétail!
J'suis pas un' fill' d'mêm' *and gav' him a black eye!"*

---

34   Lomax, *The Folk Songs of North America*, p. 335.

Someon' lâche un cri: "*Next place is Boston!*"
I grab my snatchell pis *get up*, pis oh! donc.
With my parapluie right under my bras,
I hit a pauvre homme *on the* et caetera.

Quand on va aux États, c'est pour avoir du fun.
Le diable est aux vaches en *son-of-a-gun.*
Quand ils vont aux États, *all the good* Canayens,
I[ls] se s'couent l'paroissien *with no mor'* de r'quien b'in.

Bibliography

Arsenault, Georges. *Complaintes acadiennes de l'Île-du-Prince-Édouard.* Montreal: Leméac, 1980, 261 p.

Barbeau, Charles-Marius. *Alouette!* Montreal: Les Éditions Lumen, 1946, 216 p.

Béland, Madeleine. *Chansons de voyageurs, coureurs de bois et forestiers.* Quebec City: Presses de l'Université Laval, 1982, 432 p.

Bouhier, Louis. *300 cantiques anciens et nouveaux.* Montreal: Éd. Archambault, 1948, 352 p.

Burque, Abbé F.-X. *Chansonnier canadien-français. Recueil de chansons populaires, chansons nouvelles et vieilles chansons restaurées.* Quebec City: L'Imprimerie Nationale, 1921, xx-282 p.

Cadrin, Gilles and Paul. "Traditions orales de Plamondon, un village franco-albertain," *Francophonies d'Amériques,* no. 5, Ottawa: Les Presses de l'Université d'Ottawa, 1995, pp. 93-106.

Chiasson, Rev. Anselme and Rev. Boudreau, Daniel. *Chansons d'Acadie.* Pointe-aux-Trembles, Quebec: La Réparation, 2nd series, 1944, 54 p.; 3rd series, 1948, 55 p.; 4th series, s.l., s.éd., [1976], 58 p.; 5th series, Moncton: Éditions des Aboiteaux, 1979, 60 p.

Chiasson, Rev. Anselme. *Tout le long de ces côtes. Chansons folkloriques des Iles de la Madeleine Recueillies par...* Mont Saint-Hilaire, Quebec: Chants de mon pays, 1983, 64 p.

Cormier, Charlotte. "Acadian Native Songs," *Proceedings of the Conference on the Art and Music of New Brunswick,*

Sackville: Centre for Canadian Studies, Mount Allison University. Fredericton: Goose Lane Editions, 1987, p. 53-74.

Deschênes, Donald. *C'était la plus jolie des filles. Répertoire des chansons d'Angélina Paradis-Fraser recueilli et présenté par . . .* Montreal: Les Quinze, 1982, 240 p.

Deschênes, Donald. "La Chanson locale acadienne: une expression artistique folklorique", *Francophonies d'Amériques*, no. 5, Ottawa: Les Presses de l'Université d'Ottawa, 1995, pp. 11-22.

Deschênes, Donald. "Chansons de départ pour les États-Unis", *Gaspésie*. March 1985, vol. 23, no. 1 (no. 89), p. 30-33.

Fowke, Edith. "Two Canadian Macaronic Songs," *Canadan Folk Music Bulletin*. December 1984, vol. 18, no. 4, p. 21-23.

Gagnon, Ernest. *Chansons populaires du Canada recueillies et publiées avec annotations, etc.*, dixième édition (conforme à l'édition de 1880). Montreal: Éd. Beauchemin, 1955, xvii-350 p.

Harcourt, Marguerite and Raoul d'. *Chansons folkloriques françaises au Canada, leur langue musicale.* Quebec City: Presses de l'Université Laval; Presses universitaires de France, 1956, xii-449 p.

Jutras, Monique. "Le Canada", *Le Canado-Américain*, October-December 1980, vol. 6, no. 4, p. 18.

Lanctôt, Gustave. "Chansons et rondes de Laprairie," *J.A.F.*, Vol. 33, 1920, p. 338.

Lavoie, Yolande. *L'Émigration des Canadiens aux États-Unis avant 1930*. Montreal: Les Presses de l'Université de Montréal, 1972.

LeBlanc, Barbara et Laura Sadowski, "La survivance par la chanson et la danse: Chéticamp, Nouvelle-Écosse et Waltham, Massachusetts," *Institut français. Le patrimoine folklorique des Franco-Américains*. Claire Quintal, ed. Quebec City: Le Conseil de la vie française en Amérique, 1986, pp. 105-150.

Laforte, Conrad. *Le Catalogue de la chanson folklorique française.* Québec: Presses de l'Université Laval, Volume 1: *Chansons en laisse,* 1977, cxii-561 p.; Volume 2: *Chansons strophiques,* 1981, xvi-841 p.; Volume 3: *Chansons en forme de dialogue,* 1982, xviii-144 p.; Volume 4: *Chansons sur les timbres,* 1983, xxii-649 p.

Lomax, Alan. *The Folk Songs of North America in the English Language.* New York: Garden City, 1960, xxx-623 p.

Marchildon, Daniel *et al. Trouvailles d'hier et d'aujourd'hui. Le folklore de la Huronie.* Penetanguishene: Centre d'activités françaises, 1980, 141 p.

Massicotte, E.-Z. "Nos chansons historiques: la recherche de l'or en Californie". *Bulletin de recherches historiques,* vol. 30, 1924, pp. 27-29.

Michaud-Latrimouille, Alice. *Chansons de Grand'mère.* Ottawa: Éditions de l'Université d'Ottawa, 1980, 229 pages.

Oriano, Michel. *Les Travailleurs de la frontière. Étude socio-historique des chansons de bûcherons, de cowboys et de cheminots américains au XIXe siècle.* Paris: Payot, 1980, 346 p.

Prévost, P.-É. *Chansons canadiennes. Paroles et musique de nos Canadiens.* Montreal, 1907, 114 p.

Rousseau, Guildo. *L'Image des États-Unis dans la littérature québécoise (1775-1930).* Sherbrooke, Quebec: Naaman, 1981, 360 p.

Le Temps de vivre, no. 1. Montreal: Supermagazine, 1980, 35 p.

VI

THE FRANCO-AMERICAN WOMAN

History and Mission of the
Fédération Féminine Franco-Américaine
(1951-1991)

Charlotte Bordes LeBlanc

It was curiosity that first moved me to accept the challenge of describing the work and the spirit of an organization of women on the verge of celebrating its 40th anniversary. I had become acquainted with the Fédération Féminine Franco-Américaine in 1981, thirty years after it was founded, and as I came to know its members, I often wondered about the source of their dedication and steadfastness. I wanted to find out what had occurred at the beginning, and in the intervening years, which seemed to have profoundly influenced the women of the Fédé. A close reading of the pertinent documents not only satisfied my curiosity, but gave rise to feelings of admiration, respect, and gratitude—admiration for an enterprise that so clearly expressed the intelligence and wisdom of those who undertook it, respect for the women who have remained faithful to their Franco-American identity, and gratitude toward them for having preserved and passed on their heritage. Inspired by these sentiments, I endeavored to select from the records the most significant events in the forty-year history of the F.F.F.-A., to underscore the specific contributions of each of its presidents and to convey the vigorous spirit of the organization which has never flagged through the years.

The F.F.F.-A. came into being on November 10, 1951, in Lewiston, Maine.[1] Franco-Americans were entering the new decade with a certain foreboding. Assimilating influences were gaining ground and were threatening the survival of French culture in New England. The time had come for those Franco-Americans who were conscious of their ethnic roots and desirous of maintaining their cultural heritage to gather together in the struggle for its preservation. Well aware of the paramount importance of women not only in the preservation, but in the transmission of ethnic values, the Comité d'orientation franco-

---

[1] "Le Comité de la survivance française en Amérique," *La Vie franco-américaine* (Manchester, N.H.: Imprimerie Ballard Frères, Inc., 1952), p. 265.

américaine—the all-male supreme council on Franco-American matters—had come up with the idea of bringing together into a regional federation all of the women's groups in New England and New York State.[2] The numbers alone are impressive. At that first Congress, held in Lewiston, Maine, in 1951, Gertrude St. Denis of Fall River, secretary of the provisional committee, in her report to the assembled delegates, gave what constitutes an inventory, probably the first of its kind, on the number of feminine Franco-American organizations of women which then existed in New England.

She stated that 1142 letters of invitation had been addressed throughout the six states of the region, comprising nine dioceses, and some 300 parishes, grouping 300 Ladies of Saint Anne societies, 299 Sodalities, 122 Councils of the Union St-Jean-Baptiste, fifty-four Villas of the Association Canado-Américaine, 174 affiliates of the Société des Artisans, which included both men and women, twenty-four of the Société l'Assomption, an Acadian organization, twenty-six Ste-Jeanne-d'Arc societies, fifty-three social and political clubs, nineteen alumnae organizations, fifteen cultural groups, and fifty-seven diverse organizations.[3] These varied associations were located in all six of the New England states: eighty-three in the State of Connecticut, 254 in Maine, 442 in Massachusetts, 185 in New Hampshire, 111 in Rhode Island, and sixty-seven in Vermont.[4]

In order to lay the groundwork for such a federation, a provisional committee had been appointed in June 1951, when about twenty carefully chosen women from various regions of New England, responded to the Comité d'orientation's invitation to meet in Worcester, Mass. These women enthusiastically accepted the challenge placed before them. They elected a provisional committee with Pauline Tougas of Manchester, New Hampshire as

---

2   Ibid., p. 265.

3   [The Ladies of Saint Anne grouped married women, the Sodalities were for unmarried young women. The Union St-Jean-Baptiste, the Association Canado-Américaine, the Société des Artisans, and l'Assomption were mutual benefit socieites with local councils engaged in social, cultural, and charitable activities. The Ste-Jeanne d'Arc groups were temperance societies.—Editor]

4   *La Vie franco-américaine*, p. 278.

chair.[5] The officers assumed their responsibilities with an efficiency that became the hallmark of the Fédé from that time on. A mere five months later, responding to the provisional committee's invitation, 140 delegates registered for the November convention. Here is the report given by Mrs. St. Denis at the opening of the Convention:

> Of the total, 110 societies are affiliated with the F.F.F.-A., that is to say 24 parish groups, 26 councils, 12 villas, 8 locals, 3 affiliates, 1 Ste-Jeanne   d'Arc society, 12 social clubs, 6 alumnae groups, 2 newspapers, 1 regional federation, 15 various organizations, representing altogether 47,403 members. To summarize by state: 48 from Massachusetts, 42 from Maine, 19 from New Hampshire, and 1 from Connecticut. Finally, 173 delegates have registered with the secretariat and 140 are attending this convention.[6]

The Very Reverend Thomas L. Landry, O.P., who has best articulated what it meant to be a Franco-American in those years, defined for the participants what he saw as being the precise goal of the F.F.F.-A.: "The Fédération proposes to save, to enrich and to propagate what is specifically French in every aspect of our lives which are at one and the same time Catholic and Franco-American."[7] A board of directors was elected with Alice Lemieux Lévesque as president, by-laws were adopted, and the F.F.F.-A. took its distinct place on the Franco-American scene.

From the beginning, the women of the Fédé were equal to the task set before them. Their mission would be a difficult one, for they were going against the tide of the forces of assimilation which occupied the high ground in the years following World War II. Creating a sense of unity among the scattered and quite diverse organizations was to be an essential weapon in the struggle. It was therefore necessary not only to forge ties among the various groups, but also to stimulate their interest and to remind them regularly of the role they were being called upon to play in the survival of Franco-American culture.

The biennial conventions and a newsletter, aptly named the *Bulletin*, were going to be the key elements in accomplishing this quasi-superhuman task. By means of the conventions, the various

---

5   Ibid., p. 267.

6   Ibid., p. 278.

7   Ibid., p. 279.

local groups, from one end of the region to the other, especially the officers of these societies, became acquainted with one another. The *Bulletin*, by keeping everyone informed, allowed the Fédé to launch regional projects based upon a given theme.[8]

Each president, including Pauline Tougas, of Manchester, New Hampshire, the president of the provisional committee, would consecrate her time and her energies to this cause and each has left on the Fédé the imprint of her particular talents.

The first president, Alice Lemieux Lévesque, of Nashua, New Hampshire, was an outstanding person. Her smiling wit, allied to her deep faith, her lively intelligence, enhanced by her natural eloquence and enthusiasm, formulated and communicated the ideals of the Fédération and inspired Franco-American women to follow her in the adventure of Franco-American *survivance* through its women. She it was who provided the Fédé with its *Bulletin*, that magnificent tool for reaching out to women throughout the region. First published in January 1953, the *Bulletin*, which was initially viewed as a vital link in maintaining contact among the affiliated groups scattered throughout the region, also quickly became the main vehicle for transmitting the ideas and the projects of each of the Fédé's presidents, thereby increasing the possibility of reinvigoration and emulation among the various societies. [9]

Throughout the fifties, the Fédé focused on education, and projects were initiated for its members as well as for the community, especially for young people. In 1952, the formation of study groups within the affiliated societies was advocated in order to encourage cultural maintenance. The *Bulletin* published vocabulary lists to help women maintain a certain degree of correctness in speaking French. At the 1952 convention, the delegates called for the establishment of home/school associations in all Franco-American communities. It was, however, the oral contest, launched in 1953, and open to students of French at all levels, that was one of the most important and most successful of the Fédé's projects. Writing in the *Bulletin* of June 1957, Marcelle Mainente, of Lewiston, Maine, president from 1956 to 1960, declared that the contest was the Fédé's major work, its most vital undertaking, and one in which all its groups could and should participate. The contest was held every other year

---

8   See Appendix A for a list of the conventions and the theme of each.

9   See Appendix C for a list of the editors of the *Bulletin*.

until 1974. It was unable to survive the closing of Franco-American parish schools and the lack of interest on the part of students and teachers in the public schools. The theme of the 1956 convention was Franco-American Education, upon which survival as a cultural group would depend.

Cécile Giguère Plaud was elected president at the convention held in her home town of New Bedford, Massachusetts, in 1960, at the start of a decade that would dramatically alter so many institutions, including Franco-American ones. The Fédé had to confront the changes that were continuing to take place in Franco-American communities. The struggle was becoming more and more difficult. In her message of April 1961, Cécile Plaud used the expression "*refrancisation des foyers*," that is the need to bring French back into the home thus indicating that the battle against the use of English within the family had been lost but that a last-ditch effort had to be attempted, nonetheless.[10] The convention of 1962, in Quebec, therefore focused the efforts of the Fédé on convincing Franco-Americans to retain the use of French in their homes. Cécile Plaud and her executive committee also strove to find new ways of engaging all of the member organizations in the collective effort of the Fédération. Regional committees were formed to offer all the women the possibility of taking an active part in achieving the goals of the Fédé.

Irène Lévesque, of Springfield, Massachusetts, who succeeded to the presidency in 1962, continued to exhort the women to put into practice the motto of the F.F.F.-A.: *Protégera nos foyers*. In the fall 1963 issue of the *Bulletin*, she wrote, "Let us protect our homes from the infiltration of English which threatens the existence of what is dear to us, the beautiful language of France, the language of our ancestors." Her legacy was one of discipline and the orderly conduct of business.

Flore Pelletier, of Waterbury, Connecticut, elected president in 1965, concentrated her able efforts on the development of regional committees. Convinced that to ensure efficient and far-reaching action, all of the societies had to become involved, she travelled throughout New England encouraging the formation of these committees.[11] The most successful of these was the one established by her in the State of Connecticut which continues to function to this day with astonishing vitality.

---

10   *Le Bulletin*, vol. 8, 1961, no. 3, p. 1.

11   Telephone conversation with Flore Pelletier, April 1991.

Under the leadership of Marie LeBlanc, of Manchester, New Hampshire, who took office in 1968, a membership campaign resulted in the recruitment of fifteen new affiliates. Marie LeBlanc succeeded, through her dynamism and her tact, in maintaining close contacts with all the member organizations thereby revitalizing the presence of the Fédé in all the regions.

Although the preservation of the Franco-American cultural heritage was one of the major preoccupations of the Fédé during the first two decades of its existence, the cultural enrichment of its members was not neglected. Beginning in 1964, trips to various countries in Europe, Latin America, and the Orient took place under the direction of Clémentine Poirier of Springfield. In October 1964, 126 members of the Fédération traveled to France where they spent twenty-two days in the land of their distant forebears.[12] In 1974, the Fédé organized a trip to Louisiana under the aegis of Flore Pelletier in order to establish contacts with the francophones of Louisiana and to learn more about the CODOFIL [Committee for the Development of French in Louisiana] which, propelled by former senator James Domengeaux, was giving a new impetus to the French language in Louisiana.[13]

Through the years, the Fédé sponsored concerts and exhibits of works by French and Quebec artists which helped to broaden the members' exposure to the arts. While communicating the message of cultural survival, the *Bulletin* also featured a variety of columns of interest to its readers. "Les Bagatelles de Magali," "La Vie des Cercles," "La Cuillère de Bois," all dealt with topics of the everyday life of its readers.

Marie LeBlanc's presidency can be viewed in retrospect as the bridge between what can be called the F.F.F.-A.'s youth and its maturity. The young Fédé had concentrated its action within the various Franco-American communities. For the most part, it had not ventured beyond its own people. However, the societal changes which occurred in the sixties, including the Second Vatican Council, profoundly affected the Franco-American community. With the closing of bilingual schools, the disappearance of French in the parishes and the prevalence of mixed marriages, the retention of French as the language in the family was doomed. Cultural survival would have to rely on other means. At the 1973 convention, Dr. Claire Quintal, a professor of French at

---

[12]   *Bulletin*, vol. 12, no. 4, p. 1

[13]   *Bulletin*, vol. 23, no. 1., p. 3.

Assumption College in Worcester, Massachusetts, was elected president. She would hold that office until 1981.

The activities of the F.F.F.-A. during the seventies bear witness to the open-mindedness of its leaders and members. During this period, activities were planned in conjunction with national and international events, without neglecting the Fédé's own projects. In 1976, the year of the United States Bicentennial celebrations, the *Fédé* entered into the spirit of the occasion by holding its convention in Newport, Rhode Island, a city associated with the contributions of the French to the War of Independence. Alex Haley's "Roots," made into a television mini-series, raised the country's consciousness regarding ancestry. Responding to the mood, the Fédé's president organized ethnic festivals for young people. These took place for four consecutive summers. One of them was held in Quebec in 1978 to include young Franco-Americans in a gathering of francophones from throughout the North American continent invited by the government of René Lévesque .

To coincide with the International Year of the Woman, the 1975 convention examined the evolution and broadening of the Franco-American woman's role in society. The project that year was to compile oral histories on tape of the lives of Franco-American women.

Although membership continued to be fairly high through the seventies, a decline in the number of affiliates was becoming evident. Consequently, beginning in 1980, the Fédé began to concentrate on the participation of individual members rather than on that of groups.

Marthe Biron Péloquin, of Lowell, Massachusetts, elected president in 1981, exerted a profound influence on the Fédération in her dual role as editor of the *Bulletin* for fifteen years. Convinced that individuals rather than organizations were the key to the future of the Fédération, she sought to recruit young career women as individual members. The conventions held during her term of office were essentially study sessions during which the problems and accomplishments of Franco-American women were analyzed.[14] She continued the tradition of maintaining ties with the representatives of francophone countries in Boston, in order to facilitate and encourage cultural exchange.

[14]   Proceedings of the 16th Biennial Convention of the F.F.F.-A.

In 1986, Marthe Welté Whalon of Fall River, Massachusetts, was elected to succeed Marthe Péloquin as president. She was the second French woman to have occupied the presidency—the other having been Marcelle Mainente in the 50s.[15] During Marthe Whalon's term of office, the Fédé focused on expanding its membership and highlighting the ties between the past and the present. Meetings of the Board of Directors were held in various Franco-American communities thus offering members the opportunity to come to know these communities and to enjoy the local historic sites. The main preoccupation of Marthe Whalon and her executive committee, however, was how to maintain the Fédération in light of the little interest manifested by the young in joining organizations. President of the F.F.F.-A. during its 40th anniversary celebrations, Marthe Whalon conveyed her concern as follows in the spring 1991 *Bulletin*:

> A woman at forty has reached a stage in her life when she begins to see the fulfillment of her work. She does not yet think of retirement, but she does prepare her children to take her place. The Fédé, like many other organizations, is sadly aware that replacements will be hard to find. We must therefore strive harder than ever to insure that our 40th anniversary will not be the end of the road but rather a platform for a new departure.

Having had to leave unmentioned the contributions of many women who have been the heart and soul as well as the willing hands of the F.F.F.-A., I end this brief account fully aware of its inadequacy. Although the deeds of these women are not recorded here, they are forever engraved in the hearts of their sisters. As a Franco-American woman myself, I thank these women of the Fédé for their devotion to the group, their loyalty to an ideal, and the attachment they have shown with great constancy for their cultural heritage.

Translated by the author

[This article first appeared as "Histoire et mission de la Fédération Féminine Franco-Américaine" in the French Institute's publication entitled *The Franco-American Woman*. The Appendices to the original article contained a certain number of pertinent documents relating to the F.F.F.-A. which are not reproduced here.]

---

[15]   See Appendix B for the list of presidents of the F.F.F.-A.

APPENDIX A

Chronology of the Conventions of the
Fédération Féminine Franco-Américaine

1951   **Foundation** at the second Convention of   Lewiston, Maine
the *Comité d'orientation franco-
américaine*

1953   First Convention   Worcester, Mass.

1954   Second Convention   Manchester, N.H.
Theme: *La femme dans le mouvement de la
vie française* [Woman in the French Life
Movement]

1956   Third Convention   Springfield, Mass.
Theme: *Éducation franco-américaine*
[Franco-American Education]

1958   Fourth Convention   Waterbury, Conn.
Theme: *Action féminine franco-
américaine* [The Action of Franco-
American Women]

1960   Fifth Convention   New Bedford, Mass.
Thème: *Collaboration à la vie franco-
américaine* [Collaboration in Franco-
American Life]

1962   **Tenth Anniversary**   Québec, Québec
Sixth Convention
Thème: *Convaincre et agir pour notre
refrancisation* [To Convince and to Act in
favor of *Refrancisation*]

1965   Seventh Convention   Boston, Mass.
Theme: *Le français dans la famille, à
l'école, chez les jeunes* [French Language
for the Young in the Home and at School]

1967   Eighth Convention   Lewiston, Maine
Theme: *L'enseignement du français dans
les écoles paroissiales et publiques* [The
Teaching of French in Parochial and
Public Schools]

1969   Ninth Convention   New York, N. Y.
Theme: Le rôle de la «Fédé» dans
l'éducation [The Role of the "Fédé" in
Education]

1971   **Twentieth Anniversary**   Montreal, Quebec
Tenth Convention
Theme: *Renaissance du français au 20e
siècle* [The Renaissance of French in the
20th Century]

1973	Eleventh Convention Theme: *Culture vivante* [Living Culture]	Quebec, Quebec
1975	Twelfth Convention Theme: *La Femme, son épanouissement et son action sociale* [Woman, her Personal Growth and her Social Action]	Newport, R. I.
1977	**Twenty-fifth Anniversary** Thirteenth Convention Theme: *Vingt-cinq années d'action* [Twenty-Five Years of Action]	Boston, Mass.
1979	Fourteenth Convention held jointly with that of the AFA* Theme: *La femme franco-américaine: son rôle, ses droits et ses responsabilités vis-à-vis du bilinguisme et du biculturalisme dans notre société* [The Franco-American Woman: her Role, her Rights and her Responsibilities vis-à-vis Bilingualism and Biculturalism in our Society]	Providence, R. I.
1981	**Thirtieth Anniversary** Fifteenth Convention Theme: *Trente années de volontariat* [Thirty Years of Volunteerism]	New Britain, Conn.
1984	Sixteenth Convention Theme: *La femme francophone aux États-Unis* [The Francophone Woman in the United States]	Nashua, N. H.
1986	**Thirty-fifth Anniversary** Seventeenth Convention Theme: *La Franco-Américaine: son action contemporaine* [The Franco-American Woman: Her Contemporary Action]	Springfield, Mass.
1988	Eighteenth Convention Theme: *La Franco-Américaine dans les services sociaux* [The Franco-American Woman in the Field of Social Services]	Newport, R. I.
1991	**Fortieth Anniversary** Nineteenth Convention Theme: *Histoire et mission de la F.F.F.-A.* [History and Mission of the F.F.F.-A.]	Worcester, Mass.

*   [The Assembly of Franco-Americans, a national organization founded in 1980, served for several years as a link between the French-speaking populations of New England, Louisiana, the Midwestern States, Florida, and California. Since the 1987 meeting, held in Nashua, N.H., the AFA no longer meets and thus plays no role on behalf of the French-speaking populations of the United States.—Editor]

APPENDIX B

Presidents of the Fédération Féminine Franco-Américaine

†Pauline Moll Tougas, president of the organizational committee and
        honorary president (Manchester, N.H.)   1951
†Alice Lemieux-Lévesque (Nashua, N.H.)   1951-1956
†Marcelle Mainente (Lewiston, Maine)   1956-1960
Cécile Plaud (New Bedford, Mass.)   1960-1962
†Irène Lévesque (Springfield, Mass.)   1962-1965
Flore Pelletier (Waterbury, Conn.)   1965-1968
†Marie LeBlanc (Manchester, N.H.)   1968-1973
Claire Quintal (Worcester, Mass.)   1973-1981
Marthe Biron Peloquin (Lowell, Mass.)   1981-1986
Marthe Welté Whalon (Fall River, Mass.)   1986-1991

Since 1991, the Fédération is pursuing its goals by holding an annual
meeting, chaired by one of its members who assumes the presidency for
that year:

Bernadette Bénard (Manchester, N.H.)   1992
Lillian Lamoureux (New Bedford, Mass.)   1993
Louise Champigny (Woonsocket, R.I.)   1994
Monique Blanchette (Lowell, Mass.)   1995
Monique Couture (Bristol, Conn.)   1996

APPENDIX C

Editors of the *Bulletin* of the F.F.F.-A.

†Pauline Moll Tougas (Manchester, N.H.)   1953-1954
†Marcelle Mainente (Lewiston, Maine)   1954-1956
†Alice Lemieux Lévesque (Nashua, N.H.)   1956-1960
†Marcelle Mainente (Lewiston, Maine)   1960-1964
†Charlotte Michaud (Lewiston, Maine)   1964-1967
Hilda LeBlanc (Waterbury, Conn.)   1967-1968
Flore Pelletier (Waterbury, Conn.)   1968-1972
†Marie LeBlanc (Manchester, N.H.)   1972-1973
Marthe Biron Peloquin (Lowell, Mass.)   1973-1988
Marcelle Guérette Fréchette (Kingston, R.I.)   1988-1991

Since 1991, the *Fédération* publishes the *Petit Courrier*. Marthe Welté
Whalon, of Fall River, serves as its editor.

A Franco-American Lay Missionary—Irène Farley
(1893-1961)

Marcelle Chenard

Irène Farley's life as a lay missionary spanned thirty-nine years. During that time, her involvement in the missionary movement of the Catholic Church occupied an important place in the history of Catholicism in Manchester, New Hampshire. She was a woman whose life and work were nurtured by the Franco-American community of that city. In her apostolate, called the "Missionary Rosebushes of St. Therese," and through her publications, *La Rose Effeuillée,* followed in time by *The Rose Petal,* her followers and her readers came to appreciate and support her mission. Its aim was to raise money to help the Church educate a native clergy in missionary countries and to pray so that these ordained priests would remain steadfast in their commitment. The Carmel of Lisieux honored her by naming her its North American representative in 1923. In time, she was interviewed by journalists who made her work known; yet, in her lifetime, she remained prayerful and poor, as she went about the task of collecting money for her beloved missions in her adopted city of Manchester.

Interviews, articles, her own reports and diaries provide some information about Irène Farley's life, but the results speak for themselves and show us that by dint of hard work and perseverance, she was able, with the very meager means at her disposal, to organize and administer a large network of generous and pious benefactors for the foreign missions.

Beginnings

Irène Farley was born on January 22, 1893, to Rose-Anne Beliveau and Émile Farley in St. Cyrille of Wendover in the diocese of Nicolet, Province of Quebec. She was the couple's second child, but their first to survive. Her parents had her baptized on the day following her birth and named her Marie-Anne Philomène Irène. Her mother, Rose-Anne Beliveau, was of Acadian descent. Rose-Anne's ancestors had come to Port Royal in

1644. Forcibly deported in 1755, during the "Grand Dérangement," they made their way via the St. John River to Cacouna, Quebec, in 1763, and, in the spring of 1764, they arrived at the Rivière Grégoire, in the County of Nicolet. Her father, Emile Farley, a blacksmith, was of Irish descent. His ancestors had come to Quebec City in 1710. In time, the Farley ancestors settled in St. Ambroise of Kildare parish, in Joliette, Quebec. Emile Farley married Rose-Anne Beliveau on February 17, 1890, in St. Cyrille of Wendover. He was twenty-four years old and she was twenty-five.

Irène grew up in this village, attending its local school until the age of ten. In 1903, she was awarded a scholarship to attend the private boarding school of the Sisters of the Assumption of the Blessed Virgin in St. Grégoire. Her maternal aunt, Soeur Marie-du-St-Sacrement (Victorine Beliveau), was a member of the congregation.

At this boarding school, Irène developed a love for reading, a liking for writing, a fondness for words, and an attraction for the missions. In the early 1900s, many of Quebec's religious communities were involved in missionary outreach programs in Western Canada and as far away as China. While at school, Irène was able to observe one program, the "purchase" of girl-children in the poor Chinese countryside. This program consisted of "buying" a girl-child from its parents for a dime. The religious in the mission fields solicited money from the children of Quebec to save these children from near-certain death. Each child was asked to contribute a penny to the mission fund and, in time, pennies became dimes, and dimes became dollars. With the money they received, the missionaries would "purchase" the children whose pictures they sent to the schools supporting the program. At the schools, these pictures were posted on bulletin boards for all the students to see the babies that they had literally saved from death in a faraway land.

In 1909, Irène left the boarding school to enter the Sisters of the Assumption's Normal School in Nicolet. At the end of the academic year 1909-1910, she was awarded a diploma certifying her to teach both French and English. After graduation, she set out to join her parents and her siblings in Manchester, New Hampshire, where they had settled in the meantime. Her parents were members of St. Augustine's parish in that city. Upon her own arrival, Irène found that her family was in financial need. She quickly realized that her diploma was non-transferable, so she sought employment in local shoe shops: first at East-Side, then at Hoitts, and finally at Cohas. In the evenings, she wrote a news column for *La Patrie* in Montreal, focusing on the happenings in the French-Canadian community of Manchester. This newspaper was circulated in New England cities which had sizeable French-Canadian populations. On Saturdays, she gave piano lessons, wrote *"adresses/compliments"* for individuals who were celebrating family events such as a golden jubilee or a silver wedding anniversary, and sold Larkin Company household products from their Buffalo, New York, mail order catalogue.

All of this brought her in direct contact with a great many French-Canadian immigrants. Although demanding, her numerous activities never seemed to take her away from reading. She somehow always managed to find the time to borrow books from St. Anthony of Padua's lending library. One day, Ms. Boulay, the parish librarian, suggested to Irène that she read *L'Histoire d'une âme (The History of a Soul)*, the autobiography of Sr. Therese of Lisieux. She thought Irène might like the book and she was right. Sr. Therese of the Child Jesus, born in 1873, twenty years before Irène, had lived at a time of French colonial expansion, when colonists and missionaries were leaving France, when French catholics were brought up with a sense of duty towards the missions in lands which they were colonizing. At the age of fifteen, Thérèse Martin had entered the Carmel at Lisieux to pray for priests, near and far, but especially for those in the missions so that they might stay firmly committed to their priestly vocation. So engaged was she in this, her own "mission," that one day, when her Prioress asked her to write letters to a few missionaries who had requested spiritual support, she eagerly and promptly complied.

Irène immediately identified with Sr. Therese of Lisieux. At school, she had witnessed the efforts of the Church in Quebec to keep the Catholic Church alive in North America, its missionary efforts in Western Canada and in the foreign mission fields. Two of her maternal aunts, Sr. Marie-du-St-Sacrement, S.A.S.V. (Victorine Beliveau), and Sr. St-Grégoire, a Grey nun in Montreal (Marie Beliveau), had been nurtured by a pious mother who had subscribed to the French publication of the Propagation of the Faith, printed in Lyons, France. Her aunt, Sr. St-Grégoire, while stationed among the Indians in Mackenzie, in the Northwest Territories of Canada, had sent the Farley children, at Christmas, small Canadian Indian handcrafts such as bookmarks made of porcupine quills or colorful beaded headbands. Faraway missions had thus taken on a special reality for Irène.

In 1914, a year after becoming acquainted with the life of Sr. Therese of the Child Jesus, Irène witnessed Canada's involvement in the First World War. Many of her relatives were recruited in the Quebec countryside. War meant struggle and separation. These difficult years called for courage and strength of character, two virtues that Sr. Therese of the Child Jesus was perceived as embodying. Irène and her mother inscribed their names at Lisieux that year. The sisters at the Carmel sent them pamphlets which they distributed.

In 1920, after the war, Irène's aunt, Sr. Marie-du-St. Sacrement, endowed with a practical nature, felt it was time for her niece to think about her life-long commitment. "You will be twenty-seven years old and not young forever," she wrote. As a child, her mother had asked Irène, "What will you be, my child?" "A Queen Victoria!" had been her answer. "You are the daughter of a blacksmith," had replied her mother. "In my imagination I see an incomprehensible kingdom which will consume my whole life and the kingdom will be of a divine nature," Irène had responded. Now her aunt was asking her to think about her life's work. Irène wrote her a letter stating that she "...did not feel called to the religious life, but felt it necessary to pursue it." She methodically set about to do so. Her first step was to compose a prayer to Sr. Therese of Lisieux: "Therese, show me the way. Lead me by the hand wherever I must go in order to work out my vocation." Her next step was to call on Fr. Louis J. A. Doucet, pastor of St. Anthony of Padua, to seek his advice. He told her that he felt that she would be happy in religious life and reproached her for not pursuing it.

On May 24, 1920, Irène wrote asking for admission as a Sister of the Assumption of the Blessed Virgin in Nicolet. Reverend Mother wrote back, "You should make an attempt." Irène decided to do so; she left Manchester on August 15. Six months after her admission, on February 17, 1921, Irène took the holy habit and the name, Sr. Françoise-Therese. Her novice mistress, Sr. Adèle (Béatrice Foucault), who also had a special devotion to Sr. Therese of the Child Jesus, taught the novices the hymn, "To Scatter Roses," based on a poem written by Sr. Therese of Lisieux and had them sing it in the convent chapel.

Sr. Françoise-Therese's duties as a novice included the scullery. There she felt she had observed her first miracle. She

516   STEEPLES AND SMOKESTACKS

would describe it in one of her letters to the Prioress at Lisieux as follows:

> September 18, 1921
> I went to prayers and after prayers I came back to the kitchen. All the pots and pans were washed and put away.

Sr. Françoise-Therese perceived this happening as a gentle miracle, so unaccustomed was she to having others carry out her assigned tasks. A few weeks after this declaration of faith to the Prioress, she received a package from Lisieux. The sisters at the Carmel were praying for the canonization of Sr. Therese of the Child Jesus. They sought prayerful supporters to help them. It was thus that Sr. Françoise-Therese became a proselytizer, handing out hundreds of fliers and picture cards of Sr. Therese of the Child Jesus to her companions.

In the month of February 1922, an ailing Sr. Françoise-Therese went to seek medical attention from Dr. Louis P. Normand in Trois Rivières, where she underwent some tests at the local hospital. She was diagnosed as having tuberculosis. Sr. Françoise-Therese knew that the diagnosis meant exile from the convent and she wanted no part of that fate. She remained, but her cough persisted. Her superiors sent for Dr. Bruno La Haye. After his examination, he declared her to be totally exhausted. Her superiors then asked her to leave the convent. She did so on February 16, 1922, returning to Manchester, to be with her parents. Her mother was happy to have Irène home again. She too was happy to be home. In Manchester, she went to see Dr. Robert Kerr, a tuberculosis specialist. For the next six months, she rested, exercised moderately, ate well, and slept as needed. On July 16, 1922, Dr. Kerr declared her cured. Irène wrote to the Prioress at Lisieux to express her joy at having regained her health. "I am happy to be alive and to have scars because my illness is ordinarily incurable."

She decided to seek readmission in Nicolet, but her request was denied. Reverend Mother General wrote suggesting that she seek to join a contemplative order. Irène decided to pursue this course of action, writing to two communities, the Sisters of the Precious Blood in Ottawa and the Sisters of the Visitation, also located in Ottawa. The Sisters of the Precious Blood replied favorably to her request, but she was hesitant about leading a contemplative life. While she was in the process of reaching a decision, she learned of Sr. Adèle's death. Saddened by this, Irène turned to Sr. Therese of Lisieux for help in finding her way. She waited for a visible sign. On November 20, 1922, she felt that her prayers were answered when she received a letter from the Carmel at Lisieux calling on all the friends of Sr. Therese of the Child Jesus for their support. After reading this letter, Irène felt that her prayers had been answered, stating, "I have dreamed of a Theresian vocation ever since I began to love her. Sr. Therese of Lisieux took me as a lay missionary in this country."

The following evening, which was the Feast of the Presentation of Mary, Irène Farley, accompanied by Marie-Anna Pelletier, president of the parish Sodality, went to see Fr. Louis J. A. Doucet to show him the letter she had received from the Carmel at Lisieux. The letter contained the following points:

1.   Pope Benedict XV had made a commitment to form a native clergy in foreign countries. The organization, named St. Peter the Apostle, would work toward this goal.

2.   Pope Pius XI reaffirmed his predecessor's commitment.

3.   The Council of St. Peter the Apostle wanted to have Venerable Therese as its official Protectress since she had had an attraction for the missions.

4.   S. G. Tiberghien, Secretary General of St. Peter the Apostle, had written to the Carmel of Lisieux to tell the Prioress of their intent. One difficulty stood in the way. The title was usually bestowed on a saint, and Therese was not a saint; thus an exemption was to be sought.

5.   Evidence of Sr. Therese's effectiveness as a Protectress was necessary and the Carmel was urged to help in this process by engaging the friends of Thérèse in gathering this tangible evidence.

6.   The friends were also asked to donate alms as their generosity dictated. These donations would be used for the development of a native clergy.

7. Besides their financial contribution, friends were asked to offer a spiritual bouquet.

After her parish priest had finished reading this document, Irène Farley informed him that she felt called to this Theresian vocation. She wanted to be a lay missionary. To work, to pray, and to raise money for the education of a native clergy was one thing, but to do this as a lay missionary was another matter. The Catholic Church in Manchester had no institutions to accommodate such an undertaking. Nevertheless, Fr. Louis J. A. Doucet encouraged her to try, and he promised her his full support.

Development

Marie-Anna Pelletier, the Sodality president, decided to call a meeting of its members at her home at 53 Belmont Street so that the group could hear Irène's presentation. The turnout was rather small. A second meeting was called for the following week, on November 29. On that evening, Irène Farley read her proposal to the group. It consisted of three objectives: 1. to gather evidence of the effectiveness of Sr. Therese in the life of individuals; 2. to raise money to help educate a native clergy; 3. to pray both for priestly vocations and for priests to remain committed to their vocation. Since these goals differed from those of the Sodality, a decision was made to create a new organization, "The *Cercle* [group] of Therese of St. Anthony" [parish]. In keeping with their French-Canadian tradition, the word *cercle* implied solidarity, i.e., working as a group toward the same goals, cooperating with one another, doing things together like their mothers and grandmothers had done in the Quebec countryside.

The election of officers was the next item on the agenda that evening.

The following were elected:

President	Ms. Marie-Anna Pelletier
Treasurer	Ms. Yvonne Guay
Secretary	Ms. Irène Farley

As the secretary of this organization, Irène's duties were general, though the goals were specific. In her role as a lay missionary, Irène turned to her family for help. Without hesitation, they acquiesced. The bedroom that she and Irma shared was transformed into an office. The two of them would go to their neighbors, the Desilets, to spend the night. In her role as a missionary, Irène elected to wear a simple black skirt with a white blouse. She added to this ensemble a green visor to protect her eyes from the glare and shadows caused by the electric lamp since she had a problem with one eye. It was in her home office at 442 Cilley Road that Irène methodically set about carrying out each of the group's objectives. Each objective was carefully delineated, and the means for its attainment were outlined.

Objective 1:
To Gather Evidence of Effectiveness

In the winter of 1923, the Carmelite sisters at Lisieux appointed Irène their North American representative. This appointment enabled her to sell authentic religious articles approved by Lisieux. The articles included books, pamphlets, and statues of Sr. Therese. A few short months after Irène's appointment, Sr. Therese of the Child Jesus was Beatified on April 29, 1923. This important step toward her canonization brought much joy and increased the enthusiasm of her followers. Irène Farley noted this fact by having it printed on the group's letterhead.

Office Central
des objets concernant la
Bienheureuse *Thérèse de Lisieux*

442 Cilley Road, *Téléphone* 5668-R
Manchester, New Hampshire, *États-Unis*

Irène then began to write a news column, *"Sous la Protection de la Bienheureuse Thérèse de l'Enfant-Jésus"* ["Under the Protection of Blessed Therese of the Child Jesus"], and she subtitled it, *Boîte aux lettres* [Mail Box]. This column appeared in the newspaper, *La Semaine Paroissiale*, published by the Dominican Fathers in Fall River, Massachusetts. The purpose of the column was to gather evidence on how Sr. Therese of Lisieux had intervened in the readers' lives and to give information, if requested, about devotional practices and religious articles relating to Sr. Therese of the Child Jesus. Some readers began making requests and submitting their testimony. Irène sent these on to the Theresian Documentation Center at Lisieux for verification. In the same article she would also give the readers the

particulars about their mail order, i.e., it has been sent, waiting
for a new shipment, etc. Irène also felt compelled to write her own
testimony to the Carmel. In her testimony, she described her
journey, in the winter of 1922, returning from Nicolet to
Manchester.

> During my two days in Siberian temperatures, I ceased to
> cough. The temperature for the 17th and the 18th of
> February broke a ten-year record. The cold had always
> bothered me, but this time I did not feel it. At 6 P.M., when the
> train pulled into the railroad station in Laconia, New
> Hampshire, there was no heat in the station. The next train
> for Manchester was at 4 A.M. the next morning, the 18th.
> I am convinced that were it not for the intervention of Sr.
> Therese, I would have died on this trip.

The list of testimonies grew and so did the orders for books
and statues. Irène hired Irma, her sister, to keep the records
straight since she was not a businesswoman. She had Charles, her
brother, help her with the statues. Every night after supper,
Charles and Georges Morin, a boy Mrs. Farley had adopted,
unpacked crates of statues. Each statue was checked to see if it
needed to be patched or retouched, or if it was broken, before it was
sent to its owner. Due to a high number of broken statues, Irène
and her brother Charles and Mr. Bercegol, the contact person at
Lisieux, decided to have the statues manufactured in Boston.
Charles Farley filled out the necessary copyright forms and sent
them to the U.S. Copyright Office. The initials and name C.E.
Farley were stamped on each of the authentic statues.

All went well until May 17, 1925, the day that Sr. Therese of
Lisieux was elevated to sainthood. From that day on, "fake"
statues, knock-offs of the original, began to flood the market
thereby impacting their own market and inventory. Their ads in
the *Catholic Directory*, assuring the public of the authenticity of
their statue did not remedy the problem since the price of the
counterfeit statues was lower. In 1929, Charles Farley was forced
to declare bankruptcy. Irène Farley experienced anguish over this
financial setback, although the situation had been caused by
external factors and was no fault of hers. Her supporters
understood this. The canonization of Sr. Therese of Lisieux also
meant the realization of the first objective Irène had set out to
accomplish ". . . to gather evidence of effectiveness."

Objective 2:
Donations for the Development of a Native Clergy

Raising money is never an easy task, but to raise it from poor people can be even more difficult since they have fewer resources. Irène Farley was well aware of the low wages of the French-Canadian mill workers in Manchester, having been one herself. Most mill workers earned one dollar and ten cents a day or nine cents an hour and some earned one dollar and forty-five cents a day or twelve cents an hour. She knew that they were committed to the Church and that they held the belief that to have a son become a priest would bring a blessing to his family. Native priests could be viewed as adopted sons, and as such would bring blessings upon the family. For such a cause, mill workers did donate some of their hard-earned money. Her own experiences as the recipient of a *burse* had taught her that people were generous.

She decided to raise donations for *burses* to be used to pay the room and board of seminarians. This was a practice that most French-Canadian immigrants understood. This was how the boarding schools of religious communities operated, how the country teachers lived, and how country people showed hospitality. Two parties—the recipient and the host—benefitted from this practice. Irène fixed the monetary value of a *burse* at $1,000. Only the interest on that sum could be used toward payment of room and board. The capital would stay untouched. A *burse* could thus be held in perpetuity. All the money raised would be sent to the Carmel at Lisieux. In turn, from 1922 to 1937, the sisters there saw to it that the money was distributed to various organizations, but primarily to that of St. Peter the Apostle, in Rome.

Manchester's local French newspaper, *L'Avenir National,* regularly reported on the apostolate started by Ms. Farley. On March 23, 1923, Ms. Lydia Asselin read an article in the paper about the *Cercle* of Therese at St. Anthony and brought it to the attention of her sister, Mrs. M. Halde. Together they decided to invite the women of their parish, St. Marie, and to ask members of the *Cercle* of St. Anthony to come to speak to them about the goals of their organization. The meeting was held at 3 Montcalm Street on March 18, 1923. The women filled three rooms in the house!

After listening attentively to Ms. Farley and Ms. Pelletier, they decided to form a similar organization. The ensuing discussion centered around a name for the group. Mrs. Albertine

Déry enthusiastically cried out, "The Little Flower is often represented with a crucifix covered with roses; we want to help the missions; let us call ourselves, *Missionary Rosebushes of Saint Therese.*" This is how the name "Rosebushes" came about. The *Cercle* of Therese of St. Anthony became Rosebush #2. The Rosebush would be a parish organization and the Society of Therese of the Child Jesus would be the parent organization. The members of a Rosebush would also be members of the Society of Therese of the Child Jesus and Irène Farley would be the Directress of this parent organization. The aggregate of Rosebushes was perceived as a Missionary Rose Garden.

The women of Rosebush #2 proceeded with the election of its officers.

President	Ms. Hermance Gingras
Vice-President	Mrs. Médéric Maynard
Secretary	Ms. Régina Pomerleau
Treasurer	Ms. Lydia Asselin

Irène Farley wanted as many people as possible to participate in the apostolate. She was committed to keeping Catholicism alive in North America and bringing it to foreign fields as well. Priests were necessary to achieve this goal. The concept of the Rosebush enabled her to operationalize the possibility of numbers. Each Rosebush symbolically represented a *burse* of $1,000. She devised a classification of donors. Three categories made up the classification. A **founder** would contribute $1,000 to establish a *burse*. A **benefactor** would contribute a part of that sum; thus he/she would be a branch of the Rosebush. A Rosebush consisted of twenty branches. A benefactor would donate twenty cents monthly toward the sum of five dollars which was equivalent to the cost of room and board for one month. If children made up a branch, then each child contributed a penny toward the sum of twenty-five cents. A benefactor would be an ongoing donor for a period of years. The last category, that of **associate**, consisted of a yearly donation of one dollar. When the total sum of $1,000 was attained, then the *burse* was held in perpetuity, i.e., the bishop in the foreign country would keep the capital invested and take the interest from the investment and use it to pay the bed and board of a seminarian.

Irène Farley listed each Rosebush sequentially, by parish, by city of origin, and by year. Each branch was assigned a number and a name. St. Anthony of Padua, started in 1922, was Rosebush

#1, Manchester. The official charter members of this particular Rosebush were:

Marie-Anna Pelletier	Alicia Côté
Laura Pelletier	Rachel Côté
Yvonne Guay	Corinne Champagne
Bernadette Blondin	Doris Champagne
Irène Farley	Louise Lemelin
Irma Farley	Yvonne Lemelin
Gracia Côté	Rachel Dumas
Bernadette Brown	Corinne Blondin
Bernadette Guay	Germaine Guay

St. Marie's parish established Rosebush #2. The parish itself was branch #1, its two schools—Hevey for boys and *Saints-Anges* [Holy Angels] for girls—became branches #2 and #3; Mr. and Mrs. J. M. Déry were the benefactors of branch #6. Mission banks were placed in the schools so a child could put his/her penny in the bank. One bank was represented by a little black boy dressed in blue, holding a shell. When the child placed the penny in the slot, the head of the boy would swing forward slightly in a sort of bow. At the base of the statue were the words, *Pour nos Missions*/For Our Missions. The money was collected weekly and turned over to the parish Rosarian (f.) or Rosarist (m.). This person was in charge of collecting the money and seeing to it that it reached Ms. Farley. In addition, the Rosarian/Rosarist saw to it that the group held monthly meetings to keep the members informed of their progress and to educate its membership concerning the activities taking place in the foreign mission fields. At the end of the educational program, a social was held. The members then had an opportunity to talk to the guest speaker and to chat with each other. An annual business meeting was to be held to summarize the year's activities and to present that year's financial report. Each Rosebush would extend invitations to other Rosebushes to join them for the annual meeting since it was to be a social gathering as well as a business meeting.

Each protégé was expected to write a letter introducing himself to the founder or benefactors. The content of the letter from the recipient was usually one of appreciation for their generosity, followed by a short description of his family and his country. The letters were to be sent to the Directress, Ms. Farley, and she saw to it that they reached the founder or benefactors. In certain instances she had some of these letters printed in issues of *La Rose Effeuillée*. This practice is still in effect today.

On November 22, 1923, their first anniversary, the officers of Rosebush #1, St. Anthony's Parish, held their first annual meeting which was reported in the local newspaper, *L'Avenir National*. In the report, the treasurer, Yvonne Guay, stated that Rosebush #1 had a membership of 671 persons and Rosebush #2, St. Marie, had 101 members. Three perpetual *burses* had been set up by:

1:   Mgr. Louis J. A. Doucet, Manchester, New Hampshire
2:   Fr. J. P. Clarke, New Bedford, Massachusetts
3:   Ms. Emma Leblond, Lewiston, Maine

Total contributions amounted to $4,556 at the time of the meeting.

La Semaine Paroissiale carried an article on March 27, 1924, which stated that Rosebush #2, St. Marie, had raised the sum of $350.00 toward its goal of $1,000. The first official annual meeting of Rosebush #2 was held at Hevey Hall, on Cartier Street, presided by Ms. Hermance Gingras. Irène Farley presented a progress report in the first issue of *La Rose Effeuillée* dated September 1925. Table 1 shows the data presented in her first official report to all the members.

Table 1.   Three Year Report of *Les Rosiers* / The Rosebushes

	1923 (12 mos.)	1924 (12 mos.)	1925 (9 mos.)
Money Raised	$4,975.50	$10,444.40	$7,546. 85
Perpetual *Burses*	3	36	
Seminarians in Process	20	30	
# of Rosebushes	2		
March 1924		6	
May 1924		27	
Sept. 1924		42	
Membership	772 (11/23)	1,100 (8/24)	

The increase in the number of Rosebushes in 1924 may be due to the wider publicity given to the work by *L'Avenir National*, *La Semaine Paroissiale*, and *L'Opinion Publique*, of Worcester, Massachusetts. Irène Farley placed an ad in *La Semaine Paroissiale* with the headline, "They Offer Their Life and Would You Not Give Them A Little Bit of Money?" Included under this headline was the picture of six foreign young men. This newspaper ad brought in a number of benefactors. Parishioners of St. Anne, in Fall River, Massachusetts, became Rosebush #3; the Dominican Sisters of Lewiston, Maine, became Rosebush #11; and some parishioners of St. Joseph, in Lewiston, Maine, became Rosebush #42. Month by month the list of benefactors grew. Some created fund-raising activities such as holding a card party. Others strung dried roses to make a *chapelet/* rosary beads which they labeled the Theresian *chapelet*. All the money raised was sent to the Missionary Rosebushes.

After the canonization of St. Therese of the Child Jesus on May 17, 1925, Irène Farley decided to publish her own magazine, *La Rose Effeuillée*. There was an expressed interest in the mission fields. The missionary priest was the modern man of the Church and people wished to know more about the foreign missions. Irène felt it appropriate to respond to this need by publishing the 5 1/2" by 8 1/2" paperback magazine. It contained news of the missions, the organization's financial report by month, letters from protégés, spiritually uplifting quotations, a list of devotions with the frequency for each, obituaries of members, along with various other features to keep the reader informed. Mr. Louis Paré, one of the editors of *L'Avenir National*, helped Irène with the revisions before its presses printed the edition. Then Mr. Albert Ballard saw to its publication at Ballard Press. The cost of the publication was $1.00 to its members, $2.00 to non-members. The first issue was dated September 1925. Bishop Georges Guertin gave his approval for the publication on September 4, 1925, and Irène filed the postoffice mailing forms for second class mail on October 14, 1925. The French publication was successful and, with the growth of English-speaking contributors, Irène decided to publish an English version which she entitled, *The Rose Petal*. Paul Farley, her brother, was one of the translators for this publication. Individuals in different cities collected the subscription money for these magazines which were the official voice of the Missionary Rosebushes of St. Therese.

Irène Farley was involved in a process of social change which was world-wide, and she started to note in her diary some of the impact of this change.

1926:   October 26, 1926, in St. Peter's, Rome, two Chinese priests were consecrated as Bishops of the Church.

1927:   October 3, 1927, Pope Pius XI consecrated the first Bishop of Japan, Mgr. Hayasaka. Bishop Hayasaka was the indigenous protégé of *Opus Sancti Petri*.

On December 14 of that same year, St. Therese of the Child Jesus was proclaimed the Patron Saint of Missionaries, men and women, throughout the world.

In 1927, Irène Farley began to compile a list of the adopted sons of the Rosebushes who had been ordained priests.

1927:   Jacob Mendonca, Trichinopoly, India
         Maria-Joseph Chinnappen   "   "

1928:   Benoît Peter, Rangoon, Burma
         M. J. Abraham, Kandy, Ceylon

1929:   Maria Francis Palai, Trichinopoly, India
         A. S. Pushpam
         Maria Chelliah
         Gnagni Santiago

1930:   Berchman Marianayagam, Trichinopoly, India
         P. M. Lourdes Raja, Palakarai, India
         A. Louresamy, Trichinopoly, India
         A. Soosaimanickam, Marambady, India

Each year, more names were added to the list and continue to be added to this day.

The growth in the number of Rosebushes resulted in two needs: for space and for help. The first need was met by moving the office from the Farley family home at 442 Cilley Road, to 31 Elm Street. This move occurred on January 5, 1928. This address was to be the location of the Rosebushes until March 3, 1937. That year, Bishop J. B. Peterson and Mgr. T. J. E. Devoy endowed Ms. Farley with a house at 110 Concord Street. The national headquarters of the organization would remain there until the spring of 1956 when it was moved to 117 Walnut Street. Since there was no space for an office in this building, the *Association Canado-Américaine,* a mutual benefit society with members in both French Canada and the United States, located at 52 Concord Street, provided Irène with the necessary office space.

The second need—for help—was harder to come by. Since the organization was a non-profit one, very few people were paid employees. Irma, Irène's sister, was paid for her services, but Irène conceived the idea that other women would probably like to live as lay missionaries like herself so she was inspired to form a religious society. She chose the name, Society of Missionary Sisters of St. Therese of the Child Jesus. She mentioned her idea to Bishop Guertin in 1926 since his approval was necessary to start a community. She even showed him the habit that she had designed, but he kept his silence on this issue until 1929. That year, he directed Ms. Emma Tassinari from Salem, Massachusetts, to Ms. Farley. Ms. Emma Tassinari worked with Irène Farley for approximately one year (1929-1930). At first, Ms. Tassinari lived with the Farley family at 442 Cilley Road, but Bishop Guertin had Irène Farley rent a little apartment near the Sisters of Mercy on Concord Street and the two of them moved into the apartment on April 23, 1930. Ms. Tassinari had hoped to help Irène start the religious society, but since there was no possibility of a society being formed in the immediate future, she left.

Ms. Cécile Boucher then came to join Irène in her work and stayed with her for four years. Others such as Maria Marcoux, Marie-Therese Crozet, Marie-Claire Gagné, Ernestine Paradis came and left. The dream of a religious society was not to be. Coming to that realization, Irène Farley formed the Third Order of Our Lady of Mt. Carmel in 1950. Many pious secular women became members of this Third Order of Mt. Carmel.

In 1931, Irène Farley lost a concerned bishop and a good friend when Bishop Guertin died. He had been instrumental in her receiving two Papal Benedictions for the publication, *La Rose Effeuillée,* the first in 1925, and a second in 1929. At his death, Mgr. J. S. Buckley renewed the permit to publish the two magazines until a new bishop was named. Mgr. John B. Peterson was appointed Bishop of the Diocese of Manchester on May 13, 1932. Irène Farley went to meet her bishop on July 23, 1932 to discuss her work. He assured her of his support with respect to her apostolate.

There would be more changes taking place in Manchester. The

economic situation was very depressed. The Amoskeag Manufacturing Company, the city's largest employer, had laid off a great number of employees following a prolonged strike. Life went on with people having to do with less and less. The majority of the people were patient and waited it out. Some French Canadians decided to go back to Canada and try to pick up where they had left off. For the bishop, these were difficult days since some people were dressed so shabbily that they were ashamed to attend church services. Yet, Irène Farley's supporters continued to toil nonetheless and somehow managed to donate their monthly contributions.

In 1937, another change was to take place. This time, Irène Farley was invited by Mgr. Th. J. McDonnell "to send the money she raised for the seminarians through *Opus Sancti Petri* in New York City while remaining autonomous." She went to see Bishop Peterson to discuss the matter with him and complied with this request. Joseph Lynch, Field Director of the Propagation of the Faith, wrote to Bishop Peterson regarding this new affiliation. Then five years went by with no mention made of the Rosebushes and their contributions to *Opus Sancti Petri*. Bishop Peterson wrote to Mgr. Th. J. McDonnell to express his disappointment that the Rosebushes were not being given any credit while other works were listed in their accountings. This lack of visibility did not go unnoticed by Ms. Farley.

The outbreak of World War II seemed to have given an impetus to the increase in contributions to the missions. The sons and daughters of the first generation of founders, benefactors, and associates began to send donations to the organizations. Names like soldiers Adrien Jalbert, Arthur Halde, Jean-Louis Defosses, Gérard Boucher, etc. appeared in the listing of new associates in *La Rose Effeuillée* and *The Rose Petal*. Some mothers of servicemen also contributed money to the Rosebushes, probably in the hope that St. Therese of Lisieux would protect their son or daughter. Irène Farley, fully aware of their fears and feelings during this time of world conflict, decided to coin lovely names for a branch as a living memorial. An example of this thoughtfulness is Rosebush #85, St. Jean-Baptiste, Manchester—Branch #1 *Notre-Dame des Ailes* [Our Lady of the Wings] in honor of Colonel Yves Normand, a pilot, whose mother, Mrs. Georges Normand, was the benefactor of that branch.

Table 2 shows the contributions of a few selected months for the war years 1943 and 1945.

Table 2.   **Contributions of Selected Months for 1943 and 1945**

Month	Year	Donations
January	1943	$2,688.07
February	1943	1,096.51
May	1945	1,788.50
June	1945	1,423.50

The total revenues for these years, were approximately $22,707 for the year 1943 and $19,272 for 1945. The grand total of money raised by the year 1945 was $260,000, as stated in *La Rose Effeuillée* in 1961, on p. 67.

In 1947, Lyle Terhune, in her article, translated by Mrs. Corinne Rocheleau-Rouleau, of Worcester, Massachusetts, and Montreal, as *"Des roses pour rançonner le monde,"* stated that, as of October 1947, Irène Farley had raised over $300,000, and that the total number of priests ordained was over 200.

In 1949, the year's revenues amounted to $27,824.15. In addition to this fact, Mr. Lucien SanSouci reported in *Le Phare* the following statistics up to that year.

Total money raised	$335,000
Priests ordained	235
Seminarians in process	215
Total number of Rosebushes	226

The Missionary Rosebushes were in nine American archdioceses:

Boston, Massachusetts	New York, New York
Cincinnati, Ohio	Philadelphia, Pennsylvania
Detroit, Michigan	St. Paul, Minnesota
Los Angeles, California	San Francisco, California
Milwaukee, Wisconsin	

They were also to be found in two Canadian archdioceses: Montreal and Quebec.

Every state in New England, except Vermont, had parish

Rosebushes. New Hampshire had fourteen cities and towns with Rosebushes. Massachusetts had thirteen cities, Rhode Island had five, Maine had four cities, and Connecticut had two.

The contributions of the Rosebushes were coming in on a regular basis and being sent to Mgr. McDonnell in the same manner. In 1947, Mgr. McDonnell wrote to Irène Farley to ask her "if the offering for the perpetual *burses* could not be raised to $2,000 instead of $1,000." The reason for his request at the time was that $1,000 no longer yielded the same interest that it had in former years. It might be added that the cost of delivery of services in foreign fields had also increased and political instability in many of the foreign countries caused monetary fluctuations. Irène Farley deliberated, considered the request seriously, and decided to modify it. She agreed to raise the *burse* to $1,200 and no more. The interest on that total would yield sixty dollars a year at five per cent interest.

In 1949, Mgr. McDonnell sent a second letter to Ms. Farley. This time he made two requests. The first one was "that she no longer appeal for *burses* but for scholarships of $1,200." The second request was "to let the Propagation of the Faith group together several *burses* for the support of one student so that the combined yield would cover the yearly tuition of one seminarian." Both these requests were unacceptable to Irène Farley. In the first case, a change from *burse* to scholarship meant a change in the original concept. A *burse* was meant to be a contribution for the living expenses of the seminarian, whereas a scholarship was for his tuition. The second request, that the Propagation of the Faith combine the *burses*, meant that she would lose control over the appropriation of the money raised. Without delay, she wrote these words, in French as she always did, to Bishop Matthew F. Brady: *"C'est une question de mourir ou de fleurir."* [It is a question of dying or thriving.] After she appealed to him, Cardinal Cushing wrote a letter on her behalf in which he stated that it was "impossible to establish *burses* for $1,200 and to change from *burses* to scholarships." The cardinal told her that he worried about her "dealing directly with the missionary Bishops and the Apostolic Vicars." His worry was not shared by Irène since she knew by that time that she had gained the trust of a "Third World Order" of adopted sons, friends, and missionary bishops. In fact, Father Jacob Mendonca, an adopted son, was now a bishop.

With determination and acquired American pragmatism, Irène Farley turned for advice to a trusted male friend, Mr. Wilfrid

Lessard. She respected Church authority, but she also wanted to retain control of the Rosebushes. He advised her to have legal "Articles of Agreement" drawn up as a preliminary step to forming a legal corporation. Five articles were drafted. The first two read as follows:

Article 1.   The name by which the Corporation shall be known is Missionary Rosebushes of Saint Therese.

Article 2.   The object for which the Corporation is established is: To help educate native seminarians for the Priesthood in the Foreign Missions of the Roman Catholic Church.

On April 23, 1950, five individuals signed their names to the agreement. The five incorporators were: Bishop Matthew F. Brady, Bishop of Manchester, Rev. John Foley, Rev. Napoleon Gilbert, Mr. Leo A. Gilbert, and Irène Farley. On April 29, 1950, six days later, another meeting was called, this time to set up a corporation as stated in the Articles of Agreement. The officers chosen to head the corporation were:

President	Mgr. Matthew F. Brady
Treasurer	Rev. Napoleon Gilbert
Secretary and Clerk	Rev. John Foley

This legal procedure was required by the State of New Hampshire and the forms had to be submitted to the Attorney General of the State for examination and approval since the Missionary Rosebushes of St. Therese would be registered as a non-profit organization. This procedure meant that Irène Farley would retain control of her decisions, with the approval of the officers, and would determine with them the policies of the Missionary Rosebushes. She set up one further procedure following this event. She initiated contracts. Two contracts would be drawn and would be signed by the Directress of the Missionary Rosebushes and by the bishop in the foreign mission. Each of the parties would keep one contract.

In 1951, Irène Farley received a personal endowment of $101,597.08 from the will of Ms. Marie C. Dubois, of St. Joseph's Parish, Biddeford, Maine "for whatever you need, but not for the Rosebushes." For two years, Irène did nothing with the gift. In 1953, she decided to ask a friend, Mr. Andrew Barbeau, to buy a small cottage for her in his name at the beach. She named the cottage "Rita Rose." She allowed herself a week's vacation a year at the beach. She rented it the rest of the season and donated the rental money, after paying expenses, to the Missionary Rosebushes. In 1954, she turned once again to Mr. Barbeau, this time to have him buy for her in his name the Ken-Law Hotel at the top of Mt. Uncannonic. She wanted to have the hotel converted into a retreat center for the Third Order of Mt. Carmel. This never came about.

In 1956, the City of Manchester decided to convert a portion of Concord Street into a municipal parking lot. The headquarters of the Missionary Rosebushes were affected by this decision. Irène was forced to move. She rented an apartment from Mr. Barbeau at 117 Walnut Street. In 1960, with the arrival of a new bishop, Mgr. Ernest J. Primeau, she asked Mr. Barbeau to arrange a meeting for her at 117 Walnut Street. At the meeting, Irène informed the bishop that she wanted to purchase the house from Mr. Barbeau. Bishop Primeau inspected the house, then turned to her and said, "You'd be crazy not to buy it for $25,000." Mr. Barbeau had agreed to let her purchase the house at the price he had originally paid for it. So she wrote a letter, addressed to Bishop Ernest J. Primeau, to inform him that she had purchased the house at 117 Walnut Street and that it was now the headquarters of the Missionary Rosebushes of St. Therese. The Bishop's lack of hesitation and his approval might possibly be explained by the fact that Ms. Farley had had an official meeting with him a few months prior to this, at which time she had discussed the results of the Missionary Rosebushes. Tables 3 and 4 present the statistics contained in that report.

Table 3.   Contributions by Year

1949	$27,824.15
1950	24,889.88
1951	22,860.72
1952	23,816.20
1953	24,466.28
1954	24,701.67
1955	36,718.27
1956	38,818.30

Table 4.   Results of MRB by the Year 1960

Total money raised	$800,000
Priests ordained	800
Seminarians in process	400
Perpetual *burses*	400
Total number of contributors	10,000

Ms. Farley lived at her residence at 117 Walnut Street with two associates, Ms. Madeleine Sweeney, who had joined her in 1956, and Ms. Claire Langevin, who came on November 20, 1960. Together they lived, prayed, and worked. On February 15, 1961, Irène Farley went to work, like she had done for so many years, at her office at the *Association Canado-Américaine*. At 5 P.M. that afternoon, she folded her apron, placed it in the desk drawer, and never returned to the office. The next day, she sent word that she was ill. On the night of February 16, 1961, she entered Notre Dame Hospital where she died in the early morning hours of the 17th. The day of her death was personally significant to Irène since it had been on that day, forty years earlier, that she had taken the habit of the Sisters of the Assumption of the Blessed Virgin in Nicolet, Canada. It was also the day of her parents' wedding anniversary. Later that same morning, Madeleine Sweeney carried another habit, that of the Third Order of Mt. Carmel, to the hospital since Irène was to be laid out in it. She was viewed at Letendre's Funeral Home. The funeral mass was officiated by Bishop Ernest J. Primeau at St. Georges Church, on February 21, 1961. The mass was attended by a large number of people, including many priests and dignitaries, relatives, friends, founders, benefactors, associates, and a few curious observers. The foundress of the Missionary Rosebushes of St. Therese was dead. Would there be a successor? Would the work continue?

Bishop Ernest J. Primeau initiated a plan of action to ensure the survival of the organization. He appointed Mgr. Wilfrid Paradis, Ph.D., J.C.D., D.D., to administer the affairs of the organization. His responsibilities consisted of filling the position of the Directress and taking an inventory of all the belongings of the Missionary Rosebushes of St. Therese. Both tasks proved to be very demanding and time-consuming. The first assignment, that of Directress, was offered to Mrs. Charlotte Farley, Irène's sister-in-law, who accepted it and carried out her duties as Directress and

Business Manager of the publications until 1968. Ms. Aurea Paradis became editor of the two publications. Madeleine Sweeney and Claire Langevin disassociated themselves from the organization during this transition period. By the end of the year 1961, the summary report was a good one. Table 5 shows the summation of the Missionary Rosebushes up to that time.

Table 5.   Results of MRB in Year 1961

Total money raised	$850,000
Priests ordained	800
Seminarians in process	405
Perpetual *burses*	400

The table indicates a slight increase in the number of seminarians in process compared to Table 4.

The organization had managed to stabilize itself after the death of its foundress, under the leadership of her sister-in-law. The founders, benefactors, and associates of the Rosebushes continued to support the goal, i.e., the education of a native clergy. In 1968, the death of Charlotte Farley brought another change. This time a part-time employee was hired to administer the organization and did so until 1972. There were a few disadvantages to this solution. The organization had been administered by a foundress consumed with a love for the missions, a sense of purpose and dedication, a personal acquaintance with many of its members, and a strong belief in the promise of faith. Her successors did not possess these qualities in the same degree nor had their life's commitment been that of a lay missionary. The spirit of the foundress, though felt, began to erode somewhat and many of the original benefactors had died. Donations continued to come in, but they were decreasing somewhat.

In the year 1970, the yearly donation amounted to $30,000. The goal of the organization being an ongoing one, contributions were still needed to fulfill its obligations in order to safeguard the continuity of the apostolate. Its Board of Directors decided that this continuity might be best preserved if it were in the hands of a religious community. But, which one? Two communities, the Carmelites in Concord, New Hampshire, and the Sisters of the

Precious Blood in Manchester, were proposed as possibilities. Discussions, however, pointed to the desire to keep the apostolate in Manchester. Its beginnings had been in Manchester and its first founders, benefactors, and associates had been either French-Canadian immigrants or their descendants of that city. Their generous response to the work had been enthusiastic from the onset. The Board decided to ask the Sisters of the Precious Blood, a French-Canadian order, to take on the apostolate. Their prioress, after some consideration, informed the Board that the sisters would take on the apostolate.

On March 2, 1972, Sr. Marilyn, S.P.B., became the Directress of the Missionary Rosebushes of St. Therese and held the position until the month of December 1972. Sr. Mary Agnes succeeded her in the position and is still the Directress of the Missionary Rosebushes of St. Therese. Her ties to the organization are binding ones. Her mother was of French-Canadian heritage and, at her daughter's birth, she had dedicated her to St. Therese of Lisieux. Early in life, Sr. Mary Agnes was attracted to religious life and considered entering the Carmel, but decided to enter the Sisters of the Precious Blood since that community had a lower age requirement for entry.

In the meantime, Mgr. Wilfrid Paradis sold the three properties: "Rita Rose" cottage, the Ken-Law Hotel, and the house at 117 Walnut Street, saw to the collection of a few promissory notes, located cartons of documents of the organization, had them transferred from various places like the *Association Canado-Américaine,* to the Precious Blood Monastery at 700 Bridge Street, Manchester. He also gathered data pertaining to Ms. Irène Farley's life to be compiled by Ms. Eileen Bruton. He also took care of numerous other details pertaining to the organization.

Once the new setup was in place in its new home, the Board of Directors, acting on some of the suggestions of the Directress, decided to assess the workings of the organization. The Board decided to modify and to simplify the accounting system. The status of each Rosebush was determined as active or inactive; if the status was active, then its old alpha and numeric codes were replaced by a four-digit code. The second change was to discontinue the dual publications and replace them with a newsletter, *The Rose Petal Newsletter.* The title, *The Rose Petal,* symbolically represented a continuity with the past, but it also manifested a discontinuity with the French language, Irène Farley's mother tongue.

The Board decided to try to appeal for donations to a larger number of people. Ads were taken out in the Catholic Sunday newspaper, *The Catholic Register*, in diocesan newspapers, such as the one in Albany, New York, and in Los Angeles, California, as well as in parish bulletins. The response to these ads did bring in new members. The third change was to modify the concept of *burses* to that of scholarships of $1,500 to $2,000 which could be paid in installments and at the convenience of the individual. All the money raised is now earmarked for scholarships, in keeping with the present mode of delivery of education in foreign countries. The fourth change was to increase the number of Directors to ten. The procedure of two contracts involving the Missionary Rosebushes of St. Therese with the foreign bishops was kept in place. The Directress sees to daily recording of the incoming contributions, to banking the money, to the correspondence between the adopted "son" and his benefactor(s), to the contracts between the organization and the foreign bishops, and to the publication of the newsletter, besides reporting to the Board, and doing whatever else has to be done.

The financial reports of the Missionary Rosebushes of St. Therese show an organization that is thriving and stable. In 1987, the year of the 65th anniversary of the organization, *The Rose Petal Newsletter* presented favorable results for the year.

Total money raised in 1987	$162,000
Priests ordained	48
Scholarships sent/completed	78
Scholarships in process	194

The organization listed over 1400 *burses*/scholarships since its start in 1922 and the beneficiaries were to be found in fifty-six foreign countries. In 1988, one year later, and the sixty-sixth year of its creation, the results show a decline in three categories: money raised, priests ordained, and scholarships sent or completed. However, the category—scholarships in process—shows a gain from the previous year.

Total money raised for 1988	$154,000
Priests ordained	30
Scholarships sent/completed	77
Scholarships in process	203

The harvest of the Rosebushes continues to have a productive yield. In 1989, there were 207 scholarships in the making, i.e., from $1,000+ to under $200; in 1990, 209 and, in 1991, 208. There was renewed hope for the future since 48 Rosebushes were begun in 1989, 59 in 1990, and 39 in 1991. The total sum of money sent to the missions from various sources, i.e., scholarships, masses, gifts, baptisms, for the years 1989-1991 were as follows:

1989	$184,611
1990	$238,510
1991	$271,220

These results show an organization which is stable, dynamic, effective in reaching its goals, and properly directed. The external environmental changes that have taken place over the years do not seem to have impacted negatively on its mission. The internal changes seem to have preserved its autonomy and its continuity in keeping with the spirit for which it was created.

Objective #3:
Spiritual Bouquet

The third goal which Irène Farley had initially defined was to pray for priestly vocations and to pray that priests remain committed to their vocation. The letter that she had received from Lisieux in 1922 had called on friends to offer a spiritual bouquet for the intended work. Irène Farley set about preparing an ongoing spiritual bouquet in keeping with the spirit of St. Therese who had said, "We (Carmelites) offer our prayers and our sacrifices for the apostolate of our Lord." Ten items made up the bouquet. Nine items consisted of devotional practices and one item pertained to personal generosity. The items were:

Holy Communion	*Chapelet* (5 Decades of the Rosary)
Spiritual Communion	Decades of the rosary
Masses Heard	Mortifications
Way of the Cross	Invocations/Indulgences
Rosaries (full)	Alms for Missionaries

Irène Farley led people in prayer, conducted novenas, observed the first Thursday of each month, recited rosaries, alone and with others, made the way of the cross for each new member that was recruited, and motivated members to do likewise. The list and the frequencies of these religious practices were given in each issue of *La Rose Effeuillée* and *The Rose Petal*. Irène Farley also prayed for the deceased members of the Missionary Rosebushes of St. Therese and included their names in the publications so that others could pray for them. Everyone was welcome in her small oratory on Concord Street. Donations were accepted for the vigil light in the oratory. People would drop by on a regular basis to pray, to ask her to pray for their intention, or to thank her for her prayers. She inspired people not only in their devotion to St. Therese of the Child Jesus, but also to good living.

Both publications, *La Rose Effeuillée*, and *The Rose Petal*, presented a regular feature *"Etincelles"* [Sparks] which consisted of spiritual quotations from selected writers. Among the numerous quotations presented over the years, two have been chosen to show the reader the kind of inspirational message that Irène Farley printed for her readers:

> Much prayer, much grace;
> little prayer, little grace;
> no prayer, no grace.   St. Francis of Assisi

> Our Lord does not look so much at the
> greatness of our work as at the love with
> which we accomplish it.   St. Teresa of Avila

The donations of alms to the missionaries seem to have consisted primarily of money for masses that individuals sent or gave her and Irène would see to it that the money was sent to missionary priests. She also collected cancelled stamps and the money raised from their sale was sent to the missions. In addition, she asked people to send a stamped self-addressed envelope to help defray the cost of mailings. All these requests were used as means of raising a little bit of money for the foreign priests and another way for a donor to give alms and practice generosity.

Since the Missionary Rosebushes of St. Therese were conceived as an integrating organization, at the death of one of its members, all the members of that particular Rosebush were asked to go to the wake so as to recite the rosary and to offer their condolences to the family members as well as to send a delegation to the funeral of the deceased. In some cases, this practice is still adhered to.

Though prayer is still a component of the Missionary Rosebushes of St. Therese, there are no longer any reports concerning the ten-item spiritual bouquet. In the newsletter, the reader can find requests to remember the deceased members and to pray for the dead and the living, a reminder that a novena in honor of the Little Flower will be conducted, and a note that the month of October is named "Mission Month." The families of deceased members often mention in the obituary which appears in their local newspaper that the deceased was a participant in the Missionary Rosebushes of St. Therese.

Conclusion

What can be said about Irène Farley's personal commitment as a lay missionary? Her life was inspirational to a great many people in Manchester. To this day, her memory is highly respected as that of a pious woman. As an innovator of social action outside the Church's normal structure, her role was sometimes misunderstood because the laity in those years did not play the role that it does today. Still, she reached her objectives with integrity and dedication. She touched the lives, first of immigrant French Canadians, then of the second and third generation, etc., of these French-Canadian families by drawing on their spiritual impulse and by uniting them in a religious purpose that gave meaning to their lives as ordinary people. In turn, they gave her existence a meaningful purpose. Together they cooperated, worked, prayed, and shared in contributing to and helping her to maintain her mission, which was to educate and to pray for a native clergy. Their Rosebush in the Missionary Rose Garden was a manifestation of their love for St. Therese of Lisieux, and Ms. Irène Farley was perceived as the woman who worked for the Little Flower in creating the Rose Garden for the missions.

The three objectives that Irène Farley defined in 1922 have all been attained. The first was to gather data regarding the effectiveness of Sr. Therese of Lisieux in people's lives. This objective was realized when the Church canonized her and then declared her the Protectress of the Missions. The second objective—to raise money for a native clergy—is still an ongoing goal which has helped to build an army of missionaries giving witness to the Roman Catholic Church in the mission fields. In 1888, Jeanne Bigard, realizing that a native clergy was essential to the future of the Church in the missions, had founded the work of St. Peter the Apostle (Opus Sancti Petri). Irène Farley worked toward the same end.

By responding to a given need, she became involved in a

process of international social change. She helped young men, called to a religious vocation, to become spiritual leaders in their society. The financial contributions that the Missionary Rosebushes of St. Therese sent to foreign countries helped the local economy. The letters that these adopted sons wrote to their benefactors created sentimental bonds and personal attachments. Irène Farley distributed the letters herself to the founders and benefactors. Thus, their pleasure at receiving such a letter was enhanced for having touched the hand of the foundress.

Over the years, this second objective came to be shared by individuals who were not of French-Canadian descent, but who also had a love for St. Therese of Lisieux and/or a love for the missions. This gave the organization continuity. The third objective—to pray for priestly vocations—is still pursued, perhaps more informally than in years past, but the call for prayers is still requested of all the members. The impact of the Missionary Rosebushes of St. Therese has been, is, and will be felt for many more years to come, in fifty-six countries, like Taiwan, India, the Philippines, and Guatemala. The continuity of the mission is in itself a tribute to its foundress, Irène Farley. In Manchester, her name is inscribed on a plaque at the base of the statue of Our Lady of the Interior Light outside the convent of the Sisters of the Precious Blood. Her apostolate is carried out inside by the sisters, in the same simple, loving, and dedicated manner that had come to be associated with Ms. Farley herself.

[This article first appeared as "Irène Farley, a Franco-American Lay Missionary, Including a Descriptive Study of the 'Missionary Rosebushes of Saint Therese'—Origin and Development (1922-1988)" in the French Institute's publication entitled *Franco-Americans and Religion: Impact and Influence.*]

References

Unprinted Sources

Missionary Rosebushes of St. Therese. 1985. Compilation of dates to remember, interviews, family genealogy, letters to bishops, records of properties, vocation, helpers, magazines, endowments. Compiled by Eileen Bruton. Manchester, New Hampshire: Sisters of the Precious Blood.

Interviews with: Mr. Andrew Barbeau, Sept. 12, 1984
Mrs. Annette Biron, July 10, 1984.
Mrs. Arthur Bousquet, Sept. 18, 1984.
Mr. Paul Farley, July 21, 1984.
Mrs. Irma F. Parkinson, June 25, 1984.
Ms. Madeleine Sweeney, March 16, 1985.

Archives of the Missionary Rosebushes of St. Therese, Sisters of the Precious Blood, Manchester, New Hampshire.

Archives of the Sisters of the Assumption of the Blessed Virgin, Nicolet, Quebec.

Interviews with Mr. Paul Farley, brother of Irène Farley, conducted by Marcelle Chenard August 18, 1988, and December 31, 1988.

Printed Sources

"L'Anniversaire des Rosiers de la Bienheureuse Thérèse", *L'Avenir National*, (22 novembre 1925): 1, 4.

Lucien C. SanSouci, "Mademoiselle Irène Farley: Notre Missionnaire Séculière", *Le Phare*. 11, 2 (Mars 1949): 8.

"Notre Roseraie Missionnaire", *La Rose Effeuillée*, 1ère année, 1 (septembre 1925):1-2.

"Ad Multos Annos A Nos Nouveaux Prêtres", *La Rose Effeuillée*, 4ème année, 6 (novembre 1928): 54.

"Solde de Novembre 1929", *La Rose Effeuillée*, 5ème année, 3-4 (novembre-décembre 1929): 144.

"Echelle des Bourses Perpétuelles", *La Rose Effeuillée*, 18ème année, 7-8 (mars-avril 1943): 188-189.

"Nos Aumônes de_____", *La Rose Effeuillée*, 18ème année, 7-8 (mars-avril 1943): 184-187.

"Notre Premier Moissonneur", *La Rose Effeuillée*, 20ème année, 11-12 (juillet-août 1945): 401.

"Images Rétrospectives: M. l'abbé Maria-Joseph Chinnappen et M. l'abbé Maria Francis", *La Rose Effeuillée*, 22ème année, 5-12 (janvier-août 1947): 114.

"Appel de la Vénérable Thérèse de l'Enfant Jésus à ses Amis et Protégés", *La Rose Effeuillée*, 23ème année, 1-12 (septembre 1947-août 1948): 22-25.

"M. et Mme J.-Michel Déry et leur fils, Gérard", *La Rose Effeuillée*, 23ème année, 1-12 (septembre 1947-août 1948): 79.

"Maria Chelliah", *La Rose Effeuillée*, 23ème année, 1-12 (septembre 1947-août 1948): 81.

"Gnagi Santiago", *La Rose Effeuillée*, 23ème année, 1-12 (septembre 1947-août 1948): 91.

"Nos Aumônes de _____ 1947/1948", *La Rose Effeuillée*, 23ème année, 1-12 (septembre 1947-août 1948): 126-169.

Lyle Terhune, "Irène Farley, 1893-1945: Des roses pour rançonner le monde", tr. Corinne Rocheleau-Rouleau. *La Rose Effeuillée*, XXXVI, 5-8 (janvier-avril 1961): 57-66.

"Irène Farley", *La Rose Effeuillée*, XXXVI, 5-8 (janvier-avril 1961): 67-70.

"Tout Catholique Devrait Avoir Un Prêtre Pour Fils Adoptif", *La Rose Effeuillée*, XXXVI, 9-10 (mai -juin 1961): 101.

"En 1970" *La Rose Effeuillée*, LII, 37-39 (janvier-février-mars 1971): Inside Back Cover.

Lyle Terhune (Rev.) "Roses to Redeem a World", *The Rose Petal,* XX1V, 4-6 (April-May-June 1968): 37.

The Rose Petal Newsletter. (Spring 1988): 5.

The Rose Petal Newsletter. (Spring 1989): 5.

"Sous la Protection de la Bienheureuse Thérèse de L'Enfant Jésus", *La Semaine Paroissiale,* 4ème série, 14 (jeudi, 25 septembre 1924): 7.

"Boîte Aux Lettres", *La Semaine Paroissiale,* 4ème série, 76 (jeudi, 16 décembre 1926): 12.

"L'Oeuvre des Rosiers", *La Semaine Paroissiale,* 3ème serie, 40 (jeudi, 27 mars 1927): 1.

"Religion in Quebec: Present and Future", ed. J.-P. Rouleau et al. *Pro Mundi Vita: Dossiers.* Dossier Europe/North America, 3 (Nov.-Dec. 1977): 3-31.

A Portrait of the Female Franco-American Worker
(1865-1930)

Yves Roby

The hundreds of thousands of French-Canadian migrants who flooded New England between 1865 and 1930 had one goal for the most part: to accumulate as rapidly as possible the money needed to pay their debts and begin a new life. In order to attain their goal, most of them took advantage of a view of the family regarded as a unit of production. While wives and mothers stayed at home, all the boys and girls old enough to work were sent to the factories.

Like all generalizations, such affirmations are exaggerated. They suggest that the young, single Franco-American female workers who worked in the shops left them once they married. But that is a distortion of reality. These statements have, nonetheless, the merit of indicating from which perspective the study of this subject should be approached.

This portrait will attempt to delineate the features of the Franco-American female worker, the nature of her role, the conditions under which she worked and lived, but only after having highlighted the circumstances of and the reasons for her departure from Quebec as well as those of her family, for these can throw light on the various aspects of her situation.

Motives and Circumstances of the Migration of French Canadians

Indebtedness was, first and foremost, what caused hundreds of thousands of French Canadians from the Quebec countryside and cities to flock to New England. Let us first look more closely at the countryside.

The farmers of the Richelieu Valley, the Montreal Plain, the Eastern Townships, and, to a certain degree, those of the Quebec Region, who had the advantages of fertile soil, of proximity to markets and to exportation centers, and a more adequate transportation network, were accustomed to modernizing their farms. The more progressive among them became specialized, extended the area of their tillable land, increased their herds, improved their agricultural practices, and purchased somewhat more expensive equipment. To do this, they did not hesitate to borrow at interest rates of eight, ten, or twelve percent. When times were prosperous, harvests abundant, and prices stable or on the rise, everything was fine. A poor harvest, a drop in prices, brought on anxiety. If the prices remained low for a long period of time (as they did from 1873 to 1879), if poor harvests occurred one after the other (as in 1888, 1889, and 1890), and if the competition increased in the international markets, the result was catastrophic. Merchants required immediate payment, mortgage holders became impatient. Then foreclosures took place or one had to resort to less scrupulous lenders—usurers—who profited from the times by requiring interest rates of fifteen, twenty percent or even higher. The misfortunes of the farmers had repercussions on the small proprietors and the day laborers who, in those regions, depended completely on seasonal work to meet their expenses. Many of these rural people chose to go to work temporarily in the United States in order to acquire quickly the money needed to pay off their debts and to start over again.

In the more remote areas of the Saguenay, Lake St. John, the Mauricie, or the Ottawa River and Témiscamingue, the Lower St. Lawrence and the Gaspé, a similar mechanism led to emigration. In those regions, where the soil was less cultivable, subsistence farming was practiced. Families counted on work in the forests, on roadways, on railway construction, or on fishing to make ends meet. Should the demand in Great Britain for board lumber, or on the American market for structural lumber or paper pulp slacken, or if the price of fish dropped, or the extensive public works projects slowed down, the vicious circle of seasonal unemployment, indebtedness, and discouragement began again with the inevitable consequence of a temporary migration toward the more favorable conditions of New England.

The urban centers of Quebec also contributed an increased flow of emigrants to the United States. There is no doubt that industries such as clothing, food, lumber, iron, steel, and rolling stock, which dominated the industrial landscape of Quebec, did make notable progress in the nineteenth century, but at what a price! During the lengthy recession, which lasted from 1873 to 1896, the large companies, hard hit themselves by unrelenting competition, managed to keep their share of the market only by mechanization, automation, more aggressive marketing, and by maintaining the lowest possible wages. Workers often saw their real earnings shrink. In certain industries, such as clothing and shoes, where sweatshops were the rule, the situation was worse. The contractors, who partially transformed raw materials in their shops and then passed them on to skilled artisans or to piece workers at home, competed tooth-and-nail for the business of retailers. Because the latter bought from the one who offered the lowest price, the contractor tended to decrease the cost of production by lowering the pay scale of the piece workers at home.

In normal times, the income of a working family was just barely sufficient to provide for essentials. But when, for a long period, unemployment set in, wages were lowered, or working hours were cut back, the result was hard times. Since there was at that time no welfare system, the hellish cycle of debt set in which led people to temporary exile in the States.

After the Civil War, most of the emigrants, benefiting from the rapid expansion of the railway system, flocked to the southern part of New England. The cotton, wool, and shoe industries, which were developing at a frenzied pace, exerted a powerful attraction, all the more so that technical improvements allowed the hiring of workers from rural areas. Contractors, who found French Canadians to be skillful, conscientious, docile, undemanding, and little inclined to strike, sought them out. Recruiting agents, whom they sent to the Quebec cities and countryside to vaunt the advantages of factory work, encouraged people to come as family units, assuring them that all the children who were old enough to work would find employment. Relatives and friends, who had already succumbed to the invitation, reassured the heads of families that, because of the rapid development of urban centers, they would find jobs in construction, laying sewers or water pipes, or in snow removal. Many saw there an unexpected chance to solve their problems; they believed that by putting the whole family to work, and by reducing their expenses to the strict minimum, they would be able to accumulate the greatest savings in the shortest possible span of time.

From this long introduction, what might we conclude? First of all, that at the moment of departure the migrants were experiencing a very painful situation. After years of tribulation, they were riddled with debt so that they deliberately chose to go to the "States." They could not depend on receiving help from the government and they were unwilling to accept public charity.

Their choices were quite limited. They could stay put and, if they were lucky, hope to survive as a result of long years of labor. They could listen to the propositions of the elite and head for the regions of Canada being opened up to colonization. There, a life of sacrifice awaited them. Finally, they could head for the States. They chose the last option, with hope in their hearts, placing their faith in the alluring promises of recruiting agents or the encouraging assurances of relatives and friends. They believed that their absence would be temporary. As one Mr. Saint-Germain remarked to Jacques Rouillard: "We were going to give a 'rush' wherever we had to in order to make money. After that we were coming back."[1] Although confident, they did not have the impression they were going to paradise, or to the promised land. They went to work in the United States as their Canadian counterparts would one day go to James Bay. They looked upon their sojourn, remarked Dr. Gédéon Archambault in 1884, at the golden anniversary of the Société Saint-Jean-Baptiste of Montreal, "as a term in prison."[2] What Dr. Archambault meant was that the migrants were ready to make the greatest sacrifices in order to accumulate money quickly to pay off their debts and to start over again. These sacrifices they willingly imposed on their families, because it is with their families that the majority of migrants, after 1865, came to the States.

From their already established relatives and friends, the migrants were quite cognizant of the fact that a worker could not, with his single wage, meet his family's needs, and, even less so, manage to save money. Only families with children old enough to work could hope to succeed.

> Take, for example, a man who had four children old enough to work in the mills. After a few months of apprenticeship, each one would earn at least one dollar a day. The father also, if he was hard-working . . . would be able to earn his dollar. When the month was over, he would take in quite a tidy sum: about five times twenty-four dollars or one hundred and twenty dollars.

1   Jacques Rouillard, *Ah, les États! Les travailleurs canadiens-français dans l'industrie textile de la Nouvelle-Angleterre d'après le témoignage des derniers migrants* (Montreal: Boréal Express, 1985), p. 26.

2   P.-P.-H. Charette, dir., "Noces d'or de la Saint-Jean-Baptiste. Compte-rendu officiel des fêtes de 1884 à Montréal," *Le Monde*, 1884, p. 405.

A hundred and twenty dollars at the end of the month! What a handsome sum for the former Canadian peasant. Out of that had to come rent, food, and clothing. A flat, or 5-room apartment, would cost 12 to 15 dollars per month. Food another 15 to 20 dollars. That left a surplus of 80 dollars for the other expenses.[3]

These are the reasons why observers have noted that only families with children old enough to work left Quebec for New England in the nineteenth century. Migrants without children or with very young children were an anomaly.

In those families which left temporarily, the role of women was essential.

Portrait of the Female Franco-American Worker (1865-1900)

It is especially in the mills that French-Canadian women went to work: exactly 78% worked there.[4] The textile industry, especially cotton, attracted them most. Important contingents were to be found also in the silk industry, and in the hat, sweater, and shoe shops. They worked at the more menial and lower-paying jobs.

In the mills, as we have already said, employers hired entire families. Distinctions need to be made, however. Heads of families and single men over twenty found work in foundries, in the manufacturing of machinery, and in the machine shops of Worcester, or in the shoe factories of Lynn, Brockton, Haverhill, and Lewiston-Auburn. Often they preferred to work cutting firewood, or as day laborers in the construction industry, or for the city in the construction of water mains and sewers. Wives and mothers stayed at home, at least in normal times. It is, therefore, the young who constituted the majority of the work force, and young girls outnumbered the rest. Take the case of the spinning mills of Holyoke, Massachusetts, in 1878. Almost 76% of the

---

3   Edouard Hamon, S.J., *Les Canadiens-français de la Nouvelle-Angleterre* (Quebec City: N.S. Hardy, 1891), pp. 16-17.

4   Ralph Vicero, "Immigration of French Canadians to New England, 1840-1900: A Geographical Analysis" (Doctoral dissertation, University of Wisconsin, 1968), p. 304.

workers were under 20, and 57.2% of them were girls.[5] At first glance, it appears that the female Franco-American worker was young, worked in the mills, and that her role should be studied in terms of the family considered as a unit of production.

We must remember that the migrants had only one goal: to accumulate as quickly as possible the money needed to pay their debts and start a new life. From this perspective, the individual gives way to family priorities. From the age of twelve, and sometimes less, most children, in this case the girls, had to leave school to take part in this collective effort. Parents said to themselves: "We're only here for two or three years, and we'll teach our children in Canada when we get back to our country."[6] It was an unwritten law. "When we worked," relates Ora Pelletier of Manchester, "we all gave our pay at home . . ."[7] Rose-Anna Bellemare, of the same city, says, "My last pay, I threw it on the table just before I got married. There was ten cents in the envelope that Papa said we could keep."[8] "That was the way," remembered Yvonne Dionne philosophically, in an interview with Tamara K. Hareven.[9] It has been evaluated that up to the time of their leaving home young women handed in 95% of their income.[10]

What is astonishing was not that children worked, since that was a necessity in working-class families, but the scope of the phenomenon. In their haste to accumulate savings, parents did

---

5   Peter Haebler, "Habitants in Holyoke: the Development of the French-Canadian Community in a Massachusetts City, 1865-1910" (Doctoral dissertation, University of New Hampshire, 1976), p. 68.

6   *Congrès Nationaux. Histoire et statistiques des Canadiens-Américains du Connecticut, 1885-1898* (Worcester, Mass.: L'Opinion publique, 1899), p. 203. This is a comment made by Rev. Senésac at the Ninth Congress held at Taftville in 1894.

7   Tamara K. Hareven and Randolph Langenbach, *Amoskeag. Life and Work in an American Factory-City* (New York: Pantheon Books, 1978), p. 239.

8   Rouillard, p. 118.

9   Hareven and Langenbach, p. 196.

10   Tamara K. Hareven, *Family Time and Industrial Time* (Cambridge: Cambridge University Press, 1982), p. 189.

not hesitate to break the law. They lied about their children's ages, falsified their names, and took them out of the mill temporarily when they were notified of the visit of inspectors. Thus, a foreman in Southbridge relates that he had the habit of telling French-Canadian employees that the law did not allow the hiring of children under ten; "the next day, they were all ten years of age."[11] Cora Pellerin recounts, "When I was eleven, my father had a birth certificate made for me in the name of my sister Cora, who died as a baby, because you couldn't go in to work unless you were fourteen."[12]

These children, these young girls, worked under extremely difficult conditions. Twelve hours a day, almost without interruption, they had to live as recluses, in an enclosed area, which was dirty and nauseating. Newspapers and various commissions of inquiry described in great detail the difficult conditions under which they had to work. In the weaving rooms, the steam that was used to prevent the thread from breaking made the atmosphere very humid, which caused colds and pneumonia.[13] In the summer, temperatures above 95° Fahrenheit and even as high as 120°[14] dehydrated the girls and caused them to faint. Lighting was weak, noise deafening; the girls suffered frequent headaches, eye trouble, and deafness. "When the looms were running," remembers Evelyne Desruisseaux, "we couldn't hear anyone speak. We communicated by hand or eye signals. To be heard, we had to speak directly into an ear. That's probably why I am hard of hearing."[15] The girls also complained of sexual harassment.

The work was easy, but monotonous and dangerous. The

---

[11]   This was taking place in 1872. Iris Saunders Podea, "Quebec to 'Little Canada'. The Coming of the French Canadians to New England in the Nineteenth Century", in L. Dinnerstein and F.C. Laher, Dir., *The Aliens. A History of Ethnic Minorities in America* (New Jersey: Prentice Hall, Inc., 1970), p. 210.

[12]   Hareven and Langenbach, p. 202.

[13]   Philip T. Silvia, "The Position of Workers in a Textile Community: Fall River in the Early 1880s," *Labor History* 16 (1975): 240.

[14]   "En ville," *L'Avenir National*, June 8, 1899.

[15]   Rouillard, p. 105.

bosses did not hesitate to increase the rhythm and to multiply technological changes. The speed of the work, coupled with the lack of safeguards, inexperience, fatigue, and monotony, resulted in numerous and serious accidents: fingers cut off, crushed hands, mutilated arms. Industrial diseases were a more surreptitious affliction which lay in wait for the worker after several years spent in poorly ventilated rooms, rooms that were too humid and dusty. "Not many Canadians can endure life in the mill for more than ten years or so," wrote the Jesuit Edouard Hamon.[16]

According to their collected testimonies, the girls professed themselves to be fairly well satisfied with their job. Several stressed the pleasure they found in the mill. "We'd have an hour for dinner. Some would crochet, and some would sit down and tell stories. We'd have a lot of fun."[17] "At noontime, the frames were stopped for an hour. We'd sit in the alley and eat our lunch; and if there was a good singer, she would sing and we would dance along the aisle."[18] This is not surprising, stresses Virginia Erskine, because "when you work twelve hours a day, you have to find pleasure in work. There's nowhere else to find it."[19]

Such satisfaction, though it might seem surprising today, can easily be explained. Work in the mills, even though difficult, was no more arduous than work on the farm or in the factories of Quebec where young people toiled very hard. "Some writers," recounts Lucille Caron Lagassé, of Goffstown, New Hampshire, "are saying that life was so hard, that the people complained, but I don't remember it that way. We did all right."[20] Cora Pellerin goes her one better, "When I was a little girl, I liked it on the farm in Canada. But I didn't miss it because for me it was paradise here in

---

[16]   Hamon, p. 17.

[17]   Hareven and Langenbach, p. 194.

[18]   Ibid., p. 200.

[19]   Ibid., p. 231.

[20]   Dyke Hendrickson, *Quiet Presence. Histoires des Franco-Américains en New England* (Portland: Guy Gannett Publishing Co., 1980), p. 150.

Manchester."[21] Cora Pellerin reminds us that the satisfaction of migrants should be measured, not by our criteria, but by their previous experience, by their goals, and their dreams. Certainly life in the New England mills was difficult, but even then it was a definite step upward. And, as the money came in, and the savings accumulated, joy reigned in the household.

The existence of networks of relatives and friends played an important role. The migrants directed relatives and friends to the departments where French Canadians were already numerous, to foremen who were tolerant and conciliatory; they kept them, as much as possible, away from employers who were brutal, prejudiced, and known to harass the women and young girls. These practices brought about the concentration of French Canadians in certain departments. There, relatives and friends initiated the children and young girls in the basics of their job, gave them advice, and taught them the rules of behavior that were not written down but were in force among the group. They would learn to respect the rhythm of work of the elders and not to exceed the quota of output which had non-officially become accepted within the group. Should relations with other workers or with the supervisor grow bitter, a relative would intercede to restore peace. They would be forewarned of the behavior of their supervisors. "Now there's French Charlie, he will take only pretty girls; he takes mostly French girls, too, of course. But French Charlie, he don't cheat you on your cloth; some supers are terr'ble mean that way."[22] All this gave the youngest workers particularly, great material and emotional security.

Those were some of the elements of a working person's culture which permitted them, both male and female, to fashion their environment to a certain degree, and to modify it to their advantage. These comments reveal the workers' capacity to exert pressure on the system, to increase their own power vis-à-vis that of the employers. "Workers," writes Tamara K. Hareven, "also tried to introduce some flexibility into their schedule and production by extending their breaks and occasionally interrupting work to socialize with fellow workers. They congregated at the water fountains, took longer toilet breaks,

21   Hareven and Langenbach, p. 203.

22   David Montgomery, *The Fall of the House of Labor. The Workplace, the State, and American Labor Activism,* 1865-1925 (Cambridge: Cambridge University Press, 1987), p. 144.

visited other workers at their machinery, looked out the window, and wandered around."[23]

The fact that the French-Canadian labor force was in great part composed of young and single women, and migratory on top of that, can explain to a great degree the poor reputation of French Canadians among the unions, at least during the first decades after the Civil War. When the young girls came home and aired their complaints and grievances and the strike rumors which circulated through the factory, they were quickly called to order by their fathers. The latter, invoking the authority of the Church, would remind them that in the world there are those who command and those who obey; the roles and duties of individuals were clearly defined. A good employer risked his capital to provide work for employees, a fair wage, and decent working conditions. In return for that risk, the employer had the right to expect of his employees that they would work long and well, that they would be on time, sober, skillful, honest, and keep their nose to the grindstone.[24] In the case of conflict or misunderstanding, the elders enjoyed direct contact with the employers. Ora Pelletier recalls that "The only place we could go to complain about things like that was the main office. They always listened; and if they thought you were in the right, they'd help you out."[25]

This Church teaching served the "birds of passage" well, i.e., those who hoped to return to Quebec after having accumulated the most savings possible in the shortest interval of time. Thus, there was no question that they or their children would take part in the strikes for reforms or improvements that would not affect them and, in addition, obligate them to dig into their savings and undoubtedly make new debts. Cora Pellerin, who had learned the lesson well, confided to Tamara K. Hareven, "It seemed that nobody won in the end, only that the people are out and they lost

---

[23]   Tamara K. Hareven, *Family Time and Industrial Time.* Cambridge, Cambridge University Press, 1982, p. 130.

[24]   Ferdinand Gagnon, "Le travail." Lecture given in Lowell, Massachusetts in 1873, in M.-E. Martineau, ed., *Ferdinand Gagnon, Biographie, éloge funèbre, pages choisies* (Manchester, New Hampshire: 1940) pp. 129-130.

[25]   Hareven and Langenbach, p. 188.

their wages."[26] Under those conditions, when a strike was called, one looked for another job or left.

Even in the nineteenth century, that attitude created tensions between the female workers and those migrants who, after a time, chose to live in the United States. The latter, after one or two generations, reacted much more aggressively to the progressive transformation of their work locale. They became alarmed over the technological innovations which speeded up the rhythm of work, tied them down a great deal more to their machines, and multiplied the risk of accidents. They became angry with employers who profited from every crisis to impose a cut in wages and who united to chip away at the privileges accepted in more prosperous times. Labor unions seemed to them to be more normal and natural.

You may have noted that, up to this point, married women have been rarely mentioned. In normal times, single women and widows made up the female work force, essentially because wives and mothers took care of the education of children and the execution of non-remunerated household tasks. Only a minority of them worked outside the home.[27] That is the way tradition and the Church wanted it. This situation is thus worth examining.

It was up to the man who dominated, controlled, and protected the family's interests to assure its financial security. His authority in the family and respectability in the community depended upon this. As for the woman, subject to her husband, she played a role that was both exacting and complex. She performed all the domestic tasks and had the primary responsibility for the education of children. She was entrusted with the task of inculcating in them a respect for traditional Catholic values, and she was also their first teacher of French. According to this model, the dominant socio-economic role fell to the father, while that of socialization agent was vested in the mother. The influence of the latter in the bosom of the family has been constantly underscored. "Habitually," wrote the Jesuit Edouard Hamon, "she is the one who governs the whole of that little republic, including its

---

[26]   Ibid., p. 209.

[27]   Barely 12% in Lewiston, in 1880. See Yves Frenette, "La genèse d'une communauté canadienne-française en Nouvelle-Angleterre: Lewiston, Maine, 1800-1880" (Doctoral dissertation, Laval University, 1988), p. 194.

president."[28] In addition to being the minister of finances, she was also minister of the interior. When the husband came home in the evening, she was the one who chose to tell him or not, of the children's escapades. Because of this, she had great power over the young ones. This disciplinary power sometimes extended throughout the tenement houses. "That is why, in those vast houses for workers, which sometimes numbered between twenty and thirty families, one finds an astonishing regularity most of the time. Disorders are rare and short lasting. Owing to these women, to these truly Christian mothers, the law of God reigns in the whole block with an authority which contrasts singularly with what one sees elsewhere under analogous conditions."[29] Women were cautioned, nonetheless, not to contest the limits of their role. She should stay in her place, noted one observer, because if she wants to get out of her home, she would have to neglect her duties of wife, mother, and mistress of the household. Who then would take her place? "Who will prepare meals? Who will take care of the children? Who will raise them as Christians . . .? Who will keep the house neat to make it pleasant in the eyes of the husband and the sons . . .?" In short, writes *Le National* of Manchester, on March 3, 1894, "a woman has a noble and sublime role to play in society. . . It is in the home that she must exercise it. It is there and there only that she can do good."[30]

Under those circumstances, as Evelyne Desruisseaux expresses it so well, "a woman who worked was a sort of dishonor."[31] Most men would accept it only in cases of the greatest need. Every testimony confirms this. "Women did not work the whole year long in the factory," Elmire Boucher tells us. "If the husband fell sick, the wife would go to work for three or four months, just the time for him to recuperate. Or, in the case of men who worked as day laborers, and so had nothing to do in winter, they would mind the house and their wives went to work."[32] "After my parents got married," relates Alice Lacasse of Manchester, "my

---

28   Hamon, p. 25.

29   Ibid., p. 25.

30   Evat, "Le suffrage des femmes," *Le National*, February 1, 1895, p. 2.

31   Rouillard, p. 109.

32   Ibid., p. 93.

mother just worked periodically, for two or three months at a time, when things would get too hard and my father didn't have any money."[33] "My husband," stated Maria Poitras-Lacasse, "never stopped me going to work when we needed the money."[34] In those cases, a goodly number of men seemed to prefer that their wives contribute to the family income without leaving home, by doing child-care or laundry, serving hot meals at noon to employees from the mills close by, or taking in boarders.

In the family as a unit of production, the mother's salary represented only extra income. This part-time work formed part of a complex strategy set up by working-class families to counter the constant menace of seasonal or cyclical unemployment.[35]

It must be noted that even during the years of relative prosperity, regular jobs among the blue collar workers were a rarity. So, about 20% of the workers in Massachusetts experienced unemployment between 1890 and 1900, and the typical employed worker was out of work slightly more than three months.[36] When the economy experienced a severe crisis—which happened four times between the Civil War and the turn of the century (1873-1879, 1882-1885, 1888-1891, 1894-1896)—the chances of finding a

---

[33]   Hareven and Langenbach, p. 255.

[34]   Ibid., p. 261. On this question, the attitude of married women was ambivalent. Many of them liked working in the mill, the friendships formed there, the solidarity it created, and the independence which it made possible. They would have wanted to continue to work after their marriage had it not been for the weight of tradition. On the other hand, others saw marriage as a liberation from the obligation of having to work. For five years, says one of them, "I lived the life of a vegetable." She saw her marriage as a period of rest after a hard day's work. C. Stewart Doty, *The First Franco-Americans. New England Life Histories from the Federal Writers' Project, 1938-1939* (Orono: University of Maine at Orono Press, 1985), p. 41. For the first, see Hareven, p. 78.

[35]   For an excellent synthesis of the various means used by the unemployed, see Alexander Keyssar, *Out of Work. The First Century of Unemployment in Massachusetts* (Cambridge: Cambridge University Press, 1986), pp. 151-165.

[36]   Alexander Keyssar, "Unemployment and the Labor Movement in Massachusetts, 1870-1916," in Hebert Gutman and Donald Bell, ed., *The New England Working Class and the New Labor History* (Chicago: University of Illinois Press, 1987), p. 233.

seasonal job grew slim. Thus, during the difficult year of 1885, about a third of Massachusetts workers were out of work more than four months each.[37] Employers were trying to counter the weak market by lowering wages, reducing the hours of work, or letting their employees go for more or less long periods.

What could the unemployed do then? It was useless to count on the employer. Questioned as to what he counted on doing to alleviate the problems of his laid-off workers, an industrialist of Brunswick, Maine, replied, "Nothing. They should have saved money while they were working."[38] To survive, the unemployed had to count, first and foremost, on their family, their neighbors, and on a complex strategy founded upon experience. Like the ant in the fable, they prepared for periods of scarcity by saving when they worked and by multiplying their sources of revenue. As we have already pointed out, the farsighted head of the family sent his children into the mills and asked his wife to take in boarders if the children were too young to work or else had already left the family. These methods proved effective and useful, but clearly insufficient when unemployment lasted for a long time or else hit more than one member of the family. In that case, they had to find new sources of income and pare expenses to the bone.

From the start, the mother played a major role. As we have seen, she left home for the mill. As "minister of finances," she cut back on leisure activities, a subscription to the local paper, medical care, put greater intervals between meals with meat, mended the children's clothing again and again; she invited her husband, worried and irritable over lack of work, to cut down on his drinking. If it became necessary, she accepted to sell some furniture, bring some precious articles to the pawn-shop, run up debts at the stores, with friends, or with loan sharks, and move into a less costly apartment. Mobility added to the problems of mothers. Before settling down some place, individuals or entire families went from city to city, everywhere it was rumored there was work, or chose to go back to Quebec temporarily, before they lost all their savings.

Even when husband and children worked, the life of a stay-at-home woman was hard. Nine out of ten migrant families were

---

[37]   Ibid.

[38]   Michael J. Guignard, *La foi – la langue – la culture. The Franco-Americans of Biddeford, Maine* (n.p.: Michael J. Guignard, 1982), p. 114.

tenants in those worker-houses which were called tenement houses. They were large buildings, four or five stories high which could accommodate ten to thirty families. With few exceptions, the quality of the apartment ranged from fairly good to mediocre. Numerous inquiries revealed that in too great a number of cases, the apartments in those worker-houses were too small, badly lit, poorly ventilated, and dirty; most of them, which were without bathrooms and had toilets only on the first floor, were poorly maintained and deteriorated quickly. Several testimonies are damning. In Lowell, in 1880, one of those worker-homes sheltered 396 persons in 36 apartments, an average of eleven persons per apartment.[39] It wasn't always easy under those circumstances to keep one's lodging clean and to make it look good to one's husband and sons.[40]

A woman had to be a nurse also and spend many sleepless nights caring for her family. In "the darkest hovels of the poorest sections" of New England, where they were to be found,[41] the migrants were very vulnerable to epidemics which broke out periodically. In winter, influenza, tuberculosis, and diphtheria hit hard. In summer, poor sanitary conditions brought on diarrhea, dysentery, typhoid fever, and infant cholera. The anxiety of the mother, like her disciplinary role, encompassed the whole ensemble of worker-houses and the network of relatives and friends. She was at the heart of the solidarity which developed in the Little Canadas.

The life of a Franco-American female worker, of young girls as well as married women, was a hard one in the first decades after the Civil War. She resigned herself to it and accepted to live in such difficult conditions because the whole strategy of the working family was to save up money as quickly as possible so as to go back eventually to the homeland. Such was the scenario at the moment of leaving for New England. Gédéon Archambault was right. The migrants looked upon their stay as being "like a term in prison."

---

[39]   Frances H. Early, "French-Canadian Beginnings in an American Community: Lowell, Massachusetts, 1868-1886" (Doctoral dissertation, Concordia University, 1979), p. 171.

[40]   Ibid.

[41]   Alexandre Goulet, *Une Nouvelle-France en Nouvelle-Angleterre* (Paris: Chauny and Quinsac, 1943), p. 103.

This portrait of the female worker underwent some transformation during the first three decades of the twentieth century. The third part of this essay, which is much shorter, will touch only upon the changes needing to be brought to this portrait and to an explanation of them. They come down to three: the girls were better paid, older, and more militant.

Some Minor Changes

Between 1900 and 1930, living conditions among working families improved greatly. We have seen that before the turn of the century, Franco-Americans were employed in the more menial jobs and also in the least well remunerated. On the eve of the war of 1914-1918, the situation had greatly changed. Thus, in Central Falls (Rhode Island), a study has shown that, at least in the sample taken in 1915, about 60% of the male and female Franco-American workers earned $14 and more per week, that is to say, a higher wage than earned on the average by other workers.[42] They worked in textile mills, machine shops, and in the construction trades. The others, the 40% who earned less that $14 per week, filled the jobs of day laborers or unskilled workers in the same industries.[43] It would be dangerous to generalize on the basis of a single case. However, there is little chance of error in stating that, in the whole of New England, on the one hand, the ratio of adults employed as day laborers was much lower than before 1900, and, on the other hand, the situation of blue collar workers had changed for the better. As an example of this, let us consider the case of the cotton mills.

In 1900, Franco-Americans, who constituted 44% of the manpower in the cotton industry, surpassed all other ethnic groups in number and percentage of workers.[44] In the course of time, however, Polish, Greek, Portuguese, and Italian immigrants took over an increasing number of jobs. According to the data

[42]   Louise Lamphere, *From Working Daughters to Working Mothers. Immigrant Women in a New England Industrial Community* (Ithaca: Cornell University Press, 1987), p. 132.

[43]   Ibid.

[44]   Philip T. Silvia, "The Spindle City: Labor, Politics and Religion in Fall River, Massachusetts, 1870-1905" (Doctoral dissertation, Fordham University, 1973), p. 686.

compiled in 1908-09 by the Dillingham Commission on workers of foreign extraction, Francos occupied the middle of the wage scale, after the Scotch, the English, and the Irish, but well ahead of the Portuguese, the Polish, and the Greeks. Men earned an average of $10.09 per week, and women $8.23. By comparison, the Scotsmen, who were better paid, received $12.27 and Scotswomen $8.66, while at the bottom of the scale, Greeks earned only $7.06 and $6.88.[45] The inquiry also revealed that a large proportion of Franco-Americans in the cotton industry had worked there for several years; they had lived in the United States for a long time, and had taken root;[46] that is the key to the explanation of their improved situation.

As a consequence of this, the conditions of life of Franco-American families, at least of those whose income fell in the middle range or above, had noticeably improved. Several testimonies confirmed that "their life style has changed," as Dr. J. Armand Bédard of Lynn, Mass., declared in 1912. "They don't live in large company buildings as they used to; they have become owners or else they live in elegant modern apartments; they are not piled one on top of the other . . . Conditions are much more sanitary."[47] "Franco-Americans," specifies Henri Bourassa, "have abandoned their dirty tenements and their squalid ghettos to the Portuguese, Slav, or Hungarian newcomers."[48] Since the work week was shorter, families disposed of more leisure time than had formerly been the case.

As can be seen, conditions had changed for the better. Still, most heads of families could not make ends meet on a single salary. A study undertaken in Fall River by the American Bureau

---

[45]   This applies to workers who were eighteen years of age or older. Bruno Ramirez, "French-Canadian Immigrants in the New England Cotton Industry: A Socioeconomic Profile," in *Labour/Le Travailleur* (Spring 1983), p. 137.

[46]   It is worthwhile noting that from 1900 to 1920, immigration from Quebec diminished greatly; according to some, it almost stopped altogether.

[47]   Dr J. Armand Bédard, "La langue française dans la famille et dans les relations sociales aux États-Unis," *L'Avenir National*, July 6, 1912.

[48]   Henri Bourassa, "Les Franco-Américains," in the *Bulletin de la Société historique franco-américaine* (1956), pp. 161-165.

of Labor Statistics in 1908 concluded that to achieve an acceptable standard of living, a family needed an annual income of $700. That was more than the mill workers earned.[49] So they still needed to count on the help of their children. We are especially interested here in the girls and the wives, and the role of both had changed noticeably.

Almost all young French-Canadian girls over the age of fifteen worked, notes Louise Lamphère.[50] The laws regulating child labor had become much stricter than they had been before. All the New England States prohibited the work of children under fourteen years of age. At that age, those who wanted a job needed, up to the age of sixteen, to provide a certificate attesting that they had reached a normal development, that they were in good health, and that they were physically able to do the work for which they wanted to be hired.[51] It must be said that many parents, with the complicity of employers, did not adhere to the letter of the law. "Newly-arrived families," said Elmire Boucher, "could hire out their children by simply stating they were 14. I knew some who worked in the mills at 10 . . . Nobody asked for a birth certificate."[52] "Age was only a formality," added Alma Ouellette. . . "One of my friends, who started at 10, was so tiny that she had to use a box to climb up to tie her threads. Her father worked close by and helped her."[53]

Despite all this, the contribution of children to family incomes decreased appreciably, compensated for, it must be strongly emphasized, by the greater participation of married women. Despite tradition and the teachings of the Church, which had not changed, 22.9% of married Franco-American women

[49] Keyssar, Out of Work, p. 46.

[50] Lamphere, p. 132.

[51] "Le travail des enfants," L'Avenir National, January 9, 1907; "Écoliers seront dans l'embarras," L'Avenir National, June 4, 1915.

[52] Rouillard, p. 90.

[53] Ibid., p. 140.

worked in the cotton mills in 1908,[54] and that percentage appeared to increase with time.

Mothers and wives working outside the home on a regular basis called down many admonitions upon themselves. "No matter the cost," Msgr. William Stang, bishop of Fall River, reminded his flock, "married women should not be allowed to work in the mills except in cases of extreme need. A married woman, by solemn contract entered into with her husband in the presence of God, has taken upon herself the duties of wife, mother, and housekeeper. That contract may not be broken, even by her own choice. The natural law requires a mother to give all her care and her time to her children and her home. Violation of this law would ruin domestic life and ultimately undermine the foundations of society."[55] *L'Avenir National* of Manchester queried, "What will happen to her children during her absence? Will the man have to stay at home and play the role of mother?"[56] The insistence of the elite in reminding married working women of their duties clearly indicated that in certain quarters they were held responsible for the tensions which shook the Franco-American family at the beginning of the century.

All of these transformations which affected the lives of female workers and their families inevitably resulted in important consequences. Let us consider the case of the textile industry, which at that time was experiencing profound changes.

Facing relentless competition from companies in the South, employers had to reduce their costs of production and increase productivity, which only served to provoke the demands of female workers and their shopmates. Indeed, the scientific management of work which was adopted by large manufacturing concerns such as the Amoskeag in Manchester, threatened the little control that workers had managed to exert over their work locale. But there was even worse. Every time an important drop in demand increased inventories, and a lowering of prices proved insufficient to correct the situation, employers took advantage of this to

---

[54]   Ramirez, p. 139.

[55]   "Femmes et enfants dans les fabriques," *L'Avenir National*, February 2, 1906.

[56]   "Le vrai féminisme," *L'Avenir National*, June 10, 1931.

impose on their workers cuts in pay of 10, 15 and 25%. Their unwillingness to restore the pay scale to its former level when prosperity returned provoked the anger of employees. There followed frequent violent and costly strikes in which the Francos took part more and more actively, with the approval of the female workers. Having set down roots in the U.S. many years before, and occupying skilled job positions in greater numbers than in the past, the Francos showed themselves as aggressive as others in the protection of their work conditions. In defense of their own jobs, they even protested against the influx of too many immigrants from Quebec.

Between 1920 and 1930, because of the economic problems experienced in Quebec, approximately 130,000 French Canadians took up permanent residence in the U.S. They arrived in the midst of an overheated social context. After the prosperous years which preceded World War I, the working conditions of textile workers were deteriorating. The crisis of 1920-21, the competition from the southern states, led manufacturers to impose a first cut of 22.5% in wages in 1921 and a second cut of 20% in January 1922. The male and female workers revolted. When the employers, in order to break the spirit of the unions, called in new French-Canadian immigrants as strike breakers, the latter became the target of the Francos. "Band of Canucks!" protested the people of Manchester. "You come and take our work from us! Why don't you go back home where you belong? Then we would have work."[57] "When they left the mill to return home in the evening," related Alexandre Boivin, speaking of the strike breakers, "they ran the risk of being killed."[58] Facts such as these must be known and applied to complete a true portrait of the female Franco-American worker on the eve of the Great Depression. Because of the dearth of studies, it must be added that our view of the twentieth century is more impressionistic than is the case with the previous period.

Translated by Alexis A. Babineau, A.A.

[This article first appeared as "Portrait de l'ouvrière franco-américaine (1865-1930)" in the French Institute's publication entitled *The Franco-American Woman*. It has been reviewed by the author for inclusion in this volume.]

---

[57]   Rouillard, p. 116.

[58]   Hareven, p. 323.

VII

FRANCO-AMERICANS TODAY

New England's Francophone Population
Based Upon the 1990 Census

Madeleine D. Giguère

On April 28, 1993, a national newspaper, USA TODAY, featured a Census Report on language in a front page story.[1] Using Census Bureau statistics, the article stated that in 1990, 1,702,175 persons in the United States reported that they spoke French at home. They made up the second largest foreign-language grouping in the United States with one-tenth as many speakers as the Spanish. French was the leading non-English language in four states: Louisiana, Maine, New Hampshire, and Vermont.[2]

A certain number of general statements are in order before undertaking a more detailed commentary:

• The terms "French Speakers," "French-Speaking," and "Francophone" will be used to refer to persons who reported to the U.S. Census in 1990 that they always or sometimes spoke French or French Creole[3] at home, not limited to slang or to a few

---

[1]   "Census: Languages Not Foreign at Home," USA TODAY, April 28, 1993, pp. 1 and 11.

[2]   In all there were 31.8 million home speakers of languages other than English, 14% of the total U.S. population. Of the non-English speakers, 54% of the total were Spanish, 5.3% French, 4.9 German, 4.1% Italian, and 3.9% Chinese. There were twelve states where French was the second largest language grouping, sixteen states where French was third, and seven states where French was the fourth largest language grouping. In only eleven states was French not among the first four non-English languages spoken. French was third in Connecticut, Massachusetts, and Rhode Island, after Spanish and Portuguese, or Spanish and Italian, in the case of Connecticut. Rhode Island had the largest number of Portuguese speakers of any state as well as Mon-Khmer, while Massachusetts was the state of residence of the largest number of Greek speakers in the U.S.

[3]   This census language category includes French, Walloon, Provençal, Patois, French Creole, Haitian Creole, and Cajun.

expressions.[4]

• What follows is about language use in the home and not the capacity to speak French. There is no census information on persons who speak French but do not speak it at home.[5] Thus, the figures used here underestimate the number of persons with the ability to speak French.

• For New England as a whole in 1990, there were 360,000 home speakers of French, 3% of the region's population.[6]

• We cannot assume that French Speakers are only of French or French-Canadian Ancestry.[7]

• This study uses the language of ratios. Percentages refer to the relationship of a part to the whole. Ratios relate a part to a part. Thus we can say that the sex ratio of males to females in a given population is 85, meaning that there are 85 males for every 100 females. In this mode of expression, I found that there was a ratio of 20 Francophones to French/French-Canadian Ancestry persons of first report, meaning that there were 20 French Speakers for every hundred persons in New England in 1990 who listed French or French-Canadian **first** in reporting their ancestries. Also, I found a ratio of 35 Francophones to Single French/French-Canadian Ancestry persons of the region.

---

4   Our data come from the 1990 Summary Tape File 3A5, a U.S. Bureau of the Census publication on CD-ROM.

5   Language data were collected on the long census form or schedule, which approximately one-fifth of the households in the United States received. Only household relationship, sex, race, age, marital status, and Hispanic origin were covered on the short schedule or form distributed to the entire population.

6   The language data are not reliable to the last digit and probably not to the last two digits; consequently, I have felt free to round out figures for presentation.

7   "Ancestry refers to a person's ethnic origin or descent, 'roots,' or heritage or the place of birth of the persons or the person's parents or ancestors before their arrival in the United States." 1990 Summary Tape File 3A.

• The Single Ancestry persons are those who answered **only** French or French-Canadian or their equivalents (Québécois, Acadian, Franco, etc.) to the census question on ancestry.

* * *

Looking at the numbers of French Speakers in New England, we find Massachusetts with a Francophone population of 125,000, followed by Maine with 81,000, Connecticut with 54,000, New Hampshire with 51,000. Rhode Island had 32,000 and Vermont 17,000 Francophones (see Table 1). To put this another way, we find that Massachusetts was home to 35% of the Francophones in New England, Maine 23%, Connecticut 15%, New Hampshire 14%, Rhode Island 9%, and Vermont 5% (see Table 2).

New Hampshire and Maine had 5% to 7% of their total population speaking French, Rhode Island and Vermont had 3%, Massachusetts and Connecticut had 2% of their populations speaking French at home (see Table 3).

As regards ancestry[8] of first report (see Table 4), there was a ratio of French Speakers to French Ancestry of 29 in Maine, between 18 and 20 for New Hampshire, Connecticut, Rhode Island,

---

[8]   I combined the number reporting French Ancestry first and those reporting French-Canadian Ancestry first to get the French, French-Canadian population of first report. I believe that you must use both French and French-Canadian Ancestries. Some people would prefer to add the second report of ancestry to the first report numbers. But once you add second report to the first report and add French and French-Canadian Ancestries together, you will get a double counting of some persons. The ancestries reported in the STF 3A General Profiles are a combination of first and second report of a particular ancestry. As long as you use only one ancestry, such as Italian, the total Ancestry count is correct. but when you use two ancestral identifiers, for example, French and French-Canadian, you are double-counting some persons. Luckily, Sample Tape File 3A does provide a separate listing of first report and second report ancestries, so that we can isolate the first report data. Franco-Americans are more likely to style themselves of French Ancestry than of French-Canadian ancestry, yet there are many who say they are of French-Canadian ancestry. In 1990, in places of more than 1,000 residents, more persons reported French-Canadian ancestry than French ancestry in: Augusta, Biddeford, Lewiston, Madawaska, Saco, Sanford, Van Buren, Waterville, and Winslow in Maine; Berlin, Manchester, Nashua, and Suncook in New Hampshire; Waltham in Massachusetts; Cumberland and Woonsocket in Rhode Island.

and Massachusetts, and 13 for Vermont (see Table 5). For those who listed but one ancestry, Vermont had a ratio of speakers to ancestry of 23, New Hampshire, Massachusetts, and Rhode Island ratios of around 33, Connecticut 39, and Maine 44 (see Table 6).

Summary Tape File 3A contains data only for Incorporated Places and Census Designated Places with populations of 1,000 or more. If we look at these and select the Places with 1,000 or more French Speakers in 1990, we find three cities with more than 10,000 French Home Speakers: Boston, Lewiston, and Manchester, and four cities with between five and ten thousand French Speakers: Woonsocket, Biddeford, Nashua, and Lowell. Towns of 2,500 to 5,000 include: Stamford and Bristol in Connecticut; Springfield, Chicopee, Worcester, Cambridge, Brockton, Fall River, and New Bedford in Massachusetts; Pawtucket in Rhode Island; Berlin in New Hampshire; and Auburn, Augusta, and Madawaska in Maine (see Table 7).

When we look at the percent of the population speaking French in these places with at least 1,000 French Speakers, we find quite a different picture. There are three towns with more than 73% of the local population speaking French at home: Van Buren (81%), Madawaska (80%), and Fort Kent (73%). Five cities show 20-40% of the local population speaking French: Berlin, N.H. (40%), Biddeford, Maine (35%), Lewiston, Maine (34%), Woonsocket, R.I. (21%), and Sanford, Maine (20%). Nine localities have 10 to 16% of their populations speaking French: Auburn, Maine (16%), Augusta, Maine (15%), Saco, Maine (15%), Caribou and Waterville, Maine (14%), Manchester, N.H. (12%), Somersworth, N.H., and Gardner, Mass., (11%) and Central Falls, R.I. (10%) (see Table 7).

The more opportunities one has to speak French, the more likely one speaks it, thus maintaining the language and passing it on. Ancestry or ethnic groupings foster the use of spoken French. What do we see when we look at the ratio of French Speakers to French/French-Canadian **Ancestry of First Report**? We find the three St. John Valley, Maine towns of Van Buren, Madawaska, and Fort Kent with even higher ratios (92, 89, and 82) than on a simple locality basis. These towns are unique in the proportion of the local population speaking French. Obviously, then, the opportunity to speak French is very high in these towns. It is also high among the French Ancestry persons in the next four cities with ratios of French-Speaking to French Ancestry in the fifties: Berlin, N.H. (58), Hartford, CT (54), Lewiston (55), and Biddeford,

Maine (55). There are evidently cultural communities in these cities which support the use of French (see Table 8).

If we look at the ratio of French Speakers to persons of **Single French Ancestry**, we find the three towns of Fort Kent, Madawaska, and Van Buren, Maine, with ratios ranging up to 97, pointing again to a community of French Speakers. Following is Berlin, N.H., with a ratio of 70. These four towns are relatively isolated and near a border with French Canada. In Maine, there are also Lewiston, Biddeford, Augusta, Sanford, and Auburn, all with ratios of over 50. These persons who do not report any other ancestry may have more occasion to speak and maintain their French. Their families are probably more French-speaking than are the relatives of the first-report French. The same is true for the French Speakers of Waltham in Massachusetts and New Britain and West Hartford in Connecticut, which also have ratios of 50 and over (See Table 9).

The major finding of the data on the cities of New England is that there are what I have called "New Francophone Communities" in Stamford, Norwalk, and Bridgeport in Connecticut and Somerville, Cambridge, Brockton, and Boston, in Massachusetts. These Francophone communities are neither large in numbers of French Speakers (except for Boston) nor in percent of the city's population, but they do stand out for having a substantial portion of their French Speakers who evidently did not report themselves as being of French or French-Canadian origin.

The less traditional Franco-American towns of Bridgeport, Conn., Somerville, Mass., and Norwalk, Conn., had ratios of French Speakers to French Ancestry of first report of between 66 and 70. There is also the phenomenon of ratios greater than one, found in Stamford, Conn. (160), Cambridge, Mass. (123), Boston, Mass. (122), and Brockton, Mass., (108). These figures indicate that there are more French Speakers than persons of French and French-Canadian Ancestry.[9] Possible sources of "new" franco-

---

9   These last 6 cities reported less than 4% French Mother Tongue in 1970 and still have fewer than 5% French Speakers in each city in 1990. Only Boston reported more than 4,000 French Mother Tongue persons in 1970. That year, there were 14 cities with French Mother Tongue Populations larger than that of Boston (10,500). These larger Francophone cities in 1970 were: Lewiston and Biddeford in Maine; Manchester and Nashua in New Hampshire; Chicopee, Fall River,

phones are Haiti, Belgium, Luxembourg, Switzerland, and the former French colonies.

Exploring the most likely of these possibilities, I found no published data on Haitians for cities. I did find State data in Social and Economic Characteristics (CP-2) of the 1990 Census which reported 23,690 persons of Haitian ancestry in Massachusetts, 5,000 in Connecticut, 950 in Rhode Island, 280 in New Hampshire, 160 in Maine, and 80 in Vermont. If all persons of Haitian Ancestry speak French or French Creole at home, and, as recent immigrants this is a reasonable assumption, Haitians comprised 8.4% of New England Francophones in 1990.

If we compare the data on French-Speaking in the New England States between 1980 and 1990, we find that all the states lost French speakers. The overall decline in French speakers in New England was 13%. The greatest loss was in Rhode Island, where the French-Speaking population decreased by 22% in the decade, compared with 8 and 10% decreases in Massachusetts and Connecticut. The French-Speaking population in Maine and Vermont declined by 14%, and New Hampshire's French-Speaking population lost 17% (see Table 10). The lesser decline of the Francophone population in Massachusetts and Rhode Island probably reflects the Haitian immigation. In 1990, Haitian-origin population probably made up 19% of the Massachusetts Francophone population and 9% of the Rhode Island Francophone population.

The decline in speaking French is the continuation of a trend which is documented, if imperfectly, back to 1940, and probably existed prior to that time. The documentation is imperfect because of the change in the census question between 1970 and 1980. In 1940 and 1970, the census question was "What language, other than English, was spoken in this person's home when he was a child?" Note that this question did not ask if the persons could speak the language or whether they had ever learned it. I term this a "language orientation" question rather than a "language use" question; The U.S. Census termed it a "Mother Tongue" question. One can argue that it reflected language use of the previous

---

Lawrence, Lowell, New Bedford, Springfield, and Worcester in Massachusetts; Hartford, Connecticut; Pawtucket and Woonsocket, Rhode Island. French Mother Tongue represented more than 14% of each of their city populations except in the case of Springfield, Worcester, and Hartford, which had 7 and 8% of their populations with a French Mother Tongue in 1970.

generation (around 1945 for the 1970 question and 1915 for the 1940 data).

The number of French Mother Tongue persons in New England rose from 705,000 in 1940 to 907,000 in 1970. In 1980, when the census question changed to language use in the respondent's residence, the numbers declined to 411,000 French Home Speakers in 1980 and 360,00 in 1990.[10]

In a study of the context of French language use in Maine in the 1980 Census, I found that persons were more likely to speak French if they had only French ancestry, if they lived in the more French-speaking areas of the State, if they were older, and if they were foreign-born.[11]

The number of French Speakers can also be affected by the demographic processes of fertility, mortality, and migration as well as by assimilation. My educated guess is that differences in mortality probably do not cause differences in the rates of French-Speaking within New England. Differences in birth rates among French Ancestry persons may have an effect on rates of French-Speaking among the New England States; for example, the size of French families in the St. John Valley may influence the higher rate of French-speaking in Maine.

Migration patterns undoubtedly affect the size of French-Speaking Populations. One of the best known migration patterns is that from Maine, especially from the St. John Valley, to Connecticut. It is to be noted that Massachusetts and Connecticut lost a smaller percentage of their Francophone population from 1980-1990 than the other states of the region. As always, economic opportunity plays a major role in population shifts. But so too do the new lifestyles of retirees. The decline in the number of French Speakers in New England has been accentuated by their migration to warmer climates, either on a full-time or a seasonal

---

[10]   See 1940 Census of the U.S., Mother Tongue. 1970 Census of the U.S., General Social and Economic Characteristics, Table 49. 1980 Census of Population—as quoted in InformACTION, January-February, 1986. 1990 Census of Population—Summary Tape File 3A.

[11]   Madeleine D. Giguère, "Language Maintenance—Speaking French at Home: Some Socio-Demographic Determinants." (Paper prepared for the Congrès du Conseil International d'Études Francophones, Montreal, April 16, 1988.)

basis. Even seasonal "snowbirds" may still be in the South on the early April date of the census, although they spend as many months in New England as in the South. In fact, the data indicate that Francophones of all ages have emigrated from New England. Many were no doubt answering the call of economic opportunity.[12]

The explanations for the rates of change in speaking French range from the lack of transmission of the language to out-migration in the northern states, to in-migration in the southern states, to intermarriage. If you are French-speaking, but marry someone who is not French-speaking, it is very difficult to maintain the language within the household, even though you may speak it outside the home. It is not easy to transmit the language, even with two French-speaking parents, when it is not being reinforced by the community, the school, or the church. Today, speaking French is an accomplishment, not a necessity. Knowing French does provide monetary returns for persons who teach French, engage in international relations or trade, or serve the elderly or the French-speaking immigrants and tourists. Knowing French provides one with an entry into other cultures, whether by reading, traveling, or by watching French-language television.

In a certain sense, the percentages reported here exaggerate the extent of French-Speaking. Certainly, speaking French in my house does not mean the same thing that it meant to my maternal grandmother who never learned to speak English. Today Franco-Americans are overwhelmingly monolingual in English, as our data show. In New England, only one-fifth as many persons speak French as say they are of French or French-Canadian Ancestry. Only a little more than one-third as many persons speak French as reported a single ancestry, whether French or French-Canadian. Madawaska data indicate that 20% of its population spoke English only, 76% were bilingual, and 4% spoke French only (i.e. spoke English "not well" or "not at all"). For the population age 65 and over, 13% of those who spoke French were

---

[12]   New England in 1990 was home to around 21 per cent of the Francophone population of the United States, whereas it was home to almost 50% of French Mother Tongue Persons in 1940.

monolingual in French. [13] This in a city with a very high rate of French-Speaking persons and in a census district in which there were census takers, not simply self-report forms.

Even French-Speaking Franco-Americans may well tend toward English dominance. This is understandable given that the last great wave of migration from French Canada was in the 1920s, more than two generations ago. The miracle is that Franco-Americans have kept their ancestral language for so long while living in an English-speaking world at work, on the radio, on television, on the streets, and now even in church. Not only do all Franco-American national parishes to my knowledge have Masses in English, some have no French Masses at all, and those who attend "French Masses" in some French churches may hear the Mass in French but the sermon in English. [14] Is French on the verge of becoming a ritual language for Franco-Americans, not only in church, but in public assemblies and private greetings, for example, on answering machines (including mine), "Hello/ Bonjour?" The major process affecting the numbers of French Speakers and the rates of French Speaking is undoubtedly assimilation into the greater American society.

When one considers the rates of intermarriage, the aging of the French-Speaking populations, the lack of immigrants from French Canada, and the Americanization of persons of French and French-Canadian Ancestry, the survival of the French language is a tribute to the tenacity and commitment of French Speakers.

[This essay, presented at the 1994 French Institute colloquium entitled "The Franco-Americans," is published here for the first time.]

---

[13]   "Age by Language Spoken at Home and Ability to Speak English"—1990 Summary Tape File 3A. Since there were no languages other than French and English reported in Madawaska, it is possible to use the data in this way.

[14]   There are still national parishes, such as SS. Pierre & Paul in Lewiston, in which Masses, entirely in French, are offered every day of the week including Saturday and Sunday.

TABLE 1

FRENCH* SPOKEN AT HOME: NEW ENGLAND STATES, 1990
Persons five years of age and over

Maine	81,012
New Hampshire	51,284
Vermont	17,171
Massachusetts	124,973
Connecticut	53,586
Rhode Island	31,669
Total	359,695

* Language Category includes: French, Walloon, Provençal, Patois, French Creole and Haitian Creole, and Cajun.
Source: 1990 Census of Population and Housing - Summary Tape File 3A.
MDG 6/94

TABLE 2

DISTRIBUTION OF FRENCH* SPEAKERS AMONG NEW ENGLAND STATES 1990

	Percent
Maine	22.5
New Hampshire	14.3
Vermont	4.8
Massachusetts	34.7
Connecticut	14.9
Rhode Island	8.8
Total	100.0
	(Number = 359,695)

*Language Category
Source: 1990 Census of Population – Summary Tape File 3A.
MDG 6/94

TABLE 3

PERCENTAGE OF NEW ENGLAND STATE POPULATIONS
SPEAKING FRENCH* AT HOME
Persons five years of age and over

	Total Population (thousands)	French Speakers (thousands)	Percent Speaker
Maine	1,142	81	7.1
New Hampshire	1,025	51	5.0
Vermont	522	17	3.3
Massachusetts	5,606	125	2.2
Connecticut	3,060	54	1.8
Rhode Island	936	32	3.4
New England	12,290	360	2.9

*Language Category
Source: 1990 Census of Population -Summary Tape File 3A
MDG 6/94

TABLE 4

FRENCH AND FRENCH-CANADIAN ANCESTRY
NEW ENGLAND STATES, 1990
First Ancestry Reported

	French- French-Canadian (thousands)	Total Population (thousands)	French- French-Canadian (percent)
Maine	277	1,228	22.6
New Hampshire	260	1,109	23.5
Vermont	134	563	23.7
Massachusetts	685	6,016	11.4
Connecticut	262	3,287	8.0
Rhode Island	158	1,003	15.7
Total	1,775	13,207	13.4

Source: 1990 Census of Population - Summary Tape File 3A.
MDG 6/94

TABLE 5

RATIO OF FRENCH* SPEAKERS TO PERSONS OF
FRENCH/FRENCH-CANADIAN ANCESTRY
NEW ENGLAND STATES 1990
First Ancestry Reported

	French & French-Canadian (thousands)	French Speakers (thousands)	Ratio
Maine	277	81	29
New Hampshire	260	51	20
Vermont	134	17	13
Massachusetts	685	125	18
Connecticut	262	54	20
Rhode Island	158	32	20
Total	1,775	360	20

* Language Category
Source: 1990 Census of Population - Summary Tape File 3A.
MDG 6/94

TABLE 6

RATIO OF FRENCH* SPEAKERS TO PERSONS OF **SINGLE**
FRENCH/FRENCH-CANADIAN ANCESTRY
NEW ENGLAND STATES 1990

	French Speakers (thousands)	Single Ancestry (thousands)	Ratio Sp./Anc.
Maine	81	184	44
New Hampshire	51	159	32
Vermont	17	75	23
Massachusetts	125	375	33
Connecticut	54	140	39
Rhode Island	32	97	33
Total	360	1,030	35

* Language Category
Source: 1990 Census of Population - Summary Tape File 3A.
MDG 6/94

TABLE 7

PERCENTAGE OF POPULATION SPEAKING FRENCH* AT HOME
PLACES WITH 1,000 OR MORE FRENCH HOME SPEAKERS:
NEW ENGLAND, 1990

	FRENCH SPEAKERS (number)	PERCENT FRENCH-SPEAKING (percent rounded)
Maine		
Auburn	3,510	16
Augusta	2,950	15
Bangor	1,100	4
Biddeford	6,730	35
Caribou	1,260	14
Fort Kent	1,470	73
Lewiston	12,590	34
Madawaska	2,760	80
Portland	1,160	2
Saco	2,130	15
Sanford	1,880	20
Van Buren	2,090	81
Waterville	2,210	14
Westbrook	1,130	8
New Hampshire		
Berlin	4,460	40
Manchester	10,960	12
Nashua	5,750	8
Rochester	1,850	8
Somersworth	1,140	11
Vermont		
Burlington	1,310	4

TABLE 7 – Continued

	FRENCH SPEAKERS (number)	PERCENT FRENCH-SPEAKING (percent rounded)
Massachusetts		
Boston	19,530	4
Brockton	2,830	3
Cambridge	4,150	5
Chicopee	3,460	7
Fall River	3,700	4
Fitchburg	2,080	6
Gardner	1,950	11
Holyoke	1,360	4
Lawrence	2,380	4
Leominster	1,990	6
Lowell	5,360	6
Lynn	1,570	2
New Bedford	3,490	4
Salem	1,790	5
Somerville	2,140	3
Southbridge	1,160	9
Springfield	3,150	2
Waltham	2,280	4
Worcester	2,910	2
Connecticut		
Bridgeport	1,790	1
Bristol	4,020	7
East Hartford	2,320	5
Hartford	1,910	2
Meriden	1,390	3
New Britain	1,740	3
New Haven	1,090	1
Norwalk	1,420	2
Stamford	2,760	3
Waterbury	1,630	2
West Hartford	1,000	2

TABLE 7 – Continued

	FRENCH SPEAKERS (number)	PERCENT FRENCH-SPEAKING (percent rounded)
Rhode Island		
Central Falls	1,570	10
Pawtucket	3,690	6
Providence	2,380	2
West Warwick	1,320	5
Woonsocket	8,610	21

* Language Category
Source: 1990 Census of Population--Summary Tape File 3A
MDG 6/94

TABLE 8

RATIO OF FRENCH* SPEAKERS TO
FRENCH/FRENCH-CANADIAN ANCESTRY
PLACES WITH 1,000 OR MORE FRENCH HOME SPEAKERS
NEW ENGLAND : 1990
First Report Ancestry

	FRENCH SPEAKERS	SPEAKERS/ ANCESTRY
	(numbers)	(ratio)
Maine		
Auburn	3,510	40
Augusta	2,950	45
Bangor	1,100	19
Biddeford	6,730	55
Caribou	1,260	31
Fort Kent	1,470	82
Lewiston	12,590	55
Madawaska	2,760	89
Portland	1,150	13
Saco	2,130	36
Sanford	1,880	40
Van Buren	2,090	92
Waterville	2,210	34
Westbrook	1,130	25
New Hampshire		
Berlin	4,460	58
Manchester	10,960	32
Nashua	5,750	27
Rochester	1,850	25
Somersworth	1,140	26

TABLE 8 – Continued

	FRENCH SPEAKERS (numbers)	SPEAKERS/ ANCESTRY (ratio)
Vermont		
Burlington	1,310	13
Massachusetts		
Boston	19,530	122
Brockton	2,830	45
Cambridge	4,150	123
Chicopee	3,460	18
Fall River	3,700	21
Fitchburg	2,080	17
Gardner	1,950	26
Holyoke	1,360	17
Lawrence	2,380	25
Leominster	1,990	18
Lowell	5,360	25
Lynn	1,570	17
New Bedford	3,490	24
Salem	1,790	25
Somerville	2,140	68
Southbridge	1,160	21
Springfield	3,150	14
Waltham	2,280	35
Worcester	2,910	12
Connecticut		
Bridgeport	1,790	66
Bristol	4,020	28
East Hartford	2,330	27
Hartford	1,910	54
Meriden	1,390	22
New Britain	1,740	31
New Haven	1,090	42
Norwalk	1,420	70
Stamford	2,760	160
Waterbury	1,630	18
West Hartford	1,000	29

TABLE 8 – Continued

	FRENCH SPEAKERS	SPEAKERS/ ANCESTRY
	(numbers)	(ratio)
Rhode Island		
Central Falls	1,570	37
Pawtucket	3,690	22
Providence	2,380	27
West Warwick	1,320	18
Woonsocket	8,610	36

* Language Category
Source: 1990 Census of Population and Housing - Summary Tape File 3A.
MDG 6/94

TABLE 9

RATIO OF FRENCH* SPEAKERS TO PERSONS OF SINGLE
FRENCH/FRENCH-CANADIAN ANCESTRY
PLACES WITH 1000 OR MORE FRENCH HOME SPEAKERS
NEW ENGLAND: 1990

	French Speakers (rounded)	Single Ancestry (rounded)	Ratio Speakers/ Ancestry
Maine			
Auburn	3,510	6,590	53
Augusta	2,950	4,900	60
Bangor	1,100	3,340	33
Biddeford	6,730	10,440	65
Caribou	1,260	3,110	41
Fort Kent	1,470	1,760	84
Lewiston	12,590	19,120	66
Madawaska	2,760	2,970	93
Portlland	1,150	4,700	24
Saco	2,130	4,430	48
Sanford	1,880	3,500	54
Van Buren	2,090	2,150	97
Waterville	2,210	5,170	43
Westbrook	1,130	2,900	39
New Hampshire			
Berlin	4,460	6,340	70
Manchester	10,960	24,730	44
Nashua	5,750	14,810	39
Rochester	1,850	5,050	37
Somersworth	1,140	3,010	38
Vermont			
Burlington	1,310	5,470	24

TABLE 9 - continued

	French Speakers (rounded)	Single Ancestry (rounded)	Ratio Speakers/ Ancestry
Massachusetts			
Boston	19,530	8,150	240
Brockton	2,830	2,620	108
Cambridge	4,150	1,670	249
Chicopee	3,460	13,110	26
Fall River	3,700	12,000	31
Fitchburg	2,080	8,010	26
Gardner	1,950	5,430	36
Holyoke	1,360	5,010	27
Lawrence	2,380	6,150	39
Leominster	1,990	7,100	28
Lowell	5,360	14,080	38
Lynn	1,570	4,390	36
New Bedford	3,490	9,500	37
Salem	1,790	4,890	37
Somerville	2,140	1,630	131
Southbridge	1,160	3,930	30
Springfield	3,150	11,320	28
Waltham	2,280	4,340	53
Worcester	2,910	13,150	22
Connecticut			
Bridgeport	1,790	1,380	130
Bristol	4,020	9,370	43
East Hartford	2,330	5,840	40
Hartford	1,910	2,340	82
Meriden	1,390	3,200	43
New Britain	1,740	3,470	50
New Haven	1,090	1,270	86
Norwalk	1,420	1,020	139
Stamford	2,760	768	359
Waterbury	1,630	4,940	33
West Hartford	1,000	1,840	54

TABLE 9 - continued

	French Speakers (rounded)	Single Ancestry (rounded)	Ratio Speakers/ Ancestry
Rhode Island			
Central Falls	1,570	3,340	47
Pawtucket	3,690	10,460	35
Providence	2,380	4,560	52
West Warwick	1,320	4,360	30
Woonsocket	8,610	19,830	43

* Language Category
Source: 1990 Census of Population - Summary Tape File 3A.
MDG 6/94

TABLE 10

FRENCH* SPEAKERS AT HOME:
NEW ENGLAND 1980 - 1990
PERCENT CHANGE 1980 - 1990
Persons five years and older

	1980 (thousands)	1990 (thousands)	Percent Change
Maine	94,225	81,012	- 14
New Hampshire	61,846	51,284	- 17
Vermont	19,906	17,171	- 14
Massachusetts	135,124	124,973	- 8
Connecticut	59,788	53,586	- 10
Rhode Island	40,563	31,669	- 22
New England	411,452	359,695	- 13

* Language Category
Sources: 1990 Census of Population - Summary Tape File 3A.
            1980 Census of Population quoted in *InformACTION*,
                January-February 1986.
MDG 6/94

TABLE 11

PERCENTAGE CHANGE IN FRENCH* HOME SPEAKERS
NEW ENGLAND 1980 - 1990
COUNTIES WITH 2,500 OR MORE FRENCH SPEAKERS
Persons five years and over

	1980 (thousands)	1990 (thousands)	Change (percent)
Maine			
Androscoggin	24,115	19,882	- 17.6
Aroostook	21,994	17,680	- 19.6
Cumberland	6,647	6,027	- 9.3
Kennebec	10,669	9,079	- 14.9
Penobscot	4,133	4,170	+ 0.9
York	18,077	15,796	- 12.6
New Hampshire			
Coos	8,552	6,838	- 20.0
Hillsborough	30,607	23,197	- 24.2
Merrimack	4,384	4,480	+ 0.02
Rockingham	5,158	5,239	+ 1.6
Strafford	6,055	4,836	- 20.1
Vermont			
Chittenden	5,431	4,392	- 19.1
Franklin	2,859	2,542	- 11.1
Orleans	2,838	2,451	- 13.6

TABLE 11 – Continued

	1980 (thousands)	1990 (thousands)	Change (percent)
Massachusetts			
Barnstable	2,035	2,607	+ 28.1
Bristol	18,247	13,598	- 25.5
Essex	17,443	13,045	- 25.2
Hampden	15,937	11,554	- 27.5
Hampshire	3,565	2,740	- 23.1
Middlesex	28,267	27,060	- 4.3
Norfolk	6,076	6,032	- 0.7
Plymouth	3,930	5,693	+ 44.9
Suffolk	9,058	20,319	+124.3
Worcester	27,054	19,114	- 32.9
Connecticut			
Fairfield	8,178	10,632	+ 30.0
Hartford	25,061	19,895	- 20.1
New Haven	9,755	8,792	- 9.9
New London	4,283	3,572	- 16.6
Windham	6,059	4,865	- 19.7
Rhode Island			
Kent	4,882	3,450	- 29.3
Providence	32,306	24,788	- 23.3

* Language Category
Source: 1980 Census of Population – InformACTION (January-February 1986)
          1990 Census of Population – Summary Tape File 3A
MDG 6/94

[PLEASE NOTE: The statistics listed on the next page were presented by Dean Louder, professor of geography at Laval University, at the French Institute's 1994 colloquium on "The Franco-Americans." The sources of these statistics are: Table ED 90-6, Languages Spoken at Home by Persons 5 Years and Above, by State: 1990 Census 1990 CPH-L 96 and USA 1980, Bureau of the Census; Chapter C-Tables: 60 and 172. We publish them here with Prof. Louder's permission.]

States	Population of 5 Years and + 1990	French-Speaking 1990	French Ancestry 1990	Population of 5 Years and + 1980	French-Speaking 1980	French Ancestry 1980
Alabama	3 759 802	17 965	108 069	3 322 234	9 819	94 165
Alaska	495 425	2 030	30 031	355 723	1 710	23 012
Arizona	3 374 806	13 115	183 658	2 505 455	9 264	154 539
Arkansas	2 186 665	8 210	86 244	2 111 214	4 908	83 056
California	27 383 547	132 657	1 207 805	21 969 013	112 760	1 307 235
Colorado	3 042 986	12 855	173 337	2 670 872	11 249	175 992
Connecticut	3 060 000	53 586	371 274	2 922 810	59 788	326 483
Delaware	617 720	3 753	22 427	553 319	2 326	22 749
District of Columbia	570 284	9 783	10 450	604 289	8 779	10 467
Florida	12 095 284	194 783	630 540	9 180 230	71 924	484 904
Georgia	5 984 188	34 422	183 573	5 049 559	18 543	140 420
Hawaii	1 026 209	3 921	25 650	857 400	3 936	26 437
Idaho	926 703	2 839	53 704	850 632	2 463	54 792
Illinois	10 585 838	43 070	405 863	10 586 633	35 438	486 724
Indiana	5 146 160	20 578	231 135	5 071 880	13 563	267 338
Iowa	2 583 526	7 941	114 793	2 768 363	5 483	151 103
Kansas	2 289 615	7 851	122 931	2 393 102	5 770	140 959
Kentucky	3 434 955	13 543	102 707	3 462 290	7 730	107 668
Louisiana	3 886 353	261 678	1 069 558	3 845 505	263 387	934 237
Maine	1 142 122	81 012	336 227	1 046 188	94 225	266 096
Maryland	4 425 285	39 484	148 782	3 945 488	26 129	154 728
Massachusetts	5 605 751	124 973	946 630	5 400 422	135 033	838 509
Michigan	8 594 737	39 794	828 557	8 577 824	33 673	871 877
Minnesota	4 038 861	13 693	283 632	3 764 209	10 026	303 682
Mississipi	2 378 805	13 215	103 539	2 305 754	8 132	95 185
Missouri	4 748 704	20 135	289 050	4 563 086	12 831	340 026
Montana	740 218	2 572	51 088	721 613	2 379	54 124
Nebraska	1 458 904	4 135	61 445	1 447 251	3 036	77 834
Nevada	1 110 450	5 464	71 112	744 698	3 509	54 912
New Hampshire	1 024 621	51 284	324 569	858 108	61 846	237140
New Jersey	7 200 696	52 351	189 010	6 893 400	32 448	213 913
New Mexico	1 390 048	3 402	51 538	1 191 276	3 205	48 034
New York	16 743 048	236 099	783 209	16 429 011	165 158	834 742
North Carolina	6 172 301	37 590	166 589	5 559 813	22 900	134 210
North Dakota	590 839	1 998	32 144	662 049	2 153	33 917
Ohio	10 063 212	46 075	401 474	10 011 580	32 728	464 366
Oklahoma	2 921 755	8 328	133 722	2 792 986	6 617	151 980
Oregon	2 640 482	10 854	191 189	2 435 197	8 336	195 957
Pennsylvania	11 085 170	45 515	296 616	11 117 862	34 072	336 177
Rhode Island	936 423	31 669	206 971	890 643	40 563	178 710
South Carolina	3 231 539	22 339	102 546	2 884 059	15 320	84 072
South Dakota	641 226	1 228	27 843	632 385	1 056	30 936
Tennessee	4 544 743	20 444	130 483	4 267 445	12 021	112 532
Texas	15 605 822	64 585	737 234	13 034 594	47 520	673 565
Utah	1 553 351	6 684	60 028	1 271 285	5 467	60 281
Vermont	521 521	17 171	165 697	475 452	19 906	144 528
Virginia	5 746 419	40 353	216 954	5 008 578	27 903	191 712
Washington	4 501 879	19 883	320 579	3 826 416	15 180	315 136
West Virginia	1 686 932	7 695	43 798	1 804 171	4 904	49 633
Wisconsin	4 531 134	14 242	295 039	4 358 993	10 468	323 759
Wyoming	418 713	1 558	25 079	424 510	1 560	26 396
USA TOTAL	230 445 777	1 930 404	13 156 122	210 426 869	1 549 144	12 890 949

Acadian *Survivance* in New England

Clarence J. d'Entremont

Acadian survival in New England—some will find it presumptuous of me to undertake to write about such a topic. It is of course true that many descendants of old Acadia[1] have forgotten their origins and have voluntarily allowed themselves to blend into the "melting pot." There are some who prefer not to be identified as Acadians. Basing themselves solely on persons such as these, others have made of them a general rule: *"De uno, dice omnes."*[2] I have observed that people in certain areas of old Acadia have the impression that a person ceases to be Acadian after moving to New England. More than once, when I still lived in the United States, I would be scowled at for introducing myself as an Acadian. I was considered to be a renegade, a traitor. No, the Acadians of New England are not renegades of old Acadia, just as their ancestors who came to Acadia were not renegades of old France.

It is true that living in a milieu that is not French presents a grave danger to Acadians, just as it does for the French Canadians—that of losing the heritage left to them by their forebears. The worst of these losses, you will agree, is that of one's mother tongue, which is, as Acadians would say, *quasiment inévitable.*[3] Robert Rumilly, in his book *Histoire des Franco-Américains* (1958), writes that in the United States, "the preponderance of English quickly reduces French to the role of a second language, a foreign language, a dead language, or a luxury language." Please note, however, that it is not only in the United States that one can find many Acadians who no longer speak French; unfortunately, the very same thing happens in too many

---

[1]   [The Canadian Maritime Provinces of Nova Scotia, New Brunswick, and Prince Edward Island.—Editor]

[2]   "What can be said of one can be said of all."

[3]   The expression *quasiment inévitable* can be translated as *almost inevitable.*

areas of the Maritime Provinces of Canada.

The question which needs to be raised here is whether or not there can be an Acadian survival without the French language. In other words, should we apply to the concept of Acadian survival what used to be said about the preservation of faith, namely, that one's language is the guardian of one's faith? Not necessarily. Language is certainly a great advantage; no one can deny that fact. But there are other factors which can contribute to the survival of a spirit, of traditions, and of an attachment to the past. In this regard, Rev. Édouard Hamon, in his book *Les Canadiens-Français de la Nouvelle-Angleterre*, assigns to religion a role equal to that of language as the guardian of the nationality of a people. When I was still living in New England, my purpose was to make their own history known to Acadians, in order to make them love their past and the Acadia of their ancestors.

It is true that, were one to base oneself on authors, one would have to conclude that Acadian survival is non-existent in New England. In fact, almost no historian of the Franco-Americans mentions Acadian survival. Worse than that, all of those historians, almost to a man, seem to be completely ignorant of the very presence of Acadians in New England. Brother Antoine Bernard, C.S.C., for instance, who in his book *L'histoire de la survivance acadienne,* devotes a chapter or two to each of the Maritime provinces, as well as to Quebec, the Magdalen Islands, Gaspé, and even Labrador, writes not one single word about the Acadians of New England, not only in this book, but also in all the others he has written on the history of the Acadians, except for one brief reference to La Société Mutuelle l'Assomption[4] which was founded in New England. Hamon is just as silent. In his 550 pages on Franco-Americans, Rumilly did not think he owed more than five short paragraphs to the Acadians. In the second edition of his *La Tragédie d'un peuple*, Emile Lauvrière, devotes thirty-four pages to the topic of the "Acadian renascence," in New England. In thirty-one of the thirty-four pages, he writes about the French Canadians. Only three pages refer to the Acadians. It is useless, therefore, to look for anything pertaining to the Acadian survival in New England in these works. Either their authors did not believe it to be possible, or they knew nothing about it.

---

4   [Initially a mutual benefit society founded in Waltham, Mass., in 1903, as an insurance society for the protection of Acadians. For details of the founding, see below.—Editor]

And yet Acadia has not died in New England. It lives on, if not among all Acadians, at least among a good-sized group of them who, while being very good Americans, are proud to call themselves Acadians. Those who remain attached to their country of origin, its traditions, its customs, and especially its history are quite numerous. One must not say, "*Loin des yeux, loin du coeur,*"[5] for many of these Acadians are more truly Acadian than many of their counterparts in today's Acadia.

Let us examine what has transpired since the first contingents of Acadians arrived in New England. According to my research on the demographic statistics of the Acadians in Massachusetts at the Bureau of Vital Statistics in Boston, there were a few marriages of Acadians during the decade of the 1850s, particularly in the fishing ports. There were about twenty in the 1860s. Then, in 1870, and especially in 1871, Acadian immigration started to expand, with the number of births, marriages, and deaths increasing constantly. These were mostly fishermen coming to seek their fortune along the American coast. The early ones came from Cape Breton, especially from Arichat, and then from the southern part of Nova Scotia. Consequently, Acadian women being rare at first, some of the marriages contracted were with American women. However, during the 1860s, especially in the second half of the decade, Acadian women accompanied their men at the start of the fishing season in order to come to Massachusetts to work in the cod industry. But almost all would return home to Nova Scotia at the end of the fishing season.

I studied the marriages contracted in Massachusetts between 1854 and 1880 by Acadians, from the southern part of Nova Scotia in particular, to which I added a few from Madame Island on Cape Breton. I found that during those twenty-seven years there were one hundred twenty-seven marriages of which only thirty-five, or 27.5%, were contracted by Acadian men with Acadian women. Of the other ninety-two, or 72.5%, a few marriages were contracted with persons from the province of Quebec, the rest were with Anglophones. In all likelihood, this ratio also applies to the marriages of all Acadian immigrants of the same period. It is, therefore, difficult to imagine that there could have been an Acadian survival one hundred years ago for three quarters or so of the Acadians who had married in New England.

---

5   "Out of sight, out of mind."

Those were not, however, the only Acadian families in New England. In the early 1870s, already-constituted families of Acadians began to migrate as family units to New England. In all likelihood, the lifestyle of these families continued much the same as had been the case in Acadia before their departure, at least within the home—a family does not change its customs overnight. But away from home, on the streets or in the factories, Acadians had to act like Americans. They could not do otherwise in an era when President Theodore Roosevelt was writing: "We must be Americans and nothing else;" or again when he stated that the United States must not become an immense house of polyglot boarders. This was an era when Acadians could see signs displayed in store windows, or on the walls of factories, which read: "Help wanted. Catholics or aliens need not apply." It is during this period that the Aucoin name became Wedge, Chiasson became Chisholm, Doiron became Durant, Fougère became Frazier, Girouard became Gillwar, Leblanc became White, Poirier became Perry—to mention but a few. Acadians at home, but on the street or at work, Americans only. Could the Acadian spirit survive in such an atmosphere?

It is, therefore, useless to look for any Acadian activity during those early years, since the newcomers were fishermen, factory workers, or laborers whose first thought was to ensure the basic necessities of life. I found the records of eighty-two Acadians living in Massachusetts between 1854 and 1880, and exactly half of them, i.e., forty-one, were fishermen; twenty-one, or one quarter, were hired hands or farmers; there were also thirteen carpenters, five shoemakers, and four carters. Of the remaining eight, one was a boat builder, one a mason, one a painter, one a sail-maker, one an iceman, and so forth. There were no professionals, unless you want to classify a male nurse as such.

One can understand then why Rameau de Saint-Père, during his journey to America, in 1860-61, having gone to Boston, lauded the efforts of the French Canadians to remain Catholic and to preserve their hereditary language while making no mention of Acadians, the study of whom was, nonetheless, one of the principal reasons for his journey. He does, however, name one Acadian, probably the only one he visited, namely, Louis Surette, a native of southern Nova Scotia, whose mother was a d'Entremont. He says of Louis that "he built up his own fortune, first as a sailor, fisherman, and coaster, trading from port to port along the coast, then as a store clerk in Boston," before adding, "He is at the head of an important enterprise and sends his ships to all parts of the world." Louis Surette is the only Acadian of the period to have left us, in writing, an account of his participation in Acadian affairs, as revealed by the large number of his hand-written letters, as well as many newspaper articles, which I have in my possession. Most of his letters and the newspaper articles deal with Acadian matters: history, genealogy, customs. I have the reports of Acadian meetings which took place at his home in Concord, Massachusetts, as early as the 1860s, but more especially from 1870 on.

Louis Surette notwithstanding, it can be said that, in the early period, one has to go to Maine, especially, if not solely, to ascertain the efforts of the New England-Acadians to remain Acadian. The proximity of Maine to New Brunswick made this possible. Thus, in 1880, when forty or so Acadians from the Maritimes responded to the invitation of the Société St-Jean-Baptiste of Quebec to attend their national convention, the State of Maine is mentioned. We should point out, however, that when one speaks of the Acadians of Maine at that time, we are referring especially to those people of the American Madawaska who are usually considered historically as belonging to the New Brunswick group. They are the descendants of the two thousand or so Acadians that the Webster-Ashburton Treaty of 1842 severed from New Brunswick to incorporate them into American territory. Additionally, during the 1840s, numerous Acadians of the Madawaska Region, along with French Canadians from the Beauce Region drifted to the lumber camps and mills of Skowhegan, Waterville, Augusta, and Belfast, and then later on toward Lewiston and Biddeford, where their descendants can still be found.

At the first Acadian Convention held at Memramcook, New Brunswick, in 1881—the year following the Quebec Convention—the feast of the Assumption, August 15, was chosen as the national holiday of the Acadians. It would seem that New England was not represented, and for good reason: only the parishes of the Maritime Provinces had been invited. If the letter of Rameau de Saint-Père, responding to the invitation he had received, had not arrived too late, New England might have been represented, at least the State of Maine. For, in his answer, Saint-Père wrote: "I think it would be helpful to make contact with the Acadians of Maine who are your next door neighbors. . . [They] should, on every occasion, be considered as belonging to your group." Had they been present, I wonder what their reaction would have been to the statement of one of the orators, Sir Hector

Langevin, Minister of Public Works for Canada, who told the delegates: "Do not emigrate to the United States; stay in your beautiful Acadia, especially you intelligent young men . . . don't go . . . ruin your health in the enslaving labor of American factories and mills."

At the second Convention held at Miscouche on Prince Edward Island, when the Acadian flag and national anthem were chosen, Rameau de Saint-Père's letter had been heeded. An invitation to attend had been sent to the Acadians of the State of Maine. However, I could not find the name of any Acadian delegate from that State, nor, it stands to reason, from any other part of New England. Would that have been why they believed that Acadians who had gone to the United States had already lost their identity and did not care to be recognized as Acadians any longer? Whatever the reason, from the very first session, the plague of emigration to the United States was brought to the fore when a resolution was adopted to use every means possible to stem the tide which was reaching alarming proportions.

As one can readily see, there could not have been any significant Acadian activity in New England in comparison to the activity of the French Canadians from the province of Quebec, who, more numerous and generally coming from a more developed culture, were organizing themselves and expanding rapidly. In fact, these Canadians attracted a number of Acadians into their societies by showing them the benefit they could derive for their own improvement and perhaps even for the preservation of their Acadian spirit.

It seems, then, that during the 1880s, the Acadians of New England began to awaken, especially with the arrival of alumni from *le collège* Saint-Joseph[6] of Memramcook, founded in 1864, by Holy Cross Fathers from Montreal, and those of *le collège* Saint-Louis, founded in 1874, by Monsignor Marcel-François Richard.

Confining ourselves for the moment to the Acadian Conventions, according to the reports of the time, we finally find some Acadians from the United States at the third one, which was

6   [The old system of *collèges classiques* consisted of a course of studies lasting eight years, roughly corresponding to the American high school and college systems combined. Thus, one could enter a *collège* as early as age twelve or thirteen.—Editor]

held at Church Point, Nova Scotia, in 1890. They are not identified by name; what is mentioned is the presence of a representative group from Haverhill, Massachusetts. Acadians were thus beginning to take cognizance of themselves even though this was true of a small number only.

The contacts which the Acadians of New England were beginning to set up at that time with the Acadians of the Maritimes greatly contributed to the awakening of the Acadian spirit among the former. I am referring at this point, not so much to social contacts with family and relatives, but to contacts pertaining to Acadian matters, such as history, genealogy, culture, language, in a word to anything that touched upon the Acadian issue in New England as much as in the Maritimes. Acadian newspapers, such as *L'Évangéline, Le Moniteur Acadien, Le Courrier de Bathurst* already had a number of subscribers in New England. In the voluminous correspondence exchanged before 1890 between my uncle Léander d'Entremont of Peabody, who always took an interest in the history of Acadians, and Louis Surette, whom I mentioned earlier, I find references to articles on Acadian topics published by the one or the other in those newspapers. I still have some copies of these articles. Both men also corresponded with the old-timers of their region, and elsewhere even, in order to learn more about the history and genealogy of Acadians. They then provided information to authors who were proposing to write, or indeed did write the history of the Acadians. In the case of Mr. Surette, he kept up a correspondence with several pastors of Acadian parishes in the Maritimes. All this was taking place before 1890.

Although means of communication had already long existed, travel was becoming easier between New England and the Maritimes. Already, in 1855, there was steamer service between Boston and Yarmouth, Nova Scotia. In New Brunswick, a railway opened between Moncton and Saint John in 1860; then, in 1871, it was extended all the way to Bangor where it connected with the American rail system. As for Prince Edward Island, an oceanic link was established in 1864 between Charlottetown and Boston.

In 1890, the *collège* Sainte-Anne opened its doors at Church Point in Nova Scotia and some Acadian families of New England began to enroll their young boys. The trip from Boston was easy since the *collège* was only a few miles from Yarmouth. From my own experience, I can tell you that when I entered the *collège* about thirty years later, a certain number of Acadian students from New

England still studied there: ten in 1922, twenty-three in 1923, sixteen in 1924, nineteen in 1925. That practice continued for many more years. During the first three of the years listed above, the students came from different areas of Massachusetts, namely Beverly, Boston, Cambridge, Cape Cod, Chelsea, Dorchester, East Boston, Fitchburg, Gardner, Ipswich, Lowell, Lynn, New Bedford; there were also some from Waterville, Maine, from Woonsocket, Rhode Island, and one from New Hampshire.

Among the students who attended *le collège* Sainte-Anne, at least from 1897 up to 1954, all told, the seventy who attended came from thirty-four different cities of Massachusetts. There were a few from Brownsville and Waterville, Maine, and from Dover and Portsmouth, New Hampshire; some also came from Woonsocket, Rhode Island, and from Hartford and Cromwell, Connecticut, and we must not forget that there were also a number of young Acadians from New England attending *le collège* Saint-Joseph of Memramcook.

This leads us to ask ourselves where the Acadians from the Maritimes settled in New England. At first, they chose Massachusetts, particularly Lynn and Salem, in addition to Gloucester and Boston. A little later, toward the beginning of the twentieth century, and more particularly at the end of World War I, when immigration reached its apogee, Acadians from Yarmouth County, Nova Scotia, chose the northern suburbs of Boston, beginning with East Boston; then came Andover, Chelsea, Everett, Malden, Melrose, Reading, Saugus, Stoneham, Wakefield, and Wilmington. The Acadians of Digby County chose instead the southern suburbs of Boston: Braintree, Dorchester, Milton, Quincy, and Weymouth. As for the Acadians of Cape Breton, particularly those of Cheticamp and Arichat, they settled mainly in Cambridge, although a sizeable number from Madame Island are found in Gloucester. The Acadians of New Brunswick tended to settle in manufacturing centers. Those from the Memramcook area grouped themselves in Waltham and Lynn; those from Saint Paul likewise went to Lynn, and also to Leominster and Gardner; in Gardner you can still find Acadians from Bouctouche and Saint-Antoine; those from Saint-Louis de Kent settled especially in Waltham and in Worcester. In addition, many Acadians from Westmoreland County and the southern part of Kent County went to southeastern Massachusetts, to Brockton, Taunton, Fall River, and New Bedford mainly, because of the many textile mills. Sixty years ago, there were already six hundred Acadian families in New Bedford, five hundred in each of Lynn, Fitchburg, and Gardner, two hundred in Cambridge, one hundred fifty in Newton and Waltham, and so on.

At first, the Acadians of northern New Brunswick did not emigrate proportionally in such great numbers as those mentioned above. Those who came settled in Cambridge along with those from Cape Breton, but subsequently, they were to be found in the area of Springfield, Chicopee, and Holyoke, Mass. Even though one finds today a goodly number of Acadians in New Hampshire, as well as in Rhode Island and Connecticut, immigration to these States took place after the migration to Massachusetts and was never as large.

One can readily understand why organizations for the protection of Acadians as a people did not get their start in manufacturing centers; in such locations, Acadians were chiefly laborers whose level of culture was no higher than average. At the beginning of this century, though, there were already some Acadians who had climbed the ladder of success in business. If a large number of Acadian professionals did not yet exist, we do find Acadians who had begun to exercise a beneficial influence on their own people.

The first attempt at organizing the Acadians of New England in a permanent fashion and on a large scale dates back to the early days of this century. The aim was to unite them, not so much by appealing to their patriotism, but by the more subtle means of playing up the financial benefit they might derive from joining. The goal was to create a financial institution, an insurance company which would be their very own. From this concept arose La Société Mutuelle l'Assomption. It has been said that the Acadians of New England, having already lived for a time in the United States, had become more adept at business matters than their counterparts in the Maritimes who had never hit upon this idea although they already had their own national society: La Société l'Assomption. Although this society had taken root in 1880 at the French-Canadian Convention of Quebec, which seventy Acadian delegates had attended, it was really founded in 1881 at the Memramcook Convention. From the beginning, its membership included Acadian names which, soon afterward, would be found in New England. These are the people who dreamed of adding to it a society or company for insurance protection quite distinct from La Société l'Assomption itself.

In April 1902, Ferdinand Richard, who was the secretary of

La Société l'Assomption, convened at Waltham a small assembly to which Fitchburg, Lowell, Lynn, New Bedford, and Worcester sent delegates. It was decided to meet again in Waltham, on the following August 15th to discuss the matter in convention. A very large number of Acadians from all parts of New England responded to the call. When Ferdinand Richard presented his plan of an insurance company for Acadians, he easily won the support of influential Acadians, such as Messrs. Jean H. LeBlanc and Clarence Cormier, president and secretary of the committee. Another meeting took place on May 30, 1903, this time in Fitchburg, at which it was unanimously voted to establish a mutual benefit society for Acadians. The name given to it, La Société Mutuelle l'Assomption was to distinguish it from La Société l'Assomption which had been founded more than twenty years earlier and which would later take the name La Société Nationale l'Assomption.

The new society held its first meeting on September 8, 1903, in Waltham where the national headquarters were located. The following year, in 1904, at the first congress of La Société Mutuelle, which was held on August 15 at Waltham, it was announced that the new society already numbered nine branches, seven in Massachusetts, one in Maine and one in Bouctouche, New Brunswick. It had 454 members in all. The second general meeting of the Mutuelle was held the following year, 1905, at Fitchburg. The next one, in 1906, was held in New Bedford, and during all those years, the new society spread throughout New England. Even though it had an American founding, it was penetrating even more rapidly in the Maritimes than in New England. By 1907 there were already forty-two branches in the Maritimes compared with sixteen in the United States. Then the decision was taken to transfer the headquarters from Waltham to Moncton. This took place in 1914. The transfer did not sit well with a number of Acadians in New England and two thousand of them withdrew from La Société Mutuelle l'Assomption to form a new mutual benefit society which was named La Société Acadienne d'Amérique, with Elphège Léger of Fitchburg at its head. At the start, the new organization met with great success and so did its annual conventions which were attended by representatives from all parts of New England. However, only a dozen branches were ever formed. La Société Mutuelle l'Assomption still remained too vigorous throughout New England for the newcomer to last. After a dozen years or so, fifteen at the very most, it went out of existence and was absorbed into La Société Mutuelle l'Assomption.

It is fair to say that during the first half of the twentieth century there was perhaps no other organization that did as much for Acadian survival as did La Société Mutuelle in the Maritimes, as well as in New England, when each branch held almost monthly meetings. In Waltham and Gardner, two branches existed. There was one in each of the following cities: Amesbury, Cambridge, Everett, Fisherville, Fitchburg, Lawrence, Leominster, Lynn, New Bedford, Newton, Reading, Springfield, and Worcester in Massachusetts; Bridgeport, Hartford, and Norwich in Connecticut; Berlin and Nashua in New Hampshire, and Lewiston and Skowhegan in Maine. Sad to say, these branch offices were all suppressed in the 1960s. It can be stated that those years of the first half of the century were the most beneficial to the Acadian survival in New England.

Acadian activities were faltering when I arrived in New England in the first days of 1952. Some Franco-Americans were still maintaining the culture brought from Quebec. So, I did like other Acadians and joined these organizations and societies. By appearing at meetings, and by making myself heard, people began little by little to look upon Acadians as having an identity distinct from their own, an identity which should be acknowledged. Among these organizations, should be mentioned Le Comité de Vie franco-américaine, La Société historique franco-américaine, the Richelieu Clubs, the Franco-American federations of the various New England States, and more recently the national Franco-American conferences which initiated annual voyages between New England and Louisiana. These organizations have always included Acadians among their membership. Here I wish to make special mention of *Le Travailleur*; in this newspaper, Wilfrid Beaulieu, a descendant on his mother's side of the Acadian family of D'Amours, published a great many articles about Acadians and he did so over a long period of time.

However, the society which was destined to do the most good for the preservation of the Acadian heritage in New England was not located in New England but in Moncton. I am referring to La Société Historique Acadienne which was founded in 1960. Almost from its foundation, it included twenty-four members from New England and New York. These members could not, unfortunately, attend the meetings which were always held in the Moncton area. The Société did publish a magazine called *Cahier*, but it is especially from the meetings that the members derived the most benefit.

One day, I said to myself, why couldn't we have our own meetings in New England? So, in the Fall of 1966, two of us went to the annual meeting of the Society to present our proposal. The keen interest which it generated among the members present, and the enthusiastic approval accorded to it by the executive committee, were more than sufficient to launch our project. Subsequently, in 1966, the New England group of La Société Historique Acadienne was founded. This was not a new society, but simply a grouping of the members residing in New England who already belonged to La Société Historique Acadienne.

This organization was very successful during its twelve-year existence. Within a few years, one hundred eighteen new members joined the original twenty-six. I realized very quickly that the reason they joined us was to learn more about the history of their Acadian forebears. At this point I can say that many of these members were experiencing their first contact with Acadia. They subsequently often visited old Acadia, going to the places where their ancestors had settled either before the Deportation or after it, and from which they had emigrated to settle in New England.

For twelve years, we held four meetings each year in the vicinity of Boston, at which a formal lecture was delivered. I had noticed that only one-third of the members could speak French well. Another third understood it, but could speak it only with some difficulty. The final third could neither understand nor speak the language. For that reason, most of our meetings were conducted in English. But the call to each meeting and the minutes were always issued in both languages. The lectures always developed an Acadian topic: history, genealogy, geography, customs, mores, language, literature, and so forth. There were about forty-five of them all told.

One of the goals which the group had set for itself from the start was the restoration of Saint Croix Island. We worked on that project with a will. The voluminous correspondence which I have kept is proof of this. We corresponded with senators and representatives in Washington, with the directors of the National Park Service, particularly Acadia National Park at Bar Harbor, and with individuals from Calais, Maine, just to mention a few. In November 1969, a number of us went to Saint Croix where we joined with members from Moncton who had come to meet us. We had gone there, not only to visit the island, but especially to promote the restoration project. We had agreed to meet in Calais with the authorities of the National Park Service at Bar Harbor.

In Augusta, we held a meeting, at which the Governor's administrative assistant presided, with six directors of parks, museums, the arts, and the Historical Commission of the State of Maine; a representative of the University of Maine at Orono was also present as well as the librarian of the Maine Historical Society of Portland. I believe that our group had much to do with the ongoing efforts to succeed in restoring Saint Croix Island to the appearance it had at the time of De Monts and Champlain.[7]

The greatest success of this group during its twelve-year existence occurred during the American Bicentennial Celebrations in 1976. On that occasion, then Governor Michael Dukakis of Massachusetts decided that every ethnic group in that state should have its day of celebration at the State House in Boston. The last week of May was reserved for the francophone groups. Three weeks before, the governor had issued a formal written proclamation setting aside Monday, May 24, as "Acadian Day in the Commonwealth of Massachusetts." Permission had even been obtained to fly the Acadian flag from morning to evening of that day in front of the State House, side by side with the American flag and the flag of the Commonwealth.

The New England Group of La Société Historique Acadienne was, nonetheless, moving toward intoning its swan song. After having organized, for the end of June and the beginning of July, 1979, one last excursion to Saint Croix Island, to mark the 375th anniversary of the arrival there of De Monts and Champlain and their party, there fell to me the painful and thankless task of

---

7   [Dedicated as a U.S. national monument in 1949, Saint Croix was declared an International Historic Site in 1984 to highlight its significance to both the U.S. and Canada. It is the only international site in the National Park System. Among other finds, archeological studies have identified twenty-three burial sites. Thirty-five of the seventy-seven men accompanying DeMonts and Champlain, who discovered the island naming it L'Isle Saincte Croix, died of scurvy during the winter of 1604-1605. The survivors then moved to Port Royal (Annapolis Basin) in Nova Scotia.

A commemorative plaque, dedicated in 1904 to mark the tercentenary of the island's discovery, states that Saint Croix was then "the only settlement of Europeans north of Florida." It was from Saint Croix that Champlain explored the New England coast. In anticipation of the 400th anniversary of the site, in 2004, the National Park Service is working on a management plan and environmental impact statement.—Editor]

announcing that the group no longer had the wherewithal to continue functioning.[8]

The American-French Genealogical Society of Rhode Island often publishes articles relative to Acadia in its bulletin *Je me souviens.* The *FAROG Forum,* at the University of Maine in Orono, publishes articles on the Acadian question in each of its issues. Mention must also be made of the Historical Society of the American Madawaska which seeks to establish an Acadian sanctuary in northern Maine to mark the 200th anniversary of the arrival of Acadians there, at a place called Acadian Landing.

After all that has just been stated, it is not presumptuous to speak of an Acadian *survivance* in New England. The worthy sons and daughters of Acadian immigrants have forgotten neither the tragic history of their deported ancestors, nor the more immediate past, that of their families who came to New England within the last 100 years in search of a better life for themselves and for their children and grand-children.

Translated by Rev. Alexis Babineau, A.A.

[This article first appeared as "La survivance acadienne en Nouvelle-Angleterre" in the French Institute's publication entitled *L'Émigrant acadien vers les États-Unis: 1842-1950.* The author has approved its inclusion in this volume.]

---

8   [The group managed, nonetheless, to maintain itself for a few years as an affiliate of the American-Canadian Genealogical Society of Manchester, N.H., where it was known as "L'Association généalogique et historique acadienne de la Nouvelle-Angleterre." Today, it is an independent group known as The Acadian Cultural Society/Société culturelle acadienne, with nearly seven hundred members. Its headquarters are in Fitchburg, Mass. where it publishes a quarterly called *Le Réveil Acadien.*—Editor]

From Franco-Americans to Americans of French-Canadian Origin or Franco-Americanism, Past and Present

Yves Roby

In 1976, at a colloquium organized for the purpose of discussing where things stood with regard to Franco-Americans, the assimilation process, and the prospect of an ethnic resurgence, the author Jacques Ducharme had this to say: "The 'melting pot', that prodigious American stew pot, seems to have made a *ragoût* of the Franco-Americans along with other nationalities."[1] The finding is provocative. Interpretations differ. Some ask themselves whether the *Franco-Américanie* desired and dreamed-of by the early leaders is not about to disappear; others argue that it is better to speak about a *Franco-Américanie* that is going through profound change.

The following overview of Franco-American history from 1930 to the present day is meant to provide some material for an assessment of this existential question. I readily admit that the picture proposed here is imperfect, incomplete, and impressionistic.

1. Runaway Assimilation: An Assessment

It is important, though it may seem paradoxical, to note at the outset some of the successes achieved by Franco-Americans. It should be remembered that in the area of politics, Félix Hébert

---

[1] Jacques Ducharme, "Après trente ans," in *Les Franco-Américains. La promesse du passé, les réalités du présent.* Colloquium coordinated by the National Materials Development Center for French and Portuguese, 1976, Bedford, New Hampshire, 1976, p. 17.

[Jacques Ducharme is the author of two books relating to Franco-Americans: *The Delusson Family*, a novel of his own family's emigration from Quebec to Holyoke, Mass., and *The Shadows of the Trees*, a descriptive account of the Franco-Americans of New England.—Editor]

was a senator from 1929 to 1935 and Philippe Noël, governor of Rhode Island from 1973 to 1977; that in the area of religion, Franco-Americans have been elevated to the episcopacy: Bishop Ernest Primeau and Bishop Odore Gendron, to the see of Manchester, in 1960 and 1975 respectively, and Bishop Louis Gélineau to the see of Providence, R.I., in 1972; Bishop Amédée Proulx was named auxiliary bishop of Portland, Maine, in 1975. Michael Côté succeeded Bishop Proulx as the auxiliary bishop of the Portland diocese in 1995 after Bishop Proulx's death in 1992. Bishop Thomas Dupré was named auxiliary of Springfield, Massachusetts, in 1990, and appointed to the see of the same diocese in 1995. Some successes in business, sports, and literature are equally impressive. Aubuchon became one of the important names in hardware; Leo Durocher established himself as one of the best managers in major league baseball, and Joan Benoit, who won the Boston Marathon in 1979 and 1983, captured the gold medal at the 1984 Olympics; Will Durant won the Pulitzer Prize in 1968 for his *Story of Civilization: Rousseau and Revolution*; Grace de Repentigny Metalious' first novel, *Peyton Place*, sold 8,000,000 copies, was dramatized on television and filmed in Hollywood, and, finally, Jack Kerouac's career was meteoric.

These successes, which illustrate in exceptional fashion the contributions of Franco-Americans to the American scene, cannot, however, hide the inescapable fact of the decline of the presence of the French language in New England. The signs are numerous and irrefutable.

As of 1930, bilingualism was a given, except among recent immigrants. However, it was clear that even if they were bilingual, more and more Franco-Americans had a tendency to use English rather than French. It goes without saying that the French that they neglected slipped away from them little by little. Among their children, the number of those who spoke only English increased rapidly. "What is certain," wrote Hormidas Hamelin in 1930, "is that the number of people who speak only English is extensive and increases rapidly year by year."[2] In 1935, Josaphat Benoit added, "The attitudes of Franco-American youth toward French can be summarized as follows: some know their language fairly well, but speak it as rarely as possible; most of them know very little French and speak it even less; a goodly number don't know it at all

---

2   Hormidas Hamelin, *Lettres à mon ami sur la Patrie, la Langue et la Question franco-américaine*, n.p., n.d., 1930, p. 185.

any more or no longer want to speak it."[3] Today, English unilingualism has become the norm.

From the start of the century, all observers called attention to the change in the spoken language. Franco-Americans who were in constant contact with English—the only language with any prestige in political, economic, and social circles—constantly borrowed words and expressions from it. As Evelyne Desruisseaux put it very simply: "One says many English words when one hears a lot of English spoken. One speaks like the others without even realizing it."[4] While, as a rule, the language of the elite retained its purity, that of the man in the street deteriorated. Already in 1937, Edward B. Ham, at that time a professor at Yale University, referred to the language of the working class as an "incredible jumble of French and English."[5]

Along with the language, the values, customs, and traditional attitudes were being transformed and, in some cases, disappearing. Observers noted that, with the passage of time, the Franco-American family differed less and less from other American households. According to the claims of the militants of *survivance*, "mixed" marriages, i.e., between members of different ethnic groups, were "the most devastating plague eating away at our Catholic and French stock in the United States." Almost unheard of in 1900, they accounted for about 50% of marriages in 1945 and are the general rule today. Contraception and divorce are increasing. Parental authority is attacked. "Sons born in the United States," wrote Josaphat Benoit, "are less like their parents born in Canada; they pick up from their environment ways of thinking and acting that astonish their fathers and mothers."[6] Very often, they know nothing at all of the culture of their

---

[3]   Josaphat Benoit, *L'Âme franco-américaine* (Montreal: Albert Lévesque, 1935), pp. 182-183.

[4]   Quoted in Jacques Rouillard, *Ah les États! Les travailleurs canadiens-français dans l'industrie textile de la Nouvelle-Angleterre* (Montreal: Boréal Express, 1985), p. 106.

[5]   Edward B. Ham, "Le parler populaire franco-américain," in Adrien Verrette, ed., *La croisade franco-américaine. Compte-rendu de la participation des Franco-Américains* (Manchester, N.H.: Éditions de l'Avenir National, 1938), p. 297.

[6]   Josaphat Benoit, *op. cit.*, p. 182.

forefathers' homeland. Comic strips in the newspapers, the movies, radio, television, and American sports answer their needs far better.

The institutional network, based on the national parish and envisioned as a fortress capable of safeguarding the distinctive features of Franco-American nationality was no longer playing its role; it was even in the process of vanishing. Adolphe Robert was already deploring this state of affairs in 1937: "There are parishes which disregard the traditional liturgy, abolishing high mass, vespers, the sermon, retreats, and pious associations; where the language spoken between the pastor and his assistants, and the priest with the altar boys, is English; where minstrel shows imported from the South have replaced the parish bazaars of old, and where, quite simply, the French spirit is in decline."[7] As the number of unilingual English persons increased among Franco-Americans, English became to a greater extent the language of parish life. Pastors gradually inserted it into their announcements and homilies, and, after Vatican II [1962-1965], celebrated some of the liturgy in English rather than in French. Under the pressure of circumstances, ecclesiastical authorities transformed "national," i.e., ethnically based parishes, into mixed parishes and even into territorial parishes, i.e., based on the neighborhood. The consequences were inevitable: in the seventies, of the 277 Franco-American parishes in New England, only fifty-five were still considered to be "national" parishes.[8]

The changing of the guard was, moreover, accelerating in these parishes. Little by little, Franco-American priests replaced the pastors born in Quebec. From 1929 to 1939, their number increased from twenty-seven to sixty-four, rising from 11% of the total to 27%.[9] This percentage continued to rise thereafter. These priests never espoused the "national cause" with as much fervor as their predecessors. "The theory that language is the guardian of faith," deplored Josaphat Benoit, "does not have proponents

7   Adolphe Robert, "La survivance de l'esprit français aux États-Unis," in Adrien Verrette, ed., *op.cit.*, p. 162.

8   Clarence d'Entremont, "Les Franco-Américains de la Louisiane," in *Le Franco-Américain au 20e siècle*, Comité de Vie franco-américaine, 1976, p. 56.

9   Statistics compiled from the *Guides franco-américains* by Francine Roy.

among the Franco-American clergy."[10] But could they do otherwise? Would not refusing to offer their services in English to the young Franco-Americans incapable of confessing themselves in French and of understanding the Sunday sermons in the language of their parents, prompt them to join territorial parishes?

The more educated lay people adopted the same behavior as the clergy. Professionals educated in American universities were content to remain on the sidelines of the struggle for *survivance*. They adapted readily and without balking to a clientele which was becoming more and more anglicized. Often enough, they claimed to be Franco-American only when they entered local politics or were looking for clients among their compatriots. As for businessmen and politicians, they soft-pedalled their ethnic origins as soon as their business success and their political ambitions went beyond the limits of the "little Canadas."

The parochial schools evolved along the same path as the national parishes. Two tendencies can be observed in them. First, a constant decrease in the time allotted to French, which, little by little, began to be taught as a second language, a "foreign" language. The reason for this was that, as Hormidas Hamelin remarked, "the bilingual school prepares young people to go quite naturally from French to English without noticing it."[11] That evolution came about under pressure from Franco-American parents and to accommodate a Catholic clientele of diverse ethnic origins. Second, there was the disappearance of an ever increasing number of parochial schools. A study has shown that in three dioceses of Massachusetts, a third of the parochial schools closed their doors between 1956 and 1972 and that enrollment dropped by 50%.[12] Parents who saw little difference between a parochial school and a public school simply preferred to send their children to the latter, especially if they wanted to "mainstream" their children. On top of that, because of the increase in expenses and the decrease in religious vocations, maintaining parochial schools often became prohibitive.

---

10   Josaphat Benoit, *op. cit.*, p. 187.

11   Hormidas Hamelin, *op. cit.*, p. 179.

12   Elliot Robert Barkan, "French Canadians," in Stephan Thernstrom, dir., *Harvard Encyclopedia of American Ethnic Groups* (Cambridge: Harvard University Press, 1980), p. 396.

The third pillar of the institutional network—the press—collapsed and disappeared almost entirely. In 1912, Francos were publishing forty-three periodicals (newspapers and magazines), and only twenty-five in 1935. Adolphe Robert estimates that the total readership of all these periodicals (in 1935) barely attained 50,000 subscribers.[13] Only the number of subscribers can give us an accurate count and not the number of copies printed. For instance, in 1938, the *Courrier* of Salem, Massachusetts, which had 630 subscribers,[14] was printing 2,430 copies, most of which were distributed free of charge. After the war, for lack of readers and sufficient financial resources, Franco-American newspapers, including, in 1979, the reputable *Le Travailleur* of Wilfrid Beaulieu, disappeared one after the other.

Finally, it should also be mentioned that the essential role of promotion and protection of Franco-American *survivance*, always performed by the mutual benefit societies, declined constantly. In order to survive and to recruit new members, these societies, having to focus to a greater degree on their economic objectives, allowed English to be used at meetings and in their publications and, in recent years, even allowed non-Catholics to become members, albeit on a limited basis.

Thus it is that the traditional pillars of *survivance* crumbled one after the other. The Franco-Americanism that the early leaders had dreamed of, and for which their successors had so valiantly fought, was in the process of disappearing. Why?

2.   Runaway Assimilation: Its Causes

Let us approach this question in a chronological manner, beginning with a study of the consequences of the Crash of 1929.

---

[13]   Adolphe Robert, *loc. cit.*, p. 168.

[14]   Edward B. Ham, "Journalism and the French Survival in New England," *The New England Quarterly*, 11, 1, March 1938, p. 96.

The Crash of 1929

In October 1929, an economic crisis of unprecedented magnitude struck the United States. In less than a month, the official value of stocks quoted on the market dropped by approximately 40%. The market continued its up-and-down slide until 1933; at that time, stocks were worth about 10% of their 1929 quoted value. From 1929 to 1932, the crisis affected the entire economy. Nearly 5,000 banks failed, with devastating consequences, as a result of having invested huge sums in the purchase of stocks and in financing brokerage operations. Those bankruptcies spurred investors to withdraw their savings from banks that were still solid. To meet their obligations, banks cut down on the volume of new loans to individuals as well as to corporations and even called in outstanding loans. Restriction of credit and a drop in the buying power of individuals pressured heads of industry to curtail production. Employers laid off some of their workers and cut the wages of others. For these reasons, in 1933 there were between 12 and 15 million unemployed, while from 1929 to 1932 average weekly wages of those who did work decreased from $28.50 to $17.05. The resultant loss in buying power brought on a new cut in production, and the vicious cycle began anew. No sector of the economy was spared.

New England was heavily impacted, all the more so because the textile and shoe industries were already in trouble due to competition from the southern states. Bankruptcies, unemployment, loss of revenue, indebtedness, penury were the lot of a great many people. In certain cities, such as in Manchester, N.H., where the giant Amoskeag Company closed its doors in 1935, the situation was catastrophic. In their downfall, these larger firms, which fueled the economy of medium-sized cities like Manchester, brought about the ruin of dozens of small industrial and commercial companies. "When the Amoskeag closed, oh my God!", exclaimed Antonia Bergeron, an employee. "It was awful. Then there were a lot on relief . . . Everything went slack everywhere. Business fell completely."[15]

The impact of the crisis on what may be called "Franco-Americanism" was considerable. It put an immediate end to the migration of French Canadians from Quebec to New England. As

---

15   Tamara K. Hareven and Randolph Langenbach, *Amoskeag: Life and Work in an American Factory City* (New York: Pantheon Books, 1978), p. 64.

the historian Richard Sorrell has written, "there was obviously 'a push' from a Quebec suffering from the Depression . . . However, the United States offered 'no pull'." [16] But, more was to come! In September 1930, Herbert Hoover, the President of the United States, ordered the American consuls posted in Canada to refuse a visa to any person likely to become a welfare burden on the country. The decision thus limited immigration to people assured of a job in the United States or who had sponsors capable of supporting them. One might as well say that the border was hermetically sealed. It is also probable, even though it would not be easy to provide exact data, that thousands of Quebecers, who had been living in New England for many years, returned to Quebec during that period.

The end of immigration meant that the number of Franco-Americans born in the United States and who favored a better integration of their families into American society continued to increase. In 1940, they made up 71.3% of the population as against 64.4% in 1930. This change had a considerable impact on the evolution of the Franco-American institutional network and its struggle in favor of *survivance*. As a result, "national" parishes were still being established, but at a slower pace: between 1930 and 1940 only six new parishes were created, compared to twenty-eight in the previous decade. After the defeat of the militant "sentinellists," that fact was of major importance. However, the most severe aftershocks of the crash were felt by these institutions at the financial level.

Financing parochial schools became a heavier and heavier burden on parents who were victims of unemployment and reduced wages; subscribing to a Franco-American paper was a luxury that few could allow themselves; the resources of the mutual benefit societies were strained to the limit. At the same time, the debt of parishes grew heavier, and many even found themselves unable to pay current expenses. Bingos and second collections at Sunday masses were some of the measures resorted to by pastors to balance their budgets.

Finally, the crash took a heavy toll on the values, customs, and attitudes of people. The family and the bonds of traditional

---

16   Richard S. Sorrell, "The Sentinelle Affair (1924-1929) and Militant *Survivance*: The Franco-American Experience in Woonsocket, Rhode Island" (Doctoral dissertation, S.U.N.Y. at Buffalo, N. Y., 1975), p. 66.

solidarity were subjected to strong centrifugal forces. We have noted that the duty of the head of the family was to work and put aside money to take care of his dependents. His authority in the family and his respectability in the community depended on his ability to meet his obligations. An inability to do so, according to the value code in force in the Franco-American community, created enormous tensions in the family unit. The situation was all the more stressful because the extended family, the network of relatives and friends, was unable to offer its usual support. "You can't imagine," states a witness, "the impact that the shutdown had on a community like Manchester. Complete families—fathers, sisters, everyone—were all out. There was nobody that you could turn to. I don't think before the Amoskeag closed I ever knew anyone that was on welfare . . . People were proud, very proud. If you were in trouble and didn't have any income, someone always would say, 'Well, come live with us for a while.' That's the way it happened."[17] The parish itself, normally the last resort, could not cope. Even taxed to the utmost, the generosity of parishioners was unable to alleviate all the needs. There remained the State. Putting aside their pride, Franco-Americans were forced to do as everyone else and solicit from the State what they needed to live on and put food on the table. That was a great comedown which did not go unnoticed. Adélard Janelle, an employee of the municipal welfare office of Lewiston, Maine, admitted that he was happy to get fired in 1931 by the Democrats who had recently come to power. He was finding it too painful to face his compatriots who came seeking help from the city. "It was a difficult job, because the French are proud. They didn't like it. But they had to eat. They had to pay rent . . . I was glad to be out."[18]

The War

The Second World War undoubtedly had as great an impact as the Crash of 1929 on the values, attitudes, behavior, and institutions of Franco-Americans.

---

[17] Tamara K. Hareven and Randolph Langenbach, op. cit., p. 354.

[18] Quoted in Dyke Hendrickson, Quiet Presence. Histoire de Franco-Américains in New England (Portland: Guy Gannett Publishing Co., 1980), p. 5.

Little Canadas held very little attraction for the tens of thousands of Franco-American veterans after the exciting years away from home spent in training camps and at the front. Many found the atmosphere in the Franco-American parish to be too stern and sometimes oppressive. They objected to it or fled from it. Others challenged its French character. Because their imperfect mastery of English had made them the butt of many jokes during their years of military service, they worked now, to ensure not that their children be bilingual, but that they speak flawless English. For the Franco-Americans who stayed at home, the war played a bonding role. The length of the conflict, the privations endured, the anxiety over relatives, family, and friends who had been drafted, fanned the patriotic fervor of Franco-Americans and brought them closer to their fellow Americans. The wars in Korea and Vietnam played a similar role.

In addition, the war ushered in an era of unprecedented prosperity for workers, both male and female, who willingly became part of the consumer society.

The Media

No element of the consumer society has had a greater impact than television. In 1945, the ratio of households equipped with a television set was minute; in 1990, it approximated 90%. Several hours per day, all the members of the family, but especially the women and children, are exposed to a non-stop barrage of pictures, music, ideas, values, "American" behaviors which produce an undeniably homogenizing effect. No one can doubt the effect of a series such as "Father Knows Best" on the Franco-American family.

To the influence of television must be added that of newspapers, magazines, radio, cinema, and video.

The Break-Up of the Little Canadas

Prosperity incited a goodly number of Franco-Americans to move out of the Little Canadas to the suburbs. The urban renewal programs of the federal government, developed in the late 1950s and continuing into the 1960s, accelerated this migration. These programs sought to destroy the old, poor, and even sordid neighborhoods of the inner cities, in order to build subsidized housing there. But because the rent often exceeded their means, the dislodged tenants had to change neighborhoods. Once dispersed, they either could not or did not want to re-create their ethnic enclaves.

There still are vestiges of Little Canadas in certain New England cities. There one still finds Franco-Americans, often among the poorest, or the oldest, rubbing elbows with new immigrants of Latin-American or Asian origin. The institutional network has been profoundly transformed. The decline of religious practice, from the 1960s on, has weakened the entire parish structure. Even the economic infrastructure has disappeared, the residents preferring to shop in suburban malls.

All the factors just enumerated have weakened the institutional network of the Little Canadas and are accelerating their disappearance; they have also profoundly transformed the ideas, values, customs, and behavior of Franco-Americans.

Under those conditions, does "Franco-Americanism" have a future?

3.   The Elite and the Future of "Franco-Americanism"

By the1930s, some of those who were born in the United States or who had lived here for ten, twenty, or thirty years made the normal and respectable choice of rapidly assimilating into American society. They believed that choosing to take root in the United States was the only way to ensure that their children would get the maximum benefits from all that American society offered. These people, lived, for the most part, in territorial parishes, sent their children to public schools, and, as a general rule, burned all their bridges to "Franco-Americanism." However, the majority of Franco-Americans continued to speak French and remain attached to the culture of their elders; they were ready to make many sacrifices so that their children would imitate them. The elite among them, who had played an essential role in the realization of that dream and who had clashed violently during the "Sentinellist" crisis of the twenties, remained hopelessly divided as to the means of attaining this goal.

The more radical militants, heirs of the "Sentinellists," who regrouped around Wilfrid Beaulieu of *Le Travailleur*, did not believe it possible to ensure the *survivance* of the French language, religion, traditions, and customs inherited from the ancestors unless they recreated a French Quebec in New England. Every threat to the integrity of the institutional network centered on the national parish had to be fought unremittingly regardless of whence it came. Even though the assimilating designs of the bishops haunted them still as much as before, they were more worried about the deleterious influence of the milieu. In order to prevent ethnic life from diminishing in intensity, they proposed a rather simple program: the French language must occupy the central position in the parish and its institutions. It must be the only language used in church and in the "national" societies and the major language at school. Every infraction was to be vigorously countered and the guilty were to be pilloried.

The moderate militants were just as concerned about the ravages of anglicization. How, they asked themselves, could they retain within the fold those who were tempted to assimilate, yet work to ensure that their children benefit to the utmost from the advantages of integrating into American society? To pretend that they could accomplish this by imposing ever more French and by inviting the elite to seek inspiration, encouragement, and guidelines from Quebec, appeared utopian to them. They advocated an institutional network better adapted to American reality. Some English at church, they contended, would keep young people attached to their parish. Free tuition, added to a better teaching of English, programs better adapted to the milieu, and better trained teachers, would induce more parents to choose a parochial school for their children. Finally, the training of the better endowed students beyond the elementary level, in Franco-American institutions, rather than those of Quebec, should better prepare them to assume their role in the group.

The moderate militants maintained that Francos had greatly changed. Decades of life, struggle, and hardships in a new environment had progressively modified the feelings, ideas, values, and behaviors inherited from their elders. These militants demanded that their "national" life be distinct from that of the French Canadians of Quebec and different from it in many respects. They maintained that Franco-Americans were bilingual persons who spoke French in certain circumstances and as a second language. Admittedly, they believed it necessary to inculcate in the young a love of French and to promote its use, but they refused to regard the use of English as a crime or a betrayal. Their view of things corresponded more closely to the interests and ideas of Franco-Americans of the second, third, and fourth generations, who, in 1940, made up 71% of the population.

In a country where English is the official language of use, the effects of bilingualism are unavoidable. In families where the parents were born in Quebec, the use of both languages, alternately spoken by parents and children, spread rapidly. Everywhere, at work, on the street, in schoolyards, even at home, youngsters born in the United States tended to speak English rather than French. In conversation, many even switched from French to English without realizing it. Certain people also wondered why others insisted so much on their speaking a language of so little use in communicating with the world around them. In time, English unilingualism tended to become the norm.

When the young abandoned the speaking of French, all, including even the moderates, were obviously worried. What will happen, they asked themselves, when the generation that is growing up will no longer know French? The answer was clear. Priests would have to preach in English, French-language newspapers would disappear for lack of readers, and the mutual benefit societies would die out. What was happening here and there would occur on a general scale all over New England. In the mid-1930s, this realization caused the militants to soft-pedal their disagreements and to rally behind a single program of action. Both groups urged their compatriots to a renewal, to a crusade capable of instilling in young people the cult of memory, "national" pride, and the militancy of their elders. In all this history played a major role.

Since one cannot admire or imitate what one does not know, the elite thought it absolutely necessary to teach the young that the discoverers, the explorers, the pioneers, the missionaries of their nationality had played a great role in the history of the United States, and that they themselves were not intruders in the United States, or orphans without a past. The rising generation needed to know that the French language "ties them into a whole ensemble of mores, beliefs, traditions, and especially to a glorious past,"[19] "that Quebec, the cradle of our forefathers, is not a

---

[19]   Wilfrid Dufault, A.A., and Armand Desautels, A.A., "L'esprit français dans nos écoles paroissiales de la Nouvelle-Angleterre," in Adrien Verrette, ed., *op. cit.*, p. 261.

backward country."[20] Through the study of history, "of the luminous trail extending from Clovis to Jeanne d'Arc, from Champlain to Montcalm, to Lafontaine, to Ferdinand Gagnon, and Mgr. Hévey, Mgr. Dauray, and Mgr. Prévost," this generation will know what it means to belong to the French race."[21] "We will no longer dare to require of them," declares Rodolphe Pépin, "that they be proud of ancestors they don't know and about whom no one has ever talked to them."[22]

In order to inculcate in the young this cult of remembrance, the elite invited teachers, both male and female, to teach "national" history, i.e., Franco-American history, and to organize history contests, with monetary rewards, using the *Catéchisme d'histoire franco-américaine* of Josaphat Benoit. So as to remind pupils each day of what the French heroes of North America had done and to impress upon their memory and their imagination the feats of their ancestors, they requested that the walls of classrooms be hung with the calendars of Brother Wilfrid, of the Brothers of the Sacred Heart in Central Falls, Rhode Island, and that his historical booklets be purchased. Schools were invited to celebrate the feast of Dollard[23] and the heroes of Long Sault, near Montreal, on May 24 of each year. By placing before the eyes of the young the example of young men willing to sacrifice everything to save New France, they hoped to have "the consolation of seeing at every moment and everywhere at once arise successors to Dollard, who will stand guard over our

---

[20]   Adrien Verrette, "Au service d'une survivance," in Antoine Clément, ed., *L'Alliance française de Lowell, 1937-1947* (Manchester, N.H.: Éditions de l'Avenir National, 1948), p. 257.

[21]   Adrien Verrette, ed., *La croisade franco-américaine* (Manchester, N.H.: Éditions de l'Avenir National, 1938), p. 44.

[22]   Rodolphe Pépin, "Les amitiés françaises en Amérique," in Adrien Verrette, ed., *op. cit.*, p. 140.

[23]   [Dollard DesOrmeaux (1635-1660) and sixteen companions— accompanied by four Algonquins and forty Hurons who, except for their chief, deserted to the Iroquois—withstood the attack of 800 Iroquois warriors for many days before being killed or taken into captivity. Their resistance was said to have saved Montreal and New France from destruction at the hands of the Iroquois.—Editor]

institutions."[24] Parents and teachers were invited to organize contests of French song and to patronize the work of *Les Cahiers de la Bonne Chanson* of Rev. Charles-Emile Gadbois. For "the soul of the ancestors, the hopes of their descendants, the entire glorious past, the realistic present, and the future laden with promise are all contained in the verses and refrains of the French-Canadian folksong."[25] To fuel "national" pride among the young, the elite suggested also that the feast of John the Baptist be celebrated with fanfare as well as the anniversaries (tenth, twenty-fifth, fiftieth, and centennial) of the various parish institutions. The spectators at the parade on the "national" feast day would see pass before their eyes the living reality of the Franco-American "nation," the exceptional contribution of the French to North-American life. As for commemorating the various events and outstanding dates of the Franco-American past, they would enable the young to take stock, they would reveal to them their own identity and would inspire in them, it was to be hoped, an unshakable loyalty to the accomplishments of the founders. They would say to themselves, "Are we going to pass on to our children such a glorious heritage, after having allowed it to diminish?"[26]

Measured by the yardstick of the hopes that the elite had invested in it, this program was a fiasco. French was continually losing ground, the "national" parishes were losing their parishioners to English-language "territorial" parishes, the remembrance of the life that used to be lived in the "Little Canadas" of yore was gradually fading. "Franco-Americanism" was undergoing a profound mutation; its vision, which had nourished the dreams of the founders and the builders, was in the process of disappearing. The gulf separating the young from their elders was continually widening. Hanging on with nostalgia to a past that they had labored hard to fashion, the traditional elites reproached the younger generation with asperity for not wanting to carry the torch. Their speeches, which border on incantation,

---

[24]   "Fête vraiment inspiratrice," *L'Avenir National* , Manchester, May 25, 1938, p. 4.

[25]   "La bonne chanson," *L'Avenir National*, Manchester, January 18, 1939, p. 4.

[26]   Louis-A. Ramsay, "25 ans de vie paroissiale," *L'Avenir National*, Manchester, January 15, 1940, p. 4.

most often do not rise above vilifying the "spineless," the "resigners," the "traitors," the "defeatists."

In the 1960s, some among the most militant young people revolted. They could not see how the incantational, outmoded, and sometimes contemptuous speech of certain elders could inspire a renascence of "Franco-Americanism." They refused to accept that one had to speak impeccable French, go regularly to church, and be a devotee of the cult of ancestral traditions to have the right to call oneself Franco-American. Many of them, who murder the French language and have distanced themselves from the Church, are mortified by the poverty of the "Little Canadas" and have lost all faith in *survivance* as preached by the traditional elites.

Those who participated in the FAROG (Franco-American Resource Opportunity Group), an activist organization founded at the University of Maine at Orono, supported in the FAROG *Forum* the idea that the renascence of Francos would be accomplished by the young and by ordinary people. The latter would initially have to rid themselves of the demoralizing picture of a people lacking in pride, uneducated and apathetic. They would have to recognize who they are and renew the ties with their true past from which they had been cut off. The discovery of a past capable of enhancing one's self-esteem is a source of pride and of progress as proven by the impact in the United States of the televised production of Alex Haley's *Roots*. But that past, which the young expect will enlighten their present and orient their future, is not to be found in the history being taught them. Indeed, the exodus of hundreds of thousands of French Canadians to New England, their integration into American society had been seen only through the deforming prism of the thinking of their own upper classes.

In the pages dedicated to the foundation of "Little Canadas" and to the unremitting struggle to ensure survival on American soil of the French and Catholic reality, there had been room only for the leaders: priests, religious of both sexes, and professionals. Rarely was there a reference to what the workers and their families believed, thought, said, and did. Besides, in this past, which was being taught them, ordinary people were presented as victims of forces which were beyond them and which crushed them. Their only hope of salvation: to let themselves be guided by their leaders like a flock of sheep. This image was just the opposite of the one that they vaguely perceived and that recent studies in social history proposed to them: the image of persons who were independent, dynamic, and capable to a certain degree of shaping the world in which they lived. This search for roots, which is at the origin of the FAROG's work, also explains the popularity of genealogical societies that have sprung up here and there in New England, and the attempts of all kinds to know and to make known popular Franco-American culture and even certain aspects of the intellectual culture, overlooked up to that time, for example, particularly the efforts to discover and appropriate the work of celebrated authors like Jack Kerouac and Grace Metalious.

This inquiry into the past is complementary to that being pursued by the more traditional militants of French identity and the scholars who, in research centers and universities, interest themselves in the work of the elite, and in the areas of the Franco-American past that are better known.

Thanks to the work of both, many Francos, who either do or don't speak French, who either do or don't practice the religion of their fathers, discover with pride their true place in American history and in the francophone world of North America. They understand that, together with the Yankees, the Irish-Americans, the Italian-Americans, etc., they have contributed to molding the American of the Northeast. They discover that, on an equal footing with the Acadians, the Francophones of Quebec and of the rest of Canada and the United States, they are witnesses in their own way to the French fact in North America.

Thus has history contributed to the enlightenment of all those who share the same cultural heritage.

Translated by Alexis A. Babineau, A.A.

[This text, prepared for the French Institute's colloquium on "The Franco-Americans" and entitled "De Franco-Américains à Américains d'origine canadienne-française ou le passé et le présent de la Franco-Américanie" is published here for the first time.]

VIII

THE VIEW FROM WITHIN

Arthur Milot's Memoirs: *Childhood Memories*

Claude Milot

Arthur Milot (1907-1986)

[Arthur Milot, who was born in Lowell, Massachusetts, grew up in the Pawtucketville section of that city. Having received his grade school education from the Marist Brothers at the *Collège* St. Joseph in Lowell, he then studied with the Oblates'in Colebrook, New Hampshire, and Natick, Massachusetts.

After earning his Bachelor of Arts degree from St. Bonaventure University, in 1931, he entered the field of journalism, writing first for *L'Étoile*, Lowell's French-language daily newspaper, and then for *L'Indépendant* of Woonsocket, R.I. Both of these newspapers served large French-Canadian populations in those respective cities.

He left journalism to become under-secretary for the Union Saint-Jean-Baptiste in Woonsocket, at that time the largest mutual benefit society for Franco-Americans. In the mid-fifties, he accepted a post with the U.S. Department of State as a comptroller with the Agency for International Development. In this position, Arthur Milot spent eighteen years in the French-speaking countries of Vietnam, Mali, and Morocco.

Before his death, in 1986, Arthur Milot wrote his memoirs about growing up in Lowell in the first quarter of this century. Although he was perfectly bilingual, Mr. Milot chose to write the book in French because it was in that language that he had experienced what he was writing about. In the book, he recalls the sights and sounds of his youth, but he also describes a people struggling to maintain its identity in a new land following the great migration of hundreds of thousands of French Canadians from the farms of Quebec to the mill towns of New England.—Editor]

[*Cahiers de Souvenirs d'enfance* appeared in a bilingual edition in 1992, translated and published by Arthur Milot's son Claude, who entitled the translation *Childhood Memories*. The following pages contain extracts from *Childhood Memories* with commentary by Claude Milot.—Editor]

My father's testimony is that of a witness to a fleeting moment in history. He lived the Franco-American experience. What he saw, and heard, and felt is important to us as a record of our cultural past. But what he thought of this experience is even more important to those of us who seek to define ourselves through our ancestry. [C.M.]

Quebec

While the rural Canadian population was in desperate need of money, the new textile mills of New England were seeking unskilled workers by the thousands. They promised to pay in cash anyone who was willing to work: men, women, young girls, even children. No experience was necessary and no special skills either. For many families on the edge of starvation, this was a godsend. . .

There is no doubt that the immigrants arrived poor—poor, but proud. They had foreseen with horror the coming of the day when, at the end of their rope, they would have to beg outside the church from those who were coming out after Mass. It was better to seek work in another country than to debase oneself by begging.

Emigration

The first ones who came wrote back to their brothers and cousins to urge them to take on these jobs that paid salaries in cash. Upon their arrival, these immigrants were thus assured of a warm welcome, a place to spend the first few nights, and a helping hand to tide them over until the first job and the first payday.

In spite of their efforts and their sacrifices, my grandparents were wiped out, like so many others, during Quebec's economic crisis in 1875. My grandfather tried everything to get back on his feet, including commercial ventures and public transportation. But, nothing worked. Finally, he had to join the crowd heading for the States. He had some cousins who would be waiting for him at the station in Lowell, Massachusetts. And he would be able to find work right away for himself and his children.

My father was 15 years old in 1880 when he left Canada for good with his parents and the rest of the family.

[. . .]

I never heard my mother, my uncles, nor my aunts speak about the bad times or the sadness of the departure. Grandmother had brought with her in camel-backed trunks everything she had of any value.

Settling-in

When my parents came to the States, they found a way of life dictated by emerging industries. The American population was evolving from one that had been mainly agricultural. . . to one that had become primarily industrial. Farmers had always enjoyed an abundance of fresh air and a dinner table covered with home-grown produce, but they rarely got paid in cash for their work. Having become salaried workers, they now learned to place a value on things in terms of dollars. Instead of worrying about the next crop, the former plowhands now learned to worry about the next paycheck to pay the rent, the food bill, and the suit of clothes, and to keep up with countless household needs. . .

These 500,000 or so Canadian immigrants, while happy to be able to bring Saturday's paycheck to the family, were not willing, just the same, to break with the past. They knew that with an identity all their own, and especially with their own language, they would not be the same as the other people around them. I don't know if they gave any thought to the right of survival that the old Canadians had won after the Cession of New France. At that time the English had pounced on Canada to try to transform it into a satellite where everyone would be Protestant and speak nothing but English. For the French Canadians, language had been the guardian of the faith at the same time as their means of retaining a national cohesiveness. . .

These Canadians brought with them their language, their religion, their customs, and their way of life. They lost no time in setting up organizations to preserve their culture while blending into the American scene.

[. . .]

In the United States, where they were surrounded by strange and sometimes hostile nationalities, who spoke a language they didn't understand, the Canadian immigrants grouped themselves into parishes, thus opening a new chapter in their history. With their churches, where everything was done in French, with their bilingual schools and their societies, with their newspapers, and with a whole network of professional and commercial establishments serving a homogeneous population, our parents and their contemporaries were trying to preserve their old, traditional moral values in their new, adopted American country. "It was their cultural contribution to the wealth of their new country," said the French newspapers of the day. They were especially confident that they were directing their children toward a life that conformed to an honorable and wholesome past.

Arriving in Lowell in 1880, my grandfather Milot and his family found a Canadian parish in full operation. Father André Garin, an Oblate missionary, was the founding pastor of St. Joseph's parish and the force behind its development. Soon there was a school, a convent, religious societies, an orphanage, new parishes in several Canadian neighborhoods, and a religious program run by clergy recruited from Canada and from France.

Language

Because people continued to speak French at home, in church, in school, in children's games, and even at the mill among Canadian workers, they did not feel like expatriates. Priests, doctors, who had also come from Canada, and French-language newspapermen mixed with the weavers, shoemakers, spinners, masons, and tanners who constituted the majority of the immigrants. Canadians started small businesses like groceries, pharmacies, and hardware stores in which French was spoken openly by the Canadian customers. Bakers had their bread delivered to neighborhood apartments by delivery boys who spoke French and who knew everything that was going on among the Canadians. And we were used to seeing wagons whose side panels had names like Pelnault, Bégin, and Faucher. French names were also seen on trucks belonging to the milkman, the laundryman, and numerous grocers.

In my days, that is, when I was a pupil at St. Joseph's School, Canadians had a choice of doctors on Merrimack Street: Mignault, Roy, Belhumeur, Lavallée, Laurin, Giguère, O'Brien (a

French Canadian), Lamoureux, Caisse, Rochette, and Patenaude. Maybe I'm forgetting one or two others, and I'm not even mentioning the Greek doctors who spoke French.

Children spoke French among themselves on their way to school or while at play. Even the little Irish kids had to learn to speak French if they wanted to participate. I knew several who spoke French just like us. There were some Greeks and Irish in our classes at St. Joseph's; they were there to learn French literature. The Brothers gave them a lot of attention, but those pupils spoke only English in the schoolyard. So, I don't know if those classes really helped them. On the other hand, the ones who learned our street French, swear words and all, lost no time in getting themselves understood.

We Canadians took the language that our parents had brought from Canada and quickly put it to work. Mill hands didn't know the equivalent terms being used in France, so they created their own vocabulary to fit their needs. In Lowell, for example, we worked at the "moulin" [the factory]. They said shoe *shop*, wood *shop*, going to the *shop*. But they also said "boutique de forgeron" [blacksmith shop], "la buanderie," [the laundry], and "la boulangerie" [the bakery].

. . . we never took on the Brothers' accent when we spoke French. We studied in French using textbooks and exercises in use in France. We learned the rules for participles, the litany of exceptions for plurals, the tenses, spelling, the use of capitals, and all the regular and irregular verb conjugations. Our grammar book was always within reach.

In school we spoke the same French we spoke at home or at play. It was our French . . . and not the French of the Brothers. Actually, we would have been upset had a Brother tried to speak to us with a Canadian accent. We would have thought he was making fun of us. We understood perfectly well the French spoken by the Brothers, even when one of them spoke with an accent from Marseilles. They understood us, too. . .

The Brothers forgave us our "moué pi toué" [jargon for me and you], very rustic talk, but not uniquely Canadian. On the other hand, they never forgave us a mistake in grammar or spelling on our dictations and compositions. Written French always had to be flawless. And we knew they were right. . .

Schooling

Those who went all the way knew how to read fluently in English and in French; they also knew how to write in both languages; and they knew catechism. They had a working knowledge of arithmetic and algebra and even accounting. They had acquired a knowledge of the most important events in the history of the United States. They had heard the Brothers talk about the history of France, but rarely about the history of Canada. There was no textbook on either. . .

Religion

In our day we practiced our religion in French, we said our prayers in French at home as well as in school, and we went to confession in French. Even today I feel ill at ease in speaking English in a confessional, and I will never be able to say my Act of Contrition in anything but French. . .

Our family said the Rosary after the dishes had been washed and put away in the cabinets. Everyone knelt, backs curbed under the weight of the day's labors, elbows resting on chairs, and many fingers running through hair and scratching heads. . . We recited the Our Fathers and the Hail Marys in a monotone voice, minds busy visiting elsewhere. But it was still a positive sign of faith, just like the Sign of the Cross.

Petit Canada

Lowell's *Petit Canada* doesn't exist anymore. Everything is gone: the streets with rows of grey blocks with their flat roofs and the red brick mills strung along the Merrimack for a mile. Gone. In their place there is a sort of park surrounded by low-income housing. . . The *Petit Canada* that I knew in Lowell went from the canal that was used for water power, all the way to the river, thus forming a long island covered with huge factories and housing for the workers. . .

We had to cross the *Petit Canada* to bring lunches to those who were working in the *moulins* (that's what we called all the cotton mills and hosiery factories along the river.) Along the way we saw the streets with those big, grey blocks of six, eight, even twelve tenements (today we would call them apartments). They were full of children of all ages. The tenants all hung out their wash to dry on lines stretching from one block to another. Like flags, but not as nice.

The tenements weren't fancy in any way. Only one cold water tap, and only the lucky ones with a bathroom. The others had to share a toilet off the unlit landing of the staircase. No electricity, and certainly no central heating. The new arrivals from Canada had to squeeze in the best they could while awaiting better quarters elsewhere. . .

In the Canadian community, the *Petit Canada* was the poorest neighborhood. The people who lived there dreamed of the day they would be able to move elsewhere, and saved whatever they could out of the multiple family paychecks. . .

The first time I set foot in one of the mills, I met with a neighbor named Dolly Proulx who was delivering lunch to her sisters who worked in the Lawrence and Suffolk Mills where my brother Lucien also had a job. We had had to cross a foot-bridge to get from one mill to the other. We entered an enormous room filled with weaving machinery that made such a hellish noise, we couldn't hear ourselves think. Somehow I could see the workers communicating with one another in a normal tone of voice through the horrible noise. Workers got used to it, they said. I would have been deaf for the rest of my life. We went from one room to another, all of them enormous and busy. To my great surprise no one asked me what I was doing there. We were simply going about our business like everyone else.

Family

My father and mother had uncles, aunts, and numerous cousins who had come, like them, to find work in the United States. They were everywhere: in Lowell, Worcester, Rochester, Woonsocket, Manchester, Nashua, Taunton, Providence—all natives of Yamachiche. It is not surprising that they experienced great joy when they ran into each other in their new country. They would take turns visiting each other sometimes by train, sometimes by interurban tramways. The inexpensive automobile replaced all other means of transportation after the war.

Relatives were always welcomed with cries of joy. These visits were usually unannounced, but they were welcome just the same. According to our customs, the youngsters would gather around the piano to sing popular songs, while the adults would sit in the kitchen to exchange news, go over the family roots and origins of new arrivals, discuss Canadian politics, and talk about their jobs and whatever else interests people their age.

The automobile allowed us to visit each other from city to city for a generation. But once the old people and then the first cousins died off, we each went our own way. The only thing that remains of those meetings in the old days are family albums full of pictures of loved ones.

As a student of history, my father was fascinated by the historical factors that caused the Franco-American "happening" to dissipate after only 100 years (roughly from 1860 to 1960). This one, brief statement represents the core of his thesis on the matter. In a way, he was saddended by the gradual disappearance of the French-Canadian identity, but he came to view it as the natural way of things. All the more reason, he felt, to record his memories of that period when the evolution had reached its acme. [C.M.]

. . . it was the French language with its Canadian intonations that bonded these people into a powerful historical reality that was to last a century and number a million souls. But there was a flaw in all of this. The Canadian immigrants had not been able to transplant themselves as a people into the American population, because for people to survive as a people, they need a land they can call their own. . . The idea of Franco-Americans as a people could not take root, because their descendants became Americans, on American soil, in a country that they fought to defend against all foreign enemies. For two or three generations, they were Americans somewhat different from the others, but wholly Americans nonetheless, like their descendants.

His reflections on that question are worth revisiting.[C.M.]

Times have changed. The parochial infrastructure of the Canadians who emigrated to the United States has seen its day. . . For the old-timers as well as for my father's generation, the language was the guardian of the faith. Would they have agreed to part with such a large share of their hard-earned savings to build schools and churches where only English is spoken?. . .

"What will remain?" is the question my father poses for us and for future generations. [C.M.]

Will any part of this Franco-American reality endure? A man's surname, of course, will always be a clue to his origins, even if it has been anglicized, as sometimes happens. Children will learn from their parents that their ancestors came from Canada, even if it is more trendy to boast of an ancient link to France than to Canada.

For those who unfortunately no longer speak French, their family name is all that remains to identify them as descendants of French Canadians. . .

Not long ago I crossed the park along the canal where the tenement houses of the *Petit Canada* once stood. The brown water flowed by slowly as always, but the factories that had stood there like giant red cliffs were all gone. So was the *Petit Canada*.

[This text was presented at the 1994 French Institute colloquium entitled "The Franco-Americans."]

From the Parochial School to an American University: Reflections on Cultural Fragmentation[*]

Lucien A. Aubé

The personal memories presented here are still quite vivid in my mind half a century after my graduation from parochial school. The intensity and persistence of these memories is proof of their being deeply rooted in real life experiences. To statements of fact relating to the curricula and educational objectives of three parochial schools in Lewiston, Maine, will be added the perceptions and impressions of a Franco-American confronted with the problems of adapting to different and diverse educational, social, and cultural environments. It is to be hoped that this testimony will contribute in a modest way to the history of these three Lewiston schools, and will illustrate the cultural fragmentation which has been the lot of those who have tried to live their Franco-American heritage with intensity.

In 1928, I started first grade at Saint-Pierre et Saint-Paul elementary school in Lewiston, Maine. Twenty years later, I was teaching my first course at John Carroll University in Cleveland, Ohio. But it was only around the year 1973 that a series of events led me to reflect seriously upon the cultural agonizing which I had experienced since my parochial school days. In the process of preparing to teach a course on the French influence in America, I came upon passages from the Jesuit *Relations* telling of the destruction of Huronia by the Iroquois in 1649. In a flash, I was back in Lewiston in sixth grade at École Sainte-Marie.

Soeur Marie-Thérèse would tell us about the "good Indians,"

---

[*]   My sincerest thanks to my sister, Laurette Drouin, for her efforts to obtain for me, in Lewiston, materials and testimonies which otherwise would have been difficult to procure, my daughter, Mary Elizabeth Aubé, and my son-in-law, Yves Frenette, for their helpful suggestions.

the Hurons[2]—who were good because they were the allies of the French against the Protestant English—and the "bad Indians," the Iroquois. The Hurons were all the better because many of them had converted to Catholicism. Sister described the Iroquois for us as bad, barbaric, cruel, blood-thirsty. Were they not guilty of having martyred many Jesuits, Fathers Jogues and Brébeuf, as well as Brother Lallemant?

In the sixth grade at Sainte-Marie that year, French classes were taught in the afternoon.[3] Morning classes were taught in English. Soeur Marie-Clotilde, who was Irish and spoke French with an accent, was always encouraging us to read James Fenimore Cooper's novels: *The Last of the Mohicans*, *The Deerslayer*. In these novels, the Iroquois were the "good Indians" and the Hurons, the "bad ones." And then, when we studied the history of the United States, the English, so despised by soeur Marie-Thérèse, became heroes, the Founding Fathers of Jamestown and Plymouth, of the United States of America, Cradle of Liberty, whose flag we saluted every day by reciting "The pledge of allegiance" in English, following a prayer said in French.

I was only ten years old but these discrepancies left me confused and perplexed. My classmates did not seem to share my concerns. To them, Hurons and Iroquois were Indians, and Indians were Indians, just like those they saw in cowboy movies on Saturday afternoons. Besides, I was much too timid to raise the issue in class. After all, I was well brought up and I had been taught never to contradict adults, especially if they were priests or nuns! Little by little, I came to forget all about the "good" and the "bad Indians" until that day in 1973.

In September 1928, when I began school at Saint-Pierre, I was six years old. I did not speak a single word of English. When I left

---

[2]   There were other "good Indians." I remember the Algonquins and the Abenakis. I did not know when I was young that the Abenakis belonged to the Algonquin nation.

[3]   Soeur Marie-Thérèse taught only French. In the morning, she taught a third grade. Impossible to forget that. From time to time, the dear sister would bring in "*la petite Aline*" [little Aline] from her morning class to shame us, "*les grands*," the older students who did not understand the rules governing the agreement of past participles. Soeur Marie-Clotilde taught only English and her afternoon class was a fifth grade, if memory serves me correctly .

that school the following June, I still did not speak a single word of English. In the first grade at Saint-Pierre, the objectives were twofold: initiate the pupils to the study of their mother tongue, French, and prepare them to make their First Holy Communion. The study of English—as a second language—began only in the fourth grade.[4] Testimony from *soeur Marie-Céline Bonenfant*, a Dominican, seems to confirm that, in 1928, French still maintained its priority at École Saint-Pierre et Saint-Paul. However, her testimony makes it quite clear that even at Saint-Pierre et Saint-Paul, in the early thirties, pressure from the community was growing constantly to give greater importance to English:

> With the arrival of the Dominican Sisters in 1904, "*le* **bon** *français*" ["good" French] experienced a revival. All classes were taught in that language. All the children spoke French, in school, on the street, as well as at home. This was the case until about 1933-1935 when, with the arrival of a new principal, it was recognized that there now existed a need to add some other academic subjects to the English curriculum as it then existed: (*Grammar-Reading-Spelling*). Mathematics was the first subject to be added; then American history, geography, the sciences. Finally, in 1940 (approximately), all that remained in the French program was the course in language, that is, reading, composition, grammar, catechism, religion classes: French until 1955-1960; then these were anglicized also. (Except in the high school, where the teacher at the time was French.)

In 1967, when I became principal during that last year

---

[4]   I dare assert this categorically in spite of a lack of definitive documentation. My brother Roland tells me he is "absolutely sure" that this was the case. The testimony submitted by soeur Marie-Céline, O.P. would seem to confirm my brother's certainty. The anniversary booklets are very vague on this subject: "Since 1929 significant progress has occurred at École Saint-Pierre . . . The teaching of English has been pushed vigorously and notable results have taken place in the judgment of competent people." *Album-Souvenir du 75e anniversaire de la paroisse Saint-Pierre et Saint-Paul de Lewiston, Maine, 1871-1946*, p. 29. The people who went through this experience are already senior citizens. The schools are closing, these parishes are becoming English-speaking. What is being done to preserve the documentation necessary to write the history of these bilingual schools?

that the Dominican Sisters were at Saint-Pierre, the Dominican Fathers gave catechism lessons ("*faisaient*" *le catéchisme*) in French, but the textbooks were no longer in that language. However, even at that time, the children still spoke French among themselves without our having to pressure them to do so. That is because in families, French remained the dominant language, but not absolutely everywhere.[5]

It was also at École Saint-Pierre et Saint-Paul that I was taught the importance attached to good conduct. One day, my first grade teacher, a young woman who lived two houses down the street from us, came to complain to my mother that I had been bad (*"méchant"*). Thank God, my memory has been kind to me so that—honestly—I cannot remember what great crime I had committed. The teacher had told me beforehand that she was coming to speak to my mother. Fearful of the encounter, I had curled up in a corner of the stairs of the back porch to hide. My mother found me there and reprimanded me. When my father came home from work, I was punished very severely. It was the first and the last time that there ever was any complaint about my conduct in school. "Good little boys" were supposed to be docile and obedient. Without a doubt, this "goodness," this docility, which was so valued as a virtue, both in school and at home, proved for many years to be a serious obstacle to the development of my personality and to the realization of my professional ambitions. Today, another question arises: If the notion of "good" and "bad" Indians remains so vivid in my memory, is it not because I have never forgotten what was expected of a "good little boy?"

So, from École Saint-Pierre three vivid memories remain: my First Holy Communion, what it meant to be a "good little boy," and, more to the point, not a word of English.

Since my family moved during the summer months to the recently-established parish of Sainte-Croix, I found myself enrolled in that parish's elementary school the following

---

5   From a letter addressed to the author in November 1985. Soeur Marie-Céline Bonenfant, O.P., was born in Lewiston. As a child, she attended École Saint-Pierre, before returning there as a religious, first to teach, then to serve as principal of the elementary school and later of the high school. Presently retired, Soeur Marie-Céline resides at the convent of the Dominican Sisters in Sabattus, Maine.

September. I was in store for an unpleasant surprise: I would have to repeat the first grade! The reason? Classes at Sainte-Croix were bilingual. On the other hand, it could have been worse and there might have been no French at all at Sainte-Croix. There was general agreement in the parish that the intent of Bishop Louis Walsh, the Ordinary in Portland, had been to make of Sainte-Croix an English-speaking parish.6

Another possible explanation for the fact that English was taught earlier at Sainte-Croix, starting in the first grade, may be that the majority of the people in the parish had climbed a step or two of the social ladder. They owned their homes and saw in the study of English an indispensable means of guaranteeing a still better future for their children. Whatever the explanation, I repeated first grade, but then I skipped second grade and also fourth grade. I would like to believe that it was due exclusively to my ability and my hard work that I made such great progress in school. However, the reality of the situation may not be as flattering: it seems that second grade and fourth grade were overcrowded and that there may have been more room in the third and fifth grades.

Let us observe in passing that students now enrolled in this institution at present number 375, divided into seven classes. There is a need for a larger building and for this reason of finding a dwelling for the Sisters since they are now living in two classrooms. However, it is impossible at the present time to assume the expense

---

6   See the *Programmes Souvenirs* of the 15th and 50th anniversaries of the *paroisse* Sainte-Croix. Both texts give essentially the same information. The parish was founded on October 29,1923. The first pastor was Reverend Michael F. Drain, the second, *le révérend père* Alfred René. In spite of the evident good will and the pains taken by the anonymous author of the French printed program for the 15th anniversary to be diplomatic, discreet, and charitable, the reader senses that the unpleasant memory of the clash with Bishop Walsh still lingered. There is a deep appreciation for the zeal and priestly qualities of Father Drain. However, since most of the families are of Canadian origin, they wished most ardently to be ministered to by a French-speaking priest. Unfortunately, this matter fostered for some time a ferment of dissension in the minds of the people . . . The few Irish families left the parish and the inscription "Sainte-Croix" superseded the original "Holy Cross" on the frontispiece.

which such a move would entail and we are resigned to making of necessity a virtue.[7]

I was now in the third grade. It was at this time that an event occurred which has had significant and long-lasting effects on my entire existence. To this very day, I demand too much of myself and others. Remember that I had just skipped second grade. Nonetheless, at the end of September and October the report cards which I brought home had perfect marks, 100's, in all subjects; as well as for conduct, application, punctuality, piety. Unfortunately, perfection eluded me in November. I had been given a 99 in arithmetic. As he was putting his signature on the report card, my father turned to me and said: "You could have done better." He was not joking; he was dead serious. I did not give him a single other opportunity to reproach me for the remainder of the school year. I was eight years old.

In the fifth grade, it was at church that I encountered similar moral rigor. I was an altar boy. I can see myself, as if it were yesterday, holding the paten for the *curé* as he distributed Holy Communion. All of a sudden, he shoved me with his elbow and said: "Move on to the next one." Why? you ask. Because the woman kneeling at the communion rail was wearing a dress which the *curé* considered immodest: the neckline was cut too low, he thought, or possibly he found the sleeves too short. He thus refused to give her Holy Communion.

It is quite deliberately and not haphazardly that I have chosen these incidents as typical and significant. I could also cite many others: for instance, the obligation to assist at Vespers every Sunday or being absolutely forbidden to go to the movies on Saturday afternoons.

The most vivid memories of my early years in elementary school are, then, of a training which was, by far, more concerned with religious and moral formation than with intellectual development. That should not come as a surprise, however, because at Sainte-Croix the school was most concerned with imparting to the young "that of which they have been most deprived, religious instruction and Christian upbringing."[8] Would

---

7   *15e anniversaire de la paroisse Sainte-Croix, Lewiston, Maine, Programme Souvenir*, p. 45.

8   Ibid., p. 13.

my memories be different had I continued at Saint- Pierre? I shall never know, of course. At Saint-Pierre, the stated objectives seem to have aimed a little higher. They claimed to strive for schools which "contribute to form an intellectual elite of the very first order, apostles who will spread the name of Jesus Christ, our Leader."9

As regards bilingual education at Sainte-Croix, nothing which I can recall seems to have any great significance. There is no doubt in my mind that, while I was in school, I did my very best to learn both languages as well as I possibly could. But once I had returned home, the rest of the day was spent in a French-Canadian atmosphere.

The year was 1932, the Great Depression—my father's restaurant went bankrupt. The house had to be sold and the family had to move to "*le Petit Canada*" of Lewiston. We were not very proud of this tumble down to the lower part of town, for the move was accompanied by the contempt of some members of the family and meant being forgotten by most of the friends from Sainte-Croix. So it is at Sainte-Marie that I completed the sixth, seventh, and eighth grades. Since I had transferred from another school, I was assigned to the "B" section. It was in "6B" that soeur Marie-Thérèse, besides drilling us on the agreement of past participles, spoke to us about the "good" and the "bad" Indians and that soeur Marie-Clotilde encouraged us to be proud of being Americans. It is upon suddenly remembering those classes that, in 1973, I began to ponder the meaning of this cultural fragmentation which I had experienced.

Upon graduating from the eighth grade at Sainte-Marie, a student could be awarded two diplomas, the first for English and the second for religious education and French. However, our particular eighth grade teacher was very set in her ways and her ideas. Of the twenty-one pupils in our class, only three received their diplomas in French. One of the girls, who later joined the Ursulines and in time became principal at Sainte-Marie, like me, did not receive her certificate in French . . . To this day, I hold a grudge against that nun.

It was at Lewiston High School that, for the very first time, I found myself in a totally English-speaking environment. I had

9   *Album Souvenir du 75e anniversaire de la paroisse Saint-Pierre et Saint-Paul, 1871-1946*, p. 29.

elected the business curriculum, my parents arguing that this was a more practical way to finish my education. I was totally ill at ease in this strange world and that year ranks as one of the most difficult in my life. In spite of that, I improved my command of the English language.

I was at Lewiston High School for one year. The next year I entered the minor seminary of the Blessed Sacrament Fathers in Suffern, New York. Once again, I had to repeat the first year, this time because I had not studied Latin at Lewiston High. (Languages!) But I no longer felt like a fish out of water: of the twelve students in my class, eight were Franco-Americans from New England. Two of the professors were French Canadians and the ten others were Franco-Americans. All the religious in the community had spent some time studying in Québec. But even if French was still held in high esteem in Suffern, it had lost its priority as a first language. The striving to be fully assimilated into the American way of life and integrated in the melting pot were deliberate and obvious. The superior and the professors were constantly reminding us that the study of the English language was the most important subject in the curriculum.[10]

Although I had not been awarded my certificate in French upon graduating from Sainte-Marie, it became quite obvious to me, after the very first few weeks in Suffern, that only one of my classmates, René Bélanger, who came from New Bedford, could offer me any serious competition in French. I accepted the challenge and during the next six years we battled each other for the first and second place in French. We, of course, compared ourselves to the other Franco-Americans in the other classes. Some were as strong as we were in French, others were not. Weak or strong, knowledge and skills in French were not always on a par with the knowledge and abilities these same students manifested in English, Latin or Greek. Even at that time, when I was still a student in Suffern, I had formed a very clear

---

[10]   See *Schedule of Courses, Eymard Seminary*, Suffern,N.Y., Fathers of the Blessed Sacrament, n.d. *Passim* in summary form: For six years, four English classes and five study periods per week; three French classes and four study periods per week. Over and above that: *Reading: A minimum of three hours of English per week is required* . . . *Book Report*: **One English** *report* **per month** *is required.* **Two French** *book reports are required* **per year**. (Words in boldface are mine.) These details and the wording in English illustrate that French was not neglected in Suffern, but it no longer enjoyed its status as a first language.

impression that there had to be tremendous differences in the quality of the French taught in various parts of New England. [11] It is in Suffern that I discovered that it is possible to be a Catholic in English.

Having completed six years of juniorate in Suffern, I then left for the novitiate and scholasticate of the Blessed Sacrament Fathers which, at that time, was located in Cleveland, Ohio. Every day, it seemed to me, the atmosphere was becoming increasingly anglicized, notwithstanding the fact that almost all the religious were either Franco-American, French-Canadian, or Belgian. If ever I became a priest, I would be ministering in English to people whose language would be English. Still, whenever I recited the rosary privately, I would do so in French, and even though I went to confession in English, I always recited my Act of Contrition in the language of the great Molière.

In 1946, I made one of the most important decisions in my life. That decision also brought about a traumatic change of direction in my bilingual itinerary. I left the seminary after one year of philosophy and decided to pursue studies in French at Western Reserve University [12] with the intention of becoming a teacher of French at the secondary level.

---

[11]   Every year there would be between fifty and sixty minor seminarians in Suffern. Eight out of ten were Franco-Americans. While I was a student there, well over one hundred different Franco-Americans came to the seminary. From Maine, they came mostly from Biddeford-Saco, Waterville-Winslow, Old Town and Lewiston-Auburn; from Connecticut, only from Hartford and Putnam; from Rhode Island, they were mostly from Woonsocket, Central Falls, Pawtucket, and Providence; they came from almost everywhere in Massachusetts, but more especially from Fall River, Lynn, New Bedford, Worcester, Chicopee, Fitchburg, Holyoke, and Gardner. There was not a single one from New Hampshire or from Vermont. According to my observations, the best prepared in French came from New Bedford, Fall River, Central Falls, and Lewiston. Are my observations correct and do they indicate that, in fact, there were great differences in the quality and levels of French taught in New England? If my observations are correct, what explains these differences? It goes without saying that if such a study were undertaken, Manchester, Nashua, and several other cities could not be overlooked.

[12]   In 1948, Western Reserve University and Case Institute of Technology were two distinct institutions. They merged in 1967 to become Case Western Reserve University.

First shock: I discovered that if, on the one hand, I read with relative ease the classical writers Corneille, Racine, Molière, Bossuet—on the other hand, I experienced great difficulty reading contemporary writers like Sartre, Gide, Cocteau, Montherlant. I was utterly frustrated trying to decipher their vocabulary, their syntax and their style. Only many years later did I finally understand fully why I had experienced these difficulties.

Second shock: Although the English-speaking students in the class envied the ease with which I spoke French, and although one of my professors, on one occasion, told me that I wrote French "almost with a certain elegance," I was made to feel, practically from the beginning, that I spoke an inferior French, to tell the truth, a dialect. Then to add insult to injury, I was obliged to take courses in pronunciation and phonology, just like the English-speaking students. And I, who thought that the Dominican Sisters, the Sisters of the Presentation of Mary, and the Ursulines had taught me "*le bon français*," which I had worked so hard to perfect when I was in Suffern, acquiesced to all of their demands and, two years later, thanks to the recommendation of one of my professors, I was offered, without my seeking it, a position as a lecturer in French at John Carroll University.

It was the beginning of a new life with a totally different focus, one that my life would maintain for about twenty years. I began teaching "*le bon français*" to English-speaking students in an English-speaking city. I obtained my master's degree, married an American of German descent who did not speak a word of French. The mother tongue of my children would be English. My daily life now revolved around three centers of activity: my family, my career as a professor, and the pursuit of a doctorate in French literature on a seventeenth century author, again at Case Western Reserve University, where the only French language and French culture considered legitimate and authentic were those of France itself. I was not betraying my Franco-American roots, nor had I forgotten them. My life was simply unfolding in another world. I spoke the French of la belle France and the English of Cleveland, Ohio.

I have just stated that my life had become focused in a new direction, a direction that it maintained for twenty years. It probably would have been more precise to state that my life was gradually changing its focus and was evolving almost imperceptibly toward a confluence of the three languages and three cultures which had divided my life. A very long time before I remembered my classes in the sixth grade at Sainte-Marie, faint glimmers of light had fallen on that language block I had experienced in my classes on contemporary French authors. The first of these came while I was preparing my doctoral dissertation on the *Grand Cyrus* of Madeleine de Scudéry.

Allow me to point out first of all, that if I chose to write a dissertation on a French author of the seventeenth century, it was not because I had found seventeenth century authors easier to understand when I had first come to the university. The real reason is that the choice of dissertation directors was limited at that time at Case Western Reserve. The director I preferred was a specialist in seventeenth-century literature. My own preference would have been to do a dissertation on Claudel, Bernanos, or Saint-Exupéry. I presented several drafts on these modern authors to my director. Invariably, he would find some pretext to reject whatever I wanted to do. Finally, it dawned on me that he would only accept to direct a dissertation on a seventeenth-century topic or author. Studies on baroque literature and *préciosité* were in vogue at the time, and the director suggested the *Grand Cyrus*.

Ten thousand pages, ten volumes, a dearth of original and complete editions, a whole body of criticism which considered the book unreadable and the ideas ridiculous. The project was far from appealing. But I had made up my mind that I would get that doctorate at any cost. Besides I was so well trained to be docile that I readily agreed to do as I was told. However, I had been right to hesitate in my own mind to take on this task. What a chore! The mere reading of the ten volumes required an entire summer, three months, isolated, alone, 350 miles away from my young family, buried in the library at Ohio State University. And, especially in the beginning, there were other problems: familiarizing myself with seventeenth-century print style, the absence of paragraphs, spelling variations and inconsistencies.

However, what pleasant surprises were hidden in these voluminous pages! The more I read, the more I discovered a whole world of ideas, moral and societal values, and ideals of conduct which I had known since my childhood, since my earliest year in school: self-control, generosity, word of honor, awareness of the dignity of self and of others, loyalty, devoted attachment to all that is good, and avoidance of evil. In those pages, I was discovering above all this ideal of dedication to duty and spiritual love which I too had tried to live, first at the juniorate and even more intensely during the novitiate and the scholasticate. The ideas and ideals of Madeleine de Scudéry were not ridiculous. Things were getting clearer in my mind. The difficulties I had experienced at Western Reserve while reading twentieth-century authors were caused then by their ideas as much as by their vocabulary, syntax, and style. There was a reconciliation slowly taking place between my Franco-American antecedents and my university training.

Once doctoral studies were over, numerous factors contributed to further this reconciliation. They were, however, more a matter of chance than of deliberate planning. Trips, especially two trips to Québec City, played a significant role in this. While attending a conference in that city, I was surprised to learn that French was the common language of Québec a century before it became the common language of France itself. As he was making this statement, the speaker, it seemed to me, was clearly needling some of the native French snobs in the audience. Instinctively, I was delighted. The following summer, having returned from accompanying a group of students to France, I took my family for a vacation to the northern part of Michigan. We visited, among other places, the shrine of Blessed Tekakwitha, Fort Michilimackinac, two churches founded by French Jesuit missionaries, one at Saint Ignace, the other at Sault Sainte-Marie. Still later, while on a trip to visit my family in Lewiston, we stopped for a visit at the shrine of the Jesuit Martyrs in Auriesville, New York. As these events unfolded, I did not attach any great importance to these occasions, which, on the surface, appeared to be mere coincidences.

At John Carroll, we had just dropped the language requirement. If we wanted to remain in business, we had to become creative and come up with new courses. I proposed developing culture courses taught in English and I volunteered to teach two of them dealing with the French heritage in North America. That is when it happened all of a sudden—while I was preparing for one of those courses and reading the Jesuit Relations. There I was in the sixth grade at Sainte-Marie. In an instant, everything had crystallized!

I pursued my inquiries and discovered the answer to the dilemma of the "good" and the "bad" Indians. Yves F. Zoltvany [13]

---

[13] Yves F. Zoltvany, *The French Tradition in America* (New York, Harper and Row, 1969), p. 7. See also: G.T. Hunt, *The Wars of the Iroquois: A Study in Intertribal Trade Relations*, 2nd ed., Madison, Wis., 1960.

and several other historians easily convinced me that the destruction of Huronia by the Iroquois had been economically motivated, for 'they needed to have access to pelts from the Hudson Bay area. The supply of furs from their own territories was so depleted that their very participation in the fur trade was being threatened. Even more convincing was Zoltvany's argument that the history of the United States, which I had been taught, rested solely on the Anglo-Saxon, Protestant interpretations of Francis Parkman in his authoritative *France and England in North America* and L.H. Gipson's *The British Empire before the American Revolution.*[14] Soeur Marie-Clotilde had interpreted the history of the United States from a point of view which would have caused her serious remorse of conscience had she been aware that she was presenting history from a Protestant standpoint. Soeur Marie-Thérèse's point of view, on the other hand, was obviously Catholic and French. Zoltvany eventually convinced me that the truth was to be found somewhere in the middle ground of these two partisan points of view.

To meet the demands of the courses on the French heritage in America, I found it necessary eventually to study the French spoken in Canada and to read, among others, Victor Barbeau's book, *Le français du Canada.*[15] While reading the very first chapter, entitled "Le fonds français," I finally understood the reasons for the linguistic block which I had experienced at Western Reserve.

There was one problem remaining, that of cultural fragmentation. The many years that I had studied French notwithstanding, nobody in France had ever mistaken me for a Frenchman, not even the kindest or the most polite person. On the other hand, if my accent, my vocabulary, my sentence structure sometimes left people in France a little perplexed, on the other hand, these same language peculiarities of mine did not clearly stamp me as Canadian. All I had to do to convince myself that I was not Canadian was to pay a short visit to my aunts, uncles, and cousins living in Québec. And at John Carroll, where I have been teaching for decades, some colleagues do not consider me totally Americanized. Just recently, a colleague whom I have known for

---

14   Zoltvany, *op.cit.*, pp. 8,9. See also: W.J. Eccles, *Canada under Louis XIV, 1663-1710* (Toronto: 1964).

15   Victor Barbeau, *Le français du Canada* (Quebec City: Librairie Garneau, 1970), pp. 11-22.

over twenty years was completely taken aback when I told him that I was not Canadian.

Consequently, I find myself fragmented, heir to three cultures, but unable to clearly and definitively identify with any single one of them. From the age of seven up to and until I left the seminary, I lived the dichotomy of feeling drawn by two value systems, two cultures, two languages, this dichotomy which I sensed so keenly at the age of ten without comprehending it. Then, during my years in college and at the university, a third linguistic and cultural variant was added to the mix and, without my realizing it, turned a dichotomy into a "trichotomy" if you will allow me to coin the term. From the day I started in the parochial schools of Lewiston and continued through a public high school before entering a juniorate and major seminary with strong Franco-American influences, my life has followed a path of sorts, but not always in a straight line. Rather, the path has zigzagged, alternating between going in the direction of one French language, sometimes in the direction of the other, sometimes in the direction of English, until that day in 1973 when the line started to straighten itself out and the contradictions began to resolve themselves.

Today, after many years of anguish, I understand the causes and effects of this cultural fragmentation which has so deeply affected my life and, I suspect, that of many Franco-Americans of my generation.

Translated by the author

[This article first appeared as "De l'école paroissiale à l'enseignement universitaire: réflexions sur le partage culturel" in the French Institute's publication entitled *Les Franco-Américains et leurs institutions scolaires*.]

"Tsi Gars"

David Plante

I often asked my father about the ancestry of our family. He always answered that he didn't know much beyond his grandparents. I kept asking him, hoping my asking him would remind him of something he'd forgotten. He rocked back and forth in his rocking chair in the kitchen, his head held high, as if trying to recall, but his answer was that he didn't know.

I wasn't sure he was interested. For my father, no other people of any importance existed on the Continent of North America but Francos—Francos and, as strange bed-fellows, members of the Republican party—but he didn't seem to be interested in the history of the Francos.

I asked, "You don't know when the Plantes came from France?"

"No, *tsi gars*," he answered.

"Or from where in France?"

"No, *tsi gars*."

Perhaps it had never occurred to him to wonder. Why this was so, and why I did wonder, would, I think, account for more than a difference between us as personalities, it would account for the difference between us as belonging to different generations. Why wasn't my father interested in his deep past? I will leave many questions as I go on, hoping that if they go unanswered they will at least open windows of the little clapboard house we Francos live in onto the great woods from which that house came, was cut from, sawed up in, hauled out of, built of, from pine beams to shingles; that old house whose attic, in the hot summer, always smelled of pine trees, and whose beams and joists still exuded, years and years after the house was finished, tears of resin. The fact is, we hardly ever think of the woods from which our house came.

I don't understand why my father wasn't interested, but I can suggest why I was. I say "suggest," because one never understands anyone, not even oneself some thirty-five years back. This is my suggestion: I grew up in a small Franco-American parish in Providence, Rhode Island, called Notre-Dame-de-Lourdes. *M. le Curé* couldn't speak English, only French. Many of the nuns at the parish school I went to could speak only French. My paternal grandmother never learned English, nor did the cobbler to whom we took our shoes to be repaired and our ice skates to be sharpened. But, really, I didn't grow up in a *Petit Canada*—that is, in a mostly Franco neighborhood. There was such a neighborhood, close to the church, where my father grew up. But, shortly after he married, he and my mother and their first three children moved to a new house a ten-minute walk from church, at the then edge of the city of Providence, where new houses were being built on lots. My mother once told me that when they moved into this house, beyond it were farms, countryside and woods. I recall, when I was a boy in that house, empty lots in which the neighborhood gangs played. Some of the lots, like the one right next to our house, still had trees, and on summer nights, when the glass window was open and shadows of trees were on the window screen, I was terrified of that small lot of woods. In bed at night, I sometimes shouted out, and my mother or father would come to my room, take me to the window to look, and say, "There is no one out there. There is nothing there." I recall the fresh nighttime smell of the air through the screen—a smell of wild roses that grew along the boundary between our narrow yard and the trees and of some other, acrid smell, perhaps shunk cabbage, or skunk, which I thought of as *bête puante*. But I recall, more than anything, the still trees and the moonlight through the trees, and my frightened sense that, among the old rusted automobile fenders and tires dumped in those woods, there were people who, when I was alone in my room, came up to my window and looked in. My parents didn't convince me they weren't there. Those people were hiding. As I grew up, all the empty lots were built on. I watched, from my window, a bulldozer come and clear the little woods next door. I didn't mind, because by this time it had become just a dumping ground, and all the invisible people who had inhabited it were gone.

But what I wanted to say is that, though I did go to the parish church and school, I was brought up outside the parish. All our neighbors, Irish and Italians mostly, were also brought up outside their parishes. As soon as we got back from our respective parish schools, we'd change from our school clothes—uniforms for the girls, ties with long-sleeved shirts for the boys—into overalls, and we'd meet outside to play. We were all Catholic, but we were different nationalities. Virginia was Italian, Ilene was Irish, and I was French.

Virginia's grandmother could only speak Italian. We, the gang, were often invited in, and while we sat about the kitchen table and drank minuscule glasses of wine and ate thin slices of cake, Virginia's mother translated for us stories her old mother recounted of Italy. One story was about an accident in a Roman ruin, where she had once played, and a stone fell on her. This story was meant to warn us to be careful while we played, though there were no Roman ruins in Providence. Ilene's father and her mother drank beer. Her grandmother didn't. We weren't given anything to eat or drink in Ilene's house, but her grandmother, with a brogue, told stories about Ireland. She had kissed the Blarney Stone and she recalled the green of the hills. My friends' parents—or most of them—were born in old countries, and they remembered these old countries. They had relations living there. My suggestion as to why I wanted to know where my family came from is that I was envious of my friends for knowing where theirs came from, and I wanted to know.

Here is another question: Why was I envious? Why were my friends' cultures dominant to such a degree that they revealed how base my own culture was? My parents didn't drink, certainly not wine, but not even beer. I wanted to have played in a Roman ruin, to have kissed the Blarney Stone amidst the green hills of Ireland. I wanted an old country.

Was my old country Canada? My father was born there, and was taken by his parents to Providence when he was two years old. He had many relatives there. Though he never went, my aunts and uncles did, to visit those relatives. But Canada wasn't really the old country.

My friends were first generation Americans, and I, by association with them, also took myself to be a first generation American. This was, in fact, an expression I had heard my older brothers use about themselves. We were, as a family, first generation Americans.

Canada was not America. More to the point, Canada hardly existed. Canada was nowhere.

Italy existed, Ireland existed. I had some claim, some distant claim, to make on France. Perhaps France was my old country.

But I must confess a France existed for me that was essentially different from the way the old countries of my friends existed for them. It did not at all exist in terms of personal experience of anyone I knew in my family. It was beyond recall. (My aunt Cora, whom I call *Tante* Oenone in my novels, once told me she had heard of an ancestor, a woman, who arrived from France possessing only a pair of lace gloves and an ivory fan, and my imagination worked on that a lot.) My France existed in fantasy, a fantasy formed almost entirely by reading about France. When, in my late teens, I read Chateaubriand, I fantasized about coming from St. Malo. When I read Balzac, I fantasized about being a provincial in Paris. France was my invention.

When, finally, I went to France, in 1959, at nineteen, I looked for connections. I found very few, but I did find some in church. But the most exciting occurred while, in the Luxembourg Garden, I was reading *Les Chouans* by Balzac, and, a short way into the novel, I came across a word that made all my attention quicken. My father often called his sons "gars," or "tsi gars," and I had thought that expression originated with him, or at least in the parish. I didn't know what it meant anymore than I knew what my name meant. I read (the translation is mine):

> The word *gars*, pronounced gâ, is a remnant of the Celtic tongue. It has passed from Low Breton into French, and is, in our present language, the one word which most reverberates with the past. The *gais* was the principal arm of the Gaels or Gauls; *gaisde* meant armed; *gais*, bravery; *gas*, strength. These parallels prove that the word *gars* originated in the expressions of our ancestors. The word has an analogy with the latin word *vir*, man, the root *virtus*, strength, courage. Patriotism justifies this dissertation, which will, perhaps, rehabilitate, for some people, the words: *gars, garçon, garçonette, garce, garcette*, generally banished from discourse as unseemly, but whose origin is so warlike, and which occur here and there in the course of this history. 'She is a famous *garce* (wench)' is a not well understood expression of praise which *Mme* de Stael got in a little canton of Vendômois where she spent a few days in exile. Brittany is, of all France, the country where the Gallic customs have left the strongest imprint. The parts of that province where, up to our day, the savage life and superstitious spirit of our crude ancestors have remained, as it were, most

flagrant, is called the country *des Gars*. When a canton is inhabited by a number of savages similar to those who have apppeared in these pages, the people of the country say: *Les Gars* of such and such a parish, and this old name is like a reward for the fidelity with which they strive to preserve the traditions of the Gaulish language and ways; moreover, their lives retain deep vestiges of the beliefs and superstitious practices of ancient times. There, the feudal customs are still respected. There, antiquarians discover Druid monuments standing. There, modern civilization is frightened to penetrate through the immense, primeval forests. An unbelieveable ferociousness, a brutal stubbornness, but also faith in oaths; the complete absence of our laws, of our language, but also the patriarchal simplicity and heroic virtues, make of the inhabitants of this country people as intellectually poor as are the Mohigans and Redskins of North America, but as lofty, as cunning, as hard as they. The place which Brittanty occupies in the center of Europe makes it a greater curiosity than Canada. Surrounded by an enlightenment whose healing warmth does not penetrate, this country is like a frozen piece of coal which remains hidden and black in the bosom of a bright hearth.

The frozen piece of coal in my bosom suddenly glowed. I felt in touch with my ancestry. But it wasn't France I felt connected to, it was Canada.

A couple of years ago, I received a genealogical list from an aunt of mine in Rhode Island which had been sent to her by one of those mysterious relatives—an uncle three of four times removed—who still lives in Canada. He had sent it to me, as he'd heard I was a writer and might be interested. His name, Lajoie, is the maiden name of my paternal grandmother, the daughter of a fur trader and a Blackfoot Indian. Her genealogy went back pretty far, to 1709, but that of my grandfather, Anaclet Plante, after whom my father was named, went back even further, to 1650, when the marriage between Jean Plante and Françoise Boucher was recorded at Notre-Dame-de-Québec on September the 1st of that year. Jean Plante's father, Nicolas, had died and was buried in France, at Lalleu, near La Rochelle, in May 1647, and his mother, Isabelle Chauvin, in February 1649. Jean had obviously come to America shortly after the death of his mother. My family,

I was suddenly aware, had been in Canada, in North America for a very long time.

By the way, I found, in the list, the name Francoeur, which I had chosen to be the name of my fictional family, which makes me wonder about my negative belief that nothing is inherited through blood but blood.

I was, I realized, not a first generation American, I am tenth generation North American, and I would like to know what my family, who have been gathering forces for almost three and a half centuries, have to say to me. For ten generations, and, for my great-nieces and nephews, of which I seem to have an endless number, for twelve generations—we have been on this Continent. That is a long time for a great deal to happen—long enough, I'm tempted to say, for a new species of animal to have evolved.

My North American ancestry is like an unexplored forest to me, and yet I am a product of it. I am one of those strange animals who evolved in those vast forests, but who for years thought the strangeness was embarrassing and something to be hidden. And now, I think, it is exactly what I should as a writer center on.

I would like to center that strangeness—or, if you don't like the word strangeness, the uniqueness of what a Franco is, after having developed in what he made his own country over many, many years—on the heart of the Franco. It is a very difficult heart to see, however, and that is, to me, its attraction. It is not going to reveal its secrets easily. And it does have its secrets.

Everyone knows that the secrets of a culture are best kept in its language, but I, a Franco, consider that language too private to write in it, though I admire people who do. It is a rich language, including anglicisms which, I think, shouldn't be purged. It is, as my private language, somewhere below my public language, the English I write in. I never write "skunk" for example, without hearing an aunt talk about the smell of a *bête puante*. And whenever I see cranberries I think of the word we used at home: *"atacas."* Many Franco words shine through the English, but I can't assume that this shine is seen by anyone who doesn't know the language, and that is, I'm afraid, a great many.

And yet, perhaps the greatest secrets aren't entirely closed to me. Like someone illiterate, which so many, if not all, of my ancestors were— *"qui n'ont su signer"* occurs often on copies of marriage and baptismal certificates I've seen—I must try to read the pictures, the images. And I must try to find those images that are most at the center of my culture.

I say "center," implying, perhaps, a kind of analytical study of Franco-American culture to try to reach some central understanding of it. I don't doubt that anthropological studies would reveal a great deal that I'm unaware of, but I'm not an anthropologist, I'm a novelist, which I sometimes think, however, is just a lazy anthropologist who doesn't want to do field research or construct arguments. My research is done in a chair, at my desk, with my eyes closed. I'll try to give an example of how I work. My intention is to get to the heart of the Franco culture. Within that intention, I think of images, image after image, with no apparent connections among them, of what I recall or have heard about, or have dreamed about the world of the Francos. Often, totally incongruous images occur, like a man in striped pajamas walking on stilts through puddles of water in the rain, which I have to clear my mind of. I must say, I like to have such images occur on their own. A big round table set with mis-matched plates and cups and saucers and Christmas *tourtières* and mash potato pies and platters of *tire* with walnuts and a glass bowl of oranges? Yes, but it's not, I feel, at the center. Boiled maple syrup thrown on the snow to make it solidify into candy? That's rather picturesque, and I'm against what is merely picturesque. And so I go through a great number of images, sometimes over days and days. There is, I know, one image that is going to center the true secret of the Francos. When it occurs, it will be while I am putting on a sock. This is the image that occurred to me: of Mass celebrated in a clearing in the woods. The moment it occurred, I knew it opened the heart I was trying to look into. Not that it reveals the secret. It simply embodies us.

I am, I should say, an atheist. And yet I know that Franco culture means nothing if it is not centered on the Franco God. And I say "the Franco God" trying to identify a God as unique to us, I believe, as a God is in whom a tribe has its own being, its identity. That ritual of the celebration of Mass in the woods is the real manifestation of our Canuck God. He is, I am sure, as North American as Canada's forests. I don't believe in Him, but I feel an expansion of spirit in the contemplation of Him.

And the big question—the question that offers most possibility, most promise, to the Franco—is: Who is this God? We know Him, but we know nothing about Him.

He is at our center, but it is as if He is in darkness. Is one of His attributes darkness? What are His attributes?

It would take a novel—many novels, I think—to try to come to some understanding of Him, but I think I can say now that He is not a false God, because He is an elemental God, like the woods from which our very houses are built.

Our North American pasts are our forests, pasts which disappeared into the forests, and we, I think, are so unaware, for whatever reasons, of those forests we hardly know they exist for us. As a writer, my desire is to go into them, not so much to claim a heritage as just to find out what that heritage is. My way of doing that is imaginatively, is to allow the most extravagant of images as long as I feel sincerely, with the same sense of the presence of what is larger than oneself when one is praying sincerely, that these images are true. And I'm sure the truest images will be found to be religious images of a religion that is everywhere hidden, like our ancestors, among the trees.

[This article first appeared in the French Institute's publication entitled *Franco-American Literature: Writers and Their Writings.*]

Telling Stories in Mémère's Kitchen

John Dufresne

Every Sunday afternoon throughout my childhood, through the fifties and into the sixties, our considerably extended family met for dinner at Mémère's house on Fairmont Ave. in Worcester. Doris's family and Eva's and Joan's and Lucille's and Bea's daughter, and the uncles, and occasionally the great-aunts and uncles from Lowell or Holyoke or Canada. And every Sunday, Mémère cooked brown potatoes and pot roast and boiled the life out of some string beans. And every Sunday I licked the beater that had whipped the cream for the chocolate pie and ate the blueberries that didn't fit into the shell. And when the meal was over and the dishes cleared, and Mémère's sons-in-law had drifted to the parlor to watch the Red Sox blow a five-run lead to the Yankees, someone perked a pot of coffee, set the sugar bowl and the can of condensed milk on the table, dealt the ashtrays to the aunts, and then we all sat around the kitchen and talked about the family and the neighbors. If Uncle Fred were there he'd go on about his childhood on the farm or his hunting trip to Maine. And if Uncle Fred weren't there we'd speculate about the number and whereabouts of his "illegitimate," as we called them then, children.

My job was to sit away from the table and to listen, to fetch another pack of Pall Malls from my mother's purse, bring Pépère another bottle of Tadcaster ale from the shed, and "Go see why your brother's crying, tell him if I have to get off this chair he's going to be a sorry young man." The adults talked about what on earth Georgie Barry might be up to in that enormous tent he's set up in his yard next door and about what a fine job the landlord was doing with the property—but isn't he a little strict with his kids?—about what Bunny Bourassa was doing down at Moore's Pharmacy, about where Uncle Richard picked up that funny way of talking, and about why George Lucier spends every night at the Queen Elena. Hearts were mended at the kitchen table, grief was shared. I learned that people who we thought would always be around sometimes pass from our lives. I learned about the aunt I never knew, who had Down's Syndrome, and died as an infant, and what that was like to have death come to the door and enter the wrong room. To come for the child and not the mother.

I want to talk about how those afternoons made me who I am, or who I think I am, and I'm going to do that by telling a story that was prompted by what was said around that table thirty-something years ago. But let me start out with a quote from novelist David Plante, author of *The Family* and *The Country*, among other works, novels about growing up French-Canadian not far from here, in Providence, Rhode Island. He says: "Franco-American culture is gone, and perhaps the only way to have written about it was to believe it was over even while it was being written about. *Les vrais paradis sont les paradis perdus* might have been said by Proust about an entirely different world, but it applies—with the difference that the Franco past was never a paradise."

I suppose our presence here today belies Plante's pessimism, as does the anthology *Lives in Translation: an Anthology of Franco-American Writings*, a recent collection of poetry and prose by a dozen Franco-American writers, from which that quote was taken, but his sentiments deserve attention. Are we now in danger of vanishing as a culture? Have we Franco-Americans forfeited our birthright? And if we are to be judged by the stories we tell, what do the stories say about us?

In a review of *Lives in Translation*, critic Steve Kronen wrote in the *Harvard Review* that he found in the collective work a depiction of a culture "financially and emotionally exhausted . . . tottering between bitterness and resignation." Kronen traces the Franco cultural migration from the poverty and hardscrabble farms of Quebec to the poverty and mills of New England, the trip my Pépère, and yours, perhaps, took. In the States, Kronen writes, "parents watched their children [and grandchildren] lapse from the culture, forget the language, and eventually move elsewhere." A familiar story, certainly, repeated in culture after culture, but with a difference in our case. According to Kronen: " . . . while most immigrants' tales are suffused with sadness for customs lost and keepsakes abandoned, they also shine about the edges with the promise of new lands and financial independence—if not for themselves, then for their children or grandchildren. *Lives in Translation* is written by those grandchildren, and what little lustre once shone from their elders' brows has proven to be little more than sweat."

Ours is a broken history, littered with lost tales and lost craft and lost folklore and lost community, as the recent events at St. Joseph's Parish will attest. This seems tragic to me, one of the grandchildren Kronen speaks about, one of those who was so busy assimilating as a child that I never knew I was ethnic except on St. Patrick's day among the Irish kids at St. Stephen's school. Here I stand a stranger to my grandparents' and my mother's language and the poorer for it. Part of the job of fiction writers is to pick up the pieces of our history and hold it up as a mirror to our faces to see who we are and what we look like to the world because there is a danger in acculturation not only to our own souls but to the soul of the country. Our hearts are nurtured by the past, by the language of our families, by the attitude toward life that we learned at home—and out of those elements, our characters grow. When we are finally all alike in this country then we will be spiritually doomed and barren. We will cease to grow as a people or as individuals. There are, then, matters of significance at stake in holding onto our traditions.

We each get to construct our own histories; that's what we use our memory for. And memory is not simply a recollection of the past; it's a fabrication of the past. It's a fiction, then. It's the lie that tells the truth. We are what we chose to remember, and our lives begin with our earliest memory. I am who I am because of where I grew up. Grafton Hill, known as "French Hill," was in the fifties and sixties as exclusively Catholic and blue collar as neighborhoods get. Jobs ran to the trades, factories, and public service. There were no dancers or brain surgeons, actors, or professors on the Hill. The exotic vocations were never mentioned. We knew that explorers and linguists and actors existed because we saw them on TV, but those jobs were for people who were not at all like us. We were styled to survive the neighborhood, and we learned not to set our sights too high. Our Catholicism was devout, but not reverent, decorous, but not arrogant, a Catholicism you could live with.

The first stories I heard, I heard around my mémère's kitchen, and in them I heard the voice of the neighborhood. And what I felt immediately was that stories increase your love for the world. Telling them and hearing them. These were stories my pépère told about growing up on the farm, one of nineteen children, in southern Quebec; about smuggling alcohol from Montreal to Worcester during Prohibition. Stories my mémère told about Pépère's latest drinking bout, how he shot up the radio, emptied the icebox, and hid the food under his bed. Stories my aunts told about the boys at the Jay-Dee Grille, the motorcycle boys who looked just like the Everly Brothers. Stories about people we'd just seen that morning at Mass at St. Joe's and the no-good they were up to. About "Whozee" and "What's-His-Name's Wife," and don't they have any shame and aren't they afraid they'll get caught? And who's sick, and who's p.g., and who owes money to whom. I could listen all afternoon. Gossip. I loved it. That's the writer's job: Listen to the gossip and spread it as far as you can. At the heart of all good fiction and at the heart of all good gossip is the same thing: trouble. Fiction is nothing more than gossip about made-up people.

All of the stories I heard around that table were about characters I knew, set in a world I lived in, told in a language I understood, in a voice I recognized and admired. The characters in their stories tended to be the independent ones, eccentric, perhaps quirky, like Uncle George whose life is more a spontaneous fiction than anyone I've ever met. He claimed to be pals with everyone on the Red Sox, and when he drove home from Fort Devens with a Jeep, he told us the Colonel let him use it because they were friends. And we believed him. Until the MPs showed up at the door. The characters we admired and talked about did not always do what they were supposed to do. And that is precisely why we liked and admired them. Like us, they were individuals, had their own minds. They may have behaved strangely at times, expressed inappropriate thoughts, felt muddled and powerful emotions. They were not heroes. They were the people in the neighborhood, living quiet but important, funny and often heartbreaking lives. They were a submerged population that we felt ourselves a part of. I found none of these qualities in books. I read the stories they told us to read in school, but I couldn't hear that familiar voice on the page. And I couldn't find my neighbors, myself, or anyone like us, like the Berards and the Favreaus and the Desrosiers and the Paquettes in the books, and so books meant nothing to me then. But stories meant everything.

The writer Grace Paley advised young writers to pay attention to the voices you hear in the neighborhood. She said, "If you say what's on your mind in the language that comes from your parents and your street and your friends, you'll probably say something beautiful." Most of us though don't always want to know what's on our minds or we're too busy. Any many of us consider the language of home to be different from the language of literature, politics, commerce. But only when we get back to the language of our people can we begin to tell their stories, keep those stories, let the stories escape when the time is right.

It would be the Southern voice that broke the literary silence for me. When I was finally able to hear a narrative voice as compelling as those in Mémère's kitchen, it came with a Southern accent. In the works of Flannery O'Connor, William Faulkner, Harper Lee, I found characters I recognized, the people I now write about, people who have been held out of the mainstream or who have decided to hold out. These Southern writers dealt with depravities and misfortunes of poor people which other writers, in my experience, were not doing. I found the honesty attractive and familiar. I already knew the world was a mess because I looked around me and saw men, young men, grown pale soft, and cynical, all up and down Grafton Hill, in the Diamond Cafe, the Cosmopolitan Club, Jack's, Uncle Charlie's Tavern, the AJ, the American Legion, sitting with other men in the dark watching TV, smoking, drinking shots and beers, reminiscing, wondering, some of them, where their dreams had gone. And these were the men who had the jobs, the families, the homes, who dreamed the American Dream. I saw friends, teenagers and already alcoholics and junkies, toothless and conniving. So when Harry Crews says of the South: "If we are obsessed with anything it is with loss, the corruption of the dream. And the dream was the dream of the neighborhood," I know he is speaking as well of Grafton Hill.

The first lesson I learned about telling stories was that every story has to take place somewhere, and all the interesting people are a lot like me and the people I know. That's what the reader asks, that's what the boy at his mémère's table asked: Tell me about me. All stories are particular and all stories address the problems of the individual in society. The purpose of the stories told around Mémère's kitchen table and the purpose of fiction is the same: to say, "This is what it's like to be a human being, and this is how it feels." If a story doesn't help us to understand our lives, it's a waste of time. The job of the storyteller is to look at the world one street, one three-decker at a time because it's through the particular that we come to know the general, through the concrete that we come to know the abstract, through the peculiar that we come to know the normal, through the neighborhood that we come to understand the world. Instead of "Once upon a time in Utopia," better to write "Just this morning on Caroline Street, a woman who loved her husband realized that she could no longer live with him."

People are the center of stories. Morality is not. Stories don't preach, priests do. The purpose of telling stories at the kitchen table was to try to understand and explore, not to judge. And what kind of people make subjects for interesting stories? Compelling characters, I learned, are never passive. No one of the aunts ever talked about the quiet guy on the third floor who spent all his time in the house watching television. But they often talked about Aunt Eva who also stayed in the house, but who spent her time writing letters to my father on rolls of toilet paper, ate M&Ms by the truckload, and had every issue of the *TV Guide* ever published spread out over the living room floor and furniture, who spoke a rapid-fire language, part giggle, part whine, that none of us ever understood. Compelling characters set goals for themselves and struggle to attain them despite obstacles. It's through struggle that we come to knowledge and in no other way. Aunt Eva was losing her mind, and she struggled in those letters to keep a grip on reality. She spent her weeks now at the State Hospital and came home on weekends. The letters were the way she talked to the world.

What else I learned was that there are no victims and villains in life, that we are, all of us, saint and sinner. Life is not black and white. And the purpose of telling stories is not to fix blame. What would be the point of that? The purpose is to try to understand why people sometimes behave villainously or allow themselves to be hurt. The job of the storyteller is to be honest and to witness what the people do. And here is something else I learned, and it was at odds with what I was learning in religion class. We are not condemned by our mortal sins which might, in fact, take great moral courage and steadfastness to commit, which might even be admirable, the way Aunt Bea up and left her husband, divorced him, and started a career in a time when women stayed home and took whatever life they were handed. No, we are damned by our venial sins which we can easily ignore and commit a hundred times a day, until they become part of our character—they become who we are: the liar, the vain, the greedy, the self-important. Great sins are aberrations, small sins are a way of life.

The people in stories make decisions and take responsibility for their decisions and their behavior. We will not care about, nor will listen to talk about people who point their fingers. The characters in our stories do not join support groups with other characters to whine about their misfortune and to blame their mothers or fathers or the school system or the spouse or the Republicans or society. Our characters can't get away with such nonsense. They are willful and responsible. They may, in the last resort, do whatever seems right to them, but they must accept responsibility for the act in this world and the next.

And I learned that it wasn't what characters did that made them interesting, but why they did what they did. We were always digging at understanding. We wanted to find out whatever possessed Carl Brin, say, to think he could get away with shooting his junior high teacher? What had gone so desperately wrong in his life? And what do you suppose happened at the Jacques' that the one boy turned out so wild? And why would Claire stay with that drunk she's married to this long, him with his flannel shirts and white socks and bloodshot eyes. Could it really be that she loves him? The real story I learned was below the surface, where values and morals lie.

I came to my vision of life, my understanding of the human condition in that kitchen through those stories. It's peculiar, I suppose, it's not particularly happy. It's this: We are dying and we don't want to be. We are in love with things that vanish. Everything we care about eventually slips away, everyone leaves us. We struggle against the sadness at the core of our existence by giving shape to human experience. And it is this improbable struggle against our short lives and vanishing relationships that constitutes the beauty of life. We make art, we make children, we create afterlives, we photograph, we write fiction, we sit around a kitchen table and tell each other stories. We do what we can to stop time, to comfort ourselves, to offer solace to our family and friends. That's as close to immortality as we get in this life.

One Sunday afternoon when Pépère was out of the room, the aunts began to reminisce about the old days and about life with father. Pépère was a man who kept his shiners in the bathtub during ice-fishing season, shot pigeons off the roof of his three-decker with a .22, hid all his money in cubby holes in the cellar, who refused to answer the phone all of his life. He was not a reasonable man but was a perfect character to tell stories about. Why does he do these things he does? And then one of the aunts began the story of the time they all came home from Armand Poisson's wedding in Lowell and Pépère killed the radio with a couple of rounds from his rifle, and then locked everyone out of the apartment. And then he hid the food. And thirty years later I wrote this story inspired by the fragment I remembered of the story. It's called "Surveyors."

There were six rows of twelve tomato plants each. Each plant was pruned to a single stem and tied with ribbons of plaid flannel to sturdy five-foot-tall hickory stakes. Training the vines made the weeding and the liming easier, my grandfather said. It exposed the fruit to more sunlight, which produced a richer color and sweeter taste. Glossy, elliptical Earlianas bunched in clusters on tender-vined plants. He also grew Burbanks with thick, solid skins and juicy flesh. These were his favorites. The Bonny Bests were brilliantly red, flattened and globular in shape, and often swelled in size to six inches across. He gave these away like trophies to his friends.

The littered, over-weeded lot next to his apartment building had become my grandfather's tomato garden. And every July evening in 1953, the year of the polio epidemic in Massachusetts when I was five, he and I would finish supper and sit out on the grass beside the cinder driveway and watch the garden.

He was a housepainter and a difficult man at times. Whenever he wore one of his two suits, he drank too much. Every time he drank too much, he took off his leather belt and strapped somebody. One night, after returning from a nephew's wedding in Lowell, he locked his wife and children out of the house, fired four .22-caliber bullets into the walnut body of a console radio, and hid all of the food from the icebox under his bed. That was before I arrived for the summer and before the garden was planted.

I carried his green glass bottle of warm Tadcaster ale like a chalice to our grass seats. He wore a beige straw hat with a narrow, down-turned brim and seersucker band. He surveyed the garden, his green eyes inspecting each plant in turn. He stood up, picked his teeth with the edge of a matchbook, took off the hat, and fanned his face. His thin chestnut hair was graying at the temples even then. The pleated brown-flannel trousers were zipped but unbuttoned and were held up by olive Y-backed suspenders that followed the white paths of his T-shirt straps over his large shoulders. I see the tomatoes for us, he said, and flopped away in his cordovan slip-ons to gather our dessert.

My tomato smelled of linseed oil from the touch of his short, thick fingers. He drew a yellow shaker, shaped like an ear of corn, from his pocket, took his first taste of tomato, and sprinkled salt into the bite.

He told me the Depression story. How he had lost his home, a seven-room cottage that he had built himself with the weekend help of six of his fifteen brothers. The red house sat on a shaded avenue away from the factories. It had a backyard large enough for two pear trees, a rhododendron bush, and a small vegetable garden. He wiped his stiff-bristled mustache with a handkerchief and then dried a thin pink river of tomato juice meandering down my wrist. That's why, he said, he hadn't deposited one dime in a bank for twenty-three years. That's why his savings were stashed like memories where no one else could find them—locked in steel boxes and hidden in secret cavities of floors and walls and ceilings.

Told me how when the bank foreclosed and he was out of work, he moved his family to a $15-a-month flat and wondered how he'd feed six kids. He built a two-story pigeon coop and raised homers. Taste like chicken, he said. He set squirrel traps, planted tomatoes and beans, and fished for calico bass and horned pout in the quarry pond at the old brickyards. That's when he smuggled whiskey on the trains from Montreal to Worcester. He wanted me to know that I would not be saved by my possessions. It's not what you have, he said, but how you are. The bastards can't take that away from you.

The fussy old French priests in this parish are as crooked as ward bosses, he said. Every one of them. Joe McCarthy is the only politician in this country who cares about poor people, he said. You watch, we're going to make him President.

We had seen Ted Williams play baseball for the first time that summer on my grandfather's new nineteen-inch Motorola television. My grandfather was fascinated by the explosive grace of Mr. Williams' brilliant swing and by the way he defied both pitcher and probability by always taking the first strike. Even the great DiMaggio could not do that. DiMaggio needed three strikes. That's the art, my grandfather said, giving a strike to the pitcher.

As my grandfather talked and I listened, two men stepped down from the cab of a maroon pickup. One man nodded to my grandfather. The smaller one slid a tripod from the truckbed and lifted it to his shoulder. The men are surveyors, he said. They're here to measure the property. He sent me to the house for another bottle of ale. When I returned he was talking with the young man in the sanforized green jumpsuit. The man wore a Yankee baseball cap on the back of his head so that the bill pointed skyward. He stood near the edge of the garden between rows of Burbanks and held a striped range pole with his right hand. When he blushed at something my grandfather said, he looked like another tomato plant. They're going to build a house, my grandfather said. They start tomorrow. But it's our garden, I said. But it's not our land, he said.

In the morning he dressed for work in his white bib overalls, white shirt, and white Pratt and Lambert painter's hat, and sat quietly at the kitchen table, drinking coffee. He heard the horn and walked outside and told his friend Studley to go without him; he would catch a bus to work later. He carried a galvanized tub to the garden and began a final harvest. By the time the flatbed truck delivered the bulldozer and its driver to the lot, he had filled and unloaded the tub three times. He gave me a grocery bag from Candella's Market and told me to fill it with tomatoes and give them to the driver. We have enough tomatoes. I refused. He's going to kill our plants, I said. The man is doing his job, he said.

We took our grass seats and watched the bulldozer rip the land and crush the plants into the rocky soil until there was nothing left to look at.

[This text was presented at the 1994 French Institute colloquium entitled "The Franco-Americans."]

Work Cited

Ledoux, Denis, ed. *Lives in Translation: An Anthology of Contemporary Franco-American Writings*. Lisbon Falls, Maine, Soleil Press, 1991.

Contributors

Authors

Jacquelyn Alix, P.F.M.

Born in Webster, Massachusetts, Sister Jacquelyn was educated in a parochial school in the city of her birth by the Sisters of Saint Anne. She is a graduate of Becker Junior College in Worcester, which granted her its Distinguished Award in 1986, and Annhurst College, where she obtained a B.S. in Business Administration. She also attended Babson College, in preparation for a Licensure in Nursing Home Administration, granted in 1977 by the Commonwealth of Massachusetts' Board of Registration of Nursing Home Administrators. Having entered the Congregation of the Little Franciscans of Mary in 1965, she has, since 1975, been the chief administrator of St. Francis Home—the original Hospice Saint François for the elderly, founded by her community. Sister Jacquelyn is active in professional circles as well as in the Worcester community. She has served on Worcester's Commission on Elder Affairs and she is a long-standing member of the Coalition of Women Religious Ministering in Maine and Massachusetts. In 1984, Assumption College awarded her an honorary doctorate in Humane Letters.

Fernand Arsenault, D.Th.

Fernand Arsenault has devoted his entire career to the Acadian population—as a priest, as a professor, and as an administrator. In the latter capacity, he has served as a member of the University of Moncton's Conseil des Gouverneurs and as Dean of its School of Liberal Arts. He taught at the University of Moncton in New Brunswick from the opening of that institution, after having taught at Saint Joseph's University, from which the former evolved. Deeply interested in Acadian history and the questions of cultural identity and bilingualism, he has prepared reports on these questions for both the provincial and the federal governments. He served on study groups which led to the official recognition of bilingualism in New Brunswick, duality in the province's Ministry of Education, and to the subsequent establishment of school committees for the French-speaking population of the province. Having retired from teaching in 1994, he is a member of the Mental Health Commission of New

Brunswick as well as the secretary of La Société historique acadienne.

Lucien A. Aubé, Ph.D.

Born in Lewiston, Maine, Lucien Aubé received his Ph.D. degree from Case Western Reserve University. A specialist of seventeenth-century French literature, he spent his academic career teaching French and chairing the Department of Classical and Modern Languages at John Carroll University in Cleveland. His teaching interests included the methodology of foreign-language teaching and France's legacy in North America. He is now retired.

Neil Boucher, Ph.D.

As the Director of the Acadian Centre at Université Sainte-Anne in Nova Scotia since 1980, and as a lecturer and professor, Neil Boucher is immersed in Nova Scotian Acadian questions. He obtained his Ph.D. in Canadian History from Dalhousie University with a dissertation entitled "Acadian Nationalism and the Episcopacy of Edouard A. LeBlanc, Bishop of Saint John, New Brunswick: A Maritime Chapter of Canadian Ethno-Religious History." Active in both academic and community activities, Prof. Boucher has contributed articles on Acadian questions to scholarly journals, organized exhibits, and served as a consultant, researcher, and editor for numerous projects, all of them related to the Acadian question.

Gerard J. Brault, Ph.D.

An alumnus of Assumption College, Gerard Brault received his M.A. from Laval University and his Ph.D. from the University of Pennsylvania. He has taught at Bowdoin College, at the University of Pennsylvania, and, since 1965, at Pennsylvania State University where he is Edwin Erle Sparks Professor of French and Medieval Studies. As a medievalist, Prof. Brault has published works on *The Song of Roland* and on the medieval *blazon*. Parallel to his medieval scholarship, Gerard Brault has maintained his interest in Franco-Americans, directing language institutes for Franco-American teachers of French, editing *Essais de philologie franco-américaine* (1958), *Cours de langue française destiné aux jeunes Franco-Américains* (1965), and publishing *The French-Canadian Heritage in New England* in 1986.

Armand B. Chartier, Ph.D.

An alumnus of Assumption College, Prof. Chartier has taught at the University of Rhode Island since 1971 after obtaining his Ph.D. from the University of Massachusetts at Amherst. In 1977, he published a book on the nineteenth-century French novelist, Barbey d'Aurevilly. He has published numerous articles and reviews on Quebec and Franco-American questions in various academic journals, but his major achievement is the publication, in 1991, of *Histoire des Franco-Américains de la Nouvelle-Angleterre—1775-1990*, a 400-page overview of Franco-American life and history.

Marcelle Chenard, Ph.D.

A native of Manchester, New Hampshire, Marcelle Chenard received both a B. A. and an M. Ed. from Rivier College in Nashua, New Hampshire, under the direction of the Sisters of the Presentation of Mary. She was awarded a Ph.D. in Sociology from the Catholic University of America in Washington, D.C. Since 1971, she has taught sociology at the College of St. Elizabeth in New Jersey where she is now a full professor and department chairperson. In addition to her college courses, she has taught and lectured to various constituencies and different age groups. Her research has included a book entitled *Coping With Grief: A Guidebook for the Bereaved and Those Who Work With the Bereaved* (1981); an oral history research project on Employed Women, for the Morristown (New Jersey) Historical Society; and chapters of books on the topic of social workers and volunteers within the hospital setting. Among her writings are also articles on women and faith for the French periodical *Missi*.

Rev. Clarence J. d'Entremont, C.J.M.

A native of Nova Scotia, Rev. d'Entremont was ordained as a Eudist priest in 1936. He then spent two years in Rome studying canon law. Upon his return, he taught until 1952 when he transferred to the Fall River Diocese, becoming the chaplain in a home for the elderly in New Bedford. When he retired, in 1982, he returned to Pubnico, Nova Scotia, where he was born. His principal publications include *Histoire du Cap-Sable* (5 volumes, 1981), *Nicolas Denys, sa vie et son oeuvre* (1982) and, more recently, monographs on the Nova Scotian francophone villages of Pubnico, Sainte-Anne-du-Ruisseau, Quenan, and Wedgeport.

Donald Deschênes, M.A.

Director of the Franco-Ontarian Folklore Centre in Sudbury, Ontario, Donald Deschênes received his M.A. degree in Ethnomusicology from Laval University. A lecturer at the University of Sudbury, he has taught at the University of Moncton and has directed folklore workshops for schools. Active in the promotion of native crafts and community cultural development among the Acadians of New Brunswick and Prince Edward Island, he has also published a collection of traditional songs entitled *C'était la plus jolie des filles,* and numerous articles in various folklore journals. In his present position, he both conducts research and sees to the dissemination of Franco-Ontarian folklore.

John Dufresne, M.F.A.

John Dufresne, who grew up on Worcester's "French Hill," is currently an assistant professor of creative writing at Florida International University. His published works include short stories and poems, as well as *The Way That Water Enters Stone* (1991), a book of short stories, and a novel, *Louisiana Power and Light* (1994). Prior to studying for his graduate degree, John Dufresne was a social worker, a drug abuse counselor, and an administrative supervisor for the U.S. Census Bureau of Worcester, Massachusetts. In addition to presenting papers at conferences, and judging fiction for various contests, John Dufresne has received awards for his own writing, including the PEN Syndicated Fiction Award. He was a Bread Loaf Fellow in 1993.

Frances H. Early, Ph.D.

Although an American, Frances Early has spent her teaching career in Canada, after obtaining both an M.A. and a Ph.D. in History from Concordia University in Montreal. The title of her dissertation is "French-Canadian Beginnings in an American Community: Lowell, Massachusetts, 1868-1886." Since 1981, Prof. Early has taught at Mount St. Vincent University in Halifax, Nova Scotia. She is the co-editor, with Louis A. Eno, Esq., of a bilingual edition of *Immigrant Odyssey* (1991), the autobiography of Félix Albert, a French-Canadian immigrant to Lowell, Massachusetts. The original French title of the work is *Histoire d'un enfant pauvre* (Nashua, N.H., 1909). As a board member of Mount Saint Vincent University's Institute for the Study of Women, her current research interests are focused on questions concerning women.

Charles W. Estus, Sr., Ph.D.

A professor of sociology and chair of the Department of Sociology and Anthropology at Assumption College, Prof. Estus received a B.D. from Duke University's Divinity School and an M.A. in Sociology from its Graduate School of Arts and Sciences. He obtained his Ph.D. from New York University in Social Psychology and the Sociology of Religion. In 1972, he was a visiting scholar at the Center for the Study of World Religions at Harvard University. Along with his colleague, Kenneth J. Moynihan, he received funding from the National Endowment for the Humanities to set up a Program in Community Studies at Assumption College, as well as grants from the Swedish Government and the Swedish Institute of Stockholm to study the Swedish origins of early immigrants to Worcester. These grants culminated in a large museum exhibition in 1993, and the subsequent publication of the book *gä till Amerika: The Construction of a Swedish Ethnic Identity for Worcester, Massachusetts*—in collaboration with Prof. John McClymer, Ph.D., also of Assumption College. The author of numerous articles, he taught first at Drew University, then at Clark University. He has been at Assumption College since 1968.

Yves Garon, A.A., Ph.D.

Born in Quebec, Rev. Garon studied at Trois Rivières and Nicolet before entering the novitiate of the Assumptionists at Sillery in 1937. He was ordained in France in 1943, having studied philosophy and theology in that country from 1938 on. After the war, he studied French language and literature at Laval University, obtaining a doctorate in 1960, with a dissertation on Louis Dantin, a noted Quebec critic and author who lived in exile in Cambridge, Massachusetts. Between the years 1945 and 1962, he taught for twelve years at Assumption Prep and at Assumption College. Professor of French and Quebec Literatures at Laval from 1964 to 1969, Father Garon is currently the chaplain of the Augustinian nuns of Quebec and vice-postulator of the cause of Rev. Marie-Clement Staub, A.A., founder of the Sisters of St. Joan of Arc.

Madeleine D. Giguère, M. Phil., D.H.L. (Hon.)

Professor emerita of the University of Southern Maine, and currently volunteer Director of the Franco-American Heritage Collection at Lewiston-Auburn College, Madeleine Giguère received her advanced degrees from Fordham and Columbia. Her teaching career as a sociologist was spent at St. Joseph's College, St. John's University, Boston College, and the University of

Southern Maine, where she also chaired the deparment. In the late seventies and early eighties, she served on the Maine State Advisory Committee to the U.S. Commission on Civil Rights which she later chaired. Her anthology of articles on Franco-Americans, published in two volumes by the National Assessment and Dissemination Center for Bilingual/Bicultural Education in 1981, has been a useful guide for scholars and students interested in Franco-American Studies. In recent years, her research has focused on analyses of census data regarding Franco-Americans.

Michael J. Guignard, Ph.D.
Michael Guignard is a native of Biddeford, Maine, where he studied in the Franco-American parochial school system at both the elementary and high school levels. He obtained his B.A. in Government at Bowdoin College and a Master of Arts Degree as well as a Ph.D. from Syracuse University. He was a Foreign Service officer for the United States Department of State from 1973 to 1986, serving in Washington, D.C., Naples, Costa Rica, Montreal, and Tokyo, rising to the Consular rank. Since 1986, he has been a visa consultant with a private law firm in Washington, D.C. His articles in this collection are based upon his Ph.D. dissertation entitled, "Geographic and Demographic Forces Facilitating Ethnic Survival in a New England Mill Town: The Franco-Americans of Biddeford, Maine" which he published as *La Foi — La Langue — La Culture: The Franco-Americans of Biddeford, Maine* (1982).

Pierre E. Lachance, O.P.
Born in Fall River, in the very parish where he now ministers, and whose sanctuary to St. Anne he directs. Father Lachance studied at the Collège de Montréal, before entering the Dominican Order in St. Hyacinthe. Ordained in 1942, in Ottawa, he taught philosophy, theology, and liturgy from 1944 to 1955 at the Dominican House of Study in Ottawa prior to doing mission work in Saskatchewan. From 1973 to 1978, he was an associate pastor at St. Anne's parish and principal of its school. Father Lachance has been Director of St. Anne's Sanctuary from 1959-1973 and from 1978 to the present. He has written on Fall River and its many Franco-American parishes and lectured on spiritual topics.

Brigitte Lane, Ph.D.
Born in France, Professor Lane received her Ph.D. from Harvard University in 1983. Her research encompasses the fields of oral tradition, anthropology, and folklore. She has been

especially interested in studying the passage from oral to written literature as well as the relationship between modern French literature and modern literatures in French. Her Ph.D. dissertation, published by Garland Press in 1990, is entitled *Franco-American Folk Traditions and Popular Culture in a Former Mill Town: Aspects of Ethnic Urban Folklore and the Dynamics of Folklore Change in Lowell, Massachusetts.* Professor Lane has taught French language and literature, as well as culture, folklore, and theater, at Wellesley College, M.I.T., and Brandeis University. The author of numerous articles, she is currently a member of the French department at Swarthmore College.

Michel Lapierre, Ph.D.

Michel Lapierre wrote his master's thesis on Rosaire Dion-Lévesque. He obtained his doctorate with a dissertation on Quebec literature entitled "Le rêve d'une littérature sauvage d'Alfred DesRochers à Jacques Ferron," which he is preparing for publication. He is also working on a book concerning female characters in the Quebec novel. He is a lecturer at the Université du Québec à Montréal where he teaches a course on Jacques Ferron, a noted Quebec novelist.

Charlotte Bordes LeBlanc, M.A.

Born in Woonsocket, Rhode Island, Charlotte LeBlanc attended bilingual schools in that city, staffed by the Sisters of Jésus-Marie. She received her B.A. and M.A. degrees from Boston College and completed all but her dissertation for the Ph.D. in French Language and Literature from that same institution, where she also taught until 1990. She is a founding member and past-president of the Richelieu Club of Boston, a French-language service club.

Paul D. LeBlanc, M.A.

Born in Nova Scotia, Paul LeBlanc, who came to Fitchburg, Massachusetts, at the age of twelve, knows first-hand what it means to be an immigrant. His own experience has made him particularly successful at interviewing others who share the immigrant experience. He is deeply committed to his community of people—the Maritime Acadians who have come to settle in New England. Paul LeBlanc has a B.A. in American Studies from the University of Massachusetts at Amherst, an M.A. in American History from Assumption College, and he has pursued studies at the doctoral level at the University of Maine at Orono. His work experience is a varied one: teacher of social studies, developer of youth programs, director of admissions at a private school,

student services coordinator at the University of Maine at Fort
Kent, and, presently, human resources administrator for an
environmental remediation firm in Colorado.

Béatrice Belisle MacQueen, M.A.

A native of Worcester, Massachusetts, Mrs. MacQueen is a
member of the second graduating class of Rivier College, the first
Franco-American college for women, under the direction of the
Sisters of the Presentation of Mary. She obtained her Master's
degree in French from Assumption College. After graduating from
Rivier, Béatrice Belisle worked at Worcester's *Le Travailleur* under
the aegis of its publisher, Wilfrid Beaulieu, before returning to
Rivier College to teach for two years. The mother of four children,
she later taught French at the high school level, in Westborough,
Massachusetts, for many years.

Claude Milot, M.A.

Claude Milot was born in Woonsocket, Rhode Island, where
his father worked, first as the editor of *L'Indépendant*, a French-
language newspaper, and then for the Union Saint-Jean-Baptiste,
at that time, the largest of the mutual benefit societies for Franco-
Americans. He grew up in Manville, R.I., his mother's home town,
where he lived in the tenement house built by his maternal
grandfather, attending a bilingual parochial school and
surrounded by a French-speaking community. He studied with the
Oblates for six years before attending the Catholic University of
Louvain, majoring in political science and philosophy. By then
his father had joined the Foreign Service of the United States.
Claude Milot has spent virtually his entire career as a publishing
executive with The Hearst Corporation in New York and in
Michigan. In New Jersey, where he lived for many years, he served
on the Green Township Board of Education for thirteen years, five
of them as president. He is a frequent contributor of articles on
current affairs, administrative management, and education to
various journals.

Kenneth J. Moynihan, Ph.D.

Professor Moynihan has taught history at Assumption
College since the early 70s having received his Ph.D. in History
from Clark University. His dissertation title was "History as a
Weapon for Social Advancement: Group History as Told by
Jewish, Irish, and Black Americans, 1892-1950." His teaching
specialties are Early American History, American Black History,
and Community Studies. In his capacity as the specialist on
Franco-Americans in Worcester for the college's Community

Studies Program, he has translated a number of key documents into English, among them, Rev. T. A. Chandonnet's *Notre-Dame-des-Canadiens* (1872) and Alexandre Belisle's *Livre d'Or des Franco-Américains de Worcester, Massachusetts* (1920). He is the author of numerous articles on ethnic groups, and his awards include study grants from the Massachusetts Foundation for the Humanities, the National Endowment for the Humanities, the Bay State Historical League, and the American Antiquarian Society.

Robert B. Perreault, M.A.

A free-lance writer, Robert Perreault is a native of Manchester, New Hampshire. He obtained a degree in Sociology and French from Saint Anselm's College and a Master's degree in Franco-American Studies from Rhode Island College. He worked under the tutelage of Tamara K. Hareven—interviewing Franco-Americans in French for her book entitled *Amoskeag: Life and Work in an American Factory-City*—and as the archivist of the Association Canado-Américaine's extensive collections (1975-1982). During that time, he was a contributor to its journal before becoming its Associate Director (1980-82). Author of a French-language novel entitled *L'Héritage*, and a number of studies on Franco-American subjects, he also teaches French conversation at St. Anselm's College, his *alma mater*.

David Plante

Born in Providence, Rhode Island, David Plante has lived in London since 1966. His books, which have been praised widely, include: *The Ghost of Henry James*, 1970; *Slides*, 1971; *Relatives*, 1972; *The Darkness of the Body*, 1974, translated by André Simon and published under the title *La nuit des corps*, 1977; *Figures in Bright Air*, 1976; *The Family*, 1978; *The Country*, 1981; *The Woods*, 1982. These last three books were grouped together and published as *The Francoeur Novels*, 1983; then came *Difficult Women: A Memoir of Three*, 1983; *The Foreigner*, 1984; *The Catholic*, 1986; *The Native*, 1987; *Le sixième fils*, translated by Jean Guiloineau, 1988; *The Accident*, 1991, and *The Annunciation*, 1994. He is also a regular contributor to *The New Yorker* magazine. In addition to his writing, he has been Henfield Writing Fellow at the University of East Anglia, Norwich (1977); writer-in-residence at the University of Tulsa, Oklahoma (1979-1982); writing fellow at Cambridge University (1984-85), and scholar-in-residence at the University of Quebec at Montreal (1988-1989). He is the recipient of an Arts Council bursary, an American Academy Award, and a Guggenheim Grant.

Yves Roby, Ph.D.

A professor of history at Laval University, Yves Roby is a native of Quebec. He has written extensively on Franco-Americans in many articles and in a book entitled *Les Franco-Américains de la Nouvelle-Angleterre (1776-1930),* published in 1990. Some of his articles, which have appeared in various Quebec and American journals, include: "Un Québec émigré aux États-Unis: bilan historiographique," "Les Canadiens français des États-Unis (1860-1900): dévoyés ou missionnaires?," "Quebec in the United States: A Historiographical Survey." Recipient of the Governor General of Canada's Prize, in 1972, Professor Roby has also written about the credit union movement in Canada: *Alphonse Desjardins et les Caisses Populaires 1854-1920* (1964); *Histoire économique du Québec, 1851-1896* (1971); *Les Caisses Populaires Alphonse Desjardins 1900-1920* (1975). As an American history specialist, Professor Roby is the author of *Histoire générale des États-Unis* (1976) and *Les Québécois et les investissements américains 1918-1929* (1976). Prof. Roby has also written articles for the *Dictionary of Canadian Biography,* the *Canadian Encyclopedia,* and the *Dictionnaire des oeuvres littéraires du Québec.*

Janet L. Shideler, Ph.D.

Janet Shideler received her Ph.D. from the University of Massachusetts at Amherst after obtaining an M.A. from McGill University with a specialization in French-Canadian Literature. Having taught in both Canada and the United States, she is, at present, an assistant professor at the State University of New York at Potsdam College. Her Ph.D. dissertation, entitled "The Quiet Evolution: Regionalism, Feminism, and Traditionalism in the Work of Camille Lessard-Bissonnette," is being published by Peter Lang Publishers under the title, *Camille Lessard-Bissonnette: The Quiet Evolution of French-Canadian Immigrants in New England.*

Philip T. Silvia, Jr., Ph.D.

Born in Fall River, Massachusetts, Prof. Silvia received both his M.A. and his Ph.D. degrees in History from Fordham University, after graduating from Providence College. He has taught history at Bridgewater State College since 1968. In addition to his dissertation, entitled "The Spindle City: Labor, Politics, and Religion in Fall River, Massachusetts, 1870-1905," he has written numerous articles for various publications, including *Spinner, Labor History, The Catholic Historical Review,* and *International Migration Review.* Dr. Silvia has also written about the city of

Fall River in three volumes: *Victorian Vistas: 1865-1885, 1886-1900 and 1901-1911*. He has served on many community boards and committees, and as a consultant on historical projects relating to Fall River.

Marcella Harnish Sorg, Ph.D.

As a licensed nurse, Marcella Sorg decided to study psychology at Bowling Green State University in Ohio. She then pursued graduate work in anthropology, receiving her Ph.D. in Physical Anthropology from Ohio State University. Since 1977, she has been a faculty associate at the University of Maine at Orono, where she was also Associate Director of the Center for the Study of Early Man at the Institute of Quaternary Studies of the university (1983-1987). In 1984, she was named a Diplomate of the American Board of Forensic Anthropology. Now Vice-President of Sorg Associates in Orono, she serves as a consulting forensic anthropologist for the Offices of the Chief Medical Examiners of Maine, New Hampshire, and Vermont, and is a past president of the American Board of Forensic Anthropology. In addition to the essay which appears in this volume, she has published an article entitled "Patterns of Infant Mortality in the Upper St. John Valley French Population: 1791-1838" in *Human Biology* (1983), reprinted in *Mortality Patterns in Anthropological Populations*, Wayne State University Press, 1983. She has also written numerous articles for scholarly journals and is the editor or co-editor of two books in preparation.

Richard S. Sorrell, Ph.D.

Born in upstate New York, Richard Sorrell holds a Ph.D. in History from the State University of New York at Buffalo. He has been a member of the faculty in the Department of History at Brookdale Community College, in New Jersey, since 1971. His dissertation, "The Sentinelle Affair (1924-1929) and Militant *Survivance*: the Franco-American Experience in Woonsocket, Rhode Island," was a study of the relationship between the Sentinelle Affair of the 1920s and the Franco-American community of Woonsocket. Dr. Sorrell has published a number of articles on the Sentinelle Affair, as well as on the Franco-American backgrounds of the writers Jack Kerouac and Grace Metalious. In the last decade, he has been involved in the teaching of a course on "The 1960s: Popular Music and the Counterculture," a social history of youth in America since World War II. He is the co-author, with Carl Francese, of a text on that subject, *From Tupelo to Woodstock: Youth, Race, and Rock-and-Roll in America, 1954-1969* (Kendall-Hunt, 1995).

†Mason Wade, Ph.D. (1913-1986)

From the early 1950s, Mason Wade, author of the monumental work *The French Canadians 1760-1945*—later revised and extended to 1967—had also taken an interest in the descendants of the French Canadians who had emigrated to New England. In 1967, he wrote a key article on Franco-Americans for the *New Catholic Encyclopedia* which has remained relevant to this day. As the founder of the Canadian Studies Program at the University of Rochester in 1955, Mason Wade was a pioneer in persuading American scholars of the importance of French Canada as well as English Canada. A graduate of Harvard University, Mason Wade's discovery of Francis Parkman's journals, and his subsequent publication of a biography of Parkman, marked the start of his lifelong interest in French Canada. His first book on that topic, entitled *The French-Canadian Outlook*, was published in 1946. At his death, Mason Wade had completed a manuscript on the Acadians of the Maritime Provinces.

Translators

You will find below some information on the translators of the articles in this collection. They have given unstintingly of their precious time and informed effort so that this book could appear in print. In some instances, the authors, many of whom are bilingual, translated their own texts. If there is no indication of a translation, the text was originally written in English. Some of the translators are also the authors of one or more articles in this collection. Biographical information on them can be found under *Authors*.

Alexis A. Babineau, A.A., Ph.D.

Rev. Alexis Babineau, the translator of most of the Acadian articles in this volume, is an alumnus of Assumption College, where he has spent the greater part of his career as a professor and an administrator. He earned both an M.A. and a Ph.D. from Clark University in Organic Chemistry and taught chemistry for many years before being named Campus Planner, a position he held for more than a decade. In recent years, he has been an assistant to the director of Assumption Publications, he has re-edited the books of the late Joseph Pelletier, A.A., and he has been a missionary in Kenya. In 1995, he celebrated the 50th anniversary of his ordination to the priesthood.

Madeleine Rivard Bérard, R.N.

A pianist who lived in France for many years, Madeleine Bérard was brought up in a French-speaking home in Central Falls, Rhode Island. A trained nurse, she now lives in Fall River, Massachusetts, where her husband, Maurice Bérard, practices medicine.

Gary Crosby Brasor, Ph.D.

Dr. Brasor received his Ph.D. in French Language and Literature from Indiana University. After working for Digital Corporation for many years, he was recently named Associate Director of the National Association of Scholars, headquartered in Princeton, New Jersey.

Hon. André A. Gélinas, J.D., LL.D., hon.

A graduate of Assumption College, Class of 1960, André Gélinas spent his junior year in Paris at the Institut catholique. He received his J.D. degree from the University of Michigan Law School at Ann Arbor in 1963, and practiced law in Fitchburg where he was born. Since 1985, he has been the presiding justice of the Fitchburg District Court in the Trial Court of Massachusetts.

He was the founding president of the French Institute's administrative council and, among numerous distinctions and awards, he was honored by his *alma mater* which bestowed an honorary LL.D. degree upon this distinguished alumnus.

†Raymond J. Marion, Ph.D.

An alumnus of Assumption College, Raymond Marion enjoyed a long and distinguished career at his *alma mater*. After obtaining his Ph.D. from Clark University in French and International Relations, Professor Marion taught history, chaired the department, and served as academic dean of Assumption College. Upon his retirement from teaching, he was appointed college historian. On active duty as a young Marine officer in the South Pacific during World War II, he took part in the Battles of Tarawa, Saipan, Tinian, and Okinawa, receiving the Silver Star for action on Tinian. In 1990, he received the d'Alzon Medal of the Augustinians of the Assumption, awarded for outstanding service to the college community. He passed away in October of 1995.

Jeanne Gagnon McCann, M.A.

Active in parish and cultural affairs in Worcester, Jeanne McCann obtained both her B.A. and M.A. degrees in French Language and Literature from Assumption College. A trained nurse, she is the mother of four grown children.

Henry L. Messier, M.A.

A native of Central Falls, R.I., Henry Messier was a Brother of the Sacred Heart for some forty years, teaching first in Ottawa (1927-1943) and then the Montreal suburb of Verdun before being assigned to the United States. He was the Director of Mount Saint Charles Academy in Woonsocket, R.I., St. Dominic's High School in Lewiston, Maine, and Notre Dame High School in Fitchburg, Mass., in the late forties and through the fifties. After leaving the Brothers, he taught at Oakmont Regional High School in Ashburnham, Mass. He now lives in retirement in Leominster, Massachusetts.